The
Wallaces
of Iowa

A Da Capo Press Reprint Series

FRANKLIN D. ROOSEVELT
AND THE ERA OF THE NEW DEAL

GENERAL EDITOR: FRANK FREIDEL

Harvard University

The Wallaces of Iowa

by RUSSELL LORD

DA CAPO PRESS · NEW YORK · 1972

Library of Congress Cataloging in Publication Data

Lord, Russell, 1895-1964.
  The Wallaces of Iowa.
  (Franklin D. Roosevelt and the era of the New Deal)
  Includes bibliographical references.
  1. Wallace, Henry Agard, 1888-1965. 2. Wallace,
Henry Cantwell, 1866-1924. 3. Wallace, Henry, 1836-1916. I.
Title. II. Series.
E748.W23L6 1972   973'.0099   76-167843
ISBN 0-306-70325-4

This Da Capo Press edition of *The Wallaces of Iowa* is an
unabridged republication of the first edition published
in Boston in 1947. It is reprinted by special arrangement
with Houghton Mifflin Company.

Published by Da Capo Press Inc.
A Subsidiary of Plenum Publishing Corporation
227 West 17th Street, New York, New York 10011

The
Wallaces
of Iowa

FOUR GENERATIONS OF HENRY WALLACES

The Wallaces of Iowa

by RUSSELL LORD

Illustrated with Photographs · Published by
Houghton Mifflin Company · The Riverside Press Cambridge

BOSTON 1947

The Riverside Press

CAMBRIDGE · MASSACHUSETTS

PRINTED IN THE U.S.A.

T O
RAYMOND CLAPPER
1891–1944

Late in 1943 when we were talking Ray said: 'You have stretched a large canvas for your panorama but these Wallaces are a great subject. They are great because they are natural. Tell the whole story and keep it close to the ground. That is their strength.'

BOOKS BY RUSSELL LORD

Men of Earth
The Agrarian Revival
Behold Our Land
The Wallaces of Iowa

GRATEFUL ACKNOWLEDGMENT

is made to *The Atlantic Monthly*, The Bobbs-Merrill Company, The Curtis Publishing Company, The F–R Publishing Company, Henry Holt and Company, G. P. Putnam's Sons, Reynal and Hitchcock, Inc., The Viking Press, Inc., and Whittlesey House for permission to quote from their publications.

ACKNOWLEDGMENTS

WRITING THE INTRODUCTION to Henry A. Wallace's *Democracy Reborn* (Reynal & Hitchcock, New York, 1944), I said, as of April 9, 1944:

In a collection of papers such as these the editor who makes the selections and enters the annotations should perhaps declare his position in respect to the author. I worked for him in his Department during his first year as Secretary of Agriculture. Then I left Washington to do some writing on a small farm in Maryland and to consider the continuing agrarian and industrial revolution from that quiet hill. As a free-lance writer and editor I have since been drawn back for weeks and months on end to Washington, and some of my work was for the Department of Agriculture — for the Soil Conservation Service, the Forest Service, Triple-A, the Bureau of Agricultural Economics, and the Commodity Credit Corporation, successively. But this work brought me back into firsthand visits with the Secretary, and later the Vice-President, only very occasionally; and while I like and admire him greatly, I have, I think, been a somewhat objective and not altogether uncritical spectator of his growth. For the past three years, between times, I have gathered the material and now am writing a three-generation biography of his family, an account of a century of our progress in terms of the connected doings and sayings of his grandfather, his father, and himself. That book, and this one, are to be issued by publishing houses entirely outside of the Government; and while the Vice-President and others of his family have approved of these projects in general, and have answered all questions freely, these are not 'authorized' works. The responsibility for the choice of material and for the interjected opinions is mine.

To this, at this second date of completion, August, 1946, little need be added. As each of the first nine chapters was completed, covering the years up to the Roosevelt New Deal era, I checked them in manuscript with Henry A. Wallace along with a number of other persons who were closer to the facts than I was, but always with the understanding that their corrections were to be factual only. With the same understanding, Mr. Wallace consented to scan Chapter X and the greater part of Chapter XI at points where, after my utmost of outside digging, the facts still seemed to remain in shadow of doubt. As for the final chapter, XII, which presses so closely to present events and speculations as to raise questions of some delicacy, I told him that I thought I had better write that one on my own entirely, not showing him any of the manuscript; and he agreed.

My obligations to Daniel A. Wallace — youngest son of Uncle Henry, and the current Uncle Dan of the family — are evident on many a page. I have known him longer than I have known any others of the family. We used to go on fishing trips together when he was editor of *The Northwest Farmer* of St. Paul and I was a wandering writer for old *Farm and Fireside,* later *The Country Home.* By no means the least great among the Wallaces, Dan helped me then as he now has helped me again, enormously, in the business of pressing joyous human juices out of dry or musty recitals of events, contemporary or long past.

So many other people have been generous; I could not begin to name them all. But for constant help, close-in, on research, checkup and the general struggle toward publication I must name at least Miss Mary Huss of Washington, D.C., Mrs. Wilbur Pope of Athens, Georgia, Miss F. Grace German of Bel Air, Maryland, and Mrs. U. T. Miller Summers of Houghton Mifflin Company.

R. L.

'THE LANDMARK'
BEL AIR, MARYLAND
August 1, 1946

CONTENTS

I
SPRING MOUNT

II
SEMINARY VEAL

III
THE YEARS OF THE GREAT REBELLION

IV
MORNING SUN AND WINTERSET

V
THE TORCH AND THE LAMP

VI
'WALLACES' FARMER'

VII
THE FIRST WORLD WAR BOOM AND CRASH

VIII
REAPING THE WHIRLWIND

IX
OUTSIDERS

X
WHEN THE DEAL WAS NEW

XI
DISPLACEMENTS AND DEPARTURES

XII
INTO THE NINETEEN-FORTIES

ILLUSTRATIONS

The
Wallaces
of Iowa

I

SPRING MOUNT

Let a philosophical observer commence a journey
from the savages of the Rocky Mountains, eastwardly
toward our seacoast. There he would observe in the
earliest stages of association men living under no law but
that of nature, subsisting and covering themselves with
the flesh and skins of wild beasts. He would next find
those on the frontiers in the pastoral state, raising
domestic animals to supply the defects of hunting. Then
succeed our semi-barbarous citizens, the pioneers in the
advance of civilization, and so in his progress he would
meet the gradual shades of improving man until it
would reach his, as yet, most improved state in our
seaport towns. . . .

I am eighty-one years of age, born where I now live, in
the first range of mountains on the interior of our country. ' And I have observed this march of civilization
from the seacoast, passing over us like a cloud of light,
increasing our knowledge and improving our conditions,
inasmuch as that we are at this time more advanced in
civilization here than the seaports were when I was a
boy. And where this progress will stop no one can say.
Barbarism has been receding before the steady step of
amelioration; and will, in time, I trust, disappear from
the earth. — THOMAS JEFFERSON in a letter to William
Ludlow, 1824.

1. By Western Waters

WHEN PITTSBURGH was still a pleasant small town in the
forest, a Scotch-Irish American named Andrew Finley
and his brother Joseph claimed adjoining tracts of land
on the rough, descending slopes of the Alleghenies, thirty miles
up the Youghiogheny River from Pittsburgh, to the south. They
crossed the mountains from Philadelphia afoot with a pack train

to claim these modest holdings — one hundred and sixty acres, more or less, between them — in the open weather of 1795. They were Westerners. Impatient under the exactions of Eastern landlords, they had sought new soil on which to set up in business as landlords for themselves. They were Westerners at heart and by location, for the fields they cleared lay beyond the Allegheny Divide in the Land of Western Waters where all the streams flow inland, away from the Old World.

Scotch-Irish attract Scotch-Irish. Others soon came. To protect themselves from beasts and Indians, the first families built their cabins rather closely together, and also their church and school. Their marriages brought forth abundantly of children and in time, of new cabins and more children.

In 1823 there came by way of the stone pike from Philadelphia to Finleyville, as the community was called, a gaunt eighteen-year-old lad named John Wallace. He walked erectly, but bore his body always a little gingerly because of an injury to his back which he had suffered as a boy wrestling with other country boys around home in County Antrim, Ireland. Having landed at Philadelphia, John Wallace made his way at first afoot and by stage toward Finleyville. His people at home knew members of the Finley and Ross families who had left the north of Ireland earlier and were now settled in western Pennsylvania. John Wallace wanted to farm in America; he had not determined exactly where; he was simply moving around, making love to the country, as the saying goes, before coming to a decision and settling down. Thriftily, as he traveled, he added to his belongings a small peddler's pack and sold things to the people along the way. His peddling business grew modestly as he gradually made his way westward and learned more of what was demanded and at what price. Somewhere around Greensburg, Pennsylvania, it must have been, he bought a horse and light wagon and came by nightfall to the inn by the bridge across the Youghiogheny at West Newton.

It is an old story now, and the precise dates and details are undecipherable, but people still love to tell what a greenhorn John Wallace was when he first came to that part of the country. He was so green he didn't know horsefeed. Driving into that inn yard he asked for oats. There were no oats; instead the young Irishman was given Indian corn. Those ears of corn resembled nothing that a horse could swallow, as John Wallace saw it, and he was sure a trick was being played on him. Then the horse reached over and started to nibble at the tip of one of the ears. He threw his armful of corn to the ground. 'You know more about this than I do. Do what you like with it.'[1]*

The looks and yields of this part of the country did not completely please him. Fields barely fifty years cleared of forests, bears, and Indians had been farmed so heedlessly that already the soil was dwindling in fertility. But he liked the people in that part of Westmoreland County and soon felt at home there. He had, moreover, a passion for taking hold of misused soil and building it back to fertility. At first he worked for wages, or rented land. Later he assumed the management of some of the larger earlier tracts where the settler had grown too old to work and where the sons had departed for situations and occupations more promising of gain and excitement than hill and swamp farming in the Pittsburgh hinterland.

A man of quick temper but of steady ways, John Wallace came of a long line of established farmers, great and small. A farmstead nearly three centuries old torn down only recently in Ayrshire, Scotland, still had a heavy brass knocker faintly inscribed 'H. Wallace' on the door.

That Scotch Henry Wallace was a good man, but impatient when he felt that he was being unfairly treated. The *Annals of Ayre* relate that he threw a knife at a minister who scolded him from the pulpit for not getting to church on a previous Sunday when his cart and horse had bogged down in the mud.

As far back as 1680 the family had thrown out a stem across the Irish Sea to the north of Ireland. An Irish Henry Wallace was married to the daughter of a Cromwell captain. And 'Mad Billy' Wallace married a landed woman whose place was confiscated because she was a Presbyterian. So deeply was 'Mad Billy' moved by the religious persecution of his wife that he left the Episcopal Church and put his own holdings to hazard by becoming a Presbyterian.

* All notes and references are grouped at the back of the book, following p. 584.

In 1835 when John Wallace took a wife, he married into two of the oldest established families around Finleyville. His wife's father was a Ross and her mother was a Finley. Her name was Martha Ross. It would hardly have been possible to make a union more closely and purely Scotch-Irish, and both John and Martha were strict United Presbyterians.

The Rosses and the Finleys had come not only from the same part of Ireland but more anciently from the same part of Scotland as John Wallace's people. He had known many members of both their families in County Antrim and the neighboring counties there. But the Finleys and Rosses were of a more adventurous temper, for the first of them had come to America the better part of a century before this more cautious or deliberate Wallace made the passage. He came of a relatively conservative and rooted family. Even then in the eighteen-twenties when hard times in Ireland had turned more cruelly hard, Henry Wallace of Kilrea, Ireland, struggling on his farm against conditions that were approaching famine, opposed John's going to the States. Young John himself went through sad and anxious calculation and spiritual wrestling before, in his eighteenth. year, he broke home ties and crossed the sea.

2. Gentlemen of the Midland

As SCOTCHMEN, as Irishmen, and, in the century since, as Americans, this family of Wallaces appears to have been moved characteristically not as first-wave frontiersmen but as second-wave builders and pioneers. Their decisions to move from place to place, or from idea to idea, have been on the whole not impulsive, not notably exuberant, but soberly and reasonably conservative, calculated, planned. The leading American descendants of John Wallace have followed along, as he did, on cleared ground, trying to make something better of hasty pioneer wreckage, commercial involvements, and patriarchal concepts which are comforting but which fail in the course of time to square with facts.

The Finleys were more nearly openers of new country, surgers, scrappers. Michael Finley, born in 1683, left County Armagh, Ireland, in 1734 and came with his wife and seven sons to the New World. Another of the family, John Finley, left County Armagh shortly afterwards, attempted to settle in Westmoreland County, Pennsylvania, and was killed by the Indians in nearby Cumberland County in 1758. Another John Finley, of the seed of Michael, is said to have piloted Boone to the meadowlands of Kentucky in 1769, and to have pushed on from there later beyond the Missouri to the present site of Denver and the Far West.

Randall Ross, who came from County Derry, married Martha Finley of Finleyville in 1793. Martha Ross was the sixth child of their ten. She was twenty-four years old to her husband's thirty when she and John Wallace were married in May of 1835. Randall Ross was by this time very old, getting on to ninety. Most of the younger Rosses and Finleys had departed for newer farmland or older towns. Thus a tract of some one hundred and fifty acres with thirteen corners, roughly conforming to the original lines of claim for 'Finley's Fancy,' came under the care of John Wallace and his wife; and this farm of moderate size became the seedbed of an American family as remarkable in its own way and manner as the urbane Adamses of Massachusetts were.

Before this country around Pittsburgh was fenced, cows wandering in the woods and thickets made trails to the springs. Cows, like buffalo, have a natural sense for following contours and walk as a rule on the level around the hills. John Wallace built his first home in America and then his second at the same site along a cowpath, now a road, near a never-failing spring. The spring broke out of the ground near the head of a hill. He named his place 'Spring Mount.'

Their first home at Spring Mount was a log house, large for the time and place; it measured thirty by thirty-two feet. The barn John Wallace built of native oak and maple in 1839 was thirty by seventy feet. Later he built a brick house on a stone foundation; but his first-born child, Henry, was born in the log house, on March 19, 1836.

John Wallace was an exceptionally good farmer and his wife was a great help to him. They did well, but their later lives were shadowed by the early death, one upon another, of eight of their children. They had nine children, and all save one died of consumption or closely related maladies before the age of thirty. However, their eldest son, Henry, did not die until nearly the end of his eightieth year. An ordained minister, he served as a chaplain in the War Between the States. A combination of soul trouble and lung trouble sent him West to shake it off. He stayed West, and became a really great man in Iowa. He founded *Wallaces' Farmer*, which still lives. Many say that he could have been Secretary of Agriculture, that he was proffered the post. But 'Uncle Henry,' as they called him first in Iowa and later throughout the country, declined to seek the secretariat and urged the appointment of an eminent compatriot, 'Tama Jim' Wilson, of Tama County, Iowa, who served as Secretary for sixteen years. During Theodore Roosevelt's administration this Henry Wallace served on the Country Life Commission with men of such stature as Liberty Hyde Bailey, Gifford Pinchot, and Walter Hines Page. He died in 1916.

A son, Henry Cantwell Wallace, was Secretary of Agriculture under Presidents Harding and Coolidge, until he died in 1924. His first-born, Henry Agard Wallace, having served as Secretary of Agriculture in the first two administrations of President Franklin D. Roosevelt, became Vice-President during Mr. Roosevelt's third term and Secretary of Commerce in Harry Truman's administration.

The three Henry Wallaces who will be the principal characters in this narrative stand, then, in the closely linked succession of grandsire, first-born son, and first-born grandson. The work and character of any one of them is such as invites the more formal biographer to consider him separately as a product of his own years, apart. But the lives of these three men exhibit an extraordinary sense of genetic continuance of which they were, or are, conscious and proud. They did not grow up separately or work separately. They grew close together and grew fast once their clan, transplanted from Pennsylvania, took root in Iowa. I intend to write of them together as a continuing growth through a century of amazing change.

Time was, in this country, when the pursuit of agriculture and attainment to a statesmanlike eminence proved a common working combination. The tradition still demands obeisance from time to time. Who does not recall those marvelous campaign photographs of Calvin Coolidge in a stiff white collar sheepishly pretending to pitch hay? And the Maryland Tidewater country where I live still inclines to elect as governors and senators landlords who may be photographed gazing over their own fences at their own herds or groves. It is a pleasant and harmless impersonation. They are really lawyers or financiers, not farmers or agriculturists, in the main. With the Wallaces agriculture has always come first; and it is primarily as men of the earth that they have served unofficially and officially in the councils of twelve administrations.

It tells very little that is essential to tag them, as newspapers have for the past few decades, with that demeaning phrase: *dirt-farmer.* The fact that John Wallace, the American founder of the line, was sometimes called 'The Squire' by his pioneer neighbors in upland Pennsylvania comes closer to the point. 'My father had no lack of means,' said the first Henry Wallace, writing of John, his father, proudly. This first Henry, with his passion for improved strains of clover and livestock, his wide array of husbandlike learning, his determination to dignify agriculture as an art, a science, and a way of living, would have made a splendid companion for George Washington had their days on earth coincided. The General would have classed this bearded giant from the middle country as 'gentry' — and superior gentry — at a glance. The second Henry in his turn would have been far happier in one of the earlier cabinets than he was in the cabinets of Harding and Coolidge, and the present head of the family, Henry Agard Wallace, is of a mind and character that will delight Thomas Jefferson in heaven. They have much in common.

'Country gentleman' is another set phrase or stereotype that comes to mind when you consider the Wallaces. They are more than that. They are democratic Midland aristocrats of a new sort. I say this with no thought of draping upon their rugged frames a mantle of pretension that in our oldest states has faded and worn thin. The Wallaces have made their main growth in a newer part of our country, in Iowa, where people are called

'folks,' where the word 'gentry,' if ever heard, arouses a snicker
and where the clothing of males is seldom designed to give a
tweedy, country club effect. But they are unquestionably
gentlefolk, scholars, and public characters of distinction. It is
extremely misleading to regard them, however shyly or ardently
they insist upon it, as only common men.

They burn for fellowship with ordinary folk and for a common
advance, but they do not really think that they themselves are
ordinary. They know that they are most extraordinary. They
have known it all their lives. The innate superiority of this particular strain of Wallaces, and the consequent responsibilities, is
a fact that has been dinned into the minds of their young and
especially of the first-born males from birth. They bear their
pride with a genuine humility, but they are proud. They are
possessed of a sense of family destiny that drives them hard.
Their preoccupation with questions of descent and mating, while
differing somewhat in detail from that of the leading families of
York State, Virginia, Maryland, and Massachusetts, is intense
and constant. The present leading Henry Wallace, a trained
geneticist, can tell you not only the full name and life span of
remote great-aunts or great-uncles, but also how good their teeth
were, when in the course of their lives their hair turned gray or
fell out, whether they liked to read, and whether they could carry
a tune; not to mention their major illnesses, what they died of,
or, worse, the cause of a premature decline into dotage.

Stout hearts, good wind, and sound bones mean more to the
men of this family than they do to genealogists in general. They
have increased as a family remarkably (as livestock men would
say) 'true to type.' Even in his childhood the first American
Henry Wallace, like his father, John, before him, had a keen eye
for livestock. Both he and his father respected the soil that grew
corn and wheat and fruit in season; and they treated their land
well and reverently, both of them; but both were possessed of the
stockman's feeling that grain and the like are bloodless crops,
mere intermediate products. They loved to breed and grow
blooded stock; and they were not above expressing slyly that
instinctive sense of superiority which seems to distinguish pure-
bred livestock breeders of all degrees.

When the first Henry Wallace had grown quite old, past seventy, it was one of his delights to sit in the study of his Des Moines home late of nights talking about livestock and related matters with his son, Daniel A. Wallace, a great livestock man himself. One evening, Dan Wallace remembers,[2] he and his father fell to discussing the effects of different kinds of livestock on the men who tend them.

First, Dan, we have the horse people, the studhorse men. They're fine fellows and rich livers but not much use in church affairs. You know! fine gold watch chains, horseshoe jewelry and a weakness for the bottle sometimes. But generous; nothing mean about them. They'll give you their last dollar. I like them.

Now beef cattle men are a little more substantial. Pretty good livers, pretty fair at their church duties; usually directors of banks and boards. Good-hearted but careful fellows; on the whole a very good class of fellows, Dan. And hog men run about the same as beef cattle men; only sometimes they're a little more careless in their personal habits, and, well, sort of *waxy*, Dan.

There's the dairyman. He's awful conscientious. Kind of a slave to those cows. They have to work hard to get their money, pulling tits. They get their money hard and spend it hard. Good church workers; awful conscientious. But not just the fellows you'd want to take along on a fishing trip.

Yes, it's curious how they differ, these fellows that grow livestock. But they're a fine class of farmers. I like them all.

And, Dan, if ever you find yourself among a crowd of fellows with no chins and no bellies, then you'll know you're at a horticultural convention. But they're *very* spiritual!

And he roared with laughter.

If your father weren't such a *good* man, Mrs. Wallace used to tell the children, he would have been an awfully bad man.

Those of the Wallace family who have worked through the years to compile and bring up to date the intricacies of the family

'Stud Book' — so old Uncle Henry used to mock with hidden
pride his wife's absorption in the nobler aspects of genealogy —
remark that it is far in excess of the law of averages, how, once
the family hit on the idea of naming the first-born of the main
line Henry — how often the first-born was a boy. Since 1836,
on this side of the water, this has happened nearly every time.
A sort of alternating current as to verbosity is also to be noted.
John Wallace of Finleyville was a man of very few words. He
never wrote a line for publication or made a speech. Not so
Uncle Henry, his son. Uncle Henry's son, Henry C. (generally
called Harry), reverted to reticence, as far as he decently could
as a public man. And the son of Henry C., Henry A., while
extremely sparing in the small talk of social conversation, spills
out through public channels like his grandsire all over again.

Uncle Henry's published words, including especially his periodical utterances, first in county papers and then in his own paper,
run into the millions. He was a highly articulate and rather
opinionated man.

Kinsmen and friends who have known Henry Agard Wallace
all his life say that you cannot begin to understand him until
you know something about his family, and more particularly
about 'Uncle Henry,' his patriarchal grandfather. They say that
many of 'H. A.'s' qualities skipped a generation; that he is, to
a degree almost uncanny, 'his grandfather's boy.' There would
seem, indeed, to be an unusual likeness of views, gifts, and dreams
between the first American Henry Wallace of this line and the
third. The second of the line, Henry Cantwell Wallace — the
one who died as Secretary of Agriculture during the Coolidge
administration — was possessed of the same views and visions,
but he maintained the appearance of a more stolid, more immediately practical man. He was an excellent business man and
perhaps a better executive, in the strict or immediate sense, than
either his father or his son. He was certainly also a better politician than either one of them.

'Harry' Wallace, or 'H. C.,' as they called him to untangle
the confusion attending three Henry Wallaces working together
on the same farm paper, was a stouthearted, redheaded man. As
a publisher he could spot a bad credit risk at sight; or, later, a

slippery political customer; or any man, however sincere, un-
alterably formed by nature to oppose to the hilt the ideas that
he, Wallace, and his clan championed. Harry Wallace could be
counted on to fight all such villains at the drop of the hat. He
was a quicker, more natural hater than either his father or his
son. In his zeal to preserve and advance what rival publishers
came to call the 'Wallace dynasty' in Iowa he was adamant.
His early middle years were largely given over to repairing the
family's advancing fortunes as publishers, which had suffered a
sharp setback. It pleased Harry Wallace and his father deeply
when, before his father's death in 1916, they would hear the paper
sometimes described in trade circles as 'Wallaces' Gold Mine.'

In his private and public career Harry Wallace preferred to
work in the background. Much that he did as Secretary of
Agriculture was credited to bureau chiefs and subordinates at his
insistence. The gift of words with the beat of wings to lift them
appears in him to have skipped a generation; yet in the enuncia-
tion and execution of a continuing agricultural policy he was
tenacious and plain. As Secretary of Agriculture he fought hard
against a commercial and political fumbling back toward 'normalcy.' This trend dominated the years of his maturity and cut
him down.

Almost the first public act of 'Young Henry,' as they still
called him in Iowa when in 1933 he came in his turn to Washington as Secretary of Agriculture, was to ask that the officially
painted portrait of his father be withdrawn from the sequestered
gallery of such portraits in the Department of Agriculture. He
had them hang it on the wall directly before his desk. In 1940
when he became Vice-President he asked if he could take his
father's portrait along with him. Again, as Secretary of Commerce, he still had that picture on the wall above his desk. This
son, who was born more like his grandfather, must be understood, I think, as seeking to be more like his contentious, pragmatic father and yet to maintain the light of a ripened understanding in a world that has fallen upon evil days.

Not only 'grandfatherism,' as geneticists call it, has molded
the mental and spiritual resemblance between 'Young Henry'
and 'Uncle Henry.' The chances of environment, a rare compan-

ionship between the very young and the very old, also played a part. 'Grandfather and I were very close,' the Vice-President told interviewers for *Fortune* when they undertook to analyze him in 1942,[3] 'much closer than my father and I were.' His father, he added, was hard-pressed with practical affairs. His grandfather had more time. When young Henry went to work on the family paper he was twenty-two. His grandfather was seventy-four. 'Our office was about a mile from his home. Grandfather used to have me walk up home with him at noon for lunch. Afterward I would read to him. I used to read a lot of *The Irish Homestead* . . ., George W. Russell's (AE's) paper. . . . Yes, I think you can say I got my interest in theology and philosophy and the classics from my Grandfather. He had a liberal mind. He liked to read books of philosophy and sociology and to the end of his life he was fond of new ideas, of changes. I remember he was interested in Bergson's *Creative Evolution* back in 1910. He was by no means what you would call an orthodox preacher. But he always held a firm belief in Jesus Christ as the supreme power for good in the world. He was constantly striving to find ways to apply Christian principles to changing conditions. He believed in change. He knew change was inevitable.'

The grandfather, like the grandson, was interested in nutrition or dietetics and experimented on his own person. His mental and emotional or religious life displayed a constant growth beyond confining dogma. He examined platforms and creeds, lay and religious, and spoke his mind regardless. Words just ran out of him. His manner of preaching, as those who heard him remember, was simply but deeply and naturally eloquent; commanding but reasonably humble; and nearly always self-controlled.

In the days of his ordained ministry, Uncle Henry went to church clad in the formal frock coat and trousers of the same cloth, a choker collar, and all that was then required for preachers of his creed. But he bore his stiff garb somewhat loosely and jauntily; and it delighted some deep sense of freedom in him to stride up to the church steps with a Pittsburgh stogie fuming in his face. He confronted stares of shock and disapproval. He would cast the stogie from his countenance, stomp it out, and then go in and preach to them.

He believed that solvency and salvation went together but he never worried about money as long as he had it. He had a strong pietistic streak but he had an eye on the ground, too. He never despaired, never at least for long; he could not by nature believe in ultimate evil for man. One reason that his son Harry found it well to assume management of *Wallaces' Farmer* and let his father simply write and edit was simply that Uncle Henry trusted everybody. Yet he was by birth and upbringing a man of practical faith and he did not expect too much of the mortal fruit of Adam in a hurry. Time mellowed the more ardent of his earlier pastoral or agrarian expectations but time never narrowed or embittered him. He started his farm paper as a supporter of McKinley-Hanna high-tariff Republicanism but changed his mind thoroughly and often before he died. He was less conservative in his seventies than he was when he was forty. He turned his back on Populism in its more excessive forms but he never claimed to know all the answers and he never doubted on the whole that ordinary people, given their heads, would somehow manage to work things out. He was amused by those whom the Scripture calls 'puffed up with pride,' and in the material realm he distrusted generalizations unbacked by research. He preferred if possible to try it personally and see for himself. 'The experimental attitude,' we call it now. Under all the rigidity of form, thought, and conduct which marked the respectable people of his era he did not often rebel; but he had a questioning mind.

Uncle Henry's Own Story or Personal Reminiscences [4] is the memoir of a stalwart Puritan with a quiet sense of devilment. When he started dictating these letters in the autumn of his seventy-fourth year, 1910, there were no great-grandchildren of his line. But 'I am morally certain that you will appear in due time,' he wrote, and 'you will make your appearance in a world so different from that in which I made my appearance, some seventy-five years ago, you will no doubt wonder how I managed to get through.' His letters ran on in the paper until 1919 and were republished by the Wallace Publishing Company in three successive paper-bound volumes in 1917, 1918, and 1919. For Volume I of the series his grandson, Henry A., who was then twenty-nine, wrote in his introductory note:

He lived a very full and eventful life during a most wonderful period of the world's history. Between his boyhood and old age a transformation had been wrought in the methods of living and in civilization itself. Means of transportation by land, sea and air had been wholly changed. The world had emerged from a period of hand labor to machine labor, with a revolution in the lives of working people. It was a period of invention, discovery, and wonderful progress in transportation and science, a period of world-wide evolution in agriculture. All of this he had seen; and in some of it had played a very important part.

3. Cloud of Progress

THE NICETIES of life had penetrated from the seaboard to the upland of Pennsylvania rather haltingly a hundred years or so ago. Starting together in their log house on Spring Mount in 1835, John and Martha Wallace's life would probably come under Thomas Jefferson's scholarly classification: 'semi-barbarous.'

Martha cooked their meals in pots on a crane over an open fire. The doors and windows were unscreened; flyspecked strips of paper festooned from the beams of the cabin were supposed to move with the draft that came through the chinks in the floor and walls and frighten the flies away, but they never did. Water for use in the house was lugged by the pail uphill from the spring. All possibility of infection from water, milk, meat, air, and wounds was barely suspected, for the existence of bacteria was unknown. Appendicitis, then known as inflammation of the bowels, killed a considerable number. A boil, brought to a head by poulticing, then slashed with a penknife, was commonly esteemed to be worth five dollars because it got the poison out of your system. Neurotic patients were described as 'steriky' and treated with scant compassion. Doctors traveled on horseback carrying their own drugs, lances, and 'pullicans,' for they were also dentists. Bleeding, blistering and, in extreme cases, cupping were favorite operations. The general rule for the sick was:

> Puke, purge, bleed, and sweat 'em,
> And if they die, why, let 'em.

To charm away warts you looked at the moon over your left shoulder, rubbed the wart with a piece of side-meat and intoned: 'As thou, moon, increasest, this wart decreases.' A bone from the right part of a hog's head carried in the pocket warded off toothache. If a cow fell sick and her horns were cold, that was a case of 'hollow horn,' complicated, perhaps, by 'wold in the tail.' The accepted cure, to catch the trouble at both ends, was to split both horn and tail and pack in red pepper.

Women in childbirth were more generally attended by neighbors than by doctors, and not much was made of the occurrence. The dead were not embalmed. Neighboring women washed the female dead and laid them out on a cooling-board, then dressed them for burial. Men tended dead males in like manner. It was considered only neighborly to dig a grave for a friend, and the graves were stark holes carved in naked earth, with none of the fake grass mats and lowering apparatus by which morticians have come to refine the passage of dust to dust.

People lived and died quite simply in highland Pennsylvania little more than a century ago. But that 'cloud of light,' bearing progress, was traveling faster westward all the time, and it was assuming shapes that Jefferson in another mood found unpromising. Between 1820 and 1840 the population increased from short of ten million to seventeen million, and the proportion of those engaged in agriculture fell from four fifths to three quarters. The eighteen-thirties brought turnover of mechanical inventions — the McCormick reaper, steel plows with detachable plowpoints, Peter Cooper's railroad steam engine. The tariff became a state's rights issue. Antagonism between the commercial and farming interests sharpened, with the farmers, increasingly dependent on factory tools, themselves becoming of necessity more commercially minded.

Hard roads had come through; graded railroads were being built. The waterways, choking with silt, were waning in importance. But there is still much talk of the river and its dying traffic in Henry Wallace's early boyhood. The Youghiogheny, which follows a tortuous course to join the Monongahela near Pittsburgh and so is linked by the Ohio and Mississippi to the Gulf of Mexico, was a hard river to navigate even then.

These hills had been the scene of the Whiskey Rebellion of

1794, a revolt primarily against an excise tax. A few unreconstructed veterans of that rebellion were still living in the community when Henry Wallace was a boy there; the strictest Presbyterians tended to justify a continuing flow of such traffic on
the ground that it was the economic way in which to get grain
out. The product, as Wallace's letters to his great-grandchildren
observe, is compact, bearing 'great value in small bulk.' Again,
'if the boat struck a snag and sank, the whiskey barrels could be
thrown out in the river and still float; whereas, even flour would
be damaged and wheat ruined.' Around West Newton in the
years of his youth, he added, 'Taking an occasional dram, or
even more than an occasional one, did not bar a man out of a
good and respectable society.' The current local price of rye
or corn whiskey was around twenty-five cents a gallon or sometimes as little as sixteen cents a gallon by the barrel; and it was
the general custom to take a jug of whiskey to the harvest field
along with what was called the 'piece' — a 'snack,' we would
call it now — served forenoon or afternoon. John Wallace came,
in the light of observed results throughout the neighborhood, to
disapprove of this. He never allowed a jug to be made available
in his home or fields after his boys were old enough to sit at the
table and go with the men to the fields to work; and he made a
number of character loans without interest to drinking farmer
neighbors who had let their farms and fortunes go downhill,
with the sole proviso that the man stop drinking. On at least one
occasion, it is recorded, John Wallace's cure worked wonders even
after the direst maledictions of preachers had failed.

Those people who knew John Wallace, and who saw how quietly
but completely he governed his farm and family, said he ruled
with his eyes. According to his son Henry's account, his eyes were
gray-green or a very peculiar blue.

> They sometimes beamed with kindness and love, which
> he was very loath to express; ... but when displeased, they
> bored into one as though they would bring to light every
> secret thought. Deeply religious, he said little about it.
> Very orthodox in belief, he was wonderfully tolerant in prac-
> tice. I never heard of him making a speech and I think he
> never wrote anything for publication; but he was a man of

commanding influence in the community. He became a sort of oracle in the neighborhood, and the neighbors came to him for advice and sometimes for the settlement of disputes and difficulties. He never volunteered advice unasked. He had a horror of debt. He sometimes speculated, but when he did he always bought whatever he was dealing in, and paid for it, so it was really more investing than speculating. Taking into account the circumstances and conditions, I think I never knew a better farmer. He bought a farm of which the cleared part was badly run down, and which needed drainage. He redeemed it by the use of lime and clover and feeding livestock. I think he was the first man west of the Allegheny Mountains to use tile, and was usually the first man in the neighborhood to buy any improved machinery. He bought the first grain drill, the first combined mower and reaper, and was one of the first to buy a horse rake and improved plows.

In addition to the vertebral injury that came from a fall at wrestling in Ireland, John Wallace had suffered an early sunstroke while working there in his father's hayfield and his health was never robust. He stood just short of six feet tall, and weighed around a hundred and seventy-five pounds at maturity; but his complexion was brownish-dark, never very healthy-looking; he suffered from recurrent headaches; and he had to use his head to save his back.

The granary of America had passed from Pennsylvania west. Most of the farms around West Newton were slow to adjust to a more pastoral or feeding economy, seeking instead on now narrow and depleted holdings to compete with the wide, fresh grainfields of the West. John Wallace was an active advocate of grass and livestock. He kept a flock of a hundred sheep — a number beyond all precedent there around West Newton — on his hundred-and-fifty-acre farm. Whenever his opinion was asked, he talked sheep. Sheep would clean up the brushy pastures, he showed; they were easy to keep; hardy feeders, pawing the snow off the bluegrass and getting part of their own living browsing even in the dead of winter. Less moved, no doubt, by Wallace's words than by his example, his neighbors began to increase their flocks.

To the first white New World migrants the country around

Pittsburgh must have seemed such a land as Moses promised the
Children of Israel: [5] '. . . a good land, a land of brooks of water,
of fountains and depths that spring out of valleys and hills . . .
wherein thou shalt eat bread without scarceness, thou shalt not
lack anything. . . .'

But there were natural limitations soon to appear. Many of
these farms were too steep to be plowed safely; the soil washed
away. Coal which is made to be burned, rather than limestone
which helps put strength into soil and people, predominated as
the natural deposit. And the bottoms, densely underlain with
soft coal, the remains of an immense vegetative growth for
thousands of centuries dead and crystallized, were swampy.
Life in the country around Pittsburgh was taking a form not
encouraging to good farming, even a hundred years ago, when
Henry Wallace was a boy. He recalls in his memoirs a vista that
carried a note of premonition: 'A scene I shall never forget. From
the top of Miller's Hill I looked north to Barren Run Range —
not mountains but a ridge of hills of poor soil, thrown up after
the great beds of coal, with which this section was covered —
were laid down, throwing out the coal.'

A sorry spot on the face of the earth today, Barren Run Ridge
is barren indeed. A hundred years in the life of a body of land
is as nothing — merely a clock-tick in the geological span; but
we are a vigorous people, we Americans; we have machines; and
if we take a notion to deaden or deface a landscape in the name
of progress, we can work fast. The profile of these once lovely
hills and small, sharp mountains around Pittsburgh have changed
only a little, of course, in the century since young Henry Wallace
was a boy here; but much of the life has been worked out of the
land; it looks half-dead. Mining and industry have transformed
the earth here, and have pitted, weakened, and poisoned it.

Not far from West Newton now, the new arterial auto highway
between Pittsburgh and Harrisburg strikes with deep cuts and
slow coils through these hills, with smooth and sleekly graded
multiple lanes. It is an express highway and so new that most
of the sharp banks on each side are as yet entirely bare of vegetation, raw and naked. In the deeper cuts the traveler sees black
seams in the roadbanks, seams that have been at once the life

and bane of this western Pennsylvania highland country — coal. When the road breaks out of the cuts and lets you see the country, you see still some middling-good bottom land of sound Westmoreland clay loam, but for miles on end the remaining topsoil or subsoil is of a villainous, slaty mixture with the curious habit of throwing out wet-weather springs of water high up the hills and mountainsides, toward the crests. Where this happens considerable patches of soil are likely to have washed away entirely, making 'scalds' or little 'balds' like scabby spots on the head of a man bedeviled with mange. The topsoil of the farms has been thinned by excessive plowing and washing to about half its former depth and richness. The farms here have been beaten about half-dead, and the farmsteads show it.

The coal blight has reached only indirectly the stringy farming settlement that is still called Finleyville. But Finleyville has not grown. A few roadside cottages in indifferent repair, a store that is mainly a wayside stand, dispensing soft drinks, candy-bars, and gas amid the blare of a radio — that is about all there is to Finleyville today. But the amiable proprietor of this small store knows about the Finleys and about everyone, past and present, who is related to the Finleys; and he is glad to direct an increasing if not excessive number of persons who stop and ask the way to the old Wallace place.

The place is still called Spring Mount, but it is more generally known in the locality as the Painter place today. Thurman Painter, a retired schoolmaster, bought the place from his uncle, John Fullerton, who had bought it from John Pore, who had bought it from the Wallaces when John, the father, decided to follow his first-born, Henry, to the fresher fields of Iowa in 1867.

The house the Wallaces built stands about a mile behind the store, beyond fields and swamps and occasional clumps of surviving timber, just back from the road on a small eminence, folded into the arms of three converging hills. The house is of brick on a stone foundation. The Wallaces built it on almost exactly the same site as the clay-chinked log cabin that they reared here first. This second and somewhat more spacious mansion dates from 1848, the year young Henry turned thirteen years of age and the railroad came.

They razed the old log house and used the stones of its great chimney to make the foundation for their new home. They burned their own bricks in their own kiln and built this house inside and out from materials there on the farm. They did most of the work themselves. It is a fourteen-room house and the estimated out-of-pocket cost was only six hundred dollars at the time. They built it to last and it has stood up well for nearly a century in a part of the country where agriculture has been visibly overshadowed and undermined.

The Thurman Painters who live here now like the place. Like the Wallaces who farmed here before them, they are related to the Finleys. They are glad to show visitors through the house: the strictly square rooms which John Wallace planned so that square rugs could be turned around at each spring and fall housecleaning, and made to last longer; the large cellar in which he made no effort to reduce dampness because the wool he stored there absorbed a certain amount of moisture and weighed that much more when it came up for sale.

The industrial shroud of soft-coal smoke which so often dims the sun now in the valleys of the Allegheny, the Monongahela, and the Youghiogheny occasionally reaches Spring Mount and makes cleanly housekeeping difficult but does not seem to harm vegetation.

Some of the trees in the original orchard the Finleys planted still stand and yield a little. Yard trees the Wallaces planted or tended have increased in branch and foliage overhead. Myrtle the Wallaces planted on this terraced small front yard when they built here has spread to cover the yard almost completely now. The Painters live simply and farm very lightly the remaining hundred and fifty acres or so of Spring Mount. The place is moderately productive, but probably it would be impossible to make a full living on it now.

The industrial transformation and the decay of farming on the inner slopes of Pennsylvania had definitely started in Henry Wallace's boyhood. Later he recognized that; and once he got farther inland and saw unspoiled country, he induced all the living members of his family to remove West. But there was always a sort of radiance surrounding his memories of early boyhood in western Pennsylvania before the earth there became so scorched and pitted and the sky shrouded with smoke. Those days as he recalled them seemed the morning of the world.

I I

SEMINARY VEAL

My Dear Great-Grandchildren:
You are enjoying luxuries which kings and queens, with all their wealth and power, could not possibly have secured two hundred years ago. But I wish you to realize that with all their disadvantages, people were just about as happy in those early days as you are now or ever will be; that neither education nor wealth nor comforts nor conveniences can change to any great extent the fundamental problems of existence; that nothing blesses but right living, which may be summed up in faith in the Supreme Being, and following our Saviour's rule with regard to our fellowmen: 'Thou shalt love thy neighbor as thyself.' (You may think I am sermonizing. So I am; I rather like it.) — HENRY WALLACE, starting *Uncle Henry's Own Story*, 1910.

1. A Lad of Spirit

HENRY'S GRANDFATHER and Grandmother Ross lived in a big stone house with a big stone barn within an eighth of a mile of the Wallace home on Spring Mount. Grandmother Ross's father had been Andrew Finley, who came over the mountains with his brother Joseph in 1795.

Henry Wallace's most vivid memories of his Pennsylvania childhood were memories of food. He dearly loved to eat. All his life he swerved between the sort of innocent gluttony one encounters among Puritans, and associates with thresher-trenchermen and Thanksgiving feasting, and an extreme aestheticism, combined perhaps with stomach trouble, which reduced him at times to such sparing diets as toast and tea alone. As an old man he remembered happily the days when his stomach was new

and insatiable, back there at Spring Mount: 'My! how thick
that cream was, almost like pancakes. We had milk such as you
do not get from the creamery, and cream that was cream — cream
that made the coffee taste just right. ... Then we had ham and
breakfast bacon; spare ribs and sausage, home made, seasoned
according to mother's taste, with garden herbs picked green and
carefully dried, for she always saw to that. We had first-class
bread, baked in the out-oven. ...'

From the orchard set out sixty years before by the Finleys, the
Wallaces had summer and winter apples, some sweet, some so sour
they were called vinegar apples, especially useful for making cider.
Windfallen apples of all sorts were made into apple butter. 'It
kept all winter, and we could have all we wanted.' The Wallaces
did not know anything about canning fruit, but they did put up
jellies — 'half a dozen different kinds — served always with
good, thick cream.'

Then there were wild fruits, blackberries, mulberries, dewberries. 'We did not buy them by the quart as you do now, in boxes
that do not hold a quart, but just took a bucket and went out
and gathered — I have not tasted since boyhood such dewberries
as grew wild in that section, especially on the thinner soils. They
were luscious fellows, few on a bush, and happy was the boy
who found them. ... They just melted in the mouth. O, my!'

Young Wallace learned to milk and to do light work around the
place, such as carrying the 'snack' to hands afield, almost as soon
as he could walk. Like most farm boys from time immemorial,
he learned to talk dirty almost as soon as he learned to talk. His
mother exerted a constant influence in gentling this impetuous
colt to the harness of morals, manners, and bearing. The only
time she ever whipped Henry was for using an obscene word that
he had heard from a hired man. Generally it was simply, 'I'll
speak to your father.' John Wallace never whipped his children.
He used those eyes of his. Directing a piercing gaze upon them
he would tap their ears with the tips of his fingers and utter a
few words of reproof.

At church, as a presiding elder, John Wallace sat in one of the
front pews. He took the liberal view, on the whole, on points of
rigorous dissension. 'He never objected to repeating tunes.

He used to laugh a great deal about a very strict United Presbyterian who left the church furiously angry at this innovation of giving out two lines at a time. "You have done what the devil and all his angels could not do: You have stopped my mouth from singing God's praises!" this man explained. My father was deeply religious, but said little about it. He kept up family worship quite regularly, but I never heard of his praying in public, nor did I ever hear of his making a speech. His prayers at family worship were exceedingly uniform in phraseology. I knew most of them by heart when I was a boy; but when my little sister was at the point of death he introduced two or three new sentences, and when he arose from his knees he was weeping. I think this was the only time I ever saw him in tears.'

Even before their first son was born John and Martha Wallace had their hearts set upon it that he grow to be a minister of the United Presbyterian Church. Remarkably early in life the child began to talk; and his mother always claimed that he had learned his letters by the end of his third year. These were accounted signs of promise for the ministry; but the lad had the devil in him, too. He had a quick and furious temper. He came by it honestly from both sides of the house. It is something of a quandary among many of the Wallaces even today to determine whether an outburst of righteous wrath is righteous, or simply wrath. When this boy Henry felt that fare at the family table was not up to his standard or lacking in variety, he would stand at his place at the table, livid, and declare his feelings about mush or sowbelly or whatever the offending dish might be. His father developed a neat way of breaking up Henry's unmannerly ructions at mealtime. Without saying a word he would throw glass after glass of cold water into Henry's face. 'This enabled me to get hold of myself and do some serious thinking,' the boy wrote when he was a man full grown and had come in his turn to the task of admonishing the young.

To her children at home Martha Wallace was a buoyant and fond companion. 'Henry,' she would say, 'we'll have to make a lawyer of you; you've such a knack for talking your way out of things.' Or, again, when given to do the job of sodding over a bare place in the yard her first-born displayed more speed than care, 'Henry,' his mother told him, 'that old sow there, snouting out grubworms, can do a better job of sodding than this.' Her eyes, like those of her husband, are described by those who knew them sometimes as blue, again as gray. In temperament it was as if she were more Irish than Scotch, and her husband more Scotch than Irish. 'Their married life,' as their son remembers it, 'was of the happiest. I never remember my father saying an unkind word to her or of her saying an unkind word to him. She had a most profound respect for him, but knew how to manage him without his ever knowing or suspecting it, and usually had her own way. If she feared the influence of any hired man, that man had to go.'

Filling with soil that was washing from the overplowed hilly farmland, the Youghiogheny River was becoming constantly less navigable and less fit to fish in and catch something. The river was dying. But the pike — the National Road — was lively.

A hard road, remarkably well graded for the time but bumpy, it looped down a long, steep hill from the east to cross the bridged Youghiogheny at West Newton, then climbed to the west over a series of sharp rises, visible for miles. The traffic was vigorous and various. To a boy, the Concord coaches were wonderful, for the four-horse teams that drew them were of the lighter sort of Conestoga horses that really could make time and did, no matter how rough the going or how steep. These teams brought the coaches bouncing at a gallop down the east hill, with the drivers blowing their horns. A tavern by the bridge at West Newton was where they changed teams. There coachsick ladies were given basins and tea by the kind old hostess, Mother Yowry; and the gentlemen repaired to the bar. All this, of course, was for the son of a 'strict' family of the locality to be viewed only from without; but, 'If you were right close' to the whirl of the passing coach, or the comfort stop of the coach at a tavern, 'you might see Henry Clay for he often traveled this road from Washington to Kentucky . . . or the Governor of Ohio or Indiana. Or merchants from states farther west, going home after buying goods. . . . If there were any women in that coach, they would excite your compassion; . . . too sick to eat anything.'

Less dashing than the passenger trade, but spirited, were the freighters of the highway, the Conestoga wagons, hauling dry-goods and similar stores. These wagons were stoutly made of hickory. They were 'large, broad-tired, hoop-covered wagons, the cover rising at both ends much after the fashion of the old-style poke-bonnets women wore to church when I was young.'

And there were always the drovers and cattlemen and sheep-herders driving tough, rangy stuff to the Eastern market with whoops and yells. 'During the summer season one was scarcely out of sight of these great droves. There was no baby beef; for the steer could not travel over the mountains unless he had length of limb. Hogs were bred not exactly for speed, but for ability to walk to market. The hogs were large, rangy, and at a year and a half old would develop into about three hundred pounds in weight. The brood sows were terrors, and woe to the boy who interfered with their little pigs! In order to avoid toll, for there was a toll-gate every two or three miles, the drovers sometimes left the pike west of West Newton, crossed over Budd's ferry, and came past our schoolhouse, catching the pike again farther on. It was a great day at our schoolhouse when we heard the bawling of cattle or the squealing of pigs or the bleating of sheep.'

When Henry was thirteen, the first railroad was built through this part of the country. He loved the trains: 'I knew the whistle of every B & O engine on that road. There were five of them.'

The tavern keepers and men who had pastures on the roadside to let were in despair. Henry noted the change in the livestock with the passage of time: 'The railroad has shortened the hogs' noses, shortened the legs, done away with the bristles, and put a more lovely kink in the tail, as well as changed the color from a mixed black and white to white or black, or red. ... And now, instead of cattle of indeterminate breed, Shorthorns were being introduced in our neighborhood.'

The principal diversions of his boyhood were husking bees, coon hunts, singing schools, fishing with 'swabs' in the river, and 'sugaring-off' parties in February; then he adds: 'In spite of these things, as I look back over those days, I realize that the amount of recreation and amusement was pitifully small.' Yet

life was not altogether without amusement there around Spring
Mount. There were birds to stone, boys to fight, and minor
neighborhood sagas in the making. Young Henry seems to have
led a normal boyhood in most particulars. He was, as the first-
born, probably rather spoiled; and his displays of spirit, as they
first called it, grew more trying as the family increased. To any
task assigned him the boy applied himself with ardor; but when
weights to be lifted tugged stolidly at his shoulders, when cows
to be milked swished his face with stinging tails, when sows to
be penned escaped into the garden, contentedly grunting as if
to say, 'Didn't we come it over buddy?' — then buddy blew up.
This (apart from overeating, which was accounted no sin at that
time and place) was the one form of intemperance to which he
was ever given; and it took him years to overcome it. 'Sinful
anger,' he wrote later, 'is always a sign of weakness. It is a sign
of immaturity — vealiness, if you wish to call it by its right name.'[1]

Vealy, in the vernacular of the time, bore a meaning not wholly
different from the current slang word, *corny*, which means in
general unsophisticated, crude, naïve or fake-naïve. But *vealy*
means, above all, immature. It was like *calf love* carried over into
general behavior. When a divinity student sent out for rural
practice training had preached, and the elders had paused on
the way to the carriages to appraise the sermon, they would say,
'Not bad, for seminary veal,' and then fall to talking of earthy
matters.

Of the vealy temper of his adolescence and young manhood,
Henry Wallace remained, like topers who reform, reminiscently
fond. Especially in his *Letters to a Farm Boy*, published in 1900,
he tells how he channeled his rages: 'It is all nonsense to say that
a boy cannot control his temper. Controlled temper, on the other
hand, has its uses. I endured torture from the bully of the
school because it was known that John Wallace would not allow his
boys to fight at school. I broke the rule once, and I had peace
afterward. If my father ever learned of it, he said nothing to me.
I hope the recording angel conveniently forgets to report the boy
who knocks down the bully who, by brute force, terrorizes weaker
boys. If I had the reporting to do, I would look the other way, and
if I happened to see it, would report a credit mark instead.'

2. School

THIS CHILD Henry was sent soon after his infancy to the same one-room log schoolhouse at a corner of the Wallace and Ross properties that his mother had attended before him, as a Ross. Whether, as she claimed, he already knew his letters, having learned them from glances 'upside down' at books read aloud to him at his mother's knee, he later doubted. She 'tried to make me out a good deal smarter than I really was, a common failing among mothers,' he said, but added that he had been started off to school so young that he could not remember for certain how old he was. He must have been young indeed, for they carried him to school at first on horseback; and the schoolhouse was barely half a mile away. If, as seems most likely, he entered school in the autumn of 1839, he was almost exactly three and a half years old at the time.

Into the one-room school shack at Finleyville forty to fifty children were jammed. Attendance was larger and more regular in winter than in open weather, but the space was always crowded, for its floor measured a bare twenty by thirty feet. In winter, when the center space was taken up with a great cast-iron stove flaring red, then abruptly cooling, the population pressure on that small space exceeded that of most city slums or sweatshops; ventilation was all but completely lacking; and the homely winter stench of old-time country children, the cow-flesh and manure odor which outdates bathrooms and deodorants, was high.

No one minded that; they were used to living with earthy smells, in barns and in close-shut homes, especially in wintertime. In age the scholars ranged from three to the early twenties. The smallest sat on rough-hewn benches arranged in a square closest to the stove. They were given no books at first, only paddles of pine wood about six inches wide, whittled down at one end to a handle. As homework these children were told to cut the letters of the alphabet — first capitals, then small letters — out of newspapers, to paste them on the paddles in alphabetical order, and later to make words. The parents were asked to help them in this homework.

The teachers were invariably men. Later in the community's

history when a woman teacher was employed for the first time, nearly all the males over fourteen quit school, walked out. They were not going to be bossed by a woman, they explained. This was after Henry's time as a scholar there. The teachers he remembered all were men, and most of them were harsh men with the eye of a drill sergeant and an arm ever ready to reach for that bunch of switches — preferably birch — that hung behind the teacher's platform on the wall.

'Professor' Billy Clemons drank hard in school and out. He had lost an eye; only it really was not lost; it was hidden, his scholars said, in the short hair at the back of his head. He was a small man, but a born policeman in the baser sense of the word; and he taught with a hurt, driving determination that all expression of individuality in that school should be his alone. He was mean enough when he had a hangover, but it was when he showed up drunk that he took most pleasure in humiliating the most intelligent of his charges. 'It was my ambition,' Henry Wallace wrote, reviewing his schooldays, 'to stand at the head of the spelling class, and I trembled when I saw him coming down the lane with his drunken swagger, for I knew I was destined to go to the foot that day. But what hurt me most was the way he would leer at me with his one eye and say: "Henry, you are a pretty smart boy, but you know it!" Inasmuch as most of the parents took an occasional nip at the "O be joyful," they tolerated old Billy, notwithstanding his failing, because of his real ability as a teacher; and he taught our school for a number of years.'

But Billy 'took too much tea,' as the boys said, at the approach of a Christmas season and refused to honor a custom then current in the locality, known as a Christmas treat. A committee of the larger boys presented him in due order their written demand for a number of bushels of apples, gallons of cider, pounds of candy, lest there be a 'barring-out' of his person from the school building on the last day before the holidays. Billy brought no offering and, finding the door locked, entered by way of the attic, dropping in on his scholars by way of a trapdoor in the ceiling. With whoops of joy they wished him the season's greetings and threw him out. That was the finish of 'Professor' Billy Clemons in those parts.

His successor, Harrison Markle, or 'Miracle,' as they called him, committed some offense against the person or dignity of young Henry Wallace which Wallace does not specify in his memoirs, remarking simply that he withdrew from school sometime in the 'reign of Miracle' and did not return until a successor, who was 'a man of good education,' took over. 'Miracle . . . had the funniest way of punishing both boys and girls that I ever heard of. One of his favorite methods with a boy was to make him run around the stove on all fours, and as he passed him each time, he applied the paddle. Another was to have four boys ride the offender on a rail. His way of punishing girls was likewise ingenious. He had auger holes of different sizes bored in the logs and when a girl committed a misdemeanor, he made her put her nose in an auger hole, the holes being adjusted to the height of the girls. He did not teach us very long, but he left a marked impression on our minds.'

The school's equipment was as primitive as its clay-chinked log walls. The pens were goose quills and it was years before the scholars were given a blackboard instead of slates. The texts were likewise primitive but not all of them lacked value. Henry studied Webster's Spelling Book, Ray's Arithmetic, Kirkham's Grammar; also the Western Calculator and the English Readers. Of the Grammar and the Calculator he held a low opinion, but the leading Readers, in three volumes, leading from simple beginnings to such strong meat as parts of Locke on *Human Understanding*, took a grip on his mind.

When Henry first started here to school almost all of the children were of Scotch-Irish families, and the Shorter Catechism of the Presbyterians, appended as a pious afterthought in the back of the *New England Primer*, was the regular subject of study and recitation every Saturday afternoon. But already a change was taking place in the community. The Scotch-Irish were thinning and scattering out upon larger fields of farming and other endeavor; the Pennsylvania Dutch were coming in. Some of these German children could speak no English at all when they were sent to school. They learned readily, but they could not be expected to take part in the Presbyterian drill.

3. Devotions

THE SHORTER CATECHISM of the Associated Reformed Seceders, as the United Presbyterians then were called, was a statement of dissenting principles in the form of one hundred and seven questions and answers. It derived from hard and bloody days of the persecution in Scotland when those who declared such Calvinistic doctrine did so at their peril.

'A genuine love for oatmeal porridge and a good understanding of the Shorter Catechism,' the mature Henry Wallace used to say, 'makes a well-balanced ration when you are feeding for brains, muscle, and morals. . . . I give it as my judgment to you young folks that committing and reciting intelligently the Shorter Catechism is equal to a full year at school.'[2]

But the weekend routine of Sabbath-keeping seemed a dull and trying discipline to the coltlike young. Even after Saturday afternoon catechizing was removed from the common-school curriculum, the discipline started Saturday evening. Then the boys were required to lay out their Sunday clothes and to black their shoes and their parents' shoes, and the girls were set to grinding coffee and preparing ahead of time as much of the Sabbath fare as possible. Only the unregenerate, and they were few, went out sporting on Saturday nights there around Finleyville in the eighteen-forties.

In most households the whole family rose early and clad themselves for private devotions — full family worship — in their own homes before going to church on Sunday morning. First they would sing a Psalm together, without music. Even families that countenanced violin music or fiddlejigs on weekdays would have accounted it a sacrilege to take the instrument from its case on the Sabbath. After a Psalm a chapter was read from the Bible and the family concluded its private service with a long prayer.

The Wallaces attended an old stone church in West Newton, six miles distant. They made the twelve-mile drive, back and forth, in any weather. Their church was plain within, with a high pulpit, reared half-way between floor and ceiling, with steps leading up to it on two sides. The service started with an invocation. Then a Psalm was read, followed by an explanation requiring a quarter-hour or longer; and then, without organ music or choir, the people sang a Psalm. In this singing they were led by a 'clark' or precentor, who stood on the floor at the base of the pulpit and gave out two lines at a time.

The 'long prayer' which followed was delivered extempore. Often it lasted for forty minutes. It was at this stage of the service, Henry Wallace remarked wryly later in life, that 'the Power to whom the prayer is offered receives a great deal of instruction in Calvinistic theology.' Never, even as an ordained minister of the church, did he develop great patience or reverence for rituals and forms; and the parts of his *Reminiscences* which treat of his earliest introduction into spiritual harness plainly indicate that for the most part the Sundays of his boyhood bored him stiff.

The strain of Sabbath behavior was such that, while it was expressly set down as sinful to speak that day of business or worldly matters, a certain latitude of circumlocution was generally allowed. In the churchyard and after services and on the way home the men would bring up the question whether wheat would bring as much as a dollar a bushel that year; and thus, as Henry Wallace remembered it, 'The good men veered off and were soon talking of matters belonging to this world. During my last trip to the old churchyard (in 1914) I reminded a grayhaired elder of a conversation:

'"That's a fine horse of yours, Jim. If it were not the Sabbath, what would you take for it?"

'"I never trade on the Sabbath; but if it were not the Sabbath, I would take a hundred and fifty."

'"I never talk trade on the Sabbath, either; but if it were not the Sabbath, I would give you a hundred and forty."

'"Come over and see me tomorrow."'

Every Sunday after return from church the children were drilled in the Shorter Catechism and required to learn and recite a Psalm. Henry did not like committing things to memory. He had a special fondness for the briefer Psalms, and especially the 'cursing' ones: '*May his wife be a widow and his children fatherless!*' That was spirited, easy to remember; and there it was, in the Psalms of David.

While the usual routine of churchgoing did not go deep with the instinctively religious youth, Communion, a rather extraordinary occasion in the church of his fathers, stirred him profoundly. Communion was held only twice a year, spring and fall, during weeks when the pressure of farm work was lightest and the fullest devotions possible. The discipline of approach to Communion was more stringent than that of the ordinary Sabbath-keeping. Preparation started on Friday, a Fast Day. Saturday was marked with a special service and the distribution of 'tokens.' Tokens were pieces of metal, usually of lead, small enough to be concealed in the palm of the hand, with the name of the church stamped in the metal; that was all. These tokens derived traditionally from the years of the persecution when Covenanters had to commune in secret and needed some secret means of identification. On Communion Sunday the service was especially long, but exalted, markedly ceremonious for a Protestant order, and of a highly mystical strain. There would be three or four Communion tables arranged, as were the aisles of the church, in the form of the cross. Amid solemn chanting the minister would stand at the end of the tables and pass to communicants bearing tokens 'the elements,' which are the body and blood of Jesus Christ. 'I know,' wrote Henry Wallace, remembering, 'of few more solemn scenes than the approach to the Communion tables in my boyhood. There was something about leaving your seat, coming in at the foot of the table and passing out at the other end after the service was over, which is entirely lacking where the communicants sit in the pews.'

In 1849 there came to live for a while with the Wallaces at Spring Mount another Wallace from Ireland, 'Uncle Daniel,' John Wallace's youngest brother, who was around thirty years old at the time. A man of impressive mien, lordly and disputatious, Daniel Wallace took a great liking to young Henry, who was now thirteen. To a green country boy who had never as yet been even as far away from home as Harrisburg, Uncle Daniel, with his foreign ways and views, opened new vistas into the larger world, geographically, theologically, politically — and while the boy reacted furiously against his uncle's inborn Toryism, and they quarreled like brothers, they became close friends. Sitting by the fire of evenings when John and Daniel Wallace talked, Henry learned why his father had been sending relief corn to Ireland. A plant blight, the potato rot, had brought on famine there. In two years Ireland had lost one fourth of its population through death and removal. Daniel Wallace was, in effect, a refugee in America. So, later, were 'Little Henry' Wallace and Gideon McHenry, cousins from Ireland, who stayed for a while at Spring Mount and helped with the work afield.

Old Henry Wallace, remaining on his farm at Kilrea, was grieving, Daniel said, for the blight that had come upon his country and for his sons who had gone away. Betty McHenry Wallace, his wife, was scolding, storming, and running the show, as ever, wherever she was, at home or in town. She had set up a soup kitchen by the roadway and hundreds of starving people on the way to and from market would stop for some of her free soup.

'My uncle,' Henry wrote later, recalling those fireside conversations, 'was an aristocrat.[3] He believed in the rule of the "best." My father was a democrat, believing in the rule of the people. My father was an abolitionist. My uncle believed that the colored people were best where they were, and were unfitted for freedom. Naturally, in later years, when questions growing out of the Civil War came up for discussion, my uncle became a Democrat and my father a very strong Republican.'

Repeal of the Corn Laws at the close of the eighteen-forties led John and Daniel Wallace into many a wrangle. Daniel was a free trader; John, a protectionist: 'We have coal in plenty; we have iron ore,' John would say. 'Why not enact a tariff that will encourage infant industries? Competition between industries will keep down the price.'

But most of the time they argued about religion, or about theology. Daniel was an 'Arminian,' or Methodist. He would argue for paraphrases of the Scripture and lay composition, with greater freedom of forms. John, the Calvinist, would oppose such freedoms stoutly. 'Daniel,' he would say, smiling but serious, 'this is iniquitous. You are offering strange fire to the Lord!' But always, Henry afterwards remembered and recorded, they disputed as gentlemen: 'My father would say, "Are you through, Daniel?" or my uncle would ask, "John, are you through?" Or,

"I beg your pardon," or "Allow me," or "Wait a moment, if you please."'

On one occasion Uncle Daniel, arguing, threw his considerable weight around so hard in the chair that the hickory wood splintered and the chair collapsed. Sprawled on the floor, he completed his argument without a pause for breath. Then, 'John, I believe that I have broken this chair, and will have to get it mended,' he remarked in all calmness.

4. Henry Leaves Home

JOHN, what are you going to do with Henry?' Uncle Daniel had asked one evening when they did not know that Henry was listening.

''Deed if I know,' Henry's father answered.

It was getting to be a sore question. Henry was predestined for the ministry. His mother, especially, had set her heart on that. But John Wallace had only begun to get his farm in good shape; he loved these fields and already his strength was failing. The old hurts of back strain and sunstroke hurt him more now. His sons, after Henry, as they came along were not men of the sort that Henry was growing up to be; they were slighter of build and of less rugged health. Henry was growing into quite a hand and, better, a help. He had good judgment, half of which at least is instinct, as a farmer. People who used to laugh as they picked out 'Henry's rows' in some informal contest of plowing or reaping — at first he covered more ground than anyone else but made an unfinished mess of it — respected him now as a quick, thorough workman.

When, in 1854, his eighteenth year, Henry Wallace, 'after long and very serious consideration, and a great many family discussions,' determined to devote himself 'to the gospel ministry,' his father did not object. Indeed, 'he promised any help I needed; but was very much disappointed that I did not continue on the farm. For a year or more I had taken the heavy end of the work, while he did the planning. My leaving home was therefore a grievous financial and personal loss to my father.'

Henry's profession of religion at this stage of his life seems to have been in no sense ecstatic. He simply figured out what he thought he had better do, and explained his choice dispassionately: 'My mother wanted me to become a minister, and if I had determined to become a lawyer, it would almost have broken her heart, and my father would have given me no assistance.'

Partly for family reasons, but principally because he lacked secondary-school training and credentials, it was decided that he enter Sharon College in the hills of southeastern Ohio, more than a hundred miles southwest of his home. A cousin of Martha Wallace had set himself up as president of this obscure institution. All the Wallaces knew about it was that Henry could get in there. Away he went, taking the stage at West Newton at four in the morning and coming into Wheeling, West Virginia, the following night. It was a miserable journey. Coachsick, homesick, and lonely, he changed coaches at Wheeling, standing by a lamp-post and reading a chapter of the Bible to compose his mind. Then all that night he rode by coach again, with 'the stage swinging from one side to another of the rough turnpike, churning up my stomach, and bringing on a violent seasickness.' He reached Washington, Ohio, at dawn. The hotel had no room for him; he was too sick to want breakfast. So, lugging a heavy carpetbag, he struck out on foot for Sharon College, thirty miles up in the hills of Noble County, Ohio, and with an occasional hitch by buggy arrived there by late afternoon.

Sharon College, a school of fifty students of all grades and ages, did not amount to much. Neither, for that matter, did its president and founder, a man of genuine piety, Henry's reverend cousin — who at one and the same time was bookseller, preacher, and educator, and who later found his niche surprisingly as a news correspondent covering the Civil War.

Wallace did not bother to stay the year out; he returned home early to help on the farm. Later, about all that he could recall having learned during his first year of 'college' was his first clear intimation that civil strife was brewing, and the coincident discovery that he was not a born salesman.

He and a roommate ran out of money and determined to get out into the backlands, enlighten the countryside, and gain some

cash. They filled the back of a buggy with specimens of the
Reverend's stock of books and set out. Henry chose as the
potential best-seller *The Life of Charles Bull*, an escaped slave.
A farmer weighing at least two hundred pounds called him a
Yankee and was about to do him violence, so he did not press
further to make that sale. The long day waned; neither Henry
nor his companion had sold a book. As a last hope, Henry leaped
from the buggy, approached an old gentleman who was hoeing
in a garden, and tried to sell him a copy of the *Charles Bull*
abolitionist tract. The old gentleman regarded young Wallace
with a straight glance, and said: 'I am an old man. I am preparing for death. If you have Boston's *Future State* or Alliene's
Alarm to the Unconverted, I would like one of them. Or Baxter's
Saints' Rest? No? Then you have nothing to suit me. You
may pass on.'

The year after that young Wallace went to Geneva Hall, an
academy, about a hundred miles farther westward, at Northwood,
in Logan County, Ohio. He went there for two years, from 1855
to 1857. It was a strict Covenanter School and community.
Northwood had no paved streets and its wooden sidewalks were
six inches wide. It had forty houses and three churches, all
Presbyterian but of varying creed and practice. The Old School
Presbyterian church members would not vote. In order to vote,
they argued, one must take the oath of allegiance to a Government which had separated Church and State and countenanced
human slavery. They were men who exhibited in general what
Wallace called the 'Covenanter cast' of head and countenance,
and were 'good judges of theology and livestock.' Their little town
of Northwood was a station on the 'Underground Railway' and
whatever their doctrinal differences in detail, these Covenanters
of the Old School and the New School were continually smuggling
Negroes through from Cincinnati toward the Canadian border.
Henry laughed at their excesses of zealotry, but respected them.
They were a grim sort, highly argumentative and fearful of
pleasure; but the teaching at their school was thorough and searching. 'What is education? Why are you here?' Wallace's teacher
of Latin kept demanding. Wallace got up at four in the morning
and studied hard until six or seven, to make sure he would have

his Latin lesson, down to the last nuance of proper pronunciation, right.

Henry was a raw and clumsy boy, shy and proud. He never forgot the occasion on which he was asked to tea by this Latin teacher, Dr. Sloane: 'He invited me, with other boys, to take tea and spend the evening. His wife was city-bred, fashionable and vain. I was fresh from the country, awkward and very plainly dressed. She lectured me on my lack of taste in dress and refinement in manner. He overheard it, and said: "Henry, you will find it much easier to put my wife's advice in practice if you stick close to your studies, get the foundation first, and be thorough in all your work. Your dress and manners will then come all right. Make yourself worth polishing, and the polish will come as you rub against men."' [4]

Northwood was an inexpensive academy. Everything was plain. Board and room in the country roundabout cost less than four dollars a week; and the fare, while rough, was plentiful. But Henry and a classmate, Richard Shaw, who also was studying for the ministry, were always 'hungry as hounds' and they made a deal with a near-by farmer who had a surplus of peaches. They paid the farmer twenty-five cents for the right to enter his orchard at any time while the crop was ripening. 'We were to have all we could eat or throw at each other, if we had a mind to — but we must not give any to the other boys.'

Student diversions and outside activities were simple and rustic. They had no fraternities, no athletics, no parties. Sometimes they went out and hunted wild turkeys, which were getting scarce, or shot squirrels. They raided henyards and stole chickens. They resented and punished departures from normal or conservative conduct, much as student bodies do, as a rule, today. One of the queer ones among them was a sort of Johnny Appleseed, who favored a sacklike costume and a straw hat with the sides drawn down by a string tied under the chin. 'He said he was fitting himself as a missionary to Afghanistan; and we all wished he were there. He argued that it was wrong to take the life of any animal, even of the most offensive insect. He argued that we should eat nothing that was not grown in our immediate environment. Hence, he abjured tea, coffee, spices and sugar, except maple. He refused to cut off even his hair and beard. On election night, the fourth of November, 1856, there was a struggle and much hair and gore were found on the floor in the morning. In taking off the long hair, which he had refused to have cut, they also took some of his scalp with it.'

The election of 1856 brought into the national arena a new party, the Republicans. Until then it had been the Whigs against the Democrats, and the Democrats had been in power, except for an eight-year upset, since 1832. Now Buchanan, the Democrat, defeated Frémont, Republican, 174 electoral votes to 114. 'The hour had not yet come for the Revolution that was to follow. In 1856,' Wallace adds in his memoirs, 'Abraham Lincoln was just beginning to appear as a great, potent moral and political force, looming above the horizon on the West.'

Henry Wallace was half a year too young to vote. But the student literary societies at Northwood debated: *Is the fugitive slave law constitutional? If constitutional, should it be observed? Is the Dred Scott decision binding on a Christian? Is there a higher law than the Constitution? Should slavery be abolished?*

He had credits enough to pursue courses in a standard college now. He worked on the farm at home that summer and enrolled at Jefferson College (now Washington and Jefferson), only thirty miles from there, that fall.

Jefferson College, in Washington County, Pennsylvania, was in country much like his home place, but richer at base. The coal miners and industrialists have transformed this county also during the years since, but it was 'beautiful, rolling and fairly well-wooded country' when Wallace went there to college in the late eighteen-fifties. 'The population was then almost entirely rural, and its main products were sheep, barley, and Presbyterians. The community was stocked with Presbyterians at the start. The College was founded in 1802, largely through the influence of one Dr. McMillan, a graduate of Princeton, and was one of the earliest colleges of that part of the West. The Scotch and Scotch-Irish settlers had taken their church and their schools with them as they pioneered.'

The students at Jefferson came from rather a wide area, in terms of the times. Some came from as far west as Illinois and there was a considerable Southern element from West Virginia, Kentucky, and Tennessee. Equipment was sparse, and the beginnings of scientific courses then under development were weak; but Jefferson gave such thorough drill in the classical subjects that its classes grew as the instruction progressed. There were when Wallace entered, for example, around thirty freshmen in his class, and by the time that class had graduated, in 1859, the class numbered nearly seventy. The faculty was generally competent, with two or three really stimulating teachers among them.

Strangely enough, in a college with Northern and Southern students, there was little talk of slavery or secession at Jefferson during Wallace's years there. It was between elections. The country perhaps was weary of the heights of dissension. Instead of debating political issues as had the literary societies at Northwood, Franklin and Philo, the corresponding rival groups at Jefferson, conducted discussion on more esoteric levels: *Can the unconditioned be cognized or defined? Faith and reason: their claims and conflicts. Does the* Essay on Man *prove in itself that Pope was an infidel?*

Greek-letter fraternities had been founded at Jefferson. Wallace joined Sigma Nu and took a mild part in campus politics, which centered around the literary societies, but he never kept up his fraternal connections afterwards. Two outstanding occurrences stood out in his mind years later as somehow typifying the march of implacable circumstances, the gathering storm. The first was an act of God: the great frost or freeze on the night of July 4, 1857. The ground next morning was frozen; corn knee-high stood dead afield and wheat, about to blossom, was almost completely killed. At home that summer, Wallace noted, 'my brother and I cut all the wheat on twelve acres between noon and three o'clock. This was a small patch protected by a grove of trees.' Fear of famine ran high in the Allegheny country and Ohio, and rations, pieced out with catch crops of buckwheat, were lean that fall and winter.

A wave or revival of religion swept all this part of the country in Wallace's final year of college, 1858. 'It just came. There were no professional revivalists. It just came like the wind that "bloweth where it listeth, and thou hearest the voice thereof, but knowest not whence it cometh or whither it goeth; so is every one that is born of the Spirit." Prayer meetings were better attended, the churches better filled. The Bible when read seemed to have more power over the hearers. One of the most profane students in college was heard praying in agony in his room. Many of the students were converted. The two churches just outside the town — an Associate or Seceder church and a Union church — were welded together with other such churches all over the nation, and formed the United Presbyterian Church. I have sometimes thought [Wallace concluded] that this revival was a baptism of the Holy Spirit to prepare our country for the baptism of blood that came so soon afterward.'

5. The Fleshpots of Kentucky

HE TOOK no honors at graduation. His grades were good. He had led the class in Greek; but midway in his course he had decided not to apply himself for top grades in mathematics and to spend more time at the library reading. He was given an honored place on the Commencement program, but excused himself and returned home before the exercises were held. Affairs of the farm seemed to be proceeding satisfactorily. His father was feebler, but the third son, James Wallace, was taking hold. Henry Wallace decided to go out in the world again and try to make some money before going on with post-graduate preparation for the ministry.

His *Reminiscences* hint, rather circuitously, at two main reasons for this decision. First, John Wallace, in his quiet way, had turned to his accounts of money advanced Henry in the course of his college years and had drawn now, at graduation, as had been agreed between them, a note for Henry to sign. The note was for nine hundred dollars, which Henry considered a generous underestimate. He signed it, so now he owed his father nine hundred dollars, and there was a girl he had met while he was at Geneva Hall in Ohio. She lived in Mansfield, Ohio. Having decided to try his fortunes in Kentucky, Wallace went there by way of Mansfield, a considerable detour. In Mansfield he fell in love not with the girl he went to see but with a cousin of hers, Nancy Ann Cantwell. On matters of state and intellect the autobiographical notes of Henry Wallace are generally clear and candid, but in matters touching on courtship he covers his tracks so dexterously that, while the words are there before you in the plainest English, he seems almost to be writing in code. This, for instance, to his great-grandchildren not yet born is his account of his first meeting with Nancy Cantwell: 'I fell out with my room-mate that year, and changed my rooming house, and so became acquainted with a young lady much older than myself. Through her, two years later, I had the opportunity of becoming acquainted with the lady who became my wife. Thus do the most trifling things shape our destiny. Some call it chance; some luck; I call it Providence. Just think what a difference it might have made in the Wallace family if I had not fallen out with a schoolmate over a trifling remark, changed my boarding-house; and perhaps remained an old bachelor, or perchance married a less noble woman than your great-grandmother!

'I started for Kentucky in July and stopped at Mansfield, Ohio, to visit the young lady I have spoken of, and for the first time met her cousin. I do not know whether it was a case of what novelists call "love at first sight," but the acquaintance then formed was continued by correspondence and occasional visits for about three years, when it ended in an engagement and about four years afterwards in marriage. I know very well you youngsters will want to know all about it, how I "popped the question," what she said, and what I said. I am not going to tell you; for there are some things in life too sacred to be revealed even to one's great-grandchildren, and among them is courtship, both before and after marriage. My marriage was a piece of great and undeserved good fortune.'

Nancy Cantwell lived on a modest but somewhat stately country place near Mansfield, Ohio. It was near the farms that since have been bought and restored by Louis Bromfield. The Cantwells were distinctly Ohio gentry and esteemed themselves as such. James Cantwell, Nancy's father, was a member of the state legislature and a prominent Republican. His farm was a station on the Underground Railway. Later he served as a colonel in the Civil War.

It required but a day or so in Mansfield for Henry Wallace to turn his eyes from the 'much older' young lady, and begin his courtship of Miss Cantwell. He had crossed the Ohio River into Kentucky and had found a teaching position by the day, when those of his class who remained for the formal exercises received their diplomas. But he was so short of money by this time that he had to borrow twenty dollars from an old schoolmate, and he found it expedient to set forth afoot — with occasional buggy lifts from friendly planters — from Danville to Perryville to Columbia College, eighteen miles from Perryville — in search of a paying post. The first two places had no openings, but at Columbia they wanted 'a man who could teach Latin, Greek, mathematics, English and whatever else needed to be taught — for four hundred and fifty dollars for nine months, including board, fire, washing and a Negro servant, with fifty dollars in advance to bind the bargain.'

Coming thus for his first time south of the Ohio River, Wallace was enchanted with ante-bellum Kentucky. It was, and is, a land of lavish richness, based on a natural soil endowment of phosphate and lime. Even this Green River country, which lies south of the Bluegrass proper, made Wallace's home soil, and the life he had led there, seem by comparison bleak and thin. 'Rich land, rich people; poorer land, poorer people. The quality of the homes gives a very fair indication of the soil and the character of the people,' he reflected; 'I have never before seen, and never expect to see again, the like of this!' Everyone at first was kind to him. He had planned to make the last leg of his journey, from Perryville to Columbia, afoot; but an old gentleman met on the way took him home, dined him, and placed him astride a splendid horse. A boy, he said, would come to the stables at Columbia and bring the horse home later. So Wallace, with his carpetbag in his lap, entered upon his new post, as a mounted man, rather grandly; and immediately was installed with a boy of his own as footservant and valet. He did not ask this boy if he were a slave and how he liked it. He had asked that question of a bellhop in the inn back at Perryville, and a Northern news-paper correspondent sharing the same room had warned and re-buked him sharply. 'Unless you're looking for trouble,' this other Yankee said, 'you'd better be more careful.'

Wallace learned to be more careful, in a measure; but during his nine-and-a-half months' stay in Kentucky he taught Ben McKee, his slave boy, how to read. This was done in secret, as it was against the law in Kentucky at the time. The boy learned with surprising readiness to read the simpler parts of the Scripture aloud with his surreptitious teacher and master. Their favorite exercise was the first three chapters of the Gospel of John. Wallace felt rather as if he had gained a convert to monogamy among the then Mormons; but a friendly planter whose opinions Wallace had learned to trust as realistic took him out for a stroll toward the end of his Kentucky experience, and said:

'"Now, professor, you think Ben is a good Christian nigger?"

'I answered: "I certainly do." My friend then gave me in-formation which proved that Ben had been guilty of repeated immorality. Ben was, however, like many another man who had a better chance than he. . . . I doubt if the whole life work of a Kentucky slave more than paid for the cost of his raising and keep . . . (and yet), while you might not believe in slavery, it was quite comfortable, I admit, to lie in bed on a cold morning until a Negro came in and built a hickory fire. There was something very pleasant in the snapping and sparkling and the warmth which gradually pervaded the room. . . . Living in that section of the country was a delight.'

Columbia was a very lusty village of some seven hundred souls. It had more taverns than churches and many murder trials. 'This doomed, damned town!' the County Attorney, Stuart, called it, in the course of such a trial. Stuart was famous for what then was known as Sam Brownlow style of oratory. Wallace made friends with him immediately. Stuart's extravagance of speech, in court and out, gave him delight. Of a witness named Fields, Stuart said: 'Gentlemen of the jury: If a stream of ipecac as wide and deep as the Mississippi River were to flow into the infernal regions to all eternity, it would not puke up a bigger

liar than Sam Fields.' And of another witness: 'Gentlemen,
that man has brass enough in his face to make the dungeon doors
of deep damnation.'

The 'college' was really a small seminary, predominantly
Presbyterian. In the summer of his twenty-third year, when he
arrived there, Wallace found it possible to discuss with most
of the students and faculty the slavery issue. He told them
frankly that he was a 'Black Republican'; but promised to make
no public utterances on the matter, and to distribute no tracts.
On the sixteenth of October, 1859, however, John Brown made
his attack on Harper's Ferry; and a few days later word ran
through the village that the Negroes were in insurrection there
near town. Wallace had no trouble by this time in sensing a
change in atmosphere. 'My popularity as a man had begun to
decline. I was at the postoffice, anxious to get mail by this time.
In fact, I was homesick, so homesick that I used to take delight
in looking in a store at a box of McCully's glass. McCully was a
noted Pittsburgh manufacturer of glass. That evening I found
the postoffice full of men drinking, swearing, buying powder and
shot, loading pistols and shotguns, their horses standing saddled in
the street. They said there was an insurrection, which I doubted,
but I did not stay any longer than was necessary.'

The reported insurrection was a minor case of disorderly conduct on the part of a Negro. Life around Columbia became,
notwithstanding, less amusing. 'If you folks nominate Lincoln,'
the leading Presbyterian minister told Professor Wallace somberly,
'this country will be shaken to its foundations, and this old ship
will go on the rocks.' Wallace finished his term's work and
started for Louisville on the very day that Lincoln was nominated
at Chicago. It was a stormy day he long remembered: 'A cyclone
had swept through Iowa, and we were detained at Louisville by
the worst storm I had ever seen. I saw next day a sugar-tree
grove with all the tops of trees more than a foot in diameter twisted
off from twenty to thirty feet above the ground, as neatly as you
could wring the head off a chicken. The political storm seemed
to have its echo in wind storms over a large portion of the Middle
West.'

6. Theologians

H E WAS NEVER so glad in his life, he said, to get away from any place as he was from Kentucky; and yet when he was home again he missed the South. Something shining and spacious always came into his words when he spoke of his days there, through all the torment and anxiety that was to come. At home, things seemed changed. 'There really is no returning,' DeWitt Wing has said, 'to the places you remember from your early youth; and so, in a measure, we are homesick all our lives.' Back home, at the old springhouse, Wallace found the milk did not taste the same as in Kentucky and reflected that 'climate and environment affect the quality and flavor.' It was almost with reluctance that he resumed in the autumn of 1860 his studies for the ministry. With sixty-five others he enrolled in the United Presbyterian Theological Seminary at Allegheny, which is called North Pittsburgh now. There were three professors. Reverend John T. Pressley, who taught Systematic Theology, was a tartar; no student would dare to express a doubt. 'So far as he was concerned,' wrote Wallace, 'we were in a theological cage, of which he held the key.'

The students had to preach for practice before the dour Dr. Pressley. His comments were often scorching, not to say venomous. '*Vox, et praeterea nihil*' (sound, and nothing more), he said, when the sermon lacked matter, and, when a student tried to preach with dispassion, 'It is said of the lion that when he wishes to enrage himself, he lashes himself with his tail. I advise the brother to follow his example,' Dr. Pressley said. Wallace preferred Dr. Young, who 'provided true insight into expository preaching.' But increasingly he found his course at Allegheny restrictive, cramping, and dull. He did settlement work for practice in Pittsburgh, and was amazed to find how different from country boys city gamins are. They rather frightened him. It was all 'not thoroughly satisfactory.' Of his teachers, 'I was disposed to ask questions, sometimes I feel impertinently.' And none would believe him when he predicted a great and terrible war.

Northern and Southern Democrats split that fall, with the Southerners nominating Breckinridge, and the Northerners, Stephen A. Douglas. Pittsburgh, for years a Whig stronghold,

put on 'Wideawake' parades to arouse support for Lincoln. 'The
Wideawakers' paraded in miner's costume, with capes of oilcloth,
and a miner's lamp stuck in their caps. Wallace heard the famous
stump speaker, Tom Corwin, harangue a Republican rally. As a
student of public discourse Wallace was vastly more attracted by
Corwin's way of speaking than by that of the Reverend Professor
Pressley. But even as he sat enthralled by Corwin's consummate
showmanship, he had doubts: 'I wish I could describe to you his
eloquence, his facial expression and bearing when, after describing
the threats of the South to secede, he would scream: "*Tear down
the Union, will you? Tear down the Union!*" . . . But I could not
help but feel that the effect of it would be to lull the people of the
North into a sense of security for which there was no warrant.'

Just before Christmas word came that South Carolina had
seceded. 'The gloomiest of the gloomy days of that to me
gloomy winter was the Sabbath after,' Wallace noted. He had
quarreled again with his Uncle Daniel Wallace, who was getting
more 'aristocratical' and violent in his opinions all the time.
This particular quarrel was about Wendell Phillips, whom Henry
and his father admired exceedingly as a man and orator. Uncle
Daniel's opinion about everything proceeded from a different bias.
It did not amuse his relatives at Spring Mount when Uncle Daniel
tore into their idol, Wendell Phillips. 'I think I'll just leave him
alone,' Henry told his father. 'That is right; it would be best,'
his father had said.

But Henry was in torment within himself, by this time; and
he walked in casually on his Uncle Dan at his Pittsburgh office,
and Uncle Dan had leaped to his feet with a 'God bless my soul,
it's good to see you!' and they were friends again. It was Uncle
Daniel who asked Henry to dinner at the Monongahela House
the night that Lincoln, elected President, also took dinner there
and consented to a change in train arrangements, to slip him
more safely to the Capitol through rebellious, rioting Baltimore.

'Lincoln arrived late. In passing through the hall he went
by my uncle's door, and I had a good view of this remarkable
man — tall, awkward, ungainly, homely — a man who paid
little attention to dress,' Henry Wallace wrote in 1916, remembering, at an age approaching eighty. 'He had the saddest face
and the saddest eyes that I ever saw on a human being.'

III

THE YEARS OF THE GREAT REBELLION

I went with my father and a fellow student to the old church in the country, six miles from home. It was a very gloomy day, with a cold, drizzling rain. The church was a large one, and always full as I remembered it six years before. The roof leaked. The paper on the wall was stained and moldy from the drip. There was but a handful of people there, like a few bees in one corner of a large hive. . . . It seemed to me as I sat there in the old pew that the church was a type of the nation, and the day typical of the times. One state had seceded. I felt that all the cotton states would follow, and that there would be a bitter and cruel war. I felt that everything was going to pieces, and thought of the Greek poem I had read, where the poet in describing death said: 'And we, a little dust, lie down, even our bones being dissolved.' — The 'Last Sunday in 1860,' from *Uncle Henry's Own Story*.

1. West to the Prairie

On the Sunday in 1861 when Fort Sumter fell, the son of a tenant farmer who once had worked for the Wallaces was moved by liquor and patriotic excitement to load a pistol, steal a horse, and start South. He also stole and wore on the gallop young Henry Wallace's new preaching jacket, an elegant frock coat. Henry was furious. He gave way to his temper. 'Get me a cup of coffee! Get me a horse!' he shouted to the keeper of the inn on the National Road where he had stayed for the night. 'I will catch Ben!' Off he went in hot pursuit; but sixty miles along, with Ben still leading, he gave it up, and informed the police of Monongahela City of the offense. The police rounded Ben in and brought him back — coat, pistol, and all. He was tried at West Newton and 'pardoned on condition that he would carry out his original design of fighting the rebels.'

It has not been clearly determined whether under the canons of his church fledgling ministers were supposed or permitted to bear arms. Whether Henry really felt moved to do so, as a soldier, is not recorded; but it is plain from his record of those days that he was distressed and irresolute, a young man torn from his faith in fixed spiritual moorings, restless and sore at heart. 'The smart young prep,' as they called him at Allegheny College, was fitting less and less readily into the routine indoctrination there in practice. 'The question arose in my mind whether I should go back to Allegheny or west to Monmouth, Illinois. I had seen enough of the rigid opinions of the United Presbyterian Church in Pennsylvania to convince me that I would never be an acceptable preacher in that section of the country. I would have to find some section where there were more liberal views.'

Toward autumn the question of certifying Wallace to Monmouth, Illinois, Presbytery aroused such bitter debate in the local Westmoreland Presbytery that, even though the certification was grudgingly granted, ill feeling ran high. 'My boy,' John Wallace told Henry, 'there is only one thing for you to do now, and that is to go West.'

At the West Newton station where he took the train for Chicago many neighbors were gathered, but not expressly to see him off. They were there awaiting the mail train from Pittsburgh and the first casualty lists. Amid the confusion of wartime traffic Henry stopped off at Mansfield, Ohio, and spent a day at the Cantwell home. Colonel James Cantwell, Nancy's father, was at the head of his Federal regiment afield. Nancy Cantwell and Henry Wallace came, it seems, to an 'understanding' in the course of this visit. It was not a 'ring engagement'; but she was wearing his Sigma Nu fraternity pin on her shirtwaist when she saw him off on a clanking train of mixed freight and passenger cars, drawn by an engine with a flaring, bell-shaped smokestack, for Chicago and the West.

Chicago, in 1861, was an inconsiderable city with plank walks and rickety wooden buildings, for the most part, stuck in a swamp. Three things impressed Wallace principally in open country and in cities, on this his first trip to the great Midland: mud, corn, and rats. Much of the land, he observed, was in need of drainage, and everywhere, as he proceeded southwestward, to Monmouth, which is near the Iowa border, Illinois seemed 'a vast cornfield, a state literally full of corn.' Visiting on a Sabbath in the country out from Monmouth, he sat by a stove in which corn was burning for fuel. In Monmouth old corn was down in price to ten cents a bushel and new corn was eight cents. 'The town itself was full of corn, corn everywhere. And it was also full of rats. Monmouth was a small town then — perhaps eight hundred or a thousand people. The rats chased along under the wooden sidewalks as you walked along. From my window on a moonlight night I could count anywhere from twenty-five to fifty rats gathering up the corn which had fallen from farmers' wagons as they brought it to market.'

Of his theological studies, resumed now in the raw Midwest, on the middle border, his memoirs say little. His studies were largely repetitious, but he had the good fortune to sit at length under the sort of preacher-professor whom he could completely admire. Dr. Alexander Young, who conducted the Theology course, knew more about the geology of the country around Pittsburgh, and more about the shameful waste of gases from its coke ovens, than did Wallace, who came from there. Years after, in the Roosevelt-Pinchot era, when he helped to organize movements for conservation in the middle country, he repeated the data and warnings of this earthy theologian.

Dressed very plainly, Dr. Young was working one day in his garden when a visitor from the East came by and fell into talk with him. Returning to his hotel, the visitor declared: 'If the people of Monmouth knew what they were about they would elect that old gardener as president of the college. He has more nearly universal knowledge than any other man I have ever met, East or West.'

At the outbreak of the war, Lincoln had called for an army of seventy-five thousand men, to serve for ninety days. Now, in 1862, he called for three hundred thousand men. Of the one

hundred and eighteen students at Monmouth College, seventy
joined the Union Army. Dr. David A. Wallace, the president
of the college, wrestled in prayer and announced at the opening
of the summer vacation that he would remain. Here, he said,
was his post of duty. 'Moreover, it is expected that every
member of the faculty will be at his post at the opening of the
Session, September 2. We must educate,' his announcement concluded, 'whether there be peace or war.' Henry Wallace, not
related to the president of his college, but increasingly influenced
by this David Wallace's views and character, decided to press
his studies toward ordination, then go with the Army as a chaplain, if he could. By reason, possibly, of wartime disruptions, he
was permitted to 'supply' preaching to a number of rural charges
almost as soon as he had registered as a student there. Thus,
he made his first entrance into Iowa by a circuitous route, around
floodwater, during the great rising of the Mississippi River in
April of 1862.

The swollen river was ten miles wide at Burlington that April,
and the miry roads of Iowa were all but impassable. Wallace's
first mission was to 'supply' two small congregations alternately
in the sharp hills of Monroe County, not far from the Missouri
border in southern Iowa. It was rude, new country, but beautiful, with natural bluegrass meadows, fine timber — birch, hickory,
walnut, oak, and elms in groves. Land still sold there for three
dollars an acre.

Wallace walked on the grass by the side of the miry roads to
preach to his first charges; and he always remembered what wonderful grass it was, so thick, springy, and resilient. He stayed
but a month in Monroe County. It was a sad month. Word came
that a son of the elder with whom he was staying, together with
other local boys, had fallen in the Battle of Shiloh. 'The first
duty that fell upon me, therefore, was to try to comfort the mourn-
ing, those who mourned for the dead, the sick and wounded and
the missing.'

The funeral of a frontier child at which he officiated weighed
on his mind for years: 'It was a little child. The soil in that part
of Iowa is a hardpan. The grave was dug and there was a foot
or more of water in the bottom. I saw the little coffin let down

in that water, and I said to myself: I never want to bury anyone
I love in a grave of that kind.'

If he had thought to find a greater liberality prevalent here
along the Illinois-Iowa border, he was in part disappointed; for
the Covenanters and the Seceders, strictest of all the Scotch and
Scotch-Irish dissenters, had dug in stoutly here, as always, at
the outer edge on the march of settlement. During his first
month on Iowa soil, in Monroe County, Wallace heard a member
tried who had been read out of church by the Seceders because
he had stopped by at a Methodist camp meeting to see a man
about a horse. It was not, of course, the horse-trading that was
the sin; but the 'occasional hearing' of preachments by another
sect. In spite of the suspension, the member wished to have his
child baptized. 'This the pastor refused to do, until the father
would make a public confession of his sin in attending this
Methodist camp meeting on a Monday night. So I had the
pleasure of hearing a man confess in public to one of those church-
made sins that have no little part in keeping good, earnest men
out of the church.'

Henry Wallace was ordained in April of 1863 and accepted the
united call of two small churches on opposite banks of the Mississippi River. One church was in Davenport, Iowa; the other
was in Rock Island, Illinois. He had been filling both these
pulpits as 'a stated supply,' with a joint annual salary of five
hundred and fifty dollars during the close of his student years.
Rock Island at the time was a town of some ten thousand inhabit-
ants; Davenport already had twenty thousand or so. Both of
these Presbyterian churches were poor, physically mean and
unattractive; and their congregations were jealous of each other,
always suspecting that their Reverend was giving more time to
the Illinois side of the river than to the Iowa side, or the other
way around.

The mixture of Presbyterians in both congregations brought together from all along the new border had frequent disagreements
on doctrine and conduct, in the use of tokens before Communion,
Psalm- and hymn-singing, the propriety of belonging to secret
societies and of dancing. Wallace had come to what were considered radical views in such matters. When asked privately by

anxious youngsters whether to dance were sinful, he would tell
them of a girl back in the old country, Scotland:

'Jeanie, do ye feel any sin when dancing?' the presiding elder
asked.

'I do not,' she answered.

'Then, dance, Jeanie, child, aye dance!' the old elder said.[1]

But Wallace always added that he, himself, had never learned
to dance, and had never regretted it. He had to take a middle-
of-the-road position in many matters, there in Illinois and Iowa,
at first. It would have been considered the height of impertinence
for a student 'on supply' to have suggested changes in dogma or
ritual. He felt, himself, that the distribution of tokens before
Communion, deriving from the time when the sect was in itself
a secret society, did not square with the sect's subsequent ruling
that no member of a secret society should be admitted to Communion. Again, while granting a certain 'gnarled vigor' to

> Froward thou kythest
> Unto the froward wight —

the antique version of the Psalm saying 'With the froward thou
showest thyself froward,' he held that the old words, still a part
of the service, were more or less gibberish to the American young.
Moreover, they were not 'singable.' He wanted the young, and
he wanted singing in his church. He had determined that as
soon as he was ordained he would take a stand on these questions,
and break also with the general wartime practice of not speaking
of the conflict and the corruption of the times from the pulpit.

The chance came barely a month after his ordination. The
war was going very badly for the North; so badly, indeed, that
although President Lincoln had written his Proclamation of
Emancipation, he had hesitated until September, 1862, to issue it.
Decisive Northern victories were still to come, and the home front
was in confusion, by reason, particularly, of a great inflation of
the currency. President Lincoln proclaimed May 30, 1863, a day
of fasting and prayer. Iowa had a number of Southern sympathizers, and some of them were powerful in the affairs of church
and state in Davenport. Rather than preach on Fast Day when
he needs must speak of the War, a leading Baptist minister,
with one of the largest congregations in Davenport, found it more

convenient to be away. Wallace, the youngest pastor in the city, was asked to preach in his stead.

He embraced the chance. 'I had determined that I would go the whole length. I therefore took this text: *Is not this the fast that I have chosen; to loose the bonds of wickedness, to undo the bonds of the yoke, and to let the oppressed go free, and that ye break every yoke . . . and that thou hide not thyself from thine own flesh?*

'I soon found the audience in thorough sympathy with my radical notions. I was not half through before the Methodists and even the Baptists began shouting "Amen."'

Then Wallace made his first attack on corruption in public affairs. Going beyond generalities, he charged that there was graft at McClellan Heights, a near-by military camp, and to the business men of Davenport who were in on that graft, 'Repent, and do work meet for repentance!' he cried.

It was a written address. He had worked on it hard and carefully. Printed by newspapers as far away as New York, his Fast Day sermon did much to establish the young Reverend Wallace as a man of importance in Davenport. But it aroused antagonism as well. Members of his own two congregations became more hotly divided in their opinions, not only as to ritual and politics, but as to the 'soundness' of Wallace as a man.

2. Deaths and a Marriage

HIS COURTSHIP of Nancy Ann Cantwell had advanced meantime to the point of a formal engagement. The Second Battle of Bull Run was fought on August 29, 1862. Standing next day before a newspaper office in Davenport, Henry Wallace read that among those killed was Colonel James Cantwell. 'I knew that her father was all in all to her, and that she would be in very great trouble; I therefore took the first train and went to give her what comfort I could.' His journey was to Kenton, Ohio, where the Cantwell family then lived. It was the fourth or fifth time that he had ever seen the girl to whom he now was betrothed to marry in the course of a year.

The next time he saw her was the day they were married at a

Presbyterian Church in Kenton, September 10, 1863. The
Cantwells were Episcopalians, but now that 'Nannie' was marrying this young minister she changed her sect. 'You are marrying
a shadow!' her friends teased her. Henry Wallace, grown to a
full six feet now, was having one of his spells of stomach trouble,
which seemed to coincide always with troubles in his church
or congregation. He had been living on nothing but tea and
toast for months, and was 'very thin in flesh — about 137 pounds.'
He was twenty-seven years of age now and she was twenty-four.

'Oh!' said the bride saucily to attendants, as the train came in
to bear them eastward. 'How can I go away with this strange
man?' She was a pert little thing, fine of bone, elegant in carriage.
Her height was five feet three and she weighed only ninety pounds
at the time of her marriage. She was handsome, in a petite way,
rather than pretty; spirited and humorous and proud. Scotch-
Irish like the Wallaces, the Cantwells had rather more Irish in
their blood stream than Scotch.

'When she was between twelve and twenty years of age,'
her grandchild, Henry Agard Wallace, wrote of her retrospectively
in typed *Notes on Ancestry*, 'her father spent several years in the
Ohio House and Senate and she got a little taste of social life
and a sense of the varying importance of different people. After
marriage she led the life of a U.P. minister's wife, although considering the size of her family she found a lot of time for writing,
painting and club work. Her eyes were hazel or brown shot
with yellow; straight, fine, dark-red hair. She had freckled
hands and a medium-sized nose, fairly straight, but with a
little bump on the end of it. She gave the impression of being
weak physically, but really had great endurance and vitality.
A close observer. Good with her hands. Bright and alert men-
tally. Intuitive rather than logical. Moderately original in her
methods of thinking. Good memory. Humorous. Not philosophical; wanted action; highstrung. She liked a horse that
would get out and move. She was suggestible; her thinking
processes could easily be influenced by those who cared for her.
An indulgent parent, she devoted much time to her children.
Very ambitious for her husband. Deeply religious but not pious.
Extremely sympathetic, appreciative and quick to do justice

to others, she made others believe in themselves. She was a good mixer but decidedly aristocratic. She seemed instinctively to feel that some people were much more worthwhile than others.'

After a wedding-trip visit to the Wallaces at Spring Mount, Henry returned with his bride to the banks of the Mississippi. They started their life together in one room of a Rock Island boarding house. Wallace's small fixed salary could not be stretched far, with an inflation running, and he was yet to discover the delights of acquiring easy money by speculating in land.

The war was entering its third winter. The offensive had passed to the forces of the North. Lee's second attempt to invade in the eastern sector had ended in the shambles of Gettysburg, and major action had shifted westward: Atlanta, Chattanooga, Chickamauga. But the North as a whole seemed torn, at times incurably torn, with internecine strife. There had been riots at many places, smaller replicas or variations of the draft riots in New York City.

In many ways the first winter of this Wallace marriage was the darkest winter of the War Between the States. Doubtless the troubles and differences Henry encountered in his church affairs were in some part the reflection of national cleavage and hysteria, for the war was drawing closer to the Middle North.

He had been working before his marriage to bring about a union of several weak Presbyterian churches in Rock Island, a union that would lead the joint congregations to more liberal worship and provide him and his new wife with a more spacious and rewarding living. He thought that he had the union arranged, but returned from the East with his bride only to find that the richest man in the congregation had led a petty insurrection to wreck the plan. He rather lacked ardor in his Rock Island duties after that, and did more of his work across the river in Iowa. Here he moved boldly. He dispensed with the use of tokens before Communion, admitted the singing of hymns, admitted Psalms translated into plain English. He initiated an ambitious program of social work and adult education which reached beyond his congregation to the community as a whole.

Davenport in the eighteen-sixties was a hard-drinking city, drinking even harder now in time of war. Soon growing tired of praying over sots who wept and immediately returned to the bottle, Wallace called and addressed a temperance mass meeting with a definite object. He proposed that the church people of Davenport set up, in competition with the saloons, a 'poor man's club — warm, well-lighted, with modern reading material, and games and light refreshments.' Then he pressed on. He proposed to rehabilitate a library in Rock Island which had been closed for lack of funds. To this end he promoted a lyceum or winter lecture course in a large hall above a livery stable. The idea took hold. Wallace discovered to his delight that the larger the fee a speaker charged, the more profit there was in it for the sponsoring organization. He scheduled such headliners as Bayard Taylor, Annie Dickinson — 'a brilliant woman, but a spitfire' — and the Liberator hero of his boyhood, Wendell Phillips. 'Never have I heard any other lecture equal to that,' he said of Phillips's performances in this series. 'He spoke in a conversational tone, made but one gesture, and that a slight motion of the forefinger of his right hand — and held his audience breathless from beginning to end.'

In the expository style of preaching that he was developing, Wallace gave preference to a conversational tone. The orthodox high boxed pulpit of his Davenport church cramped and irked him. 'It ·seemed to stand as a barrier between me and my people. I asked the trustees if they would tear away the pulpit except the platform and give me a little stand that I could move from one side to the other. This was regarded as an innovation, offending the prejudices of some of my people. The most serious objector, unfortunately, was the richest man in the congregation.'

So it had been in Rock Island. There, too, it was the richest man who withdrew. But that rich man was a non-resident, and so was not subject to Presbyterian church discipline; and this rich man of Davenport remained in residence but stubbornly stayed away from service. He said that he could not return until that upstart had been driven from that pulpit. Wallace could not ignore the challenge to apply church discipline, in which he had little confidence or belief, so he had the Session cite the truant to appear. The recalcitrant member appealed to the

Presbytery and finally to the General Assembly, which ignored the appeal as trivial. So this certain rich man and another, with certain of their relatives, transferred attendance to another church. But Wallace now was beginning to attract to both of his churches increasing audiences of clerical and working people; and his churches actually showed a better record financially after their richest initial contributors had taken their souls for more soothing treatment to other pews.

The war entered its fourth year in 1864. The dead and mangled were now to be numbered by the hundreds of thousands. There were many Cantwells in the service. Each week or month seemed to bring to Nancy Wallace the news of some cousin, uncle, or other relative dead or wounded. And in 1864, Henry Wallace's brother, James, died of consumption, the first of seven brothers and sisters to die of the same disease, one by one, before their thirtieth year. James's death was a heavy loss to Henry's father and mother and to the family as a whole. They had thought him the vigorous member of the family in contrast to the oldest son, Ross, who had always been 'delicate' and saved from the heavy chores.

James had taken the lead in all the farm work, and was hewing logs to build a barn on a farm which his father had recently purchased when he took a severe cold which settled in his lungs and killed him.

'It was a most crushing blow to my father,' wrote Henry. 'He had a great ambition that one of his sons should take the old farm and maintain the family and the old name at that place. I had gone. Ross was evidently in decline. We had leaned heavily on James. The two other boys were unable to take his place.'

Nancy and Henry Wallace took the first train to Spring Mount when news of James's death came in a letter from the family. There was nothing they could do to help hold Spring Mount and John Wallace's new farm together as a continuing family property. It was too late. Henry advised his family to change soil and climate, come to Iowa, start anew. But it was now too late for those of the Wallaces still at Spring Mount to take a new hold vigorously atop fresh soil.

3. To the Front

EARLY IN 1865 Wallace applied for an appointment in the Christian Commission, a non-denominational body, formed during the war to perform religious, social, and hospital services for the Northern Army. The ministers who went on such service were loaned, ordinarily, by their congregations for a six weeks' tour of duty. They received no pay from the Government, but the railroads let them ride free. The work might vary from safe and harmless Y.M.C.A. frivolities to tending the wounded on the line of action. Wallace asked to be sent to the front. 'I am anxious to see something of actual war,' he said.

His orders came through in February, 1865, just six weeks before the end of the war. He took his wife with him as far as Ohio and left her with her people there. In Philadelphia he reported to the national headquarters of the Commission and was shipped to Baltimore with a mixed cargo of Union replacements, religious and social workers, and paroled Confederate prisoners returning South. Wallace was like a boy on an outing. 'This was the first time I had ever traveled on a canal boat. Every bunk and berth was occupied, and we had to sit around on our "hunkers" or on the floor.' Wallace talked for the greater part of the night with a paroled Confederate — 'a brilliant fellow' with whom he spoke 'as freely as though we had been comrades.'

Proceeding by steamboat southward from Baltimore to Fortress Monroe, Wallace fell in with the eminent evangelist, Dwight L. Moody, who was one of the leaders of the Christian Commission. Wallace had enjoyed, in a measure, a previous acquaintance with the Reverend Moody on missionary boards in the Midland, and had formed a distaste for Moody's 'religious hysterics.' [2]

The evangelist had been so distressed by the smutty singing of soldiers that he had commanded them to surround him and sing a hymn. 'There is a fountain filled with blood. Sing!'

They started singing, for the most part mockingly. Without his evangelistic partner, Sankey, Moody 'never could sing a bit,' Wallace observed. He had no more music in him than a crow. A lurching Irishman broke into the ragged roaring, asking:

'Mister, what branch of the Church do you belong to?'

'To no branch! To the root!' Moody cried.

The Irishman howled and came in with his fists up. Protestant soldiers had to keep the Catholics back and protect the evangelist all that night. Moody, Wallace noted, seemed proud of this; and all that he said he planned to do when assuming command at his new station sounded 'exceedingly dictatorial, arbitrary and impatient.'

A cold February was turning into a stormy March when Wallace arrived at his station before Richmond at the extreme right of the Army of the James. Richmond and Petersburg were under siege. Both Grant and Lee were waiting impatiently for summer weather and firmer ground to throw their forces into a decisive action. It was a quiet front and morale was low.

'I had expected,' Wallace wrote, 'to hear more or less skirmishing going on, but in three weeks I did not hear a gun, except the firing off of guns that had been brought in by deserters from the Rebel Army. The breastworks of both armies were but a short distance apart. On a clear day we could see the church spires of Richmond. The swapping of tobacco and provisions was constantly going on between soldiers [of the North and South]. Desertions from the Confederates were frequent and desertions to the Confederates almost as frequent. In the neighborhood of our tent there were three Connecticut regiments made up largely of bounty-jumpers who had deserted from their own regiments for the bounty, amounting to $500 or $600, given by the cities of some of the eastern states.'

The Colonel of one of these 'broken home' regiments, having had all manner of Methodists and Congregationalists pray over and preach before his idle rogues to no good end, entreated Wallace: 'Come over and preach the good, old-fashioned United Presbyterian doctrine of eternal torment!' Wallace did; but that was no good either. Desertions continued. The men crouched in the mud under improvised tents in foul March weather, and spoke most blasphemously of Virginia's 'sacred soil.'

On Saint Patrick's Day, March 17, 1865, Abraham Lincoln, together with Grant, Stanton, Sheridan, Meade, Hancock, and Ord, the leading officers of the armies of the James and the Potomac, visited this sector. It was a bright, sunny day. Irish

Catholics among the troops competed in climbing a greased pole and in trying to catch a shaven, soaped pig. 'Father Abraham' and the generals rode up and down the lines. This was the second time that Wallace had seen Lincoln. He was less impressed than he had been before. 'Lincoln is probably the most awkward man that ever rode a horse,' he wrote.

Wallace spent his twenty-ninth birthday, March 19, in a makeshift tent, fighting a terrific rain and wind storm that rose to its height on the twenty-first. War, he reflected, is a dull business. But the weather was turning more open now, and things were stirring. Only in the vague way that men at the front know where they fit into large stratagems did Wallace know exactly what was up, though he knew several generals. Years afterwards, when memoirs had been written, maps drawn, and varying views resolved in the wisdom of hindsight, the contemplated action seemed in essence simple. Grant had determined to withdraw a considerable part of his Army of the James, three divisions, from the right of their line, before Richmond, and throw more strength across the most probable point of the enemy's attempt to escape westward, at his left, around Petersburg.

Provisioning in the Army of the James was a rather random business. This Christian rookie, Wallace, of no particular rank or command, proved a good forager from the first. He and his companions in that leaky tent got hold of a cook who was a wonder. 'What that man could do in the way of temporary needs of the moment,' Wallace exclaimed, 'no one was able to find out! He could make the most delicious biscuits that I ever ate except in Kentucky. He was amazingly fertile.'

General Harris, commanding three regiments, the Tenth, Eleventh, and Twelfth West Virginia, himself a United Presbyterian who loved good fare and conversation, found Wallace's tent a pleasant place to visit and often stopped by. One night he said:

'"We are going to move tomorrow. There will be something doing the next three weeks. I have three regiments and no chaplain. Would you care to act as volunteer chaplain until the end of the war or of your term? I don't want you to give me a hasty answer, because you may get a bullet."

'I told him at once that I would go with him, and he said:

'"Report to me at five tomorrow morning. I have provided a horse and blankets for you. You can mess with me and sleep in my tent."'

At daylight next morning they started. The first day's action was a feint. Two thousand foot soldiers and a pontoon corps commanded by General Mickey made a fifteen-mile march to the Chickahominy with intent to mislead the enemy into thinking that by linking the banks with a bridge there Sheridan's cavalry would strike over that bridge. 'A detachment of Confederates,' Wallace's notes of the action relate, 'was evidently marching in parallel columns with us, as occasionally we could see their videttes standing at a distance on a high place; and once in a while a shot would be fired and a man would fall.'

They camped that night on the bank of the Chickahominy, then marched back, 'the pontoon corps taking the pontoons with them. We did not go back to our old quarters, but went direct to the James River; and before we reached it saw the whole Twenty-Third Army Corps, comprising some fifteen or twenty thousand men, in motion. Cavalry, infantry, artillery — all in motion. Something was going to happen and I was glad that I had an opportunity to see it. We marched all night, past Painted Rock, on to the left of Richmond, to the east of Petersburg.'

The march continued a day longer, 'from the extreme right to the extreme left, and through the different army corps, whose numbers I have forgotten. That night the General [Harris] said to me:

'"Chaplain, I think there will be some work in the morning. I want to write a letter to my wife. I suggest you had better write to yours, though I don't know where we can post them."'

They both wrote letters to their wives. Wallace mounted to ride and post them. He had a friend on the Christian Commission, attached to the Ninth Corps, who was handling soldier mail. But: 'It was dark and I missed the way. (I never could find my way, anyhow.) On inquiry I got back on the right road, which happened to be a corduroy road, and put spurs to my horse.

'I remember the horse falling. I remember hearing his hoofs

as he got up and started away. I followed, not knowing where I was going. I remember asking some soldiers if they had seen a horse. I became unconscious.'

It was evidently a case of concussion. He was out on his feet. They found him wandering around and took him to the tent of Reynolds, the man he had been looking for to mail his letters. 'On waking, I found him and some others bending over me in great alarm.'

The days that followed remained forever strange in his mind. He could remember parts of them with uncanny clarity — the sound of a voice saying certain words, the sharp outlines of a face or action, the smell and feel and sound of things. He was in some skirmishing, but remembered none of it. He remembered the men of his regiment throwing up breastworks; he remembered meeting troops from West Newton and talking with Bob Fulmer, an old schoolmate; but no fighting.

General Harris saw that he was a little 'off' and requested him to go back to City Point to the hospital.

Wallace went, after some argument, but proved a cheerfully recalcitrant patient. Making friends with a young theological student from Boston, another 'walking case' at the hospital, 'I took a notion to go back and see the boys up in front of Richmond, and went. Wherever I went my young friend went with me.'

They were truly 'walking cases,' but they took such lifts as offered. Returning from Richmond they 'missed the boat, but got a skiff, went over to Bermuda Hundreds, crossed the neck, and caught a boat as it came around the bend. That was Saturday.'

Saturday, April 1, 1865: 'I shall never forget that night. I was commending myself to my Maker by my cot in the hospital at nine o'clock, when I heard the first gun in the attack on Petersburg. It was followed by cannon after cannon. The gunboats on the James joined in, and during the entire night, whenever I was awake, the windows were rattling. I arose at six, got some breakfast from one of the cooks, and started off for the battlefield, taking the railroad (which was not much of a road, being laid up and down without grading), and always listening to the roar of

the cannon. When I thought I was about opposite Petersburg,
I left the track and started off. Singularly enough, I struck my
own division, which, after swinging around to Seven Forks and
Hatcher's Run, had moved up to attack Fort Gregg, on the south
of Petersburg, while the New England regiments attacked it in
front.'

By the time he got there the battle was over. The dead lay
all about, and the wounded were many. Wallace came again
upon the company from West Newton and asked about a cousin.
'He had been killed and buried. There was too much to do to
look after a dead man. I would not like to say how many men
there were at that field hospital with severe wounds. I was
busy assisting the surgeons all afternoon until about ten that
night. I can still see the pile of legs and arms that lay outside
the operating tables.'

4. In Pursuit of Lee

O N THAT SAME DAY, Sunday, April 2, General Lee sent a
telegram to President Davis at Richmond, saying that
both Petersburg and Richmond must be evacuated at
once. Jefferson Davis read the message in church and left before
the service ended. He was, in effect, no longer President. The
Confederate States had no capital city or offices of central government from that time on. It was a wild and tragic Sunday in
Richmond. Committees of citizens undertook to destroy all
liquor, lest the Yankees swill it. The gutters of Richmond ran
with the stuff, even as the retreating military burned tobacco
warehouses and blew up the iron-clad rams in the river; and di-
vers bands of soldiers and civilians reeled around seeking pillage.
Next morning the Federal forces entered the city.

The flight and pursuit of Lee and his shattered forces westward
to Appomattox, where Lee surrendered, was in effect the final
engagement of the war. The course of the pursuit was a jagged
seventy miles, with the lines of march roughly parallel, and the
Federals striking wherever they happened to establish a glancing
contact with the forces of the enemy heading west. There were

innumerable small engagements, or collisions, and great slaughter; for the action was now entirely out in the open, and both sides had attained to a deadly skill in open warfare.

Wallace had by this time recovered from the head wound and General Harris had replaced the horse which had stumbled from under his chaplain over a log in the corduroy road. Wallace's notes on the week's pursuit are far more clear than his recollection of the action before Petersburg.

'Monday was a clear, bright day. The sun never shone lovelier. The peach trees were in full bloom. The bands played their most soul-inspiring airs. The flags waved in the breeze. The battle and the carnage, the groans of the dying and the wounded on their weary way to the field hospital at City Point, were in marked contrast to all this.'

General Grant rode with General Harris and his attendants, Wallace among them, on the first stages of the chase. 'It was to be a long chase and a weary one. General Grant was a particular friend of General Harris. They rode together at least two or three hours of the day, Grant on his famous black horse, with a cigar in his face, whether smoking or not, said but little, and then on general subjects — nothing about the fall of Richmond, which had then taken place, although the army did not know it until the next day.'

So they marched for the first day and night. Every once in a while couriers would gallop up to Grant, and he would fall behind to receive their dispatches, then gallop to his place at the head of the line again.

On the third day Wallace happened to be standing within a few feet of General Grant when two or three cavalrymen came through the pine woods and handed the General a message which he read aloud. It was from Sheridan, telling Grant that if he would push on a brigade as fast as possible to the high bridge over some creek, Lee could be intercepted and the whole army captured. The General at once put spurs to his horse and Wallace did not see him again until after Appomattox.

The war was going to pieces fast. Wallace marched on with his corps as far as Farmville. There he set forth with his corporal's guard, foraging. They came to an old house with a locust tree in the yard. A cannon ball had torn a limb from the locust tree but had not harmed the house. 'There were a woman and three or four grown-up daughters in the house. While my boys were getting a chicken — and from subsequent experience I suspected it was the one Noah took into the ark — I interviewed the ladies. They did not seem to be particularly afraid of me. I assured them that there was no danger to them. They could not understand where all this army that was passing through came from. They seemed to think the North was a great city, which could pour out men.

'A drizzling rain came up. There were no tents — at least I had none. There were plenty of fences, however. The best thing I could do was to take a blanket, fasten it to a fence rail, drive in a couple of stakes and fasten the other end to them. I then went to an old straw stack, gathered up some coarse straw, and made me a bed. In the meantime, after an hour or two of cooking, we undertook to eat that rooster; but I could feel it revolving in my stomach all night. I regretted my bed, for the next morning I found it was plentifully supplied with chiggers. They were strangers to me although possibly I was not altogether a stranger to them. I had chigger sores for a month afterwards.

'The next morning the army resumed its chase. A number of men in my brigade had been wounded in the skirmish the day before; quite a number had been wounded in the Battle of Harper's Farm, and had been taken to Berksville. I walked back to help look after them instead of going on to the final surrender at Appomattox. On the eighteen-mile walk back I met a very jubilant-looking darkey; in fact, he came out to meet me at a crossing.

'"What do you people think about these doings?"

'"Massa, the white folks can't think for crying and the black folks can't think for joy."'

In Berksville Wallace fell to work amid horror. More than three thousand of both armies with capital wounds were crammed into improvised hospitals, mainly two long railroad sheds, largely open to the weather, with the crudest of operating equipment, knives, tables, basins, lint, and inadequate anaesthetics.

'It is no pleasant thing to see capital wounds so treated. It is no pleasant thing to have a wounded man say to you: "Chaplain, won't you take this dead man away?" I don't dare to try to describe that experience.'

He was much impressed with a Southern white woman he met in a rickety one-horse wagon with a Negro driver. Learning that her husband she was looking for had been captured and sent on to Richmond, she settled down to help care for the wounded. 'I watched that woman work with us in the hospital the next two days. They told me she never slept. Her husband was out of her reach, but she turned in, and, with the most wonderful courage and endurance and devotion, ministered to the wants of Federal and Confederate alike. I knew the Southern people fairly well, but I think I never saw any woman with more courage, devotion and endurance, or of a better spirit.'

He rode with the wounded on a jolting freight to Richmond, helping make them 'as comfortable as possible. It was the worst night's travel I had ever endured; you hardly knew whether the train was on the track or off it.

'It was a great relief, on our arrival in the early morning at daylight, to go down to the James and wash off the "sacred soil" of which I had accumulated considerable in the last week; to count the number of chigger sores, and then get aboard a steamer for Fortress Monroe, and home.'

I V

MORNING SUN AND WINTERSET

What is West? It is a form of society rather than an area. A new environment is entered, freedom of opportunity is opened, the cake of custom is broken, and new activities, new institutions and new ideals are brought into existence. — FREDERICK JACKSON TURNER in *The Frontier in American History.*

1. Interim

HE MADE HIS WAY homeward through a welter of disorganized transportation and communication. He saw Grant — 'silent, self-contained, reticent' — on the train from Richmond to City Point.

Four days later Wallace got off for a meal stop at Alliance, Ohio, and met General Mickey, whom he had come to know in Virginia. 'Lincoln was shot last night in the theater in Washington,' General Mickey said. Wallace could not believe it. But all along the way papers were coming out with the news of a wounded President, and the news of the President's death reached Nancy Wallace at Kenton while Wallace was still traveling. She was with child and greatly agitated. Mails and the telegraph were overladen and slow, and she had not heard from her husband for three weeks.

'She was almost distracted, waiting every day for a letter,' said Wallace, telling of his homecoming. 'When she saw in the papers that Lincoln had been killed, she ran to my brother-in-law's store crying that the Rebels had killed Lincoln, that they were going to kill all the great men, and Mr. Wallace would be the next one. My brother-in-law said: "I guess not. I have just had a telegram from him. He will be here in an hour."

'As long as she lived, she never heard the last of "killing all the great men."'

They were hoping that the Wallace luck would hold and that their first-born would be a boy, to be named Henry, the second American Henry Wallace of the line. But the child, born a few weeks later, was a girl, and weakly. Because of slight stature and fragile form Nancy Wallace suffered horribly in childbirth. The child, named Mary, died after a three-day illness in her third month.

'A most grievous blow. She was a most affectionate and devoted mother,' Wallace wrote somberly. 'Partly to distract her mind from her sorrow, and partly because we did not find boarding a satisfactory life, we rented a small house in Rock Island, on the river bank, and went to housekeeping. There she was comforted by the birth of our oldest boy, Henry Cantwell, the next year.'

This was on May 19, 1866. Called 'Harry' in the family, in order to distinguish him from his father, Henry Cantwell Wallace led in his early boyhood a life more constricted, less simple, and less spacious than his father had led as a boy. The house, on the banks of one river city facing another river city across in Iowa, was small. It was not a tranquil home or time. The Reverend was worn down by a constant denominational bickering, by an irritating petty supervision of his family's every action, and by continuing illness and death within the family.

Back East the old home place and farming tradition were passing out, with none of the family fit to go on farming there. Wallace's favorite sister, Martha, died of consumption in 1865. In 1868 Ross, the second eldest son, died. In 1869 the Wallaces offered Spring Mount for sale. John Wallace and his wife Martha, together with their three surviving children, removed to a rented house in Rock Island, to be near Henry. Nancy Wallace's widowed mother and a brother also came to live in Rock Island. They all leaned heavily upon him. He was the central pillar of remaining strength in the Wallace clan. And now his health, too, was failing. 'Bowel trouble,' they called it, with a possible complication of 'lung trouble.' The attacks would come almost invariably on Sunday evenings, after he had preached two sermons. Pain would take sharp, rending hold on his chest or bowels. His arms and legs grew cold and it would take hours to get them warm again.

He had not smoked as a youth or as a divinity student. As an ordained minister, in his thirtieth year, he started smoking Pittsburgh stogies and kept at it incessantly, wherever he went. This was criticized. He promised his people, wryly, not to smoke in church, and added (no one ever knew whether he was serious or joking) that a doctor had told him Pittsburgh stogies had an antiseptic effect on the lungs. He was a furious and messy smoker, scattering ashes upon his clothing and on the floor. This too was criticized, even at home, for Nancy Ann Wallace was a finicky housekeeper. 'Now, Blossom,' he would say mildly when she scolded. He called her 'Blossom,' in the family. She called him 'Mr. Wallace,' or 'Your Father.'

The Western march was under way with a rush again, now that the war had ended. This point on the Great River where the Wallaces were stationed was a passage point for a considerable part of the migration. Crossing on the ferry went prairie schooners and families afoot. The boy Harry could sometimes hear them singing:

> Cheer up, brothers, as we go
> O'er the mountains, westward ho —

Then:

> O'er the hills in legions, boys,
> Fair freedom's star
> Points to the sunset regions, boys —
> Ha, Ha, Ha-ha!

They were Americans and they smelled new land. Inflation still was running high, but out beyond the middle of Iowa new soil still was cheap, and the turnover was rapid, on a rising market.

At first to eke out his salary in time of inflation, and then for the gain and joy of it, the Reverend began toward the end of 1869 to play around in the land market. Cautious John Wallace, his father, loaned him a thousand dollars at six per cent interest, and advised him to put it in bonds. 'I shall put it in land,' said the Reverend, and went out to look for his land. His first deal, in which he had a partner, one Thompson, was on a quarter section, in which he held 'an eighty,' or half share, in Scott County, Iowa, down the river on the Illinois border. 'We

bought at $11 an acre — bought it cheap because about seventy
acres of it was a bare slough needing drainage. We spent $11,
rented the improved land next year for $2 an acre in cash and
one third of the crop; had the slough mowed on shares, and
realized $12 an acre net rent for the cultivated land. This may
seem large rent, but the ground was already broken.'

The township, Cleone, in Scott County, was almost entirely
German. Few could speak English. Wallace's partner, Thompson, spent a good deal of time there on the ground. He was a
vigilant steward, seeing that the crop was locked in the granary,
while he carried the key until threshing time, and then superin-
tended the division of the grain. 'Thus there was no danger of
any of it getting away from us,' wrote Wallace. 'Prices were
good. I remember being offered $1.97 [a bushel] for barley, and
holding for an even $2.00. I sold it afterward at $1.60. I comforted myself with remembering that my father had been holding
his wool for a dollar. I advised him to sell it, which he was
afterwards glad to do at fifty cents. So I was not the only
unwise farmer.'

He had, nevertheless, formed 'a taste for making easy money.'
With only ten dollars in his pocket he bid for and took title to
a three-hundred-and-twenty-acre tract at the end of Burlington,
giving a sixty-day note for $1000. The land, which had city-lot
prospects, cost him only a little more than $3.00 an acre. Before
the note matured he sold it at $12.50 an acre. Then he put part
of his winnings in Adair County land at $2.50 an acre, did some
breaking and sold it the next year for $10.00 an acre. He bought
and sold this particular piece of Adair County without ever seeing
it or setting foot upon it. But he was traveling around Iowa now
by train and buggy quite a little, courting the country before
deciding where to settle down; and of all the country he saw,
the adjacent counties of Madison and Adair, in central Iowa,
south from Des Moines, pleased him best. Even careful John
Wallace, having moved the remaining members of his family
West in 1869, took the fever a little and allowed his son Henry to
buy in his name some of this fine, fresh Adair County earth. In
1870, when the first income tax was collected, the Reverend Henry
proudly paid a somewhat larger tax than his father, Squire John.

2. Affairs of Earth

IN THE WINTER of 1870-71 he resigned his charges in the cities by the river and accepted a country call to Morning Sun, in Louisa County, a riverbank county of Iowa. This village is down the river from Davenport, and some twenty miles north of Burlington. It was at the time a village and community of farmers. Most of them, having come from a community of the same name in Ohio, had replanted three Presbyterian churches, a United Presbyterian and two Covenanter edifices on this new soil.

The people of Morning Sun were carrying on a number of old family feuds, originating back in Ohio. 'These good people,' Wallace continued, writing of his new location and duties, 'think it their religious duty to "visit the sins" (real and fancied) of the fathers upon the children, at least to the second generation.' He knew the locality, in a general way, from his trips to religious conferences and from his land-buying. He could estimate the difficulties in advance. But it was good farming country there around Morning Sun; the people were at heart 'wonderfully friendly,' and his health had broken sharply that winter. 'Go,' his father advised. 'Buy a small farm, look after it. Keep out-of-doors as much as possible and your health will be restored.'

So the Henry Wallaces and their son Harry, a lad of eleven now, went to Morning Sun and lived on a small place at the edge of town. The Reverend Wallace was out in the country again. He put by his ministerial garb almost entirely, and wore his frock coat only when preaching or when attending formal church sessions. He stopped writing his sermons to be read from the pulpit and preached extempore. He dug in the garden a little, and walked for miles around the country, hunting, fishing, and talking with farmers. Informally he revived the vanishing practice of pastoral calls. 'My habit of hunting and fishing gave me the opportunity of knowing everybody who had any sport in him. I stopped once for a cup of water at the house of a parishioner and the old lady who opened the door took me for a tramp. When I told her who I was the lightning change in her expression was very amusing. There was nothing too good for me after that. If I asked for water, she would give me milk, and had I asked for butter she would have offered me honey in a dish. I made it a point to talk farming to the farmers.

'I got the idea that if a man wants to preach effectively to country people he must do so in terms of farm life. I sat at my people's feet, so to speak, and learned enough about farming there to ask intelligent questions. One farmer, for example, one day called to my attention the fact that if the pasture grass was closely pastured down, blue grass would come in of itself, and that blue grass was the best pasture grass in the Mississippi Valley. I found later that this theory was absolutely correct.

'Once when hunting wild turkeys, I fell in with a hunter, rather famous in the neighborhood, who was also a very successful bee-keeper. He said to me: "Why don't you keep bees?" I replied: "I would, if I could get a hive that would not swarm on the Sabbath." He sold me a hive of Italians, very gentle, and showed me how to divide them so there would be no occasion to swarm. I set them out under a cherry tree in the front yard, and thereafter kept bees. This kept me out of doors and was profitable. It was unusual in that staid old United Presbyterian congregation, surrounded by still more staid and rigid Covenanters, for a preacher to do so many unministerial things, but my people endured it.'

The church itself was a square stone building, 'of studied ugliness,' and the acoustics were 'rather trying to a man whose lungs, as mine at that time, were not of the best.' Some people did not like his new, plain style of speaking without manuscript or notes, but most of them liked Wallace. Sabbath after Sabbath they filled his church.

Slowly, as his health improved, he became less abrupt in pronouncing judgments, more mellow; and they called upon him to settle land squabbles, arbitrate wills, pray over their sick, and decide such questions as whether a man should marry his dead wife's sister. But Wallace could be short when he felt that he need be. He would stride into stuffy sickrooms and throw up windows. (Faulty ventilation was much on his mind at the time, because of the malady ravaging his father's family.) On one occasion, when a Methodist divine had prayed a hysterical woman into a nervous spasm, 'This is not a praying case!' Wallace pronounced sternly and told them to call in a doctor and stop that other preacher if he came back.

They were touchy people, the farmers around Morning Sun. They had to be handled gently, as a rule. Wallace developed for most of them a deep fondness during his six years there. He discovered within himself new skills in 'making some salve for sore heads and doing some anointing.' One such need of anointment was brought upon him by Harry and John, 'degenerate sons of the pastor,' and the prank they played upon a 'peculiar member of the congregation, afflicted with a habit of which he was entirely unconscious. He had a habit of drawing in his breath while I was preaching, and emitting it slowly. The boys got to calling him "Hoo, Poo!"'

Hoo-Poo lived at the edge of the timber. His farm was part prairie and part woods. His fences were imperfect, so his cows were belled. He was always on the alert to keep them out of his corn. Harry and John would slip out to Hoo-Poo's place at night, carrying cowbells. Other boys joined the sport. They deployed with their cowbells in the corn and on the timber side and ran poor Hoo-Poo all over hell's half-acre, night after night. But there is no such thing, perhaps, as a perfect crime or prank.

'One of the boys,' their father related later, 'dropped his hat in the cornfield. It had church papers in it, so the offenders were located. He had heard what they called him, so he was doubly offended. Naturally, the man quit coming to church. The session summoned him. He refused to attend. They laid the matter before me, confessed that they had blundered, and asked me if I would not try to get him back to church. I studied over the matter, borrowed a horse one day, went out past his farm, where I saw two men plashing a hedge, that is, cutting a hedge of two or three years' growth half-way down, and banding it across, not to kill the plants, but to compel sprouts to grow up thickly, and fill any vacant places there may be. I suddenly became very greatly interested in plashing. I told them that I had control of a farm belonging to my father that had just such a hedge on it, and that I did not know how to fix it.'

The owner of the place, in charge of the job, was glad to enlighten him. 'After getting a lot of valuable information, I asked him to whom I was indebted for it. He told me who he was, and I said:

'"Why, bless me! You are a member of my church."

'"Well," he said, "I was; but I declared I never would enter that church door again."'

Wallace threw his leg over the arm of the saddle and argued. 'I tried to use the old argument that boys will be boys, even if they are the sons of preachers or the elders, and that he could well afford to overlook it. The more I talked, the more excited he became. Finally I looked him squarely in the eye, and said:

'"I am thoroughly ashamed of you."

'"I'd like to know why," he said.

'"Well," I answered, "when you became a member of the church you made a fair-and-square bargain, as follows: *If they have persecuted me, they will persecute you.* Now you are getting what you bargained for, and you are whimpering about it like a baby." He thought about it for a minute and said: "Well, now, there may be something in that." He and his wife returned to the church, and one or two members of his family joined the church at the next Communion season.'

Life was rarely dull at Morning Sun. Wallace grew in strength and in peace of mind. But: 'I had more trouble in getting in touch with the Covenanters, notwithstanding the fact that I held them in highest regard. There were two congregations of them, one in town and one in the country, made up of the best farmers and the best people, on the whole, in the community. They were somewhat shocked at my ways of hunting, fishing and getting acquainted with all sorts of people. They were particularly shocked when I felt compelled to oppose their pet project, that of securing an amendment to the constitution of the United States, especially recognizing the Divine Name and the authority of Jesus in things governmental and political as well as religious. Knowing that I had been educated partly in a Covenanter college they could not understand why I opposed a principle which seemed to them self-evident, and some of the survivors think to this day (1915) that I am a sort of renegade and heretic.

'I said what I thought. I told them, for example, that an amendment to the constitution of the United States required a two-thirds vote, and that this would be an impossible task: that it would disfranchise Jews, Unitarians, Free-Thinkers, and change the constitution of our government. I said that an amendment to the constitution is useless unless accompanied by proper legislation; and that while I believed that good would come of the discussion, I did not believe that it would ever amount to anything. Furthermore I told them that the people always get as good a government as they deserved — that the main object of the churches should be to convert sinners and build up character, and that in the proportion that this was done we would have a Christian government, not merely in name but in fact.

'As they refused to vote until the constitution was changed, it will be seen at once that our views were widely different, and for the life of them they could not understand me,' Wallace concludes, somewhat somberly, his account of arguments with Covenanter adults. He proceeds to tell with gusto of a shocking speech he made to their young when they were forced by courtesy to ask him to say a word at one of their church picnics. In brief:

"I have been looking at those tables until my mouth waters. I am sure your mouths are watering too. This is not the Sabbath. This is a picnic. I will not keep you five minutes from those tables. But I want to tell you a story about a little boy sitting on a fence. A stranger came up and said:

"'Sonny, what are you doing?'"

"'I'm chawing terbacker.'"

"'You oughtn't to say *chaw* but *chew*, and you oughtn't to do either. I'd like to know what you are chewing tobacco for.'"

"'To get the juice out of it,' said the little boy."

'Now [said the Reverend Wallace, concluding his parable to the Covenanter young], I wouldn't advise any of you to either chaw or chew; it's a nasty, dirty habit. But I think I can tell you how to get the juice out of today. Get at those good things on the tables. Then make the swings go; play, wrestle, but don't fight; do whatever you like in getting rid of your surplus energy. That will get the juice out of today.'

The years at Morning Sun were happier far than the years that he and his family had spent in the river cities. But he had his troubles. He could not, for the life of him, stay out of public or

political affairs. He was fearful and almost fiercely scornful of
politicians. He burned to exert sway and influence, but was unready to assume the thrall and responsibility of public office. He
was caught up in a local row as to the location of a county seat,
and so: 'In 1875 I unfortunately got into politics.' Swearing he
would ne'er consent, he finally agreed to run for the Iowa Senate
in a district comprising his own county, Louisa, and the neighboring county of Washington. His account of the half-hearted campaign he made seems to show that while he did not really want the
job they put him up for, he hated to be beaten:

Washington County had a Republican majority of about a
hundred; Louisa County, in which I lived, of about six or
seven hundred. A county seat fight was going on in Louisa
County. A lot of land speculators had located a new town at
the junction and had built a courthouse. Wapello, the old
courthouse town, was rather dead at the time, and was cut
off from a good deal of its territory by the river, which was
not always crossable. As it came the turn of Louisa County
to be represented, they put me up against my will. Each
side of the county seat matter was anxious to have me champion its side. I told them that I did not want to take any
part in the controversy, that I would not make any speeches.
I did subsequently make a speech in Washington, which was
a failure, because the state committee had sent me the usual
'dope'; in other words, had told me what I should say. As I
did not know anything about it, and cared less, there was no
heart in it, and I made the poorest speech I ever made in my
life. Finally the Columbus Junction folks sent a committee
to see me, and to tell me that if I did not take one side or the
other I would be beaten. I replied:
'Then I will be beaten, for I have given my word that I
will take no part in the controversy and I won't do it. I don't
care to go anyhow.'
Louisa County that year polled the largest vote in its history, the extra voters coming from different parts of Iowa and
from Illinois. The result was that three weeks after I was
supposed to be elected, I was found to be defeated by twenty-

three votes, although I carried Washington County over any other candidate. I was sincerely glad that I was defeated, although my wife was gravely disappointed. She had always had political ambitions for me, her father having been active in politics. . . .

This was my first and last venture into politics; for I have ever since refused to run, although twice urged to be a candidate for United States senator (the last time when election seemed absolutely certain) and once or twice for governor. I do not say that it is wrong to go into politics; but that a man should engage in politics, if at all, only from a high sense of duty, and under no obligations save to his country and his God.

His father, John Wallace, had died in 1873. Of the seven children, there were now but three living, Henry, John, and Margaret, together with the widow, to inherit the estate. The widow, Martha, and her daughter, Margaret, died in the winter of 1876. Henry's lung trouble seemed to have improved now but John was ailing. Henry and John made a trip across the Rockies to California, in an effort to raise John's spirits and improve his health. Henry had a gorgeous time, conversing on boats and stages with all sorts of odd, rough characters and 'thoroughgoing agnostics,' rebuking them for their profanity: 'Either there is a God or not,' he would argue. 'If there is not, it is foolish to talk about Him disrespectfully. If there is, it is dangerous to offend Him.' 'You're a devil of a preacher,' one rough customer responded, to Henry's delight. John seemed to improve a little. They put some money into land options around Riverside, California; and visited at Santa Barbara an 'older' cousin of Nancy Cantwell, married now to 'an old Forty-niner named Cook.' It was this Mrs. Cook who had introduced Henry to Nancy. The old Forty-niner turned out to be 'the oddest man I ever knew. The morning after we reached there, his breakfast was a great, big, raw potato, with the ends cut off, but otherwise intact.'

Everything in the Far West struck Wallace as simply wonderful. But: 'John evidently was not getting better. He took only a mild interest in things that interested me profoundly.' They

went home. 'The four children had all had the measles while I
was gone. While I was having one of the best times of my life,
my wife was having one of the hardest.' After spending a month
with Henry's family, John returned to Adair County in the hope
that life in the open air in Iowa would do for him what California
had failed to do. The Reverend and Mrs. Wallace made a pleasure trip East to Niagara Falls and from there on to Philadelphia
to attend the Centennial of 1876.

Returning, they could see at a glance that John, the last of the
children of John and Martha Wallace, save Henry only, was soon
to die. 'He had lost heart, and all that there was left to do was to
take the best care of him until his death.'

John died in the autumn of 1876. Henry brooded. 'After his
death I was despondent, I think for the only time in my life. I
liked to look at the photographs of the family, nine of whom had
died in the last twelve years and, with the exception of my mother,
all with some sort of lung trouble.'

He was aroused from this despondency in a singular way. 'I
went around to the drug store one morning and saw on the
counter a large poster telling of the villainies of the Republican
candidate for Congress. "Liar," I thought, was written all over
that poster, and down the middle. . . . The idea of charging a man
with licentiousness in Siberia on the eve of election made me
righteously angry. I said to the druggist: "Satan himself would
not own the man who wrote that."

'A fellow who was sitting there got up, white as a sheet, and
walked out. The druggist said: "That's the man." I said to him:
"Hold on, my friend. I owe you an apology. I will take it all
back. The devil *won't* be ashamed to own you."

'I made up my mind right there to stop brooding over what
could not be helped, and to do something worth while. Next day
I worked at the polls — for the first time in my life.' The maligned
Republican was elected.

Now Henry fell ill again, losing appetite and weight. A doctor
friend came to him and said:

'I want to have a square talk with you. I will give you six
months to live if you continue in that pulpit. It's either out of
the pulpit or into the boneyard.'

Wallace had about come to the same conclusion himself. He asked: 'Well, what shall I do?'

'Get as near Heaven as you can without going out of the State of Iowa. Go to Winterset and spend your time looking after your farms in Adair County, and keep out of doors.'

So in June of 1877 the Reverend Henry Wallace resigned his ministry and went with his wife and four children — Harry, Josephine, Harriett, and John — to establish himself as a landed man in southwestern Iowa. It was a trying departure. 'My wife was greatly concerned about my condition, and I was pretty blue. The train from Burlington was full of preachers. They regarded me as practically a dead man. I can see that peculiar expression when they shook hands with me and said:

'"Brother Wallace, how do you feel today? Do you cough much?" The more noted they were for their piety, the longer their faces were, and the more solemn their countenance. . . .

'To the most solemn of the whole lot, I said: "You needn't select a grave or employ an undertaker. You needn't even appoint a committee of condolence to my widow: for I shall not die, but 'live and remember the works of the Lord,' and don't you forget it!" I was so disgusted that after we left Burlington, I went to the rear of the car and sat on the steps all the way to Keokuk, just to get away from them.'

3. Man of Property

THE MOVE to Winterset in his forty-first year he always regarded as one of the principal 'turning-points' of his life. He established his family in a farmhouse with fairly large grounds and a garden and rode out in a buggy to supervise his holdings in Adair, the county adjoining. Winterset, the county seat of Madison County, had then in the late eighteen-seventies a population of twenty-six hundred and was a pleasant town. Farming and civilization were rather well developed in Madison County by that time. 'The farming was fair, so far as corn was concerned, but there had been little if any study of scientific farm problems. The land was supposed to be inexhaustible in fertility. The schools were fairly good, and the society good for a comparatively new country. The people were sociable and unusually free from class distinctions.'

To the west, Adair County, where most of Wallace's holdings lay, was fresh and raw, without trees and mostly prairie. The wave of western migration which had seeded Madison County in the eighteen-fifties had been slowed down by the panic of 1857 and the war. That was one thing. Again, Madison County was on the dividing line between the tree country and the open prairie — partly wooded and partly open. Adair was without timber; the earlier settlers from the East preferred as a rule to farm near trees. Trees, such as there were in Madison County, made them feel more at home, and provided them with fuel.

After the war, however, a swelling movement out to the open prairie southwest in Iowa resumed. Adair County was filling up. 'The State of Adair' was country to lift the heart of a man who wanted some room around him, no trees to fell or stumps to grub, and no rocks to dull his plowshare when he farmed. Most of the prairie at the point where Wallace operated was not flat; the fields had gentle lift and drained rather easily; and the roads were generally good, for they followed the ridges.

In came the settlers with 'the germs of future Iowa agriculture' in their wagons, as Herbert Quick says in *One Man's Life*, his autobiography, of this stage of Iowa's development. 'The prairie grass made a beautiful hay, so fragrant, so sweet and juicy, so free of mold and dust. Primitive Iowa was a wonderful hay country,' he writes, and 'the great bird festival of the grasslands was on. I have seen the golden plover, or prairie pigeon, running over the new-turned prairie in such numbers that the surface of the earth seemed to be moving, as with their black bellies and beautiful gold and silver spangles they sought their food.' [1]

Wallace's approach to the raw prairie was more husbandly and matter of fact. But he always distrusted overuse of the plow and had a decent respect for grass. His father before his death had installed improvements on the family's three farms in Adair, and a fourth farm which John, Senior, had bought and improved as an absentee owner came also into Henry's care. 'I am inclined to think,' he wrote with caution, knowing how fiercely such claims are disputed, 'that I brought in, in 1877, the first Shorthorn bull ever brought into Adair County, the first pure-bred hogs, as well as the first imported Percheron horse. Like many others, I began at the wrong end — the breeding of livestock instead of growing feed for them, the study of animals instead of the study of soils and methods of cultivation. I made some serious mistakes. I was executor of my father's estate, and had more money than was good for a new beginner, and of course threw some of it away; not in buying land, for every land investment I made turned out well, but in managing it. I made too many improvements, brought into cultivation too many acres, and could not always get renters who were satisfactory or who could handle livestock as it should be handled. If I had had less money to use, it would have stuck to my fingers a whole lot closer.'

His situation was more secure, perhaps, than that of the ninety-and-nine of Iowa farmers; but times were hard. For the days of the post-Civil War boom had ended; the Government proposed to resume specie payments on New Year's Day, 1879; and the nation was in panic. Wallace hauled wheat thirty miles to Winterset and sold it for thirty-seven cents a bushel. He sold fat hogs that year for two cents a pound. But he made money, he noted, on cattle grazed on the prairie with a herder to tend them. He found he could grow a calf to weaning time for ten dollars, and winter them on grain and wild prairie hay. He grew cattle up to two and a half years old, and sold them at three cents a pound at a profit. Meantime he went ahead working to establish clover pastures. Everyone said that clover would not grow in that country. Wallace grew it.

An adventure in the milk business, which he led at the time, proved not so happy. Wallace saw the need of a local creamery and built it. He struggled on with it for a year or so, with his farmer-patrons adulterating their product, turning in dirty stuff, and denouncing him as 'a bloated bondholder' when he complained. The Babcock test for butterfat content had not yet been invented; sanitary and refrigerating equipment was very crude. Wallace declared in shutting down the business that neither cow nor man in Adair County had been educated up to the dairy business as yet.

Times stayed hard. Discontent was mounting. Asked to make the main speech at Fourth of July exercises in 1878 in the courthouse yard of Winterset, Wallace planned to repeat 'The Coming Man,' a whimsical address he had delivered for the amusement of the people in other places. 'You had better not,' a friend advised. 'You are expected to say something worth while. The people are not in the mood for fun.'

This was the night of July 3, 1878. Wallace was forty-two years old at the time. He sat by the sickbed of his youngest son, Ross, who was soon to die of a spinal ailment, and wondered what to say. He was up until two or three o'clock in the morning writing a speech entitled, 'The Perils of the Republic.'

Next day he delivered it in full voice, and was astonished at the sensation he aroused. The first part was general, and was well received, but without excitement. He ripped into machine politics, called for better schools, and insisted that elementary agriculture should be taught along with the three R's. Then: 'There must be less loyalty to political parties and factions. We must have less of these doctors — these politicians — who are doping the public under pretense of curing evils; these old grannies with their paregoric and catnip tea in the shape of greenbacks — seeking to soothe the present discontent, causing people to forget the incipient growing pains of the country!'

His blast against soft money aroused a local tempest, and 'never was a man more astonished than I. I was not aware of the fact that at least half of the people of the county were Greenbackers, and believed fiat money to be the efficient means of salvation. They whom I had tried to score appeared quite insensible to my maledictions, but the Greenbackers were furious, and while the Republicans applauded, the Greenbackers expressed their disapproval in a most emphatic way.

'*The Beacon Light* of Winterset came out with a sharp, vitriolic, slangy editorial roasting me to a finish. Next day in a store a farmer asked me:

'"Mr. Wallace, what is good for hog lice?"

'"Take a barrel of rainwater, put in a copy of *The Beacon Light*, let it stand over night, and sprinkle your hogs with it the next morning. That ought to kill all the lice and make the nits sick."

'The young fellow named Koutzman who edited *The Beacon Light* got word of this, and the next day denounced me more fiercely than ever. He said I was a discredited minister of the gospel who happened to have a little money and was pretending to teach agriculture to the farmers, of which subject I was absolutely ignorant. Of course *The Madisonian* (the Republican paper) defended me. The leading Democratic paper expressed dissent, rather mildly at first, but with increasing earnestness as the weeks went on. Betwixt them all I got to be known to about every man, woman and child in the county, and in some of the adjoining counties.'

He was getting into public life in his own way now, with no strings on him; and he was greatly enjoying it. In the spring of 1879, on his way to mail a letter, he ran into Colonel J. B. Cummins, editor of Winterset's *Madisonian* (R), and made record of their conversation afterward:

'It seems to me you ought to make a better paper than you now are making.'

'What's the matter with my paper?'

'Why, comparing it with other papers, it's good enough; but all of them are poor, and from the farmer's standpoint your paper is not much account. I don't see anything to build up this town except agriculture. Your subscribers are mostly farmers, and all the advertising you get is for the purpose of reaching farmers. Therefore, if I were you, I would talk less politics and more farming.'

The Colonel did not receive this suggestion with cordiality, and Wallace thought that was the end of it. But a week or so later they met on the street again, and Colonel Cummins said: 'I've been thinking over what you said. What will you take to run a page in *The Madisonian* for a year?' Wallace answered: 'You want agricultural matter, and I want an organ. I will edit the page for a year if you will keep me supplied with stationery — but I must have absolute control of the page.'

This time the Colonel was cordial. He had thought the page would cost him money. Wallace started his career in agricultural journalism. 'I wrote on creameries, on dairying, on harrowing corn, about which I knew very little, and on seeding down to grass. I told them that their lands would run down eventually, unless they went to grass; that having gone to grass, the next improvement was to have something to eat it; at which the cow and her calf were most efficient; that to get the full benefit they must milk the cow, sell the cream, and feed the skim-milk to the pigs.'

Everything went well for several months. Then Wallace attacked 'the unwillingness of politicians to forward the agricultural interests.' His editor said that would have to come out. 'Cut that out and I am through,' said Wallace. The publisher asked if he might have copy for one more week. Wallace got up another batch. 'I thought he would give in. I was really running a bluff. But the next issue announced that Mr. Wallace's copy was not satisfactory, and hereafter the page would be edited by a practical farmer.'

But now, an addict to printers' ink, Wallace was determined to go on. He bought a half-interest in the second Democratic paper in the county, a sheet with four hundred subscribers, extremely obscure. He knew nothing about the publishing business and paid 'about twice as much as it was worth.' But he was again a lay minister with an 'organ' — *The Winterset Chronicle*. And: 'I then started out as an independent Republican or free lance, ready to meet all comers and goers in the journalistic field. In about ten months the subscription list increased from four hundred to fourteen hundred, and I began to see that while I knew nothing about journalism, my partner-editor knew nothing or would do nothing, and that the foreman was really doing all the work of the office. So I bought out my partner and had it all to myself.'

The Chronicle was quoted fairly widely throughout Iowa, but the competing local press ignored it. Wallace saw the need of 'some advertising,' and arranged to obtain it free. The offices of the Republican *Madisonian* and the free-trade Democratic *News* fronted each other on Winterset's public square. Wallace wrote a piece describing one Godell, the Republican editor ('a very nice man, by the way'), sitting there chewing high-tariff articles into spitballs and shooting them across at Brother Palmer, the Democratic editor, while the band played 'Hail Columbia.' The next week he had Palmer shooting low-tariff spitballs back, while the band played 'God Save the Queen.'

All this made talk. 'It was too much for them,' Wallace noted happily. 'They both commenced to abuse me, which is exactly what I wanted them to do; and this had no little influence in boosting our circulation. . . . Nothing is so harmful to the sale of a paper or a book as to have it absolutely ignored, and abuse is often much more effective than praise — so it was abuse I wanted.'

Wallace's *Chronicle* made life no easier for Judge William H. McHenry of Des Moines — 'a gentleman of the old school, thoroughly honest and upright, but rather given to gushing over real and imagined sufferings.' Winterset was having a spell of local Prohibition, and the Judge, as Wallace saw it, was much too easy on bootleggers.

'So just for fun I wrote an article in the paper, stating that Saint Paul, in writing his letters to the churches, laid great stress on "bowels of mercy," but that if he had lived in Winterset and attended Judge McHenry's court when a liquor seller was to be convicted, the judge could have supplied the apostle with "bowels" enough for Antioch, Ephesus, Corinth and the seven churches of Asia; in fact, more bowels than ever before went under one human vest.'

The Judge got back at him. He was running for office again. Wallace went to hear him. He pointed to Wallace in the audience and said:

'You have here a man named Wallace, who poses as the very essence of all righteousness. If you will look at him closely you will see the wings sprouting from his shoulders. When he gets to heaven, if he ever does, he will ask the Almighty to tell the Lord Jesus to get off His throne and let him sit there.'

But Wallace, as the saying of the time went, 'had not been brought up in the woods to be scared of hoot owls.' He kept after the Judge on his weak and merciful side, and not long after, a friend, rocking with laughter, came to Wallace in the office of his *Chronicle* to report:

'Yesterday, in Des Moines, Judge McHenry fined a bootlegger five hundred dollars, fined a bootlegging druggist two hundred and fifty dollars, and sentenced a man convicted of rape to the penitentiary for seventeen years.'

Wallace's articles were being copied now throughout Iowa and

the adjacent Corn Belt states, and people were beginning to speak
of him as 'Uncle Henry,' a title which is a sort of accolade expressing the feeling that the man who bears it is kin to the whole striving human family.

In his own home and community Uncle Henry Wallace was not
an especially 'strict' man; but he retained in a number of curious
particulars some of the most rigid principles of a rigid Puritan
upbringing. He never took the name of the Lord in vain; and he
permitted no one to do so in his hearing. He saw no harm, however, in declaring in the course of a campaign against some charla-
tan or demagogue that his purpose was 'to put the fire under
that scoundrel's tail.' When driven to what in a man of different
principles might have been a profane invocation, Uncle Henry
would explode into a thunderous verse or phrase of Scriptural
malediction, quoted verbatim, or seek outlet by way of a feebler
expedient: 'Whatsayshe or whatsays!' Until quite late in life he
remained a close conformist to completely Puritanical ideas of
proper Sabbath behavior. 'The only time my father ever chastised me physically,' Daniel A. Wallace, his youngest son, remembers, 'was occasioned by my infringement of the edict that the
Sabbath day was not a day to read or to play "grievous" games
such as mumble-peg.'

Even so, life in and around the Wallace home in Winterset,
Daniel A. recalls, was robust, gay, and little inhibited, on the
whole. The Wallace young had a good time. In hitherto unpublished notes on Winterset days, prepared in 1939 for the family
records, Dan Wallace wrote:

> My two older brothers, Harry and John, were active in
> outdoor sports — fishing at Backbone or North River, horse-
> shoe pitching, baseball and the like. They sometimes took
> me along. Both were good hunters. A picture published in
> one of the Winterset papers showed Harry and two other
> local hunters surrounded by nearly one hundred prairie
> chickens.
>
> Father was a good shot, too. He had two very old muzzle-
> loading shotguns. I saw him kill two prairie chickens with
> one shot. He was always on the lookout for bee-birds because

he thought they killed bees, but later he decided that he had done the bee-birds a great injustice.

Harry was a very fine skater. I remember with envy his carving figure-8's on the ice; and he and my sister Josephine were crack performers down at the roller-skating rink where they speared wooden rings off the racks as they 'rolled through the air with the greatest of ease.' This song, 'The Man on the Flying Trapeze,' by the way, was one of the frivolous songs that Mother used to sing with relish and zest. Father, I think, considered the song just a bit below the dignity of a preacher's family; but he said nothing. The tops in music, in his opinion, were the good old Psalms. But he loved to hear Mother sing 'Old Susan.'[2]

4. Agriculturists

A FARMERS' MEETING in Des Moines in the spring of 1879 had brought together for the first time three men whose growth was never completely separable from that time on. They were only fledgling patriarchs then, but they grew into the three great founders of modern agriculture in Iowa, and in some part throughout the nation. They were James Wilson, of Tama County (pronounced *Tay*-ma), more generally known as 'Tama Jim'; Seaman Asahel Knapp of the county just east of Tama, Benton County; and Uncle Henry Wallace of Winterset, Madison County, and the adjoining 'State of Adair.'

They felt at once that they had much in common. They were all successful practical farmers and ardent stockmen, lately come to this new soil from east of the Mississippi. They were close to the same age, all in the middle forties. Wilson, born in Scotland, was forty-four. Knapp, born in upstate New York in the hill country, was forty-six. Wallace had just turned forty-three. They were bearded men, all three, with the close-cropped side and chin whiskers that the mode of the time sanctioned for farmers, professional men and politicians, especially, in middle life. They were men of substance and dignity; they knew their Bible and how to quote it effectively in lay discourse, but they had grown beyond

the limits of a too formal sanctity; they enjoyed good earthy stories and a belly laugh. But the real and enduring bond between
them was that each, in his own way, separately, had seriously
determined to restore stature and dignity to the calling of agriculture.

Tama Jim [3] was the son of John Wilson, his first-born of fourteen children. Born in Ayrshire, Scotland, August 16, 1835, James
Wilson came to America with his parents in 1851, and remained
with them in Connecticut until 1855 when he came West and, at
Grinnell College, Poweshiek County, Iowa, completed twelve
years of schooling which had started back in Scotland. In 1861
he acquired a farm near Traer in Tama County, and was married
to Esther Wilbur the year after. Elected in 1868 to the Iowa
House of Representatives, he became Speaker of that body in 1872
and after that served a term as a congressman in Washington,
from 1873 to 1877. Now he was back in Tama County, farming.

Seaman Knapp [4] had come to the first stages of an agricultural
career remarkably similar to that of Henry Wallace at the time.
He had been born in 1833 at Schroon Lake when that eastern
village in upstate New York was in many ways a frontier post.
His family background was much the same as Wallace's — frugal,
proud, temperate, puritanical, staunchly religious. When he
was sixteen he borrowed money, attended Troy Conference Academy in Poultney, Vermont, transferred from there to Union College in Schenectady and graduated in 1856. The same year he
married Maria E. Hotchkiss, a teacher, and they taught together
at Fort Edward Institute in upstate New York. He taught Latin
and Greek. She taught art and the modern languages. They
were paid three hundred dollars a year, jointly, with board; and
yet by the end of seven years of teaching they had bought and
paid for a half-share in that Institute. Knapp loved the classics,
but there was a decided business streak in his make-up; and he
had modern views of education. He and his wife bought and ran
the near-by Troy Conference Academy. It had been a poor little
school when they had attended it as high-school students. They
made it over into Ripley Female College and drew pupils from
wealthy New York families. Young ladies, however elegant,
Knapp held, had bodies under their crinoline and their bodies as

well as their minds should be exercised. He taught the girls how to 'play ball' — a sort of softball of his own invention — in the schoolyard. Playing ball with them, he fell on stones and hurt his knee. Complications set in to wreck his health. The Knapps gave up their school and rode into Iowa on a jolting day coach with two children. With every bump and swerve of the train Knapp, with crutches beside him, gritted his teeth to keep from moaning with the pain.

This was in the spring of 1866. During the next two years Seaman Knapp was pastor of a Methodist church at Vinton. He walked on crutches and preached sitting on a high stool. Then he was named superintendent of a school for the blind at Vinton. He taught the blind from his thirty-sixth year until his forty-second, and at the same time worked to restore his health by diets, water cures, and exercises adapted from the Swedish. His wife taught music at the same school.

His knee healed. He could walk again. His recovery to health and return to farming from preaching coincided in time remarkably with that of Henry Wallace, and as to the proper manner of farming they held the same ideas. After 1875, having bought and moved to a small farm near Vinton, Knapp began to express on the face of our earth, not in words alone, his ideal of diversified farming. 'Fine stock was the money crop,' a daughter wrote later [5] of the Knapps' Iowa farm. 'Berkshires and Poland China hogs brought fancy prices. For the home there were cows, chickens, eggs, milk, butter, honey, cherries, currants, grapes, strawberries, and a splendid garden with every vegetable grown in that climate. Yes, father was a real farmer, now, and the editor of *The Western Stock Journal and Farmer*, an agricultural paper. This meant conventions, farmers' institutes, meeting the influential farmers, men like James Wilson, the beloved "Tama Jim," who afterwards was Secretary of Agriculture ... and Henry Wallace.'

They were good farmers, but more than that, they were agriculturists; and each of them, when first they met in the spring of 1879, was working, on the side, as an agricultural columnist or the editor of an Iowa country paper. Tama Jim was doing a column for a Toledo, Iowa, county-seat weekly. Knapp, who had not yet acquired his own paper, wrote a weekly page for *The Gate City Ga-*

zette; and Wallace was covering agriculture for *The Madisonian* of Winterset, for that deal was still on at the time of his first meeting with Knapp and Wilson. That very week, in fact, Wallace had turned in his 'last' copy, daring the publisher to print it as it was written or fire him.

He told his troubles to these new-found friends and fellow-columnists, not to Wilson and Knapp only, but to other farm scriveners and future allies of such caliber as C. F. ('Father') Clarkson of *The Des Moines Weekly Register*, John Scott of *The Davenport Gazette*, E. C. Bennett of *The Waverly Republican*. These men had seen some of Wallace's articles and approved of them; they told him they thought he would be fired. Wilson asked Wallace: 'Isn't there some paper in your town with a small subscription list, that you could buy cheap?'

Tama Jim at once became Uncle Henry's friend, colleague, confidant; and, later, some say, he was Wallace's Secretary of Agriculture, for sixteen years. Wallace went back to Winterset, bought a half-share in the decrepit Democratic *Chronicle*, then a full share. The papers fulfilled 'Wilson's promise that they would give me a state reputation inside of three months.'

Harry, the eldest boy of the family, was now fifteen. He was beginning to sport around the country a little, with ribbons on his buggy whip. 'To give vent to Harry's surplus energy, I told him that if he would stick type and help us in the shop, I would pay him three dollars a week, of which sum he could possibly save enough to go to college.' So Harry entered the publishing business almost as soon as his father did, and within a year or so, with the paper making some money, they bought and consolidated into their *Chronicle* the rival Republican *Madisonian* of Winterset.

Iowa had a State Agricultural Association, formed in the early eighties. As Uncle Henry became more familiar with the nature of this organization he came to hold it in contempt. 'There was no agriculture about it, but a good deal of politics and, I suspect, not a little graft.' The Association seemed a fake farmers' 'front' for the railroads. County delegates were provided railroad passes and slept free in Pullmans sidetracked in the railroad yards of Des Moines during the annual state meeting. 'A splendid reunion for the boys who were known to be "all right,"' Wallace wrote. Nevertheless, a man writing agricultural news could not ignore this gathering of tame farmers; so Wallace, Knapp, and Wilson all were there.

Father Clarkson, the editor of *The Register*, liked the smell of this no better than did Wallace, Knapp, and Wilson, and he invited the three of them with some others to an oyster supper at his house. This group considered themselves the true representatives of agriculture and the group at the Aborn House engaged in electing officers only the nominal representatives.

They formed what came to be known as the Agricultural Editors' Association of Iowa that evening at Father Clarkson's oyster supper, and later the same evening — 'about the time we got down to nuts, raisins and coffee' — the host proposed that they organize the Farmers' Protective Association, to be made up of farmers in the state, who would agree to pay a membership fee of one dollar a year 'to be used for a fighting fund.' To Wallace it seemed about the wildest scheme he had ever heard of, but he made no objections.

The Farmers' Protective, incorporated immediately, jumped into a fight against the Eastern barbed-wire monopoly at once. The directors contracted with a Des Moines manufacturer to furnish its members Iowa-made barbed wire at cost plus a reasonable profit. An Eastern company, Washburn-Moen, of Worcester, Massachusetts, took legal action, 'and the first thing we knew our Washburn-Moen machinery was taken out of our Des Moines factory,' Wallace wrote.

Farmers joined the new Association to the number of several thousand. 'We were just then fencing up the state, and it involved a clear saving of five cents a pound.' The Eastern opposition, feeling that it could stand a temporary loss better than these farmers, put down the retail price of wire and at the same time tried to cut off from the farmers' factory, wholesale, its supply of smooth wire. A friendly merchant bought materials for the Association wholesale and transferred it to the Association warehouse under cover of night. But by this time the Association was almost bankrupt, and had to put pressure as a bloc upon the Iowa Legislature for a relief appropriation. The Legislature appropriated three thousand dollars. The 'combine' enjoined the

State Treasurer from paying it. The farmers carried the case to the Supreme Court and retained A. B. Cummins, who later became Governor of Iowa and United States Senator, as their lawyer. A patent case, it dragged on for years.

Except for the day that he appeared in the Justice's Court at West Newton to testify against that rascal Ben who had stolen his frock coat to ride to Fort Sumter, this was Wallace's only experience with the ways of the law up to that time.

Uncle Henry Wallace was not by nature quarrelsome, but all the exactions of the railroad interests upon Iowa agriculture enraged him, and this pettifogging action between the farmers and the iron fence 'combine' stirred his blood. As the Farmers' Protective Association became prominent, there was some evidence that the same forces which controlled the State Agricultural Association would be glad to enter the Protective and bore from within. Wallace, at least, held that suspicion. 'We saw some dark days,' he wrote, as one of the Protective's directors. 'I remember at one of our meetings a director proposed that we should charge the Association with our railroad fare, and hotel bills.' Tama Jim objected: 'Mr. James Wilson rose to his feet and said that if we were to appeal to the farmers of Iowa, our hands must not only be clean, but there must be no ground for suspicion of anything else, and announced that he would resign if the motion passed. I made the same announcement.'

His years as editor of *The Iowa Homestead*, an involvement which proved at once so productive, yet almost ruinous, were entered upon casually in 1883. Together with Knapp and Wilson, he had considered buying this farm paper, jointly; but they could not figure it worth more than ten or twelve thousand dollars. The publisher of a county newspaper, J. H. Duffus, whom Wallace knew but slightly, stopped him on the street in Des Moines one day and said he was thinking of offering the Gue family, who owned *The Homestead*, fifteen or sixteen thousand dollars for a half-interest.

Wallace told him: 'I do not think it is worth that much.'

'If I get it, what shall I do for an editor?' he asked.

'I replied: "If you haven't enough brains to edit it yourself, buy brains," and suggested Mr. James Wilson and Mr. S. A.

Knapp. I was greatly surprised some time afterward to receive a letter from him, saying: "I have bought all the stock of *The Home-stead*, and I have elected you editor. Send on your copy." I could do this at the time without much difficulty; for we had consolidated *The Madisonian* and *The Chronicle*, and I had nothing to do except to furnish a page of agricultural copy each week and look after my tenants, of which I had three, farming about a thousand acres. I thought it was merely a temporary matter, and thought little of it. It occurred to me two or three weeks afterward that I had better go down and look into it. I went to the office.

'"How much will you take for a year of such matter as you have been furnishing?" Mr. Duffus asked.

'I said: "You have paid more for this paper than it is worth. I will furnish you the matter for a year for five hundred dollars." He took me up so quickly it made my head swim, saying: "Here's a check for two months in advance."'

Wallace was now forty-seven years old. 'Some day, when I have nothing else to do,' he wrote in 1915, an old and seasoned journalist nearing eighty, 'I will look over my first effort at editing an agricultural paper, but I will put it off as long as I can, for I'm sure I shall be ashamed of it.'

5. Land Grant Colleges

'WE MUST EDUCATE, we must educate,' ran a sentence in the Fifth McGuffey Reader, 'or we perish in our own prosperity.'

The passion for education that had prevailed in all our successive pioneer settlements was taking a new bent in Iowa when Henry Wallace's children were growing up there, and he was among the strongest champions of the new trend. Every passing year of his life confirmed in him more deeply the opinion that country people should be ministered to and educated in country terms; and every year increased his impatience with the stolidity and stupidity with which agriculture was taught, if it was taught at all.

The Land Grant Colleges were an established fact in our country now, but they did not as yet amount to much. The Morrill Act, first proposed by Senator Justin Smith Morrill of Vermont as early as 1857, made land grants to the states, permitting them by the sale or use of these tracts to establish agricultural and mechanical colleges, under some sort of extremely mild Federal supervision. The bill was passed by Congress in the prewar Buchanan administration, but President Buchanan vetoed it. In Civil War time, with Southerners not in Congress voting, Senator Morrill brought in his bill again. Again it passed, and on July 2, 1862, with the Union forces under McClellan retreating from the slaughter of Malvern Hill, President Lincoln signed the Morrill Act. Eleven million acres of land — twice the area of Senator Morrill's home state, Vermont — were thus turned over to agricultural educators.

In pushing for the passage of this Land Grant College Act, Andrew Dickson White observed that Justin Morrill 'did a service which deserves to be ranked, and which future historians will rank with those of Hamilton in advocating the Constitution, of Jefferson in acquiring Louisiana, and of Clay in giving us a truly American policy.' [6]

Some few of the states struck oil or mineral deposits under their quota of this eleven million acres of American soil, and this made their little agricultural and mechanical colleges filthy rich for a while. But most of the land was sold as topsoil after the Civil War on a low market. The 'cow colleges,' as academicians called these agricultural and mechanical institutions for many years, were badly housed and miserably endowed. In general, they were cringingly taught and administered during the first quarter-century of their existence. It seemed to make little difference how much money they got for the land that they put on the market in order to rear their buildings and pay their staffs. They were mediocre schools, in the main, at first; and it could hardly have been otherwise. For where were they to turn for good professors and trained agricultural deans or leaders?

George Washington, Thomas Jefferson, and, for that matter, Lincoln, who signed the Morrill Act offhand with many more pressing matters on his mind, had all paid the customary verbal tribute to agriculture as the most basic and sacred of pursuits; but this was the first actual move toward making American agriculture a learned profession. Initial teaching, research, and administrative staffs had to be recruited from the ranks of professional botanists, veterinarians, chemists, geologists, and the like. Many, indeed most of them, were feeble specimens, inclined to be apologetic because they had strayed from the fields of 'pure' science — cringing, toadying, responding with false smiles when their well-established colleagues in purely academic and scientific lines made sly jokes about cows and manure.

This did not please Henry Wallace, Seaman Knapp, or James Wilson. It made them furious; but they were mature men now, and, in their various ways, subtle politicians. They moved together quietly and between them practically took over the Iowa State College at Ames; but it required a little time.

As far back as 1848, two years after Iowa was made a state, pioneer farmers had petitioned the State Legislature to establish a college of agriculture. In 1868, with Land Grant funds and sanctions, this was done. Henry Wallace's brother John, come West to die, spent a year at Ames and was one of the first students in this new school. He was preparing to study medicine, and took no agricultural courses, but his report to the family on the agricultural instruction at Ames made his brother, the Reverend, ponder.

Later, when Uncle Henry, Tama Jim, and Knapp first became acquainted, they found they all felt the same about that agricultural college. Knapp told a story, humorously scathing, about a professor of agricultural chemistry there who did not know enough to feed his own wife and puny infant properly: 'They have engaged a wet-nurse,' Knapp's story ended.

In other states strong new teachers and deans had somehow been found or had simply arisen from need and native ingenuity and learning. Not only New York and Michigan, but also Illinois, Massachusetts, and Kansas, unquestionably had better agricultural colleges than the State of Iowa where the tall corn grows. Very early in its history Iowa State had a chance to annex and employ, it seems, a Dean of Agriculture of great stature. Isaac Phillips Roberts might almost have sat for a composite physical, mental, and spiritual portrait of Wallace, Wilson, and

Knapp. Curiously, his name is never mentioned in Wallace's *Reminiscences* nor, so far as I have been able to discover, in any of the written works of Knapp and Wilson. Probably this is because Roberts did his work in Iowa from 1870 to 1874,[7] some years before Iowa's agricultural Big Three had joined forces and had begun to worry about the Agricultural College.

Isaac Phillips Roberts had never gone to college. He held no degrees. Born near Ithaca, New York, on a farm, he worked as a farmer and carpenter and went West to the vicinity of Ames, Iowa, to farm there and grow up with the country. By 1869, when the Iowa State College had been for a year established, Isaac Roberts was esteemed locally as one of the best and wisest farmers in those parts. The campus and grounds of this raw, new college were at first badly tended. Their appearance became a laughingstock among the farmers and a reproach to the professoriat. The college asked Roberts to be its Superintendent of Grounds. He soon had the college farm and campus looking fitter, richer, and clean. This was his entrance into the field of agricultural education and agricultural extension. Students followed him afield and he started teaching.

Meantime, back at Ithaca, Ezra Cornell and Andrew Dickson White were having all sorts of trouble trying to build an agricultural faculty for their new Land Grant College, a recently added arm of Cornell University. They tried agricultural lyceum speakers who turned out to have 'political ambitions,' Dr. White reports in his memoirs. They tried a good native farmer; he was inarticulate. They imported an English agriculturist, one who emerged from his suite around ten in the morning and walked around languidly, tapping at plants with an elegant rattan cane. He 'did not inspire confidence. "He don't know nothin' about corn and he don't believe in punkins," a plain farmer commented. The difficulties,' Dr. White concludes, 'were extremely vexatious.' Then someone brought up the name of Isaac Phillips Roberts. White and Cornell jumped at the suggestion, brought Roberts back to his home country in 1874, and made him the first Dean of the College of Agriculture there.

White ends his sketch of this period of early trial and error with 'Vivid remembrance of the strong feeling of hope and of courage which arose as the first work of Professor Roberts began, evidently, to be a success. . . . He was admirably competent to . . . arouse attention and to excite ambition. Soon strong helpers appeared about him, men like L. H. Bailey and others who were brought into various professorships as the Agricultural College grew.'

'For several years prior to 1890,' says Uncle Henry Wallace in his memoirs, 'there had been a great deal of dissatisfaction among farmers with reference to the Iowa Agricultural College. Mr. Chamberlain, of Ohio, was president of Ames. The college was nominally an agricultural college, but very little agriculture was taught. There were few agricultural students. . . . Horticulture, under Professor Budd, was quite strong. The engineering department was fairly strong. But the college as a whole was scientific rather than agricultural, and the science was not well applied.'

He proceeded to enter into the record an instance of grotesque incompetence that had come to his attention in 1886, the year after his son Harry had entered as a student of agriculture at Ames. Hog cholera broke out in the herd of one of his Adair County farms. He went to Ames for advice on what to do. A Professor Stalker, head of the veterinary department, was not much help. He told Wallace there was some hog cholera in the country roundabout, but that they had had no experience with it there on the college farms. Uncle Henry looked up his son Harry and they had supper together.

'How are things at home?' asked Harry.

'We have a bad dose of hog cholera.'

'We have it here, too,' said Harry Wallace.

'Stalker says you have not.'

'Stalker,' said Harry, 'doesn't know.'

The two Wallaces looked up Professor Stalker and took him for a walk out to the college barns. 'We saw hogs lying around in all stages of the disease — well, dying and dead. "Well, I didn't know it," Stalker said. And he was head of the Department of Veterinary Science!' Uncle Henry exclaimed.

Even so, affairs were looking up, there on the agricultural campus at Ames. There were a number of new men on the staff who came up to the somewhat exacting requirements of Knapp,

Wallace, and Wilson; and the first of these new men was Knapp himself. His appointment came in 1880, a year after he, Wilson, and Wallace first had met. Applying pressure quietly, Tama Jim, who was in his third term of service as a congressman in Washington, and Uncle Henry, there on the ground in Iowa, drew upon the support of the three leading farm organizations of Iowa — the Farmers' Alliance, the Dairymen's Association, and the Improved Stock Breeders' Association — and prevailed upon a politically minded board of trustees to employ Seaman Knapp, bring him in from his herds and groves and peaceful meditations, and, under the somewhat spacious title of Professor of Agriculture, put the college on its feet. Knapp went to work and in three years they made him President of the college. In that same year Seaman Knapp took a hand in the making of history. In January of 1883 he wrote the first draft of the Hatch Act, the second leg of the triad under which all federal-state instruction, research, and extension in agriculture is administered today. The Morrill Act took care of resident instruction. The Hatch Act, passed finally in 1887, provided for co-ordinated state and federal research; and the Smith-Lever Act of 1914 authorized and arranged for co-operative extension teaching. But it was Knapp, drafting the Hatch Act, who put on the law books the most spacious authorization for the dispensation of public funds: The purpose of this Act is 'to aid in acquiring and diffusing among the people of the United States useful and practical information on subjects connected with agriculture, and to promote scientific investigation and experiment respecting the principles and applications of agricultural science.'

In 1885, to the astonishment of everyone, Seaman Knapp resigned as President of the college and removed his family to Louisiana, where he took a business position as promoter of a large land company there. He had lived for thirty-two years in the East and for twenty years in Iowa. He went South to make money, but he could not keep his mind on it; and a few years later, a man in his early sixties, he became the great advocate and founder of agricultural teaching afield to the striving mass of farmers in the South. It is extraordinary, but no one of this Iowa trio of agriculturists hit his real stride or found the position on earth he really wanted until he had passed the age of sixty.

V

THE TORCH AND THE LAMP

I am a great believer in Providence, by which I do not
mean anything supernatural or special. I believe that
every life is a plan of God, and if one acquires character,
integrity or complete wholeness or soundness — that is,
becomes what farmers call a straight up and down man
— there will be in due time and at the right time an opening that will lead him into the line of business which he
should follow. — *Uncle Henry's Letters to the Farm Boy.*

1. 'The Homestead'

HENRY WALLACE of Winterset had worked for only a few
months as editor of *The Iowa Homestead* when the paper
changed hands. J. M. Pierce, a fine figure of a man, of
proud demeanor and of fiery temper, paid twenty thousand dollars for it. Until that time Pierce and Wallace had never met.
'You paid eight or ten thousand too much,' the editor told his
new publisher on their first meeting. 'You can't afford to pay
very much salary under those circumstances.' He made in his
usual cavalier manner a casual deal with Pierce, bargaining
principally for freedom. 'I will continue to do the editing for ten
dollars a week, but in case you make a success, I shall want the
privilege of buying stock when the time comes, for what it is
worth.'

'As a business man,' Henry A. Wallace wrote later of his grandfather in his typed *Notes on Ancestry*, 'he was not much good.'
In the strict sense this is true. Uncle Henry was a man of good
judgment when it came to improving in his own way his own
properties, whether that property were a piece of land or a publication; but for written contracts of partnership, stock-sharing,
and so on, he maintained until the end of his days a frontier-

like disdain. The only fire insurance that farmers needed during
his youthful days on the Pennsylvania border, he would say, was
a verbal understanding between themselves that if a house burned
down, the neighbors would pitch in with labor and material and
help the loser rebuild, and if a man's word was no good, writing
it down did not make it any better, except for lawyers. He was
never a man to suspect his associates in an enterprise or to require rigid agreements — until afterwards. If Uncle Henry had
obtained at the very first a clear-cut, written agreement of his
alliance with *The Homestead* it might have spared everyone concerned with it years of grief.

But that was not his way. He had, it appears again and again
in all his dealings, a pioneer's aversion to being hired. He did not
like being a hired man, even of the Church. His readiness to
strain his resources to acquire ownership and management of a
county paper for which he had consented to write for nothing is
typical. For nearly ten years now he had managed to wear no
man's collar, not even the Church's, and he had managed in hard
times, without giving much thought to it, to raise a family of five
and still thrive. He loved later to tell the story of a sharp-spoken
sister who admonished him midway in the process: 'Henry, I
know the Good Book says be fruitful and multiply and replenish
the earth; but I am sure, Henry, that the Good Lord did not, intend for one man to do it all by himself.' 'O ye of little faith!'
Henry had replied.

With Seaman Knapp gone South, and with Tama Jim in Washington completing a third and last term in Congress, Wallace
proceeded singlehanded with the crusade to sting the Iowa State
College authorities at Ames into a less apologetic regard for
agriculture. One of the first cartoons to appear in *The Homestead*
under Wallace's editorship was called 'A Barnyard Scene.' It
showed a cowering little Shorthorn bull, completely dehorned,
in the process of being gored to death by other bulls with Texas
horns labeled *Ethics, Economics,* and so on. 'And this,' the
editor exclaimed, 'in our bull's own barnyard!'

He continued in residence at Winterset mailing his articles to
The Homestead office in Des Moines, writing for his own Madison
County paper, and overseeing in a general way the tenant-man-

agement of his thousand acres in Adair County near-by. As time went on he wrote more farming and less politics for his own little paper, and more and more politics for *The Homestead* which increased under his guidance in circulation and prestige.

Pierce, the principal owner of *The Homestead*, and Lucas, a partner and business manager, had property in the Eighth Congressional District of Iowa, a long district lying along the route of the C. B. & Q. Railroad across the state. (The 'Q,' they called this railroad in those days; it is more generally known as the Burlington now.) Pierce and Lucas felt that the Burlington was bleeding the district. They could get no satisfaction from their Congressman, Colonel W. P. Hepburn, on this score, so they proposed to their editor a stratagem to smoke the Colonel out of Congress.

'I said,' Wallace recorded loftily, later, 'that while I would not go into any political movement, I would do what I could to educate the public as to the needs of the hour.' So saying, he jumped with joy into what was assuredly a political movement. Soon he was in it, avowedly, up to the eyes. The truth is that while he disdained and distrusted most politicians, he was a man who could neither take politics·nor let it alone.

He helped to rig up an innocent-sounding letter from an invented character who expected to go into the grain and lumber business at a shipping point on the Burlington. This fellow was planning to make shipments to many other points on that road. The rate list which the company's promotion division sent the prospect, together with the assurances that the Burlington was his obedient servant, etc., made valuable material in the campaign to defeat Colonel Hepburn, the 'railroad Congressman.' *The Homestead* followed up by a mail canvass of every man in the Eighth District who paid four hundred dollars or more a year in taxes.

The deeper Wallace dug for facts on the railroad rate structure of pioneer Iowa, the more his articles smelled of torchlight and less of the lamp. It was a maze of inequities, a tangled and inchoate little world of trade stimulants and trade barriers, with 'more favored' and sharply less favored cities, county seats, junctions, and trading zones. The rate on flour, for instance, from Kansas City to Des Moines was ten cents a hundredweight, and the same rate prevailed from Saint Paul to Des Moines; but the nearer the shipment approached Des Moines from a point beyond half way on the haul the more the rate increased. Local rate discriminations were no less 'intolerable,' Wallace wrote. 'Hogs had to be shipped from Creston back to Council Bluffs or Omaha in order to get the lowest rate from there to Chicago through Creston. All that was needed to stir up the community was to publish these rates given us by the railroads.'

This was in 1885. To radical farmers of the Midland, the Progressives or Anti-Monopolists, the Farmers' Alliance people and the Grangers, forming now into a somewhat more coherent political wedge to be known as the People's Party or Populists, such rates were not simply inequitable; they were iniquitous. Wallace was with them on that. On his own Adair County properties he had paid, one year, twelve dollars an acre tax on land then valued at only eleven dollars an acre. With counties without railroads bidding against other such counties for rail facilities, this was not at the time uncommon; nor was the outcome uncommon. 'The legislature had enacted a law,' he explained, 'requiring the railroads to give stock to the amount of these taxes. This they easily avoided by organizing an independent line, getting control of it, allowing it to be foreclosed, and thus wiping out the stock. I remember that I paid six hundred and sixty dollars in taxes to the road from Creston to Fontanelle, and received stock therefor which I was glad to sell at six cents on the dollar.'

In the storm accompanying *The Homestead*'s airing of freight rates Colonel Hepburn was defeated for re-election to Congress; and this made a considerable stir among House members who had considered the Colonel a strong 'railroad Congressman,' unbeatable. Under spur of the Grangers at the height of their political ascendancy, the House had passed a bill to establish an Interstate Commerce Commission, but the bill had failed of passage in the Senate. Now Tama Jim, in his last year as a Congressman from Iowa, took the floor in the House and made a speech bidding his colleagues in the upper chamber to take note of the fall of Hepburn. Whether this turned the tide or not must remain debatable; but the Senate passed the Interstate Commerce Law. Tama Jim always felt, and his partner Uncle Henry Wallace at the Iowa end flatly stated, that 'establishment of the Interstate Commerce Commission was a direct result of the defeat of Colonel Hepburn.'

In 1885 Iowa elected a new Governor, Larabee, supposed to be tied irretrievably to the railroads' cause. But Governor Larabee came out for a state law establishing two cents a mile passenger fares, decreeing complete revision of freight rates by a Board of Railroad Commissioners, and abolishing that petty currency of corruption — passes. Uncle Henry put *The Homestead* behind the Governor and helped to re-elect him in 1887. 'We went into state politics in earnest,' he wrote, reviewing the victory. 'We sent a *Homestead* representative to every county to secure the names and addresses of the tax-payers. This cost us a thousand dollars, in addition to railroad fare, which was paid for by advertising the railroads in exchange for mileage books — with which, it must be said, they were reasonably liberal. The next thing was to pick out thirteen members of the previous legislature whose records were bad — seven Republicans and six Democrats, and to assail their records. We managed to defeat six Republicans and six Democrats, and would have defeated the seventh Republican had it not been that a mail sack intended for distribution in his county was carried to Chicago, and did not reach the people until after election. However, he did just what we wanted him to do after that.'

Among the benefits he claimed for the Iowa Rate Law, passed in 1887, was a reshuffling in part of the rural-urban structure, a partial decentralization of industry. 'The result,' he wrote a quarter-century later, 'has been to develop in Iowa a large number of cities of from ten to twenty or thirty thousand, where manufacturing, wholesaling or jobbing can be carried on quite as profitably as in the cities which before had the advantage of greatly reduced rates.'

By 1888 he was a new sort of state political boss, without a machine, with scant funds, but with a mixed and trusting following of wild-eyed agrarians and conservative farmers. He called on Governor Larabee and urged him to run for the Senate. The

Governor reared up and said he was tired of public life; that 'his family needed looking after, and that he did not want to subject them to the Washington influence'; and finally: 'Mr. Wallace,' he said, 'I have about concluded to own no man my friend who insists upon my going to the United States Senate!'

Then came to Wallace the editor of the leading Democratic paper in Iowa, confiding: 'You can just as well be Senator as not.' Now it was Wallace's turn to sidestep. 'I told him that I would not consider the matter for a second; that I was a Republican and not a Democrat; . . . that I never expected to go to the United States Senate; but if I did I would go as an anti-monopoly Republican.'

With the Populist tide now rising rapidly, almost anything could happen in Iowa politics and before his spell of playing politics had ended Uncle Henry felt impelled to back up a little and take stand on steadier ground. Instinctively he inclined to join up with hell-raisers of the earthy variety; but he had come to enjoy a solid reputation, too. And it must be added that while he was for the unorganized little man against the big combinations, in principle, he never developed great intimacy with or personal compassion for little persons who kept crying that the world was against them and that they simply could not get along. He fought the barbed-wire fence combinations. He fought the railroad monopoly. He fought for the dairy co-operatives and insurance co-operatives against the commercial combinations which sought to put them down. He developed liberal ideas on a world scale and enlarged in such thinking to the end, but there was always something of the conservative landholder and proprietor at the root of his thought and being. Landlords should be fair to their tenants; landlords and tenants should be fair to day-hands; but renters and day-hands there would always be. In summary of his particular cast of mind Uncle Henry wrote at the end of his life that high places made his head swim, so much that he did not dare look down from a height of even twenty feet: 'I never could keep my head if I went much above the earth's surface. (Nor I might say ever since, if I go too far ahead of the convictions of the best people.)' [1]

2. Silos and Spires

STILL PREPARING at Ames for the peaceful pursuit of agricultural teaching and research, Uncle Henry's oldest, Harry, was bored with it and in love. His girl was one of the best-looking and smartest of early coeds at Iowa State College. On a visit home to Winterset at the end of his sophomore year, 1886–87, Harry found that one of his father's tenants, handling a rich three hundred acres of the family holdings, had given notice. 'How much has that fellow made in the five years he has farmed that place?' he asked.

His father estimated somewhere between $2000 and $2500, a house, and a good part of a living, clear, for the five-year period.

'How would you like to have me for a tenant — on the same terms you have been renting for?' asked Harry. Holding no high opinion of the agricultural instruction at Ames and reflecting that a lad so young had time for college later, the head of the family closed the deal at once.

The place was north of a village named Orient, in Madison County. Harry moved out, batched it alone in one of the two tenant houses, and formally proposed marriage to May Brodhead, of Muscatine, Iowa. Born in New York City, Miss Brodhead was of New England strain. Her people, strong Methodist Republicans, felt that she might form too frivolous and aristocratic notions at select girls' schools Eastward, so they had sent her out to pursue courses in the arts and music at the public State College of Iowa, in which State her father had met and married her mother in 1865. When not at Ames she made her home in Muscatine with her Aunt Jennie, Mrs. Jane Wilson — her mother's sister.

May Brodhead knew nothing of farming. But redheaded 'Harry' Wallace, riding in from twenty-eight miles west behind a spanking trotting horse, 'made farming seem most romantic.' He was a dashing suitor and a proper one. 'Please, ma'am, can I have your niece?' he asked May's foster mother, Aunt Jennie, with May, blushing properly, at his side. 'But, May, you're so young, hardly twenty!' Aunt Jennie protested. 'You were only twenty when you married,' said May.

Her aunt taught her to cook and make bread that summer. She and Harry Wallace were married on Thanksgiving Day, November 24, 1887. He sold two pigs and bought a surrey, with room in the back for the bride's trunk. They drove the twenty-eight miles out to the farm. 'The house wasn't much,' as Mrs. Wallace remembers it.[2] 'A little story-and-a-half tenant house, nice enough, but with none of the conveniences, and not a tree near it — nothing but a windmill. But it was a good farm.'

Uncle Henry was delighted with this first daughter-in-law. 'Harry was young, barely twenty-one, but his choice was worthy and based on true affection. Neither his mother nor I made any objection,' Uncle Henry wrote. The fact that both the parents of the bride had died of tuberculosis by the time she was four did not appear to have caused the Wallaces any qualms about the mating. Because his own line had survived, in him, after removal from Pennsylvania to Iowa, Uncle Henry had formed the opinion that tuberculosis is probably environmental in origin, not hereditary. The swampy, miasmatic airs of Pennsylvania, the primitive dread of ventilation which marked the days of his youth there, and the uncontrolled pollutions of barn and houseflies — these were the ways in which one 'inherited' tuberculosis, Henry Wallace said. Harry Wallace, specializing as a student in dairying and bacteriology, thought so, too.

May Brodhead's father, John Avery Brodhead, was a scholarly, lovable man of Anglo-Saxon, Holland Dutch, and Huguenot French lineage. He entered the Federal Army as a private and came out of the war as a captain, having meantime married Matilda White, of Iowa, in 1865. The ninth of ten children of a Methodist minister, Tillie White liked writing verse and painting pictures better than housework. Upbraided at fourteen for not being more helpful, she is remembered to have sighed and said: 'Oh, I don't think I was born to work, Mother; but just to read and muse and think.' Too old for active service in the Civil War, her father, the Reverend James H. White, served as chaplain at the Rock Island Arsenal, near Davenport, where the Wallaces had known and esteemed him. Tillie White nursed Confederate prisoners at the Arsenal as a worker for the Christian Commission. She learned to do the heaviest of hospital drudgery cheerfully;

but after the war she resumed her interest in poetry and painting. A few of her pictures were hung in New York shows and sold.

May Brodhead resembled her slim, dapper father and had her mother's sturdy sense of duty. She had spunk, together with a robust whimsicality of spirit which pleased her father-in-law. 'You Wallaces!' she would mock, when his tone became somewhat too patriarchal. 'You expect too much of your women. I'm not a Wallace. I only married one!'

Looking into the question of a family coat-of-arms, May discovered that the Wallaces had one and were keeping it dark. Their crest was cartoonlike in its directness and simplicity. It displayed an ostrich about to swallow a horseshoe, with the inscription *Sperandum est* (To him who wills all things are possible), or, more freely, Nothing is impossible. This delighted her. The motto on the Brodhead crest was *Non sine pulvere palma* (Not without dust in the hand) or, Nothing comes easy. The two mottoes together made an ideal statement of principles for a farm couple.

On October 7, 1888, in that small tenant house, five miles out from the village of Orient, Iowa, and fourteen miles from the county seat of Creston, she bore the first of her six children, a boy. The infant was named not Henry Brodhead Wallace, which would have been in strict accord with the established procedure in the Wallace family, but Henry Agard Wallace. This was his mother's wish. One of her earliest American ancestors was the knightly Arthur Agard, said to have been 'Sir Arthur' in England. He came to America well before the Revolution. One of his direct descendants, Noah Agard, fought with General Washington's troops. Mrs. Harry Wallace was proud of her Agard blood and wished to keep the name alive.

In 1942, Conklin Mann, editor of that lively genealogical quarterly, *The Record*, New York, announced researches showing that Franklin D. Roosevelt, General Douglas MacArthur, and Prime Minister Winston Churchill were seventh cousins once removed. The disclosure aroused a mild flurry but no great astonishment. Traits of resemblance may have seemed obvious to the public mind. When, bearing on into a veritable tangle of New England genealogical trees, Conklin Mann proceeded in 1943 to show that 'the second ranking American executive, Vice-President Henry Agard Wallace, is also related to Mr. Churchill,' this seemed more surprising. The relationship is through Henry Agard's mother and goes back to James Clark, a planter of Connecticut, who is the many times great-grandfather of Wallace and Churchill.

Conklin Mann shows that the Wallace-Brodhead cross which produced Henry Agard Wallace led to a substantial dilution of the Scotch-Irish infusion in his veins: 'He is fifty-three per cent Scotch-Irish, by way of Pennsylvania; thirty-seven per cent of New England extraction; six per cent Dutch and French Huguenot, and four per cent New York English,' the Mann analysis concludes.

When the findings of *The Record* appeared in the daily Press and reporters sought the Vice-President's comment, he replied that he had sympathy for 'the nostalgic glow and sense of romantic association with great events and 'gentle persons of the past which genealogical research encourages,' but — smiling — 'as a geneticist, I know it's the bunk.'

Young Henry's early upbringing was neither notably humble nor privileged. Harry Wallace, his father, did most of the field and barn work himself, with the aid of a married hand who lived with a wife in the other tenant house on the place. When there was company the hired man's wife sometimes helped Mrs. Wallace cook and serve. The Harry Wallaces had just about as much money, which was little, as hundreds of other farm families in Adair County. Apart from the fact that they had more books in their farmstead, more papers and periodicals, and a greater interest in music and the world of ideas, their isolation was as complete, and their means of recreation were as limited as that of their neighbors in general. A trip to town was an event. Young Henry A.'s first remembrance is of riding in a sleigh to Creston in his mother's lap with a musty buffalo robe to cover him, head and all, from the weather. That must have been when he was about three years old, in 1891.

Business and family perplexities were never discussed in the presence of the children; but children have a means of divining trouble in a household; and Henry's first impression of his grandfather was that of a bearded giant, as kind and wise as the king of a clan could be, but often sad and worried. Later he found out why. Uncle Henry had waded deep, too deep for his private taste, into the chaotic waters of agrarian reform politics. He wanted out, as the Midland saying goes; but he fiercely resented the pressure that aroused business interests were putting on the counting room of *The Iowa Homestead* and that his partners, hold-ing the majority of the stock, were putting on him. Uncle Henry was entering, in consequence, upon another of his spells of indeci-sion and rebellion. A colt no longer, a skilled and spirited lead-horse in his prime, he liked the feel of harness tightening upon him no more than he ever had; and the whole Wallace team suffered with him until at the end of five years' kicking, and rearing he managed, at a considerable cost, to stand free.

The quarrel at *The Homestead* office became a bitter one before it had ended. It started quietly as no quarrel at all with an agreed realignment of editorial policy entirely in keeping with Wallace's initial pronouncements of what a farm paper ought to be. He wrote for his memoirs: 'In 1889 Mr. Pierce came to my room and asked me if I did not think it was time to drop the anti-monopoly discussion in the paper. He said: "We have won our fight [as to the railroad rate law] and it might be well to let the matter rest a while until the excitement quiets down."

'I thought the matter over, and finally told him it would probably be as well, and then turned my attention to purely agricultural matters. In fact, I felt that if the paper was to have a permanent success, it must be devoted more largely to agricul-ture and livestock.'

Had he suspected then, as he did later, that Mr. Pierce's sug-gestion was advanced under pressure from the railroads and other large advertisers, Wallace would almost certainly have bucked. And yet, it appears, he would have been bucking against his own inclinations and a change of heart; for he had become disillusioned as to the complete reality of the great reformation in which he had led so earnestly. He had come to doubt the readiness of the electorate to support such reform. In the heat of the fight he had insisted that the new Iowa railway commissioners be elected, not appointed. Later: 'Looking back, I think this is one of the greatest mistakes I ever made. I believed that so great was the

interest in the enforcement of the new Iowa rate law that the
people would see to it that just and upright men were put on the
ticket. Experience has shown that the people will not maintain
the interest they should in such offices.' Also later, and from the
same eminence of the years, 1913, Wallace pointed out, defensively
but truly, that while as editor of *The Homestead* he had crusaded
in the field of politics, he was always non-partisan in his choices
of candidates to support or to assail. The determining issue was
generally the candidate's record as to monopolies. 'It was not
really so much of an agriculture paper as an anti-monopoly
paper,' he wrote, and added with a touch of bitterness: 'The
management soon found out that anti-monopoly was the winning
card.'

It was in all likelihood still the winning card there in the agricultural Midland, as the eighteen-eighties passed into the nineties,
so far as farm-paper circulation was concerned. But it had never
been a winning card in point of paid advertising; and the leaders
of industry who woo opinion by buying space in the papers were
now no longer complacently willing to let wild agrarians have
their little romp. Another, and a crucial, national election was
pending. Cleveland, having served as President from 1885 to
1889, was again the Democratic candidate for 1892. The margin
of strength between the two old parties seemed narrow. Third-
party fervor had mounted to a point where it could no longer be
regarded with tolerance. Soft-money agitators, shouters against
Wall Street, and similar 'sons of the wild jackass,' for twenty years
at work or longer, had lighted a political prairie fire which was
spreading South and East. In the South, Tom Watson and other
agrarian rebels had fires of their own going. They were inciting
rural revolution, bloody, if need be. Meetings had been held at
Ocala, Florida, at Cincinnati, and again at Atlanta, to bring about
a political 'marriage of the Corn and Cotton' and wrest control
of the national government from the 'plutocratic East.'

'Men of the country!' cried Tom Watson, 'Let the fires of this
revolution burn brighter and brighter. Pile on the fuel until the
forked flames shall lap in wrath around this foul structure of
governmental wrong — shall sweep it from basement to turret,
and shall sweep it from the face of the earth.' [3]

UNCLE HENRY AND 'TAMA JIM' WILSON

Many other exhorters, strange and ardent, arose in the farm country. Northward, there were 'Coin' Harvey, 'Sockless Jerry' Simpson, and 'Brick' Pomeroy, a Greenbacker editor who issued as a sideline alluring tracts with such titles as *Hot Drops* and *Meat for Men*. In South Carolina there was 'Pitchfork' Ben Tillman. 'Send me to Washington,' he told his constituents, 'and I'll stick my pitchfork in Cleveland's old ribs!' Kansas had Mrs. Mary Elizabeth Lease — she who told the farmers to 'raise less corn and more hell.' During the summer and autumn of 1890, in her thirty-seventh year, she made the same speech, or much the same, in one hundred and eighty different places from the Northwest to Florida.

'Money rules!' she cried, 'and our Vice-President [Levi P. Morton] is a London banker. Our laws are the output of a system that clothes rascals in robes and honesty in rags. We were told two years ago to go to work and raise a big crop. We went to work and plowed and planted; the rains fell, the sun shone and nature smiled, and we raised the big crop that they told us to; and what came of it? Eight-cent corn; ten-cent oats; two-cent beef and no price at all for butter and eggs — that's what came of it.... We want the accursed foreclosure system wiped out. Land equal to a tract thirty miles wide and ninety miles long has been foreclosed by the loan companies of Kansas in a year.... The people are at bay. Let the bloodhounds of money who have dogged us thus far beware!'

Her outcry was as old as civilization. Only the fact that here was a woman and a mother brazenly exhorting the rural needy made it new. 'Woe unto them,' cried Isaiah, 'that join house to house, that lay field to field, till there be no place, that they may be placed alone in the midst of the earth!' And the prophet Micah: 'Woe unto them that covet fields, and take them by violence; and houses, and take them away; so they oppress a man and his house, even a man and his herds.' As one who through all of his conscious life had known by heart the wails and imprecations of the Old Testament agrarians, Uncle Henry Wallace was not surprised or shocked by the violence of Populist campaigners. He knew, moreover, that often their complaints were tenable and that the reforms for which they screamed were just. Even so, he did not like all this screaming and breast-beating. The 'religious' manifestation of the People's Party movement, which other writers and commentators of the period found so moving, appealed to Uncle Henry Wallace little, if at all.

'The Farmers' Alliance was born in Heaven,' and 'It is next in importance to the church of the living God,' preachers in Georgia declared from their pulpits.⁴ 'The Populist platform,' Tom Watson wrote, 'is sacred. It is sacred because it gives hope to our despair, gives expression to our troubles, gives voice to our wants. Our wives have knelt and prayed for it. Our children have learned to love it. Not a church in all the land where God's blessing has not been invoked upon it.'

Watson's final flourish was of course campaign oratory. The great body of conservative churchgoers and their clergy would no more have blessed and prayed for Tom Watson and his 'wool hat boys' in the eighties and nineties, than they did for the Non-Partisan Leaguers of Arthur Townley, the Farm Holiday strikers of Milo Reno, or the poverty-stricken hill men who flocked to the standards of Huey Long in later years. Populists were 'radicals,' it was said. Basically, they were. Basic conditions out in the open country were radically wrong. Even the most docile of farmers felt at times the crying need for radical changes. Herbert Quick of Iowa remembered his patient father refusing to deliver wheat at the elevator for less than cost: 'I'll haul it back first and give it to the poor!' He remembered his Grandmother Coleman at the time when it cost less to burn corn in the cookstove than to haul it to town and sell it and haul coal: 'Something sinful in this. When I think of all the folks in the world that are hungry, it seems a sin to burn up victuals.' By no means only the shiftless, the reckless, or the born bellyachers among farming people South and West joined up with the militant Grangers, the Alliance shouters, and the Populists as these movements rose and fell successively. But many, soon after they had joined, found themselves uncomfortable in the company of political Holy Rollers, loud-mouthed incompetents, and incurable malcontents. Profoundly aware as he was of the causes of agricultural dislocation and distress, and sympathetic as he felt, Frederick Jackson Turner, the frontier historian, felt moved none the less to apologize for the Populist's 'primitive approach' to 'the complexity of business interests in a developed society.' 'There was too much emotion in it,' Vann Woodward, Tom Watson's most sympathetic biographer, had to admit. The zeal of the movement, as William Jennings Bryan said later, approached 'the zeal which inspired the Crusaders who followed Peter the Hermit.'

That was too much zeal for Uncle Henry Wallace; he simply could not stomach it. This may seem strange in a man so religious; but the shouting and twitching manifestations of religion, it must be remembered, he had always held in scorn. His own spiritual approach to the problems of the day and the hereafter was the rational probing, expository approach of the devout but cool Presbyterian. He had no more use for the torchlight evangelism of Tom Watson and Mary Lease than he had for the camp-meeting excitations of Dwight L. Moody. His private remarks about barkers for political medicine shows verged on the sulphurous. For the suffering meek who were led to expect a new heaven on earth right away he maintained a sort of scornful compassion, but he gave no evidence of a sense of companionship with such persons. 'People get just as good government as they deserve,' became one of his favorite sayings. He could not see that passing new laws, or even 'changing the system,' would permanently enrich either sloppy farmers — soil miners — or the land they served. So more and more, after his first impetuous advances toward the successive political New Deals for agriculture which his son and grandson were later to administer, Uncle Henry Wallace put his faith in education, not politics.

Some years before, in the late seventies, his friend, 'Father' Clarkson of *The Register*, had made the same considered retreat. Herbert Quick describes somewhat wryly the retreat of Clarkson:

'Governor Clarkson had warmed this Grange serpent in his bosom. It was stinging him, opposing the Republican Party. . . . Two years after his ineffectual stand against the banners [of the Greenbackers] at Hickory Grove, his fears were justified by the political developments which made Peter Cooper a candidate of the Greenback Party for the Presidency. . . . I never heard of him again in politics; but he was for many years the "Father" Clarkson of *The Register* who did a good work in the advocacy of better farming methods.'[5]

So complex and so interwoven with urban commercial interests was Corn Belt agriculture by the eighteen-nineties, however, that the editor who undertook even the simplest campaign of rural education might not find peace. A line was drawn between what 'helped business' and what 'hurt business.' It was quite all right to educate farmers to raise more food and fabric. But education in marketing — that was something else.

A centrifugal cream separator had now been invented and was on the market. A Chicago manufacturer of separators and other dairy equipment sent a high-powered sales force into Iowa to promote the establishment of creameries all over the state. Farmers sent queries to *The Homestead*. Wallace, as editor, answered their queries in his columns. He said in effect that such creameries were generally an equipment-selling dodge, that to call them 'co-operatives' was a misnomer and that projects such as these, sold on the basis of 'half-truths,' with the equipment priced at two or three times what it could earn, would surely fail. A successful creamery, he advised his readers, required: 'Educated cows, that is, cows educated to give milk; educated farmers . . . and an educated butter-maker and manager. . . . Under these conditions and with a sufficient volume of milk (at least four hundred cows, and six hundred would be better), the farmers in a community would be justified in putting from three thousand to thirty-five hundred dollars in buildings and equipment.'

The Chicago company sent word that 'unless the editorial tone of the paper was changed, they would have to cancel their advertising.' Mr. Pierce (Wallace continues in his memoirs) 'came into my room in a bad humor and wanted to know why I was knocking the advertising end of the paper. . . .

'I told him that I was running the editorial end, that its tone would not be changed, that I would tell the farmers of the West the truth about the creamery business, as I had had experience in it myself, with the loss of about five thousand dollars.' Mr. Pierce stomped out of the office.

Now came an emissary from the creamery people, direct: 'He was about the smoothest proposition I ever met. He gave me some very elegant bouquets. . . . At Marshalltown a week or two before, organizing a ten-thousand-dollar creamery, a physician, he said, had told him, "Unless you can get Wallace's endorsement, I must cancel my thousand-dollar subscription." He said [this agent] that he did not know any other man in the whole United States that seemed to have the confidence of the farmers as I had it; that I could wind them around my finger. "And now we can work together to our mutual advantage," the agent said to me. I told him I would tell the farmers the truth.'

Thus Uncle Henry in his *Reminiscences*, twenty years later. Such tales grow more definitely clean-cut in the retelling. Even when the contending parties are, each from his own side of the story, scrupulously exact and honest, the truth about an editorial-advertising wrangle of this sort rarely emerges plain and whole. Here, once the issue was joined, a not unusual compromise was effected. *The Homestead* sent out men from its advertising promotion staff and published (as Wallace saw it) 'a glowing report, which must have deceived many farmers and led to the fooling away of a good many thousand dollars. As editor of the paper, I had only a minority interest in the stock, about thirty per cent of the whole. The only thing that I could do was to insist that this creamery report should not appear as an editorial but as correspondence.'

Pierce had thirty-five per cent of the stock, together with virtual command over another block of thirty-five per cent held successively by business partners and advertising managers with whom he quarreled more fiercely and constantly than with Wallace. Pierce, 'a man of some good qualities, but of a most violent temper,' Wallace notes, 'never opened the mail of Mr. Stewart, who was the advertising solicitor, until he had finished all the other mail. The reason he gave was it made him so angry that he could not do anything the rest of the day. . . . Life in that office was anything but serene. It was an open question whether purgatory was more comfortable.'

The friction between Pierce and Stewart exploded into a libel suit, based on an exchange of personal letters at Christmastide, 1891–92. Pierce proposed that for the sake of peace Wallace join with him in voting Stewart off the board. And for the sake of

peace Wallace agreed. Pierce's chief financial backer was put
on the board instead; and still there was no peace in *The Homestead* shop. As it always seemed to happen when he became entangled in quarrels, lay or spiritual, Wallace's health failed. In
1891, upon advice of his doctor, he made a trip abroad with his
wife. To help defray expenses and feel at the same time not
wholly useless, he was glad to accept an assignment from Ben-
jamin Rusk, then Secretary of Agriculture, to report on methods
of flax-growing in Holland, Belgium, and Ireland. Tama Jim
Wilson was back home in Iowa now; but he still had his lines out
in Washington; and it was Tama Jim who arranged this pleasant
and useful tour of duty for Uncle Henry.

Uncle Henry, meantime, with a flash of his old spirit, had accomplished by some cagey political maneuvers in the field of
educational administration, a vast improvement. He and Tama
Jim had both been named to a board of farmers charged to help
select a new head for the faculty of the Agricultural College at
Ames. On behalf of the faculty, Professor Budd, whose department of horticulture was one of the strongest on the campus, came
to see Wallace privately and urged him to take the post.

> I told him I did not want it, [and] telegraphed James
> Wilson, then retired to his farm near Traer, Iowa: COME
> DOWN ON FIRST TRAIN. IMPORTANT. That evening he came
> to the office with his grip in his hand and said: 'Where do
> you want me to go?'
> 'Nowhere,' I answered ... 'I want you to be Professor of
> Agriculture at Ames.'
> 'I am not fit for it,' he said. 'Do you think so?'
> 'In one sense, no,' was my answer, 'and in another sense,
> you are. You have not had an agricultural college training
> but you are educated on agricultural lines. You can teach
> general farming, heredity, stock breeding and feeding, at
> which you are an adept; and you can get money from the
> legislature as no other man can. If we can make the change
> at all, we can get two college-bred men to take up the scien-
> tific end of it.'
> After talking the thing over until midnight, he said:

'Well, if you say so, and I don't have to bat an eye or crook a finger to get the place, I'll accept it.'

'Don't let anybody know what you are here for,' was my reply, 'but wait until you hear from the board of trustees.'

What to do with these committees [of farmers] when they got together was a thing that bothered me a good deal. The day before, I discovered that some of the Dairymen's Committee and some of the Alliance Committee were ready to oppose anything that I wanted. I therefore wrote out on my own typewriter a memorandum of what I thought the committee should do, gave it to my assistant, and told him to slip it into the Alliance member's pocket and wink at him. . . .

At the close of the meeting I said: 'The Secretary of the Alliance, which is the largest committee, can doubtless prepare a statement, which we will accept as the action of the joint committee.' The next morning he made a statement . . . simply an enlargement of the memorandum I had prepared, leaving blank spaces for names. Someone proposed the name of Mr. [W. M.] Beardshear for president of the college; and as he was principal of the high school, within a block of my residence, I cheerfully assented, and it was unanimous. There was a great deal of maneuvering as to who should name the professor of agriculture. I declined to do so, but finally someone suggested James Wilson. I opposed him, on the ground that he did not have an agricultural college training, that his experience had been mainly political, and that while he was an excellent farmer, we ought to get some man of broader culture. Those who differed with me evidently figured that I was fishing for the place for myself, and became quite vehement in their advocacy of Mr. Wilson. After making two or three talks on the subject, I said I was not going to stand out against the opinion of the rest, and would offer no further resistance. . . .

The professorship of agriculture at the time was roughly equivalent to the deanship at an agricultural college of today. C. F. Curtiss (later Dean Curtiss) and David Kent were named as Professor Wilson's assistants; and the new professor at once invited young Harry Wallace to return from farming, complete his course, and assume the duties of a third assistant professor, with special charge over the dairy barns and herds.

3. Professor's Son

THIS WAS IN 1892. Harry Wallace made the removal with his wife and two children. His son, Henry A., was four years old and his daughter, Annabelle, two. They lived in a forlorn and chilly little rented house by the Northwestern tracks at the edge of Ames. The winds whipped in from over open prairie, piling shaking masses of tumbleweed along the tracks and in the house yards. The family had to get along with almost no money until, having crammed two years' work into one, Harry Wallace became Assistant Professor Wallace. After that they had thirteen hundred dollars a year more. As a sideline, Professor H. C. Wallace wrote for, and sometimes stuck type for, *The Farm & Dairy*, a paper that he and Professor Curtiss began publishing as partners at Ames in 1893.

Cleveland had been elected President for the second time. The Republicans had been foretelling, in such an event, a financial panic, which actually had advanced to its initial stages before the votes were cast and counted. Now, in 1893, the year of Cleveland's second inaugural, business confidence collapsed; and, because of Uncle Henry's involvement as a minority stockholder of *The Homestead*, all property held in the Wallace name was put to hazard. *The Homestead* was in the midst of making sizable, confident additions to its plant. Viewing the situation upon his return from Europe, Uncle Henry found himself 'in the very worst kind of shape. I had seven or eight hundred acres of land, but it was mortgaged. The dividends from *The Homestead* were cut off in order to pay for the new building. My salary was scarcely sufficient to pay living expenses. Altogether my name was on about thirty thousand dollars' worth of paper, apart from a mortgage on the farm. Those were dark days.'

One of his notes fell due and he could not pay it. 'Who asked you to?' his banker demanded wearily. 'Your note is not worth ten cents on the dollar now, but it's worth just as much as any man's note. . . . What's going to happen? I don't know. We may get through. If not, then universal smash, a wiping out of all debts, and beginning anew.'

'This did not happen,' Uncle Henry reminisced later about the eighth national spell of depression or panic he had lived through up to then. 'The country pulled through, but with fearful losses for men who were heavily in debt, and great fortunes for men who had plenty of cash and credit. This is always the case in times of panic; the rich become richer, the fairly well-to-do lose, and the poor become poorer.

'The fact that I could no longer control the editorial policy of *The Homestead*,' he confessed, 'gave me grief which I cannot very well describe.'

The urge to publish, which in him had succeeded the urge to preach and minister, was working now in the Wallace blood stream, even to the third generation. He did not realize it, but the rootstock of a great periodical, *Wallaces' Farmer*, about to restore him in spirit and fortune, had sprouted and was growing. The original planting was made by Newton B. Ashby, a lecturer and organizer for the Farmers' Alliance who had lost faith in the Alliance and its management. He came as a boarder to the Wallace household in Des Moines and married the second daughter, Harriett. A pamphlet study tallying railway votes in the State Senate which he issued after resigning from the Alliance aroused a great uproar just at the time when, as Uncle Henry saw it, the Alliance organization in Iowa, having 'come up like Jonah's gourd in a night, had perished in a night.' By a printer's mistake, some say, and some say through Big-Party connivance, the study was given to the papers under an Alliance imprint. Newton Ashby went to the print shop, destroyed the entire issue of the pamphlet, and made a statement explaining that his was simply a month's work of investigation, undertaken, free lance, for the sum of fifty dollars. But his disclaimer never caught up with the news story and the hotheads cried it forth that Ashby, like Wallace, had sold out to the Plutocrats.

Moving to Cedar Rapids with his wife, Ashby borrowed money

and became majority stockholder and editor of *The Farmer and Breeder*, a weak and struggling agricultural paper dating from 1875. His partner-printer, a strong Democrat, worked through the party organization to obtain for Ashby under the second Cleveland administration appointment as Consul to Dublin, a post congenial to his tastes and training, and a job that he badly needed. The only proviso that the printer made was that some-one take *The Farmer and Breeder* out of his shop and off his hands if Ashby went abroad. The appointment came through in 1893. Then it was that quiet Harry Wallace with the help of his brother John, then a student at Ames, and with Professor Curtiss as a partner, took over. They changed the paper's name to *The Farm and Dairy*, and removed the shop to Ames.

No word in *The Farm and Dairy* smacked in the least of torch-light. A quiet little paper, it instructed its readers in the latest practical findings of the College and Experiment Station and led them gently toward the lamplit heights of the higher learning in agriculture.

In 1894, toward the beginning of his fifty-ninth year, Uncle Henry Wallace was ill again. It was 'serious trouble in the back of my head, caused by rush of blood; and the doctor told me it might be fatal if not looked after in time.' The doctor prescribed change, and a rest from 'thinking and talking in public.' So Uncle Henry and his wife made their second voyage abroad and paid a three months' visit to their daughter Harriett and her husband, Newton Ashby, at the consulate in Dublin.

Back at Ames young Henry Agard Wallace, the first-born grandson (who still is called Young Henry, or 'H. A.' for short, in Iowa), was learning to read at his mother's knee at home. His mother, who was a skillful and devoted gardener, also gave him his first lessons in plants. The first teacher to make an enduring imprint on his mind and character was not in the strict sense of the word a teacher, but a tall, shy Negro student, later a research assistant there at Iowa State. He called himself George Wash-ington Carver. His parents had been slaves owned by a white Missouri family named Carver. His father had been killed and his mother forced to flee during Civil Wartime guerrilla disorders in Missouri. No one could ever tell George Carver exactly how old he was. But if, as his parents' owners guessed, he was born in the summer of 1864, he must have been about twenty-seven years old when, after years of wandering in Kansas and Iowa, he enrolled in the Agricultural College at Ames.

Together with Booker T. Washington, George Washington Carver was to become one of the great men of his race. His horticultural, genetic, and chemical researches at Tuskegee Institute in Alabama and the influences that he brought to bear in the field of Negro education have made a real difference for the better in the South. Working in Alabama, and out from there, until his death early in 1943, he was made subject to a mingled acclaim and a peering public curiosity. White people gladly called him 'Doctor' Carver, avoiding the title 'Mister.' They approached him as if he were in part a saint, in part a scientist, and in part a performing bear.

He lived a long and highly useful life, but not on the whole a happy one. At Ames, however, he was happy. During his four years there as an undergraduate and a year as graduate assistant, from 1891 until 1896 in all, he expanded in his being like a corn plant in August.

The years before that he did not often care to think about or talk about. While still in his 'teens he traded work for schooling as a houseboy in the home of a colored blacksmith in Fort Scott, Kansas. He saw a mob beat out the blacksmith's brains, pour oil on the body, and burn it in the public square. Then he fled and took to the road in Kansas, picking up such work as he could and such schooling as was open to a 'black boy' along the way. He became an accomplished launderer and developed that trade as a sort of cottage industry at towns where he stopped.

Having saved a little money, he presented himself to a Presbyterian seminary at Highland, Kansas. 'We don't take niggers here,' the principal, a Doctor of Divinity, said. Carver retreated to what was then called 'the Great American Desert' in western Kansas. He took a homestead claim on one hundred and sixty acres of semi-arid land, built a sod house, put in crops, and starved out of there with thousands of other first-wave farmers in the drought of 1888.

It was then that he came into Iowa walking with a bundle con-

taining a change of linen and a classified collection of Great
Plains cactus plants. At Winterset and later at Indianola, he
remembered gratefully, he first began to look upon himself as a
human being. Until then many white people had been kind to
him; they had praised him and said that he 'knew his place.' He
did not know his place. He had been looking for it, and here in
Iowa he began to feel that at last he had found it. He was six feet
tall, lean, and not yet twenty-five; but already his head was
beginning to bend low. A white boy he met in Winterset told
him, quite without condescension, that a good way to get away
from bent shoulders and a slouching gait is to walk at least two
miles daily with the hands clasped behind the back and a walking-
stick thrust between the elbows. Carver performed this exercise
daily. It took the kink out of shoulders rounded from bending
over the washtub and again bending to botanize or do work afield,
and it lifted his heart.

Finding that Negroes were allowed to attend a white Methodist
church in Winterset, he did so with a becoming diffidence and the
minister's family, the Mulhollands, asked him home. He and the
Mulhollands exchanged lessons in singing and painting. They
urged him on to improve his painting under the instruction of
Miss Etta Budd at Simpson College in near-by Indianola. After a
year of this Miss Budd sent him on as a student with special
recommendations to her brother, J. L. Budd, Professor of the
Horticultural Department at Ames.

Writing of the Iowa State College of Agriculture and Mechanic
Arts as it was in 1891 when Carver came there, Rackham Holt,[6]
Carver's biographer, calls it, a bit extravagantly, 'an eminent
institution, [which] prided itself on being excelled in agriculture
by no other college,' and 'the seed bed from which sprouted three
men who were to rule the agricultural destinies of the United
States for twenty-eight years.' These three were Professor James
(Tama Jim) Wilson, Professor Harry Wallace, and his boy Henry
Agard Wallace — 'at the time only a small twig being bent in the
right direction.'

Under Tama Jim as Director, agricultural teaching and research was in fact moving fast toward eminence at Ames; and no
more engaging picture of a Midland Land Grant College in its

early days survives than the record made in letters that George
Carver wrote then and later. To earn his way he took work as a
kitchen hand in the college dining hall. There was some attempt
at first to observe the curious American convention which holds
that it is all right for colored people to prepare and handle food if
they do not actually sit down beside you at the table and eat with
you. They segregated him with other colored help to eat in the
kitchen. Hearing this, a resolute lady abolitionist for whom
George Carver had painted flower portraits while he was in
Indianola smacked on her hat, boarded a train to Ames, and ate
with George and the help. That ended that. He was given a
place among the other students in the dining hall. 'That day
marked the end of his isolation,' his biographer, Holt, records,
and 'George could not later recall that anyone at Ames was ever
unkind to him.' He used to recall, years afterward, the fun they
had there in the dining hall with a student game as old, most
likely, as the oldest college. One had, by the rules, to exercise
at the table impressive new words, denoting learning. Here at
Iowa's Agricultural and Mechanical College, the language to be
displayed was not only classical but scientific. Bread was
Triticum vulgare, pepper was *Piper nigrum*. Salt was *Na C one*;
sugar, *C twenty-two H twenty-two O eleven*. A freshman game, to
be sure; even sophomores came to disdain it; but to George
Carver it meant admission in fellowship to a student body; it
meant that at last he belonged.

Soon he learned to speak up in class fearlessly and to share his
own natural learning, which was great, with the professors and the
class. The Agricultural College was small in those days. Most
of the students and faculty knew one another, in class and out.
The Director of the College and Experiment Station, Tama Jim,
had an especial interest in genetics — though the name had not
been coined at the time. He liked to talk with Carver about the
possibility of applying the principles of mating superior plants to
a practical improvement in livestock. 'I have been more intimate
with Mr. Carver,' he wrote later, when the Mississippi Agricultural and Mechanical College was trying to hire his Assistant
Botanist, 'than with any other student on the campus. He has a
passion for plants. In cross-fertilization and propagation he is by

all means the ablest student we have here. . . . He understands the anatomy and physiology of animals thoroughly, and the effect of different feeds.' Tama Jim was the only one at Ames from whom Carver would accept loans or favors. 'George,' he would say in his clipped, Scotch way, 'here are two dollars. Go get a new pair of shoes. Not a word out of you! Go! Get out!' George spent many weekends at the Wilson farm near Traer; and he was a constant visitor of Professor Harry Wallace, out at the dairy barn and at his home in Ames.

Like his father before him, Harry Wallace held advanced ideas as to the eternal relationship of fertile soil, vigorous plants, strong animals, and healthy people. 'A run-down farm is like a run-down man,' said Uncle Henry. 'Civilization depends upon a vital topsoil,' said Harry, his son. 'Mr. Wallace [H. C.],' said George Carver, writing in 1936, 'was one of my beloved teachers, and while his special subject in the Agricultural and Mechanical College was dairying in all its phases, he was a master of soils. Many are the invaluable lessons I learned from him. He set me to thinking along lines practically unknown at that time, but which are now found to be almost, if not quite, as important as the exploding of the theory of spontaneous generation by Justus von Liebig more than a half century ago.'

As a student George took a leading part in such mild sports as croquet and swimming and was one of the leading spirits of Eclectic, a speaking and debating group. His portraits of flowers took prizes at the state show in Cedar Rapids. As a research assistant he created new hybrids that held, Tama Jim believed, great promise of practical benefit for Iowa. Carver collaborated on a number of Station publications. Naturally gay and ardent, he responded to kindness with unnumbered acts of courtesy and zeal. Even the gruff and terrifying General James Rush Lincoln, Commandant of the Cadet Corps, was moved to make special citation of this 'most gentlemanly and efficient cadet, rising to the rank of captain through merit alone.' George had himself photographed in his uniform, erect, proud, straight as a sword.

To Henry A., the grave young son of Professor .Wallace, George Carver was the closest friend outside of anyone in his own family in early youth. Starting in 1892, the six-year-old boy and the six-foot man were often to be seen walking together over the fields or through the woods.

Throughout the greater part of half a century, as long as Carver lived, they maintained a correspondence that was both intimate and technical. As Secretary of Agriculture, Wallace made a special trip to Tuskegee, Alabama, to visit his old teacher and to talk with the students there. Immediately, publicity-boomers and president-makers of Wallace's staff saw in the thing a 'natural' and began to play it up. Wallace had no taste for that sort of politics. His sense of attachment to George Carver as a friend, scientist, and teacher was to him a sentiment personal and inviolable, not to be explored or exploited. He continued to write intimately to Dr. Carver; but when as Vice-President he was asked to send a message to a meeting celebrating a Carver anniversary he wrote with a certain reticence that was no less moving:

> Because of his friendship with my father and perhaps his interest in children George Carver often took me with him on botany expeditions, and it was he who first introduced me to the mysteries of plant fertilization. He seemed to have a great sympathy with me. Though I was a small boy he gave me credit for being able to identify different species of grasses. He made so much of it I am certain now that, out of the goodness of his heart, he greatly exaggerated my botanical ability. But his faith aroused my natural interest and kindled an ambition to excel in this field; his praise did me good, as praise of a child often does. There is no doubt it is the gift of the true teacher to see possibilities before the pupils themselves are conscious that they exist. Later on I was to have an intimate acquaintance with plants myself, because I spent a good many years breeding corn. Perhaps that was partly because this scientist, who belonged to another race, had deepened my appreciation of plants in a way that I could never forget. Certainly because of his faith I became interested in things that today give me a distinct pleasure. I feel I must pay him this debt of gratitude.

The young man sows his wild oats; he squanders, wastes the energies which, if conserved, would have tended immeasurably to promote his happiness. He usually does not realize it until it is too late; neither does the farmer realize what soil robbing is until the soil rebels, refuses to yield up the stores of fertility. . . . Both are simply yielding to the inexorable law that wrongdoing brings with it the penalty.

We scarcely expect to get a subscription from some men until the yellow clay spots begin to appear on the hillsides, until the land crusts in a dry time and puddles in a wet time; until the owner finds out by experience that there is nothing the matter with the soil, but with himself and his methods of farming. Then he begins to think and study, gets over his foolish prejudice against book farming, and gets it pounded into his head that good farming is simply obedience to moral law. Both moral and natural law have the same origin and similar penalties for their violation. — From an editorial by Uncle Henry in *Wallaces' Farmer*, June 23, 1905.

1. 'On a Fool's Errand'

A SECOND VOYAGE to Europe in 1894 improved the health but did little to compose the mind of the editor of *The Iowa Homestead*. One of the contemporary parables that he started writing in 1895 for the guidance of farm youth[1] may be taken as an indication of an actual encounter and conversation on shipboard. 'I noticed on the passenger list,' he wrote, 'the name of Thomas Hardman, Esq., an old schoolmate. An ocean steamer furnishes one of the best opportunities to study human

nature and find out what men really think. Tom Hardman was
not free to talk about himself at first.   I felt my way gradually . . .
told him of my own hopes and ambitions in the line of newspaper
work; that my aim was to aid in developing a class of farmers
mightier than Caesar's legions, more invincible than Cromwell's
Ironsides, the stay of their country in war, its balance-wheel in
peace when other classes lose their heads. . . .'

All this idealism, as Uncle Henry's story goes on, soon gets too
much for this hard, rich man; and he lets Uncle Henry have it:
'Henry, you've been a fool all your days . . . a fool on a fool's
errand.   You have helped men into place and power, and they
have kicked you; you have given scoundrels your confidence, and
they have betrayed it, and slandered and abused you in order to
make themselves believe that they owed you nothing.   You and I
are as far apart as the poles.   You believe in God; I do not.   You
believe that there is a future; I do not.   You believe that there is
such a thing as sin; I do not.   If there is a sin, it is that of perpetuating the race in such a cursed world as this. . . .'

Then Thomas Hardman, Esquire, relates the story of his success,
and it is really villainous.   He hated his father and mother and
they hated him.   He hired out to a farmer, loaned him money for
ten years: 'The tenth year he had hard luck.   His crops failed, his
hogs died of cholera, and his cows aborted.   Times were hard;
neither the banks nor loan companies were advancing money, and
I foreclosed and took the farm subject to a mortgage of $2000,
which cut out the homestead rights and his wife's dower.   I
farmed, and he hired out.   My credit was now established.

'I soon got tired of skinning grangers.   They squeal when they
are skinned.   They have a lot of old fogey notions.   They think
the Ten Commandments are binding and that Christ talked business on the Mount. . . . I came to the city, made new plans.   The
first thing I did was to find a corporation lawyer after my own
heart, and agree to give him a slice on the sly. . . .'

Uncle Henry interrupts: 'Do you mean to tell me that there is
no relief in a corporation for minority stockholders?   I myself am
a minority stockholder in a newspaper corporation; differences
have arisen, and there is trouble ahead for the majority.'

'"None whatever," he replied, "unless you can prove the most glaring fraud. The majority can defraud all they please if they have the right kind of lawyer. The danger of being caught in a fraud in a corporation never troubles me. I never give it a moment's thought.'"

Uncle Henry concludes: 'I looked at him in amazement and replied, "Tom, this is the first time we have met for forty years. It will, in all probability, be the last. I will not put in words what I think of you and your methods. They are not new. They are as old as the Egyptian oppression. They are the methods of scoundrels in all ages. The Prophet Micah described just such scoundrels as you when he wrote — *They oppress a man and his house — even a man and his heritage.* He described you to a dot as one — *who . . . eat the flesh of the people, and flay their skin from off them; and they break their bones, and chop them to pieces as for the pot.* It is men like you that are corrupting the very foundations of public morality, and fast bringing about the same conditions of things which the prophet described when he said — *They build up Zion with blood, and Jerusalem with iniquity. The heads thereof judge for reward, and the priests thereof teach for hire, and the prophets thereof divine for money.* You are a typical Hardman, the meanest, lowest and most dangerous that I have ever met."'

Having told off the Hardmans, the Richmans, the Cheatems of the world in similar sketches, he was kinder but stern to the chronic Hardups and the Featherheads; and finally he sketched not altogether uncritically but with considerable self-satisfaction his own sort of people, the Goodmans and the Brodheads. The Goodmans, it is plain from the context, personify his mother's people, the Rosses; and it is equally plain that he had taken his daughter-in-law's maiden name, Brodhead, to stand for the leading characteristics of his father, John, and the Wallaces in general: 'The difference between the Brodheads and the Goodmans is that the Brodheads think things out. The Goodmans feel their way to conclusions, "walk by faith," as it were, while the Brodheads walk more or less "by sight." The Brodheads are not all rich, by any means. Few of them, indeed, are very rich. You will frequently find them handling great enterprises for other people, but themselves only in moderate circumstances. It is very seldom, indeed, that you will find them poor, or even in limited circumstances, and never except when some misfortune has happened to them which no foresight possibly could avoid. They do not take kindly to what is known as practical politics; that is, to office getting and holding. When a Brodhead and a Featherhead compete for the first time for nomination in any party, the Featherhead has the better chance of winning, because he will do things a Brodhead will not do, and can be used by designing men, which a Brodhead cannot. When you get a Brodhead into the legislature or Congress, however, and he has a chance to make a record, and people get to know him, he is likely to become a statesman and stay in office as long as he likes.

'The Brodheads are not always popular. They are often supposed to be aristocratic and exclusive, for the simple reason that they will not allow themselves to be hail-fellow-well-met with everybody. They try to keep themselves out of the dirt, that is all, and I like that feature of their character. They are often blunt in speech and abrupt in manner. That is a fault. They are sometimes blamed for being insufficiently enthusiastic in a good cause, with being deficient in holy zeal at revival times, and political zeal during campaigns. There may be ground for criticism, but I have always noticed that when a real crisis comes in church or state, the men who criticize them for lack of zeal go to them for counsel.'

The depression of 1893–97 continued. Business was dragging bottom. The Wallace name was on what still passed in financial fiction as thirty thousand dollars' worth of property. *The Iowa Homestead*, losing subscribers, was mailing copies to people whether they had paid up or not. Wallace had argued against this, vainly; and he wondered now how many subscribers stopped paying because they did not have the money, and how many stopped because they had lost confidence in *The Iowa Homestead*.

In London he learned from an Iowa friend there in residence that Nat Hubbard, the son of a rich railroad lawyer, traveling, had remarked over brandy and cigars that *The Homestead's* 'active support is not worth anything any more, but its silence is valuable and worth buying.'

At the consulate in Dublin, where Newton Ashby had the leading Iowa papers mailed to him, Uncle Henry found even the con-

servative *Des Moines Register* discussing a proposed twenty-six
per cent advance in freight rates; but in *The Homestead* not a word.
Then: 'Nat Hubbard's statement occurred to me, and the
question arose in my mind: Has it been purchased? If so, the
people of Iowa will hold me responsible.'

He returned to Des Moines and in October, 1894, wrote a paragraph summarizing the rate issue and suggesting that farmers send
postcards of protest to the Iowa Railroad Commission. *The
Homestead* management threw his paragraph out. He wrote it
again, made it longer, and insisted, 'This must go in.' They
voted him down in directors' meeting.

They had built him up as a great crusading editor. He was a
hard hired man to fire. Deliberately, he gave further provocation.
'I saw that I would have to get out, but that it was to my interest
to be "fired." Every day for weeks I expected that my head
likely would be found in the basket.' The directors removed him
as editor at a meeting in late February, 1895, dating the discharge
March 1 — three days' notice and pay.

And so it was at the beginning of his sixtieth year he faced his
remaining years flat broke and unemployed. He was an editor
without a paper and at the same time a minority stockholder still
obligated for nearly one third of the losses, past and future, of the
publishers who had thrown him out. With no ready money, he
hardly knew where to turn. All the land and property that he and
his family held in title were mortgaged to the hilt in time of panic.

Those who knew him best then have spoken of him since as
'a lion in torment.' Scriptural maledictions of great force
resounded from the walls of the home he had bought in Des
Moines, to be nearer to his work on *The Homestead*, and the deep-
toned chest notes he had developed in preaching could be heard
by the neighbors. The Wallace family hastened to gather.
Harry and John, his sons, had plans. The family had a farm
paper of its own now, *The Farm & Dairy*, at Ames; and the head
of the family should be at the head of it, they said. Money?
It would take very little. The paper was small, but was breaking
even. Professor Curtiss would sell the Wallaces his share of it on
a note without endorsement; and whatever further money might be
needed they could seek in the same way, as 'character' loans.

Years later, Harry Wallace told a friend, Dr. H. C. Taylor: 'I knew that my father would die if he did not have an outlet for his convictions, a platform from which to speak.' [2]

In February, 1895, the same month that the name of Henry Wallace ceased to appear as editor of *The Iowa Homestead*, his sons' little bimonthly at Ames took the name of *Wallaces' Farm & Dairy* (note the plural apostrophe); and on their masthead the name of Henry Wallace led all the rest. In a leading editorial rather curiously entitled 'A Word Personal' Uncle Henry told why he was no longer editor of *The Homestead*. He bid especially for the support of *Homestead* readers in this new venture, asking them to subscribe at the introductory rate of twenty-five cents a year, and to send in the names of other *Homestead* readers. 'We got names by the thousands,' he reported happily. 'Large numbers stopped their subscriptions to *The Homestead* and raised clubs for us.' In the third issue of *Wallaces' Farm & Dairy* he announced a publishing platform:

'The voice of this paper will not be that of a corporation without conscience or soul but of a living man responsible at once to public opinion and to that higher law by which all men are judged. Its supreme aim will be the advancement of agricultural interests in the West and especially in the State of Iowa, and its point of view on all questions that are primarily agricultural or matters of public opinion will be that of the farm. While one object in conducting newspapers is to make money, that is not the sole object. The man who has no higher aim in conducting a newspaper than to make money will go wrong as soon as his paper obtains power and influence, and nothing can prevent it. It is not human nature to resist temptation to make money illegitimately, if there is no higher motive than the making of money; and downfall is only a question of time.'

The Homestead fired back. 'It advertised us,' said Uncle Henry. 'I harbor no bitterness. That year, 1895, is one of the most memorable in my life. It brought me what seemed to be one of my greatest troubles, and witnessed the beginning of my greatest success.' But he wrote this years later. There was a raging bitterness between *The Homestead* people and the Wallaces at the time. Uncle Henry sued Pierce to get the value of his stockholdings out of *The Homestead* and got a settlement of thirteen thousand dollars, about one third of the money he figured he had invested. He sued Pierce again for libel and won a verdict of fifteen thousand dollars and costs. 'I could not have carried on the litigation,' he explained in his memoirs, 'but for the financial aid of some splendid friends who loaned me the money to pay the lawyers' fees. I learned a great deal about laws. Even if you win, you usually lose. But the litigation did bring my antagonists to the point where they were willing to buy me out . . . and it was indirectly quite helpful to us in another way. The newspapers were reporting it. . . .'

People took sides and talked. An important advertising agency asked for a cut rate on a considerable block of space, to be secured under long-time contract and resold to clients at increasing rates as the publication grew. 'It took a lot of nerve for us to turn down this offer,' Uncle Henry wrote when the lean years had ended, 'but the boys talked it over and told him it would not be right to sell advertising space at one price to one man and at another price to another man. Really, turning down this offer was a very shrewd thing from a business standpoint, although we did not fully realize it at the time. It made that firm understand that we had confidence in ourselves, and that we would treat everybody alike. They sent us a nice lot of business right along, at the same rate we got from other advertising firms.'

In the 'Battle of the Standards,' the presidential election of 1896, the Wallaces stood with the Republican 'gold bugs' for the election of William McKinley, and ran a good big share of the campaign advertising that Mark Hanna's headquarters was putting out. That Republican campaign was quite a help in keeping their paper going. They ran Democratic and Populist advertising, too, of course; and took no strictly partisan stand editorially; but the reader could gather, plainly enough, that the Wallaces did not think much of William Jennings Bryan, at the time. As for Populism, the crest of that wave had passed. Business was picking up. An era of relatively good feeling which economists later tagged 'Normal period, 1897–1901,' was just over the hill.

By the end of its first year it was plain that the Wallaces' farm paper would live and grow. In January, 1896, they moved their

printing plant from Ames to Des Moines and started to publish
weekly instead of twice a month. Professor Harry resigned his
professorship to head the business side of the paper full time. His
younger brother, John, covered all of Iowa on a bicycle soliciting
livestock advertising and subscriptions. Daniel, the youngest
son, helped around the shop and, serving as his father's secretary
and field man, grew to be one of the few who claimed they could
read Uncle Henry's hurrying, scratchy handwriting. Their
mother became 'Aunt Nancy,' writing what coarser farm editors
called 'she-stuff,' homekeeping hints and notes on the amenities
of life. They shortened the name to *Wallaces' Farmer* and added
under it in boldfaced type a standing motto: *Good Farming . . .
Clear Thinking . . . Right Living*.

Time heals all sores. Or maybe it is just that publishing, like
politics, makes, unmakes, and remakes strange bedfellows. The
present reassembled combination of *Wallaces' Farmer* and *The
Iowa Homestead* carries at its masthead Uncle Henry's ringing six-
word declaration of principle to this day.

2. Secretary-Maker

PARTISANS and friends of the Wallaces in Iowa even now claim
proudly that, much as Mark Hanna was the president maker
of his era, Uncle Henry Wallace, far more loftily and nobly,
was the maker of Secretaries of Agriculture. He made three
of them if you count in his son and grandson, they say; and he was
twice offered the post himself.

There is no written evidence that all of this is true. Neither,
so far as I have found, is there any first-hand memory of a conversation in which Uncle Henry told any living person that he
could have been Secretary of Agriculture, but passed the honor on
to his old friend, Tama Jim. He did, however, once remark to his
son, Harry, that he might have been Secretary but did not go after
it when it was right there in his lap, because 'No Wallace has ever
held a public job beyond Justice of the Peace, and I didn't want to
mar the family record.' Harry Wallace remembered this and
repeated it to James G. Mitchell,[3] who was serving as attorney for

the Wallace interests in 1920, when Iowa Republicans tried vainly to get Harry to run for Governor.

The proffer of the secretariat to Uncle Henry, if it .was made, came early in 1897 through A. B. Cummins, the Des Moines lawyer who, having argued and won the Wallace-Pierce libel suit and carried the verdict to a successful confirmation before the Supreme Court, had become a man of influence in Washington. 'In January or February, 1897,' Wallace notes in *Reminiscences*, 'I had occasion to go to Mr. Cummins' office. He said to me: "You are the very man I want to see. I have been down to Canton to consult with Major McKinley about the formation of his Cabinet. He has it all selected with the exception of the Secretary of Agriculture. He said he was thinking of appointing Professor Wilson, whom he had known in Washington when they were both members of the House some years before. He asked me three things," said Mr. Cummins, "how it would please the politicians, how it would please the farmers, and whether Professor Wilson would accept. I told him it would be entirely satisfactory to the politicians, that I thought it would be satisfactory to the farmers, but that I did not know whether Professor Wilson would accept. Then the Major asked me to go to some intimate friend of Wilson's who had some idea of his standing with farmers, and find out whether it would be satisfactory to the farmers, and whether he would accept or not."'

There may, of course, have been long, meaningful pauses in the conversation before, having sounded out Uncle Henry, Cummins asked him to sound out Tama Jim. No such pauses are indicated in Wallace's crisp report. He proceeds to say that he wrote Wilson asking him to come to Des Moines, and wrestled with him in argument from morning until eleven-thirty at night.

'Finally he consented, saying:"If I fail, I will blame it all on you."

'I replied: "*Mea culpa*," which, you know, means "Mine the blame."'

So thoroughly has it been established in Iowa folklore that three of its Henry Wallaces have been offered the secretariat of agriculture that serious students of government, publishing annotated theses, have, together with hurrying journalists, repeated the statement flatly as a fact. It probably is true, but it cannot be proven; and the nearest descendants of the first Henry Wallace say that, so great was his regard for his friend James Wilson, he would not have made it known if it were true. The other time when he is supposed to have said 'No,' was to President-elect Taft. But again there is only circumstantial evidence. Tama Jim's biographer, E. V. Wilcox, records preinauguration rumors that Taft was going to wipe Roosevelt's Cabinet slate clean, and then, Wilcox says, there came a deluge of 'letters, telegrams, petitions and delegations insisting that Tama Jim be retained.' [4]

It is known that Taft considered replacing Wilson, who then was seventy-four. Uncle Henry was consulted and called to Washington about that time; and immediately he started sending wires back to his own and other papers in the Midland to help stir up a 'Keep Wilson' agitation.[4] The upshot was that Taft appointed an entirely new Cabinet except for one member, Wilson; and Tama Jim served with high usefulness as Secretary of Agriculture until the age of seventy-eight. He was sixty-two when he first took the post. In a sixteen-year term of duty, unprecedented at the time, and never since equaled, he transformed the Department from a puny and almost disregarded arm of government into the strongest and farthest-reaching of its kind on earth.

While the halls of Congress were known to him, bureaucracy was a new proposition, and the prospect frightened him at first. But not for long: 'My work at Ames makes the work here go more easily,' he wrote Uncle Henry in 1897. 'I took charge of my work at the College with great hesitation, but I have no hesitation in taking hold here. I find in many directions places where I can infuse some prairie breezes into these abstract sciences, and set them to do something for the fellow who works in the field with his coat off. I am endeavoring here to ascertain what the aim and intention of each division is, whether it is trying to help the farmer who is struggling in the field or merely doing something that will interest brother scientists.'

The dreary, whispering tone and content of the Department's annual reports appalled him. Robust agricultural journalism of the early Iowa order broke its way into the urban press through Secretary Wilson's annual reports. The Department became not only better known but far more widely popular. From a full heart Wilson chanted praise of production, production, production: 'All the gold mines of the entire world have not produced since Columbus discovered America a greater value of gold than the farmers of this country have produced in two years.' Again: 'The earth has produced its greatest annual dividend. The sun and the rain and the fertility of the soil heeded not the human controversies but kept on working in co-operation with the farmer's efforts to utilize them. The man behind the plow has filled the nation's larder, crammed the storehouses, and will send liberal supplies to foreign countries.'

O happy land and time! Having touched bottom in the summer of 1897, prices turned upward. Land values resumed a rise which for some years to come would make it again possible for Midland farmers to farm badly, skin the land, show a cash loss as well as a soil loss each year, and yet at the end of twenty years sell out and retire to the Coast with a competence.

'Every sunset during the last five years,' Tama Jim reported shortly after the turn of the century, 'has registered an increase of $3,400,000 in the value of farms in this country.' And: 'There was never a country so rich as this. There was never a country so prosperous. There was never a country so productive as this. There was never a country where labor was so richly rewarded. There was never a people so contented as ours. There was never a country in which human beings lived so well. . . .

'The farmer's standard of living is rising. He is becoming a traveler. And he has his telephone and his daily mail and newspaper. His life is healthful to body and sane to mind, and the noise and fever of the city have not become the craving of his nerves, nor his ideals of the everyday pleasures of life. A new dignity has come to agriculture, along with its economic strength, and the farmer has a new horizon, far back of that of his prairie and his mountains, which is more promising than the skyline of the city.'

Tama Jim was a high protectionist without doubt or quibble and a resolute pioneer expansionist at the same time. 'There are no bad acres,' he exclaimed. 'We have no useless American acres! We shall make them all productive. We have agricultural explorers in every far corner of the world searching for crops that have become acclimated to dry conditions like our own in the West, and we shall in time have plants thriving upon our so-called desert lands.'

'Poetry. wedded to patriotism,' E. V. Wilcox, his biographer, called it, and added: 'The patriotism of Secretary Wilson was not limited to the idea of America for the Americans only. It included also those who chose to come to us with the intention of becoming loyal citizens. But his slogan was "America First." It went against the grain with him that we should depend upon the rest of the world for anything. . . .'[5]

How long ago and far away it all sounds now! With Spain smacked out of the way in the Caribbean, with money somewhat easier to get, with the westward march of the plow renewed upon the High Plains country and with the thrall of Manifest Destiny mounting, the threats and shrieks of the dispersed Populists subsided. An evangelical and idyllic tone was to pervade now for a while in discussions of agriculture and country life. *O fortunatus nimium, sua si bona norint — Agricolas!* This classic expression of the period carried over to be inscribed irremovably in true fresco on the wall of the Department of Agriculture's main building during the Hoover administration — a somewhat unsuitable time. 'Which means,' said the second Secretary Wallace (H. A.), translating wryly: 'If the farmers only knew how well off they are they wouldn't be bellyaching all the time.' Tama Jim Wilson could hardly have picked a better year to start being Secretary of Agriculture than 1897 or a better one to retire than 1912.

Those were good years, too, for getting ahead in the farm-paper business. Certain of success now, the Wallaces skimped and borrowed every cent they could, plowing the money back to the roots of their growing property. 'Everything all of us had went into the "pot,"' Uncle Henry wrote. 'Each of us drew out what he had to have for his family living expenses. At the end of three or four years, however, we had gotten over the hill, and paid up most of our debts, and were making money. Then we had a settlement. I had been getting three thousand dollars a year as editor of *The Homestead*. So the boys credited me with that amount each year from the time we started *Wallaces' Farmer*, and it was paid to me as fast as we had money to spare. Each one of

them was also credited with a small salary. I don't remember
just when we began to pay our salaries regularly, but I think it
was before 1900.'

Not long after that, with *Wallaces' Farmer* paying dividends as
well as salary, Uncle Henry found himself for the first time in his
life with enough ready money to bother him. All of his days he
had been an easy mark for nearly anyone, however shiftless,
dissolute, or abandoned, who came asking alms outright or a loan
which by reason of the nature of the borrower would never be
repaid. This was known; it was also known that he had money
now, and that the doors of his home and office were always open.
Callers with hard-luck stories came in numbers. Uncle Henry
would lecture them severely about the sinfulness of improvidence,
then impatiently give them his nearest fistful of bills or silver in
order to be rid of them. The boys told their father that he really
ought not to do this. 'I shall make other arrangements,' he told
them majestically. He went to his banker and arranged for a
trust fund, starting immediately. Into this fund went everything
he had made or would make in his lifetime. Out of it came a
moderate annual annuity for himself and his wife — 'enough to
live in comfort'; and the remainder was disbursed in annual
amounts to designated causes and charities, with small annual
beneficences to the children. The arrangement pleased him so
greatly that he was never through advising well-to-do friends of his
own age to make similar arrangements. 'Just think!' he would
tell them. 'You will never have to worry about money again as
long as you live.'

'The happiest years,' as Daniel A. Wallace, the youngest son of
his household, remembers them, 'were along there in the early
nineteen-hundreds, with all the lawsuits settled, a paper of our
own going, no business or political brawls to upset Father's digestion or trouble the goodness of his spirit, and with money coming
in regularly. The agrarian uproar had died with the Populist and
Granger breakdown. Now everything was farmers' institutes,
Chautauquas, Acres of Diamonds stuff — self-improvement. It
was a big time for Gospel Seed Corn Trains, and Co-operative
Creamery demonstration tours. Father loved it. He and Harry
helped to organize trains and demonstrations. They brought

P. G. Holden, the corn evangelist, on from Illinois and arranged for *Wallaces' Farmer* to pay part of his salary as an Extension man for the College. Father went out and trouped for the New Day in Agriculture all over Iowa. And Mother, with the family pretty well grown up and out from under foot, was having just as fine a time with her women's club work, advancing culture. Mother was a strong believer in culture.'

He tells of a particularly wonderful summer when his mother went off to Europe alone and left Dan and his father to fend for themselves.

'One summer there, she wanted Father to take her to Europe again and visit some art museums, but he was too busy; so she fixed it for Father and me to take our meals at a nearby boarding house while she made the trip herself. We saw her off to the train and she gave us a lot of instructions. "Write that down, Dan," Father would say absent-mindedly, and I would write it down. I knew what was on his mind. A man brought up as a preacher has to do a lot of eating around, and now that Father had a good big house of his own, he would stay and eat there. He liked his freedom.'

When her train had pulled out and they were walking home, Uncle Henry said: 'Dan, can you, perhaps, make coffee?'

'Yes, Father.'

'And fry eggs, or perhaps some ham?'

'Yes, and pancakes, Father!' said Dan.

All that summer the two of them bached it. They never went to that boarding house. 'Sometimes there were ants in the maple sugar we put on the pancakes, but there was nothing whatever the matter with Father's digestion when he was happy, and that was an idyllic summer, all except the end of it,' Dan Wallace recalls. 'We ate whenever we felt like it and lay around talking and scattering cigar ashes all over the place wherever we liked. I asked Father if it would be all right if I asked in some of what he called my "typical minister's son's friends" for a game of poker; and, "Certainly, Dan; have your friends," he said. We had company almost every evening after that. Some of my poker companions were distinctly proletariat, from the wrong side of the tracks. Father was delighted with them and they loved him, just

as everybody else did.   Cards were all Greek to him, but he liked
to watch us play and to join in the talk.   He had more than any
other man I ever knew a natural sweetness, innocence, and gaiety
of spirit.   We had a wonderful summer.

'But one night toward the end, strange visitors appeared.
Father said: "Bed-bugs, Dan!"   We got out of there and into
another bedroom.   Bed-bugs weren't as unusual or disgraceful as
they are now, if you had grown up with the State of Iowa, as we
had.   Just the same, I thought I had better not have any more
help come in to make beds and so on until I had solved the problem.   Otherwise, Father and I agreed, word might reach Mother
through some of our relatives; and, "that would be unfortunate,"
Father said.   So we put off doing anything about it and kept
changing bedrooms until we were out of bedrooms; and just then
came a cable from Mother saying she had sailed; and we had to
call in all the women of the family to help us.   Father was scared.
"What will your Mother say, Dan?" he kept saying.   She was
furious.   All the women in the family were furious.   They said
I had corrupted Father, which was silly, because Father was perfectly incorruptible, and as long as he lived he used to talk about
what a marvelous time we had that summer.' [6]

3. Corn and Charts

A T THE TURN of the century the Harry Wallaces moved three
times in four years.   'In the nineties our circumstances
were almost sharply necessitous, and I hardly remember my
father when he was not working,' his son, Henry A., recalls.
'Father went at everything with a steady intensity.   Whether it
was advertising contracts, a circulation problem, or a question of
editorial or shop organization, he did it all.   When it came to key
decisions and action in business he was worth all the rest of us put
together.

'I remember in 1898 shortly after he had resigned his professorship at Ames and moved us into another rented house — 1619
Seventh Street in Des Moines — he took us walking, my mother
and sister and me — one Sunday afternoon beyond the outskirts of

the city. Des Moines was putting up a row of rather ugly little two-story homes; and I remember my father saying, " If we could get hold of $900 we could build a house like that of our own." The next year, 1899, we rented another house, at the corner of University and Thirty-Eighth Street. It was old and dilapidated but it had an acreage. And in 1902 Father bought ten acres and built a mansion — 3780 Cottage Grove Avenue. It cost $5500! That is the house in which I grew up.'

Des Moines' suburbia was beginning to give itself airs even then, in young Henry's opinion. Instinctively he set himself against country club standards. He maintained a manner and appearance aggressively rustic, to his mother's dismay. Boys neatly combed, cleaned, and buttoned seemed to him hardly human and for girls he had at the time no use at all. It was all right for girls and women to be dainty, but it took a lot of work to keep them that way. He knew this because by this time he had three sisters and it was his job to pump water up to the attic tank which supplied the family bathroom at 3780 Cottage Grove Avenue. Saturday, with other womenfolk of the family there to visit, was his heaviest day.

He did not mind pumping, however. He found that it had a calisthenic effect on the arms, chest, and shoulders which helped him with the rather rowdy gang that he chose to run with. They were public-schoolers, like himself, but they came from all the wrong parts of town. And his closest friend in the gang was the son of a washwoman whose husband was a Swedish sailor.

At home he tended garden, cared for the chickens, milked the family cow, and fed a pen of hogs. His mother was always after him to change from his work-clothes after breakfast (or at least change his shoes) so that he would not smell like a farm boy in school. He never argued about it, but went to school smelling the way he pleased. His city teachers were a little sniffish about it, but they uttered no formal complaint. By this time his mother had five other children to look after so she let Henry have it his way.

Suburban gangdom did not long attract him. He found an increasing pleasure in being alone. Alone is perhaps not the word for it exactly. He has said in the years of his maturity that no discerning person should feel lonely out-of-doors. One of his most revealing papers, a fifteen-minute radio talk that he gave when he was Secretary of Agriculture, he entitled simply, 'The Strength and Quietness of Grass.'[7] From his earliest boyhood he had found plants companionable.

One of the first things George Washington Carver helped him learn was to classify the grasses. Corn is a grass bred to grow high and bear grain by Indians, selecting desired strains, trying them in new soils and climates, and crossing one strain upon another for ten thousand years or more. 'The finest corn breeders who ever lived,' young Henry Wallace wrote in one of the many articles that he published in *Wallaces' Farmer* on the subject,[8] 'were the forerunners of the Aztecs in the highlands of southwestern Mexico. They caused grass to do a thing it had never done before. How these early corn breeders worked on the wild prototype of corn to make it the plant which it has been for at least ten thousand years, is a mystery which baffles the best scientists.' The article proceeds to trace the past ten centuries of blending and adaptation of long-season soft or 'gourd' corn on the one hand and short-season or 'flint' corn on the other, 'a wonderful piece of work,' and all performed by Indians as they moved up into North America, encountering shorter growing seasons on the way. A thousand years — ten centuries — why, that would date the beginning of systematic agriculture in North America back to the time of the Crusades, young Henry A. Wallace reflected; and back beyond that lay ten thousand years — one hundred centuries — of unexplored inter-American sciences, economics, religion, history. The classics droningly taught in schools, the ancient history and languages of Greece and Rome, took no such hold on his mind.

The Indians called corn 'Our Life.' In Iowa it is called 'King.' It is one distinctive native grain of America, the mainstay of its primitive agriculture. The whites on their march from Jamestown and Plymouth to the Rockies had taken 'corn' from the Indians and planted it. In so doing they imposed upon themselves, in the great middle country particularly, a pattern of agriculture which uncovered the earth to the beat of the weather and so made their whole structure extremely vulnerable to the ravages of time. At the same time these Midwestern corn planters imposed

SOME OF THE FIRST HYBRID SEED CORN
Henry A. and Uncle Henry, July, 1914

upon themselves an economic overreliance upon corn in the grain and corn on the hoof which laid them open to the storms and lulls of commerce, and led them in time of panic to lose their land to traders, as well as to the streams and the sea.

'It would sometimes seem,' Henry A. Wallace wrote in the fourth decade of the present century,[9] 'that tobacco, corn, and cotton, all plants that we took from the Indians when we took their continent, have taken rather a horrible revenge on us under our clean-culture, straight-line methods of culture.' But back in the first decade of the century there was little or no such talk or thought.

He might now, if he were to return to genetic researches, Wallace has said, work hardest on such grasses as make sod. He recalls prophecies announced by Arthur Mason of Illinois a quarter-century ago: that 'agricultural regions with cloudy streams must be temporary,' and that the only way to prevent this 'slow bleeding to death' was to abandon clean-tilled corn culture altogether, matting the prairie with a solid sward of leguminous grass, and feeding it to livestock dehydrated.

And yet, even while acknowledging that too much land for the good of the country has been plowed and worked, Wallace remains true for the most part to his first love among all the plants of the prairie, to the giant grass and grain-giver, Indian corn. Delivering in 1938, at Michigan State College, a memorial lecture to Frank A. Spragg,[10] the great plant breeder, he said: 'This year there will be planted at least fifteen million acres of hybrid corn and if we have ordinary weather, the total yield of corn will be at least one hundred million bushels more than would have been the case if the same acres had been planted to open pollinated corn. . . . Looking ahead we can be fairly certain that in 1945 there will be well-adapted commercial strains of hybrid corn for practically every section of the Corn Belt, and that it will yield at least twenty per cent more than the average open pollinated corn as grown in the respective parts of the Corn Belt. The twenty per cent of the corn land which is most poorly adapted to corn and most likely to be hurt by erosion, can be taken out of cultivation and returned to grass.'

He told how he first became interested in breeding corn: It was not, he said, until about 1890, within the span of his own lifetime, that 'the people of the Corn Belt began to think seriously in an organized way about improving their corn. Up to that time Corn Belt farmers in their corn breeding operations had improved upon the Indians chiefly by substituting a later type of corn from the East for the earlier types which the Indians had grown. . . . After 1890 came thirty years of enthusiastic interest in corn shows. Standards of corn beauty were evolved which had nothing whatever to do with yield but which gave great satisfaction to several thousand corn farmers. The agricultural colleges held corn shows and trained farm boys to act as judges. In this way an immense interest in corn was stirred up, and while the corn show doctrines were utterly misleading, the eventual outcome was good. The powers of observation of thousands of farm boys were firmly fixed on corn. It is not surprising that after a time some of them began to dig deeper than the superficialities of the corn show.

'Perry G. Holden, the great corn evangelist, proved in this respect to be an interesting study in dual personality. He had graduated from the Michigan Agricultural College in 1889, with the benefit of rigorous training in botanic observation by Doctor J. W. Beal, a student and follower of Agassiz. . Mr. Holden used the corn show mechanisms to get hold of many hundreds of Iowa farm boys. He could place corn samples with an air of great finality, as though he really knew which ones were best. And yet he must have had twinges of conscience about the whole matter, because in 1904 he encouraged me to plant on an ear-to-row basis thirty-three ears of corn which he had placed in a corn show. . . . Of course, I found that Holden as a corn judge didn't really know anything about the yielding power of the different ears. But Holden as a stimulator of boys was a tremendous success. He whetted my eagerness to see how the different ears of corn would yield. I shall never forget my debt of gratitude to him.'

If ever a disciplined scientist, a born publicist and promoter, a politician and a gifted teacher can be said to have dwelt in reasonable harmony within one skull and skin — that is P. G. Holden. 'The Corn Man,' they called him in Iowa and throughout the Corn Belt. Slim, bespectacled, and bearded, dynamic and persuasive, he was hailed in his time, almost reverently, by the more ardent of his co-workers in Agricultural Extension in the Midland as 'a missionary declaring the glory of tall corn.' He had performed botanical research, taught college-grade science, served as a county superintendent of schools, worked for a beet-sugar company, and organized the largest seed-corn business in Illinois as manager before he came to Iowa in 1902. In Iowa he became Director of Extension for the State College and resigned to run for Governor, unsuccessfully, in 1912. *Wallaces' Farmer* championed his Boys' Corn Clubs, a forerunner of the 4-H Club movement, and supported him for Governor. He was a frequent visitor at the Wallace home from 1902 onward.

Fourteen-year-old Henry, experimenting as usual, put a ring of wood ashes around a cherry tree and his father took him to task. The question was not whether the potash in the ashes would benefit the tree, but whether they should be put in a ring the circumference of the whole tree, to the full spread of its branches, as Henry claimed, or closer to the trunk. Holden said the boy was right. 'It was the first agricultural controversy I ever thought I had won,' as Wallace recalls it, 'so I decided this new professor really knew something and was all right.'

Admitting Holden, with justice, to the company of the immortals among 'the maize finders' at that period, Paul de Kruif in his book *Hunger Fighters* also admits young Henry Wallace to that high company and describes him as a premature scientist — 'A thin boy whose face was too earnest for his age.' A little later on he says Henry's 'super-serious face had become a hundred times more serious,' and wonders if, even in moments of triumph, this Wallace 'ever laughed out loud at all.' We may suspect overdramatization in De Kruif's imaginative description, but there can be no doubt that when confronted with the earlier manifestations of 4-H (Hand-Head-Heart-Health) evangelism Henry pulled a wry face and did not lead the cheers for the Professor.

The trait that bothered him most about Holden, whom he greatly respected and liked, was this: Why should a man so well equipped to seek the truth wear himself out by spreading too thin a popular mixture of the true and the inane? All this talk of 'pure' breeds, types, and show-ring standards, what did it come to? The 'thoroughbred' fetish as to horseflesh and people, the 'purebred' fetish as to cows, hogs, dogs, and hens, and all this conventional concern as to the purity of corn varieties — Henry had his doubts. Cur dogs, or hybrids, he noted, ordinarilv had more vigor than dogs of the accepted 'breed' types.

The same Dr. Beal who had taught Perry Holden in Michigan was the first scientist on record deliberately to inbreed our* corn. He made his crosses at Michigan State in 1881 and demonstrated what he called 'the buoyancy of hybridization.' He crossed corn plants as dissimilar as the draft horse and the mustang, or the Newfoundland dog and the Pekingese. He did this by pulling out the tassels of plants he chose to be exclusively female and letting the pollen from yellow corn, for instance, fertilize the silks of these carefully 'pure' white strains or 'varieties' near-by.

Haphazardly, but in accord with Nature's large intent, the wind had been breeding corn hybrids from time immemorial. The male flowers of corn are borne, as Beal's technique has indicated, in the tassel; the female flowers are borne in the ear; and the pollen visits around between plants. When the tassels ripen and open the pollen floats on the air or is borne by the wind where it listeth (although generally not for great distances, in any effective way), and a pollen speck must land and mate at the tip of every strand of cornsilk before there can be a full ear.

The Indians did not care what color their corn was. They were content if it was fit to eat. Much of the earlier seed corn the white man took from the Indian grew 'calico' ears, with grains of various colors, according not only to its own mixed nature but to the nature of chance visitation of pollen from fields near-by. This did not look right to the early white pioneer corn breeders. With a passion for standardization that was in part aesthetic and possibly in part moral, they located plantings of white corn as far as possible from plantings of yellow. Then they selected rigorously to impress upon the offspring some 'type' they had in mind.

Old Jake Leaming of Ohio went along with a prevailing super-stition, or at least the chemists called it that, until they discov-ered caroten. Jake Leaming held with those who said 'yellow corn has more strength to it; the hogs like it better.' He was against stalks which bore their ears so high that a man had to climb and hunt them. He liked ears that leaned out 'to shake hands with you,' so he chose such ears for seed. He wanted early-maturing corn, so, as he walked in his clean-tilled fields in the late summer, he spied on the redheaded woodpeckers. The woodpeckers know which ears have ripened first. Jake Leaming would tie pieces of string to the plants the woodpeckers visited and at husking time, if the ear was also a thing of beauty, he would save that ear for seed. He used the instinct of the birds to make corn ripen earlier on fields that were still to be planted long after he should be dead.

Leaming was one of the great corn varieties of the period. Reid's Yellow Dent, first developed as a chance hybrid in Illinois, was another. A farmer named Robert Reid coming West from Ohio in 1846 brought with him in his wagons the seed of a corn named Gordon Hopkins and failed to get a good stand of it at his first planting in Illinois. He replanted in the rows at places where the first planting had missed with a yellow flint corn, locally called Little Yellow, the seed for which he obtained from Indians. The resulting intermating of Little Yellow with the reddish semi-gourd dent type from Ohio became the foundation of the seed that Robert Reid's son James developed during a lifetime as Reid's Yellow Dent.

James Reid picked corn for its looks; he was a shy, dreamy man. The ears of corn he sent to the shows had the clean outline and the slight, graduated taper of Greek columns. They were almost as uniform in their appearance as if an architect had drawn them with exact instruments to the same design and scale. His corn took sweepstakes at the World's Fair in Chicago, and his name became famous in the Midland. It is recorded that rather plain farmers, seeking perfection, paid as high as one hundred and fifty dollars a bushel for the seed of his best show ears. But James Reid himself never cashed in on the show-corn craze, which was not unlike the tulip craze of another era. He died poor.

From the beginning of recorded time on this continent Indian corn has been especially the object of celebrations and ceremonies by which man praises continuing birth and renewal. It is such a beautiful plant; it grows so fast and makes grain so bountifully that man may well revere it as an annual tree of life. Modern machinery does not dim the wonder of its growth. Rather late in

the spring — 'when the leaf of the oak is as big as a squirrel's ear,'
the Indians said — the planters bury the seed. Then in a few
warm days the miracle of the resurrection is repeated, transform-
ing the face of the land. 'How beautiful,' wrote Thomas Carlyle,
in England, 'to think of tough, lean Yankee settlers, tough as
gutta-percha, with a most unsubduable fire in their belly, steering
over the Western mountains, to annihilate the jungle, and to bring
bacon and corn out of it for the posterity of Adam.'

Iowa, in particular, Paul de Kruif has written, is 'the real corn
state, the one corn land laid down by God and the glacier for the
particular purpose of growing maize to turn into meat on four legs.'

Varying sects, cults, and rituals as pagan in their way as earlier
rites to gods which cause the frogs to croak, foretelling rain, were
growing and multiplying on all sides in our great Midland when
Henry A. Wallace was a boy. It all went on under college auspices, more or less; and it all took the tone of hard-fisted practicality and science. A committee of corn judges sought to compose such differences. They drew up a score card for corn shows,
a mathematical statement of the ideal ear. So many points per
cent for straight rows; so many for well-filled tips and butts; so
many for deep, wedge-shaped grains. Some of the points of
beauty these corn cranks stressed were, it will be observed, func-
tional. So are some of the points on the score cards by which livestock is judged today; and there is always an attempt to rationalize every show point, or justify it, on that score. But many of the
points are entirely 'fancy,' bearing no relevance whatever to the
rustic adage, 'Pretty is as pretty does.'

As manager of the Reids' big seed farm in Illinois, Holden had
helped to develop Reid's Yellow Dent. In Iowa as a public
servant he boosted no one variety above another, but he preached
with zeal that the clean-cut, streamlined, deep-grained beauty of
the Reid type was beauty that paid. He went farther. You
could see virility in one ear of corn above another, he told his
Corn Club youngsters, training them as judges. 'This ear has
vigor, constitution; note the fine, strong middle!' he would say,
placing that ear first. To the preternaturally skeptical Wallace
this did not make sense. A fine, strong middle of what? Good
girth at the barrel of hogs or cattle might indeed denote superior

constitution and virility. But when it came to corn, what vital organs or processes could possibly be affected by the shape of the ear? Heft, maybe, but not shape. He raised such questions shyly, quietly, but with an intense, prying persistence. Holden was not offended. He had been a research man himself. 'If you don't believe me, why don't you check my judgments with an ear to row yield test?' he asked.

Wallace made his first such test planting in the spring of 1904. The story of the genetic revolution in seed corn has become a legend now, and it is part of the legend that Wallace, at sixteen, showed up Holden and the other judges simply by planting a few seeds in the back yard. The fact is, he ran a five-acre test on thirty-three ears.

To plant breeders the contests that they arrange between plants afield are more exciting than human contests waged over an inflated pigskin amid organized cheering. But it is a laborious and solitary affair. And five acres is about the size of five football gridirons.

Holden supplied the contestants for this trial — thirty-three lovely ears of Reid's Yellow Dent from a corn show. During the winter Wallace gave each ear a number, tacking a placard into each cob at the butt. Then he shelled by hand half of each ear, put the seed from each in a numbered sack, and stored the half-shelled ears for future use or discard.

In the spring he went out to his five acres and marked off the prepared ground in rows: Two rows for each of the test ears.

He divided the field into a north and south half, detasseled the rows representing the even numbered ears and in the south half detasseled the rows representing the odd numbered ears. Five acres is quite a stretch of ground when you cover it, stepping and stopping, stepping, stopping and bending, again and again. Once through for the planting, once through for thinning, three or four times through for cultivating and weeding — the procedure thus far as for ordinary corn. Now comes the work of detasseling. The tassels for most varieties ripen irregularly over a period of two weeks; to pluck them too soon hurts the plant's growth and to pluck them too late permits them to shed undesired pollen. Conscientious detasseling, therefore, requires a trip down the corn rows every day for three weeks or so; and the hand labor required to do this runs about thirty hours to the acre. Finally there comes the longer labor of harvesting, weighing, checking the crop of each such row separately, and computing the yield of each in terms of bushels to the acre. This was the part of it most fascinating to Wallace, for his interest in mathematics had dated from a day in the fourth grade when they came to a primary arithmetic lesson in ratio and proportion. Too eager to wait for the crop to dry, he figured cob weight and moisture loss in, too, and arrayed his sums in terms of relative acre-yields of air-dried shelled grain, later to be verified. The findings were astonishing. These ears, which looked so much alike, varied as yielders from thirty-three to seventy-nine bushels to the acre, and the ear Professor Holden chose as the very best proved one of the ten lowest yielders.

Three years later, in 1907, writing one of his first articles for *Wallaces' Farmer*, young Henry reviewed the findings, verified many times now in his own experience and in that of others. Nubbins may be better seed ears than show ears; and he raised a rude question: 'What's looks to a hog?'

By this time corn breeding had taken a startling new turn. Inbreeding, orthodox agronomists called it. Arguing backward from human statutes which had certainly never been openly tested scientifically, they held that in-and-in breeding of plants and animals can result only in degeneracy and rapid enfeeblement of the strain.

Plant genetics had taken, none the less, a revolutionary trend. In 1906, with Wallace a freshman in agriculture at Iowa State, Dr. George Shull at the Carnegie Institution Station for Experimental Evolution on Long Island, mated some corn plants to themselves to see what would happen. Dr. Edward East, later of Harvard, but then a research worker at the Connecticut Agricultural Experiment Station, tried the same idea independently at about the same time. They tied bags over the tassels of their corn, collected the pollen and applied the pollen borne on a given stalk to the silks of the same plant. Their initial results announced in 1908 and 1909 were similar. They found that seed from plants thus inbred displayed more than Beal's 'buoyancy of hybridization'; that the result was a genetic explosion, exhibiting the widest, most amazing variations, including an occasional sharp lift in yield.

Shull had no interest in the practical possibilities of this discovery. He reported his findings and went over to recording and hastening the processes of evolution in the Evening Primrose and Shepherd's Purse. But East, and later Donald Jones and H. K. Hayes, of the Connecticut station, worked on, trying to see what could be done to fix the character of high yield and other desirable agricultural characters in these strange new inbred strains.

All through the Corn Belt other experimenters — Kiesselbach in Nebraska, Hoffer in Indiana, Richey at the United States Department of Agriculture, and an increasing number of others — started work on the same problem. Wallace made a few backyard inbred crosses and became fascinated. But he did not go over to inbreeding all at once. The method was exceedingly laborious. He was not sure that it was practical; and between courses at Iowa State and covering agricultural news from there as correspondent for *Wallaces' Farmer* (he made his own way entirely in the senior year by writing at space rates) he had too few hours for plant breeding. That is one of the reasons he decided not to take a graduate degree. He would rather do graduate work in his own way, he told his father, and work it over toward a paying seed-corn business than go on with scholastic routine toward Master's and Doctor's degrees. So he took the plain degree of Bachelor of Science in Animal Husbandry with honors in 1910, and left college.

He was not a big man, in terms of the campus, either in high school or in college. In point of scholastic grades he was preeminent, graduating as top man in the College of Agriculture, and when a subject interested him his work was brilliant and original. He was quietly popular and joined a house-club, Hawkeye, which later became a chapter of the Delta Tau Delta fraternity; but he never appeared to take deeply to heart the fraternal bond.

When the exactions of a course or teacher seemed to him arbitrary or out of reason, he was inclined to argue as an equal and to display without recalcitrance a mildly rural antic streak. In high school he had a history teacher whom he suspected of grading themes according to length rather than content. Experimentally, he submitted a brief, crisp paper, and noted the grade: 88 per cent. Then he wrote a long dull one, and the good man trustfully graded it 95 per cent without ever having reached the final page on which his pupil had entered irrelevant reflections about a lone red cow grazing on the billowy prairie and ruminating on the vanity of history and long themes.

But this same teacher, N. H. Weeks, Wallace remembers gratefully as 'the first to arouse me to consider the iniquity of tariffs.'

After he left college, the professor he most venerated was kindly H. D. Hughes, who backed him, smiling, in his young assaults on the standpat pronouncements of conventional agronomists. 'Hughes did not want to hurt people,' Wallace said in his Spragg Memorial lecture on genetics, 'but at the same time he wanted to wake them up.'

In 1909 Wallace began to puzzle about measuring the precise influence of rainfall and temperature on corn yield. He ran across a book by H. L. Moore of Columbia University dealing with the application of calculus to the problem, and hired a Drake University professor of mathematics to explain it all to him. Then he devised some mathematical short cuts, using a key-driven calculating machine. Excited by his calculations, he decided the college at Ames needed a strong course in biometrics and for one time in his life became a college teacher. For ten Saturdays in 1913 he taught a class of professors and postgraduate students, and he wrote the first draft of a pamphlet, *Correlation and Machine Calculations*,[11] on the basis of this course. G. W. Snedecor, the Professor of Mathematics at Ames, worked with him and later joined with other professors in making the biometrics work at Ames probably the best in the United States.

These initial adventures in conventional scientific composition did him no good as a writer and speaker. It was years before he worked the ponderous passivity and the pretended Olympian detachment of such jargon out of his style.

In the social sciences, in questions of relationship between soil and nutrition, and in advanced genetics Iowa State had at the time little to offer; neither less nor more than any other college in the land. For a college graduate Wallace is to an extraordinary extent a self-made technician and educated man.

He made some good friends in college. Most of them were on the faculty, and after he went back to Des Moines he continued to see his friends at Des Moines and occasionally to carry on some work project with them.

John M. Evvard, an eminent research man in animal nutrition, joined the staff at Ames in 1910, the year Wallace graduated, and he and Wallace became friends at once. They argued about diet. Evvard believed in meat. Wallace at the time was shy of meat. It was not a cultish or ethical choice, but remembrance of butchering days on the farm repelled him, and a man's instinct, he argued, may be a guide in personal food choice. Evvard had no respect at all for man's food-choosing instincts. He had shown by experiments that animals, given choice of grass or feeds rich in minerals or poor in minerals, invariably choose the richer food; whereas man cannot smell, see, or taste the difference. Wallace's unguided interest in nutrition had led him as a student first to fast and make notes. Now for a while he tried living on soy beans and corn meal, with every portion weighed and measured to assure the needed proteins, carbohydrates, and calories by which adequate diets were figured at the time. None of these experiments were successful. John Evvard showed him why. 'I think I can claim,' Wallace said, years later, 'to be one of the first to know what vitamin deficiency is.'

In the summer of 1909, his twenty-first year, he made his first trip west of Iowa. The idea was his own; the trip took three months; and the reportorial series he wrote, 'On the Trail of Corn Belt Farmer,' covered the experiences of Midlanders who had migrated to sites as far removed as irrigated farms in California and the Matador Ranch in the Texas Panhandle.

In the summer of 1910, having graduated, he took a solitary walking trip over Iowa, covering prairie, hills, and the river country, talking with people, considering them in respect to their inherited traditions, their adjustments to the living landscape and the ground at their feet. He found startling differences between people of Northern and Southern extraction, between hillmen and prairie-cove farmers, between riverside people and people of the open plain. He made notes and computations and returned to Des Moines to announce to his father and grandfather the epochal finding that for the first time in history land over Iowa in general was priced too high. His grandfather and father agreed, agreed that it *was* epochal and put it in their paper bluntly. An epoch had ended when a man had to pay up to a hundred and fifty dollars an acre for Grade-A land. You could not farm land in an ordinary year and hold on to it out of the earnings at that price.

But the years 1909–14 were not, in the light of all that was to follow, bad years for farmers or for businesses depending directly on farmers having money. This, indeed, was the 'parity' period that farm relief acts were later to seek to re-establish. Quite by chance in this five-year stretch before World War I the prices paid to American farmers for their crops and the prices they had to pay for the things they needed to farm and live had been jostled into a fairly reasonable trading relationship, so that farmers could deal with the cities and the cities with farmers roughly on a par.

The national life jogged on placidly, with continuing mild reforms. Arrival of the first parcel-post package at the offices of *Wallaces' Farmer* was celebrated by the editors with acclaim. They had campaigned for this measure which, together with R.F.D., was expected to bring farm producers and city consumers into direct trading connection and greatly diminish middleman tolls. For those farmers who were born storekeepers and merchandisers the reform did make a little difference for the better, but for most farmers it brought no change at all. And with really big traders having more and more to say about running the country, such minor poultices as Rural Free Delivery (which is not free), somewhat easier farm credit policies, and Federal aid to agricultural extension teaching might not, it began to appear, be enough.

Coming in like a lion, Theodore Roosevelt had frightened conservatives a little and had fanned the cooling ashes of militant progressivism in the Midland. To a friend in Iowa who wrote to ask him for a correct inside slant on this Roosevelt, Tama Jim wrote confidentially:[12] 'At every Cabinet meeting we are better pleased with him. You would be utterly surprised that he feels about trusts just about as you do. One day he had me take luncheon with him and questioned me very extensively along that line. He will go as far as a wise man should go. He will be a much more conservative man than the majority of people think. The heavy weight that is on his shoulders calls out all the conservatism that is in his nature. But let me tell you, you are going to hear some squealing among the machine politicians. He will have straight men or none.'

One of T. R.'s straightest men was Gifford Pinchot, the conservationist. Tama Jim had esteemed Pinchot and as Secretary of Agriculture had stoutly supported his forestry programs for ten years. The conservation movement that Roosevelt and Pinchot started with a Conference of Governors at the White House in 1908 never came in the public mind to more than an agitation to protect public lands from exploitation and to preserve woodland. But the movement gave voice to a new leadership which considered woodland, range land, and farmland, soil resources, water resources, and human resources as a living, working whole. Whether their special concern was soil, trees, wildlife, ore, or water, these early conservationists cleared ground for an ecological approach more enlivening and revealing than that of the completely partitioned scientist. 'The key [to continued soil fertility],' Dr. Thomas C. Chamberlin of Illinois said, 'lies in due control of the water which falls on each acre. The solution essentially solves the whole train of problems running from farm to river and from crop production to navigation.' 'To skin and exhaust the land,' Theodore Roosevelt proclaimed, 'will result in undermining the days of our children.' And in Iowa Uncle Henry Wallace, taking up a theme announced by his old friend Governor Hoard of Wisconsin, wrote: 'The race [Americans] has been a race of timber barons, of coal robbers, soil robbers, and robbers of every good thing, robbers even of health. But really good land will always respond to the man who understands soils and climates and grains and grasses. It is kept in store for just that kind of fellow. . . . The good land was not made to be worn out in twenty years, or fifty, or five hundred.'

The first President Roosevelt also appointed a strong Country Life Commission, which held thirty hearings throughout the country. His commission was charged to analyze with human understanding the entire farm problem, from soil waste to spiritual waste. Liberty Hyde Bailey of Cornell was chairman. Walter Hines Page, Gifford Pinchot, Kenyon L. Butterfield, and Uncle Henry Wallace were the commission members who took the most active part in the investigation and report.

The Country Life Report expressed the prevailing spirit of rural idealism in a lofty, even dedicated, tone.

The goal ... is a new and permanent rural civilization. Upon the development of this distinctly rural civilization rests ultimately our ability, by methods of farming requiring the highest intelligence, to continue to feed and clothe the hungry nations; to supply the city and metropolis with fresh blood, clean bodies, and clear brains that can endure the strain of modern urban life; and to preserve a race of men in the open country that, in the future as in the past, will be the stay and strength of the nation in time of war, and its guiding and controlling spirit in time of peace.[13]

To feed the hungry and clothe the naked everywhere is an instinct that goes deep with good farmers. In the earlier days of our country this instinct had in the main accorded with the business thing to do. The opening of all of our land to farming, the extension of railways, and the rise and growth of our gigantic industrial structure were financed in large measure by European capital. As a young nation, in debt, we could pay in goods; and we did. Our exports were predominantly agricultural goods; but now times were changing and young Henry A. Wallace, with his charts before him, was wondering what would happen when the time came that Europe owed *us* money. How then could Europe pay, if not in goods? And how in goods, over ever-rising tariff walls? He argued these questions with his father and grandfather. Lifelong Republicans, both of them, and at the same time agrarians, they were not in principle high-tariff men, but had simply become more or less reconciled to the idea, as a workhorse becomes broken to harness. When, however, in 1909, the very year of the Country Life Commission's exalted report, Congress passed the Payne-Aldrich Tariff, sharply raising schedules, the faith of even the two elder editors in the Grand Old Party as a true supporter of agriculture was jolted. The Democrats when in power had done little better, as *Wallaces' Farmer* pointed out. A Democratic Congress had passed the patched-up Wilson-Gorman Act which Cleveland vetoed with the comment: 'Bought, bought, bought, in every schedule a tariff of perfidy and dishonor.' And now with the

Payne-Aldrich performance before them, the editors of *Wallaces'*
Farmer agreed sadly that the prevailing governmental process of
greasing the farmer as a producer and hamstringing him as a
trader still went forward in the sacred name of *laissez-faire*.

In 1912 young Henry made his first trip to Europe and stopped
on the way for a four-day visit in Washington. It was his first
visit there. He stayed as a guest in the apartment of Tama Jim
Wilson, the Secretary. At the time the Wallaces were backing
Roosevelt in his runout on the old-line Republicans and Secretary
Wilson was standing for President Taft, his chief; but this caused
no rift between old friends. Tama Jim sent twenty-four-year-old
Henry Wallace around his greatly growing Department. 'Sit,
my boy, at the feet of the wise old bureau chiefs,' he advised.
Wallace met most of the great institutional figures of the period:
Milton Whitney, Chief of Soils; B. T. Galloway, of Plant Industry;
Marion Dorset, of Animal Industry, who developed the serum that
prevented hog cholera; David Fairchild, the plant explorer. Plant
explorers were heroes to young Henry, and he was especially anxious to discuss foreign corn with Dr. Fairchild. They did not get
around to talk about that, as Wallace recalls it; for Dr. Fairchild
had just taken a train trip and spent the hour denouncing the
menace of Pullman toilets which spread filth and disease over the
face of this land. But Fairchild has always remained a hero, and
a lucky one, to Wallace, because 'he saw the whole world and did
his own work with plants, in the Department and without, and he
was never bound to conventional routine.'

In his swing of Europe, which followed, he visited England,
France, Germany, Holland, and Belgium. He bought his ticket
cut-rate as part of an inexpensive students' tour, but left the party
before it had completed its rounds of the Continent, and poked
alone into the work of experiment stations that were doing some
work with Indian corn. He went from there to visit some relatives
in the north of Ireland. Then, going on to London, he took rooms
alone in Bloomsbury and spent two weeks in great contentment,
exploring the metropolis and writing his impressions of the journey.

'There are cycles in all things,' he wrote upon return in the family paper, referring specifically to the swing from the utility corn
standards of the simple Indians to the show corn of the white man,

and now the apparent swing back toward utility standards on a plane of scientific fact. To square the cycles of past experience with current problems seemed to him the most fascinating of all pursuits. As time went on he extended his observations and calculations to the weather, to yield and price cycles, to the birth rate of states and countries, to election returns, and to such changes in state policy as marked, for instance, the abrupt turn in nineteenth-century Britain from high protectionism to free trade. Some of his calculations, he has since admitted, were 'simply what happens to the human mind when it is left alone with some figures in an office.' But he observed a rigid self-censorship in such matters. Few of his blowsier speculations got into print; and the incidence of hits to misses among his public prophecies was cannily high.

Afield and in the shop, Wallace's approach was scholarly; but it was almost invariably pragmatic. He had followed with admiration the work of Shull, East, Jones, and the earliest hybrid corn breeders, but he did not see that their work yet connected with yields afield; and their tabulated results seemed to him too much like running races with oneself around an adding machine. What he wanted was a hybrid that would consistently outyield under field conditions, year after year, the best commercially offered open-bred seed, and he bent all his efforts in corn breeding to that end. At the same time, working for *Wallaces' Farmer* as a reporter and editor, he trained himself as a statistician and forecaster in the corn-and-meat trade, the largest single trade in our country.

He read widely, but usually for information rather than pleasure. He had no time for novels, then as now; and his taste for poetry seems to have been a slow growth from the delight he took in the musical prose of George (AE) Russell, a poet operating under the guise of an agrarian reformer and the editor of *The Irish Homestead* at that time.

All of the Wallace men liked solid reading; partly, perhaps, a survival of their Puritan bent and training. In any event, romances and works of the imagination were for women, they felt, and of rather doubtful value even for them. It is said in the family that when young Henry first went calling on Miss Ilo Browne of Indianola he carried with him a modern classic on permanent agriculture in China, King's *Farmers of Forty Centuries*, and read it to her aloud. 'Henry has a girl, and it seems to be very serious,' Uncle Henry wrote his son Daniel, who was homesteading a claim and starting in the farm paper business on his own by this time, in Minnesota.

The family was amazed at the speed of young Henry's wooing. He and Ilo Browne were married in Des Moines on May 30, 1914. The groom behaved with a dazed radiance suitable to the rôle. As they left the church to drive to the reception he entered the car ahead of his bride, closed the door before he thought, and left her standing there for several seconds, until the gibes of onlookers reminded him that he was no longer a single man. The girl was cheerful, calm, and regal. They went to housekeeping immediately in a small place of their own at 4331 Harwood Drive, Des Moines.

The Brownes' lineage was remarkably like the Wallaces'. Ilo Browne's father, successively a school teacher, merchant, and dealer in Iowa land, was born near Fort Palmer, only a few miles from West Newton where the Wallaces had started farming in Westmoreland County, Pennsylvania. His father, David Browne, had farmed, run a brick kiln, and built brick houses as a contractor in the first half of the nineteenth century. The Brownes were United Presbyterians and they married United Presbyterians. James Browne, Ilo's father, married Hattie Lindsay of Saint Charles, Iowa, in 1877. He was an elder and Sunday School superintendent in the United Presbyterian church at Indianola until his death in 1911. A quiet man of distinguished bearing, he was liked and respected in Indianola. He did well there and left a moderate fortune to his heirs.

4. Bequest

I REGARD IT as a great mistake for any man to be educated intellectually beyond his moral capacity,' Uncle Henry Wallace told a convocation of students during Farmers' Week at the New York State College of Agriculture, Cornell University, during February of 1912. He twitted these Easterners mildly for an assumed pride in place of birth and race.

You will risk failure if you take to yourself credit for being born of good old New England stock, or of Dutch, or even Irish or Scotch-Irish. They were really good people, and did their work well, without your help, and you are entitled to no credit. They had also their weaknesses, and you inherit them, some of them at any rate. With two parents, four grandparents, eight great-grandparents, to say nothing of your more remote ancestry, you are likely to be pretty well stocked with weaknesses. If you are taking to yourself any credit for having been born in New York State, I stand in fear for you. Really, you have nothing to do with that. That is your good fortune, but not your merit.

Toward the conclusion of the same address he said:

The recent ages have given us no greater man than Abraham, the ranchman; than Moses, who combined in himself the physician, the statesman, the warrior, and the sage; than David, who has voiced the joys and sorrows, the hopes and suffering of humanity, as no man ever has before or since. Passing by these great names of Holy Writ, the world has never produced a second Socrates, nor has the widest range of human speculation passed beyond Plato and Aristotle, whose thoughts we are still thinking today. The Victorian Age never produced a Shakespeare or a Milton or even a John Bunyan. If men were really evolved from the monkey, the period of evolution must have been suspended many thousands of years ago. . . .

It will be a fearful mistake to assume that an additional sheepskin, even with a 'cum laude' or 'summa cum laude' will insure your success in the twentieth century. You have this great advantage in entering upon your life work in the twentieth century: that if by making the best of your heredity and environment you become really big, your power will be vastly multiplied by the machinery of organization, just as the power of the farmer and the mechanic has been multiplied for the past half-century. For this is a century of big things — big trusts, big banks, big railroads, big newspapers, big universities, a vast and complicated network of organizations; and the man who is big enough to go to the head and hold his position has a power for good, and also, alas, for evil, hitherto unparalleled in the history of the human race. . . .

You will make a great mistake if you imagine that by pure intellect, by pure eloquence, by great ability as a writer, or an organizer, or an executive, you can do anything that is really worth while. You may acquire fortune, fame, the power of adjustment over the lives and good fortunes of men; but as soon as your grave is nicely rounded, and you have furnished the text for the penny-a-liner in the newspaper; before there is time to rear over you a monument of marble, the world will forget you; or, if it remembers you, it will be only to throw stones and fling curses at your monument, if you have been its oppressor. . . .

If you study the history of the last twenty, fifty, one hundred, five hundred, one thousand, two thousand, five thousand years, you will find that the world cherishes the memory only of these men who have been altruists, who, whether in literature, science, business or the church, have aimed to do good to their fellowmen.

Really big men are now realizing that abiding success can be secured only by methods and practices that will help the common man. . . .[14]

In 1912 the Democrats had come into power again after a long fast — so in 1913, Tama Jim Wilson's unexampled sixteen-year tenure as Secretary of Agriculture ended. He was seventy-eight years old now, a year older than Uncle Henry, and free at last to make a journey long planned, a visit back to the farm where he had been born in 1835 — 'my father's farm in Ayrshire where the land ran down to the sea.' He and Wallace had always planned to go abroad together, and at last they could.

'This was my fifth trip to Europe,' Uncle Henry wrote in his *Reminiscences*. 'I had been working very hard for a couple of years and needed a rest. The Secretary was an exceedingly tired man and needed rest more than I did. We started out with the idea that for once in our lives we would lay everything else aside

and be boys again.   My ostensible object in going was to attend
the Pan-Presbyterian Council in Aberdeen, Scotland . . . a treat:
I think the most distinguished, ablest, most polished, and most
thoroughly educated set of men I have ever met.   Neither the
Secretary nor I gave very much time to the council, however. . . .'

The Governor of Iowa had asked them to investigate the land-
lord-tenant situation in Scotland.   They made the investigation
in a whirl of personal visits, especially in Ayrshire, the birthplace
of Secretary Wilson, and the county from which the Wallace ancestors had gone in the latter part of the seventeenth century to
the north of Ireland.   Then: 'We spent two or three days, visiting the home of Burns, the monuments, the Highlands, and the
statues of Tam o' Shanter and Scouter Johnny, his boon companion.
We studied the statue of Tam's wife, with a curious look on her
face, as though she suspected where Tam was, with whom he was,
and what was going on.   The Secretary recited Tam o' Shanter
before the statues.   We then went to the Brig o' Doon, to the top
of which we climbed, and there the Secretary sang, " Ye Banks
and Braes o' Bonny Doon."'

Edinburgh University gave the Secretary an LL.D., his ninth.
'We were the only two men there who did not have robes of office,
but wore Prince Albert coats and silk hats.'   Adding stockmen's
canes to their formal attire, these vigorous old gentlemen from
Iowa attended the Royal Agricultural Show at Bristol: 'This gave
us the opportunity of meeting with all sorts and conditions of
folks — ladies, lords, dukes, earls, counts, members of the royal
family, tenants, etc., etc.   It gave us the opportunity of seeing the
best of the livestock in England.   We spent two days at this
show.'

Here for a while they parted.   The Secretary went to Galloway
to visit his father's people, and Wallace went to England to visit
friends in London and to spend a day or two with Ambassador
Page, whom he had learned to know and love when they worked
together on the Roosevelt Country Life Commission. . . . He and
Wilson later met in Dublin where they began a tour of investigation in Ireland. . . .

'Sailing for home, we celebrated the Secretary's birthday (his
seventy-ninth) on board ship the day we landed.   It was a hard

trip in some ways; we both became too interested to rest very much. Altogether, however, it was a pleasant and profitable trip, and we came home feeling fine.'

Harry Slattery remembers calling on the travelers at Gifford Pinchot's residence on Rhode Island Avenue in Washington. Here, on a scorching summer day, they had taken up temporary quarters in order to prepare their report. This they were doing; and, in deference to the heat, they had stripped down to red flannel underwear and were drinking, as a stimulant to concise dictation of the report in question, steaming hot tea.

A man of seventy-seven now, Uncle Henry weighed two hundred and twenty pounds, but his great frame and more than six feet of height bore it bravely. He had in his middle years lost the sight of one eye completely (no one could say exactly how); but his unimpaired eye was as good as two; he read even fine print easily without eyeglasses. An old friend of the Wallace family, DeWitt C. Wing, remembers calling on Uncle Henry at this culminative stage of his career: 'His son Dan and I spent a long evening with him in his Des Moines home. We found him reading. He wore a loose robe and slippers, smoking a stogie. He was lying on a couch and writing on a pad. He called to Josephine, a daughter, to bring him a small bottle out of a drawer in his dresser. Uncle Henry chose to celebrate a little. Later, in showing us how he operated his exercising chair, he was as happy and amused as a child. . . . He had much pleasure in telling me how he edited *Wallaces' Farmer*. He had fifty-two pasteboard-box files on shelves. Subjects for treatment, articles that he had written for them, and new information that he had accumulated were filed according to the months. It was basic seasonal information to which he'd add something new and different, year after year. Basic information was always good. He constantly improved and added to it, so that month after month, he always had plenty of ideas and facts drawn from many reliable sources.' [15]

His greatest delight was a column feature he wrote for every issue of *Wallaces' Farmer:* 'Uncle Henry's Sabbath School Lesson,' it was called. Never probably in the history of American farm journalism was there another circulation builder and circulation holder to compare with it. The paper had to copyright it, after a while, to prevent too wide a reprint by rival concerns and publishing literary pirates. Uncle Henry wrote it in all faith and with a burning simplicity. The topography, the crops, the wars, the passions and tragedies and ecstasies of the people of Bible Land were real to him, and living, and he wrote of them in terms of living reality for his own people. Ribald cowhands as far away as Texas, who could not bear the smell of plowed loam or the hated 'nesters,' as they called farmers, became life subscribers to *Wallaces' Farmer* on the strength of this one feature alone. Iowa farmers and their wives read it to their children as sufficiently sacred literature while jogging along in their buggies to Sunday School and church.

Uncle Henry worked out a perpetual rotation system for these dispatches from the Scriptures. He prepared on the basis of weekly publication a twenty-year advance supply. Each lesson accorded in general with the time of the year and the growth of the seasons. His Christmas and Easter lessons, derived from the newer Gospels, were as radiant with universal love, faith, and tenderness as his accounts of Old Testament battles and conquests were realistic and gory. He had laid by, his grandson Henry believes from years of close companionship with him, especially from 1905 onward, all belief in a literal eternal hell. He believed that earthly hellfire, personal torment, followed wrongdoing. Land became sick, the body of man and his spirit sickened; health was broken, homes were broken, and whole nations were broken when man did wrong; but the mercy of God and His compassion were infinite and forever enduring. Man has in him the seeds of perfection visibly growing and there would be, literally, a life hereafter. This was his faith.

When, on September 8, 1915, the first of the great-grandchildren to whom he had been dictating his *Reminiscences* appeared in the person of Henry Browne Wallace (see Frontispiece), the head of the clan and his grandson Henry were drawn more than ever closely together. 'I remember well,' the Vice-President told reporters from *Fortune* somberly in 1942: 'Grandfather was profoundly disturbed for fear we would get into the war. We were out driving in the country the day the *Lusitania* was sunk and we drove back into town and heard the newsboys crying the headlines. Grandfather was deeply upset. He had to get on a train and come to Washington to see Wilson about it, to try to keep us out. He had been through one reconstruction and he knew what it meant. If you will go back into the files [of *Wallaces' Farmer*] you will see that I wrote something in January, 1919, on the inevitable costs of the war that were still to come. That was from Grandfather's teaching. The costs came. They will come after this war, too. Grandfather was a great and strong man. He had a great deal to do with my training and my thinking.' [16]

In the closing letter of the serial series, *Uncle Henry's Own Story of His Life*, by Henry Wallace, Editor of *Wallaces' Farmer*, he dictated on November 3, 1916, an account of a trip East.

He told of stopping off between Chicago and New York for a day or so, then of breaking his journey at the sanatorium at Markleton, Pennsylvania, in the county adjoining the one in which he was born. 'My object in visiting it had nothing to do with my health; for I am well and in no need of either doctors, medicine, or sanatoriums. But in a previous visit there I had made the acquaintance of a very interesting man, at one time wealthy, but not so now. While at a bridge party one evening, a blood-clot formed on one eye, which destroyed its sight, probably forever. It seems that some religious people regarded this as a judgment of God. But a few weeks afterward, while attending prayer-meeting, he lost the sight of the other eye in the same way. He has lived at that sanatorium the six years since — blind, lonesome beyond conception.'

He had become interested in the man on a visit to Markleton the previous summer with his daughter, Josephine, and was deeply attached to him. The man had written him several urgent letters, asking him to stop even for a day. He did so, 'Glad that I could relieve the monotony of life for him for even that short time.'

Wallace's next objective point was Washington, D.C. Before he left he had a long talk with Leigh Hunt on the state of the world: 'In the course of our conversation I suggested that there could never be world peace so long as any one nation or group of nations controlled the great seas. I suggested to him that when the Lord made this world, He made about three fourths of its surface water,

which no man or nation had the moral right to control; that the
present war, which is killing off the best people on the other side,
bankrupting the nations, and imposing on posterity for a hundred
years a most crushing burden of taxation, was mainly a war for the
control of trade and traffic — Germany feeling that she could
have no outlet for her manufactures and commerce so long as
England controlled the seas, and England realizing that she must
control the seas in order to keep open her trade with her widely
scattered colonies.'

Mr. Hunt was so much interested in Uncle Henry's view that he
suggested he talk it over with President Wilson, and agreed to
arrange an interview.

Uncle Henry described the interview as follows:

At six I called on the President in the Blue Room of the
White House, and he received me most cordially.   I told him
that this war must end some time; that he was the one man
who could attract the attention of all the world; that probably
the time would come when he would be able to suggest as the
basis of lasting peace the freedom of the seas and their policing
by an international fleet, so that for all time to come, the
nations of the world, wherever they might be located, could
freely trade with each other without fear of molestation.   I
said to him that this was only a vision of mine, a dream; that
I made it to him merely as a suggestion, saying that it would
not be practical until every woman's heart in the warring
nations was broken, until the nations themselves were bankrupt.   I said to him that when that time came, surely the
common people of these nations would not permit themselves
to be crushed under an added burden of taxation, if the ends
for which the navies were built and maintained could be subserved without it; and that if the people once came to clearly
see this, they would overturn the government that insisted on
breeding men for the shambles, to carry out the ambitions of
their leaders.

The President said to me: 'Of course you do not expect me
to give you a definite answer on this point.'   I said: 'Certainly
not.   It is not a plan, simply a vision, which may mature in

time, and if it does mature will give us world peace for all time.' He followed me out into the hall when I was leaving, talking to me on agricultural matters. He listened to me most attentively.

On February 22, 1916, while sitting in a pew of a church in Des Moines, waiting to speak as a guest minister, he had a stroke, a cerebral hemorrhage, and died instantly. He was one month short of eighty years old.

He delivered his last sermon to his own family in his will:

I. I desire to express to my children and grand-children my mature conviction that life is worth living, if it is lived worthily, [and] that the supreme and perfect example of worthy living is the everliving Jesus of Nazareth, who was God manifest in the flesh. . . .

II. Religion is not a philosophy but a life. God cannot be apprehended except by faith in the Father of All, manifested in the details of daily life. I solemnly warn you against a materialistic philosophy. Men who sincerely believe in the fundamental teachings of Christianity, but who are naturally lacking in emotion, fail to enjoy the full comfort of a Christian life, because they lack the emotional experiences which others enjoy. I have passed through this experience. It was, I think, characteristic of the members of our family who have gone before. I began to live more worthily when I came to realize that feelings are largely matters of health and circumstance, and that the passing cloud is no proof of the lack of sunshine above the clouds. The attitude of God towards us as revealed in His Word is the important thing, and not our present realization of His feeling towards us. . . .

III. There are possible temptations against which I must warn you. The family has been prospered in many ways beyond anything which I hoped or could have expected. It has prospered in a material way, and enjoyed a reasonable measure of public confidence because we have never thought of wealth or social usefulness as ends in themselves, but merely as a means of enlarging our possible usefulness to the community at large. Any serious departure from this policy will

be fatal to the best interests of the family. The temptation
to amass wealth for the sake of wealth, the temptation to gain
position, political or social, for purely selfish purposes, comes
naturally with prosperity. Avoid all this. Keep clean in
speech, clear in mind, vigorous in body and God will bless you.

IV. I am aware that it is quite unusual to discuss such
matters in a last will. I have departed from the usual
custom. Any help that I may give my children and grand-
children in the supreme work of life is of far greater real value
than any worldly possessions I may hand down to them.
Having acquired a competency several years ago, I have, as
my children all know, contributed to some worthy objects,
and divided the rest among them each year, thus distributing
my annual income, save that needed for a life of comfort.
I have found great satisfaction in this, and advise them, after
seeing their children well started in life, to follow my example. It will save them from many temptations, and give
them a saner view of the real object of life.

His sons and grandsons continued to run his name at the head of
the editorial masthead until they had published all of his *Reminiscences* and other collected papers in 1917; and his Sabbath Lessons
continued until 1938.

VII

THE FIRST WORLD WAR BOOM AND CRASH

... Prices of farm products have been beaten down as far as possible, while prices to the consumer have increased as well as the prices of practically everything the farmer has to buy. 'Farmers' Unrest a Grave Danger, Officials Find,' says a rather startling headline, first column, page one, *The New York Times*. ...

What is the matter with the farmer? Why is he dissatisfied? The answer is easy. The farmer is getting tired of being made the goat. ... This does not mean that he promises to make a disturbance, or try to overturn the government, or start a new political party, or confiscate property. Nothing of that sort. ... It means simply that ... he sees it is time for him to study the business game and see how to play it for himself. ... Especially it means that he is tired of being double-crossed not only by other business interests but by people who are in positions of authority in government. ...

If we were asked to name one man who is more responsible than any other for starting the dissatisfaction which exists among the farmers of the country, we would instantly name Mr. Hoover. ... — H. C. WALLACE in an editorial, *Wallaces' Farmer*, Feb. 12, 1920.

1. Redheaded Gamecock

HARRY WALLACE,' Gifford Pinchot once remarked, 'was a natural-born gamecock. He was redheaded on his head and in his soul!'

Gifford Pinchot became the nation's first Chief Forester in 1905. 'Harry and I were within a year or two of the same age,' he recalled in 1914; 'young Henry was around twenty, and Uncle

Henry was in his seventies, when I first came to know the family on visits to Des Moines.

'The Wallace family is an institution. Uncle Henry was one of the most admirable characters I have ever known. His old age was a perfect pattern of how a man may decline in years without declining in happiness or usefulness. To me, he was almost like a father and I think and hope he thought of me as almost a son.

'I remember stopping off in Des Moines for a visit, during the Ballinger fight, shortly before I was fired as Chief Forester by Taft. The Wallaces were with me in that fight. I was dog-tired and discouraged. Uncle Henry and I were walking down a shaded street of houses. We saw a comfortable-looking middle-aged man sitting in his shirt sleeves with his feet on a porch-rail, reading a newspaper. "That's what I'd like to be," I said. "Come back in three years and you won't see him," Uncle Henry told me. "That's all it takes, as a rule. for these retired Iowa farmers to be bored to death."

'His oldest son, Harry, was a devoted admirer of Theodore Roosevelt. That bound us in an intimate bond. I had always been drawn to Harry, but it was not until the First World War, when he waded in to head off false moves by Hoover and others up in the Food Administration, that I got mv first taste of his real quality.

'He was not a hasty or a showy man. He was a man so firmly rooted in quiet possession, so humble of mind in the truest sense, and yet so conscious of his own latent strength, that he could afford to be, and was, slow to take offense. But there was never any question where he stood. When it came to a matter of principle, you could count on him to stand up with you and fight to the last ditch. He stood up like a church!'

A gamecock with a redheaded soul that stands up like a church would be a tempting item for The New Yorker's 'Block that Metaphor' department. Even so, everyone who worked with Harry Wallace recalls in him, with terms similarly mixed, an engaging and quietly intricate compound of the flesh and the spirit. 'My father,' Henry A. Wallace said recently, 'was a curious combination of worldly impulses and a strict, high sense of duty. He loved high living; he had an Irish heart but a Scotch conscience.'

The boyhood of Harry Wallace had been brief. He grew up fast under rather hard conditions at a time when the family was poor. He married young, at twenty, in hard times, and his thirties were years of ever harder work and heavier family responsibilities. When he led in the founding of *Wallaces' Farmer* he had little thought of restoring in this way the family fortune. It was principally to provide a sort of vocational therapy for his father, and a sounding board for the Wallace family principles, he told his friend, H. C. Taylor,[1] that he made the move which took him out of college teaching into publishing full time.

When, thanks largely to his shrewd, propelling management, *Wallaces' Farmer* started making money in quantity, none enjoyed it more than Harry. For the first time in his life he began to allow himself regular hours off duty for sport and pleasure. At the age of forty he took up golf. Soon he was turning in a fairly consistent score of from 84 to 88 over a stiff course. He induced his son Henry A. to take up the game at the same time, but Henry was no better at golf than he was at tennis, at first. Naturally ambidextrous, he threw himself into court games both sides against the middle with headlong clumsiness and no attention to form. On the links he was even worse, addressing himself to the ball contemptuously, tearing up turf, hating the game intensely. By reason of the love he bore his father he learned the rules and made the rounds with his parent, but after the fourth round of effort at the country club links he gave his clubs away.

The pleasant thing about it, he recalls, is that in this period, when his father was beginning to take time off for golfing, fishing, hunting, and playing the guitar of evenings, they became really intimate, as father and son, for the first time. On trips to a Wallace summer home in Colorado the father would fish while the son climbed mountains. But they were often together between times and Henry discovered in his father an endearing minor vice. Harry Wallace chewed tobacco like a gentleman, in very small quids, tucked under the lip or into the back recesses of the jaw. His jaw never moved in this sort of chewing and he never spat. He swallowed the juice, and when he exercised heavily, the nicotine and oils came out in his perspiration and stained his golfing and hunting sweatshirts brown. By this time, in the 'teens of the present century, the day had passed when old-timers like Tama Jim and the elder senators and Supreme Court justices could make the tall brass cuspidors of officialdom ring with no thought of indelicacy; but still a number of the sons of that generation chewed on in more seemly secrecy, and not even their wives knew that they chewed.

In the years of his maturity Harry, or H. C., was a solid chunk of a man, with a round body, never very fat. He was muscular and wiry and he had a round, firm face. He weighed about one hundred and sixty pounds. He was not tall, only five feet eight; but he walked and sat so erectly that he seemed taller than he was. He drank alcoholic beverages, but moderately. He carried that shock of red hair with an air of dignified cockiness. Even his eyebrows were red. On rare occasions when he permitted himself an open display of anger, old Forest Service men who were with him in the fight against the Fall crowd will tell you, 'H. C. just clamped his lips tight and tossed his mane.'

His eyes, a heathery gray behind pince-nez glasses, could be by turns blandly non-committal or glow with a guarded friendliness. He was a correct and careful dresser, well-tailored without being foppish. In his middle forties when he took to riding early of mornings, in order to keep his weight down and his flesh hard, he cut a handsome figure as a mounted man. Bowling and poker were two of his other diversions at that period and in Washington later. He bowled around 175, on the average, and had good card sense, not only in poker but in the economic-political game. In this larger game he drew almost the worst cards imaginable, but he played his hand with a rare combination of patient calculation and an all but reckless daring.

Harry Wallace was rather an earthy man. With his fondness for rich fare, well-to-do homes and establishments, and all the amenities and comforts, he might in an earlier manner of spea .ing have become a 'sport.' But for all his Cavalier tendencies he was at heart a Roundhead. His family training and a pervading sense of family responsibility shaped his every final action, if not his every thought. His business success did not, as business success so often does, persuade him that anyone who really tried could be successful. He never forgot the struggle he had as a tenant on his father's property; he had started to raise his own six children at a time when corn, if it sold at all, was bringing the starvation price of fifteen cents a bushel, hogs were down to $2.75 a hundredweight, and land, reacting in value from speculative excesses after the Civil War, was a drug on the market.

In the ups and downs of the price cycles land passes fairly constantly into 'strong hands'; absentee ownership rises; tenancy increases. Harry Wallace had seen this separability of land ownership and operations proceed apace in Iowa, and he felt it to be an evil. He believed that the responsible care of land and a solid substructure for democracy could be developed only with the greatest risk and difficulty unless the greater number of farming families own the land they till. 'Land speculation by non-farmers,' he would say in his speeches to farmers, 'is a curse, injuring both the man who farms and the consumer who must buy what he produces. Sometime perhaps we may find a way to keep the speculator from meddling in farm land.'

'*Sometime perhaps we may find a way* . . .' This was typical of his more cautious first approach to agrarian and commercial reform. Later, when he tried to hew a way through to 'equality for agriculture' by passage of a law designed 'to make the tariff effective for agriculture,' the conservatives of both major parties marked him down as a radical. The truly radical, or liberal, thing to do would have been to abolish tariffs. The proposal to dump subsidized farm exports abroad with heightening tariff walls retained against imports here was no bold move leftward; it was rather an involved agrarian concession to the ruling mores of a protected business structure.

Swinging over as the years advanced from the old-time Republican belief that high tariffs help agriculture, Harry Wallace came to doubt and then to disbelieve, though he never went the whole way through to the other side. As a member of the Harding administration, he became indeed something of an apologist for tariffs. He expressed his doubts, however; and even among confirmed Midwest Republicans these doubts were mounting, confusedly, year by year. Something had happened. The protective economic rigging which had swaddled our infant industries and helped to open up the country was not working in the old way.   Only here and there, far between, over the period of 1900–15 had statesmen or economic and business forecasters foreseen such change.   Strange to note, Tama Jim Wilson's first chief, William McKinley of Ohio, was one of these few.   Either that, or some passionately anonymous free trader operating for the moment as the presidential ghost writer led McKinley clearly to state in a speech on September 5, 1901, the day before he was assassinated:

> Isolation is no longer possible or desirable. . . . We must not repose in fancied security that we can forever sell everything and buy little or nothing. . . . Reciprocity is the national outgrowth of our wonderful industrial development under the domestic policy now firmly established.   What we produce above our domestic consumption must have a vent abroad. . . .
>
> The period of exclusiveness is passed.   The expansion of our trade and commerce is the pressing problem.   Commercial wars are unprofitable.   A policy of goodwill and friendly trade relations will prevent reprisals.   Reciprocity treaties are in harmony with the spirit of the times. . . .

These words would seem to indicate, at least, the seeds of an awareness that Europe might soon owe us money in balance, and that a creditor nation might not be able to collect its bills from foreigners over heightening tariff walls.

By 1915 this change had taken place.[2]   In September, 1914, we owed Europe a bare five hundred million dollars.   By September, 1915, Europe owed us fifteen million dollars.   Three months later it was a hundred and thirty-two million dollars, and America was on the march to a towering creditor position in a changed world.

Shooting wars and revolutions announce themselves emphatically.   Yet it is possible to live through a shooting revolution with the shooting not far away and never realize what is going on, as the Grand Duchess Marie, in her memoir, *The Education of a Princess*, recalls that she did not.   In the final days of the old régime at Saint Petersburg she knew of course that there were strikes and street disorders; she knew that there was pillage and killing; but until the Czar and his immediate family were blown back into the dust by a firing squad, she did not realize that it was a revolution.[3]

We are told on every hand that the First World War, the inter-war New Deal, and now the Second World War, are but successive stages of a world revolution and it is needless to labor the point. Yet the technological revolution in the United States has provided thus far no period of rest between upheavals where one might stand back and observe, 'Why, that was a revolution!' There have been points of false repose, imagined lulls. We have just turned in the previous chapter from some account of a period in which most Americans expected an endless and comfortable continuation of progress without pain. But all the while the cycles of change were whirling and clashing faster and harder.

The Wallaces were pre-eminently outriders and leaders of the agricultural revolution in this country. Events had thrust them out in front. Their views and choices were more often ruled by events, doubtless, than their views and choices changed events; but there they were, out in front of a loyal following, with decisions to make fast — troublesome decisions.

Harry Wallace came to leadership in the family at an especially troublous and confusing time. When his father was born, three quarters of the American people were gainfully employed in agriculture. When he, Harry, was born, fewer than half of our people were on farms. By the time his son, Henry A., was born, the proportion of those on farms was down to 40 per cent, and a rapid downward trend toward fewer than half of that was plainly on the cards. In Uncle Henry's youth it had required about three *hours* to grow and harvest a bushel of wheat. Now, in Harry's prime, a new working tieup of internal combustion motors and the combined harvester and thresher, was ready to do the same work in three *minutes*.

America's agricultural progress was a projection and a high-geared speed-up of what had been going on more or less the world over. In the middle of the eighteenth century, when the Wallaces farmed in Ireland, it required the farm work of from 75 to 95 per cent of the people in the most advanced civilizations of the world to provide food and fabric for the 100 per cent. The year 1850 stands as a sort of dividing point in the passage toward industrialization and interdependence; fewer and fewer farmers fed more and more people from that time on. This process made much faster headway in the United States than in any other considerable nation on earth. The Civil War stepped up the process in the United States. The Union Government's mobilization alone withdrew from farming pursuits a million men — the largest army ever brought together by any nation on earth up to that time. In the North and West, especially, where machinery remained more readily available than in the South, the men and women left on the farms had to use it, and did use it, more and more. Thus, even shorthanded, the North and West produced a greater wheat crop than in the previous years of peace.

But it was not until after 1910, when tractor power began to replace horseflesh afield, and the automotive transformation of our highways and living patterns really hit its stride, that the full impact of the machine revolution reached American farms in great number, hastening production, speeding displacement, raising new standards, new problems, and unexampled hopes.

Agriculture, like urban industry, has its instances of workers seeking to wreck or sabotage some new laborsaving device, then embracing the use of it; but such instances in the advance of mechanized agriculture in America are relatively few. With a constantly expanding acreage under the plow, together with a constant drain of their young to cities, American farmers, once they got started replacing flesh, blood, and bent human backs with iron hands and power, made faster and more eager progress in this direction than American industry had accomplished. A few brooding backward-lookers held that the old sweat-and-blood pioneering manner of toil was more pleasing to God and productive of sturdy virtue than all this sudden speed and ease; but these were very few. The general wrench in parting from the old-time pastoral ideology did not come with the sale of the sleigh and buggy and the purchase of a Ford, the substitution of the combine harvester for the old twine binder, or the advent of the telephone and electric lights. The most acute moral conflict which has marked, and still marks, agricultural progress has come from agriculture's reluctant adoption and use of the existing large-scale trade mechanisms. To that revolution in trade mechanisms which brought on the rise of tariffs, the growth of corporations and monopolies, and the rise of central banking throughout the nineteenth and early twentieth centuries, our farmers were far from acquiescent, as a whole. They were loud and sometimes violent in their protests, partly for moral reasons, but especially because these growths were pinching farmers back in number and influence, and building up city people in wealth, freedom, and power.

The Wallaces, more than most of the farmers who read their paper, did not like to see farmers, already a minority group, shrink still further in number. And yet, if mechanization is the price of progress, what was the alternative? Retrogression to a peasant status, or, as they expressed it in their gloomier moments, to 'barbarism'? What, then, to do? As editors, they raised the question bluntly and printed thousands of farmers' letters in response.

'Abolish capitalism!' screamed the hotheads. The Wallaces did not care for that. 'Use the weapons of industry against industry,' cried a larger group, farmers' organization zealots; and this, though generally with moderation, was the line that Harry Wallace and, to some extent, his son Henry were compelled to take by the increasing force of circumstance. To induce a scarcity of goods through monopolistic manipulation was wrong, they said; but if that was the game, then let agriculture, too, restrict production. Tariffs were iniquitous in principle, but if industry insisted on maintaining them, then agriculture must have a 'tariff equivalent' measure. It was, indeed, a sort of paradoxical 'liberalism' they advocated. Philosophically inconsistent, bristling with contradictions, it was essentially a program of compromise. But, coupled with a drive toward greater efficiency in production and distribution, it was an action program and the only one that sensible and conservative agrarians could in some part agree on and see hope in at the time.

Among men in general, and moralists in particular, a 'sauce for the goose, sauce for the gander' approach to reform instills a fighting spirit that may be somewhat at odds within itself, uneasy, defensive, touchy. This will appear in the account of the years to follow. It took the better part of the succeeding quarter-century to arrive at a farm program that squared on the whole with the Wallace conscience.

2. Country Come to Town

WALLACES' FARMER fought for the agricultural interest primarily, but its editors were never indiscriminate business-baiters or scorners of all things urban. It was not in their nature to be so. A decent respect for the rights and privileges of property was in their blood. Through their own enterprise in a highly competitive business they had accumulated, in terms of that time and place, a considerable amount of property themselves. As civilized men educated to think objectively in the applied sciences that enter into agriculture and its relation to the national and world-wide interest, they liked the association with men of all callings and all shades of political and economic persuasion that the city of Des Moines provided and they liked the quiet fields close by. They were, in a word, *rurban*. Dr. Charles Galpin of the United States Department of Agriculture made up this word from the roots of *rus* and *urb* a quarter-century or more ago; and it is one of the few useful bits of sociological verbiage ever coined.

The rurban reformation of America which has followed so fast upon the development of rapid highway transportation began under horse-and-buggy conditions when specialized functions of the old-time all-inclusive agriculture started removing to urban or semi-urban situations, in cities and towns. Plow and machinery making, for example, removed from the old farm shop to larger special shops and then to factories. So also, in large part, breadmaking, buttermaking, and the processing of most foods and fabrics went to town. With the founding of the Land Grant Colleges and the quick growth and elaboration of specialized research and teaching centering in the Department of Agriculture in Washington, there came a further centralized clustering of special farm-born talents cityward. Many farm boys left home to study farming in college. Most of them became agriculturists and never came back. The first stage of the removal, quite generally, was to a State College locale or a near-by city on work more nearly commercial, but generally intermeshed with the scientific findings of the Department and the colleges. Here it was sometimes possible, if one had the time and capital, to farm out from town on the side. But the next centralizing tug that the urban trend exerted, often irresistibly, on these educated agriculturists, took them for the most part out of farming altogether, to Washington, D.C.

There is, by and large, more money in being an agriculturist in Washington, more chance of fame, more stimulating associations, and a far wider terrain — increasingly international — over which to pursue facts and advance notions.

An intermingling of the rural and urban has worked, of course, both ways. Even as agricultural leadership has become more centralized, city callings, city outlooks, city businesses have been moving out into the country, beyond the suburban rim. Improved means of transporting persons, ideas, and electric power have speeded a decentralization of industry and a citification of the countryside. Uncle Henry called the turn on this outward trend at the very opening of the century. He foresaw factory smokestacks and then dynamos amid cornfields. He also foresaw more and more people doing their work in cities but living and working for part of their living with one foot on the land. This phase of the urban transformation has gone so far now that anyone with eyes may see a resettlement sketched out on the landscape along almost any hard-surfaced road in the parts of the country that have been longest settled — a working redesign.

To dramatize the displacement of human flesh and brains from full-time farming by the advance of machines, as the moving picture of John Steinbeck's *Grapes of Wrath* has done with such sharp effect in recent years, is to suggest only in the simplest terms the whole change, and to do so in terms that inevitably seem to pronounce a moral judgment. Was it immoral for the machine farmers to make more and more wheat cheaper and cheaper on bigger and bigger holdings in western Kansas? How about the present snow-balling of comparable practices and displacements in traditional farm homeland, the Corn-and-Hog Belt? Then it might be argued that everything was wrong which happened in the eighty-year lifetime of the first Henry Wallace to slash down again and again the number of farmers relative to the whole population. Going far back beyond that, it might be shown that it was immoral for the first nomads to stop being nomads, to domesticate themselves and plants and animals, so that other families might live in cities and be fed and clothed from the countryside, by trade. And it was surely a wicked contriver who set humming the first great technological revolution in agriculture, trade, and industry by inventing the wheeled vehicle or again a ship with sails. All these changes have been upsetting, disruptive. It may be that a people, by an acceleration of such changes, can be carried too far for their own happiness, safety, or comfort, but to denounce them all as immoral is to hold that civilization in itself is sinful and a sad mistake.

Within the span of a century a people more than three fourths rural in situation and occupation have become a people distinctly more than three fourths urban or suburban; in Clare Leighton's poignant phrase, most Americans find themselves 'fed from fields they do not know ... from lands and rivers that are only names to us'; and it is evident that the change has brought some loss and pain. But it is also evident that the great body of the American people, on farms, in villages, and in cities alike, have embraced the change, enjoyed it, and benefited by it vastly. Consider any aspect of technological advance you may choose: medicine, transportation, entertainment, education, power and lighting, home and community equipment. Or consider more particularly the still-changing field of agriculture itself. And it can hardly be doubted that people live more fully and completely in this country now, with a far better chance to develop a special bent or purpose, than was true of Americans in general a century ago.

Always in our march from dominantly pastoral to dominantly commercial and urban standards we have as a people gazed wistfully backward and moved forward with pleasure. We have bewailed the continuing displacement of people from the land; we have bewailed the diffusion of occupations which used to be simple farm occupations. We celebrate continually in popular song and story an incurable heartache for barefoot bliss, the old oaken bucket, and the little red school. But the plain fact seems to be that most people found unmitigated rustic simplicity relatively dull and dulling and departed willingly from that sort of life. It is also a fact that circumstances which repeatedly have forced farming families off land they loved and away from ways they cherished have sometimes — indeed often — done them a favor. To work too small a piece of ground with inadequate tools and capital for a living is a hopeless occupation for the young and hopeful. Even for those of riper years who have developed a compensating philosophy such farming is seldom idyllic. To be pushed out of this sort of farming into other callings has proven as good for some people as it has proven bad, even heartbreaking, for others.

The quickening changes of rurbanization have come to the American open country hardly less than to our people in towns and cities. Diversity in sources of income, diversity in interests, a quick advance in the art and science of agriculture, together with an enormously greater liveliness of mind and spirit, have come as a result. Urban drawbacks, urban evils, urban ugliness have extended in some part along with the improvements; but a net general gain is plain. American country people have as a whole taken all these changes in their stride gladly. It is doubtful if any amount of moral remonstrance or any acts of 'Backward, turn backward' lawgiving will induce them to return willingly to simple homespun aspirations and ways.

The essential nature of the agricultural (or rurban) revolution is obscured by counting heads and shouting the score in such terms of social-scientific jargon as 'farm' and 'non-farm.' Such arbitrary terms of demarcation no longer hold; and that ponderous misnomer by which the census designates 'persons gainfully employed in agriculture' does not count in agriculturists, as distinguished from farmers, at all.

As the wilder, unreconstructed agrarians claim, the rising influence of the college or government agriculturist, in the fields of economics and politics, especially, has served somewhat to soften or moderate the immemorial conflict of interest and opinion between farm and town. A militant Western farm leader told me angrily in 1930 that if the peasants of France had only had a nice Land Grant College and Extension system to soothe and soften them, farmers would never have had the guts to march for freedom on Paris to the tune of *La Marseillaise*.

That may be. Harry Wallace, though a Land Grant graduate and an ex-professor, never had perfect faith in the intent of all the leaders of that great system to represent the agricultural interest aright. He spoke most sharply on occasions of 'kept professors' passing cards to Big Business under the table; and Harry's boy, Henry, in his young manhood, went out and made speeches against the Hoover candidacy, which the State College crowd was covertly backing, from the same platform with that shouting rabble-rouser of the Midland, Milo Reno. Young Henry liked the spirit of these nonconforming farm rebels, but he seldom placed great value on their judgments.

Farmers in general suspect, and often have cause to know, that agricultural leaders, lay or professional, who go to town to represent agriculture in the marts, the courts, in Congress or its lobbies, in college or Department circles, or in the Cabinet, soon find it more pleasant and rewarding to get along with the big, smart men of the ruling order, and proceed from that, consciously or unconsciously, to sell agriculture down the river with the greatest amiability and ease. This has been said in Iowa even of the Wallaces, Harry and Henry; but it has been said remarkably seldom and believed by only a passing few.

Iowa farmers knew these Wallaces not only by what they wrote in their paper but face to face in the rough-and-tumble controversies of railway rate hearings, co-operative marketing endeavor, and the furor attending the rise and growth of the American Farm Bureau Federation.

Traditionally, the editor of *Wallaces' Farmer* served as Secretary of the Corn Belt Meat Producers' Association, an outgrowth of the organized fight Uncle Henry had led for fairer freight rates and against packer domination in the eighties and nineties. 'H. C.' was Secretary of the Association now. 'H. A.' became its statistician, and as such was called in 1915 to Washington to be an expert witness before the Interstate Commerce Commission in the Western railway rate case. Clifford Thorne, a keen lobbyist and the Association's lawyer, was so impressed with the way young Henry handled figures and comported himself in a court of inquiry that he tried to hire him away from *Wallaces' Farmer* and his corn farming, and make of him a farm organization man in Washington. But from this, his second trip to the capital, young Henry returned with the feeling that there must be something peculiarly sterile about a city given over almost entirely to governing, with no immediate business or agricultural roots. He determined never to live in Washington if he could help it.

Neither Henry nor his father was the natural-born public speaker, preacher, or orator that Uncle Henry had been, but Harry Wallace was a good downright talker, especially when the subject stirred him and he stood up to speak extempore. He used few gestures and no tricks of voice, but his self-possession and complete command of his subject inspired respect and he had a good platform presence, quietly rugged, yet a shade patrician.

At banquets, to which livestock men are excessively given, his talks were suitably red-blooded and jaunty, adhering to the accepted tradition that some after-dinner stories are suitable with ladies present, others suitable with gentlemen present, and still others suitable for livestock men only. A devout Presbyterian churchman and a Y.M.C.A. leader, Harry Wallace was rarely profane in his language, but he was never what his father used scornfully to call a 'goody-goody,' unaware of uproarious incongruities between conventional pretense and the biological facts and urges. 'It is really too bad,' Harry once remarked to his friend and closest professional crony, Dr. H. C. Taylor, when in course of a three-block walk they passed three stunning-looking women, 'too bad, really, that we superior and high-principled males are so limited in our genetic possibilities!'

Young Henry A. Wallace told no jokes, either gay or grim, in his early speeches on farm subjects throughout Iowa and states near-by. He was at first by all accounts a miserable speaker; he looked miserable and sounded miserable whenever he had it to do. 'His attitude on the platform at these little farm meetings,' Donald R. Murphy, the present editor of *Wallaces' Farmer & Iowa Homestead* remembers, 'was always one of nervous awkwardness as if he hated to make a speech, but was determined to do it. And back in the hall, where I generally was, farmers would turn to each other and say: "Is that young Wallace? He is a *young* fellow, ain't he?"'

That was around 1913, when young Henry was twenty-five. Most of his first talks were about corn. He had grown a small, straight mustache, but soon decided it was more of a trouble than an adornment and shaved it off. Standing five feet ten and weighing, normally, around one hundred and sixty-five pounds, he had an outdoor look — a tanned face, strong legs, wide shoulders, and an extraordinarily deep chest. For a young man his face was unusually grave. As an editor, a market statistician, and an active farmer driving out six miles from Des Moines in an old Winton car as a reversed commuter, he worked unreasonably hard, and often he was tired. On his farm of eighty-seven acres he was building both a hybrid pedigreed seed business and a supplementary income from dairy products delivered direct to Des Moines customers on a milk route of his own.

Even in 1913 when he made his first hybrid crosses of corn by hand as a pastime, he had planned to go into the seed business in earnest. In the years 1914 and 1915 when he became a husband and then a father, he made the turn from a shotgun method of experimenting toward a methodical commercial production of seed. He had saved some two thousand dollars by the time of his marriage, but his salary as assistant editor of the family paper was modest, and he had no other property or means. Ilo, his wife, had inherited a farm near Indianola, but that was too far away for proper supervision; so they sold Ilo's farm and bought the first forty acres of this farm near-by. His father, Harry Wallace, bought the adjoining forty or so and young Henry set out to make the eighty pay. He knew little about dairying, but he thought that a dairy plant adjacent to fields of seed corn could be made to utilize the stalks or stover of the corn as by-products and sustain at the same time the fertility of the soil. The dairy side of his enterprise was later abandoned, but cows helped meet expenses while he was founding, under the trade-mark of 'Hi-bred,' the first commercial hybrid seed corn farm in the United States.

He confessed from the first to an impatience with Experiment Station genetic methods and standards and soon abandoned hand-crossing of hybrids as far too laborious and fussy for a man with limited time and practical aims. The experimenters were doing a great and brilliant work, he wrote,[4] but were 'rather too much concerned with comparing the yielding power of the cross with the parents, rather than with the best yielding variety of the locality. Could I find some cross which in Iowa would consistently beat Reid's Yellow Dent?'

'The method I used was to plant one acre to Reid's, another to Johnson County White, another acre to Eureka, another to Mexican June, etc., until eight different acres had been planted to eight different varieties. Through the center of each of these eight plots I planted four hills each of twenty other varieties, most of which were rather early and many of which were flints. These twenty early sorts were all detasselled, and this gave me 160 different combinations....'

This was only the beginning of that exploration. He grew in all nearly three 'hundred crosses of the standard North American strains, with strange intermixtures of strains from Russia, Australia, Hungary, China, and Argentina. Most of the crosses proved worthless, but all that showed any promise in point of yield, vigor, earliness, resistance to disease, or adaptability to impoverished soils were tested for a second year or longer.

He arranged with Professor Hughes at the College and occasionally with other interested breeders to share the labor of these tests. He experienced setbacks. Some first and second generation hybrids showed an exciting 'nick' of desired characters and the nick seemed at first to stick. It seemed for a while, for instance, as if a cross between Boone County White and Silver King was the answer to nearly everything. But then, 'In spite of all our selection it got poorer and poorer. About one in every ten of the young plants as they came up in the spring would have white leaves and of course these albinos died before they were three weeks old. About one in every fifteen ears was a freak, having a cluster of four or five nubbins without kernels at the place where there should be one good ear. I saw that I was fooling away my time with this cross.'[5] Then he began to try a great variety of crosses.

But the longer he worked by the shotgun method the more his findings thrust him back toward the basic findings and methods of Shull, Jones, and Hoffer of Indiana, precisely interweaving proven inbred strain on inbred strain to achieve fixed characters and sustained yield. By a like elaboration of a 'nick' between Reid's Yellow Dent itself and merged Mexican varieties Wallace found the way to breed the corn superior to Reid's that he was seeking. He worked out new types of corn houses with artificial dryers so that the seed could be delivered to customers in a highly viable condition and germinate evenly to make a solid stand.   But there were as yet few customers for hybrid seed.   'Mule' corn, farmers called it, and grumbled that even if you paid a big price for the seed, you would have to buy new seed from the hybrid breeder all over again next spring.   This is true: the natural crop of hybrid seed makes inferior seed stock.   Seed must be renewed in continually manipulated strains from the breeding farm each year.   It was also true that the early hybrid seed breeders had not bothered to breed corn of presentable appearance.   'Breed first for vitality; let appearance take care of itself,' Wallace said again and again. The first highly productive generations of his Reid-Mexican mixtures made ears which seemed grotesque to the conventional eye. Young Henry defended even the strangest among them in a front-page article,[6] closing in the true Wallace manner with a Scriptural reference: 'Any good farmer seeing these plants and these ears would laugh them to scorn.   Can any good come out of these nubbins?   The question is to invite a sneer.   It is about like "Can any good come out of Nazareth?"   The answer is much the same.'

With a sedate sense of showmanship he proposed a yield contest between the grain of his misshapen corn children and grain from the smooth, columnar ears of an openbred variety which had just won sweepstakes at the International Grain and Livestock Show in Chicago for a current 'King' of the old-time seed-corn showman, Peter Lux.   His challenge was not accepted.   Some of the old-time corn men were genuinely hurt by this young man's mockery of beautiful ears.   A bit contrite, Wallace explained editorially that he really had nothing against beauty, that he hoped in time to help rear inbreds of aesthetic charm as well as vigorous and rewarding yields at harvest.   He joined with the College at Ames and adjacent state colleges in promoting corn yield tests and certification for both inbred and openbred corn, of widely various breeders.   He praised the insight of George Krug, an openbred corn grower, who selected sound ears for seed largely by the feel of them, by lifting them and considering by their 'heft' the solidity of grain and cob.

Every annual publication of comparative yields proved the superiority of inbred strains, and Krug's selections worked over by inbreeders became a godsend, especially to the State of Indiana, where he farmed. As time went on Wallace entered into an informal partnership with Simon Cassady and made arrangements with other growers in an effort to meet the developing demand for hybrid improvements on Reid's, Krug's, and other openbred varieties of proven worth.

As a seed farmer he was by any standard of measurement successful. His experience with cows was not so happy. The soilage system of cutting and hauling corn stover as cow feed proved expensive and toilsome; the cost of the feed he had to buy was high; and while he had nothing against cows, he did not understand the creatures and care for them as naturally and lovingly as he cared for plants, especially corn. Building his cow barn in 1915, he ran into the beginning of the wartime shortage of labor and materials; and hardly had he housed his herd of forty than both bovine tuberculosis and contagious abortion appeared in the herd. This required the usual tests, provisions of isolation, loss, and slaughter. Wallace had no heart for the mess. He knew something about plants, but when it came to this cow business it seemed to him that no one knew anything, really, about the most vital questions. Truly, as old Tama Jim Wilson had said in his closing report as Secretary of Agriculture: 'We need chemists and bacteriologists to help elucidate milk problems that are to a great extent as much of a mystery today, though large progress has been made, as they were when milk was churned in a goat's skin on the back of a camel during the journey between tenting places in the days of Abraham.' [7]

Wallace studied the spotted and ravaged inner organs of his slaughtered cows with an all but morbid interest. He was morally certain that the tuberculosis, which had killed all of his grandfather's brothers and sisters, afflicted an uncle — John P. Wallace — with bone trouble, and attacked his own wife, Ilo, during the first year of her marriage, had in some part, if not in large part, been transmitted into the human bloodstream through the milk of tubercular cows.

Agricultural colleges in the great dairy states, particularly, were naturally resisting this suspicion, and the first findings which indicated that it was true. It might hurt business. For years the dairy industry and most of the professoriat opposed publicity, remedial legislation, and protective measures. It was years before discovery that cows with contagious abortion can give people undulant fever was admitted, confirmed, and acted upon. In 1916 Henry (H. A.) Wallace and his father, Harry (H. C.), a trained dairy specialist, had no suspicion of the relationship between aborting cows and undulant fever in humans; but they did suspect that the reason Ilo Wallace had to go to Colorado and shake off that touch of tuberculosis even while she was carrying her first child, Henry, in 1914–15, traced to unpasteurized, uncertified, contaminated milk.

Hers was a light attack, soon healed. Back in Des Moines she rode out with her husband almost every morning to help with the milking at four-thirty, and she drove the wagon on their milk route when help could not be found. Her husband was doing a full day's work at the office and working morning and evening at the farm. In 1916 he, too, was taken with tuberculosis. The trouble had been coming on for some time. His weight had lapsed to one hundred and forty pounds and he suffered passing seizures of chill and fever which he ignored. Tuberculosis was naturally suspected; but this Henry A. Wallace had for years maintained (and still maintains) that no matter what the source of tubercular infection may be, the proper protective diet will enable anyone to resist it, throw it off; and he would not go to a doctor. The harder he worked the worse the trouble grew. He still insists that it might have been undulant fever, not tuberculosis at all; that the afternoon temperatures of 100, 101, and up to 102 degrees which he ran at the time were undulant in nature; and that he experienced no discomfort in his lungs or bone. But three doctors, two of them insurance doctors, said it was tuberculosis. In the light of this diagnosis, together with a passing return of similar trouble in 1925, it was not until 1931 that examining physicians would accept Henry A. Wallace for life insurance at the normal rate. From both attacks he recovered quickly, but he had to spend four months in the Colorado Rockies during the spring and summer of 1916 and for the first two months of this four months' illness he was flat on his back.

Even when bedridden he continued his writing for *Wallaces'*

Farmer by dictation and continued to make his computations and charts. The grip abstract mathematics had acquired on him during his later years in college he brought to bear now on earthy problems of supply and price; and he inclined at the time to attribute to his findings a degree of infallibility which he was later to repudiate in part. 'I once believed in statistics,' he confessed to a seminar of agricultural economists at Ames, years later, and wryly added: 'I do not know but what it is just as well for one to go through the experience. In like n..anner it is no doubt a good thing for every college student to become a Socialist at one time or another. It is possibly a good thing for every economist to become a statistician. But I hope he does not impute to statistics mystical values.' [8]

Of all the economic writers he read at this period he was most impressed by Thorstein Veblen's *The Theory of the Leisure Class* and later *The Theory of Business Enterprise*. Though he found it rather difficult to 'penetrate the heavy protective coloration' of Veblen's style, he was persuaded that the Veblenian approach made 'the analyses of both the statisticians and the classical economists rather beside the point.' Later, in 1936, he predicted that in the twenty-first century Veblen 'will rank higher than he does today.' He met Veblen, who then was teaching at the University of Missouri, at a Midland economists' meeting and was pleased to find that Veblen, like himself, when young, had passed through a period of strict belief in statistics, and had used this approach exclusively in a study of wheat prices in 1891. Talking shop with Veblen, Wallace found him plain and easy to understand, and he figured that Veblen wrote the way he did to 'keep from being fired too often.' [9]

At other economic meetings and seminars Wallace heard the polite wrangling of agricultural economists who adhered to the classical dogma — T. N. Carver of Harvard, J. E. Boyle of Cornell, B. H. Hibbard of Wisconsin, and many others. He found it all rather interesting but futile. 'They reason too nearly in a vacuum. . . . It seems to me that economics of necessity must serve some deeper end in human life,' he said. He was more attracted to 'the almost Messianic complex' and vigor of advocates of applied farm management studies, notably W. J. Spillman of the Department of Agriculture and George Warren of Cornell. These two college mavericks did not believe you could 'look into your own mind for a notion as to what was good farm management, and correct it by your boyhood memories.' They thought that one should go out on the farm and get firsthand knowledge.

'Interestingly enough,' Wallace went on to say, retrospectively, in the seminar account of his experience in economics, delivered at Ames in 1936, 'Dr. Spillman is the philosophic father — in so far as it may be said to have a philosophic father — of the Agricultural Adjustment Act, and Warren is quite strongly opposed to it.

'My first vivid impression with regard to economics came with the high hog prices in 1910. Professor B. H. Hibbard, who had influenced me most as an economist during my college course, suggested that the increased production of gold probably had something to do with the price level in the world, and that the high world price level in turn influenced prices. The animal husbandry men told of a shortage of hogs due to cholera.' Then, 'A year or two later I found myself on a farm paper writing how splendid it was to raise hogs [and] . . . hogs were down to $6 a hundredweight. I determined to discover just what it was that made hog prices. I got to studying corn prices and corn supply as well.'

His initial approach, by way of calculus, now had broadened: 'There is such a thing as life, and the mathematics of life is as far beyond the calculus as the calculus is beyond arithmetic.' But he still has his first worn copy of Thompson's *Calculus Made Easy*, with this engaging motto on its flyleaf:

> What one fool can do, another can.
> —*Ancient Simian Proverb.*

By 1915 he had worked out the first short-cut method of computing corn-hog ratios that proved of practical use to farmers. Next to the Sunday-School lessons, reader surveys indicated that his articles on corn and hog markets were probably the most closely read articles in *Wallaces' Farmer*. Professional forecasters in Chicago and elsewhere began to read his articles before they issued prophecies. He seldom missed.

This pleased Harry Wallace, as a business man, as an editor, and as a father, deeply. 'Our Henry has the best mind in the Wallace family for the past two hundred years,' he boasted to Dr. H. C. Taylor. And that, for a Wallace speaking of a Wallace, was praise indeed.

3. A Dispute with Mr. Hoover

As is generally true when a major war breaks out, our financial and productive mechanisms did not immediately respond. The New York Stock Exchange, indeed, shut down for a few days in 1915, as if stunned. Then it revived in faith, took off and soared. Cotton, the most speculative of commodities, made a slow start toward the unprecedented expansion which culminated in a crop of two million bales of thirty-five-cent cotton in 1919. Wheat led the boom and rise. Internal land and population pressures had pushed attempts at wheat-growing on to the semi-arid high plains, and in 1915, with the capricious weather of the plains favoring, America produced its first billion-bushel wheat crop.

These and the ensuing vast increases in wartime farm production were performed shorthanded. The outcry of farmers in *Wallaces' Farmer* and the farm press in general was as loud and insistent then as it was again in the nineteen-forties. There is more than an immediate grief and problem behind such outcry. Farmers do not like to see those of their calling and interest diminish in number. They do not like to see sons who might like to farm crowded out of the business of farming. Yet whenever their sons go off to war, or are drawn by high wages and the prevailing excitement into the mills and shipyards, farmers have little choice save to bring in more machinery and so to pre-empt in a measure the acres those boys might till if they were to return to the land.

Again, there was little confidence, among the mass of the farmers in the South and West alike, that the Department of Agriculture and the wartime Food Administration were in the hands of men who would give a fair break to the farming interest. Having for sixteen years joined in the Government, informally, with their own Secretary of Agriculture in Washington, the Wallaces were particularly inclined to be critical of this stranger, David F.

Houston, whom Woodrow Wilson had appointed as Tama Jim's successor in 1913. Secretary Houston was by training a historian of finance and economy, not an agriculturist. He had, it is true, served for a while as President of the Texas Agricultural and Mechanical College; and he had been most useful to the Wallaces' old friend, Seaman Knapp, in helping put benefactions of the General Education Board, a Rockefeller philanthropy, behind extension of Knapp's farm demonstration programs in the Cotton South. David Houston was still a member of this Rockefeller Board, from which Congress in 1914 refused to accept further aid to agriculture, when President Wilson made him Secretary of Agriculture. 'Whether or not Mr. Rockefeller's money is tainted, as is alleged,' said Congressman James H. Byrnes of South Carolina in the course of the 1914 debate, 'certainly this government is big and prosperous enough to engage in this helpful work without entering into partnership with him.'

Before assuming the secretariat Houston relinquished what agrarians called his 'Standard Oil connections,' but a certain part of the oil smear stuck. *Wallaces' Farmer* remarked editorially that President Wilson's Mr. Houston, while doubtless an estimable gentleman, was wholly innocent of any knowledge of practical farming; and it was widely suspected throughout the farming country that the new Secretary was not 'rural-minded.' Agrarians, however intellectual, when they use this term generally take the tone of one pronouncing a curse. Mr. Houston was indeed not notably 'rural-minded.' As Secretary of the Treasury, to which position he was shifted in February of 1920, he had much to do with a cold-blooded deflation which bore particularly upon agriculture; but most of those who worked closest to him when he was Secretary of Agriculture testify that he was an excellent administrator, with sound, if overconservative, ideas about building up farm income on the business side. He died as chairman of the board of a great insurance company in 1940.

An old friend and admirer of the Wallaces, Walter Hines Page, was largely responsible for Houston's appointment as Secretary. Later, when war broke out, and an American mining engineer, Herbert Hoover, gave the embassy in London great aid in taking care of Americans stranded on European excursions and getting them home again, it was Ambassador Page who introduced Mr. Hoover into the higher wartime counsels of the Wilson Administration and later pressed for his appointment as Food Administrator.

When Herbert Hoover's name began first to appear in the papers as the wonder-worker from Iowa, the Wallaces had never heard of him. He had been born in that state, of course, on a farm near West Branch, in 1874, but had soon gone from there to study at Stanford University, and then to work in far parts of the world, South Africa, China, India, Australia, Russia, as a mining engineer. The Wallaces could not see how that experience plus even the Belgian Relief chairmanship equipped a man to be American Food Administrator, with large powers of wartime governance over agriculture. They had a question mark on Herbert Hoover from the first.

In the ensuing account of strife it should also perhaps be recognized that agriculturists of Land Grant College antecedents or training incline to look with a jaundiced eye upon anyone of other training and experience who is thrust by circumstance into a position of agricultural power. This may be a protective response to the general contempt visited upon agricultural students and professors in the early decades of the Land Grant College movement; a defensive drawing-together; a continuing, though decreasing, impulse to strike back. There is something about it, also, akin to the attitude which duly graduated and postgraduated medical men exhibit, quite actively, toward quacks who practice without a license. The agricultural profession has formed, in less active measure, its own standard, its own defense and pride. 'A rather testy self-consciousness,' Whitney Shephardson called it in a Rockefeller study in 1927; and his phrase is in a measure just.

Compared with most agricultural commentators and partisans, Harry Wallace and his son, H. A., writing in their paper and making speeches, were at first scrupulously fair, almost kind, to Houston and then to Hoover. Consider in comparison, for example, the taunt of E. V. Wilcox, Tama Jim's biographer. On taking office Secretary Houston had announced: 'Heretofore the Department of Agriculture has, of necessity, concerned itself mainly with problems of production. . . . We have been suddenly brought face to face with the fact that in many directions further production waits on better distribution.' To this Wilcox answered: 'Like Silvius, the sighing, simple-minded swain in Shakespeare's *As You Like It*, he thought that no one had ever been in love before him or at least had never had as bad a case!' A stout partisan of the Iowa or Midland element in the controversies of the time, Mr. Wilcox seemed to imply that Tama Jim had already attended to the distribution problem. If that is what he meant to say, it is largely nonsense. Secretary Wilson's governing passion had been for production. He acknowledged the need for better marketing, but that was about all. One of his most devoted students at Ames, H. C. Taylor, who later became the first chief of the Bureau of Agricultural Economics, has preserved for the record an affectionate scolding given him by Secretary Wilson when he, Taylor, wrote to ask what the chances were for a young man specially trained in economics in the Department.

'Your aspirations are high, holy, and noble, but three times a day you will want bread and butter,' the Secretary replied. Continuing, in a letter dated January 31, 1898, he advised Taylor to specialize: 'Make yourself proficient in some one line: Soil Physics, Biology, Plant Physiology, or Pathology. . . . I am turning away the half-baked fellows who do not know how to do anything well. I remember you very kindly and have great hopes of you. Specialize now, for a while, and let me hear from you again.' This was written, of course, in the first of Secretary Wilson's sixteen years as head of the Department of Agriculture; but there is no striking evidence that during his entire term of service did he consider economics a bread-and-butter farm subject or a basis for agricultural planning. As the dismal science then was taught and promulgated, he considered it no science and of no use.

David Houston was the first Secretary of Agriculture to bring to the post formal training in economics and finance, even though, as Josephus Daniels says in his memoir, *The Wilson Era*, it was 'finance as taught at Harvard.'

When America actually entered the war on April 6, 1917, President Wilson called Hoover back from Paris where as head of the Commission for Relief in Belgium he had been doing a difficult job effectively. Since 1914 his Commission had administered the relief and rationing of ten million people in German-occupied Belgium and northern France. In May of 1917 the President appointed Hoover as Food Administrator, but it was not until three months later, August 10, that Congress passed the law that authorized him to put his Food Administration to work.

In the two war years before America declared belligerence, our foodstuffs, fighting preponderantly on the side of the Allies, had been in insatiable demand overseas. There was virtually no limit to what the governments of accessible foreign belligerents would bid or pay. Food prices at home had risen accordingly to a point where, in the opinion of some economists, the United States would probably have chosen to erect some kind of a wartime control over food shipments, sales, and prices, even if this country had not declared a shooting war.

Hoover's new task was obviously one of some delicacy here at home. The farm or producing element, having tasted of high prices and good profits for the first time in many a year, wanted more. The major consuming element in this country was used to cheap food and wanted more of it. Consumer demand had to be in some part met and in some part soothed by a sales or advertising technique that Mr. Hoover, doubtless to his own greater happiness, had not been called upon to exert in half-starved Belgium.

He is a man neither apt nor trained in the art or craft of public cajolery. He had to have help on that. Skilled help rushed in eagerly. 'Food Will Win the War' was the most memorable slogan the advertising men created. It lived in the farm mind to embarrass Hoover in his years as President during war's aftermath, but it had both farmer and consumer appeal at the time. Various inferior versions of the Mother Goose rhyme about licking the platter clean were boiled down to caption-size for posters and consumer primers, civilians were acquainted with reasonably painless ways of participating three times daily in the War to End Wars. The restrictions and sacrifices he was asking Americans to undergo must have seemed picayune to Hoover, who had seen and ministered to widespread and shocking conditions of malnutrition abroad.

In Europe seventy million men had been withdrawn from productive labor to kill and destroy. War blocked or clogged most of the established landways or seaways by which grain and fats, particularly, had come in quantity before the war to offset generally deficiencies of these foodstuffs on the Continent. Continental soils, and the soil of Britain, hard-worked, were showing signs of depletion, with a lowering both of yields and of nutritional value in the product. The very elements of earth for which plants and people most hunger are the ones that in wartime go principally into explosives and are blown into thin air from the bomb pit or the mouths of guns.

Wheat was the foodstuff most immediately in demand. The Allies were begging and bidding for six hundred million bushels of our wheat when we entered the war. Hoover and his right-hand man on grain, Julius H. Barnes, acted decisively, even radically, to get the grain flowing to our ports and then across the Atlantic. Through the Food Administration Grain Corporation the entire American grain trade was nationalized, with decreed maximum prices and licensed handlers. 'All private speculation has been stopped. . . . The Allies will be supplied with every bushel of surplus wheat that can be made available to them. . . . American mills will be assured of a steady normal supply of grain to grind; and neutral buying will be under our absolute control,' Julius Barnes, President of the Grain Corporation, announced in 1917.

Corn and hogs presented a far more intricate problem. German food administrators, faced at the outbreak of war in 1914 with a like problem of inducing the use of grain and potatoes as human foods direct, or through livestock, hogs especially, had blundered badly, in the opinion of competent observers such as Gustav Stolper, viewing then and later the nutritional consequences. In his book, *German Economy, 1870–1940*, Stolper cites 'the famous story of the hog massacre' as 'a relatively minor incident' but 'significant of the sort of error to which every planning system is probably exposed.' Elsewhere in his book Stolper remarks that 'a definite shortage of fats,' in both World Wars, 'will in the long run have devastating effects on the health of the German people, particularly the young generation.'

Early in his experience in provisioning warring Europe, Hoover observed that a shortage of fats in the diet induces among any

people excesses of moroseness and unrest.   In an article entitled
'The Great Fat Fight,'[10] published in *The Saturday Evening Post*
after Hoover had read and authorized it during his 1928 campaign
for the presidency, George Barr Baker reviewed the situation in
1917 thus:

> The only quick way to make fats was through hogs.   It
> takes years to make dairy cows, whereas hogs can be matured
> in nine or ten months.   It was the only hope. . . . There had
> been a 15 per cent increase in the number of hogs in the two
> years before, under the greater prices brought about by the
> war . . . [but] the Allies, scrambling for food supplies . . . had
> bid up the price of corn relatively high to the price of hogs . . .
> [so] our farmers continued to kill hogs by the hundreds of
> thousands and to sell their corn. . . . We had fewer hogs than
> even before the war.   Even brood sows were being
> slaughtered.

In order to get more swine for 1919 consumption Hoover had to
induce increased hog breeding and a diminished slaughter of breeding stock immediately.   He was willing to guarantee a 'cost plus'
price in order to get what he felt he simply must have for European
provisioning, both as a humanitarian and an administrator with
the eyes of the world upon him.   'Cost plus,' so generally used in
allotting industrial war contracts, meant cost of production plus a
'reasonable' profit.   But what was the cost of producing hogs,
and what was a 'reasonable' profit?   Hoover asked the Department of Agriculture to help him set up a commission to determine
the cost of hogs.   With the choice of this seven-man commission
left largely to Midwest farm organization people, Harry Wallace's
Corn Belt Meat Producers in particular, young Henry Wallace
was named as statistician of Hoover's hog price commission of
inquiry in November of 1917.

During the previous summer and earlier that fall Henry had
been publishing notes and articles on the corn-hog ratio approach
to price determinations in *Wallaces' Farmer*.   The core of his
original approach to the question, later enlarged and developed in
his book, *Agricultural Prices* (1920),[11] was that you cannot simply
average what it costs a number and variety of men to produce

hogs, mine coal, make soap, render special services, or anything at all and get at an administered price that has practical meaning. 'Even in industries so well controlled by man as coal mining,' he argued, 'where the weather does not enter in, there are some mines that can produce a ton of coal for two or three dollars, while other mines cannot produce a ton of coal for less than six or seven dollars. The North Dakota wheat farmer, in a year of rust, may produce wheat at a cost of four or five dollars a bushel, whereas a Kansas farmer in the same year may produce wheat at a cost of only a dollar or a dollar and a half a bushel. Shall both the Dakota farmer and the Kansas farmer be paid cost of production plus a reasonable profit for their wheat? There is no such thing as a standard cost of production; . . . it is a will-o'-the-wisp.'

The infinite ranges and varieties of capacities and experience that would have to be figured into what might be called a 'just' price from this approach, if any sane statistician were to try it, he went on, would drive him crazy. His 'ratio approach,' on the other hand, he urged, while 'rough and ready,' was relatively simple; it was not downright arbitrary; it began by invoking common experience: 'Over a long series of years, cost of production plus a reasonable profit is roughly expressed by the relationship that exists between a raw product and the finished product. In rough form it may be most easily grasped in the case of corn and hogs. . . .'

The ratio method derived from a rule of thumb observed and followed by sagacious Corn Belt farmers as far back as 1870. 'Without any statistical investigation' they 'grasped the ratio idea.' They figured that they would make money raising hogs if the sales price of the hogs per hundredweight was as much as the cost of ten bushels of corn. Working as a statistician, Wallace refined this method to weigh in, at varying prices through the year, the corn that it takes to 'condense corn' into hog meat, and also the varying amounts of corn fed in each successive month: with 2 per cent of all the corn going into the hog or its dam in each of the first three months of feeding, 3 per cent the fourth month, and so on up to 20 per cent the tenth month, when feeding tapers off again to 15 per cent in the twelfth month.

Applying this weighting to recorded prices of Chicago No. 2

corn, Wallace recommended to the commission and went with its members to Washington to recommend to Hoover that the way to get an increased supply of pork was to offer 13 bushels of corn on the basis of Chicago corn and Chicago heavy hog per hundred-weight, live weight, as the price for hogs when they came to market the year following. The 13-bushel ratio, Wallace stated, was 13 per cent over the historic ratio, but it had to be that much in order to encourage enough corn to go into hog meat in the amount needed.

Hoover did not care much for the ratio idea. He would have preferred a flat minimum guaranteed price. 'But,' George Barr Baker continues in his *Saturday Evening Post* account of the bicker, 'the farmers' representatives insisted that the hogs could not be got without it, and Hoover had to have the fats.' On November 3, 1917, Hoover caused to be issued by the Food Administration a public statement concluding:

'As to hogs farrowed next spring — 1918 — we will try to stabilize the price so that the farmer can count on getting for each 100 pounds of pork ready for the market, thirteen times the average cost per bushel of corn fed into the hogs.

'Let there be no misunderstanding of this statement. It is not a guaranty backed by money. It is not a promise by the packers. It is a statement of the intention and policy of the Food Administration, which means to do justice to the farmer.'

There *was* misunderstanding of the statement, a serious misunderstanding, occasioning debate in *Wallaces' Farmer* and elsewhere for the better part of fifteen years to come. Note that Hoover in this statement did not mention Chicago prices. Designedly or not, this gave him or his economists an out. Food Administration circulars put out at the time to encourage a spurt in pork production did, however, mention Chicago prices, emphatically. The one thing on which both sides of the controversy agree is that the promise to 'try' to get a 13-to-1 ratio price for hogs stimulated production, produced the hogs, abundantly. The Wallace adherents say that the Hoover people used this device to give the desired flick to pork production and then did everything in their power to get out of paying for it on the basis indicated.

In the fall and winter of 1918–19 the Food Administration, by refiguring the data in the light of corn prices at the *farm* and hog prices at Chicago, tried to whittle the price down to $2.50 a hundredweight below the 13-to-1 price as originally figured. A new committee of fifteen hog producers went to Washington to protest. 'They went down to defeat,' [12] young Henry wrote in his book, *Agricultural Prices*, 'scarcely realizing what the Food Administration had done to them. When the facts became known, widespread indignation among the farmers of the Corn Belt compelled the Food Administration to abandon the hypocritical pretense of living up to the 13-bushel ratio and come out flatly for a $17.50 minimum, which was really a ratio of 10.8 bushels. The Food Administration was able thus to repudiate in part its definite obligation to hog producers, because there were no thoroughly organized farmers with leaders trained to think in terms of statistics and economics.'

He did not care, he added, 'to create a prejudice against the Food Administration. It probably did its work as efficiently as any branch of the Government during the War.' The incident revealed, however, not merely 'chicanery'; it taught a lesson: 'the extreme disadvantage under which farmers labor in bargaining with other classes of society. It is hoped that as farmers learn to follow the example of keen business men and employ trained experts to look after their interests, and as farm leaders become better trained in statistics, this disadvantage will disappear.'

Into his editorials on the subject Harry Wallace put more thump. The editors of *The Des Moines Register*, among the first to detect in Hoover possible presidential material, made light of Harry's editorial stating that Hoover had already caused more farm discontent than any living American, and twitted the Wallaces for having, with their ratio price plan, given Hoover a 'bum steer.' In an editorial sedately captioned, 'A Mistaken Daily,' Harry Wallace replied:

> . . . We should have said he was more responsible for the dissatisfaction than any one hundred other men. . . . Mr. Hoover's deceit in dealing with the farmers was in fact the impelling motive for the organization of the Farm Bureau in its later and stronger form. It was Mr. Hoover's effort to

bamboozle the farmers that brought them to see at last, if
they were to secure economic justice at the hands of other
interests and at the hands of the government, it would have
to come through an organization of their own strong enough
to compel it. . . .

Instead of keeping his promise in good faith, Mr. Hoover
undertook to juggle the figures and fool the farmers. He
tried to treat his promise as a scrap of paper. He got even
more hogs than he expected or hoped for. If he had been
frank about the matter and said he had overpromised and
could not make good, the farmers would have accepted their
loss with the same good will with which they accepted many
other losses. But Mr. Hoover did not do that. He seemed
to look upon the farmers of the West as a bunch of 'rubes.'
He seemed to think that he could pull the wool over their eyes;
and therein he was mistaken. He could fool them with his
promises, but he could not fool them into thinking that he was
keeping that promise, when in fact he was not. And it was
the realization that they had been deceived, imposed upon,
made the goats, that convinced the farmers that the time had
come to stop fooling, that they must organize so strongly
they could make their voice heard by the powers that be.[13]

In the arguments and clashes between the educational and the
more militant business promoters of the Farm Bureau as it rose to
power, there was never any doubt about where Harry Wallace
stood: He held that the influence of Washington, the Land Grant
colleges, and the co-operative state-federal Agricultural Extension
Service, created by the Smith-Lever Act of 1914, had been technically invaluable in stimulating production, but the same educational system, he found, was turning out to be just so much
soothing syrup, when it came to helping farmers band together
and getting a better price. In the fight for higher fixed prices in
wartime the farmers had been tricked, in his opinion, and bested.
This made him angry and he was further irked by a lack of audible
protest from the ninety-and-nine of the people who were supposed
to be working for agriculture in Washington and in the Land Grant
college hierarchies.

The Wallaces' friend, W. J. Spillman, did, in a sense, enter pro-test. As head of the office of Farm Management in the Department of Agriculture, Spillman, in another way of saying it, was recalcitrant. He gave out at the request of Congress some cost of production figures that his office had compiled over a period of more than ten years. Previously, Spillman had been so ill-mannered, by bureaucratic standards, as to question the pro-priety of using Rockefeller funds in federal extension teaching, and had helped to draw the bill which put an end to that practice, at the time when David Houston, a man of Rockefeller antecedents, became Secretary of Agriculture and Spillman's boss. They did not care for each other. In 1918 when Spillman gave out his figures, farm organizations clamored for more, and Congress asked the Secretary to comply. Acidly, the Secretary, replying, re-gretted premature publication of 'data [which] constitute no basis for proper action in this difficult matter. . . . I am taking steps to see that further studies, if made in this field, shall be satisfactory.' This is a situation in which a scientist and a man of honor is expected to commit a sort of *hara-kiri*, for the time being, at least. Spillman resigned and went for miserable pay to do uncongenial work on a popular farm paper, *The Farm Journal;* and the Secretary wrote him an unctuous letter, all according to form.

That same autumn, 1918, Harry Wallace launched in continuing editorials and responsive letters from farmers and farm organiza-tion men a proposal that farmers set up their own farmers' uni-versity, one they could trust. He started by saying that farmers could afford to put twenty or thirty million dollars of their own money behind it, and still be better off. That was large money, in his mind; for he was exceedingly Scotch in matters of finance, private or public; but this was a time when farmers had money, remember, and also a time when organized agriculture, in some-thing of a boom spirit, was entertaining ambitious notions of unitedly becoming a big business itself. To this end, Harry Wallace wrote on September 27, 1918, 'The agricultural colleges are not helping the farmer; in fact, they are hindering him. And the Department of Agriculture is worse, much worse, both in its sins of omission and commission. . . .'

It is doubtful if he considered it likely that such a private national farmers' university, stressing marketing, would come to pass; but he found it a stimulating prospect to consider, and the expressed shock and anger of the established agricultural savants at such a proposal seemed to give him a grim amusement. 'The more we think of that farmers' university, the better we like it,' he wrote, and continued in subsequent issues of *Wallaces' Farmer* to think about it some more:

As it is, the farmer threshes around wildly but gets little or no relief. Like a baby that is suffering from a misplaced pin, he waves his arms wildly and kicks his legs and roars. He knows that something is hurting him, but he does not know exactly what it is, and he does not know how to go about it to get rid of it. . . .

There is little hope of the farmer getting from the agricultural colleges the knowledge he most needs. . . . College emphasis has been placed almost wholly on greater production. . . . One reason is the colleges are supported by all the people. They are continually needing more money. To get it they must go to their various legislatures which are composed principally of people from the towns. . . . Let any college take up in dead earnest the work of teaching farmers more about the things we have spoken of . . . the money supply would be shut down.

Our agricultural college people are timid, as a rule. . . . They like to be on good terms with the powers that be in the state and nation. They think mostly in the same old college lines . . . and they do not encourage those younger men within their own ranks here and there, who see that there is something radically wrong with agricultural economic conditions. . . .

Perhaps what we need first is not a farmers' university, but an institution of research. Perhaps we should start with $100,000 or $200,000 on that. . . . There is one thing dead sure. Unless the farmers of the United States do something of this sort, they will degenerate into mere hewers of wood and drawers of water.[14]

It should be observed, and often has been since, that the Farm
Bureau movement was born and grew not principally in the ranks
of the lowly and dispossessed among farmers, but among land-
owning farmers who wanted to go on owning and working land at
a better profit, in the main. It was officered and led, from the first,
by the squire type in the South and East and by the equivalent
owner or banker-farmer type in the Midland. The school of
thought standing most aggressively for a large business approach,
as distinct from the public service propaganda inducing and instructing farmers to grow more and trust to God for a sustaining
price, was strongest in the Midland; and although he worked
mainly in the background, it is not too much to say that the most
influential national leader of the big business approach at the
outset of the Farm Bureau movement was this then private
citizen of Iowa, Harry Wallace.

At the first national organization meeting, when delegates from
twelve states formed the American Farm Bureau Federation, at
Chicago in February, 1919, 'The best qualified men in the country
should be hired to manage each of the various lines of work,' he
said. 'This Federation must not degenerate into an educational
or social institution. It must be made the most powerful business
institution in the country.'

Men from New York State, where the framework of the Federation had been led under milder college auspices, demurred.
'We do not need any such sums of money as some people think,'
H. C. McKenzie said. 'All we need the first year is funds to
conduct the work on a very conservative basis.'

Kentucky was with Harry Wallace. J. S. Crenshaw spoke:
'The organization movement has been sweeping Kentucky like a
prairie fire. Kentuckians have been signing ten-dollar membership checks as fast as they could get hold of their checkbooks.
Kentucky does not want a ten-cent policy! We would be ashaned
to go back to our people with any ten-cent proposition.'

Midwestern speakers expressed in general a respectable determination not to be radical combined with a blazing determination
to get more money. Harvey Sconce of Illinois made plain the
view that farmers were not laborers, but capitalists, in such
endeavor. 'It is our duty in creating this organization to avoid

any policy that will align organized farmers with the radicals of other organizations.' He spoke with distress of thousands of current strikes by dissatisfied labor; then went on: 'We shall organize, not to fight or antagonize anyone, but to co-operate and construct, managing the affairs of agriculture in a broad business manner, following the policy that most of the ills complained of by the individual will disappear when business is done in business ways.'

J. R. Howard, the Iowa farmer Harry Wallace had been backing for the presidency of the Federation, was elected at this first national meeting. He closed his keynote speech with this declaration: 'I stand as a rock against radicalism, but I believe in an organization which strikes out from the shoulder.' It typified the mood of the movement that the Federation voted a salary somewhat more than that of the Secretary of Agriculture for its farmer-president, fifteen thousand dollars a year.

With his father more often out of the office now on farm organization matters, Henry A. Wallace took on more of the writing and editing. With his wife's help he kept the milk route running and the seed business growing and himself turned out from three to twelve columns of copy for *Wallaces' Farmer* a week. In addition to these labors he composed an extended scientific paper, 'Mathematical Inquiry into the Effect of Weather on Corn Yield in the Eight Corn Belt States,' published in the Government's official *Monthly Weather Review*. The walls of his small office were nearly covered with charts. Always by his desk stood two implements, such as would drive most writers to distraction — a dictaphone and a computing machine. He had a typewriter, too, and could write fairly rapidly with two fingers, but he never learned to love the instrument. Typing, he complained, is too noisy and too slow. To him, as to his grandfather, dictation came as naturally as breathing. On familiar subjects, well thought out, he could turn out as many as two hundred words of nearly finished copy a minute. Exploring new grounds, or taking special pains to be clear and accurate, he learned to dictate very slowly, leaning over the machine, almost embracing it as a musician embraces a 'cello, thinking, forming a phrase or so, stopping, thinking, starting anew. Through it all he turned the thing on and off with the flow and

pause of the thought as naturally and easily as a good driver con-
tols the beat of a motor and the progress of a car.

Thus with tools of the machine age about him and with all the
old assured and comfortable ways of life dying, while prices
boomed and the mounting lines on his charts foretold disaster,
Henry Agard Wallace worked to render statistics into terms of living reality, and learned to be a writer in his own way.

'Land at $500 per acre,' he wrote, as a geneticist, 'demands
that we produce more hog feed per acre. Corn is a living thing and
can be changed.' But was there not some limit to what land
might be made to yield in the face of such exalted valuations, high
taxes, and high interest charges? Late in 1918, on December 20,
and early the year following, on January 31, 1919, he published in
Wallaces' Farmer two extraordinary articles. The first he called
'Fundamental Land Values.' It was a practical study of land
prices in Polk County, his home county of Iowa. He sketched the
first sharp price rise, dating from 1897 to 1909 or 1910: 'In England, France, Germany — everywhere — business began to pick
up and prices began to advance. Some said the change was due to
the repudiation of Bryan and free silver in 1896, while others found
the cause in the vast amount of gold mined in the Klondike and in
South Africa. Some even thought the war with Spain in 1898
had its influence. . . . The advance in farm land seemed perfectly natural, it was in keeping with the advances in prices of
farm products, and the prices of these, in turn, were in keeping with
everything else.' From 1910 to 1914 there was a period of pause
and doubt. 'Thoughtful persons then began to shake their heads
in a knowing way. They said the productive power of land did
not warrant such extraordinary prices. . . . Opinions of this sort
seemed to have some weight, and for a time land values advanced
less rapidly.

'Then the Great War came on, and the productive power of land
began, without question, to exceed its selling value. This became
fully apparent in 1917 when the United States entered the war.
The crops of 1917 returned 10 to 15 per cent on the value of the
land, whereas the normal rate had been 3 or 4 per cent. Manifestly if war values were permanent, the land would double and
treble in value. Of course war values would not continue in full

force: nevertheless there was small likelihood of values going as low as they had before the war. There was a wave of speculative buying of farm land in the Corn Belt in 1917, which possibly would have become a mania if it had not been for the need of money for Liberty Loans.' And again, 'Thoughtful people began to question if land were not dangerously high.'

Abstaining from praise or blame, he proceeded to consider actual price and productivity figures on 'pasture and wasteland': 'The relationship between cattle values and pasture values is close and, on the whole, ordinary Polk County pasture land is worth as much as a 1000-pound grass-fed steer on the Chicago market . . . if grass-fed cattle after the war are worth on the average $10 per hundredweight in Chicago, we would expect ordinary Polk County pasture with a little timber on it to be worth about $100 an acre.'

By the same method Wallace evaluated plowland — a calculation 'far more complex.' Here rise in price was roughly from $50 an acre in 1897 to $110 in 1906 to $220, on the average, in 1916. Weighing in all factors, he concluded that 'plow land in corn at $220 an acre was probably on a firm foundation in 1916. What about it now [1918] at $250 an acre? What should it be worth now that the war is over? Of course I will not undertake to prophesy this, but I will say that *if*, as an average of 1920 to 1925, the price of corn [December 1 on Polk County farms] is 80 cents; if labor with board averages $40 a month; if machinery is worth about twice what it was before the war, then $250 and no more will be a justified price for Polk County farm land.'

Actually, of course, considerable holdings of black soil in Iowa and other Corn Belt states were still changing hands at $400 or even as high as $550 an acre at the time. Wallace continued: 'The three battling figures are land values, farmhand wages, and crop prices. The whole nation is vitally concerned in the fight. Low or even stationary land values will ruin thousands of young farmers who have tried to buy high-priced land with a small payment down. Farmhand wages cannot justly go below $40 a month (with board) as long as everything is as high as it inevitably must be during the next five years. On the other hand, the prices of farm products cannot go too high, or city labor will strike for higher wages, and they cannot get higher wages unless business is prosperous.   For a period of a year or perhaps two or three years farm prices may be pressed far too low.   By organization farmers can prevent a low price area from being pushed too far. . . . The whole price level will depend somewhat on international action in regard to the war debt.   Many longheaded people think that it will be to the interest of the nations to keep prices high in order that the debt may be paid off on an inflated currency.   Certain it is that any sudden dropping of prices generally will cause serious business depression, widespread unemployment and misery to nearly all classes.'

His second article, published some forty days later, was in the form of an unsigned editorial, brought up to the first page of the paper, and illustrated with charts.   It bore the cryptic heading, 'Farming Depression in England Following the Napoleonic War,' and started thus:

> The Napoleonic War of one hundred years ago bore much the same relation to the world of that day as the Great War bears to the world of today.   All the leading nations were involved directly and the United States was indirectly drawn in.   England prosecuted the struggle with great vigor. . . . Every man who could be spared became a soldier or sailor. There was the same sudden rise in prices.   Farm products practically doubled the pre-war average. . . .

The Napoleonic War was more drawn out than World War I, but the really critical period was concentrated in the four years from 1810 through 1813, and for purposes of comparison Wallace figured that 1810 corresponded roughly to 1915, 1811 to 1916, 1812 to 1917, 1813 to 1918, etc.   With this as a basis he charted wheat prices for both wars.

The post-Napoleonic war chart revealed a swift descent from $4 and $5 wheat in wartime (the average price was $3.86 a bushel for the year 1812) to a bare third of that average in 1814, 1815, and 1816.   By 1815 British farm receipts decreased one hundred million pounds and the value of farming stock fell off nearly one half.   With quotations from British farm writers and historians of that period, Wallace drove home the human consequences of agricultural deflation: 'The poor-rate quadrupled, the county rate increased seven-fold, and a very large proportion of this public burden was borne by agriculturists.' Again: 'Farms were thrown up; notices to quit poured in; numbers of tenants absconded. Large tracts of land were untenanted and often uncultivated. . . . Bankers pressed for their advances, landlords for rents, tradesmen for their bills. Insolvencies, executions, seizures, arrests, and imprisonment for debt multiplied. Farmhouses were full of sheriffs' officers. Many large farmers lost everything and became applicants for pauper allowances.'

Inexorably, Wallace bore on, depicting agricultural decline proceeding from grain to meat products, and a period of agricultural prostration from which Great Britain did not recover for more than twenty years: '. . . By 1822 livestock was also down. Matters improved temporarily in 1825, but real prosperity for farmers did not begin again until 1837. . . .'

He pointed the moral for the present: 'It is a common remark that a true comparison cannot be made between the war which has just closed and the wars which have preceded it; that the recent war was on such an infinitely large scale that no fair comparison is possible. We are not so sure about this. We incline to the belief that in a general way the effect of the reconstruction period which we are now entering will be just about the same as followed previous wars.'

More than half of the two hundred and twenty-four pages of his *Agricultural Prices*, 1920, are taken up with tabulations and charts. The text is clipped in style, meaty, almost aggressively shorn of ease and grace. Many of the sentences — including the last one in the book — break off with a brusque 'etc.' Intending it to be a somewhat cold-blooded analysis of what makes prices, Henry Wallace states doubt in opening whether 'idealistic social workers, representatives of organized labor, and many farmers [who] would like to do away with the speculative system of registering prices, substituting price-fixing legislation,' could do a better job than the speculators do. 'There is nothing angelic about speculators' but 'they perform real service,' and provide 'such a delicate system of registering prices that we believe even the most virulent opponents should allow the system to run a good many years yet, in order that they may study its functions more carefully.' [15]

Others of his 1920 proposals are less negative, foretelling, indeed, the line of action that first his father and then himself were soon to take:

> Farmers . . . will find it necessary to practice sabotage in the same scientific, businesslike way as labor and capital. They will reduce the size of their crops at strategic moments, because they know that small crops ordinarily bring a better return than large crops. Of course if farmers should practice sabotage in the same heartless, efficient way as capital and labor, our society will be imperilled . . . [but] . . . when farmers also practice sabotage, labor and capital will be forced to come to an agreement with farmers on production and price methods. . . .
>
> Is there not a possibility that capital, labor, and farmers, by placing themselves in equally powerful bargaining positions, may come to see the futility of sabotage as a price-sustaining force? Once farmers are able to meet the other classes of society on equal terms, all three classes ought to unite on production as the source of profit, rather than on clever bargaining. This involves close-knit organizations of both farmers and laborers under the leadership of men well educated in general economics, in strategic bargaining, and in production. There must be men who . . . perceive the legitimate physical difficulties which our society faces. The labor leaders must come to see that there is a point beyond which labor cannot go on raising wages and reducing hours. Farm leaders must come to see that there is a point beyond which farmers cannot go on reducing acreage and raising prices. Business leaders must come to see that the common people will not stand for curtailment of production to two-thirds factory capacity to secure abnormal profits, when by running the factory to full capacity the business will give normal profits. . . .
>
> What is the best means of overcoming the food shortage resulting from drought? . . . Is it practical to build government warehouses to store wheat in years when the acre yield is more than fifteen bushels, and from which wheat will be

drawn in years when the yield is less than thirteen bushels. . . .
It should be possible to meet our physical handicaps in the
way of drought, floods, and accident, in the spirit of doing
what is best for society, instead of using the crisis for individual or class profit.' [16]

So, as the World War entered upon the long Armistice, Henry
Wallace, entering upon his early thirties, foresaw deflation,
depression, and widespread misery, with crop contraception and
sabotage on a grand scale, and the beginning of an Ever-Normal
Granary.

4. The First Secretary Wallace

WITH THE SIGNING of the Armistice late in 1918, on November 11, there appeared little reason, on the surface of
events and prospects, for American agriculture sharply to
apply production brakes.   So many underfed or famished foreigners stood in crying need of food and garb immediately, and such
huge additional vacuums of foreign demand remained to be filled
when the blockade was lifted, that American farmers were led by
instinct and by most of their economic and business forecasters to
expect stimulating economic weather for some years to come.
The demand was enormous and actual.   The catch was: how to
collect?

It was all kept out of the papers until some years later, but on
New Year's Eve, 1918, fifty days after the signing of the Armistice, Great Britain canceled her American pork orders for January,
1919, and two days later France and Italy canceled theirs.   On
December 31 also, Herbert Hoover, as American Food Administrator in Paris, received private word from the Allied Food Council
that Marshal Foch would not for a second contemplate lifting the
blockade against the enemy and neutral countries until peace had
been actually made.

The commitments thus canceled added up to 396,800,000 pounds
of pork, a perishable product, for the month of January, 1919,
alone.   This pork was already crossing the water on shipboard or

rolling in freights to American ports.   Already, under the stimulus
of promised prices, American hog production had been speeded up
to two and a half times normal, and the goal set and accomplished
for 1919 was three times normal.   The orders of the Food Administration, George Barr Baker wrote later, 'could not be counter-
manded.   [That] would have precipitated in the producing sections of America a panic that would have ruined, almost overnight,
the farmers of the country, the farm banks, the packing houses,
large and small. . . . The slightest public knowledge of the threat,
in the early months of 1919, might well have been enough to
precipitate disaster.'

Baker laid bare a number of other forces which were moving
more or less darkly at the moment in the background of the mar-
ketplace.   Britain's cancellation, it appears, was in some part an
effort to cover herself in case of abrupt discontinuation of credits
from our Treasury, with which she had been paying for our pork.
Among Hoover's other grave troubles, as he struggled to maintain
the now promised $17.50 a hundredweight for the 1918 hog crop,
was a concerted drive of the Wilson Cabinet, led by the Secretary
of the Treasury, Carter Glass, to do away with all price hoists
immediately and give Americans cheap food again.   On January 16 Secretary Glass sent word to Edgar Rickard, Hoover's
chief aide: 'It is the view of the Treasury that a fall of food prices,
while causing some loss of profit to the raisers and packers of food,
would be a benefit to the general community, and have a stimulating effect on industry.'

Replying to Glass on January 24, Rickard said that the withdrawal of foreign purchases for one month would put down the
price of hogs $5 a hundred below the promised $17.50; and added:
'Happily Mr. Hoover has been able to repair the withdrawal of the
British orders in January by securing some partial amelioration of
blockade conditions and increased shipments to neutrals.   Had it
not been for these unsupported January orders, it is probable that
a price level of 35 per cent below present prices would have been
established, and this will take place in February unless a solution
can be found.'   The Food Administration, Rickard continued, had
been properly solicitous of consumer interests, but now opposed
securing 'low price levels at total injustice to the American farmer

... by the play of international action excusing itself as co-operation from the American Treasury.' If the Treasury would advance the Allied Governments for February and March, Rickard concluded, sums 'probably not exceeding,' in the final balance, more than forty or fifty million dollars, this 'would save the American swine producer that amount in February alone.'

Thus, early in 1919, a policy of pushing continuing crop 'surpluses' at home by continuing additions to already towering foreign loans was in formation and under way. On January 29 Glass agreed to extend further credit in support of Hoover in his dilemma. In Paris, Hoover now threw himself with all his heart, as a Quaker and humanitarian, and with truly heroic effort as an administrator on the spot, into a race to break the blockade before cheap food sentiment at home brought an end to supported food prices there. It was a close race. He and his supporters later claimed they won it. Even his most captious critics, when the facts at length were brought to light, were inclined to admit that while the performance fell short of perfection, Herbert Hoover fought a game and skillful delaying action in the face of vast difficulties to support his price promises to farmers, and at the same time to feed and cover the hungry and needy of Europe.

On February 11, 1919, President Wilson, then in Paris, received a wire from his Secretary of the Treasury, Glass. It said that the Cabinet unanimously recommended 'immediate discontinuance of all price stabilization' and that 'Congress appropriate money to indemnify producers, packers, and dealers for their losses.' Hoover protested that this would involve indemnities to fifteen million individual Americans, with private losses in terms of prices far exceeding any sum that might be doled out from the Treasury in indemnity. He persuaded Wilson to hold off on ending price controls at home until March 3. Ten days after that the Brussels Conference moderated the blockade enough to open important new relief channels for the piled-up stores, and so avoid an immediate crash of prices.

Not privy to these secret inner arrangements of the administration as the Wilson Democrats floundered toward demobilization and freer prices, the Wallaces could sense none the less a succession of what they called 'price drives' forming against agriculture and growing in impact. Constantly they warned their readers, editorially, to go slow, pay debts, batten down the hatches of their enterprises against storm, raid, and disaster. And organize; above all, organize!

In his annual report for 1919, written toward the year's close, before he went on to a more congenial post as Secretary of the Treasury, Wilson's first Secretary of Agriculture, Mr. Houston, tempered a still-optimistic outlook for American agriculture with a cautious afterword of warning against mounting land prices and rampant speculation: 'Consolidate the gains already made; prepare for the period of competition which is to be expected.' The President appointed E. T. Meredith, a friendly rival publisher of the Wallaces in Des Moines (*Successful Farming; Better Homes and Gardens*), as interim Secretary of Agriculture. Meredith proved a competent and popular head of the Department during the remainder of the Wilson administration. Meanwhile the expansion of our tilled domain and an excited upbidding of agricultural lands continued.

But land prices began to break in August of 1920; so did farm commodity prices, sharply, in some lines. Agricultural distress and outcry, as may be noted from Harry Wallace's editorial of February 12, heading this chapter, soon grew sharp. The short or lame-duck session of Congress, the Sixty-Sixth, passed a bill directing the War Finance Corporation to assist in exporting farm products, and passed, contrariwise, the Fordney Emergency Tariff, hoisting tariffs higher. President Wilson vetoed the tariff measure on March 3.

The nineteen-twenties came in with a campaign year. Harry Wallace withheld the commitment of his paper to either party until after the summer conventions, but quoted T. C. Atkeson, Washington representative of the Grange, 'a man of ripe judgment and wide experience,' on his editorial page approvingly: 'Herbert Hoover, of all the men suggested as a possible presidential candidate of either the Democratic or Republican party, is the most objectionable to the farmers of this country, and the most vulnerable.' Wallace added: 'His dealings with hog and milk and beef producers gave evidence of a mental bias which causes farmers to thoroughly distrust him. They look upon him as a typical autocrat of big business — able, shrewd, resourceful, and ready to adopt almost any means to accomplish his end. Farmers do not underestimate Mr. Hoover's ability, but they fear it.' [17]

After the conventions and the announcement of the platforms Harry Wallace went out to work for the Republicans, whose candidates were Harding and Coolidge. He told members of his family, privately, that Harding was 'sporty' rather than steady and responsible by nature, but he seemed willing to listen to reason in the farm cause; and the responsibilities of the presidency might be counted upon to steady him. For the most part *Wallaces' Farmer* retained on its editorial page its traditional non-partisanship, or freedom at least to praise or attack politicians of either party. To a correspondent complaining of the Wallace 'grouch' against the 'Hooveresque Democrats,' Harry Wallace replied:

'Guilty! No one in a position of authority with this administration seems to have any use for the farmer other than to get him to produce up to the limit and then force him to sell just as cheaply as possible. Hence our grouch . . .

'It is not a matter of partisan politics. It is simply a matter of securing economic justice for the farmer. When that is denied him, we get cross. Political partisans all look alike to us when they fight against the farmer, and we shall hit them a whack every chance we have.' [18]

He had a hand in framing the farm plank of the Republican platform, and wrote or contributed largely to Harding's campaign speeches on the plight of agriculture. With the idea of making campaign promises of either stick a little better afterwards, regardless of which side won, he led officials of the Iowa Farm Bureau Federation, which by now had one hundred thousand members, to call into a quiet caucus at the Hotel Savoy, Detroit, in the fall of 1920, all members, Republican and Democratic, of the Iowa delegation in the Congress. Senator Cummins was not there, but Senator Kenyon was, and so were all the Iowa members of the House. Harry Wallace and others made strong, definite statements of what agriculture had to have in the years of war's aftermath, and beyond. They secured with remarkably little trouble a bipartisan pledge of allegiance from the greater part of the delegation. It is a neglected fact in agrarian history, and one worth noting, that in forwarding this maneuver, just prior to accepting the post of Secretary of Agriculture, Harry Wallace led in founding the Farm Bloc. The Bloc changed in nature and membership and grew much stronger later, naturally, as times grew harder over wider areas.

On March 11, 1921, *Wallaces' Farmer* repeated at the head of its editorial page the curious, inverted caption, 'A Word Personal,' with which Uncle Henry had announced the founding and purposes of the first issue. The editor knew, he said in opening, how an old friend felt who lately had written him of leaving the family home and moving to town for a time. Then —

> Like him, I am about to leave the surroundings in which I have spent twenty-six happy years and move into a strange place and an unfamiliar atmosphere. That is to say, I have accepted the invitation of President Harding to become Secretary of Agriculture.
>
> It has long been a tradition of our family not to seek politi cal office. Not that we consider the seeking or holding of a public office as discreditable or unpraiseworthy; quite the contrary. But in our case the opportunity for service seemed larger outside than in it. In becoming the head of the United States Department of Agriculture I do not feel that I am breaking this tradition. I did not seek the office directly or indirectly, as a large number of my friends who have wanted to help me to it will testify.

Gifford Pinchot, who was visiting the Wallaces in Des Moines when the Harding offer reached them, is among the closest of witnesses to that. In a preface, entitled *Appreciation*, to Harry Wallace's first and only book, *Our Debt and Duty to the Farmer*,[19] 1925, Pinchot wrote: 'He was extremely reluctant to accept, but . . . I urged him as strongly as I could to take the place, believing that in so doing lay the line of greatest usefulness. . . . When the new Secretary first went to Washington, I was . . . of some small service to him, because of my knowledge of Washington affairs. After he was warm in his seat, he was wholly master of his work, and needed to call on no man for assistance . . . completely fearless . . . he utterly despised the corruption that sprang

up in Washington during his service there, and had the courage to
let his contempt for it be known.'

Concluding his editorial of farewell, Harry Wallace expressed
both doubt and resolution:

> I go to Washington with less reluctance because from the
> beginning President Harding has taken an advanced stand
> for a sound national policy as it relates to agriculture, and I
> am sure he will do everything the Chief Executive can do to
> promote that end. Therefore he has a right to the help of
> every one of us as we can help best.
>
> As to *Wallaces' Farmer* . . . this will make no difference in
> the paper. . . . My absence will impose an additional burden
> and a real sacrifice upon my brother, John P. Wallace, to
> give the business of the paper more confining attention for a
> while at least. But it is a burden he is fully capable of bear-
> ing and a sacrifice which he makes willingly.
>
> So far as the editorial conduct of the paper is concerned, the
> responsibility will rest upon my son, Henry A. Wallace. He
> has been in the editorial work for ten years, and has been
> doing more of it than is generally realized. That he is fully
> equal to this larger responsibility our readers will discover for
> themselves. . . .
>
> I wish it were possible for me to acknowledge personally the
> many expressions of confidence and good will that have come
> to me from all parts of the country. . . . As for my work in
> the Department, that must speak for itself. . . . I will do the
> best I know. If I fall short of what it is fair to expect of me,
> the failure must be charged not to lack of an earnest desire,
> but to my own personal limitations.
>
> HENRY C. WALLACE

Among the telegrams of congratulation was a pleasant one from
Herbert Hoover, jocosely remarking that *now* Wallace, too, would
be at the receiving end of a brick and dead-cat barrage. He
expressed the hope that they would enjoy working together. Mr.
Hoover had, of course, just become Secretary Hoover of the Department of Commerce and he had some farm relief plans of
his own.

Secretary Wallace moved his wife and daughter to Washington, renting an apartment at the Mayflower Hotel, and took over from Secretary Meredith on March 4, 1921. One of his first official acts was to recall Dr. W. J. Spillman, banished to farm paper writing in Philadelphia by Secretary Houston, and create for Spillman a special post under their mutual friend, Dr. H. C. Taylor, in the Bureau of Markets and Crop Estimates. An intimate of the Wallace family since the nineties, Dr. Taylor had come into the Department from the University of Wisconsin in 1919. A bold believer in putting out facts and figures that would help farmers adjust production downward, as well as upward, in pursuit of better profits, Taylor did not go as far as Spillman or, indeed, the new Secretary were thinking, at the time. Harry Wallace was about persuaded that some counterpoise such as the Peek-Johnson ratio-price plan, which later was written into a succession of McNary-Haugen bills, must be enacted to the end of obtaining for agriculture, through subsidized exports, tariff-equivalent benefits. Spillman was beginning to conceive of far more elaborate devices, designed to induce a harvest balanced to paying demand. This planning developed years later into the Triple-A (Agricultural Adjustment Administration) approach to 'parity prices.'

The first Secretary Wallace took office about eight months after American agriculture had entered quite definitely upon a sharp and most damaging depression. A total farm income which ran between six and seven billion dollars a year during the prewar years 1910–14 and stepped up to around nine, twelve, and fifteen billion dollars, successively, in the war years, 1916, 1917, and 1918, came to a peak of nearly seventeen billion dollars in 1919. The 1919 index of prices paid to producers stood at 250.5, around two and a half times prewar. The break came sharply during the Harding-Cox campaign, with the July 1920 index ten points under the June index, the August index 15 points below July, and the September index 15 points below August. The 1920 index as a whole stood at 200.5, twice prewar. Toward the end of the year there was a short flurry of industrial price declines, with an extraordinarily quick recovery. The pinch delivered to agriculture came abruptly from the relative rigidity of industrial prices, wages, taxes, and practically all of the costs of farming. The pinch of disparity prices was sharpened by a decreed and managed deflation of credit, agricultural credit in particular. Between October of 1919 and December of 1920 the average rate of rediscount at the twelve Federal Reserve banks was stepped up successively from 4.19 per cent to 6.48 per cent, and at Kansas City to 7.41 per cent. At the same time the general economy was stimulated by the floating of a Victory Loan. The diminished issuance of bank credit which resulted from these maneuvers was much more marked in the agricultural West and South than in more industrial areas. In the agricultural Northwest little banks started popping, bankruptcies and forced sales multiplied, and this wave of distress was just beginning to reach into Iowa and approach the Midland in general when Harry Wallace became Secretary of Agriculture.[20]

Toward May of 1921, with the purchasing power of the farm dollar down to seventy-eight per cent of its prewar value, Wallace renewed with some insistence a suggestion he had made to Harding during the campaign: That the President call a National Farm Conference, with still-comfortable Eastern conservatives facing distressed, roaring Westerners, to examine conditions and suggest action. Hoover was against it. Mellon was against it. Harding demurred. Ask him some other time, he said. He was by nature a man inclined to wait things out, or put things off, or overlook them; and it honestly distressed him to take any action that aroused active disharmony in his Cabinet.

Here was surely one of the most mixed, inharmonious official families ever to sit around the same table: austere Hughes in the chair of State; Mellon of the Treasury, cold and timid but determined and inscrutable; blustering Denby of the Navy; Weeks of War. Then, as Attorney-General, the unspeakable Daugherty of Ohio; as Secretary of the Interior, sly, corrupt Fall; for Labor, honest 'Puddler' Jim Davis, of Pennsylvania; for Agriculture, Wallace; for Commerce, Hoover. What a collection!

Hughes, Mellon, Hoover, and Wallace were, in their various ways, lone wolves of the Harding inner circle. They stood head and heart above the extracurricular games and goings-on of the gang at the little house on K Street. Hughes and Wallace were quietly compatible. They saw a great deal of each other, by choice, of evenings, apart from formal social occasions. Wallace's conversations or conferences with Mellon, outside of Cabinet meetings, were strictly businesslike. There was the matter, for instance, of Land Bank credits. These twelve regional banks, set up in the Wilson administration, had been given by law five million dollars to initiate rural credit in each district, with the idea that this, together with private credit, would increase credit tenfold — fifty millions in each district, six hundred millions in the country as a whole. A ruling by Mellon, the incoming Secretary of the Treasury, had, as Wallace saw it, hamstrung these provisions so as to allow a base loan of only one million dollars in each district, with a probable expansion of only one hundred and twenty millions the country over. Respectfully but persistently, he protested against this to Mellon, with some effect.

On the Hill, Wallace put his influence steadily behind an act, passed in 1923, to establish twelve Federal Intermediate Credit Banks. These banks were planned to increase short-term credit by rediscounting agricultural paper maturing within three years. With a proper degree of indirection (for an Executive office, short of the President, is not supposed to suggest or to initiate legislation, unless called upon by the Congress to do so), Wallace pushed vigorously for new laws governing dealing in grain futures, packer and stockyard regulation, and federal warehousing, all of which measures he had advocated and worked for previously as a private citizen and farm organization man.

But soon he was forced to see that all such patchwork reforms, entered upon the law books and counted triumphantly as agrarian victories, did not get at the heart of the farm trouble. The scrap heap of agricultural hope and property grew higher as each month passed. George Norris stood far more free than Wallace was free to state the case bluntly at the time. Norris had just come by right of seniority to the chairmanship of the powerfully strategic Agricultural Committee. Credit makeshifts which provide no market for the additional goods they help bring into being are worse than useless, Norris held; they simply invite the farmers already half-broke to go broke the whole way faster: 'In time their interest would only eat up all the substance,' he said. A lonely fighter, never happy under the wraps of party lines, Norris was intensely indignant when the new Republican Congress, the Sixty-Seventh, passed in a rush the Fordney Emergency Tariff, which Wilson had vetoed. He said it was a plain case of forcing an already distressed element in the population, the farmer, to pay to industry an additional levy or subsidy.

The Farm Bloc now had about twenty members that its leaders thought they could count on, centering around Senator Kenyon of Iowa. The members met often of evenings to lay their plans. On the floor of the Senate, George H. Moses, that caustic Old Guardsman from New Hampshire, described the Farm Bloc as a combination of twenty lawyers, one editor, and one well-digger. Pat Harrison of Mississippi retorted hotly that Moses spoke for a much older bloc — 'the manufacturers' bloc . . . better oiled and more greedy.' Southern and Western 'sons of the wild jackass' were beginning to get together.

No one who had observed the somewhat socialized functioning of Hoover's Food Administration in wartime could have failed to be impressed by the doubtless enormous savings that were made through large-scale elimination of competitive duplication of function. The Government became, in many instances, the one middleman. Purchases and deliveries made in single sweeps and enormous quantity must, it stands to reason, have vastly reduced unit costs of distribution. Guarded reference is made to this in Food Administration reports; and the total figures are all there, in bulk, set down to the last decimal point. But they are so arrayed that, while complete, it is extremely difficult if not impossible to derive from the great mass of data compact and telling evidence as to the comparative wastes of the alternative system of normalcy or free enterprise.

Senator George Norris did not like or trust Hoover any more than Secretary Wallace did. The Farm Bloc became, indeed, in the years that Norris was most active in its battles, almost solidly an anti-Hoover bloc.

Norris's own first farm relief bill, hastily drawn and introduced also by Representative Sinclair in the House, amounted, nevertheless, in many particulars, to a proposal for re-establishing a Food Administration. It proposed to set up a federal farm financing corporation, a gigantic public middleman, working without profit.

This corporation would be empowered to buy up surplus agricultural products, ship them abroad on idle ships of the United States Shipping Board, and arrange for sales abroad. It aimed further, domestically, to promote producers' and consumers' co-operatives, to socialize the ownership and operation of elevators and storage warehouses, and to reduce by such consolidations and short cuts the costs of distribution, passing the savings along, forward and backward, to both consumers and farmers. When it was pointed out that railway rates would still exact high levy from producer and consumer, Norris replied that he was perfectly willing to re-socialize railroads too. All this veered considerably to the left of what Harry Wallace and his advisers believed or wanted. They let Norris and the bloc advance the measure pretty much alone.

The Norris Export Bill provided that the corporation, with a hundred million dollars' capital stock and power to issue five hundred millions in bonds, would be limited to a five-year life after which private enterprise might be given a chance again. Hoover, who had sent word obliquely that certain of the aspects of this public corporation plan seemed sound, but that he could not speak openly for fear of embarrassing President Harding, testified mildly against the bill at the Agricultural Committee hearing. 'I hesitate greatly at the Government going into any more business,' he said.

The fight came in the July heat of 1921, before air-conditioning. Lodge of Massachusetts moved for a recess. The bloc blocked it. Debate began. The imperturbable Vice-President, Calvin Coolidge, presiding, quietly encouraged the agrarians to believe that on the crucial day of debate one of their men would be recognized to speak first, then slyly evaded his promise by staying away that day and letting Charlie Curtis of Kansas preside. Curtis walked to the chair, thumped the gavel, and called recognition to Senator Kellogg, of Minnesota, who brought in an administration substitute measure. It was a simple measure, authorizing the War Finance Corporation, under Eugene Meyer, to advance one and a half billion dollars to banks and trust companies so that farmers might borrow still more money to ride along on until farm prices picked up.

Norris spoke. He said that the whole thing was a 'conspiracy' on the part of Meyer, of Hoover, and of Mellon — with 'a halo of regularity around it' — elaborately rigged by 'somebody higher up.' A tired man, warm, tense, and angry, with too many fights on his hands at once, he continued this fight for two days longer. 'Keep Government out of Business?' he said. 'The Government is all right in business when it will take a risk for financial men that they are not willing to take themselves. The Government is all right in business if the middleman and the banker and the trust company can get their rake-off. Then it's all right. Then it's a virtue. If they're eliminated, it's a crime, it's foolish, it's reactionary, it's populistic, it's dishonorable, it's unpatriotic! . . .

'It's all wrong if the farmer gets into it! Then it's a crime! Then it's bad governmental policy!' [21]

He stood breathing heavily and then, asking the Senate's indulgence for not being able to speak further, he collapsed and was carried into a near-by committee room, exhausted. The Congress passed a substitute measure and adjourned. The President sent word that he thought the country needed a rest.

5. Getting Warm in the Chair

BY THE END OF 1921 Secretary Wallace was, to adapt Gifford Pinchot's phrase, not only warm in the chair, but getting warmer. Under his firm and quiet hand the Department was humming along evenly in its thousands of somewhat sequestered ways of applied physical research. In the more aggressive line of applied economics Harry Wallace's presence and encouragement gave the more unorthodox economists, such as H. C. Taylor, W. J. Spillman, Charles Brand, M. L. Wilson, and younger men, such as Mordecai Ezekiel and Howard Tolley, a constant stimulus. There were fights and feuds, to be sure, simmering and popping, in this outwardly placid atmosphere of research and the peaceful extension of scientific teaching. There always have been, and there always will be fracases, even in the quiet competitions of the college classroom and laboratory. In the larger governmental arms which engage in action and educational programs side by side, inner dissension heightens. Harry Wallace handled warring aides in the same sure, confident manner of Tama Jim Wilson. He went even further than Tama Jim in assigning able men to important chiefships or special assignments, sparking them with ideas to supplement their own, then crediting the whole result, if it came out right, to them; or backing them up, silently and steadily, if it didn't. Men who have been in the Department a long time observed that under most secretaries they often felt that they were ghosting for a passing figurehead as Secretary; whereas, when you worked under H. C. Wallace he was up there in the front office, from eight in the morning until six in the evening, coolly taking the heat of blasts from the White House, the Capitol, and elsewhere, absorbing the blame with neither haste nor worry, passing the credit to subordinates — ghosting for them.

Blasts from without help a good deal to hold a department or any large organization together. Interdepartmental raids and rivalries are unquestionably deplorable in many particulars; but it does cut down on interbureau rivalries and internecine jealousies within a department of the Government when another department tries to make a raid on the whole works. I do not think that this is peculiar to governmental bureaucracies. The same thing can happen, for instance, in a big magazine publishing corporation, between the various contending elements therein — editorial, advertising, promotion — the same inner stiffening, shoulder to shoulder, when any other big concern sets out to raid or decimate their business. Insurance, railroading, merchandising, publishing, big business in general has its own private bureaucracies, its own power-hungry bureaucrats contending. Conversely, American governmental bureaucrats are simply Americans. They are people operating in a competitive society, engaged in making a living and a reputation in the business of government, motivated by much the same mixture of impulses to seek power and consequence and to give unselfish service that animate the generality of private enterprisers. It is really astonishing that those who hymn most loudly the stimulating effect of competition, tooth and fang, should express so violent a sense of woe and outrage when the enlivening effects of the same spirit become manifest among those who make government part or all the business of their lives.

Two major raids on the Department of Agriculture's bureaus

and functions were taking form even as the members of the new Harding Cabinet sat down for the first time together around the table with that all too amiable man, already confused and afraid, in the President's chair. The principal functions which two or more of Wallace's fellow Secretaries set out at once to take away from him, if they could, were, it happened, the parts of the job that were closest to his heart: (1) the conservation of natural resources, and (2) agricultural marketing.

Uncle Henry Wallace, surveying in his time the waste and decimation of farm land and forest, of streams and wildlife, of oil and minerals, used to speak sadly of 'the voiceless land.' In him, in Gifford Pinchot, in Harry Slattery, and other younger men of Theodore Roosevelt's following, including Harry Wallace, the plundered land found voices of defense. They coined or adapted the word 'conservation' to express their purpose, and practically everything that they did together at that time centered around the fighting standards of Gifford Pinchot's Forest Service.

The rights and wrongs of the controversy which has simmered between the Departments of Agriculture and the Interior for the past forty years and come to an open embroilment at least once in every successive administration are still much in dispute. An entire book has been published relatively recently by that redoubtable Secretary of the Interior, Harold Ickes, to show that the suspicion of corruption which attended the transfer of the Bureau (then a Division) from Interior to Agriculture in 1905 was unwarranted; that the move was simply an outcome of clashing personalities, with T. R. favoring the Pinchot men because he was fond of Pinchot. It has been a long dispute, definitely helpful at first, in that it sharply aired important differences in approach to land use and exposed a scoundrel here and there; but as it goes on repetitiously, from administration to administration and from generation to generation, it becomes more and more a waste of time and energy which might really be better devoted unitedly to the cause both sides profess, conservation.

Certain facts are not in dispute. In 1891 forest 'reservations' were first set aside by the Federal Government. In 1897, when the first federal laws were passed for the administration of forest 'reserves,' it was ordained that these laws be administered in the

Department of the Interior. In 1905, when President Theodore Roosevelt named Gifford Pinchot, a graduate of Yale in 1889 who had studied forestry methods abroad until 1900, as the first Chief Forester of the United States, the small new division was placed under Secretary Tama Jim Wilson in the Department of Agriculture, and was made a full Bureau in 1907, when Pinchot rechristened his forest reserves 'National Forests.' The administration of the National Parks and of Indian Reservations remained functions of the Department of the Interior, then as now.

Harry Slattery, one of Pinchot's foresters when there were only eighteen men in the whole new service, became Secretary of the National Conservation Association, a Pinchot offshoot, set up independently to probe waste, promote basic national savings, and perform a little helpful lobbying if need be. Slattery dug up what he conceived to be plain evidence of a plot to steal from the people government coal and timberlands and water-power sites in Alaska. Pinchot, in Agriculture, originated attacks on Secretary of the Interior Richard A. Ballinger. This soon brought on a joint investigation of the Interior Department and the Forest Service in Congress. In the hearings Louis D. Brandeis, of Boston, retained by *Collier's*, presented the case against Ballinger and came into national prominence for the first time. Norris took an active part in the hearings. In 1910 Taft dismissed Pinchot. The Congress took no action on the evidence that had been presented against Secretary Ballinger, but Ballinger resigned.

That was in 1910. Now it was 1922. Pinchot was Commissioner of Forestry in Pennsylvania, prior to becoming Governor of that state in 1923. Slattery, still Secretary of the National Conservation Association, still pursuing lines of inquiry which had opened with the Ballinger persecution, discovered that oil reserves on public land which had been transferred to the Navy, under Secretary Daniels in the Wilson administration, had now been secretly transferred from the Navy to the Interior. Secretary Fall wrote the order of transfer with Secretary Denby's assistance, and President Harding signed it.

Denby as a Congressman had been denounced by T. R. himself for attempts to shield or whitewash Ballinger. Then there was Harry Daugherty of Ohio, with Standard Oil connections, also one

of the Cabinet now, Attorney General. He seemed to be in on this
friendly inner arrangement. Distinctly, to a T. R. Progressive,
all this smelled of plunder.[22]

The antecedent record of Mr. Fall, this new Secretary of the
Interior, as a guardian or conservator of natural resources, was un-
reassuring, to say the least. As a Senator from New Mexico,
from 1916 onward, he had opposed conservation measures. As a
New Mexico rancher and attorney he had openly declared war on
the United States Forest Service as early as 1910. The Service
has still in its files a handwritten letter from Fall.[23] Their rangers
and supervisors found that he was running too many sheep on the
Alamo (later the Lincoln) National Forest. By the fraudulent
device of entering two thousand of his sheep under name of a son
and another two thousand under name of a herder in his employ,
Fall planned to graze — or overgraze — four thousand more sheep
than his proper share on the national domain. The letter from the
Forest Service served official notice that this would not be tolerated. Replying on the letterhead of his Tres Ritos Ranch, Fall
wrote that the Forest Service would 'rue the day' and promised
'punishment.'

Barely two months after he became Secretary of the Interior in
March of 1921, Fall had drawn up for the President's signature an
Executive Order, transferring the Forest Service to the Department of the Interior. Secretary Harry Wallace told President
Harding that it could not be done. Slattery, meantime, had started
investigating the transfer of the oil leases to the Navy. He kept in
touch with Secretary Wallace. At a public meeting held at the
Ebbitt House on March 10, 1922, Slattery spoke in outright attack
both of the transferred oil leases and the contemplated transfer of
the Forest Service. Wallace did not attend the meeting, but he
sent a stenographer to take down Slattery's speech for the record
and then took the record to Harding. The President tried to
evade a decision. Fall stood pat. Asked in a press conference if
he cared to reply to Slattery, 'I won't answer Pinchot's and
Wallace's stooge,' said Secretary Fall. Harding took refuge in a
compromise, backing Fall in the transfer of the oil leases, but deny-
ing him command of the Forest Service, at least for the while.

Fall pressed for victory on both counts. The question came up in Cabinet meeting. 'A row ensued' that almost 'blew the roof off,' Wallace confided to Senator Norris.[24]   Wallace was a rare and close confider. He never, for instance, told his son, Henry A., anything about the inner details of this conflict. The facts on what he said at that Cabinet meeting when he almost blew the roof off have been slow to gather into the whole story. But, piecing together what one associate knew for certain with that of another, together with Harry Slattery's gathered testimony of the entire uproar, it finally appears quite definitely that Harry Wallace coolly dropped a bomb into the President's lap as he sat there at the head of the Cabinet table with his official family gathered around.

Secretary Wallace told them that if the Forest Service were transferred, he, Wallace, would resign from the Cabinet, call public mass meetings at places such as Omaha, Chicago, and Kansas City, and put the case against Fall and his colleagues — forests, oil, and everything — before the whole country.

That quieted for a while the situation as to the Forest Service; but the agitation as to the oil grab was getting out into the open now, and ever warmer. Slattery, having heard of the 'plot' through a clerk in the Navy Department, had told Senator Norris and Senator Robert La Follette about it. They urged Slattery to keep digging into it, and he did so gladly. 'The times were tense,' he remarked with reminiscent pleasure years later, speaking at a conservation testimonial dinner given in his honor in Washington.[25] 'When we conservationists started to question his activities, Mr. Fall decided he would use some rough tactics. He had a two-gun man named Baracca who had passed several men over the Great Divide. Mr. Fall sent him around to see me, with a threat. I kicked that gentleman out of my office.'

At the same commemorative dinner, June 25, 1932, Senator Robert La Follette, Jr., said: 'It was Harry Slattery who first called attention of the transfer of the Naval oil reserves to my father. And in order that it may be on the record being made here tonight, I wish to read a letter which my father wrote to Admiral Griffin and to Josephus Daniels, dated April 19, 1922, in which he says: " I will regard it as a favor if you will talk as freely to Mr. Slattery as you would to me, were I able to see you. . . . I do not intend to see these Naval reserves despoiled for the benefit of private individuals and corporations without a vigorous protest being made on the floor of the Senate."'

And Slattery, on the same occasion, describing the Senate fight on this issue, spoke of the elder La Follette in terms reviving the zealotry and ardor of the earlier Progressives: 'He would lie down at times with a great military cloak around him, like a general on the field of battle, prepared to renew the fight that was being carried on in the Senate. . . . "We will win this fight tomorrow, or eventually we will win it," he said.'

Once the oil deal had been thrust by investigation into public notice, Harry Wallace did not worry as much about it as he had before. He was not one to talk much, either in meeting or out of it; he wanted to help and save his President; and he did win Harding's confidence in the hard, straight way, to a rare degree. The Naval oil scandal, Wallace observed drily, in an unsigned dispatch to *Wallaces' Farmer* some months after Harding's death, was only one phase of Secretary Fall's drive on conservation policies. More immediate in Wallace's mind, even then, was the unrelenting drive of that unsavory inner cabal — Denby, Daugherty, and Fall — to persuade President Harding to transfer the Forest Service back into the Department of the Interior, where in a sense it had started. Of this drive Wallace wrote: 'There is as yet [February, 1924] no evidence . . . to show that either Denby or Daugherty has been culpable or at fault in any way other than in a possible question of judgment, and that has not been determined. To force the resignation of either of them under the present showing would be to put a stain upon them which could not be removed. . . .'

Secretary Fall had already resigned and was subject to criminal charges and imprisonment. Denby and Daugherty resigned from the Cabinet shortly after. Wallace's Washington dispatch to *Wallaces' Farmer* continued: '. . . So far as Fall is concerned the case looks very bad. Whether guilty or not, he did not have very high ideals of conserving interest in the great natural resources. For two years he tried to have the National Forests transferred from the Department of Agriculture to his department, and was bitterly fought by Secretary Wallace, although little concerning the struggle appeared in the papers. Wallace finally won, although for a time the issue semed doubtful.' [26]

VIII

REAPING THE WHIRLWIND

The sufferer from sciatica or similar disease may secure temporary relief from paroxysms of pain by hot fomentations and may lessen the frequency of acute attacks by medicines which stimulate the organs of elimination and have a quieting effect on the nerves. He gets no permanent relief, however, until the cause is discovered and removed.

The farmer may find some relief by cutting down expenditures, by reducing production and marketing costs, and by readjusting production, but until farm prices rise to a fair ratio with prices of other things, correcting the present disparity, agriculture will continue to suffer economic injustice. — Secretary HENRY C. WALLACE, *Our Debt and Duty to the Farmer*, written in 1924.

Farmers' feelings had been deeply stirred when certain of their prices fell in 1921 to one-fifth of what they had been in 1920. To reach the land of social justice they constructed an ingenious craft of strange appearance, christened 'McNary-Haugen,' which was sunk in 1928 under the plea that it was a pirate ship.

These farmers who started building price boats after the price smash were of many kinds. Older farmers who had lived during the farm agitations of the eighties and nineties were familiar with the doctrines of populism, free silver and greenbacks. But the old-time correctives did not meet the situation. Bimetallism, trust-busting, railroad baiting, were beside the point. — Secretary HENRY A. WALLACE, in *New Frontiers*, written in 1934.

1. Ingenious Crafts

GEORGE NELSON PEEK was not brilliant. But he was a good, smart man in a fight; a hard man to push over, as they say in the West. An industrial agrarian of magnificent stubbornness and simplicity, he plowed just one furrow — 'Equality for Agriculture' — and plowed it straight. 'When I was a boy on a farm in Illinois,' he said in one of his countless speeches on Farm Relief, 'my family moved from one farm and later from a second one because we could not make the grade. I said to myself at the age of eighteen that I would not count on farming for a living, but go to town, make my money there, then come back and live in the country the way I wanted to live.

'That is what I was doing in 1920 when the rest of the country started putting the screws on agriculture again. Then I got mad and came out of my hole to fight.'

Born in 1873, George Peek found that one year at Northwestern University was all of college that he wanted. By the turn of the century he was well along toward making a fortune in the farm implement trade. During the First World War he was Commissioner of Finished Products on Bernard Baruch's War Industries Board. At the close of the war he became president and general manager of the Moline Plow Company in Illinois, with Hugh H. Johnson, another Baruch man, as his general counsel and assistant manager. Their offices were in the small city of Moline. There, in the course of a conversation over sales charts, Peek put into a nine-word sentence the common-sense refrain he was later to use so often in his long fight for parity prices: 'You can't sell a plow to a busted customer,' he said.

Of Scotch-Irish breeding, born in Oklahoma, Johnson was a West Pointer who did not go on with the military in peacetime, but took it up again and rose from second lieutenant to a brigadier in wartime. He helped Peek draw up the first forceful pamphlet stating the case of 'Equality for Agriculture.' The largest part of it was an illustrated chart showing how many bushels of wheat it took to buy a plow prewar, and what an awful pile of high-cost wheat it took for a farmer to do business with a plow company after the fall of prices paid farmers after 1920.

The Peek-Johnson idea was to restore the purchasing power of farm commodities to a prewar level by segregating exports from domestic supplies and dumping the exports at a surplus-disposal price abroad. This was essentially the plan soon to be brought forward as the McNary-Haugen plan.

Such sales tactics were not unknown in industry. Peek and Johnson, as manufacturers of farm machinery, can be assumed to have heard of 'dumping,' a device disposing of a price-depressing surplus at a lower price in foreign countries so as to sustain domestic prices of the same plow, car, or whatnot at a desired level here. They did not see why the same idea would not work for crops. Admittedly the administration of such a plan, involving the output of millions of different farms, was far more difficult and elaborate than a stroke of sales policy quietly arrived at around a board of directors table and put into effect by a firm or firms. The farmers, Peek and Johnson argued as their plan developed, must be given the centralizing power of the Federal Government to put this plan into motion. But it need not cost the Treasury anything, once the plan was operating; for the farmers with domestic prices so sustained could afford to split between themselves the loss taken on their dumped exports, by payment of an 'equalization fee.'

Peek and Johnson issued their first pamphlet in 1921, unsigned. They addressed it as an open letter to James R. Howard, of Iowa, President of the American Farm Bureau Federation. Iowa and the middle country were by no means wholly ready for the idea then; but many farmers were ready for it; and they began holding mass meetings, talking 'Equality' or 'fair ratio' prices, especially in the acutely distressed Northwest. Within a few weeks the industrial authors of the pamphlet published a second edition, signed, and Peek became the leader of a seven-year drive. Writing as editor of *Wallaces' Farmer*, Henry A. Wallace declared for the fair-ratio idea, and said that the plan should be tried.

Henry C.'s name still appeared on the masthead of the magazine, ranked equally with that of Henry A. as 'Editors,' but with this note immediately under: *Beginning March 4, 1921, and continuing as long as he is in public service, Henry C. Wallace is relieved from responsibilities with the conduct of Wallaces' Farmer.* This, as the Wallaces saw it, left the younger Henry free to write and print what he felt or pleased about the administration of which his father was a part; and he did so with an increasing vigor. He dissected and disapproved of Harding's first favorite among postwar measures, the Ship Subsidy bill; he tore into the Fordney tariff; and he was at times disrespectful to the pronouncements of Herbert Hoover, Eugene Meyer, and Julius Barnes. *Wallaces' Farmer* became more closely read in Washington at this period than at any time before or since. Secretary Hoover, in particular, was known not only to read it often, but to clip it, and brood over the clippings, and complain. On one such occasion President Harding detained Secretary Wallace after Cabinet meeting and showed him a clipped editorial on the tariff, asking smilingly, 'Are you for me or ag'in me?' The Secretary, who was trying hard at that time to win the President's consent for a Farm Relief Conference, explained that he had no editorial responsibilities for the paper, at the moment; and the President accepted the explanation in all good nature. But Secretary Wallace made the one admonitory suggestion that he ever advanced to his son, as editor, from Washington. 'Have a heart,' he said.

For the while, young Henry withheld his strictures; but he kept advancing in his editorial columns strange new ideas that conventional people found disturbing. He produced a fairly complete plan for governmental crop insurance against the hazards of the weather, and in further articles enlarged on ways for an 'ever-normal granary' according to 'the Joseph plan.' [1]

As far back as 1912 he had written: 'Every year somebody must play the part of Joseph in carrying the crop. The farmer can hold his grain, if he is prepared for it, with the loss only of rattage (which he can soon reduce to a minimum at small expense) and the use of the money, or the interest, and insurance on the grain while in storage. We shall come to this by and by, and the farmers will be prepared to play Joseph by simply holding their grain and refusing to sell on a market glutted with wheat from the great grain-growing sections, which must be threshed out of the shock and sold at once.' [2] Grain trade and general business statisticians rushed into print to reply, in general, that this was a wild suggestion, sadly like the emotionalized 'hog-holding' agitations which were part of the Granger rebellion. Steadily, over a decade, Wallace's editorials argued for withholding, for farm storage and state storage, producing figures to show that it generally paid. Then in 1920, while browsing through the Des Moines Public Library, Henry A. came upon a book, *Economic Principles of Confucius*, written as a thesis by a Chinese graduate student at Columbia University, Chen Huan-Chang. Chapter 30 described the workings of a 'constantly normal granary' which had operated with general success to moderate the alternations between glut and famine in China two thousand years ago. Wallace changed the term to 'Ever-Normal Granary' and started plugging editorially for an American adaptation of the idea.[3]

In 1921 *Wallaces' Farmer* started a corn acreage reduction campaign week under the slogan of 'Less corn, more clover, more money.' This campaign, which aroused a general shocked disapproval, was the opposite of governmental wartime acreage drives — Ringgold County, Iowa, alone, for instance, had run up 'Liberty Acres,' planted to wheat, from 5000 acres to 24,600 acres in a single year. *Wallaces' Farmer* now presented the figures of corn supplies at hand and diminished market prospects and argued hammer and tongs month after month for voluntary acreage reduction. It was an unpopular effort. George Peek, for one, just naturally hated it; and in Washington, too, it was accounted a wrong and sinful idea. But, alone at the editorial controls now, Henry A. kept at it. 'After everything has been taken into account,' he wrote in his issue of September 16, 1921, 'the fact remains that we have far more corn than we need. Corn Belt farmers should plant 8,000,000 fewer acres of corn in 1922 and 8,000,000 more acres of clover to be used chiefly for green manure to restore the fertility which has been wasted during the emergency.' It is really extraordinary when one comes to examine the whole record, how far out in front, alone, Henry A. was more than a decade before the 'New Deal' farm program.

So was his father, in Washington. Outwardly, Harry Wallace appeared to be enjoying his life and work there. He was admirably equipped and trained to be Secretary. It gave him quiet pleasure to feel the economic and marketing arms of the Department, particularly, taking strong new bent and direction under his hand. He had his fights and troubles, of course, in quantity: battles of packer administration, which function he had asked for and in large part taken over from the Federal Trade Commission upon assuming office; endless skirmishing and occasional sharp showdowns with the Fall crowd, who were after his Forest Service; delicate decisions to be made in matters of departmental action on Rio Grande land frauds, in which some wealthy Texans who had been the President's boon companions on a campaign journey there were involved. But Harry Wallace was never a man to let a fight trouble him unduly, as long as he saw a chance of winning it. As for his differences with Secretary Hoover, he felt that he was winning. From the outset Hoover had contended, and before a House Agricultural Committee of the Sixty-Eighth Congress, had bluntly stated, that: 'The Department of Agriculture should tell the farmer what he can best produce based on soil, climatic, and other cultural conditions, and the Department of Commerce should tell him how best to dispose of it.'[4] In a few words, Commerce wanted all of Agriculture's marketing functions, here and abroad.

This view of agriculture was, of course, anathema to Harry Wallace; and he hastened to strengthen the economic fortifications of his Department at every point.

Hoover had come into Commerce as a department almost completely moribund, and had thrown himself with great energy and skill into extending its personnel and programs. The far-flung system of trade or commercial attachés that he developed so quickly the world over served real uses in many instances, and may again. President Harding, like most Protectionists, was exceedingly anxious to expand American exports notwithstanding; so in this matter Hoover had the President's ear.

Like most such conflicts, this one often became a race to the President's ear. Wallace, on the whole a more sociable fellow than Hoover, was somewhat better equipped to get to that eminent receptacle when the President was feeling relaxed and friendly. Wallace played poker or bridge with the President, though never at the little house on K Street; and golfed with him fairly often. He genuinely liked Warren Harding, and was rather sorry for him at the same time. And the President liked Harry Wallace; he called him 'Hank.' Hank told good Scotch jokes, as Uncle Henry had before him. He had a meaty, earthy humor.

Examining the memoirs which certain of Secretary Wallace's aides committed to paper and filed in safe deposit at this period or a little later, it is at first a bit difficult to understand why, in the initial stages of contention with Commerce, Interior, the Treasury, and so on, Wallace and his economists placed such fervent emphasis on the need of a National Agricultural Conference. Another conference? Already the House and Senate had set up a Joint Committee to investigate the ills of agriculture. What could a citizens' group or aggregation of outside experts add to that?

It could do a good deal, as Wallace saw it. It could fasten news attention on the woe of the agricultural West and South, bring to light bold new ideas of tariff amelioration, startle the whole country into considering the seriousness of the farm complaint. Again, this conference, called with permission of the President by the Secretary of Agriculture, and considering the matters of marketing and distribution primarily, would in some measure serve public notice that to improve the marketing of farm-reared necessities at better prices was a function of the farmers' own Department, and not Hoover's. That was the bureaucratic politics of it, as Harding was fully aware.

It was a happy Wallace who on a balmy, almost springlike morning in Christmas week, 1921, hurried in from the golf links to phone his chief aides and economists. At the last hole the President had glanced up from his putt, smiling. 'Go ahead with your Agricultural Conference, Hank,' he said.

The Secretary phoned Pittsburgh, where H. C. Taylor, whom he had just appointed as his Chief of the Bureau of Agricultural Economics, was attending the regular Christmas-week meeting of the American Farm Economic Association. Wallace put Taylor in charge of the Conference program and suggested that he get the ideas of such less orthodox college economists as George Warren, Richard T. Ely, and John R. Commons, who were attending the same Pittsburgh meeting. Taylor returned with plenty of ideas. The dates for a five-day conference were set from January twenty-third through the twenty-seventh, 1922. Invitations were issued to a wide variety of men prominent in agricultural and related industries, and nearly four hundred came.

By the time the agenda had cleared the Secretary's office, from which it had to be cleared from the White House, it became fairly evident that if there were to be any fireworks, it would not be in the open. That was the price of holding any such conference whatsoever; and it had to be paid. But 'practically all of the notes that have been struck in subsequent agricultural policy were sounded in one way or another,' Chester C. Davis wrote, in a Department Yearbook article, 'Agricultural Policy Since the World War,' in 1940.

The Farm Conference was held at the same time as the Disarmament Conference. It was a meeting of rather headstrong and widely differing men. Samuel Gompers was there. So were George Peek* and General Johnson, with their 'fair-ratio' price plan. Henry A. Wallace was there. As Secretary of the Corn Belt Meat Producers Association he had written a forceful speech against the Fordney tariff for A. Sykes, the Association's president, to deliver. He showed the speech to his father, the Secretary. It wouldn't do; the President didn't want any mention of tariffs at this conference, the older Wallace told the younger, reluctantly; and a couple of professional ghosts in the Bureau of Agricultural Economics set out at once quite eagerly to prepare a more suitable declaration for Mr. Sykes.

The conference opened with a general session, addressed by the President and then the Secretary. The President said, rather too soothingly to suit the general temper of the conference, that self-help was the answer to the farm difficulty: 'This conference would do the most lasting good if it would find ways to impress the great mass of farmers to avail themselves of the best methods. . . . In the last analysis, legislation can do little more than give the farmer the chance to organize and help himself.' That was precisely the Hoover attitude at the time.

In the twelve section meetings which followed, most of the discussion was off the record and much of it was hot. The transcript of a preliminary huddle of representatives of Northwestern agriculture and business which has been preserved by Dan A. Wallace, brother of the Secretary and uncle of Henry A., gives, doubtless, a fair representation of the sort of alternation between rather wild and extremely soothing suggestions that went on behind closed doors. This parley was held in the Secretary's office. The soothing element included, almost without exception, the Land Grant College deans and extension directors of that area. And some of the sharpest cries of pain and anger came, not from farmers, but from business men of Saint Paul and Minneapolis. General business had begun to suffer audibly from the farm débâcle out that way.

For all the timidities which hedged the discussion and smothered the pronounced complaints, it was an historic occasion, of its kind.

Going back in his mind through the changes which led him at length to get out of the Republican Party, Henry A. believes that the process of change started quite definitely that week early in 1922. If a man could not be an insurgent against high tariffs; if, even as a member of the President's official family, his Secretary of Agriculture could not obtain an open hearing for such insurgents, thirty-three-year-old Henry Wallace decided that old-time Republicanism had become too hidebound for any good use.

He felt, however, that the great range and turbulence of warring plans and emotions which the Harding conference exhibited inwardly were helpful, forcing men of widely different prejudices to look at facts more closely, and to consider what fetishes must be given up or composed to achieve a general gain. Writing years afterward: 'As I look back,' he said, 'I realize that conference was conducted by men who were strongly imbued with the old pioneer spirit. They were rugged individualists, and proud of it. In the main, they had a right to be. Yet here they were, appealing for collective, rather than individual action. They found themselves up against a situation unlike any the pioneers, with their self-sufficient economy, had ever faced. They saw business and industry, though boasting of individualism, profiting by shrewd use of a delegated governmental power — federal subsidies in the way of tariffs, State and local franchises of one sort or another — largely at the expense of the rest of the population. In such a situation, what could one man or one farm do to protect his rights? . . . The George Peeks, the Frank Murphys, the Bill Hirths, the John Simpsons wanted — quite unwittingly — to modify the farmer's rugged individualism for his own good. They didn't think of it that way, of course; but that is what any move to use the centralizing power of government amounts to. It was a new use for the pioneer spirit, and it could appeal only to those whose feeling of social injustice was strong enough to dominate their traditional individualism.

'Out of this 1922 conference came thirty-seven legislative recommendations; but there was not, as my father had hoped, any very definite and fundamental program of farm relief. One of the recommendations, however, looked a long way ahead, for it directed Congress and the President to "take steps immediately to

re-establish a fair exchange value for all farm products with that
of other commodities. . . ."

'I have known few men so determined and so little deterred by
setbacks as George Peek in his long battle for the farmer. . . . At
the 1922 conference he was his customary battling self.' [5]

And Peek did not go home. This was really the most important
point about that Harding conference in terms of an historic continuity. George Peek grumbled that that big, sedate affair had
not been *his* idea of a real conference. He grinned a little and set
his jaw, and said he was mighty comfortable in that big suite of
his at the Shoreham, and stayed on. With his Baruch backing,
his influential friends around town from the days of his War Industries experience, and the general liking and confidence he inspired
among all who had dealings with him, he kept the heat on, even to
the White House, for a further conference about fair-ratio prices.

In a multigraphed memoir entitled *A Farm Economist in Washington*,[6] *1919–1935*, Dr. Henry C. Taylor relates circumspectly
some of the maneuverings of the weeks following. Peek, whose
method of pressing a point has been described as that of an elephant playing football in slow motion, kept coming to Wallace
and his economists for a decision about this further move toward
Equality for Agriculture. The Secretary had to avoid commitment until he could reach and persuade the President; but he felt
he could do that after the next Cabinet meeting by staying over
for a moment for a quiet word with the Chief. Taylor tells of attending a lobbying dinner Peek was giving — an elegant affair at
which Gray Silver, Washington representative of the American
Farm Bureau Federation, Fred Wells representing the Grain
Trade, and Hugh Johnson were also present: 'After the dessert
the cigars were passed and Silver was asked for his opinion of the
plan for Equality for Agriculture. . . . The Silver Eel left nothing
to be desired in the way of getting off without expressing an opinion . . .'

The Silver Eel; that was what people who did not trust him
called Gray Silver. He was also engaged at the time of this discussion in leading a shift of the Farm Bureau's position from favoring public ownership of Muscle Shoals to turning the whole thing
over to private bidders. The pretense here was to provide cheaper

fertilizer; the real prize was power. 'If I were inclined to be suspicious,' said Senator Norris at a hearing, ironically, 'I would say, "Ford has bought you. You have sold out."'[7] The tug and strain backward and forward of developing circumstances on the avowedly militant but conservative American Farm Bureau Federation was at this period, before the price smash had reached the Middle country in full force, exceedingly severe.

Dr. Taylor continues with the Peek dinner: 'Fred Wells made statements which to me were clearly noncommittal but not without elements which might easily be interpreted by the authors of the plan as hopeful. It then came my time to speak in this round table and Peek asked for my views and asked if I thought the Secretary of Agriculture would call in a group of representative men to consider the plan.'

The next day Wallace secured Harding's consent to the calling of the conference that Peek demanded. It was held in Washington, in the office of the Secretary of Agriculture, in February, 1922. A stenographic record was made of the discussion, but kept secret. The list of those invited by the time it cleared the White House was, quite properly, nicely weighted with those who adhered to Hoover's ultraconservative view. In addition to Peek and Johnson, the President of the American Farm Bureau Federation, James R. Howard, and Silver, his Washington representative, the conferees were Wells from Minneapolis, General Charles G. Dawes from Chicago, Otto Kahn from New York, Judson C. Welliver, representing the President, and Julius Barnes, representing (as the Wallace element wryly put it) Herbert Hoover.

The group exhibited a preponderantly hostile and critical attitude toward the Peek-Johnson proposal. As General Johnson said years later, 'Harry Wallace was the only man at either of those first two price-ratio conferences who would give us as much as a pleasant look.' Otto Kahn was more sympathetic than most of them; he granted that the plan had some merit but he urged that nothing be done for six months or so, in which time things might pick up. Howard and Silver played cagey. Julius Barnes said bluntly that he had his opinion of a Secretary of Agriculture who would take the time of busy men in considering such a plan.

Peek went back to Moline for the time being. Wallace and his

economic aides plugged along for the while, reshaping the system
of Farm Outlook Reports, so that farmers who wished to do so
could study the surplus score and voluntarily reduce acreage.
Young Henry Wallace, out in Des Moines, took a leading part in
the parleys which led to the establishment of these Outlook Reports, and in strengthening the Department's annual Yearbooks
on the economic side. ('With the exception of his son, I was
Secretary Wallace's closest economic adviser,' Dr. Taylor writes
in his memoir of the years 1922–24.) Secretary Wallace's annual
report for that year, 1922, advances markedly a line of argument
and defense which his son was stressing in *Wallaces' Farmer*, and
which he was to stress as a public man, but with a varying emphasis, later. In opposition to the idea that there can be no such
thing as overproduction, the Secretary said: 'There is overproduction, so far as the producer is concerned, whenever the quantity
produced cannot be marketed at a price which will cover all production costs and leave the producer enough to tempt him to
continue production.'

By 1923 hog prices were below prewar, and the Corn Belt began
to feel something of the same savage price-pinch which had laid
hold first in the Northwest wheatlands, notably in Montana. In
Iowa young Henry Wallace tried to persuade the Iowa Farm
Bureau to come out flatly for price-ratio legislation, but its leaders
still were unready to do so. Goaded ever so lightly, it seems, by
the Secretary in Washington, Congressman (later Senator) Dickinson of Iowa, a man easily goaded, went out to his home state and
made some flaming 'equality' speeches to Farm Bureau audiences
which earned him the title of 'the hell-raiser for Agriculture.'

2. Stings and Ire

PRESIDENT HARDING had transferred the oil leases from the
Navy Department to the Department of the Interior some
three months after his inauguration in 1921. It was done by
Executive Order. Outcry in Congress, with Vice-President Coolidge presiding, led the Public Lands Committee to start to probe
the transaction well within a year. With Wallace pressing at

Cabinet meetings for an airing of the leases and a showdown, and with an investigation on the Hill brewing, it is almost inconceivable that the Fall gang should have been so insensitive to the prospect of exposure as to push on with their peculations as they did. The President, it is evident from all accounts of that period, was far less insensitive to fear and apprehension than these men who claimed to have 'made him.' Most of the photographs that were made of Warren Harding from 1922 onward give him the look of a driven and haunted man.

But still he was pressed for more booty. Interior already had the handling of power sites and timber lands, pasturing and oil leases on Indian reservations and Naval reserves, national parks and other public lands, in the United States and in Alaska. The fur resource was another one that they plundered. In 1922 and 1923 Secretary Fall lifted all barriers and restrictions in connection with the killing and trapping on the public lands he controlled, and he was eager for control of the even greater public land holdings managed by the Department of Agriculture's Forest Service.

In March of 1923, with Farm Bloc congressmen notably in the forefront of the investigation and outcry, Secretary Fall resigned. It is certain from what he told his intimates that Secretary Wallace did not realize the full extent of Fall's thievery at the time; and he never went nearly as far in attributing active and proven complicity and guilt to Daugherty and Denby as did Senator Walsh, Senator Norris, and many others then and later.

Secretary Hoover sympathized with Fall, believing, at least at first, that he was an innocent man being framed by stronger, unscrupulous men. When Fall resigned and Harding issued a statement in praise of him, Hoover wrote Fall a public letter saying that the Department of the Interior 'has never had so constructive and legal a headship,' and he expressed the hope that Fall would return to public life 'as there are few men who are able to stand its stings and ire.'

By this time the Secretary of Agriculture was referring brusquely in conversations with his aides to the Secretary of Commerce as 'that man Hoover.' The agricultural economists were especially angered by charts and statements put out by the economists of Commerce to show that farmers were not really badly off now, and that things were getting brighter every day. Their own studies told the agriculturists a different story. The millions of War Finance money poured out in farm credits had only added to the certain bankruptcy of thousands more farmers, as they saw it; and things were not going to pick up for agriculture if nothing else was done. In the early spring of 1923 Secretary Wallace made up his mind to move boldly, even defiantly, against the administration policy of seeking to minimize the farm crisis, seeking simply to sit it out.

As Chief of Agricultural Economics, Dr. Taylor had always taken the position that his bureau should seek and publish facts for the advance of the general welfare and not enter into action programs to affect prices. The Secretary had several times argued with him — 'chided me gently,' Dr. Taylor puts it in his memoir. Now Wallace, still gently, pushed Taylor for action: 'One morning in the spring of 1923 [Taylor recalls] Secretary Wallace sent for me and said, "Suppose the Norris Bill were passed. How much wheat would have to be gotten rid of to put wheat on an import basis and make the protective tariff effective?"'

Taylor brought in the answer in a few days: 'About fifty million bushels.' Wallace did not press him for further action immediately; but he did call in as a more active legislative consultant Charles J. Brand. Brand had gone as a marketing man from the Department to the Pittsburgh office of the aggressive California Fruit Growers Exchange. He had been seeing a great deal of Peek and was convinced of the equity of the fair-ratio proposals. Peek and Wallace, between them, set Brand to thinking in terms of the first McNary-Haugen bill. Wallace recalled him to the Department and sent him to Europe in 1922 as an Agricultural Commissioner to look for market outlets. In May of 1923 when Brand returned from Europe Secretary Wallace told him to consult with Peek, Johnson, and others and actually draft an export-forcing bill for presentation to the Congress. In the same month of May word was given forth that the President and Mrs. Harding, with a party of aides and Cabinet members, would start in June on a long tour of the West and Northwest. This trip was to include a visit to Alaska, farther north than any President had ever been. President Harding was extremely tired, the newspapers reported. By this journey he would be spared the worst of the summer heat of Washington. He would at the same time see the country, meet his countrymen, and lay before them in nineteen scheduled addresses his conception of America's place and future in postwar world affairs.

In the party which left Washington on June 20, 1923, were Secretary and Mrs. Hoover, Brigadier General Sawyer, the president's personal physician, and Mrs. Sawyer; two Presidential secretaries, George R. Christian, Jr., and Judson Welliver; together with a number of other aides and invited guests. Secretary and Mrs. Wallace, it was announced, would join the party at Denver from where Secretary Wallace was inspecting Forest Service operations at the time.

As the train cleared the Cumberland Gap and entered the Middle country correspondents reported that the President already felt more relaxed and free from care. By unremitting toil before departure (*The New York Times* reported solemnly) he had completed the manuscript of twelve of his nineteen major speeches; the other seven had still to be completed; but there would be time for that en route.

Next day, June 21, in Saint Louis, President Harding delivered his World Court speech. He declared for the principle of a World Court, but said it must stand apart from the League of Nations. Even this set Senator Johnson and other resolute isolationists to roaring as the presidential train pushed west.

The President's farm speech at Hutchinson, Kansas, on June 23, was suitably sympathetic and noncommittal; so were the shorter speeches he made extempore from the rear platform or while demonstrating that he could drive a grain binder. Advocates of farm relief in Washington who had hopefully felt that this trip, from Kansas northwestward through the stricken, deflated wheatlands, would impress the President with a fear of farm revolt, were disappointed. There had been some early rains; the country looked good from the car window; and when the party put foot to ground to attend a fair or roundup, the hardy North-westerners were generally so glad and proud to have a President with them that all he heard was booming talk about this 'God's country' and a boundless, buoyant future. This was remarkably true at Helena, Montana's capital, Chester C. Davis remembers wryly. Davis was there to greet the Harding party. He was Commissioner of Agriculture for Montana. The plainsmen put on a great show for the President and the President made a most genial talk, loudly cheered. Yet nearly half of Montana's wheat farmers had lost their lands and homes in the postwar land crash, even then.

One of the speeches that had not been satisfactorily concluded before departure from Washington was a scheduled address on Conservation, set for July 2 at Spokane. With Hoover and Wallace on the same train with the President, after Denver; with representatives of National Park Service pressing for a withhold-ing or 'sanctuary' policy as opposed to Agriculture's contention that conservation means cultivation, sustained yields, wise use, a number of intricate interdepartmental differences were brought to a somewhat more definite solution and much in the way that Wallace wanted. He wrote most of Harding's speech at Spokane; and was able to reassure his anxious foresters that they would not be delivered into the noxious maw of the Interior. Wallace had gained, at least, the President's personal (and anxious) promise to countenance no such dismemberment of the Department of Agri-culture at this time.

The party spent two days in the Yellowstone National Park, relaxing amid the serenity of untroubled nature. Over the Fourth they witnessed pageants and parades of progress at Beecham and Portland, Oregon, and sailed on the transport *Henderson* from Tacoma on July 5. On Sunday, July 8, with bands playing, they landed at Ketchikan, Alaska.

On July 10, Chicago wheat broke to a dollar a bushel. Front-page headlines in the home press during the following week tell of the President getting some rest at last, and having a real outing in far frontier towns, parks, and forests. But at home trouble and contention mounted. *The New York Times* headlines for two days in July read:

July 13, 1923:

REPUBLICANS FEAR
RISING RADICAL TIDE

Conference of Western Leaders Seek Way
To Convince Farmer He Is Prosperous

July 14, 1923:

SCOFFS AT DANGER
OF WHEAT SURPLUS

Eugene Meyer, Jr., Declares Facts Do Not
Justify Forecast of Overproduction

This was in answer to a report by a committee Wallace had appointed to examine the wheat situation. Mr. Meyer spoke as Managing Director of the War Finance Corporation.

On July 16 the news from Alaska was that President Harding had driven a golden spike at the juncture point of a new rail line. On July 17 it was reported that the presidential party had abandoned a contemplated side trip because Mrs. Harding was 'worn out.'

Let it suffice here to compress from headlines the events which led in the days succeeding to what Gaston Means, a convicted liar and felon, described in a 'ghosted' book as *The Strange Death of President Harding*. The following outline is from *The New York Times*, which covered the maze of developments in straight news fashion with none of the extravagant surmises which swept the country by word of mouth and appeared in print then and later:

Back in Seattle on July 27, the President read a scheduled address: HARDING PREDICTS PROSPEROUS ALASKA; STATEHOOD SOON. This was on a Friday. It was expected, a further dispatch said, that five million persons would hear him by radio when he made another address on world affairs in San Francisco the following Tuesday. But over that weekend: HARDING HAS ATTACK OF PTOMAINE POISONING ... Drops Yosemite Trip; Will Go Direct to San Francisco and Rest There Two Days. His illness, Dr. Sawyer announced, was 'not serious.' To stay in bed for a day or so would put the President on his feet.

The party moved on to San Francisco with the President abed. The immediate presidential attendants took suites at the Palace Hotel on July 29. From there it was announced on the thirtieth that Harding 'suffered new symptoms and complications,' and a consultation of physicians led Dr. Sawyer to advance a new diagnosis, acute indigestion affecting the heart. On the thirty-first *The Times* carried a banner headline: 'PRESIDENT HAS PNEUMONIA: CONDITION NOW GRAVE. Mrs. Harding stays by President's Bed.'

Under the San Francisco date line August 1 the crisis was reported passed. The patient had enjoyed a good sleep. He had given out his speech, a defense of his World Court straddle. From Northampton, Massachusetts: 'HARDING WORN OUT, COOLIDGE HOLDS.'

On August 2: 'HARDING GAINS, JESTS, READS PAPERS.'

On August 2 at 7:30 P.M., Pacific Time: 'THE PRESIDENT DIES FROM STROKE OF APOPLEXY.' At 2:47 A.M. Eastern Time, next morning, Calvin Coolidge was sworn in as President by lamplight with his father administering the oath of office at Plymouth, Vermont.

The widely various diagnoses issued during the President's illness and a complete confusion in reports of the exact circumstances of his last moments gave rise to countless rumors. Between August 3 and August 5, for instance, *The Times* reported that Mrs. Harding and two nurses were with her husband, and that she was reading to him when he died; that General Sawyer was also in the room; that the General may not have been in the room, but was just outside the door; and finally, that Mrs. Harding and General Sawyer were both in the room, with no nurses, when President Harding died. Coupled, later, with the Teapot Dome scandal and the like, the manner of his passing gave rise to assertions that he took poison, that his wife and personal physician poisoned him, or that if they did not poison him, they permitted or abetted his death by neglect or malpractice.

But the general opinion of those who were with Harding on his tragic final journey seems to repudiate all such melodramatic guesses.

It is all too safe and easy to accuse the dead. Calvin Coolidge's simple diagnosis of President Harding's illness remains, when all is said, the most plausible: 'Worn out.' The equally stereotyped phrases, 'Worried to death' or even 'Frightened to death,' also make sense. Those who made that trip with Harding, who still live to speak of it or who spoke to persons still living, seem all to have recalled it with pity and horror. He was a truly lovable man, they say, and almost beside himself in the face of anxieties and responsibilities which had grown too much for him. 'God!' exclaimed one aide who was close to him and fond of him, 'that was a lucky death!'

A number of rumors attending the journey to Alaska and its termination touched on the controversy as to conservation policies and the pressure brought to bear by Wallace and his followers upon the President on that score. Certain of these stories still are repeated, although I have found it impossible to trace any of them to source. In the course of writing this book I have been told that Harry Wallace, in forcing a showdown on preserving the Forest Service where and as it was, went so far as to threaten to resign his post and let the presidential party go on to Alaska alone, while he called a mass meeting at Kansas City or Des Moines to lay bare the iniquity of spoilers in the Cabinet. Again, I have been told that by the time the party reached Alaska poor Warren Harding was in such anguish of spirit that he would ask Harry Wallace to come to his rooms at night and pray with him.

Harry Wallace did threaten to resign and tell all, but that was in Cabinet meeting, some months prior to the Alaska journey. If there is any truth to the praying legend, he never breathed a word of it to any member of his family. So we may set that down as symptomatic of the stress of the time and possibly untrue. Having come home after the funeral for a day or so of rest at Des Moines, the Wallaces were plied with questions. Those of the family who talked with them then, and other friends, remember that the Secretary was extremely grieved and depressed. He said that the whole thing had been 'tragic beyond words'; and that was about all he had to say.

It is strange; but never until then in our history had a President
been more popular, probably, than Harding was at the time of his
death. His passing was loudly and lovingly lamented. The death
of a President while transient on a long journey, and the consequent transcontinental trek of the corpse to Washington, then to
Marion, Ohio, took a powerful hold on the public imagination,
and the press responded with the usual burst of emotional obitu-
ary writing that had to be sustained by overwriting for more than
the conventional and proper time. All along the route of the rail
cortège people stood, bearing and strewing flowers in silent tribute,
deeply moved. Parents held children high to see the casket
through the car windows. Souvenir-seekers put pennies on the
track and carried these coins, mashed, as charms or luck pieces, in
token of an historic time. At Chicago the crowd numbered three
hundred thousand. Thirty thousand saw the body as it lay in
state at the Capitol in Washington. Hundreds of thousands of
others saw the procession from the White House to the Capitol,
with stricken Woodrow Wilson hunched down in one of the leading cars. The bands played *Lead, Kindly Light* and *Nearer, My
God, to Thee.* (These had also been William McKinley's favorite
hymns.) The body was at length removed to the soil of Ohio and
entombed in relative privacy at Marion on August 10, 1923.

3. Lone Hand

HARRY WALLACE went back to Washington to take up the
cudgels again. Reviewing the situation and prospect
some years later, Dr. H. C. Taylor summed up thus:

Wallace's counsel was gaining strength with President
Harding, but unfortunately Harding died just at the time
when he was most needed, if effective action for agriculture
was to be secured. A new President came into the White
House. He knew not the land beyond the Alleghanies. New
England agriculture had not suffered. Neither was it politically important. The Coolidge ear was inclined toward the
advisers with whose language he was familiar. Wallace made

little headway in showing him the needs of agriculture. The
effort for effective legislation in the winter of 1923 and 1924
not only failed of the aid which it needed, but suffered from
the opposition of the administration. Thus Wallace's carefully laid plan for educating the business men and the administration, as a basis of effective action, failed because of an
accidental change in the administration. Speculate, if you
like, whether it would have been wise to push harder at an
earlier date, even though it meant breaking with the administration. That Wallace had the courage to move without the
administration, when he lost hope of educating the President,
was demonstrated when he led the movement for the export
commission in the fall of 1923.

Plainly Dr. Taylor had been shaken completely loose by the impact of events from the down-the-middle or stand-pat position that he had expressed to Wallace the previous spring.
At Wallace's assignment, Charles Brand had in the intervening
months arrived at a second draft for the bill which more or less
suited both the industrial promoters of forced farm exports and
the Department's farm economists. Now, in September, 1923,
the Secretary called Taylor in again:

> [Again] the Secretary asked me if I could not find some
> means of helping to solve the farmer's problem. He said,
> 'We have done what we can do as a Department of Agricul-
> ture but conditions are not improving. In fact, the bad
> effects are accumulative and more of the bad results of defla-
> tion are showing now than a year ago when price ratios were
> even worse.'
> ... He agreed that the work of the Department must be
> from the national point of view, but added that all legisla-
> tion was not from the national point of view; that labor, in-
> dustry, and finance used effective methods of securing legisla-
> tion to promote their own class interests. He said, 'Further-
> more, while we as Department workers should adhere to the
> national point of view, which we are certainly doing in striv-
> ing to save agriculture from destruction, it does not follow
> that farmers as a class must adhere to the national point of

view when other groups are not doing so. In fact, unless farmers as a class get busy and *fight* for their rights, we in the Department will not long be able to take a national point of view because the point of view of other interests will dominate us.'

Wallace assigned Taylor immediately to make a swing of the Northwest, the wheat country especially; to sound out the existing demand and fervor for an export corporation bill; and to render concrete and untrammeled on-the-ground report by wire at each stage of the journey. Taylor set off on this mission eagerly. He reached Fargo, North Dakota, his first main stop, on October 2, 1923. There the College people told him that all that was needed was more farm credit, so that this part of the country could work over from wheat to corn and livestock. Then: 'At noon I was taken to a luncheon with the Kiwanis Club. The key speaker had for his topic "Optimism." It appeared from his statement that an organized effort was being put forward to get everybody in an optimistic state of mind regardless of the facts of the present depression here.' A little later, having talked with farmers in western North Dakota and eastern Montana, he wired Wallace:

Farmers here ask that you tell the President that while four years ago bankers urged that farmers borrow money to buy hay at forty to fifty dollars per ton to hold breeding stock which would have sold then for seventy-five dollars per head, bankers now find it necessary to force the sale of breeding stock at half the former prices. Feed abundant for which there is no market except through livestock. Cattle needed for breeding purposes are shipped out to the great detriment of the country. . . . The opinion of all groups and individuals met here is against price fixing but solid for an adequate protective tariff made effective through export commission.

At Helena, Montana's capital, the Commissioner of Agriculture, Chester C. Davis, had arranged for the Secretary's emissary to have dinner with the Governor and some others. Secretary Wallace remembered a pleasant and stimulating conversation with Commissioner Davis at the time when the Harding party

had passed through there four months ago on the way to Alaska.
So Davis arranged this dinner of nine places: The Governor, the
Presidents of the State Farmers Union, the State Farm Bureau,
the State Wheat Growers Association and his statistician, a Land
Bank Director, M. L. Wilson, farm management demonstrator of
the College of Agriculture at Bozeman, Dr. Taylor, and himself.
Wilson and Taylor were friends and associates of long standing in
the old office of Farm Management and in the projects centering
from Dr. Richard T. Ely's Institute of Land Economics at the
University of Chicago. Davis and Wilson were working hand and
glove together, between the State Department of Agriculture and
the Land Grant College, for an active program of farm price-
relief. The names of Davis and Wilson will recur often in this
account of progress.

Uneasy at first and anxious to get away and clear his desk for a
trip to Washington, Governor Joseph M. Dixon, having dined,
arose and, turning to Taylor, asked him if Secretary Wallace really
'had any plan for helping the farmer.' Taylor started to explain
the Secretary's somewhat recalcitrant point of view and purposes.
Then, Taylor notes, 'The Governor sat down and entered into a
round-table discussion. Two hours later he again arose, stood at
the head of the table and said, "I have always looked upon the
tariff as a failure so far as agriculture is concerned, but if it can be
made effective it would be a great thing."' Taylor wired Wallace
the gist of this, adding: 'Ideas of everyone present in line with
previous telegrams. Governor Dixon will be in Washington
twentieth and wants to see you.'

So it went. President Coolidge had sent as investigators to the
same Northwest country Frank Mondell and Eugene Meyer, both
of whom shared Hoover's unalterable conviction that an adequate
extension credit would bring the Northwest through its crisis of
deflation and drought. Mondell and Meyer had been holding
meetings with business men and bankers to present this point of
view. From Oregon Taylor wired Wallace:

> Sixty farmers Wasco County passed a resolution requesting
> the Secretary of Agriculture to recommend to the President
> that price ratio be re-established on a prewar basis by means

of an export corporation to take care of the surplus. Meyer-
Mondell meeting making hit with city business men, but
greatly damaging standing of administration with farmers.
Northwestern Wheat Growers solid for export commission in
spite of Meyer's proposed help. President can save bad results from Meyer-Mondell trip only by coming out for export
commission.

Taylor had hardly taken to the field on his inquiry when word
of his doings reached Secretary Hoover. 'Hoover remonstrated
with the President. The President remonstrated with my father,'
Henry A. Wallace recalls in a reticent footnote in *New Frontiers*
(1934). 'My father conveyed the President's remonstrance to
W. A. Schoenfeld, serving as acting chief in Taylor's absence.
When Schoenfeld wired Taylor that his presence was urgently
required in Washington, Taylor replied, "I left you in charge of
the bureau. Why don't you run it?" Taylor finished his trip.'

Both of the Wallaces, the father as Secretary, the son as editor,
had taken the bit in their teeth now. They were bringing all possible heat to bear on the icy, cagey man in the White House. Young
Henry kept hammering editorially against the stand-pat policies
of Secretary Hoover; it did no good. Ray Tucker, who was covering the White House for the United Press at the time, recalls an
enlightening incident of Hoover's touchiness and the pallid calm
of Coolidge. Hoover took one of young Henry's editorials to the
President and complained. 'Do you mean to say,' the President
asked, 'that a man who has been in public life as long as you have
bothers about attacks in the papers?' 'Don't you?' Hoover
countered; and mentioned a particularly scathing article on
Coolidge by Frank Kent in the *American Mercury*. 'You mean
that one in the magazine with the green cover?' said the President.
'I started to read it, but it was against me, so I didn't finish it.'

Taylor's name was anathema at the White House by this time,
and he knew it; but he had the bear by the tail now and was enjoying the run. In California, at his intended point of terminus, he
had a wire from Secretary Wallace, saying that the President
insisted that he come in and report. Taylor returned, remarking
ironically, 'The suggestion of going with the Secretary to the
White House thrills me and it makes me feel fine to know that we

have an open-minded President who wants to know the truth.'
He reached Washington on October 29. 'Wallace,' he notes,
'told me not to be surprised if he were ignored by the White House
and the call came directly to me, in which case I was to go. Time
passed. No call came.'

Responsible correspondents were predicting that the President
would express his displeasure with Wallace by asking him to resign. But that did not happen either. On November 14 in a
speech at Chicago Wallace endorsed the export corporation in
principle. On November 30 in a report, 'The Wheat Situation,' he
went farther and endorsed the principle of a fair-ratio price. And
now, with Charles Brand's draft of the Department's bill about to
go to the Congress as the first McNary-Haugen bill, Secretary
Wallace authorized Brand to go before a House caucus, with one
hundred and fifty present, to explain and defend the measure.
Toward the turn of the year Wallace was so pressed with work
that he could not return to Iowa for Christmas. Grumbling a
little about even having to think of Christmas on the fifth floor of
an apartment hotel in mild, misty Washington, he wrote his customary one-page holiday greeting to the readers of *Wallaces'
Farmer*. He told first of his homesickness for the crisp air, the
snow, the open fireplaces of Iowa Christmases, and went on to
more serious matters:

> During the past year and eight months I have had unusual
> opportunities to know the condition of agriculture throughout
> the country. I suppose I hear from more farmers directly
> than any other man. I know of their difficulties. But more
> and more I have been impressed with this, that those who
> have looked on their farms as homes and have taken root
> there with the idea of bringing up their families, have had the
> fewest financial difficulties and have come through this trying
> period with the fewest worries. While those who have had
> more in mind the thought of piling up fortunes quickly and
> have sold one farm and bought another every time they could
> see a profit, not only have suffered more financially, but have
> had less satisfactory lives, both they and their wives and
> their children. . . .

During the last twenty years there has been more downright speculation in land than in anything else I know of and
it reached its height during the war years. Thousands and
thousands of men, farmers, bankers, and business men have
gone broke during the past two years as a direct result of
their land speculations, their desire to get rich quickly.
It is a good thing that we are through with this period of
feverish speculation. Those who are so fortunate as to own
farms can now get down to the real business of making them
desirable homes. Those who do not own farms will find it
easier to acquire them as they are freed from the competition
of those who buy only to make money by selling again. Men
and women who love farm life, who love to work with growing
things, can look ahead in confidence.

Just as the ancients made their midwinter festival the occasion of rejoicing over the lengthening day, with its promise of
return of the sun and seedtime and harvest, so we can rejoice
that the turn has come in our period of agricultural depression. This is not to say that there will not be occasional times
of discouragement. Nor is it to say that our troubles are all
swept away with a magic wand. That sort of thing does not
happen in this world, else we would be a spineless lot of creatures incapable of the joy of living. We can say with reasonable assurance, however, that we are well started on the way
to better things for the farmer, and we can observe this
Christmas time with thankfulness and good will.

Entering upon the year 1924, conditions did indeed look somewhat brighter for agriculture. The worst of the deflation had hit
farmers, and the ones who were still on their feet at least knew
where they stood. Prices were not much better, but the ratio of
what it cost to farm and what the products brought had jostled
into a rather more equitable relationship, and this ameliorating
condition was to continue until the general crash of 1929. The
tempered optimism which Harry Wallace now expressed as to the
farm situation was a little like that of a man who has been run
over by a stampeding herd and is happy to find that he is still
alive; but during the remainder of the Coolidge administration
farm distress was not, on the whole, as acute and the farm outcry

was not as vociferous as it had been from 1921 to 1924. It became less intensely localized and more outspread. The Northwest, which went through the wringer first, felt less acute distress now, or had grown numb to it. Much of the water had been pumped out of realty values at a horrible human cost. As deflation continued southward and eastward, farmers there came better to understand what the one-crop wheatland West had been through; and successive McNary-Haugen bills gained notably in Southern and Midland interest and support.

The first such bill, introduced in January, 1924, brought George Peek back into town to lobby; and young Henry Wallace came to Washington also, to lobby for the measure from time to time; and the bill when at length it came to vote in the House on June 3 was defeated. The vote was 223 to 153. In July the McNary-Haugenites, headed by Peek, organized the American Council of Agriculture, and laid definite plans at a meeting in Saint Paul for what young Henry Wallace called 'a marriage of the corn and cotton,' a strengthened agrarian political coalition between the South and West. Secretary Wallace called Chester C. Davis in from Montana, and put him to work as contact man between the Department and the Hill. Davis's job was to promote inter-regional coalition and to help frame a more inclusive bill.

Early that summer Secretary Harry Wallace, who had never loved writing, decided that the time had come when he should write a book. He asked Nils Olsen of the Bureau of Agricultural Economics to help him on it; but he wrote a great deal of it himself, and under increasing difficulties as the summer wore on. The sciatica he mentions in token of the economic affliction of the country in the quotation at the head of this chapter was a figure of speech which suggested itself naturally; for he had suffered intermittently from sciatica since his early manhood, and now he was having the sharpest attacks of it he had ever suffered in his life. By the time he finished drafting his eleventh, the next-to-last chapter, in October, it was agony for him to sit at a desk and hold a pen. The physician at the Mayflower Hotel, where the Secretary had an apartment, said that an operation, relatively slight, would probably relieve the pain and enable him to do more effective work. He put his manuscript aside. The doctor ordered him to rest for a few days in his rooms before going to the hospital. He rested little; the pain grew more intense. Propped up in bed, he conferred with Taylor and Brand, approving the new draft and changed strategy of the McNary-Haugen bill. Then he went to the hospital. His illness seemed now to trace to an infected gall bladder, the after effect, probably, of an attack of typhoid fever he had sustained more than twenty years before while he was a professor at Ames.

The operation, which included the removal of the appendix as well as the gall bladder, seemed to be successful; but within a week complications developed; and his wife wired Iowa for his brothers and sons to come East. He died before their train had crossed the Iowa border, on October 25, 1924. He was fifty-eight years old.

'It was paralyzing news,' Dr. Taylor recalls. 'I have never sat in a meeting where a group of intelligent men manifested such lack of power to think or act as in the meeting of Bureau Chiefs the next morning after the death of the Secretary. Our leader whom we could always count on was gone and we were stunned.

'Many said that the situation in Washington killed Wallace,' Dr. Taylor's memoir continues. 'Others made it more definite and personal. Mrs. Wallace feels that her husband was a martyr to the cause of agriculture. She preferred an unofficial funeral service in Washington, but she had no choice in the matter. An official funeral was arranged at the White House. As we sat in the East Room listening to the funeral service there was little consolation in the thought that Wallace was again welcome to the White House.

'But consolation came two days later at Des Moines, when thousands of people from all over the state and from beyond marched solemnly by the casket under the dome of the Iowa Capitol, bearing silent testimony that the spirit of Henry C. Wallace yet lives and will continue to live in and through the lives of his followers.'

Gifford Pinchot sent a tribute to be printed in *Wallaces' Farmer*, and reprinted later in the Preface to Harry Wallace's book:

How much he did to prevent the attempted capture of the Federal Power Commission by the enemies of conservation;

how large a part he took in defeating efforts to take possession of and destroy first the natural resources of Alaska and then the National Forests of the United States is still unwritten history. But I, as one to whom the inside story was known, pay him my earnest tribute for the performance of a duty that was anything but easy, and the achievement of results so great that the United States will forever be his debtor. In him every farmer has lost a true and powerful friend, and the people of America, a man who would gladly have given the last drop of his blood and the last ounce of his strength in the service of his fellow-men.

Henry A. Wallace promised in a brief editorial: 'The fight for agricultural equality will go on; so will the battle for a stable price level, for controlled production, for better rural schools and churches, for larger income and higher standards of living for the working farmer, for the checking of speculation in farm lands, for the thousand and one things that are needed to make the sort of a rural civilization he labored for and hoped to see.

'He died with his armor on in the fight for the cause which he loved. He had earned the right to say in his last hours, with John Bunyan's Valiant:

> '*I am going to my Fathers, and though with great difficulty I am got hither, yet now I do not repent me of all the Trouble I have been at to arrive where I am. My Sword I give to him who shall succeed me in my Pilgrimage, and my Courage and Skill to him that can get it. My Marks and Scars I carry with me, to be a witness for me that I have fought His battles, who will now be my Rewarder.*

'And of Valiant it is spoken further:

> '*When the day that he must go hence was come, many accompanied him to the River-side, into which, as he went, he said: "Death, where is thy sting?" And as he went down deeper, he said: "Grave, where is thy Victory?" So he passed over, and all the Trumpets sounded for him on the other side.*'

I X

OUTSIDERS

Agricultural colleges and economists were as a whole indifferent to the problem. During the early years their leadership was negative and their attitude scoffing. . . . [Their] discussion of the agricultural situation was revealing; of the tariff, straddling; and of the surplus problem, vague. — CHESTER C. DAVIS, reviewing Agricultural Policy since 1920, in the *Department of Agriculture Yearbook, 1940.*

1. Coalitionists

FACING THE ELECTION of 1924 (which he won handily over John W. Davis of West Virginia and New York, 382 electoral votes to 127), Calvin Coolidge felt obliged to call another agricultural conference. Thoroughly rigged, and tame, the conference was held in November in Washington. It issued a report recommending higher tariffs on farm products, even if this called for a contraction of agriculture to domestic self-sufficiency plus provisioning 'only such foreign markets as shall be profitable.' A bill, vaguely drawn to these ends, seemed to Farm Bloc members an oblique bid to let Secretary of Commerce Hoover take over farm surplus disposal again, as he had in wartime. The Bloc was strong enough to slap this bill down in the House.

Meantime, in the Department of Agriculture, rumbling Governor Howard M. Gore of West Virginia had been appointed by the President as interim Secretary to fill Harry Wallace's place. Gore called in Dr. Taylor, raised his salary five hundred dollars annually, praised his accomplishments and indicated in the friendliest manner possible that Taylor should be seeking wider fields. Grimly amused, Taylor pretended to be obtuse. He kept

259

on doing what he was doing and collected for his memoir news dispatches such as these:

> The President, sharing the views of Secretary Hoover, who declined to go from the Department of Commerce to the Department of Agriculture, will attempt to break down the bureaucratic clique which is alleged to have employed the official agencies of the department to combat Hoover's policies on farm relief. . . . Use of the official agencies to propagandize for the McNary-Haugen bill, which the President opposed though the late Secretary Wallace sponsored it, is charged as part of the campaign which was waged against the Hoover policies having pre-eminence in the administration program.
>
> It was indicated today at the White House that the President had shifted his list of potential choices from 150 to four or five. It is announced that the new Secretary would be found in a man in accord with Secretary Hoover, not because the President is permitting the Commerce head to do his Cabinet picking, but because he and Mr. Hoover think alike on the farm question.

This dispatch by Robert Barry from Washington to *The Public Ledger*, Philadelphia, on January 19, 1925, ended by stating that 'Names of prominent officials of the Department of Agriculture who are slated for removal by the White House were not available today. It was indicated, however, Mr. Coolidge was very much aroused over some of the tactics brought to his attention.'

Next day *The Public Ledger* ran an editorial:

THE WHITE HOUSE *vs.* BUREAUCRACY

> . . . Herbert Hoover's farm ideas square with those of the President, but are cold poison to the farm blocs, farm lobbies, and bureaucrats who went overboard on the McNary-Haugen bill last winter. . . . In their opposition to the administration policy they were as busy as rabbit-chasing puppies in high rye. Price-fixing à la McNary-Haugen was handpolished in the Department and preached on Capitol Hill by palpitating bureaucrats.

If the administration's farm program is to have a China-
man's chance, the next Secretary of Agriculture must swing
the axe and let the heads fall where they may.

A month later (Dr. Taylor continues in his memoir), Gore
called him in again, and said affably: 'You know, I spoke to you
about a promotion. If your resignation were in, that would be
easy, but unless it is in my hands, the President and Hoover would
look upon your promotion as a slap in the face.' He went on to
say that the prospective appointee, William M. Jardine of Kansas,
was close to Mr. Hoover in sympathies and views, and would be
bound to dismiss Taylor if he, Gore, did not.

Smiling to himself, Taylor played a little upon the genial Governor's known rapture at the very thought of hill-billy independence.

'Mr. Secretary, you are a West Virginian, aren't you? Then I
can best explain my position in this matter by telling you that my
ancestors were Kentuckians.'

'My God, yes! We mountaineers never sneak out the back
door,' cried the Governor. He said no more to Taylor about
resigning.

But Secretary Jardine, who came into office March 4, did.
Ordinarily, the Department workers would have welcomed 'Bill'
Jardine as Secretary. He was a reasonable and amiable man.
His years as Dean and Director of Agriculture and then as President of Kansas State Agricultural College had smoothed his manner and skill as an administrator to a truly professional degree.
As an agriculturist he had acquired technical experience in Idaho,
in Utah, in Illinois, and as Cerealist in charge of dry-land grain
investigations for the Department during Tama Jim's administration, from 1907 to 1910. His brother, James Jardine, then head
of the Oregon Experiment Station, was esteemed as one of the
ablest agricultural research men of his time and he is head of Research for the Department now.

Secretary Jardine brought with him from Kansas as aides,
moreover, two of the most competent men ever in the Department,
to head, successively, its Office of Information: Nelson Antrim
Crawford, now editor of *The Household Magazine* at Topeka, and

Milton Eisenhower, a brother of General Dwight Eisenhower, who became President of Kansas State College in 1944. The appointment of William Jardine as Secretary would, then, probably have been pleasing to most people in the Department had he not come in tagged beforehand as 'Hoover's man.' As a Land Grant College president in Kansas, Jardine had deprecated the need or farm desire for McNary-Haugen measures, but that was not unusual. As a matter of fact, most Department workers, apart from B. A. E., either shared that feeling or did not care. But Harry Wallace had, as a fighting Secretary, so won the liking and allegiance of practically everyone in the Department, that any new Secretary whose first obligation was to get rid of Wallace's most faithful and ardent economic associates was bound to be somewhat unpopular; and Jardine was.

Dr. Taylor respected the new Secretary's attainments and the gentlemanly way in which he made the parting gestures. ('He said that I had done a great work in building the Bureau, but that a condition existed which made it necessary for me to go.') So Taylor resigned more or less gracefully, getting out just a bit ahead of the official boot. Likewise, Charles Brand, draftsman of the first McNary-Haugen bill, resigned. Taylor went to a research post and professorship in the Institute of Land Economics at Northwestern University; Brand, to be head of the National Fertilizer Association. Both of these comfortable ports in a tempest had been made ready, while Harry Wallace was still alive, to welcome Secretary Wallace's chief economic aides, in event of need. Taylor and Brand both made the passage early in 1925.

In the same winter thirty-six-year-old Henry A. Wallace somberly turned to the dictaphone in his Des Moines office to dictate the rough draft of a closing chapter for *Our Debt and Duty to the Farmer*, the book his father had left unfinished. He worked by correspondence with Nils Olsen, his father's collaborator in Washington. They wrote what they knew, from close association with the author, to have been Harry Wallace's final views. 'The last chapter follows the thought as outlined by my father. The ideas throughout are his,' Henry A. Wallace noted, in concluding the draft and sending the book to its publishers, the Century Company, on December 1, 1924.

Released from the bonds of administrative responsibility and scrutiny, the avowedly ghosted last chapter (XII) develops a long-range program for America's agricultural future which goes far beyond the tentative pleadings of the chapters preceding. The closing argument runs in effect thus:

> The time has passed when our farmers can treat land wastefully, sell out on the rise, and retire well-to-do; and we have no longer a fresh soil frontier. Conservation of our natural resources becomes of paramount importance. Many of our past difficulties have arisen from our haphazard policy of land utilization. We have acquired large bodies of virgin land without considering the market for their output or their suitability for farming. Unplanned expansion has benefited the manufacturing and commercial classes, particularly real estate interests, but has often injured large sections of the farming industry. All our land should be classified according to its best use. Much of it should be reforested. Leases on farmland should be drawn to protect the tenant and restore fertility. The State might well reduce tax burdens on land reforested, and on land put in process of rest and restoration under permanent pasture or leguminous cover.

Through their drives to cut grain acreage and increase legumes, the Wallaces, working largely apart from the State College and Extension staffs, had for a number of years been pushing for a spread of the practices they preached in Iowa. In 1921, through the columns of their paper and in person, they urged on the officers of the Iowa Farm Bureau Federation a positive scheme for the allotment of tilled acreages in staple crops by counties; and in 1923 they caused to be brought before the State Legislature a law to remit taxes on land planted to soil-building legumes. By 1924 young Henry was going around the state as a sort of one-man extension staff for *Wallaces' Farmer*, promoting contests among Smith-Hughes high-school students in agriculture, with prizes for the boys who would get the most land out of corn and under clover. The gain from this change was threefold: (1) Matted with grass, the soil would not wash away; (2) as a legume, clover has the power to take free nitrogen from the air and store it as fertilizer in the soil; (3) so much land out of corn and in clover would decrease corn surpluses, strengthen corn prices, and tend toward a better balanced agriculture and economy.

The remainder of the Wallaces' argument in the final chapter of *Our Debt and Duty* is crisply stated:

> For a long time there will be hundreds of millions of dollars in interest charges coming to this country every year in excess of what we owe in interest to the outside world. This situation can be disguised for a long time by continued heavy foreign loans. It is undeniably true, however ... that such exports may in effect be thrown away, or worse than thrown away so far as the United States is concerned, unless we are willing to import large amounts of manufactured goods.
>
> During the next decade or two the United States must adjust herself to her position as the world's greatest creditor nation. The economic forces of world trade balances will be against continued large exports of wheat and meat. ... If at any time in the twentieth century extreme need arises and a strong patriotic or price stimulus is applied, the farmers of the United States can again produce a large surplus for export. The tendency of the immediate future, however, is strongly in the opposite direction. ...
>
> Men of vision must arise soon if the United States is to be saved from the state of becoming a preponderantly industrial nation in which there is not a relation of equality between agriculture and industry. They must act in the faith that it will be good for the entire Nation if agriculture from henceforth advances on terms of absolute equality with industry. They must ever keep before the mind of the Nation the long-time view both materially and spiritually. They must set the minds of the farmers on fire with the desire for a rural civilization carrying sufficient economic satisfaction, beauty and culture to offset completely the lure of the city.
>
> Farm leaders who possess this ideal will find it necessary to fight at times. In both the political and business worlds are men who hold sincerely to the short-time point of view.

These men enjoy wealth and social position, and our farm leaders in their broader contacts will hesitate to oppose them. Unfortunately some of our farm leaders will find themselves in such financial straits that they will in effect sell out. Other farm leaders may be unnecessarily violent in expressing their point of view. The problem is to clarify. continuously the vision of a well-rounded, self-sustaining national life in which there shall be a fair balance between industry and agriculture, and in which our agriculture shall not be sacrificed for the building of cities

The Hoover plan, to state it roughly as of 1924 and 1925, was to loan farmers' co-operatives considerable sums of money and let them handle the surplus problems without the aid of the centralizing power of government. Hoover stated his stand ably and in good temper in the leading article of *Farm & Fireside* for December, 1925:

There have developed two major schools of thought in attempts to find a basis of better commercial organization of the farmer. One of these schools believes it can only be accomplished by direct governmental action and therefore places the question in the political field. The other school holds the belief that organization must be created among the farmers outside of the government, through co-operative action of different kinds, this group advocating that the government offer such assistance as it can in the stimulation and creation of such better organization but not to administer or regulate it.

The critics of the first school believe that action by the government to fix or control prices or buy and sell commodities will bring the greatest cataclysm of disaster to the farmer that we have ever witnessed. ... Aside from all the obnoxious weeds of bureaucracy and socialism that it implies, these plans contain one fundamental weakness so far as the farmer is concerned — that the consumers of any one agricultural product outnumber producers six to one and that in the long run the majority is bound to control the political machinery and to use it against the farmer. ...

There is much difference of opinion as to how far and by what methods the government should or could move and assist.... All the propositions seem to agree upon the creation of some kind of a board representing agriculture which shall assist and support co-operative organization in the industry. The division of opinion is largely over the powers of such a board.

In the chapters of his book which he wrote or scanned himself, the first Secretary Wallace had said that Hoover's view of such matters was mistaken and mischievous. 'The mistaken belief that by the mere organization of co-operative enterprises the farmers can be lifted overnight from the valley of depression to the peak of prosperity has prompted some curious suggestions of federal participation. I do not know of anyone who has had an important part in the conduct of any successful co-operative for any length of time, nor anyone who understands the fundamental principles which co-operative associations must observe to succeed permanently, who favors Government activity of the sort contemplated by these mischievous bills.... Some go so far as to put the Government squarely into the business of promoting so-called co-operatives. They would set up a great federal overhead agency and secondary boards of various kinds and would have these boards assume control of a number of highly important activities such as the dissemination of market news. This and other services are already carried on efficiently by the Federal Department of Agriculture....'

Here was the old line of battle, dating from Food Administration days. The period of entrenchment was over; now a sally was planned. The then Secretary and his marketing or legislative aides had noted with interest how strongly the Southern cotton co-operatives and congressmen of the Cotton South had been attracted to 'Hoover bait.' The McNary-Haugenites perceived that they must make some concession to the Southern view in the redraft of their own defeated measure.

'The Marriage of the Corn and Cotton,' for which Henry Wallace spoke editorially, never quite came off in any permanent sense. Even so the farm coalitionists of the nineteen-twenties made better time and greater headway than had their fathers who tried to unite West and South during the Farmers' Alliance or Populist movement of the eighteen-nineties. Populism was a Third Party movement; this was not; but it might have come to much the same end had it held firmly together on other than agrarian issues. Again there was a formally announced betrothal between the great crop-growing regions, with plans to set up housekeeping in Washington. In the eighteen-nineties the anti-Negro, anti-Semitic, anti-Catholic fulmination of the South's Tom Watson contributed measurably to a break in the Alliance. In the nineteen-twenties the nomination of a Catholic Democrat, Al Smith, proved disruptive. But it was an exciting and meaningful courtship while it lasted.

Chester C. Davis made the initial approaches southward. He interested leading officials of the Cotton Co-operative and Staple Cotton Co-operative associations there. In July of 1924, the month after the first McNary-Haugen defeat, insurgent agrarians, most of them Republicans, held a large mass meeting in St. Louis. Quite a few Southerners came up from the cotton country. They joined with the Westerners in forming the American Council of Agriculture. Peek was President; Davis, the chief field man and Washington representative. The Northwestern Grain-Growers came in heartily. The next Haugen bill to reach the floor of the House was again defeated; but the margin of defeat was narrowed from seventy votes, as in 1924, to thirty votes.

George Peek continued most active in the Middle country. In January of 1926 he, Henry Wallace, and others induced Governor Hammill of Iowa to call at Des Moines a conference of eleven other governors of middle and northwestern states. Governor Lowden of Illinois began to become more prominently identified with McNary-Haugenism. He went around the Corn Belt making speeches, crying shame that a time should have come when 'farmers must shudder to hear the rain on their roofs at night, for fear that a bounteous harvest will bankrupt them.' Frank Lowden declared further for the 'go to grass' movement Wallace was urging, and he stood as a believer in the big co-operative philosophy. This was the time when Aaron Sapiro was going around the country and dazzling farmers with a limitless vision of establishing, co-operatively, their own merchandising system, with all duplication of functions eliminated, with a big cut in distribution charges, with scientific grading, packing, labeling, and advertising opening and sustaining an insatiable consumption. Sapiro cited the success of the California Fruit Growers, on the whole a sound success, made possible as to lemons especially by shrewd organization of virtually a natural monopoly of suitable soil and weather, protected by a tariff wall. It is entirely natural that a resident of California such as Herbert Hoover should have had such faith in big co-ops as the sovereign remedy for farm surpluses; but the Corn Belt, the Wheat Belt, and the Cotton Belt had equal reason to feel that modern advertising, packing, warehousing, and merchandising, co-operative or otherwise, would not in themselves solve the surplus problem.

The conferees at Des Moines organized an executive committee of twenty-two, with George Peek as Chairman. They joined in lobbying and in the other forms of pressure politics with a Corn Belt Committee of Farm Organizations and with the American Council of Agriculture. Frank Lowden was their candidate for the 1928 Republican nomination. Some of them were willing to take Hughes if they could not put Lowden over. 'Stop Hoover!' was the one aim on which they all but unanimously agreed. Shortly after the Des Moines meeting Lowden made a speaking tour in the South.

With the Council leading the action these three Northern pressure groups sent representatives to a meeting of farmers and co-operative leaders at Memphis in March, 1926. 'The Memphis meeting,' Henry Wallace wrote in a reminiscent chapter of *New Frontiers*, published in 1934, 'paved the way for another session in Washington. It was then that amendments suitable to the South, and patterned after the Dickinson bill, were tacked on to the McNary-Haugen bill. In the next vote on the bill in the House, Southern votes for the first time joined Western votes in support.'

As Secretary Hoover had remarked in his wire of greeting when the first Secretary Wallace joined Harding's Cabinet, it is more fun to practice pressure politics from without than it is to sit in there as a responsible public man and take it. Into this same book, *New Frontiers*, in 1934, Henry A. Wallace, after a year at the receiving end, as Secretary, entered a thoughtful passage about 'Hot Spots, Pressure Groups, and News Drives':

Those who in the past have sought a change in the rules have not limited themselves to wishing for it, or to passing fervent resolutions. They have worked for the change, sometimes openly and fairly, sometimes secretly and deviously. It seems to me essential that we understand how these things are done. We should reject the bad and make use of the good technique, but we ought to be aware of the existence of both. . . .

Congressmen, Senators, and the people who are in administrative positions are fully familiar with the technique of these drives. But 99 per cent of the people who depend for their understanding on what they read would be amazed if they could see the method at first hand. The injudicious use of these methods may eventually cause the United States to follow Rome into history. In so far as these methods are used to awaken a sleepy Government to its fundamental responsibilities, there can be no sound criticism.[1]

As the McNary-Haugen agitators advanced, judiciously and otherwise, in their effort to arouse sleepy legislators to fight at least a delaying action, there began to appear a real chance that rising rural resentment, South and West, might be welded into at least a partially unified sentiment which would bury the 'bloody shirt.' Wallace became intensely interested. He and his uncle, John P. Wallace, the business manager of the family paper, made a number of trips to Washington to lobby for the cause. Young Henry called on Southern congressmen such as Lister Hill of Alabama and Alben Barkley of Kentucky, arguing that in the face of common problems the South and West should make common cause. With Senator Hill, who was then a congressman, Henry already had a friend in common. Lister's brother, Luther Hill, had married an Iowa girl, and they lived in Des Moines. The main thing Henry bore down on, Lister Hill remembers from their first conversation, was 'the true nature of the slow strangulation of enterprise in both the West and South through the iniquitous system of freight rate differentials.' Wallace and Hill became fast friends and have remained so to this day.

Wallace attended the Southern and Western parley which followed the Memphis conference. When in Washington he stayed at the Lee House or the Hamilton Hotel where Chester Davis, Bill Horton, Frank Murphy, and the other sons of the wild jackass stayed. The nature of the concessions the McNary-Haugenites made to bring the South more fully into the movement is sharply indicated in Davis's 1940 *Yearbook* report, reviewing 'Agricultural Policy Following the First World War':

> The bill was redrafted to provide that co-operative associations might organize to administer the export transactions of a particular commodity, backed by the equalization fee to spread the costs over all producers presumably benefited.

This applies particularly to the redraft of 1927. Comparing the successive drafts, of 1924, 1927, and 1928, Davis adds:

> The mechanism for implementing the plan varied considerably, but ... at no time did the advocates abandon what they considered the essential ideas, (1) that the centralizing power of the Federal Government should be used to assist farmers to dispose of the surplus abroad and raise prices to a desired level in the domestic market, and (2) that the loss of the segregated exports was to be paid for by the farmers themselves by means of an equalization fee....
> The supporters of the measure clung stubbornly to the principle of the equalization fee, but retreated temporarily from the fair-exchange principle, and, instead, offered a bill in which the existing customs duties were made the measure of the price benefits.[2]

'Stubbornly' is a word nicely chosen. George Peek was a mighty stubborn man. And many of the Farm Bureau gentry, as they came in behind the measure, held stoutly to the idea of getting something from governmental action without the indignity of demanding a direct handout. The Cotton South-

HARRY WALLACE AS HARDING'S SECRETARY OF AGRICULTURE

erners, as they came into the push, were generally never as ardent to stand free of subsidy as were the Midwestern originators of the movement. And when equalization computations had to be figured in on a co-operative bookkeeping basis which involved in the end rice as well as cotton, along with gestures toward peanuts and tobacco — all this, together with wheat, corn, wool, cattle, sheep, and swine — the opposition could and did say that only God, George Peek, Henry Wallace, Chester Davis, and Einstein understood what it was all about.

The paper I worked for, old *Farm & Fireside*, edited at 250 Park Avenue, New York City, took that view. George Martin was editor. Wheeler McMillen, senior associate editor on the staff, a born conservative, not to say a reactionary, and an able one, was writing most of the economic leads and editorials, just as he does now as editor-in-chief for Joseph Pew's *Farm Journal*. But I had an occasional go at McNary-Haugenism, too, on the more general ground that it had become far too complicated to be workable, in the closing years of the nineteen-twenties. McMillen argued with an all but religious zeal that chemurgy, the new magic of the test tube, would open new frontiers and dissolve crop surpluses in a suitably expansive American manner, without governmental intervention. Wallace and Davis, especially Davis, had been hopeful of developing paper from cornstalks and were receptive to the idea of making gasoline from grain; but they regarded this tub-thumping for chemurgy as the sovereign balm and remedy for farm distress as a peculiarly offensive red herring, with a strong industrial taint. Staff members of *Farm & Fireside* who sat in the galleries of Congress to hear McNary-Haugenism debated returned to the shop reporting that young Henry Wallace was there, too, listening and watching, looking awfully sour, and regarding *Farm & Fireside* men as minions of Morgan, with a bad smell. I must confess that I was not greatly drawn to this Henry Wallace by the reports which reached me through my colleagues in the farm-paper business at the time.

It is hard now to figure how much of the increased vote-gaining power the coalitionists displayed in 1927 and again in 1928 arose from the wider base of operations they had chosen, and how much of it came from the simple fact that President Coolidge, addressing the American Farm Bureau Federation at Chicago in March of 1925, declared flatly, in accents unmistakably Hoover's, that he would veto any McNary-Haugen bill that passed. This left the congressmen free to placate the countryfolk with the heat coming in on the White House, not on them. In February, 1927, the bill passed both houses, 43 to 41 in the Senate; 214 to 178 in the House. Coolidge vetoed it. The McNary-Haugenites went at it again. This time, it was provided that financing by the equalization fee would be resorted to only if storage operations failed to maintain domestic prices. This bill passed the Senate in April, 1928, 58 to 23; and the House in May, 204 to 121. Coolidge vetoed it. On May 25, 1927, the Senate voted 50 to 31 to pass the bill over the veto. There things stuck, with the fight turning toward the convention floors and the forthcoming election.

Vice-President Dawes had engaged in a published correspondence, favoring the export corporation principle, with Sir Josiah Stamp. When, in the event of an impending tie in the Senate, Peek and Davis went around to see the 'General' at the Metropolitan Club the night before the 1928 test, he said that he was against the bill as then drawn because it departed from the equalization fee; that it would be simply another raid on the Treasury. The measure passed, anyway; but that was simply political dumbshow. McNary-Haugenism, as such, was a dead issue, in so far as chance of enactment went, from 1928 onward. In directing attention to agricultural trouble, and in rallying agricultural support toward the idea of no tariffs, or tariff-equivalent handouts for all, the agitation was of value. But the new team, West and South, got all tangled up in its own traces, and a continual succession of what Davis called 'counterplans' and what young Henry Wallace called 'red herrings' or 'another rabbit out of the hat,' cut the ground out from under McNary-Haugenism even when Congress was bouncing the last two bills up to the White House for veto and back again.

Practically all the powers ever written into the Norris and then the McNary-Haugen bills, together with the powers proposed under the Grange-backed McKinley-Atkins bill of 1926, not to mention the Dickinson bill of the same year, and others, were written as rather minor parts into the Farm Act of 1933 — once. the supreme point of crisis, demanding almost any kind of roughshod action, had come.

The McKinley-Atkins bill followed a device once recommended by Alexander Hamilton, dug up and refurbished as a Farm Export Debenture plan by Dr. Charles L. Stewart of the University of Illinois. In backing this proposal, the 'conservative Easterners' of the Grange, Wallace pointed out rather wearily in an editorial, did not shrink from accepting an outright subsidy. But he was still reported as regarding the Eastern farm-paper men who spoke for the plan as paltry tools of Wall Street. I did not know him then, neither did I know Davis; but, judging from what they wrote and said about those among us who could not see McNary-Haugenism or Al Smith as the agrarian savior, they struck me as exceedingly gloomy, wrathy, and suspicious men.

Later, I learned that, strong as they were for export dumping when the McNary-Haugen push started, they knew what had happened to foreign trade walls against dumping in the four-year period of the agitation. 'Export dumping,' Wallace wrote later, 'would not work with European importing nations desperately trying to protect their own farmers' prices.'³

And, walking with Peek to try to line up Vice-President Dawes at the Metropolitan Club in Washington that evening in the spring of 1928, Chester Davis recalls telling Peek: 'George, this is the last heat I trot. We can't dump surpluses over the sort of tariff walls they're rearing over the water now.' George Peek plodded on, putting his feet down slowly, firmly, as if there were a plow before him. 'The hell we can't!' he said shortly. He never changed.

2. Corn Belt Hamlet?

I FIRST SAW Henry A. Wallace in 1927, but then we did not meet. It was at a picnic-speaking ground in South Dakota on a torrid July afternoon. I was making a Western swing for *Farm & Fireside*. Wallace was on one of his economic stump-speaking tours. The editor of a regional farm paper makes a great many speeches as part of his job. Henry's early speeches, like Harry's before him, were more nearly lectures than speeches. 'So decent, so earnest,' one of Henry's staff had told me of his first appearances on the platform, 'so determined not to make a speech!' The friend said that Henry was just as likely to make one of his shirt-sleeve economic lectures with the greater part of his shirt-tail out, and nobody minding. I could see why that was, even from a distance, there on that sorry-looking picnic ground. He was not there to blow himself up or put himself over; he was not even thinking about himself; he was simply there, talking, slowly, entirely extemporaneously, trying to tell those people who trusted him and his family and their paper why a war that was over, eight years after it was over, should reduce them here, four thousand or more miles away from the scene of the actual fighting, to ruin. They listened to him with an almost painful attention. They were in trouble, those people, in deep trouble. They needed all the help and guidance they could get.

Drought and deflation had hit hard here, all at once. The crash had been so abrupt that farmers burned out and broke were still able to get shiny new cars on credit; the car and sales companies did not dare drop their quotas abruptly at the time. So the farmers came, many of them, in big new cars; but they had the look of broken men in their flapping, dirty denims; and their gaunt women, sitting tensely with them on those rough board benches, right out in the blaze of the sun, were brave. Something about that whole 'picnic,' some air of unexpressed fear, even of desperation, touched the heart. It was toward three in the afternoon and the temperature stood at a hundred and three degrees. I was there to interview a country banker who thought he had an answer to the tenant problem; he had driven me out into the country for a breath of air. But never a breath of air stirred anywhere, so we had turned in here, and sat in the car and talked, while Wallace, patiently and somberly, talked to the people. 'The world is changing; we must change too' — that is all I recall of his lecture. I meant to go up and be introduced to him afterward, but by the time I found out what the banker thought was the cure for tenancy, Wallace had gone on across the Plains to make another talk. I followed his writings in *Wallaces' Farmer* more closely after that.

Shortly after he came to the editorship he started a personal column called 'Odds and Ends,' more offhand in style than his formal editorial pronouncements, highly individual, and generally meaty. Editorially, he took little part in the 'Stop Hoover' drive of the McNary-Haugenites or in whipping up the anti-Hoover farm march that Midwestern Republican agrarians put on at the 1928 Kansas City convention. He favored Lowden for the nomination and went on to Kansas City ahead of time, but returned before the show opened, remarking in his 'Odds and Ends' that week:

At this writing, it looks as if Hoover had been headed off. . . . The longer the balloting continues, the better chance Lowden should have. . . . The more that open-minded delegates think about the matter, the more they will become convinced that Lowden has a better chance to win against Smith than any other candidate. . . .

I met Lowden for a few minutes in Kansas City, and was greatly impressed with his vigor. It would be interesting in case the Republican convention this week turns down the cause of Equality for Agriculture, in both the platform and the nominee, if Lowden would give the voters of the South and Middle West a chance to vote their convictions by running on a separate ticket. He says that he will not do this, but let's wait and see how the convention finally ends.[4]

When Hoover bore off the nomination of a tightly organized convention, George Peek, Chester Davis, and other disgusted McNary-Haugenites went on to the Democratic convention at Houston. There, to the tune of *Sidewalks of New York*, they obtained from the Democrats a more promising farm plank together with a candidate for whom they cherished no special hope or fondness, Alfred E. Smith. Wallace did not go to Houston, but later that summer, when Governor Smith came through the Midland campaigning, he went to Omaha to hear him speak. He thought that Al Smith was a most engaging speaker. 'I was intrigued!' he said years later, when pressed by reporters to recall the day that he became a Democrat. (Actually he did not bother to change his registration in Iowa from Republican to Democrat until 1936, but he voted Democratic from 1928 on.) 'I was especially intrigued by his support of McNary-Haugenism, and I really thought Al meant what he said at the time. Later I was informed that he had been posted quite substantially by certain folks who knew more about the farm problem than he did, and while he had a grasp of the words he wasn't quite up to grasping the content of the bill. It does make a difference whether you are only repeating words or whether you understand what you are saying. However, he had it all down on the backs of envelopes, and sounded as if he meant it. The following day I defended him before the Farmers' Union and the next day I went up to the Methodist Conference and defended him to the Methodists.'

It was Rexford G. Tugwell, Professor of Economics at Columbia University, who had coached Governor Smith on McNary-Haugenism; but Wallace and Tugwell did not know each other at the time. Wallace's defense of Smith before the Farmers' Union was by no means a glowing endorsement. It was a rushed reporter who put in his mouth the words, 'The farmer of the United States can best serve his own ends by throwing his influence to Smith.' Wallace protested mildly in his 'Odds and Ends' the week following, adding:

Things like this are exasperating, but they are kind of funny, too. Some day I may learn never to say anything about politics unless I read the statement from a typed slip. What I said was (and I am quoting from the records of the official stenographer):

There is no reason why farmers should get wrought up about either one of them. We do not owe either one of these parties anything, and there is no reason why we should work our heads off for either one of them. Certainly, it may be good hardheaded sense to throw influence one way or the other. I honestly think that Hoover will carry Iowa by 200,000 votes. In view of that fact, I think it would be a fine thing for farmers who are thinking about the welfare of Iowa agriculture, if they would plunk their votes solidly for Smith, in view of the fact that there is that much margin.

Of course, this was just saying over again what we have been saying in *Wallaces' Farmer* about the desirability of making the Corn Belt doubtful territory, and making both parties feel that the farm vote is worth bidding for.[5]

But the word had gone out under headlines that a Wallace of Iowa had turned from Republicanism; and in each speech thereafter he did turn further. He did not like the way in which Smith's religion, Catholicism, was used to smear him as the campaign grew hotter. He did not like the carefully documented record Hoover uncovered to claim that in clearing the postarmistice surpluses of 1919 he saved farmers from catastrophe. And he rather enjoyed riding around in the same automobile with Milo Reno and other agrarian wild men, raising his voice against tariff-fed industrialists who were out to skin farmers further and increase their own unseemly corpulence by hoisting tariffs some more. That, far more than McNary-Haugenism, *per se*, was the line Wallace took in this 1928 campaign; and he was in some part non-partisan, for, in his quiet way, he tore into high-tariff Democrats and Republicans alike.

Joseph Knapp, the president of Crowell Publishing Company, which put out *Farm & Fireside*, along with *Collier's*, *The American Magazine*, and *The Woman's Home Companion*, was ardently for Hoover. He loaned Edward Anthony, who then was head of the Company's promotion department, to Republican National Headquarters in New York City; and when need appeared for some special farm-front material, stressing Mr. Hoover's really heroic efforts to make our former allies take the war foodstuffs they had ordered, Anthony called me in to help on it. I worked with George Barr Baker on the curiously entitled series, *The Great Fat Fight*, two pieces in *The Saturday Evening Post*, May 12 and 19, 1928. Baker signed the articles. My heaviest part in their making was to dig out facts Mr. Hoover had caused to be stored in pinprick-sized type appended to Surface's somewhat forbidding compilations: *Wheat Production in the World War* and *Pork Production in the World War*. A pre-release on May 10 on the news services (*ASSERTS HOOVER PREVENTED PANIC: Saved Farmers from Collapse in 1919, Writer Says*)[6] made quite a stir. It made an especial stir among Midland adherents of the Wallaces and haters of Hoover. By the time both articles, which Mr. Hoover read and verified in manuscript, had been published and circulated, Iowa foes of the Great Engineer were fit to be tied. They got out pamphlets and broadsides of denial and abuse. In comparison with most of the other McNary-Haugenites, Henry A. Wallace in his extended editorial, 'Facts Farmers Should Know,' was mild:

> ... To speak bluntly, the federal government lived up to its contracts with the manufacturers during the war, and fell down on its contracts with the farmers. The attitude of those responsible is particularly revealed in their astonishment that farmers should expect anything better than a deal like this.
>
> This point of view can be defended by advocates of an increasing industrialization of the country, on the ground that the important thing is to get cheap food, and that the welfare of the farmer is always to be made a secondary consideration. This is understandable and honest, even though it may be short-sighted. It is much more aggravating to farmers when this straightforward plan of argument is not taken and when the attempt is made to indicate that the breaking of the war contracts with the farmer and the holding down of food prices was in some way a step taken for the benefit of agriculture. Of course, farmers still have some votes, and if they can be soothed into forgetfulness of their grievances every four years, the job of soothing them expertly is bound to pay fairly high dividends in the political field. . . .
>
> There is no question about one point. Hog prices did hit the toboggan in October of 1918. The Hoover apologists insist that this happened because the people knew that the war was about over and were reducing purchases on that account. The farm groups have a different theory.

The editorial, dated May 18, 1928, continues with a seven-hundred-word blow-by-blow recital of the 1920 Wallace-Hoover controversy, sufficiently sketched in preceding pages, and quotes Harry Wallace's summary editorial at the time:

'This is typically Hooveresque. The impression is given that he controlled the market from October 1, 1918, to October 1, 1919, and therefore made good his promise, notwithstanding all the criticisms which have been made. [The facts are] . . . Mr. Hoover calmly claims credit for these higher prices which followed immediately after his control ceased.'

Henry A. closed his 1928 editorial thus:

> . . . The Food Administration people, after having got credit for holding down prices and getting cheap food, are now attempting to curry favor on the other side of the fence by asserting that the sole aim of the Food Administration was to protect the farmer and keep farm prices high. There must be something wrong with one story or the other.
>
> Facts are facts, and when the voters of the country know the real truth of the story, they are not likely to be enthusiastic about casting ballots for Mr. Hoover. The spirit of fair play is still abroad in the land.

Observe at this point that Henry A. did not put quite the same thump and bite into his observations on the changed hog-payment base as he had in his first book, *Agricultural Prices*, written in 1919, nearly ten years before. He had mellowed a little and somewhat changed his mind. This process continued. In March of 1944, when I had written into this book as far as the middle section of chapter VII, I sent him a letter of query. Replying March 10, 1944, from the Office of the Vice-President, he said he had reread his statement of the situation in *Agricultural Prices*, and added:

> In 1919 when I wrote this I was not familiar with other aspects of the situation which forced Hoover to abandon his guarantee of 13 bushels of Chicago corn for 100 pounds of Chicago hogs. Hoover may have been caught in a jam which made it impossible for him to carry through his guarantee or he may have had a change of heart which made him question the economic wisdom of this approach, although he was undoubtedly sold on the approach at the time. My criti-

cism today of Hoover would be that he tried to squirm out
of his guarantee by subterfuge instead of coming out flatly
and saying that the situation had so changed that he could
not do what he said he would do.

It has been many years since I have had any interest in
this matter, and since I have become familiar with the
problems of government administration I have a much
kindlier feeling for Hoover, although I still question his
wisdom in giving an implied guarantee and then pretending
for a time to live up to it when he really was not. Looking
back on it now I feel that the plan which I recommended
to the Food Administration, while undoubtedly effective in
bringing about increased hog supplies, also had inflationary
possibilities of a serious nature.

By 1929, with his father for four years dead, there still was
talk among friends and partisans of the Wallace family depicting
young Henry as a sort of brooding, scientific Hamlet, borne down
by his father's death in the political-economic conflict. The
basis of such talk was plain enough: young Henry's strong sense
of family, his youth of relative solitude, self-chosen, his delvings
into the remotest fields of mathematics, genetics, comparative
religion, meteorology, and economics. All this fitted in. Reading
his editorials and articles during the period from 1924 to 1929, I
found a somber undercurrent to nearly everything he wrote. I felt
that he must be, indeed, a broody young man, having little fun.

Shortly after the election of Hoover over Smith, I made a
Western trip for my paper that took me through Des Moines, and
dropped in at the *Wallaces'* shop to see if I could get some story
tips from the managing editor, Donald Murphy, who had helped
me in this way before. I was heading for Minneapolis to interview a wild-sounding Plains economist, one M. L. Wilson, who
had just returned from Russia announcing another world revolution in mechanization and wheat. In Des Moines I had only an
hour before the best train westward; and when Don Murphy
suggested that we step into the next office and visit with Henry,
I declined. But he heard us talking and came into Don's office.
Don introduced us; the three of us fell to talking shop; I let that

train go; and, still talking, we went to a near-by tea shop for lunch. Wallace and Murphy were much interested in a Forum type of letter column which we were developing from George Martin's personal editorial page, 'Our Letters to Each Other,' in *Farm & Fireside*. Formerly on this page the editor did most of the talking; now we were letting responding readers do most of the talking, even a certain amount of sharp reviling of us Park Avenue farm editors. I had been running the department for about three years then, and impressed with the fact that continual dog-fights in type become repetitious and tiresome, we had turned a bit toward offering praise and cash for non-professional poetry and philosophy of postcard length. We talked about that at luncheon, I recall, and I can still remember Henry Wallace's amused horror at anyone deliberately laying himself open to reading tons of amateur poems, or poems of any sort. But he and Murphy agreed that the closer you can get a whole farm paper into the tone of unstudied personal letters, the better; and the more of the paper you get written at you, by the people afield, the less stuffy and preachy the paper is likely to be. Wallace and Murphy were putting more emphasis on letters, and on material of general interest rather than specific advice. They agreed, in general, that the County Agent system relieved farm papers measurably from the almost impossible task of guessing what specific information hundreds of thousands of different farmers wanted.

We left the tea room and started back toward the office. It was a gorgeous day, sunny and gay, with high clouds lifting like white mountains around the rim of the prairie. 'Whether I ought to or not,' said Wallace suddenly, 'I'm not going back to that adding-machine right away. I'm going to steal some time and take you out to my seed corn.' Murphy warned him not to do anything his Puritan spirit would repent of later. Wallace laughed boyishly. 'Not only that, I'm going to take a Company car. Get back in there and slave, Don; we're off for an hour in the country,' he said. We got into a light pickup truck and he drove fast, once we reached the edge of town. It is about three miles out to his seed farm. In answer to my questions he said that he had no stock in *Wallaces' Farmer*, serving simply as editor, but he held a controlling interest in and was president of this seed business, which he himself had founded and organized. I asked him how the business was doing, and he said they were managing to make some money, depression or not. He gave the impression of being vastly more interested in and happy about his seed business than in editing and speechmaking; and the more nearly I came to know him, the more I believed that this was true. They had told me at the shop that his Uncle John, succeeding his father as president of the publishing firm and its business manager, was very proud of young Henry and had a high regard for his ability, but inclined fondly to treat him as if he were still a youngster who had to be told what to think, write, and rewrite. Henry was, in fact, by this time a man just past forty; he looked older than that, I thought, in the office; but barely thirty as we walked afield. He showed me a new poultry shed where his first-born son, Henry Browne Wallace, just turned thirteen, was trying some experiments with hybrid chickens.

We looked at a recently built commercial seed dryer of his own designing. He was proud of his dryer, and he had a right to be, for it put him momentarily well out ahead of competing commercial growers in delivering seed of high viability at a low handling cost. We went on to some test patches where he was manipulating genes in weird combinations: 'This part of it I do more from idle curiosity than for money,' he said. It was all so far ahead of my earlier slight experience in double-pedigree corn breeding on my father's farm in Maryland that we soon found ourselves talking about something else. The man I found myself talking about with Henry Wallace has suffered enough already, and entirely undeservedly, from getting his name in print, so I shall not mention any names. The story, itself, is a fascinating and tragic one, and Henry Wallace's interest in it illustrates certain aspects of his character which I found surprising at the time.

The friend of mine in question is a geneticist, a highly skilled and devoted research worker in the special field of plant inbreds, crossed widely. All he asked was ground and seed and daylight hours enough, there at State College, to develop corn strains that would resist attack of the European corn borer then marching in. He gained very little from this effort. That little came in three ways: partly from the Department of Agriculture in Washington, partly from the State Experiment Station, and partly from the College. He worked all hours seven days weekly and had neither time nor money for many diversions, including girls. In the manner of an absent-minded professor he did for a while, however, pay attention to a rangy-looking coed, talking to her interminably, she complained, about his precious corn plants, and escorting her to an occasional fraternity dance. The lady appears to have been something of a nymph. Months and years after my friend stopped seeing her, and had almost forgotten her, she got herself tangled up with a professor of veterinary medicine who had formed the perverse habit of giving horse medicine to coeds to excite their fancies; and she was found in a quarry pit near town one morning, shot to death. My friend, returning from his work afield that evening, was shocked to hear of the tragedy; and not believing it could really be the girl he had been fond of, he was sufficiently guileless to call up the police and ask if it were really she. They asked him who wanted to know. He told them. They came out and got him and threw him in jail.

They had absolutely no evidence against him; but he was only a poor, uninfluential research assistant; and they held him in jail for weeks, with the press, the tabloids especially, describing his criminal swagger (he had no swagger), and the tough way he kept demanding cigarettes (he did not smoke). The College fired him, still with no evidence; the State Experiment Station fired him; only those in charge of research in Washington had sense and character enough not to give in to the clamor that he be dismissed completely. Well, the police at length rounded up the murdering veterinarian, and released my friend; but the ordeal of testifying at the trial was still before him; and the College and Station officials of that State refused to re-employ him, on the ground that she had been a bad girl and he had known her and had thereby brought bad publicity down on his own head and that of dear old State. Letters written by his friends to the President of State in the hope that he might be goaded into an act of simple justice received no reply. Presidents and dignitaries of adjacent institutions were written to and visited to see if they would hire my friend, reinstating him to the place he had fairly won in the realm of science; No! They all knew his work (as Wallace did). They all said he was a wonder, and had been a comer. But no; the unfavorable publicity! They blanched at the very thought.

One reason the thing was so on my mind at the time of my interview with Wallace was that I had just sat through the next-to-last act of the tragedy with this friend of mine. A mild but stubborn man, he had refused upon release from durance to go somewhere else and finish his requirements for a Ph.D. degree. He had the right to stay and finish, and he stayed; right through the trial and conviction of the murderer, working or dwelling in solitude except when he was in the witness chair. I had run him down in his laboratory one evening, and we drove out into the country. He still had two months to do on his Ph.D. and was sticking it out; but the next week was going to be a hard one; for three days from then, there at the State penitentiary, they were going to electrocute the professor who did the murder.

Wallace broke in at one point to express some grim-lipped estimates of certain of the deans and dignitaries I had mentioned. When I finished, he stood with his head down as if meditating, muttered something about 'the inhumanity of man to man.' Then he asked, 'Do you think he would take a place with us here? We could use him here. He's good.' If it came to commercial plant breeding, with no chance of complete scientific reacceptance on a college or institutional level I thought my friend would go off somewhere, and develop the plant strains he had planned for the general welfare, as a commercial seedsman, himself. 'Yes, I guess so,' said Wallace. 'It won't do any harm to tell him there's a place here for him, anyway, if he wants it. I'll write him as soon as I get back to the office.'

We started walking back through his corn rows to the car. We had been getting along all right, better than I had thought we would; but I still had something on my mind. 'Did you know,' I asked him, 'that I worked with George Barr Baker on that defense of Hoover as a friend of the farmer that you and your friends threw up such a counterbarrage about when it came out in *The Post*?'

Henry Wallace stopped walking, dropped his head and looked at me intently under those shaggy brows. Finally he smiled. 'Do you know,' he said slowly, 'I hope I never again feel as intensely antagonistic toward any one as I did then. I felt, for a while there, I felt, almost, as if Hoover had killed my father.' We started walking again:

'That was nonsense. A fight for ideas would never hurt or kill my father. He loved to fight for ideas; he lived for it!... He had a bad case of typhoid when he was a teacher back at Ames and later, when he was under great strain, some of the after effects of that illness settled in his gall bladder; that is what he died of.

'I still think that Hoover's ideas about helping agricultural recovery, and general recovery, are about 99 per cent wrong. They by-pass the tariff issue; they sidestep the debts. They'll never work. The smash we've had already isn't anything to the smash that will come. But I am coming to believe that Hoover honestly thinks he's right, and is trying to do the best he can for agriculture and for the country. I think that his Farm Board is well-intentioned; and you'll find that we are going to back the soundest part of it editorially in *Wallaces' Farmer* in every way we can.'

We drove back to Des Moines and I took a later train. I had not the remotest idea then that I would ever be writing a book about him and his family, but what he had said about his father and President Hoover so impressed me that I made some notes about our conversation on the train. I did not see him to talk with again for nearly four years, in March of 1933, when he came to Washington as Secretary of Agriculture for Franklin D. Roosevelt. Much had happened in the meantime as he foretold.

In late July of 1929 *Wallaces' Farmer* announced with a mild flourish that its editor was going to England and Denmark, and then press on to Hungary and Central Europe, filing dispatches for every issue regularly as he traveled. Reaching England in late August, he would attend an international conference on agricultural economics; in Southeastern Europe he would look into corn strains that were said to resist the European corn borer. Shortly

before leaving, in the issue of his paper for June 14, 1929, he had
published a sharp and gloomy leading article on the tariff:

> The new tariff bill as it passed the House will do the
> farmers of the United States tens of millions of dollars of
> damage every year. As to why the farmers of the Middle
> West should allow their own congressmen to vote against
> their economic interests is a great mystery which can only
> be explained by going back to the emotions growing out of
> the Civil War. But we are now coming out from under
> the shadow of that conflict. Another war has been fought,
> and it is time for our farmers to begin to think clearly. . . .
> The Fordney bill was bad enough, but the Hawley bill
> will increase the farmer's disadvantage. Farmers should
> petition their congressmen to let the Fordney bill stand.
> The Hawley bill is an iniquitous affair which should reso-
> lutely be turned down by all congressmen who have the
> interest of agriculture at heart. . . .

Once aboard the *Leviathan*, outward bound, his editorial correspondence took on a lighter character. He had not been to Europe
since his first trip in 1912. Traveling second class with a party of
ten agriculturists, arguing endlessly in the jargon of economics
and sociology, playing deck tennis between times, might not have
seemed the height of enjoyment to everyone; but it suited him.
Filing 'Odds and Ends' from shipboard, he wrote:

> The most important member of our party is Leonard K.
> Elmhirst, a wealthy young Englishman who became so much
> interested in agriculture in attending Cornell University that
> he is willing to pay the transportation expenses of some thirty-
> five men to bring them together for a two weeks' conference
> at Dartington Hall, his home in southwestern England.
> So far our trip has been one glorious vacation and I
> wish every Iowa farmer could have as good a time as I am
> having right now. Occasionally I try to do a little serious
> work but always I find that the really important thing is to
> play deck tennis or shuffleboard.
> Dr. H. C. Taylor, who fought so vigorously for agricultural

justice while chief of the Bureau of Agricultural Economics under my father, in Washington, is the champion at ship golf. However, Elmhirst and Case, of Illinois, sometimes beat him. I refuse to play the golf game because I look on golf in all its forms as a dangerous time-killing vice.

Our best sport is conversation at meal time. Elmhirst tells us about his experiences in India, about working with Rabindranath Tagore, the great Hindu poet, in getting the Hindu boys and girls started in a kind of Four-H club work. Case may then tell us how the 400 combines in the State of Illinois are used not only on oats, wheat, and soybeans but also on clover seed. Warren and Pearson, who are very proud of the farming in New York State . . . speak of actual surveys proving that Western farmers do very poorly under Eastern conditions. . . . Cornell people seem to be especially sure that they have their work organized on the right basis. . . .

Our second-class quarters are splendidly comfortable and we don't have to put on dinner clothes every evening as they do in the first-class. I am quite sure I am not a first-class person in the steamer sense of the word.

Other Americans on their way to this informal postwar conference were Dr. O. E. Baker, land and population statistician, and Dr. Carl Ladd, later Dean of Agriculture at Cornell. They made a short tour of southern England before proceeding to Dartington Hall. Wallace's dispatches tell with some wonder of pastures so fine they rent for as high as $35 an acre a year; of moorland ponies, thin and ill-sustained, selling for from $3 to $10 each; of the ruins of Stonehenge; and of the exclamation of Dr. George Warren, 'the most level-headed man in our party': 'Blessed is the nation which has no past, but which can keep its face resolutely turned toward the future.' To this Wallace added in his dispatch:

And yet, somehow, every time I step into a cathedral and smell that ancient stone church odor and look up at the high arched ceiling and then toward the altar with the stained-glass windows behind it, I cannot help understanding how many of the people must have wanted to worship God in this way.

From the conference he filed correspondence of quietly startling import: That the farm hands' union in England had been able to secure an eight-hour day; that tenants there held long leases and were paid for improvements they made on their own initiative; that, 'Landlords find ownership a luxury and many are asking that the government buy all the farm land and become the national landlord. . . . From 1919 to 1927, one fourth the landlords of England sold out. They were glad to get from under a system where they had so little to gain and much to lose. The tenants who became owners are not so happy because they have discovered what we have learned in the Corn Belt, that there is no worse landlord than borrowed money, or, as Doctor Taylor puts it, "The lendlord is worse than the landlord."'

Wallace was much taken with, though he did not succumb to the blandishments of, J. P. Maxton, of Oxford, who read the main paper proposing land nationalization. At first, 'I looked on him as a very learned, dignified individual. Later when I had played tennis, baseball and cricket with him, I realized that he was one of the most impudently human, bright young fellows in the world. The vaudeville stage lost an artist when it let Maxton become an agricultural economist.'

Also, he liked George Dallas, 'a former organizer of farm laborers, now a Member of Parliament for the British Labor Party, which is now in power. A Scotchman, he stood for election in different parts of England and Scotland, but was elected from Northampton. We are all quite fond of him. Laboring men here, he says, have a tough time of it because, if they lose their jobs, they also lose their homes. Wages in the city are fully twice as high and the brighter boys go to the city, but right now unemployment makes it rather bad to go to towns. However, the dole paid city people out of work is $5 a week, or almost as much as the farm hand wage. There is no unemployment dole for farm hands. . . . Dallas has no hard feelings against the farmers who employ labor, because he realizes that they must have fair prices for their stuff if they in turn are to pay higher taxes.'

The tone of the conference was in some part solemn. Opening it, Elmhirst 'said the war had left a trail of fear which made official international gatherings too formal to permit of satisfactory understandings.' Even the lighter diversions of the conferees aroused serious reflections. On a field day toward closing, Dr. Pearson, in overalls, astounded the British by making seventeen runs at cricket, and Wallace and Dr. J. I. Case, economist, demonstrated hog-calling. ('I suppose that never before have the walls of a Norman castle reverberated to such din as Case and I let loose.') Wallace reported further:

> The economic forces of the next fifty years are such as to make for much irritation between England and the United States. I am very anxious therefore to see our people and the English meeting each other in friendly games. . . . It seems as though nearly every one of the English economists of my age was injured in the war. Allen, the Canadian, lost his left arm. Jones, from Wales, had a badly twisted leg. And so it goes. We of the Middle Western United States do not know how much we missed in the way of human grief. However, one of the British economists makes the point that there is a greater total of suffering after a war because of economic distractions than there is during a war. If this is true, then we of the Middle West have paid our full share.

Wallace's liking for sharp argument, conducted under rules of civility, but without gloves, appears again and again in his reports of this conference: 'Ashby, of the leading agricultural college in Wales, is good to listen to, because he speaks his mind freely. He says he can't understand why the United States Government should want to crowd farmers off of poor land into the cities and at the same time build a Boulder Dam to make more farms. He says it is high time that the governments of the world should begin to realize that economic forces can be controlled.'

After Case of Illinois had read a carefully prepared paper on cost accounting, Ashby 'took violent exception and challenged Case by saying: "If 2000 farmers are improved by your cost account work, does it not also follow that 2000 other farmers who are not clients of the college, are positively harmed by the increased competition?" Ashby thought that we had been looking at the agricultural problem in altogether too narrow a way, and that it was high time for the government agencies to consider the social results to the great mass of farmers by their efficiency propaganda. It was an interesting point, but at that time tea intervened, so we all buzzed about it over the teacups. The Englishmen were very apologetic, feeling that Ashby had jumped Case too hard. Personally, I was glad the issue had been raised, but I feel that Case was not as guilty of the narrow cost-accounting point of view as some of the others, both American and British.'[7]

While Wallace was still in England the proposal to raise American tariffs anew from Fordney to Hawley levels — the move he had warned against so sharply before leaving — was still to reach the Senate; but it became increasingly evident from the trend of the debate that the measure would become a law. Wallace recalled this years later, testifying extempore before the Senate Committee of Commerce, in January of 1945, when summoned to defend his fitness for the post of Secretary of Commerce:

> ... When we exported so much more than we imported, and refused to accept goods, a day of reckoning was inevitable. When we raised the tariff a second time that day of reckoning came.
>
> I was attending an international economic conference in England in 1929 at the time that bill had been introduced. I know the effect it had on the economists on the Continent; the effect it had on the British and the other representatives there. I knew they felt as a result that they would be pushed into taking countervailing measures, which later on they did. That is when the world tailspin really began with a vengeance.[8]

Wallace went on to the Continent. In Germany he spent, experimentally, the equivalent of a nickel for a glass of beer and could not finish his nickel's worth. Beyond the polite pretense of touching his lips to brew, vintage, or distillation as a gesture of good will and social amenity, he does not drink, and has never used tobacco in any form. At Prague he visited his sister, the wife of the Swiss Minister to Czechoslovakia. He planned to go on from there across Russia to Siberia and Japan. But '. . . then the whole thing went to waste because I got a cablegram that afternoon announcing that *Wallaces' Farmer* and *The Homestead* had merged. I thought I had better go home.'

It was around a two-million-dollar deal. He had not been consulted about it and did not know that the thing was to be done until it had been done. Trade circles had sniffed wind of some such combination coming up. On paper it would be a powerful one, and in ordinary times, logical. Those ancient antagonists, Uncle Henry and James M. Pierce, were long since dead now; and their sons and heirs had not kept up the feud, except in a purely commercial competitive way. Dante Pierce, a most dynamic son of old James F., was a good friend of Henry's, and all the Wallaces had other friends on *The Homestead* staff. Dante Pierce was running *The Homestead*, with a plant more spacious and magnificent than *Wallaces'*, valued at upwards of a million and a quarter dollars, and all this went into the trade. The Wallace plant, while less imposing, had built up a job-printing and electrotyping business, esteemed at the time and since as one of the best west of Chicago. They did all the electrotype work for Meredith's *Successful Farming* and much such work for the Pierce papers, as well as their own. So, in the still-spacious expectations of farm publishing in that era, the price, in terms of total prospect, was probably not far out of line. 'I am sure,' Dr. Tait Butler of *The Progressive Farmer*, Memphis, wrote to his editor, Dr. Clarence Poe, in North Carolina, when the deal was pending, 'that Mr. [John] Wallace does not think the Pierce properties worth over one and three-quarter millions, but he is anxious to consolidate the farm paper interests in Iowa and Wisconsin and leave the field to his son and his two nephews. I had a letter from him today [May 10, 1929] in which he stated that they were still working on the proposition, but had not made much progress, although he was confident they would still work it out.'

The merger was announced in the issue of October 26, 1929.

Wallaces' had bought *The Iowa Homestead,* lock, stock, and barrel. Henry A. Wallace was to edit the wedded publications, with a circulation of two hundred and fifty thousand. The Wallaces were ready to move into the *Homestead* building by the time Henry got back to Des Moines. Dictating 'Odds and Ends' for the issue of November 16, 1929, he said:

> I find it rather sad to move from my dingy old office in the *Wallaces' Farmer* building to a well-lighted efficient office in *The Homestead* building. The day I moved was exactly five years from the time my father died in Washington. As I looked out of the windows of my old office, I called to mind how my uncle and brother and I journeyed to Washington just five years before, to the very hour. Then I looked at the pictures on the wall which my grandfather had gathered together. There were the autographed photos of President Roosevelt, Gifford Pinchot, Liberty Hyde Bailey, *et al.* There was the old davenport upon which my grandfather used to lie and rest for half an hour after eating. There was the corner of the office where my father sat at his desk in late February, in 1921, just before setting out for Washington.
>
> And now I am in a well-lighted, larger room, with a terrazzo floor and a look of cleanness and efficiency. There are no pictures to remind me of the past and I must set my face toward the future. . . .

3. M. L. Wilson

THE DOWNSWIRL of prices and values was abrupt after the autumn of 1929 when the depression became general; and agriculture, having taken it first and hardest, had to take it hardest all over again. It was a fantastic experience, going around the nation as a farm reporter out from New York in those days, looking for successful farmers to write about, so as to encourage the others, and also to encourage advertisers to place their goods in paid space before an element of the population which was loudly protesting that, having been going broke fairly steadily for a decade, they now were headed down the drain for fair.

Fifteen-thousand-dollar-a-year promotion men in New York City were inquiring anxiously of the office's Italian bootblack how to grow potatoes, if worse came to worst; while Park Avenue farm reporters on field trips were panhandled by displaced farm operators near great, rotting stacks of wheat, out around Fargo. It was completely fantastic to be getting $400 for articles instead of the old top of $150, making more money than we had ever made in our lives; yet daring, alas, no longer to carry canes, like real New York journalists, when we walked abroad, because carrying a stick attracted too many metropolitan panhandlers, certain of whom were surly when denied. Those were strange years.

I traveled far and talked with a great variety of people. As the depression spread and deepened, we staff men were given greater and greater latitude in finding and reporting wilder and stranger cures. President Hoover's Farm Board, encountering increasing difficulties, through no special fault in zeal, was considering and even suggesting unofficially the plowdown of every third row of cotton. In making loans or grants to market gardening co-operatives the Board was quietly specifying a reduced acreage as conditional to the loan, and in some instances was even specifying that the operator apply less fertilizer. Even the driven New Dealers, when their turn at the wheel came, never went so far as to induce farmers by grants, loans, or payments to make American soil less fertile. The Farm Board's conditional loans were nevertheless strictly consistent with the end in view, an immediately decreased production, and in a mad sort of way it did make sense.

Administrators trying to gain this end by means of admonition or verbal suasion only got nowhere. When the winter wheat crop of 1931 was not yet seeded, doughty Alexander Legge, the Farm Board's chairman, and Arthur M. Hyde, Mr. Hoover's Secretary of Agriculture, went out to western Kansas to make speeches. They stood on a platform in the center of eleven and three-quarter million acres of winter wheat land, a third of the entire American wheat acreage, and shouted and coaxed for a

diminished seeding that fall. From the audience came objections.
Why should not the high-priced, humid wheat areas do the reducing, if reduction there need be? Why should the most expansive low-cost production area be asked to reduce?

'It's always the biggest hog that has its feet in the trough,'
Alex Legge recalled from his younger days on the farm. 'Does
Kansas want to be that kind of a hog?' he asked. A press association represented Mr. Legge as having said flatly that Kansas
was a hog with both feet in the trough. The press and people of
Kansas thundered with outrage and indignation; and even with
the tractor-powdered dust already rising to darken its sky and
prospect, western Kansas slapped a little more winter wheat than
ever into its soil that fall. 'We were ridiculed,' said Secretary
Arthur Hyde afterward. 'We aroused a storm of wrath and
derision. But that trip had its uses. It started thought on new
tracks.'

So it did. But simply to suggest reduction of sowings without
implementing the reduction — as economists were learning to say
around that time — was of no use. Simple stubbornness did not
keep these high plains sodbusters defiantly expanding their
plowlands. It was need. And need in varying measure kept
nearly all American farmers doing the same thing. Starvation
prices, brought on by 'superabundance,' do not invariably, in
their own good time, bring on a diminution of agricultural plantings, as Adam Smith supposed when he wrote his *Wealth of Nations*. Panic prices are likely to reduce the planters, in person and
number, but not the planting. Desperately low prices for nearly
all agricultural products prevailed in this country from shortly
after the World War, around 1920, until the more general crash
of prices in 1929. Yet at the end of that predepression period
American farmers were scratching desperately at a little more
land than they had been tilling in 1919, at the peak of the wartime
boom. Taxes had not come down, interest charges had not come
down, land values were as yet incompletely deflated. Nearly
all the fixed operation and consumer charges against modern
farming stayed high. But if wheat, or hogs, or tobacco go to
half-price, as many farmers explained at the time, 'you've got to
try to raise twice as much to stay in business.'

Between 1920 and 1925, over our country as a whole, nearly a hundred thousand farms ceased to be operated by their former tenants or owners; but still the total acreage under cultivation increased. Between 1925 and 1930 more than two hundred thousand farm homes were abandoned — more farm families than are found in all New England, New Jersey, Delaware, and Maryland — but the farming survivors kept spreading out, trying to beat more and more crops out of the land.

The State of Montana provided a high stage of preview, exhibiting gigantic forces of change at work. As early as 1924 half of the wheat farmers of Montana had lost their farms. Chester C. Davis was there suffering through it as State Commissioner of Agriculture when the Harding party passed through in 1923. So was Milburn Lincoln Wilson, head of agricultural economics at the State Agricultural College at Bozeman, Dr. H. C. Taylor's guide when he made his inspection trip through the Northwest in 1924.

'We saw what was left of the old pioneer order,' Wilson said when I went out there to see him in 1929 after talking in Iowa with Henry A. Wallace, 'a pitiful remnant scratching at sections and half-sections with inadequate equipment. All the eggs in one smashed basket, and that basket too small! Great blocks of land had passed into the hands of loan and insurance companies that did not know what to do with it. And on all sides we saw good farmers — young men, many of them lately married, with the beginnings of a family — caught, starved out on the lower sections of the ladder that leads to farm ownership, with no chance to climb.'

Born on a half-section homestead farm near Atlantic, Iowa, October 23, 1885, M. L. Wilson is around three years older than Henry A. Wallace. He shifts from economic jabberwocky, such as 'delimiting the periphery of the maladjustment,' into plain American-English quite as readily and naturally as Wallace does. 'Don't blow me up too big in what you write,' he told me at our first interview. 'I'm just a Montana farmer who saw hard times ahead of time.' Later: 'You can put me down as a scientific humanist and conditioned optimist,' he said. Like Henry A., the first time you meet and talk with him, and often afterwards,

M. L. Wilson seems a simple and forthright yet exceedingly complex man. They are quite different in a variety of particulars. Wilson, for instance, without any elaborate artifice or the least insincerity, is the more gifted showman and mixer. He loves to tell yarns and laugh. But in terms of blood, soil, and spirit, this Wallace and this Wilson are cast in remarkably the same mold.

Milburn is Wilson's given name; not the kind that you can call a man familiarly. At Iowa State College and later they nicknamed this ambling countryman from his initials, and ever since then nearly everyone who knows him speaks of M. L. Wilson as 'M.L.' One of his earliest memories is jogging to church in the family buggy while his mother read the latest of Uncle Henry's journalistic Sabbath Lessons from *Wallaces' Farmer* aloud. 'The Wallaces helped form my mind and character, just as they did for hundreds of thousands of other folks in Iowa. When I went to Ames to study agriculture in 1902, I was not the first boy in my neighborhood to go to college, but I was the first to go from there to an *agricultural* college. Young Henry, as we called him, came there as a freshman when I was an upperclassman. We knew each other, but not so well, then.'

Wilson, '07, took most of his courses in the science of growing useful plants — agronomy. Little that bore on the social sciences or the humanities was offered by the Land Grant Colleges thirty or more years ago. He did, however, take a course in philosophy which set him to reading more widely. He was offered upon graduation a job on the college staff, Instructor in Agronomy. But he had an idea that the way to learn about farming was from farms and farmers — 'lots of different pieces of land, and lots of different men, in lots of different situations' — not from neat little experimental plants or from books. Looks should follow, not precede, the experience. 'When I worked for W. J. Spillman, later, I found that was his main idea.' The science of farm management should be derived from the compiled experiences, the trials and errors and triumphs, of the people themselves. 'I don't mean to say I had the idea all set and clear in my mind. I just knew I wanted to see a lot more new land and farms. I was only twenty-two years old and I was especially interested in big farms.'

So he turned down the college post and did a quick turn of mixed farming as a tenant in a part of the country new to him, Nebraska. That part of the country had not quite settled down. There was talk of grand new stretches of land just west. Government land — free! Wilson sold out his teams and tools at a profit. 'In 1909 I came into Montana with another fellow and took out a homestead, and the first thing I did was buy the biggest steam engine I could find. There weren't any gas tractors in 1909. But I had a steam engine. I was rather aggressively machine-minded.'

He came to the Montana upland in 'good years' — years of rain. The land rush upon the northern high plains was at first a scattered push of farmers with Midland wheat and seed corn in their wagons, and plows for the grassland, and visions of furrows stretching straight for miles without a bend or quiver. In 1912 Congress passed the Three-Year Homestead Act and plains homesteading doubled. The railroads got out special posters shouting: 'Montana or Bust!' '320 Acres Look Good to Me!' 'Get a Free Home in the West!' One great colored poster showed a plow tearing sodland into an upflowing furrow of bright golden dollars. 'From Buffalo Days to Boom Days,' was the cry. Here and elsewhere on the short-grass frontier the rains those first few years were so abundant that the settlers felt, and some agricultural professors published it as fact, that plowing of itself can make a naturally semi-arid region humid. 'The man was a stoic,' Wilson wrote, reviewing the experience in a college bulletin later, 'if he could not enthuse over the crops of 1915–16. Wheat on sod without exceptional treatment yielded fifty bushels to the acre and was sold for two dollars a bushel.'

On came the migrants hopefully. Claim entries at Havre, Montana, mounted to seventy-five hundred in the year 1917. The occupations of the settlers ranged from deep-sea diver to cowhand to milliner. Fewer than half of them were experienced farmers and even some of the experienced ones were 'shotgun farmers,' as the pioneer saying goes: 'He fills his shotgun full of seed, shoots at the ground, and cusses the country if he doesn't get a crop.'

In 1917 a drought set in. It held almost without a break

through the World War years. So for all the slain grass and the headlong overplowing, Montana did not share in the plunder of wartime wheat prices as other parts of the great plains did. The slogan, 'Montana or Bust,' had lapsed into a disgruntled byword, 'Montana *and* Bust,' in many parts of Montana even before the firing ended overseas.

'As a matter of fact,' says Wilson, 'we hit some trouble even in the early years of rain. This was a new country, different from where we came from. The old seeds weren't right for it, or the old ways of culture. It was plain we were up against new propositions. We had to design a new pattern of occupation for Montana. The State Agricultural College at Bozeman called me in on some dry-land farming investigations to find out how we could work out an adjustment here, and farm so as to stay.' After that he became Montana's first county agricultural agent and its first State leader of Extension. In 1920 when he was thirty-five, he took leave and entered upon work for a Master's degree with Richard T. Ely and John R. Commons at the University of Wisconsin. His subject was economics, with stress on land economics. But the facts of Montana's situation were by this time such, says Wilson, smiling, 'that a man really needed a long serene view of things to keep on working there.' Also, in the early nineteen-twenties he spent three summers at the University of Chicago. Philosophy was his study. He took James Hayden Tufts' course on the Evolution of the Idea of Justice and Eustace Hayden's on Comparative Cultures and Religions. Tufts, especially, was a working philosopher. For some years Chief Justice of the Labor Court in Chicago, Tufts was concerned not only with the sources of man's heightening aspirations but with methods of bringing the value of philosophical implications into daily life. From Hayden and Tufts, Wilson derived something of an anthropological concept of human patterns and behavior, considering vast human settlements and dissettlements with a far view. 'I only went to summer schools in Chicago. When I would get back home, out to Montana, and go out among my old friends there, I was so struck with new slants on two contrasting cultures, Indian and White, existing side by side there, that I could see Montana with new eyes.

'Tufts had the feeling that we were developing a city civiliza-tion. He saw the greater rewards and the greater minds, speaking generally, piling up in towns. He said that wasn't healthy and that (this had quite an effect on me) if nobody else could do anything about it, the Government ought to. And then, of course, I had also been sitting under John Commons. John's an institutional economist in the field of labor. I began to make some applications of that to the field of agriculture.

'I didn't want to get too far off the ground with my ideas. In the summers of '23 and '24 I took work with Warren in his farm management department at Cornell. A lot of people never understood George Warren. There was a side to him that the fellows who only saw him over the adding machines or through the index figures never saw, and a side to him that the "gold bugs" never understood. He had a distinctly philosophical approach to the physical and physiological attributes that influence farms and farming. I also took some History of Philosophy under Dean Creighton in the Arts School. He was a purely idealistic philoso-pher, a good offset to Tufts and Warren.'

When Wilson rode into Montana as a settler, he had been barely old enough to vote. Now he was getting along toward the middle years, nearly forty. From 1924 to 1926 he divided his time between Montana and the Department of Agriculture in Washington. He was in charge of farm management and cost accounting for the Department. This brought him closely in touch with W. J. Spillman, perhaps the most fertile-minded agri-culturist of his day. As an agronomist at the outset of his career, in 1900, Spillman independently discovered Mendel's law of heredity. As a farm management specialist Spillman spoke as early as 1904 for agricultural planning, both in particular and in the large. Now in his closing years he was working on a highly mathematical treatise, relating the exponential yield curve to fertilizer experiments. More particularly, Spillman was discussing with associates such as Wilson, Howard A. Tolley, H. C. Taylor, and Mordecai Ezekiel in the Bureau of Agricultural Economics a variety of political devices to balance American farm production to paying demand.

Many measures which have come to be thought of as New Deal

measures were taking form largely unregarded in the United States
Department of Agriculture back around 1924. The devices which
Wilson took a lead in developing were: tenant rehabilitation,
experiments in regional land planning, balanced harvests by the
domestic allotment (later the Triple–A) method, and subsistence
homestead projects of rural-urban design.

Wilson did not, as is sometimes claimed for him, invent the
new social machinery in field and township by which the Agricultural Adjustment Agency (Triple–A) or the Soil Conservation
Service's (S.C.S.) self-governing districts now operate. But he
played a large part. He did not, singly and alone, invent the
subsistence homestead colonies of the Roosevelt New Deal.
He adapted such devices from previous proposals and existing
models out on the ground. He visited and talked with literally
thousands of different people who already had something of the
sort in mind or going and were trying to work it out. In the
councils of the planners in Washington, Wilson worked almost
always in the background, but with marked effect. In formulat-
ing new working compromises between our agrarian and commercial hopes and influences, he proved a most productive social
architect; and in a continuing sense he was Wallace's chief collaborator in evolving new economic-democratic social mechanisms
that would stand up in the field.

He was thinking in terms of what we now call 'farm security'
even before he tackled the so-called 'crop surplus' problem. But
he had been forced to consider the economic, social, and spiritual
wastes of a 'surplus-ridden' society and 'plan both ways at once,
against the middle.' As he said: 'We face a dilemma. We must
either resolve this dilemma or acknowledge that men are the
slaves, not the masters, of their own machines. In the First
World War rush the first tractors and combines crowded out and
for the most part swept away the old-time family farm in Montana. New, faster tractors and implements are coming not only
here but the country over all the time. In Montana we went
through the whole thing in a whirlwind. We had to stop and ask
ourselves: Suppose we got the biggest farms, the biggest and best
machinery, the highest technical efficiency imaginable — where
would we be?

'There was only one possible answer: technological displacement, technological efficiency, would continue; but this other
kind of thing, subsistence farming, probably sustained by part-
time industry, has to be given a place.'

The somewhat recalcitrant Dr. H. C. Taylor had been thinking
along like lines when he and Wilson first became companionable,
as professor and summer student, at the University of Wisconsin.
When William M. Jardine, having just succeeded Taylor's friend
and hero, Harry Wallace, as Secretary, bounced Taylor ever so
gently out of the Department, Taylor, nothing daunted, went
West again. He got in touch with Wilson. He also got in touch
with Beardsley Ruml and others he knew on the board of the
Laura Spelman Rockefeller Foundation. In 1924, when a systematic rehabilitation of tenants by Government grants or loans
would certainly have seemed a rather advanced form of state
paternalism, which it is, Taylor and Wilson turned to private
philanthropy for funds. John D. Rockefeller, Jr., liked the idea.
He made the loan. His personal check for one hundred thousand
dollars reached Montana in time to get things running for the
crop year 1925. Later, Mr. Rockefeller advanced, in endowment-
loan, another fifty thousand dollars, likewise repayable at five
per cent. The checks were drawn to 'Fairway Farms, Inc.,' a
non-profit corporation with nine directors. Five of these directors
were college professors and four were farmers and mortgage bankers. The purpose, Taylor and Wilson stated, was to establish
'a corporation that would work with distressed farmers, not
against them; that will give a definite purchase contract, a long
time to pay, sound guidance, and actual financial help over the
hard places in bad years; in short, a corporation that will work
to turn the tide against tenancy and restore as the buttress of
our national structure the free-hold, one-family farm.'

Wilson remained in Montana as head of the rural economics
division of a hard-hit State Agricultural College, working with
diminished enrollment on cut salaries; and he served without pay
as manager of eight Fairway farms established in various parts
of Montana by the end of the crop year 1926–27. These farms
were not only experiments in tenant rehabilitation. They were
experimental plantings in applied economics. They were, as

nearly as I can determine, our first definite American experiment in regional land use. Montana has widely varied soil, climatic, and crop areas. The purpose here was to find in each area the size of the holding, the amount of capital and equipment and the crop scheme which might enable a tenant not only to pay interest on his debt to the corporation, but gradually to retire the debt and own the farm.

But the drought had not relented throughout Montana. Neither had deflation. The Fairway Farms experimenters had accumulated data of sensational import; but when it came to rehabilitating tenants to ownership under the climatic and economic weather then prevailing, they never really had a chance. Late in 1927, I met Wilson by his arrangement in a small hotel just around the corner from the Grain Exchange in Minneapolis. He had a dollar-and-a-half-a-day room there. We sat in that room and talked for the better part of a day and a night.

He was forty-five years old then, and much younger-looking than he is now. He was almost boyish-looking, in fact. I recall how I labored to keep the talk on what I thought was the main track; how Wilson would pause and stare out the window and then take the talk on some wide circuit that seemed to have nothing whatever to do with the theme. But all you had to do, I found later, was to wait it out; and back he would come to where he had started, in a sort of conversational spiral that adorned the argument and lifted it a notch. Many another interviewer has found Wilson a baffling subject in the years since. That long, slow sweep of the arm describes more nearly than words the way he thinks. He thinks in cycles, but the cycles link, and in the end the point is made with force and clearness.

On a card hardly larger than a postcard he had written a table of figures summarizing the first five years' finding at Brockton, the largest and most completely mechanized of the Fairway Farms. They were growing wheat at Brockton for less than twenty-five cents a bushel, and with only three minutes of human labor for each bushel. (It is ordinarily figured that peasants, working by hand, put at least three hours' labor in growing each bushel of wheat.) Using the largest power equipment then obtainable, with sixty horse-power caterpillar tractors, the most

SECRETARY HENRY A. WALLACE AND UNDER-SECRETARY
REX TUGWELL, JUNE, 1934

efficient size for a one-family wheat farm in that locality was found to be no less than three thousand acres. And the capital outlay required to use and maintain the equipment on such a unit was $11,460 *a year.*

'But how many farm families can stand up to that outlay?' I asked. He answered absently: 'I don't know. Not very many, I guess.' He leaned his chair back against the wall, put his hands behind his head, and went on talking, slowly:

All our inherited, romantic notions about the separateness of American farming and of the American farm home stand opposed to these great changes that are at our door. People will continue to stand in the middle of a world revolution in agriculture, arguing that agriculture cannot be standardized over wide areas, that farming cannot be industrialized, that country people cannot live in towns and go out to their business — that they must live, in relative isolation, out on the land.

My view is that we stand *now*, here in America, in the midst of a revolutionary mechanization of agriculture that will touch in one way or another upon the lives of nearly every one of us.

It will remove from agriculture all but the ablest of those now engaged in it. It will wipe out the remaining differences, distances, and distinctions between country and city people. Within twenty-five years the increased mechanization of agriculture and improved communication will make of the American farmer a town or a city dweller.

All this was seventeen years ago. Wilson went on:

He will live in a house like everybody else's house, with a druggist perhaps as his right-hand neighbor, or a merchant, or perhaps another farmer, on his left. He will enjoy more conveniences, perhaps more money and certainly a great deal more time and leisure and self-improvement than most city people have now. . . .

You know, I've been changing my mind, these past few years, considerably, about the 'independence' of the diversi-

fied, one-family farm. I know all the advantages. I had
them myself when I was young. But I know also that the
average family-farm income, counting in all that the place
provides in the way of a living, is less than $1500 a year.
That's the income of a whole family — a man, a woman, and
maybe a grown son. I keep thinking about that $1500.
What kind of 'independence' is that? . . .

The place I'm most interested in, right now, is Utah, with
its farming towns and villages. I was out there recently.
I saw farmsteads along streets. The families who lived
there weren't making, many of them, any more than $1500
a year. But because their houses were together and because
a great deal of their work was shared or consolidated, those
families had leisure. And all the civilized conveniences —
electric light and power, running water, and so on.

I got to wondering what would have come out of it, if
my mother, laboring most of her life on our old homestead
there in Cass County, Iowa, could have been a farmwife in a
village like this. She was teaching school when she married
my father. She was a trained musician and an artist. But
it kept her so busy taking care of all of us out there in the
country, under isolated conditions, without conveniences,
that she never had time to go ahead with her music or to
paint. She used to play for us sometimes, but she never
knew any new pieces. She played the same old pieces over
and over for us until she was eighty years old.

Until her youngest boy had grown up, she hardly knew
what it was to have a minute she could call her own. When
she was getting on toward seventy, I conceived the idea of
getting her an easel and the materials for painting. You
wouldn't believe the joy she got out of it! And her paintings
had real beauty and feeling; they weren't just the usual
thing.

She was a woman of genuine artistic ability, with .a fine
mind. Between the time that she was twenty and the time
that she was seventy, that side of her never really had a
chance to live at all. I don't believe that any amount of
$1500 'independence' is worth that price.

There were two breaks in the day's conversation, a call from Victor Christgau, then a Minnesota congressman, and a visit with some leading brokers on the Grain Exchange. Wilson and Christgau were drafting a bill for the establishment of economic experiments like the Fairway Farms, region by region, throughout the country. The Christgau bill died in committee, but the text of it even now is worth reading. It makes plain that Wilson's principal initial interest in farm legislation was not simply to raise farm income; he saw it primarily as a device for national planning, with the people participating and growing in understanding on a grand scale. He did not care for the sort of overhead planning he had seen in Russia the previous summer. 'Those little Communists strutting! It has to be planned from the ground up,' he said. This was to his friends, the grain men, in their sumptuous office at the Exchange building. In that time of bitter need they listened to Wilson as to a father. But they were naturally more interested in what the price of wheat would be than they were in national planning. 'I've got bad news from over there in Europe,' Wilson told them. 'The Old World doesn't need, or won't take, our surplus grain. I look for a feed price on wheat for some years to come.' 'But isn't there anything to be done about it?' one of the brokers demanded nervously. 'Well, yes,' said Wilson, 'and we ought to be working on a plan.'

4. Professional Brainstormers

HENRY A. WALLACE had written in a memoir on farm relief: 'Beginning in the fall of 1931 M. L. Wilson of Montana became a propagandist for the idea of the domestic allotment plan. He knew that the support of business men as well as farmers would be necessary. He wanted to familiarize all classes of society with the idea so that the plan could be put over in the next administration.

'W. J. Spillman, a brilliant economist, had published a book, *Balancing the Farm Output.* Several men took up Spillman's idea, notably John D. Black, Beardsley Ruml, and M. L. Wilson.'[9]

Wallace, himself, was familiar with the Spillman plan from

1927 onward, was thinking ahead on it, and in some particulars was ahead of Black and Wilson. It seemed to him to fit into a possible national expansion of the 'back-to-grass' drive he had put on in his paper around 1924. That would be a soil conservation approach — and result. He had for many years known Spillman, who was an agrostologist, or grass specialist, as well as a mathematician of rare endowment,. When Secretary Harry Wallace returned Spillman in 1920 from the banishment ordained by Secretary Houston, Spillman was given a free-lance status within the Department and worked principally on a highly mathematical and technical research bulletin, *Use of the Exponential Yield Curve in Fertilizer*.[10] He considered this the most important work of his life and as Dr. Ramsay Spillman, his son, insists, W. J. Spillman is not to be credited or blamed for all the political convolutions his domestic-allotment idea later underwent. But in 1926 Spillman wrote some farm-paper articles on the problem of making up to agriculture the drain and loss imposed by tariffs, and worked this book over into the small book Wallace has cited as seminal for so many of the agricultural planners.

America, Spillman's reasoning ran, had become a high-tariff country. We were likely to stay so for a long time. We must turn our eyes from the old dream of a world to feed and clothe, of infinite markets endlessly expanding, and cultivate our own garden, and plan. This need not mean complete retreat to a domestic basis of production. Rather, we must adjust production so that our surpluses above domestic need can be sold on the world market at an advantage.

Dr. John D, Black, who had just come East from the University of Minnesota to teach agricultural economics at Harvard, was impressed by this reasoning. He worked out a production control plan, with allotments of acreage, and presented it before Congress at those hearings which led to the Farm Board's enabling Act. Farm Board lawyers found his plan unconstitutional, as Black's friend, Henry I. Harriman, a wealthy Boston business man, trained in law and experienced in the operation of public utilities, had previously suggested. Allotments could only be made to stand, Mr. Harriman told Dr. Black, on a contract basis, entered into directly between the producers and the Government.

Spillman's proposal was for an intricate allotment system, sustained by taxes collected from local dealers. Black held that a revised plan should be tried at first on two crops only, wheat and cotton; and that individual allotment rights should be made transferable, so as to permit a continued migration of crops toward regions that can grow them best and cheapest. These and other suggestions Black entered as a chapter in his book, *Agricultural Reform in the United States*, 1929.

Attending Leonard Elmhirst's international farm conference in England that summer, Wallace found foreign economists discussing the Spillman-Black plan with interest and some apprehension. It suggested to them a nationalistic withdrawal, in large part, of American farm products from world commerce.

Like devices were by no means rare in Europe; but Europeans were generally applying them in reverse, with bounties to support *increased* produce grown at home and a consequently greater degree of self-containment. By that time no less than forty foreign countries were applying agricultural price-supporting measures. Around 1930, when American farmers were taking forty cents a bushel or letting wheat go back to earth unharvested, French, Italian, and German farmers were taking supported prices running upwards of $1.25 a bushel for wheat; and England was setting up a system of 'deficiency payments' with like intent. In general, these European governments made up to their farmers the difference between the open-market or world price of wheat and a 'fair' price — enough to keep the farmers fairly happy and conservative, and growing wheat. It may have been economically unreasonable for those crowded Old World countries to grow more wheat on more and more patches instead of importing it; but fearful memories can be more compelling than reason, and there was abroad a haunting expectation of renewed war.

With world markets closing against us, the American need seemed plainly for less production, rather than more. Our allotment plan, as Wilson redesigned it with wheat in mind especially, called for governmental intervention to make up the difference between fifty-cent wheat and dollar wheat, broadly speaking, in return for a *decreased* planting, farm by farm. It was a rather modest version of the European idea, turned around.

Continuing in *New Frontiers*, 1934, a quick retrospective account of the highly involved marriage of minds whereby our Agricultural Adjustment or Farm Act of 1933 was conceived and brought into being, Wallace wrote:

> Wilson did a good job of interesting many important leaders and groups. . . . His presentation was brought to Governor Roosevelt by Rex Tugwell, and in a campaign speech at Topeka, Kansas, in September, 1932, the Democratic candidate described the essentials of what later became the Agricultural Adjustment Act.[11]

It was, indeed, an extraordinary job of quiet, open propaganda. One wonders sometimes how Wilson, away off there in distressed Montana, working almost alone on a $3600 salary which had been cut one-fifth, got so much done. His travel time and money were extremely limited. He could never pay more than two dollars a day for a hotel room, however great the city. But letter mail was only two cents in those days, and Wilson had friends the country over, and one of his best friends, W. R. Ronald, was a near-by country newspaperman with a printing press. Wilson, Ronald, and Henry Wallace formed a small supporting committee, together with Louis Clark of Nebraska and R. R. Rogers of New Jersey. Clark was a mortgage broker, and Rogers an insurance executive with large holdings in distressed land. The first important recruit to this group was Henry I. Harriman of Boston, Black's Boston lawyer friend, and President of the United States Chamber of Commerce at the time. Harriman had heard from Dr. Black at Harvard of the domestic allotment principle, and was interested, partly because it foretold the legalization of open production quotas or price covenants, such as was later attempted for industry under NRA. It foretold a large 'out' from under the Sherman Anti-Trust Act. Harriman made a trip to Montana to inspect two hundred thousand acres of distressed ranchland in which he had become interested and Wilson went to work on him out there. Harriman was persuaded. He became an energetic voluntary *liaison* agent between agriculture and industry and between East and West.

Sensible that plenty of relatively radical planning involving land use was under way, insiders surrounding Agriculture's Secretary Hyde in the Hoover administration pressed him to formulate a more conservative land program, and helped him get one up. They produced, with President Hoover's approval, a plan to withdraw especially worthless marginal land from cultivation by governmental rent or purchase; and this won fairly general conservative approbation, including that of some large holders of the most worthless foreclosed tracts. The idea of retiring relatively worthless land to forestry or recreational purposes was sound enough, incipient New Dealers within the Hoover administration and without argued; but it did not go far enough. The most pressing 'surplus' was obviously produced in large part on the better land. Marginal retirement, nevertheless, was as far as the agenda went for a Land Use Conference called by Secretary Hyde in Chicago during November of 1931.

Somewhat prior to that, in midsummer, *The Country Home* sent me to the West Coast to look into a rumor that co-operating growers of canning peaches were paying, from pooled funds, bounties to members who would pull up producing trees by the roots. It was more than a rumor; it was an organized effort. Tractors with chains were going sturdily about this strange business on some of the richest land in California. Destroy and gain! Then there was California's pending pro-rate law. Given *carte blanche* by that most conservative of Extension Directors, B. H. Crocheron, I was provided with temporary space in their Extension Service offices, and given the opportunity to see in all frankness the purposes and intent of the proposal. A child of the great co-operatives there, and especially the citrus growers, this measure provided what amounted to economic-quarantine stamps, allotted by acreage. No box or hamper of produce could leave the member's holdings and enter into commerce without such a stamp. Quite elaborate measures were proposed to 'by-process' the part of the crop not marketed raw into citrate of magnesia, fountain drinks, and so on. Some progress had been made in this; but most of the by-processing was still by Nature's simple method — the excess stuff fell to the ground and rotted.

In California Wilson had Howard Tolley, then head of the Giannini Foundation, interested and working. In Washington he had, among others, Mordecai Ezekiel, economist for the Farm Board. It was Ezekiel who had most to do with including in the Farm Board's closing statement the assertion that without production control price maintenance was impossible. Wilson also had lines out to his old friends at the University of Chicago and the University of Wisconsin. Passing through Chicago on my way back East that August of 1931, I was admitted to a more or less off-the-record Conference on Economic Policy for American Agriculture at the University of Chicago. It was principally a gathering of outsiders; around eighty conferees, a widely diverse and worried lot. Farm Board and old-line Department of Agriculture economists were invited, also, and some of the boldest came. Henry Wallace led a discussion on 'hard' versus 'soft' money, with lively interjections from self-announced 'radicals' as various as John R. Commons and John A. Simpson, of the militant Farmers' Union. Howard Tolley led the talk on agricultural planning, with regional experiments and farm allotments. The best existing summary of the conference was broadcast by Wilson and published by the University of Chicago in a pamphlet called *Land Utilization*. 'Agriculture as well as industry must have a new economic philosophy,' he argued, and 'land-use planning must be the foundation of any farm-relief program.' He proposed five major steps: (1) repeal of the Homestead Act, (2) state and regional land classification programs, (3) withdrawal of marginal lands from production, (4) enactment of the domestic allotment plan. Finally:

> The last step in the program which I recommend is parttime farming and decentralization of industry.... Since our land retirement program contemplates releasing families from poor agricultural lands, it is logical to ask: Will these join the already overcrowded ranks of the unemployed? They will be useless unless industry also adopts a new policy.[12]

One of the board which sponsored this broadcast and pamphlet was R. G. Tugwell, Professor of Economics at Columbia, who had just been drawn by Raymond Moley into Franklin D. Roosevelt's pre-convention 'Brain Trust.' Tugwell had never met Wilson, but he liked this line of reasoning, and he wrote Wilson a letter saying so. In the spring of 1932, Wilson and Tugwell met in Washington. Beardsley Ruml brought them together. Wilson described with circumambulatory gestures how farmers' committees would grow in economic education and well-being through voluntary application of the allotment principle, with all key decisions sustained by referenda. Wilson and Tugwell took to each other immediately, though they did not then or later see eye to eye in every particular.

Wilson bore on, proselyting, telling his story repeatedly to economists, writers, politicians, industrialists, farm leaders, bankers, and insurance executives with distressed landholdings. He always talked for crop allotments in the first part of his speeches and for 'a new pattern of country living,' subsistence homesteads, in closing. Told of an extemporaneous talk that Governor Roosevelt had made late in 1927 at Cornell University on 'the possibility of establishing small industrial plants in areas now given over wholly to farming,' Wilson said, 'That's my man for President!'

Fellow workers, first pushing crop allotment drives and then subsistence homestead projects, were to find his patient, stubborn insistence on democratic participation in planning impractical and annoying at times. Wilson believes in expertness and high-grade civil service decisions as deeply as anyone, but, 'it's safer to let the people in on it, from the first, and check up. When you try to move things faster than the awakened will and understanding of the people, it isn't good education and it isn't democracy,' he said, and says. He was in Washington for a short while lobbying with Henry Morgenthau, Rex Tugwell, and other fledgling New Dealers to see if the Republican Congress would not act before adjournment and make crop allotments operative by March, 1933. Word came that the Farmers' Referendum provision which Wilson had written into the measure had been thrown out in committee. He quietly got on the train and went back to Montana. 'I wasn't much interested in it without that,' he explained.

It was a sad show, that last lame-duck session of Congress in our history. Governor Roosevelt's advance emissaries got a taste of representative government in its most irresponsible form.

Marvin Jones fought coolly and ably through infinite intricacies
to assert and clarify a defensible principle for sustaining the
general welfare by farm relief. So did La Guardia of New York.
For the majority, the session was merely an exhibition, a chance to
strut and speak a piece before the holidays, or retirement. A wry
Republican lame duck, picking his teeth in the corridors, guffawed:
'The Democrats have a way to make hogs use birth control!'

So it went. Peanuts, rice, butterfat, and a variety of other
odd regional clutterings were jammed into the allotment act,
hauled out, jammed in again. At one point a persuasive attempt
was made to take out hogs and put in goats. With each new day
proceedings soared farther beyond the confines of sane decorum.
Small wonder the farm organizations sought to remove the administration of this bill as far as possible from the hands of
Congress, endowing instead with dictatorial powers the incoming,
and then unknown, Secretary of Agriculture.

5. Gyrations

THERE IS no use pretending,' said Walter Lippmann in
his syndicated column, when proposals which later culminated in the 'voluntary' domestic allotment act were
placed before the lame-duck session of Congress, 'that this is
not the most daring economic experiment ever seriously proposed
in the United States. But what other remedy is proposed for
the plight of agriculture that might be substituted for this one?'
Three weeks later, still sympathetic, but more apprehensive,
Mr. Lippmann noted that the bill had now embraced the expedient
of a 'temporary dictatorship . . . authorizing the Secretary of
Agriculture to levy any tax he considers necessary, and to change
the tax whenever he considers it necessary, in order to make
wheat, cotton, hogs, and tobacco as valuable as they were before
the war.' Two weeks after that, in mid-January, Mr. Lippmann
icily washed his hands of the whole business: 'This bill is a
package of dynamite quite sufficiently charged to wreck the
Democratic Party and blow up the Roosevelt administration,'
he wrote.

The Jones Bill came out of the House mangled and died in committee. Then the statesmen all went home. The Farm Board's chairman, James L. Stone, successor to Mr. Legge, wound up his sad duties with report to Congress of a loss on operations of $360,000,000, and the remark:

> Devices other than stabilization are required. Prices cannot be kept at a fair level unless production is adjusted to meet market demands. Any method which provided higher prices and did not include effective regulation of acreage or of quantities sold, or both, would tend to increase the present surpluses, and soon break down as a result. To be of lasting help, any plan must provide a system of effective regulation so that our millions of farmers can plan and adjust their production on a dependable basis, instead of competing blindly with each other.

No wonder a hurried copyreader on a New York newspaper wrote in as a subhead over this portion of Mr. Stone's statement: 'Favors Allotment Plan.' The degree of difference between that and the Republican stand was not very wide, perhaps, but it was important. Mr. Stone, speaking for Mr. Hoover, advanced to the very point of embracing the allotment, or a similar approach to social control of the crop birth rate, farm by farm, but at that point hauled up short. He showed that agricultural production must somehow be regulated, but failed to say by whom, or to indicate how the farmer was to be persuaded to submit to it.

Wilson now was working in the East. Wherever he had friends in editorial offices he would generally make a call. He came into the offices of *The Country Home* in New York and enchanted our editor with a tip on still 'another revolution,' the imminent perfection of the rubber-tired tractor and field machinery. It would speed production and displace hands faster and faster, he told us calmly. He had seen the model of a combine harvester designed to run thirty miles an hour; but it wasn't perfect yet; no springs; it 'jolted the teeth out of the fellows who tried it.' And pretty soon he was talking about another sort of machinery, his 'voluntary domestic allotment' plan. We ought to go see 'my friend Ezekiel,' and 'my friend Henry Harriman,' and 'this friend of mine, Tugwell, right up here at Columbia,' and have an article about it, and stir up a lot of discussion, for this was 'the coming thing,' he said.

The editor raised the standard objection: 'It will take an army to enforce it.' 'We've got the army, the farmers themselves, and all we need in the way of paid help for it are the Extension people,' Wilson answered. The same idea was beginning to reach and stir the whole national staff of agricultural extenders, from county agents upward, at the time. There was a lot about it that settled college and field workers found unattractive, but Extension was pretty much in a stalemate as to economic action and policy, and badly needed 'a new horse to hop,' as one candid state leader put it.

Not without dissent within its editorial councils our magazine ran an article which I wrote. Wheeler McMillen followed it up by helping arrange an air interview with Wilson out of Chicago in February, 1932. I was sent to ask the more friendly questions. McMillen was there, with no less friendliness personally, to make it tough for Wilson. For example: 'Of course, you would not agree with the belief of many, Mr. Wilson — that the peculiarities of human nature, in Congress as well as on the farm, are likely to defeat the purposes of your plan?'

Wilson: 'Well, we shall do the best we can to make the details accord with human nature. That's the problem we have to face continually in whatever we undertake.'

In an opening three-minute summary Wilson said that America faced a situation without precedent in our history: 'For the first time we have no great hungry foreign market calling for our goods. A growth of nationalism throughout the world has resulted in a buyers' strike on the part of European customers who formerly took about one-quarter of our wheat, half of our cotton, and approximately one hog in ten.' The result was 'a sort of creeping economic paralysis' with not only farmers suffering. 'Agricultural prices have been deflated twice as much as the prices of manufactured products. Agriculture cannot recover until a reasonable balance is re-established. Neither can industry. Economists have estimated that if farmers now had even the purchasing power they had in 1929, about half of our industrial unemployed would be at their jobs.' Industry, he concluded, had developed control measures 'which have limited, to a degree, the competitive forces. . . . Nature is not curing the present situation. It will not cure it. To cure it, we must put on the brakes, take stock and plan.'

I had with me selections from a large stack of letters readers had sent to our Forum columns in response to the *Country Home* article. I read one from F. L. Moore, an Oregon farmer, for Wilson to answer on the air: '"We farmers have been led to expect great things of the allotment plan, but it looks as if by the time they get through with it at the Capitol its originators will have to get out the fingerprint records in order to recognize their child."'

'Well,' said Wilson, 'I think the plan is still recognizable.'

'Is it as good a plan as it was?'

'No.'

'What, in your opinion, is the most serious change?'

'Elimination of the referendum by which the producers determine whether they want the plan or not.'

McMillen asked: 'Suppose a majority of the farmers decide not to come in. Then wouldn't the whole scheme fail?'

'If a majority of the farmers did not come in, I should say that the plan would fail, and ought not to be in effect for any commodity.'

McMillen pressed him on points which plainly were points of weakness: Wouldn't consumers object? Would it actually be possible to administer such gigantic adjustment machinery, with four million farmers at the receiving end, by volunteer farm committee aid alone? Or anything like alone? Wilson replied equably that consumers ought to be willing to pay, even on food, 'a small excise tax,' similar to the tax on tobacco, if that would help to restore prosperity. As for getting along with volunteer plus Extension help in administration, he hoped so, but only time would tell.

During friendly talk in a hotel room while I was trying to keep Wilson and McMillen from arguing philosophically and help with the script-writing, Wilson remarked with an air of detached profundity: 'The Greeks had no machines, but lots of philosophy.

We have many machines but are bankrupt in philosophy.' To close the script I read him a letter from Mrs. Charlotte Stevens, R.F.D. 6, Conway, Arkansas:

> '"Heaven knows we need the money, but this plan promises more than money; it promises leisure; and here is one farmer's wife who is signing up for it. Under the allotment plan we can rest part of our land each year, and we can find time to rest, ourselves. We can use the time that we used to spend in speeding up production in living and developing our own possibilities as human beings. We will have more time for our children, and more time for reflection, books, music, travel, sociability, and even art."'

Wilson got off the bed where he had been sprawling and came over to the typewriter. 'Tell her this,' he said, and dictated his answer slowly as I typed:

> That is exactly what is happening as a result of co-operative organization of farmers in Denmark now. And it is one of the finest things I see as promised by the planned reduction of useless labor contemplated by the domestic allotment plan. What good is there in working more and more for less and less? What good is labor-saving machinery if it only drives you and your family harder and harder, trying to cultivate more and more land? The allotment plan introduces into agriculture the same idea as shorter working hours, and a higher standard of living, in industry. It does so in such manner as pro-rates the shorter working hours, and the higher income, to all farmers who co-operate.

'A mild man with wild ideas,' McMillen said afterwards. There was some truth in that designation. Wilson had broken very largely with the past. But past certainties were breaking up all around us. Circumstances were compelling even the most careful 'and doubtful to see that some of the wild ideas of our economic yesterdays become, under pressure of immediate need and ferment, relatively reasonable and mild.

We had lunch on that whirling visit to Chicago early in 1932 with a fairly hard-bitten city editor of no particular political faith.

He told us some of the news he was not printing: that the winter inrush of migrant unemployed field labor into the slums of Chicago, always a problem, had now become a menace; they were not asking alms now, they were sticking people up in greatly increasing number, and taking an occasional life. The mass of ordinary residents with low means, too, were becoming relatively so much more lawless that the biggest milk companies had, without news announcement, taken their delivery trucks off night routes, and were delivering milk and bread in daylight only. Most of the holdups by night, the city editor told us, had been by unarmed people, working in masses without any particular plan or organization; and often as not the people took milk and bread and did not touch the money the driver had collected, he said. From recent travel I knew that this did not represent merely a local situation or one exclusively urban. In the Midland and West, and occasionally even as far east as Pennsylvania, farm mobs, quietly ominous, were bidding in neighbors' foreclosed property at 'penny sales' and riding the authorities sent to prevent these sales out of the neighborhood with rope nooses around their necks. In the Southern cotton country, even to the richest delta, desperate croppers and tenants were taking what they needed, singly and in groups, from store shelves, and the storekeepers generally did not dare lift a hand to prevent it.

And there had been, of course, that pitiful march of the war veterans on Washington, and the tear gas, and then in a sort of shamed attempt at restitution those veterans who would go had been quietly shipped to public lands in Vermont, where they were fed, clothed, and sheltered in return for doing conservation work. In Hyde Park, New York, a lame man with a long head talked with his first group of consultants, nicknamed his 'Brain Trust' by the press, about establishing improved veterans' work camps the country over, and a Civilian Conservation Corps for the indigent young.

Wilson bore on from Chicago, seeking interest and support from the Agricultural College and Extension people at Saint Paul, Minnesota, and Ames, Iowa. On the way to Ames he stopped in Des Moines to talk with Henry Wallace. Neither of them had met Governor Roosevelt at the time, but through Rex Tugwell they were in touch with him. In the initial stages of campaign planning the Governor asked Dr. Moley to get him some help on a farm plank. Moley, teaching at Columbia University, was glad to. He knew that George Warren's Cornell economists, through Warren's former student, Henry Morgenthau, Jr., were already in touch with the President-intendant, and that Warren was strong for controlled currency manipulation through a device he called the Commodity Dollar. Moley was conservative on the subject of 'funny money' and eager to find for the Governor a farm relief measure other than that. Moley recalled that his colleague at Columbia, Dr. Tugwell, unlike these wild Cornellians in that he was a 'sound' man on money matters, had written a largely disregarded memorandum on farm policy for the Smith campaign of 1928. So Moley took Tugwell as a Brain Truster up to Hyde Park.

Mr. Roosevelt and Dr. Tugwell liked each other from the first. Ordinarily a cool customer, the Doctor became engagingly boyish from the first in his respect and affection for 'the Squire.' To read *Looking Forward*, the President's book of campaign speeches, and then to read Tugwell's *The Industrial Discipline*, finally completed the same year, is to see how quickly, and from what widely different points of view, their ideas interacted. 'The fluidity of change in society has always been the despair of theorists' — that was one new idea in Tugwell's book, inserted and elaborated after conversations at Hyde Park. But Tugwell's book's most quoted sentence, 'Liberals would like to rebuild the station while the trains are running; radicals prefer to blow up the station,' was written long before. As a whole, *The Industrial Discipline* makes heavy reading, but the ultimate argument is reduced to seven words, 'Income has to be dissociated from jobs,' and the book clearly predicts, with occasional fatalistic premonitions of futility, such self-policing of industry and agriculture, in turn policed by the Government, as has since been tried in the United States.

In the spring of 1932 Henry Morgenthau, Jr., touring the Midland in the interest of the candidacy of Franklin D. Roosevelt, had stopped by at the Wallaces' offices in Des Moines. Morgenthau then was publishing *The American Agriculturist*; so the two young men talked mainly about the farm-paper business, which was in poor shape at the time. The Wallaces had come to a friendly understanding with Dante Pierce, whose *Homestead* they had bought, principally on credit. The Wallaces and Pierces had thrown their forces together on the combined *Wallaces' Farmer and Iowa Homestead*, which Henry was editing while Dante Pierce took the helm with John P. Wallace on the business side.

Henry and Dante got along especially well together, and Dante still (1946) carries Henry's name on the masthead as editor-on-leave. This has put Wallace in a curious spot at times; for *Wallaces'* has at times been very critical of his programs. Though Wallace does not own a share of stock in the paper, his personal attachment to Dante Pierce is such that he has refused to dissolve this purely sentimental association. *Wallaces'*, having gone through the legalities of a sheriff's sale on December 7, 1935, satisfied, by common agreement, a mortgage totaling $2,224,742, yielding a deficiency judgment for $1,231,742 to the Pierce Corporation, headed by Dante M. Pierce. The paper started doing well again as soon as farm prices and farm lineage picked up, and has been doing well ever since.

By 1932 Wallace was devoting the greater part of his time and thought to his seed business. He was president and general manager of that. Cornell University had offered a fee of $150 for Wallace to give a lecture on the farm situation at its summer session that July; but Wallace had been so pressed for time, between his seed-breeding and editing, that he had felt compelled to say no. Shortly after Morgenthau passed through Des Moines, however, he phoned from the East, saying that Governor Roosevelt wanted a visit from Wallace at Hyde Park. So Wallace thriftily reopened negotiations with his friends at Ithaca, accepted the $150 lecture or expense fee, and went to Ithaca first. In *Wallaces' Farmer* for September 3, 1932, he turned the trip to further account by writing his leading article about it. The heading was: 'SIZING UP EASTERN ATTITUDES; Editor Talks With Governor Roosevelt at Luncheon Meeting.' The article ambles along amiably for nearly two pages, relating talks about gold with Warren, Pearson, and others at Cornell; also 'a nice talk with Professor James Rogers of Yale . . . [who agrees] with [Carl]

Snyder of the New York Federal Reserve Bank, that the important thing from a world point of view is to keep credit increasing steadily at the same rate as the long-term rate of growth of goods, thus avoiding recurring periods of speculation and depression.' The editor's talkative travelogue is some twelve hundred words along before he gets to Hyde Park. Then:

> ... The Hyde Park home of Governor Roosevelt is a lovely old estate with a beautiful avenue of trees and acres and acres of timber. ... My first impression was, 'Here is a family which has had money and culture for generations. ... The day I called on Roosevelt was after two days of the Walker hearing. Reporters were buzzing in and out, telephones were ringing and telegrams were being sent. I had to wait a half-hour past the appointed time to see the Governor, and I feared I would find him so much wrapped up in the Walker case that he would have no interest in agriculture. I had heard that his legs were paralyzed, and I feared that he would be completely tired out. Imagine my great surprise, therefore, to find a man with a fresh, eager, open mind, ready to pitch into the agricultural problem at once. First he read a letter from Governor Woodring of Kansas, giving suggestions for the agricultural speech which Roosevelt is to deliver at Topeka the evening of September 13. ...
>
> Henry Morgenthau, Jr., publisher of *The American Agriculturist*, and I ate lunch with the Governor. The Governor is quite skeptical about inflation as a cure for our troubles, and Morgenthau wanted me to tell about the Honest Dollar sentiment in the Middle West. Later, I discovered that certain Columbia University professors are very close to Roosevelt because he took his law work there — and that they are responsible for his slant on certain technical economic questions, including inflation.
>
> Roosevelt does not have the extreme pride of personal opinion that has characterized some of our more bull-headed presidents. He knows that he doesn't know it all, and tries to find out all he can from people who are supposed to be

authorities. He is such a likable, humorous man that he is better fitted than most to draw the right kind of men to him.

We spent a good bit of our time talking about the way in which Hoover in his acceptance speech had again shut out any possibility for the farmer getting out of the mess he was in, except by long years of low prices. I told him I thought the Republicans had been inconceivably blind in their attitude toward the tariff, the lending of money abroad, and the building up of manufactured exports at the expense of agricultural exports. I wanted him to attack Hoover as to some extent the cause of the world-wide depression. He showed no personal animus against Hoover whatever, and diverted the conversation to a discussion of Henry Field, Brookhart, and Murphy. He then asked about George Peek, Bill Hirth, Frank Murphy, and the other last-ditch fighters for 'Equality for Agriculture,' the men who went down battling in 1928.

Through all of this discussion he displayed a knowledge of and a sympathy for the agricultural problem which surprised me considerably. He has land in Georgia, and has given much thought as to just how to manage his own land to make the most money. His Georgia friends had told him how the joint stock land banks down there were up to the trick of foreclosing the farms and selling them at the earliest possible moment, while at the same time they bought in their bonds at 30 or 40 cents on the dollar. He seemed to be as indignant about this as we are out here in Iowa.

Morgenthau tells me that Roosevelt's infantile paralysis caused him some trouble four years ago, when he first became Governor, but that since that time he has been steadily improving. I understand he has taken out $500,000 worth of life insurance recently, so I guess he is in excellent shape. He still gets his exercise chiefly by swimming. He must do considerable of this, because his mental reactions are those of a man who spends lots of time out-of-doors.

When I came back to Des Moines and tried to tell my friends about the Eastern situation, I found no simple story to relate. Mills, Meyer, and the R.F.C. are all doing their best to loosen up credit, but there is a great variety of opinion as to how long the credit loosening policy will last after the election is over.

The only really encouraging thing which has happened in recent months is the canceling of 90 per cent of the German reparations. The credit inflation and the rise in the stock market have not yet increased the dividends or put men to work or stopped the foreclosing of mortgages. These things will probably come by next spring, but there are still some bridges to cross, and it is my opinion that the people in the East are just as much up in the air as we are out here.

Immediately before the Democratic National Convention in the early summer of 1932, Wilson, back in Montana, got a wire from Tugwell asking that he fly to Chicago. The question of a farm plank pressed for settlement. Governor Roosevelt wanted to hear, through Tugwell, more about that domestic allotment plan. Tugwell flew West as Wilson flew East. They met in a Chicago hotel room. Time was short. Tugwell still chuckles recalling a companionable struggle to hold Wilson's cycles of conversation within urgent limits and answer the Brain Trust's questions by phone to Hyde Park that night. It was done. The Governor slipped a brief but hearty acceptance of the allotment principle into his address of acceptance at Chicago, and expanded the idea later, under a more direct guidance from Wilson and Wallace, in his Topeka address.

In this speech, delivered in September, 1932, the commitment was made more definite, but not bindingly specific. The candidate said he favored a means of making the tariff effective for agriculture, and added that the plan must raise the price of farm products without stimulating further production; he committed himself thus to production control but to no one — or fixed — approach or method.

Wallace had met Roosevelt for the first time on August 13, 1932, at that lunch with the Governor and Henry Morgenthau, with no others present, at Hyde Park. Shortly after that, Tugwell took Wilson for the first time to talk with the candidate and his first string of Brain Trusters on the porch at Hyde Park. They plied Wilson with questions, and he answered them slowly, with an occasional circuitous anecdote which suddenly came to the point surprisingly.

Wilson had made his presentation, and answered these questions so many times by now that as a rather searching inquisition drew to an end, he seemed tired, those who were present say. But then he shook off his weariness abruptly and, according to his established outline, went on:

'Now, Governor, that's the way I see it on the farm business side. But here's another way that fills in on the other side, the side that's closest to my heart. Out in Utah . . .'

When Wilson had finished, the Squire of Hyde Park is reported to have thrown up his head, lifted his eyeglasses from his nose with a sweeping gesture, and then with a characteristic quizzical hunching of the eyebrows, he asked with a joyous laugh: 'Have you been telling me your plan, Mr. Wilson; or have I been telling you mine?'

Late in January, 1933, little more than a month before Roosevelt's first inaugural, Moley made it known from advance guard offices of the new order in Washington that the President-elect had asked Henry A. Wallace, R. G. Tugwell, and M. L. Wilson to draw, as a committee of three, working plans to reorganize the Department of Agriculture as an instrument of active national planning. That should have been hint enough as to the forthcoming new setup in the Department's secretariat; but most prognosticators kept guessing wide of the mark. Some said Morgenthau wanted the portfolio of Agriculture above all else and that his neighboring Squire, F.D.R., would deny Morgenthau nothing. Others held it would be Tugwell; but this received little credence, because Tugwell was accounted not only a city fellow, but a New York City Columbia highbrow; and Tugwell stated freely that, after the exhibition of lame-duck legislative pranks he had witnessed as a professorial lobbyist, the very thought of going to Washington, himself, seemed repulsive.

Wilson was mentioned, too, by the form makers; but was generally estimated to be too retiring of nature and obscure. Hardly anyone seemed to think it would be Wallace. As late, in fact, as two weeks before the inaugural Kiplinger's 'confidential' Farm Letter from Washington stated flatly that Cully Cobb of Georgia would be the next Secretary of Agriculture.

The question, actually, had been virtually settled when Wallace and Tugwell visited the President-elect at Warm Springs in the first week of December of 1932, though no direct offers or proffers were made at the time. Wallace received the letter that asked him to be Secretary, he recalls, on February 12, Lincoln's Birthday, just as he was setting out to drive through a blizzard to make a speech; and he rode through the blizzard there and back, with a storm of thoughts and emotions contending within himself, before he came to a decision.

Returning to Des Moines, he sat down to his dictating machine in the offices of *Wallaces' Farmer*. Departing from the traditional heading with which all editors of *Wallaces'* from the first had announced new ventures or departures — 'A Word Personal' — he said:

ODDS AND ENDS

This is the last time, for a while at least, that I shall be writing this column. I am going to Washington, March 4, to serve as Secretary of Agriculture in the Cabinet of President Roosevelt.

I remember how my father left home twelve years ago to take a similar position under President Harding. He accepted a Cabinet place because he felt keenly the need of trying to restore the agricultural values smashed in the decline of 1920–21 and because he feared there would be a much more serious smash later on unless both the Government and the city people of the United States became aware of their debt and duty to the farmer. To this cause he gave his life. . . .

While the situation of the world and of agriculture is far more desperate today than it was then, I have an advantage he did not have — a chief who is definitely progressive, entirely sympathetic toward agriculture, and completely determined to use every means at his command to restore farm buying power. . . .

Of course, every sensible man must realize that the new administration will labor under a terrific handicap. It is fairly easy to put out a fire before it gets much of a start. To put it out after wind and time and neglect have fanned it into a flaming rage is a task of greater difficulty. The new administration must make up for twelve years of lost time. . . .

Fortunately for the nation, President Roosevelt has exactly the right kind of temperament for this kind of a situation. He rises to emergencies fearlessly and optimistically. And so, I shall be working under a courageous man with a kindly heart. . . .

I will try to do my part in Washington. No doubt I shall make many mistakes, but I hope it can always be said that I have done the best I knew.

X

WHEN THE DEAL WAS NEW

This great nation will endure as it has endured, will revive and will prosper. The only thing we have to fear is fear itself. Our distress comes from no failure of substance. We are stricken with no plague of locusts. Plenty is at our doorstep, but a generous use of it languishes in the very sight of the supply. Primarily this is because rulers of the exchange of mankind's goods have failed, through their own stubbornness and their own incompetence, have admitted their failure, and abdicated. The money changers have fled from their high seats in the temple of our civilization. We may now restore that temple to the ancient truths.

Restoration calls, however, not for changes in ethics alone. This Nation asks for action, and action now.

I am prepared under my constitutional duty to recommend the measures that a stricken nation in the midst of a stricken world may require. The people of the United States have not failed. In their need they have registered a mandate that they want direct, vigorous action. They have made me the present instrument of their wishes. In the spirit of the gift I take it. — Selected from FRANKLIN D. ROOSEVELT'S first Inaugural, March 4, 1933.

1. Green as Grass

HENRY A. WALLACE was midway in his forty-fifth year when he came to Washington as Secretary of Agriculture. The seedbed of his mind and character was fertile and well stocked. The first evidences of full growth were vigorous but by no means formed. He bore himself at first so meekly and with such an air of hating to appear in the least important that in the clutter of events surrounding that stormy inaugural he was shuttled around by guards from one entrance to another and all but missed being admitted in time for the inaugural address. He and Miss Frances Perkins, the new Secretary of Labor, arrived together, just in time.

In his first Inaugural, President Roosevelt, having declared unemployment 'no unsolvable problem,' passed immediately to a linked problem, 'a better use of the land.' He promised 'definite efforts to raise the value of agricultural products . . . preventing realistically the tragedy of the growing loss through foreclosure . . . [and] the unifying of relief activities which today are often scattered, uneconomical, and unequal.' It had been contemplated that the Congress would be called into a three-day short or extraordinary session only to deal with the banking crisis. In the first two days of the new administration, however, Wallace and Tugwell proposed a somewhat longer session, to cope with further emergency relief measures, with a new Farm Act first.

On the evening of March 8 the President told Wallace to call a farm leaders' conference, lock himself in a room with the representatives, and not come out of that room until they had agreed unitedly on a plan of immediate action.

The call went out by wire that night. Despite the difficulties of getting cash for railroad or plane travel during the banking holiday, fifty representatives of farm organizations and farm papers were in Washington for the announced opening of the conference on the morning of March 10, and they remained closeted with Wallace and his chief aides for the principal part of a day and a half.

With Andrew S. Wing, then managing editor of *The Country Home*, I was in Washington, from March 8 onward, with a slightly different aim. We were there ahead of the birth of the Blue Eagle to examine the probabilities of legalized industrial production and price schedules. Business men were already alert to such a prospect. A friend in the electrical supply business, for example, had me bring George Soule of *The New Republic* to dinner. He wanted advice. His company and others, already operating on allotted and agreed production and sales schedules, under what might have been called illegal gentlemen's agreements,

in large measure, wanted to know if they could follow legal procedures that the Farm Act might establish, come out into the
open with production and price control, and rope in a few stray
recalcitrants in that trade who persisted in operating outside of
the crudely established price umbrella.

Henry I. Harriman's Chamber of Commerce associates were
meantime envisaging, as has been indicated, some sort of Act that
would sanction all but universal trade agreements nationally arrived at. More to the point so far as Wing and I as Crowell employees were concerned, Joseph Knapp, the president of our
company, had called in lawyers and was conceiving an industrial
recovery act of his own with great vigor and not a little common
sense. In Washington, accordingly, Wing and I did not tarry
long in the main tent of the farm leaders' emergency huddle that
second week of March; we spent more time in the Chamber of
Commerce offices downtown.

On March 9, the day before the farm conferees reached the
city, Wing and I had lunch with Wallace and Tugwell in Wallace's
office. They both said that the formulation and passage of an
industrial recovery countermeasure to agricultural adjustment
was necessary and inevitable; but both were apprehensive lest it
be so drawn or administered as to make industrial goods so scarce,
relatively, that industrial prices would outbalance and outrun
farm products prices on the next price rise. Tugwell flatly expressed repugnance at administered programs of farm and industrial scarcity alike. His language, conversationally, was refreshingly unlike the elegant academic embroidery of his latest book,
The Industrial Discipline. Wallace was no less downright in his
hatred of reduced production; but was glumly and completely
determined that in the field of agriculture, first and particularly, it
must be done. He was searching, characteristically, for a moral
justification. I said it was rather far-fetched, but the nearest I
had found to an emotional or moral justification was the letter
from a cotton-stricken Arkansas farm wife M. L. Wilson had
read at the end of his Chicago broadcast. Less headlong human-
workhouse competitive expansion to grow more and more for less
and less; a better-ordered rural production and leisure. In her
own words: *'We can rest part of our land each year, and we can find*

time to rest ourselves. We can use the time that we used to spend in speeding up production in living and developing our own possibilities as human beings. We will have more time for our children, and more time for reflection, books, music, travel, sociability, and even art.'

Wallace fired up to that. 'That is fine. It is true. We must make a religion of that!'

Tugwell gave forth a sort of muted groan. 'My God, Henry, no!' he said earnestly. 'Rationalize it any way we have to, we can't make a religion out of growing or making fewer goods with this whole country and the whole world in bitter need.'

Wallace looked sidewise at Wing and me, with a slow smile, half sage, half impish. 'They get awfully scared here when I as much as mention religion,' he told us. 'But on this I guess Rex is right.'

I recall no more of that luncheon conversation. Too many things were happening all at once. As we went out, Paul Appleby, who had just come on as Wallace's first outer-office aide, said, 'H. A. wants you back in there a minute,' and I went back in. The Secretary told me that they were going to be shorthanded, with work piling higher daily, and little chance of adding much extra help, formally, until the Farm Act, with appropriation provisions, had passed. Meantime he was borrowing volunteer aides and information men. Cason Callaway of Georgia was sending up the editor of his La Grange newspaper, Paul Porter, to get up some material on a cotton-reduction program. Dante Pierce was lending Donald Murphy for a day or so, also E. R. McIntyre and Arthur Thompson from the staff of *Wallaces'* for a somewhat longer spell. Could I stay on and just make myself useful, generally, attending any conferences I cared to, performing some sort of liaison with New York magazines and book writers who were descending fast on the capital; working some with M. L. Wilson on a wheat program?

That same afternoon, March 9, 1933, I telephoned Tom Cathcart, then editorial director of *The Country Home,* who said I might stay in Washington for a while, anyway, continuing to handle the Forum mail column and to send up occasional pieces from a Washington base. Milton Eisenhower, Chief of Information, assigned me a desk and a typewriter in the same room with John R.

Fleming, with whom I had done Extension editing in Massachusetts and, later, Ohio. My wife came down from New York City, where we had lived for nine years, and we found an apartment in Washington. We stayed in Washington and I worked in the Department of Agriculture steadily, even furiously, day and night, for a little more than a year.

By March 12 the farm leaders were on record as to what they wanted, or thought that they wanted. Most of the old McNary-Haugenites were still for export-dumping, first and forever. They also wanted parity prices, or fair-exchange value. The Farmers' Union, unrepresented at this first emergency huddle by its most passionate and clamorous leader, John Simpson, wanted cost of production or cost of production plus. The Grange still saw some hope of export debentures. The Farm Bureau was fronting for the domestic allotment measure, but many of its leaders hated control of production downward quite as ardently and confusedly as George Peek did.

Midway in the conference, toward noon of March 10, Wallace came out of it to deliver by radio briefly his first address from Washington as a public man.

Time was short, he said. 'Agreement will have to be immediate. We can't legislate next June for a crop that was planted in April. There are honest differences of opinion. No plan can be perfect. One plan, for example, turns out to be unconstitutional. Another had administrative difficulties that would defy the wisdom of a Solomon. Another plan may help the wheat people a little more than it helps the cotton people, or vice versa. Our job will be to get a compromise — to comprise the most satisfactory features of each into a program.'

The outcome was accordingly not only an omnibus measure, but a fantastically elastic omnibus. The measure as drawn sought to legalize almost anything anybody could think up. To deal with the banking crisis Congress had just given the President discretionary powers unparalleled, probably, by any other peacetime law in our history. Now those who were drawing or considering this Farm Act did the same thing for the new Secretary of Agriculture, or inclined to do so. In origin the bill was primarily agrarian, with Charles J. Brand, who had made the initial drafts of McNary-Haugen measures for the first Secretary Wallace, called in first again now by the second Secretary to make suggestions. Fred Leé, like Brand, close to the Peek line of persuasion, as a lawyer, worked at Peek's insistence on the measure. Peek did not like the sight or sound of Jerome Frank, that spiritual legal wheelhorse of urban and Frankfurter antecedents who had just been drawn into the Department. But Frank, the impending author of *Law and the Modern Mind*, got a number of expansive modern notions into the first draft of the Farm Act of 1933, nonetheless. It was a scramble. About a year later, still trying to keep some show of peace between his old-time farm-leader colleagues and new men whom they regarded as urban interlopers in the Department of Agriculture, Wallace wrote:

> There have been many weird stories as to the author-ship. . . . Some said Mordecai Ezekiel. Some said it was all a Red plot of Rex Tugwell's. Occasionally I was suspected of having something to do with it. As a matter of fact a great many people contributed to the drafting. . . . The legal job was done chiefly by Fred Lee, for many years legislative counsel for the Senate, and by Jerome Frank, who later be-came General Counsel for the Adjustment Administration, Ezekiel, Tugwell, and myself from the Department; and George Peek, Chester Davis, and Charles Brand, among others saw to it that the bill carried out the wishes of the farm leaders' conference. . . .
>
> At one extreme were the left-wing farmers, whose griev-ances could not be denied, demanding $1.50 wheat and $10 hogs inside of six weeks. At the other extreme were the most hardboiled among the middlemen, who insisted on the right to run their own business as they pleased regardless of the consequences. Each group seemed so sure it was right that I knew it would never be possible to secure much co-operation from them. Consequently, when the job of administering the law did come along, I knew we would be living in a veritable hell, and I thought it best to say as much before Congressional committees and other groups. I didn't want anybody harboring any illusions about the new machinery.[1]

The actual first draft and first submission of the bill took five days, from March 11 to 16. Marvin Jones introduced it as Chairman of the House Committee on Agriculture.

The two months' interim between then and May 12, 1933, when Congress passed the first Agricultural Adjustment Act and the President signed it, was a time of seemingly interminable and hopelessly confused conferences, official and semi-official, day and night. Triple-A had still no official form or being, but by administration invitation George Peek, Charles Brand, and others pre-chosen for initial key positions sat in with already appointed Department officials and aides to the Secretary, and took an active part. Lively storms were brewing, on the surface of the negotiations and under the surface. Adherents of bluff George Peek would nod his way mournfully as he plodded into conference, and tell you, 'There is the man who ought to be Secretary, and there' — nodding to the more diffident figure of Wallace, who sat to one side of the council table, more often than not in his shirt-sleeves — 'there is the man who is!'

Peek in those days, at sixty, did look more the part of a Cabinet member, in terms of portly certainty and a certain seasoned caginess, than Henry Wallace did, at forty-five. He was a good and able man, and remarkably disinterested. He used to say, and say truly, that he was 'in politics for agriculture, and not in agriculture for politics.' But a new type of public man, younger and intellectually more flexible, was on the up; and it seemed to most of us minor aides and beginners in the new bureaucracy that this Wallace, striking off daily new patterns of candid public address and behavior, and with an increasing unself-consciousness, grew visibly, daily and weekly, like one of his own Iowa corn plants, stretching in the sun.

He had come to Washington with the appearance of a man borne down by worriment and gloom. He came only, he told some of his family and friends in Iowa, because he felt that it was an obligation. He liked free-lance genetic research and seed development. He disliked large-scale organization, even in publishing, and he disliked especially being seated above many other men and women to act as boss, empowered to hire and fire. The Department he was taking over had, at the time, 40,794 employees, with

10,794 of them stationed in Washington, within a block or so of his desk. 'What sort of job is this, anyway?' he asked, smiling in mild exasperation at the end of his first few days in office. 'All I do except talk to people is sit here and sign my name.'

But there was more to it than that, really, and he came to grips with the main job quietly and familiarly during that knock-down and drag-out initial argument about the form and powers of a Farm Act. He set out calmly to compose so far as possible the differences of excited minds, to get an Act that he felt could be administered, and then to press ahead. Once he had his action-program outlined, by the end of the first week, even, it was striking to see him change. His step lightened; his smile became less strained, more friendly and warming; he gave greater play to a sense of humor which seldom is boisterous, more often ironical, and sometimes sharp enough to cut. He found that he could eat a peck of trouble daily and thrive on it. He began to enjoy his new work.

President Roosevelt had set new forms and precedents as to press conferences. Wallace followed the pattern with a greater native candor or lack of guile. So much so, that seasoned correspondents gasped and brought a pause in proceedings to ask if *that* was on the record, or off. 'Off or on, as you please,' Wallace would say, negligently sprawling, with his feet in the wastebasket, at first. 'The legal department wants that off,' Frank objected, upon occasion. Even anti-Frank Fred Lee, sitting in as Peek's personal lawyer, would nod in shocked or amused assent. 'All right, then, off,' Wallace agreed, grinning. 'But I do think we ought to call these things by plain names and try to get the real force and impact of them straight.' At his first really important press conference, he passed around copies of the monumental draft of the new Adjustment Bill. Some sixty reporters, ruffling the leaves of this document in hasty anxiety, grouped in seated semi-circles or stood around his desk. They fired questions at the Secretary fast. Cabinet members are not protected from rude treatment so closely as are Presidents, either by rule of procedure or by an invisible aura of high office. Of the complete and true inwardness of this enormous new mass of legal language most of these correspondents knew nothing or next to nothing, then.

They knew that it was important; they knew they would have to do some fast, rude digging before phoning something to their papers, or writing something, so they pressed Wallace hard.

'Here on this page, *processing tax* — what's that?'

Wallace said it was 'an excise or *sales tax on food and other essential farm products*,' generally to be collected at points where the product went through some convenient bottleneck in the course of mercantile processing.

'*Adjustment payment* — what's an adjustment payment?'

'That's our *bait*. Money paid out from processing taxes to induce farmers to co-operate in our programs,' Wallace said.

'And over here in the Second Part of the Act — the marketing part: *Licensing power?*'

'*That's our club behind the door.* The Act provides governmental licensing by which firms or combinations of firms may enter into marketing agreements, with the idea of diminishing the wastes and losses of ungoverned competition, with the consent of the Government, among themselves. The Government is the umpire. If it decides they are not playing fair, it withdraws the license, and the deal is off. That's a rough way to put it, but that's about it.'

Talking offhand, or from notes hastily scrawled on trains or in cars, Wallace, at his earlier press conferences, mixed colloquialisms with scientific language amazingly and quite without design. Amid developing intricacies of plans to untangle maladjustments in pork production, 'Now, take the sow end of the pig thing ——' he would say. Or as to dairy marketing, 'The butter folks are on the hot spot.' What a mess! Approaching composition of a speech, pamphlet, or article, he would try his thoughts in the rough on the correspondents, and now and then the mixture of his metaphors would be nothing short of majestic. Once he had the Ship of State breasting a brave course over the mountains and prairies to New Frontiers. Again: 'The youth movement has been the backbone of every strong arm movement in this country.' But you could always understand what he meant.

He changed the Secretary's office in the administration building of the Department of Agriculture only a little, outwardly, from the way it was when Arthur M. Hyde, his immediate predecessor, had sat there dispensing iced buttermilk and faintly rebellious statements. The furniture remained just where it was. But the general change in that room and throughout the Department in point of mental excitement and a rising spirit was enlivening. No incoming Secretary of Agriculture has ever encountered in the light of hard facts greater immediate or prospective burdens. None, however, had come to the post with the same technical equipment. As a plant breeder and economist Henry Wallace ranked among the first in the country. At his conferences with bureau chiefs he could talk their language, putting questions about chromosome counts or multiple correlations which gave trouble to the most learned. His working experience as a seed farmer, editor, writer, and speaker for the farm cause served him well. And now in range of thought he manifestly began to grow beyond the encased agrarian outlook — not precipitously, always with evident twinges of growing pains, some discomfort, and with an occasional spell of ardent backsliding, but fast. Free, adventurous, and eager minds launching thoughts and speculations from broader than simply rural backgrounds, minds such as Tugwell's and Frank's, delighted and at times enchanted Wallace. The Peek adherents said 'bewitched.' But Wallace, like all his clan, has a strong, argumentative nature which cleaves to fundamentals, holds stoutly to the essence of old and established faiths and is not swept from its moorings either by enchantment or bewitchment. It would be almost impossible to overestimate the good that mental and emotional jousting in Washington with minds and free spirits of the first caliber did him — and this went far beyond companionability with men in his own Department. The record of his past shows plainly, however, that he had engaged in like jousting with superior minds and spirits, contemporary and of the past, ever since he learned to reason and to read; and he was well on the way toward enlarging deeds and concepts by the time he became a public man and a figure of importance on the national and world stage.

Behind his main desk there in the Secretary's office he had bookcases and a large additional table overflowing with new books, pamphlets and clippings about genetics, government, anthropology, hog and steel prices, history, the weather, and philosophy. From the office walls he removed all previous decorations and tokens and replaced them with four: (1) a cartoon by Jay N. Darling ('Ding' of Des Moines), celebrating the solid plowboy qualities of the first Secretary Wallace; (2) a boldly colored work by an unsigned native American artist, showing a pioneer missionary striding forth, the Bible open in his hand; (3) an American Indian — done in crude symbols in clay — glorifying the place of tall corn in an advanced rural civilization, the Mayan; (4) an oil portrait of Secretary Harry, officially painted when his father sat in the same chair.

There were many tales of the unaffected simplicity with which the new Secretary entered upon public office. He was delightfully green. Instead of pushing the buttons on his desk he would stick his cowlick out the door and call to Appleby, once of *The Des Moines Register*, now Assistant to the Secretary, 'Can you spare a minute, Paul?' He would duck out of the big limousine loaned him by the taxpayers, dismiss the chauffeur, and climb with a sigh of relief into the six-hundred-dollar car of any acquaintance who happened to come driving by. He played tennis once a week on a public court. The first time out, his new shoes hurt him, so he took them off, played barefoot and walked back from the official limousine upstairs to his office, the guards saluting him as he ambled back to work with his shoes in his hand.

When the New Deal still was shining new and understaffed, he drove himself to the point of exhaustion. He was so tired one Sunday afternoon that Donald Murphy of *Wallaces' Farmer*, visiting from Des Moines, made him leave his office and go for a walk in Rock Creek Park. The Secretary sat on the first rock they came to, started to talk, fell asleep, and slept for two hours while Murphy sat there guarding him.

At first he shied off when Edward Crockett, Negro 'messenger' to all the Secretaries of Agriculture since Houston, rushed in to help him with his coat. But soon he submitted, with an absent-minded appreciation of Edward's honest pride in keeping the Secretary looking as a Secretary ought to look.

Wallace's attempts to sidestep the trappings with which Fate had fitted him came, of course, to nothing; the escape was neither permanent nor important. He soon wore a high hat when the occasion demanded, as if he did not know he had it on. In the office he pressed bells, commanded, and said, 'Secretary Wallace calling.' At conferences he no longer slid off to one side of his big desk, as if maybe it looked a little too pushing to sit in commanding position at the middle. He sat in the middle, now, when the conference or call was official, and spoke with authority. As for the limousine, the state and diplomatic dinners with eleven kinds of forks and spoons, all the artificial and somewhat necessary ritual implied in the salutation, 'Mr. Secretary' — he bore such magnificence without thinking about it, as part of the job. But he still did not like to act important. And he uttered a mild complaint about state dinners: 'Because, by protocol, the seating is ranked, you never get to meet any new folks.'

The pressure on his door, heart, and mind were at times terrific. Soon Appleby, first guardian of the door, phoned down to Virginia, where he had edited a paper before he came to Washington, and persuaded Benham Baldwin, who was running a successful store there and getting on smoothly with contentious or troublesome customers, to come to Washington as second outer-office aide. But still there was no proper or possible way of turning aside in any considerable part that eternal bane of all public men — 'important' figures who have no business to impart, but merely want to be able to go home and say, 'I told the Secretary.' As soon as the Farm Act draft, including provision for marketing agreements, was made public, there came a determined succession of business men, some of them really important, to call on the Secretary of Agriculture and get a favoring line of agreement for their product and profit. Actually, a determined push was made by big oil operators, prior to the founding of NRA or, indeed, the passage of the Farm Act, to have oil declared a basic agricultural commodity. Wallace told them their product might have been an agricultural commodity once, but that had been rather too long ago.

More legitimate pressure never relented. 'One moment,' Wallace wrote of this period, later, in a chapter entitled 'The Thirteenth Year' in his 1934 book, *New Frontiers*, 'we concentrated on new personnel for AAA; the next moment we devoted to deciding just how the new machinery ought to fit together. The corridors of the administration building were crowded with

farmers, farm leaders, processors, and reporters, each with dozens
of insistent questions, few of which could be answered then and
there. From early morning until midnight, and often later,
delegations of dairymen, cotton growers, wheat growers, cling-
peach producers from California, and many others filed in and out
of our offices, seeking the way to make the new machinery whir
into action in their behalf. Those were hectic days. Somehow we
got through them, though it was a rare day when an irresistible
desire didn't crash into an immovable fact, with heavy damage to
frayed nerves.' [2]

The Secretary himself, to the casual eye, seldom gave outward
evidence of anger or agitation. One learned, though, in working
with him under pressure, to watch for the stiffening of the muscles
in the corners of his eyes. His eyes in themselves at times give
striking evidence of what he is thinking; he has a singularly unguarded glance when he brings it into full play, direct. He can
look right into people and see with an awful clarity what they are
after. What he sees sometimes saddens him. I recall one among
many highly skilled legal contenders. He came representing a
great food-dealing concern, fresh from the drawing room of a Pullman. He had his appointment and his argument carefully mapped
out and he was important enough to see the Secretary, beyond all
doubt. It was the end of a hard day. Wallace was drawn and
gray-looking, but he listened carefully. That man put up, force-
fully, a most skillful argument. The decision he wished would
have made him and his associates literally millions of dollars without their further turning of a hand. Wallace stood up quietly and
spoke softly just one word — 'No.' The lawyer persisted. Wallace raised one hand slightly, staying the pleading. Then, with the
other hand supporting him on the desk and his head bent wearily
forward, Wallace said, 'Unless we learn to treat each other fairly
this country is going to smash.' He was rather an awesome man
to work for at times, but always perfectly natural, friendly, and
charming, not in the least self-righteous. The evening after this
particular occasion I remarked on these qualities to Paul Porter,
who had a typewriter next to mine. 'Yes,' said Paul, 'I never saw
anything like it. Don't it beat hell? He's a Christian!'

George Peek kept a diary. Later, having served successively as first administrator of Triple–A and the first president of the Export-Import Bank, he wrote a three-part memoir of revelations, 'In and Out,' for *The Saturday Evening Post* and then, with the collaboration of Samuel Crowther, issued a book *Why Quit Our Own?* The earlier chapters establish factually that Wallace wanted Peek as head of Agricultural Adjustments, but also wanted to have Frank as head of the legal division. Talking with President Roosevelt, together with Wallace, at the White House on April 5, Peek was offered the post of Administrator, and countered by saying that Bernard M. Baruch 'was the best man in the country for the job.' Peek continued: 'He [the President] said he had talked with Baruch and that he could not take it but had strongly recommended me. I said I had come down here at Wallace's request, and had tendered my services to be helpful, but that I could not take the job without a lot of things being understood, because I felt that he [the President] alone must outline the policy....' Peek then presented the President with a five-point memorandum that was against lowering tariffs and decried in the next breath crop birth control. 'The President again asked if I would administer the bill, and I said that my views were in conflict with those of the Secretary, and that a general understanding was necessary.'

This was on a Wednesday. Peek agreed to call again on the President Friday, when Governor Lowden and Mr. Baruch would also be there. My more random notes of the period are not so precisely dated as George Peek's, but I am certain that it was at this juncture that Peek agreed to come out by night to the administration building of Agriculture for another shirtsleeve wrestling match with M. L. Wilson. Wilson's specific assignment from the Secretary and from the White House was to convert Peek to the idea of acreage restriction that night. They sat alone in a big, lighted room off the Secretary's office, with the door open, and argued. At times Peek seemed to waver, but the pioneer in him hated restriction; and a foreign dumping of surpluses, the core of McNary-Haugenism, was a personal rock of ages against which even Wilson, for all his skill in homely persuasion, could not prevail. Toward midnight Peek arose and went away, slightly smiling, and calling in a cheerful good night to Wallace and others still working.

Looking worn and rumpled, Wilson wandered into the Secretary's office. 'Did you ever,' he asked Wallace plaintively, 'try to
corner an ornery old sow in a fence-corner? First you whack her
on the left side of her head, and she turns; then you whack her on
the right side; then zip! she's gone, right between your legs!'

Here Wilson paused: 'Just the same, I'm fond of George.'

Quite often, Wilson had better luck than that, or seemed to for
a while, with even hardier individualists than George Peek. This
was especially true when he advanced as his first thrust of approach the second or reserve line of his agricultural thinking —
'the Utah idea, subsistence farming sustained by part-time industry.' It is extraordinary what an emotional appeal a vision of
a little white house with green shutters, forty acres, or four acres,
and a mule, exerted upon widely diverse and often powerful persons at the time of the 1933 bank holiday, and during the continuing spell of widespread unemployment afterward.

'We seek the security of the earth,' Clare Leighton has written,
'when all around us trembles.' Joseph Knapp, largest owner of
the Crowell publications, was not trembling. Other people attend
to that for 'Uncle Joe.' But he was certainly amenable to Wilson's vision of a part-time modern peasantry semi-removed from
the tumult and strain of commerce. Likewise, he was for 'Ducks
Unlimited,' with no piddling restrictions on the bag. And he was,
as has been told, sincerely interested in seeing something resembling Agricultural Adjustment carried over into industry. So in
April of 1933 the Old Man, as they call him in the Crowell shop,
came with three aides from New York to talk with M. L. Wilson
and Secretary Wallace. The Knapp plan, proposing in essence
to induce general business adjustments by cheap governmental
credit, was being circulated in typescript. Many New Dealers in
Agriculture (including Jerome Frank and Tugwell) liked that idea
better than the plan furthered by Henry I. Harriman and the
United States Chamber of Commerce, later NRA. I took the
Crowell delegation in to introduce them to Wallace. With his
customary air of amiable diffidence Wallace came from behind his
desk to shake hands. He said a few words of praise for certain
features of the Knapp plan. Then we all sat down.

'Young man,' said the Old Man, abruptly, 'you're tired. But

you're young. I envy you. You have the greatest power and the greatest opportunity in your hands at this moment of any American who ever ——'

He broke off abruptly, and 'My God!' he cried, 'what's that?' A white rabbit had come out from under a radiator, gently ambling and nibbling at the carpet. 'It's a rabbit,' said the Secretary. The Old Man passed a hand across his eyes. The rabbit misbehaved. The alert colored messenger, Edward, came scurrying to scoop up the rabbit with one hand and the droppings with the other. They went away. The Secretary explained that the rabbit belonged to his son, Bob, and it was sick; so he had brought it down to have a friend in the Department, a vet, look it over.

Everybody laughed and there was some attempt to get the talk back on the subject of the Knapp plan; but no go. The Old Man rose abruptly. 'Can't you see this man's tired?' Then to Wallace: 'God bless you!' They passed into the anteroom. 'Now,' said the Old Man, 'where do I find Wilson?' We took him up to Wilson's office as chief of Triple-A's new wheat section, and they talked for the better part of an hour. From this and subsequent conversations grew the report of the Thomas A. Beck–J. N. Darling–Aldo Leopold Committee on Wild Life Restoration, and from this came J. N. ('Ding') Darling's breezy spell of service as chief of the Biological Survey. But that visit was Uncle Joe Knapp's last appearance in Washington or anywhere else as anything like a New Dealer.

2. Tugwell and Others

ON APRIL 7, two days after the first White House attempt to appoint Peek administrator of the Farm Act, with the understanding that he would administer crop control as an underlying policy, Peek, Baruch, and Lowden called again on the President, as scheduled. 'The President,' Peek wrote in his diary afterward, 'said he had read my five-point memorandum and was quite in accord with it [but] he and I disagreed on the question of restricted production as a national policy.' Passing that over, Peek argued for paying farmers what need be paid to induce co-operation, not from a tax levied on processors but from a 'one hundred million appropriation, [the] Treasury to be reimbursed by tariff duties on agricultural imports, especially fats, oils, and black-strap molasses.'

The conversation was apparently hasty and completely inconclusive, but Peek departed pleased, because 'Bernard M. Baruch and Governor Lowden agreed to be of any help they could in an advisory way.' He accepted the post of administrator, appointed Charles Brand his co-administrator, and paid his own entire salary over to Fred Lee to stand by as personal legal aide. This he did from the very day of his appointment, after an unsuccessful first push to get rid of Jerome Frank. From his memoir:

> ... Mr. Frank was a good lawyer but, as I later discovered, he was more concerned with social theory than with law and he was so certain of his own cleverness that he thought in such manner as to carry out the theories he held. Practically all the young lawyers who swarmed into Washington dangling Phi Beta Kappa keys were enveloped in the delusion that they carried with them the tablets containing a new dispensation. They were going to inform the established lawyers and the Supreme Court what the law really was. Mr. Frank was slated to be Solicitor for the Department of Agriculture. Mr. Farley killed that projected appointment.
>
> Shortly after I accepted the position of Administrator, Brand and I went to the White House with Secretary Wallace. ... During the conversation I objected to Jerome Frank's acting as General Counsel for AAA. I advanced among other reasons the thought that he had had no experience with farm organizations and farmers, that he had been a city lawyer and that his personality was such as not to inspire the confidence of farm leaders.
>
> In all this Brand concurred. ... The President agreed with our point of view and told Wallace in our presence that he had better get rid of Frank by having him transferred to some other Department, and suggested Justice. Upon our return to the office Wallace sent for Brand and me and when we arrived at his office we found Frank there. Wallace said

he had told him what the President had said, and we thought
that the matter was settled. The next morning Wallace sent
for me again. He was in great distress and appealed to me
to retain Frank in the face of what the President had said.
Against my better judgment I yielded. . . . ³

So Triple-A started off as a house divided against itself, and in
more ways than one. On May 15, 1933, three days after the Farm
Act passed, Peek issued a crisp statement of policy, starting, 'The
sole aim and object of this Act is to raise farm prices.' From this
restricted view of the Act, and from a firm dislike for the measures
of physical restriction that went forward headlong during the six
months that he administered Triple-A, Peek never deviated.

Wallace assigned to Tugwell, as Assistant Secretary, responsibility for all the old-line bureaus of the Department, and took over,
in effect, the administration of Triple-A himself. It was an anomalous situation, certain to crack wide open; it was simply a matter
of time. Brand resigned in about four months, on September 30;
Peek hung on, fighting doggedly, from May until December.

From the first, Wallace took a much longer view of the Farm
Act's possibilities and functions than did any of the farm leaders
or, indeed, any of the 'planners,' apart from Wilson. In his ex-
planatory broadcast upon passage of the Act, he picked up the
word 'interdependence' from the President's Inaugural Address,
and developed the theme that the Act was a 'Declaration of Interdependence.'⁴ He challenged agricultural processing and handling
industries to take advantage of that part of the measure legalizing

. . . trade agreements, openly and democratically arrived at,
with the consumer represented and protected from gouging.
This . . . Act makes it lawful and practical for them to do
so. It provides for a control of production to accord with
the actual need, and for an orderly distribution of essential
supplies. . . .

Current proposals for government co-operation with [gen-
eral] industry are really at one with this Farm Act. Unless
we can get re-employment going, lengthen pay rolls, and
shorten breadlines, no effort to lift prices can last very long.
. . . Our first effort as to agriculture will be to adjust pro-

duction downward, with safe margins enough to provide enough food for all. . . .

We do not propose to reduce agricultural production schedules to a strictly domestic basis. Our foreign trade has dwindled to a mere trickle; but we still have some foreign customers for cotton, tobacco, and certain foodstuffs; we want to keep that trade and get more foreign trade, if we can. The immediate need is to reorganize American agriculture to reduce its output to domestic need plus that amount which we can export at a profit. If the world tide turns, and world trade revives, we still can utilize to excellent advantage our crop adjustment and controlled distribution setup. We can find out how much they really want over there, and at what price; and then we can take off the brakes and step on the gas.

The first sharp downward adjustment is necessary because during the past years we have defiantly refused to face an overwhelming reality. In consequence, changed world conditions bear down on us so heavily as to threaten our national life. . . .

That was the business part of the talk, delivered May 13, 1933. Further, 'We envision programs of planned land use . . . [and] look to a decentralization of industry, but in this respect we shall have to make haste slowly,' he said. 'We do not need any more farmers out in the country now. We do need there more people with some other means of livelihood, buying, close at hand, farm products; enriching and making more various the life of our open-country and village communities.'

Observe from this that Wallace, recoiling from the brutal compulsion of reducing agriculture's physical output in time of dire physical need, already contemplated using the discretionary powers vested in him to adjust AAA to larger and more soundly defensible purposes in the end. His phrase 'sound land use' plainly foretells the soil conservation principle to which AAA administrators were forced to repair [less willingly, on the whole, than Wallace] after the Supreme Court decision of 1936. His remarks on the open country as a doubtful refuge for the indigent and dispossessed foretell, in some measure, the establishment of the Farm

Security Administration. In particular, his insistence that agricultural adjustment is a piece of social machinery that may spur as well as retard farm output suggests, six years or so ahead of the event, the incalculable aid that Triple-A was to render in provisioning the Second World War.

In a more urbane paper, written before he wrote this Farm Act action talk, Wallace displayed candidly an astonishing duality of outlook. 'Whether, in inviting me to address the Franklin Institute,' he said in Philadelphia on May 9, 'you distinguish between my activities as Secretary of Agriculture and my activities as a scientist, I have no means of knowing; but I hope I have thus far escaped the sort of fame enjoyed by a certain gentleman who is known as an economist and a journalist; and who is referred to by economists as a highly successful journalist, and by journalists as a highly successful economist. I would not have you carry the parallel too far, however. Some such dual rôle may be forced upon scientists, before we are out of our present economic disorder. . . . I have no patience with those who claim that the present surplus of farm products means that we should stop our efforts at improving agricultural efficiency. What we need is not less science in farming, but more science in economics. We need economic machinery corresponding in its precision, its power, and its delicacy of adjustment to our scientific machinery. Science has no doubt made the surplus possible, but science is not responsible for our failure to distribute the fruits of labor equitably. We must charge that failure squarely to organized society and to government.'[5]

In substance, if not in style, this 'Challenge to Science' address of Wallace's suggests the underlying philosophy of Tugwell. He and Wallace were living and working closely and constantly together at this time. It seemed a strange friendship, perhaps inevitably impermanent; but, though developing circumstances often have strained the bond between them, they have retained a warm regard for each other, and meet whenever they can. In addition to administering efficiently the old-line bureaus of the Department, and making such excellent younger chief appointments as Lee Strong to head entomology, and Knowles Ryerson to head plant industry, Tugwell was obliging the White House by fronting, within the Department of Agriculture, for a law that would make the provisions forbidding falsehoods on Food and Drug labels or wrappers apply with equal force to paid advertising in all its forms. All the publishers as well as the entire advertising trade were up and roaring; they had the mark on Tugwell from the minute he proposed that measure; and some of the most powerful among them were openly threatening to cut him down. There were, of course, other reasons for Tugwell's general unpopularity. 'The trouble with Rex as a public man,' said Wallace on one occasion, 'is that he *exhibits* disdain.' They were friends; and the combination was not so strange as may have appeared to outsiders: Tugwell, cool and debonair, with curt manners when tired or annoyed; Wallace, the rumpled pioneer, ardent, shy, and folksy. Wallace is deeply religious and makes no effort to hide it. Tugwell is a skeptic who believes in trying to do something about things anyway. Wallace at times confronts the modern mess with the fervor for righteousness possessed by his preacher-and-editor forebears. Tugwell fights cagily, coolly. Wallace wades in, swinging. But Tugwell and Wallace have two important things in common: respect for the scientific attitude and contempt for the lower levels of political ingratiation and behavior. When they were thrown together in the New Deal's first high-handed shuffle, they discovered an astonishing likeness of outlook and a companionship rare to both.

For a while Wallace, Tugwell, and Jerome Frank, who threw over some sixty thousand dollars a year in corporation law to be a New Dealer, had adjoining rooms at the Cosmos Club. When Wallace brought his family on and took an apartment at the Wardman Park Hotel in May, Tugwell and Frank rented a furnished house on Tracy Place, at the edge of the embassy section, hired a housekeeper, and invited in to live with them, gratis, a shifting stream of Felix Frankfurter's young lawyers, who, as was usual in the confusion of the moment, were on the pay roll all right, but had not been paid.

The young men who 'volunteered in peacetime,' as they said in the early spring of 1933, were not really young men any longer. We were, for the most part, postwar men, in our late thirties or early forties, old enough to be the fathers of young men. But we felt quite young and that spring we performed amazing feats of endurance. A New Deal had been declared. All kinds of lost meanings were about to be restored. Tugwell kept pretty much the same mad hours as the other green officials, yet he was usually more collected, and far less expectant of ideality soon to be attained. The pace told on him somewhat. At the end of the first three months in Washington, he had lost nine pounds and looked ill. Hay fever, the Washington summer, life in a bachelor encampment with typewriters going all night, and strings of casual lodgers and excited visitors penetrating to his very bedside had him down. One visitor, whom Jerome Frank had known when he legally advised the rich and mighty, had the habit, when struck with an idea, of telegraphing at once. Returning to Wilmington after a visit to the Frank-Tugwell household, he wired Frank: 'BEWARE COMMA JEROME BEWARE STOP THIS MORNING AT YOUR BREAKFAST TABLE I SAW THE FACE OF ROBESPIERRE STOP THAT MAN WOULD WILLINGLY GO TO THE GUILLOTINE FOR AN IDEAL AND TAKE HIS FRIENDS WITH HIM STOP BEWARE.' Frank showed the telegram to Tugwell one torrid night as they started home through holiday traffic. Usually a careful driver, Tugwell swung a corner without signaling, and grazed the curb. He said it was a hell of a life when idiots came crowding in to look at you and then just say what they saw in the papers. 'Well,' said Frank, 'you drive like Robespierre.'

The most amazing furor, amounting in places to outright hysteria, centered upon the debonair head of this Rexford Guy Tugwell at the time. Chicago formed an anti-Tugwell Club. *The Wichita Beacon* warned parents not to let children get hold of his books.[6] The members of a church in Oregon petitioned the President to remove him from public office because of the urbane and approving way in which he had written about American wines. 'He is not a graduate of God's Great University,' cried 'Cotton Ed' Smith of South Carolina in the Senate. This was about the time that Tugwell was summoned to face trial by a Senate committee and prove that he was not a 'Red,' unfit for promotion from Assistant Secretary to Undersecretary of Agriculture, as the President and Wallace wished. Paul Porter, who comes from Kentucky and understands political behavior instinctively, coached Tugwell for that hearing. The public relations specialists of the Department, having wrung admission from Tugwell that he had tended and reared a Holstein heifer in his youth, prepared statements which made that heifer, as Porter said later, the most overworked heifer in the history of the United States. The intended picture of Dr. Tugwell as a 'dirt farmer' did not get over. He attended the hearing in immaculate white and departed, only slightly ruffled, with an air of what seemed to be well-bred amusement. ('Tell Rex,' said the President cheerfully to Henry Wallace after the Senate had confirmed the promotion, 'that I was surprised to hear he was so dirty.') Tugwell protested mildly enough his dislike of Russian absolutism and his essential conservatism: 'I really would like to conserve,' he said, 'all those things which I grew up to respect or love and not see them destroyed.' But hardly anyone was persuaded. The devices that marshal public opinion, right and left, are as little given to reservations and shades of meaning as traffic lights. Red is red.

To intimates and co-workers Tugwell is a friendly, considerate man; but he does not as a rule unbend in public. As is well known, he is a handsome man. When a Hearst paper in Washington gave its lady readers a chance to choose by ballot the best-looking New Dealer, he got the most votes. At lunch-time on the day the result was announced some associates in Agriculture tried to pull his leg, and he responded with words which showed that while in the strictest sense of the term he may be no farmer, he at least grew up in a small country town with comfortable access to a livery stable.

Around Sinclairville, New York, there are many Tugwells and Tylers. The two families came together from Surrey, England, in 1852. They landed in New York City and pushed on to Chautauqua County, in the lower western tip of the State. They intermarried. Tugwell carries on the male side the blood of both strains. His grandfather on the Tugwell side was a cattle trader. He had a big house in Sinclairville with a barn behind it and sixteen buggy horses; he was known as a good man in a trade. The son who helped him most in the business, Charles Henry Tugwell, married Dessie Rexford. Rexford Guy Tugwell, born July 10, 1891, is their one surviving child.

When the boy was thirteen, his father bought a fruit farm at the edge of Wilson, a village on the Ontario lakeshore, and the family moved seventy-five miles north. The elder Tugwell started a can-

nery there, which he still operates. No members of the household
had to toil in the fields, wash at the well, or worry about small sums.
The cannery made money most years and quite a lot of it during
the First World War. The family now is moderately well-to-do.
Rex Tugwell worked around on the farm, but only when he felt like
it, and he bossed the help for his father in summer when school was
over. When, at sixteen, he entered Masten Park High School in Buffalo with the class of 1911, there was nothing country-looking about
him. For a year he was both high-school student and reporter,
covering the police courts and City Hall for the Buffalo *Courier*.

At one stage of Rexford's high school career, the principal wrote
Mr. Tugwell that the boy was so unappreciative of educational advantages that he might just as well be taken out of school and put
to work on the farm. Only one thing in those years appears to
have implanted in young Rexford the seeds of statesmanship. He
heard William Sulzer, later Governor, make a speech about the
rights of the downtrodden, and entered college determined, perhaps
more than most youths, to amount to something.

Scott Nearing, who taught economics at the University of
Pennsylvania when Tugwell entered there in 1911, used to say
that of all his students only two, Rex Tugwell and Big Bill Tilden,
the tennis player, were certain to go far. By the end of Tugwell's
sophomore year he was managing editor of the college paper, editor
of the literary magazine, a member of the prom committee, and
had been toastmaster at the sophomore banquet. Few of his
classmates knew him well.

It was in his sophomore year that he wrote the Whitmanesque
declaration which was uncovered and widely circulated by those
opposed to the Pure Food and Drug Amendments — the lines
that start:

I am strong,
I am big and well-made,
I am muscled, lean, and nervous.
I am sick of a nation's stenches,
I am sick of propertied Czars. . . .

and say at the end:

I shall roll up my sleeves — make America over!

In 1914, his third year in college, he abruptly dropped all student activities and ceased to strive for campus honors. Simon Patten, to whom Frances Perkins also has acknowledged allegiance, had been at work on him. He married and settled down to serious work in the university's Wharton School of Finance and Commerce. Upon his graduation, Pennsylvania made him an instructor in economics. He resigned from the Pennsylvania faculty in 1917 with a number of others as an aftermath of Scott Nearing's dismissal for seditious observations. He did not resign because they had dismissed Nearing. Nearing, he felt, had asked for it and could take care of himself. Tugwell's protest was against the little red hunt in a teapot which the trustees started afterward, to the shame and discomfiture of elderly scholars and useful scientists in the Economics Department.

After Pennsylvania, Tugwell went to the University of Washington and taught economics there for a year. During the last months of the war he managed the American University Union in Paris. It was a long way from the slaughter, but he saw enough of waste and cruelty to depress him profoundly, and he returned in 1919 to his family at Wilson an ill and somber man. The doctors said that he would be well thereafter only if he could live in the country, do light work around the garden, and write only a little. He lived that way for a year and helped to build for himself and his wife, on his father's farm near Wilson. a second and smaller house. Picking up in health, he took an in   ictorship at Columbia University and completed the thesis anu other requirements for his doctorate. The University of Pennsylvania made him doctor, and Columbia raised him from instructor to assistant professor in 1922. In 1926 he was made associate professor, and in 1931 a full professor.

At Columbia he was a favored person, always given his head. He taught a light schedule and sometimes none at all, as he made studies here and abroad, and worked on his books. In his lectures he liked to expose the pretensions of classical economics. The eight weeks' trip to Russia which gave him so much trouble later was made in 1927. His official report, published with that of other economists and observers in *Soviet Russia in the Second Decade*, was sympathetic to the Russians' planned march away from family-line Czarism, but critical of that regimentation of opinion which remains an essential part of the Russian system. Tugwell took his family along as far as England that summer, and left them in a leased cottage in the Thomas Hardy country of Dorset. Hardy is his great man of modern literature. When he was through in Russia, he joined his family at the Dorchester cottage, visited all the places his hero knew, and composed his least-known and most revelatory pamphlet, *Meditation in Stinsford Churchyard*. Some scant excerpts from it may tell as much of Tugwell as of Hardy:

> Hardy's was a kind of depth that is like the rootedness of a culture. The roots were deep, well nourished, and gave the trees safe anchorage against the winds of change; the fruit was an authentic product, full, ripe, completely nourished. It had the bloom and flavor of northern-grown and fully-ripened apples. . . .
> It rains too hard; it freezes too soon; the pests come when the crops look best. There is a sense of all this in Hardy. The kernel of life is soon consumed and there is nothing much to show.
> A certain deep loneliness resides in man which has awakened pity many times. It may be largely out of pity that poets have turned again and again to comforting those who find, at intervals, the victories a little dull, or feeble, or impermanent. Never mind, they say, there will be flower and fruit and childhood always. Your thought, your hands, even the dissolution of your body is part of a cycle. . . . And whatever you do, even if you only are, you have a contribution to make without which the race would be, by a significant measure, much the poorer.
> Hardy had not this kind of pity. Fate had the power to anger him. It was pure anger, however; there was no whine in it; and no particular softness for the weakening of others. There are bleak winds that blow from eternity. But for all his large defeatist principles, he lived as though he were important, as though it always mattered what he did.

'He must be thrilled!' Frank R. Kent said of Tugwell in his column, 'The Great Game of Politics,' in *The Baltimore Sun* on July 21, 1933. 'Though only forty-two years old, the Professor has for years been studying, writing and thinking along these lines, imagining a world organized, directed, and managed in accord with his theories, a civilization molded to his thought. . . . What a transformation for this young man from his cloistered college center to the center of power in the world!'

This was an understandable reaction on the part of veteran politicians and political writers alike. They knew all the old rules and usages and thought they had the game covered. This new President had appeared in advance to be a competent technical politician who would observe the old rituals; and look what had happened: Washington suddenly full of eager-faced, immature technicians and academicians with lean bodies and no bellies, running around hatless, acting rather breathlessly mysterious and important, calling one another and the President by their first names, and more often than not, reaching his ear more readily than any of the old political hacks. There were some wild talkers, too, among these newcomers, especially at cocktail parties, saying what a mistake it had been to open the banks so quickly, instead of socializing the whole financial system; and loose talk such as that. Looking back now, I can see plainly that this strange new species of New Deal political animal was not only unbearable to the orthodox species, but in some ways, rightly so. We did not know the rules and amenities. Even as conscientious and careful an operator as Wallace at first continually instructed Congress what to think and do, and how to do it. That simply is not done by Secretaries to the President, not bluntly and directly, anyway; and there is sound reason why, traditionally, the legislative arm should initiate and pass laws, with the executive arm charged solely with administering laws so conceived and passed.

But the circumstance most unbearable of all, probably, was simply that of all these zealous novitiates in governmental action few, very few, had ever been elected to anything; and had never even tried to be. Even now, having sniffed of the Washington atmosphere, few, almost none, showed inclination to enter the arena, seek nomination, and stand for advancement by public

election. They had not come up through the onerous ritual of an
elective democratic process, ringing doorbells, slapping backs,
kissing babies, doing services for constituents, placating or fighting
free of a boss; and they did not fancy it. Within technical realms
of government work, this may be a point of strength; much government work, in fact, is rigidly screened from partisan activity or
bias by means of the Civil Service. But most of these unelected
fledgling New Dealers were operating beyond strictly technical
lines; they were up to the eyes in action programs and in active
policy-making. In this, their lack of a definite mandate and their
lack of definite political experience proved decidedly a weakness.
They were bound to arouse a mounting resentment and rebellion
on the part of Congress, particularly; and they did.

During their first weeks in Washington, well before they had
brought their families on and settled down to steady work, Wallace
and Tugwell were made aware that this would happen. Democratic
Party leaders gave a large dinner at the Sulgrave Club, black tie,
men only, with the new lads there to meet the old-timers. The
Vice-President, John Garner, was toastmaster. As the evening
wore on, he became somewhat garrulous, and at the end he gave
forth a puzzled, grim sort of statement of his true inner feelings
that was not in the least amusing and was somewhat embarrassing
to old hands and new alike. He said it was all new to him, all this
handing the top cards to boys who had never worked a precinct;
and it could not possibly come to good for the country or the party.
If this was what the President wanted, for the while — all right.
The old fellows would try to go along; but there would have to
come a showdown sometime soon.

So the boys were warned, impressively. And they inclined to
steady down, those who saw they were in for quite a stay, or
wanted to stay, in Washington. They learned to mind their
political manners better, many of them, and to exhibit less of a
gay impetuosity to hardened observers. Even so, the halls and
paths of Washington, and the buildings and mall of the Department of Agriculture particularly, maintained a campus atmosphere more markedly than in any previous administration; and,
cheered by the robustious example of that deep-laughing Man in
the White House, the newcomers relieved the strain of earnest and

monumental endeavors by occasional boisterous ,outbreaks of
somewhat intellectual mockery or horseplay. They had a good
time, and acted as if they were having a good time, while engaged
in important affairs of state in a time of crisis. This was irritating,
in a measure, not only to the elected representatives, uneasy at
having surrendered perhaps too abjectly so many of their pre-
rogatives to the executive arm; but irritating to business people,
who had also said in panic, many of them: 'It's beyond us; *you*
take it!'

It may now be said in review and condonement that the early
New Deal days were days of somewhat fantastic excesses, first excessive despair and then excessive hope. In 1933 even so seasoned
a political correspondent as Ray Tucker was writing, under Ray
Clapper as desk man for the United Press in Washington, flaming
features with headlines such as, PERHAPS A LEADER HAS
ARISEN and NINETY DAYS THAT SHOOK THE WORLD;
and even Roy Howard's Scripps-Howard papers were running
these headlines as banners across the top of page one.

Washington had indeed become the world capital in point of
hope and ferment. More news of sweeping change was being made
daily, as Clapper remarked dryly, 'in the South Building of Agriculture alone, than in the Kremlin.'

The Brain Trusters, major and minor, were fair game for
satire. Those I worked with in Agriculture, notably Mordecai
Ezekiel and Louis H. Bean, were able and brilliant, with no
ideological bias, and not notably academic in manner. The
highest type of well-trained civil servants, they worked as economic advisers to Wallace under constant pressure. In this vast
field he was a hard taskmaster. He knew mathematics thoroughly
and used it constantly, with an almost perfect memory for figures, down to the last decimal point. But Wallace never sent
a figure to print unchecked. 'I think that's right, but check it
with Louis Bean,' he told a reporter, relative to some exceedingly
daring high-trapeze work estimating corn and hog yields five
years ahead. The reporter took it to Bean, who was busy. 'It
took me a year to weigh in all the factors on this estimate, including weather,' Louis complained wearily. 'How do you expect me to confirm it in five minutes?'

'I've got to telephone this in two minutes,' said the reporter. 'So snap out of it, Doctor, and go into another trance.'

Ezekiel wrote a book on the potentialities of abundance. '*$2500 a Year for Everybody*,' it was called. Earlier than most agricultural economists he developed the concept that full employment and adequate pay in industry would do more to dissolve agricultural 'surpluses' than anything else. Of all the suspected despoilers of wealth and culture among the then New Dealers, Mordecai Ezekiel, born of an old Richmond family, had the most engaging manners and genuinely disarming approach. A rich and notably conservative lady from Baltimore who was placed next him at dinner was greatly taken with his ardent arguments that $2500 a year is not too much for every one to have, and quite possible. 'What charm!' she said. 'What earnestness! I am quite transported. I shall follow him. Yes: twenty-five hundred dollars a year for everyone!' Here she paused and added more thoughtfully, 'But not for the colored people.'

And there is a story about Frederic C. Howe, the most lovable of all the elder New Reformers.

Born in 1867, he had been in political reform since the days of Mark Hanna and the Thompson reform administration in Cleveland. When Triple-A was formed Wallace made him consumer's representative, the head of a special section, with the job of securing consumer representation and co-operation in the matter of pushing up food prices. For his first big speech he asked for thirty minutes of radio time, and was tremendously excited. He said he would write and deliver an explanation and justification of Triple-A price policy that would make the program fifty million city friends. 'Write the best speech in history; we'll okay it,' said Alfred Stedman, Director of Information for Triple-A. Fred Howe kept talking about that speech, reciting parts of it to everybody he met at the Cosmos Club, where he was quartered. 'I'll know when the moment comes to put it down on paper,' he told me at dinner there one July night, 'and then!'

Sure enough, the moment came that evening. He jumped into a taxicab, went alone to his office, turned on the lights, and sat there dictating from nine o'clock in the evening until one o'clock in the morning. He was getting along into his sixty-sixth year, but he still had plenty of fire. He put everything he had into that speech, and in the morning he was worn but radiant. 'Twelve cylinders full!' he said. 'The best I ever did, the very best, I'm certain!' But, unhappily, he had failed in every take to shove down the little lever that makes the needle bite the words into the record; so all he had was blank records. 'And that,' as the more unregenerate of the agrarians used to say, 'is what happened to the cause of the consumer in the Department of Agriculture.'

Amid such sallies and forays it was a simple pleasure to go in and take statements from blunt George Peek. 'I have known few men,' Wallace wrote in *New Frontiers*, 1934, after Peek had left the Department to be special adviser to the President on foreign trade, 'so determined and so little deterred by setbacks as George Peek in his long battle for the farmer.'[7] While Peek later said that Wallace had not been really active with the Mc-Nary-Haugenites in the culminating stages of that fight, and spoke of him disparagingly, as by no means the man and fighter his father was, I never heard Peek, in the height of the bitter departmental fight preceding his leaving us, say a single word that revealed either personal dislike or contempt for the Secretary; and the same was true of the little he said about Tugwell.

I was working on statements for both Peek and Tugwell at the time. It was quite a stretch; but there was a sort of covert liking between them. They respected each other's fighting qualities, at a distance. In fact, the sharpest thing Peek said about Tugwell, personally, in his printed reminiscences was: 'That young man kept out of my way.' George Peek was capable of nurtured and enduring animosities; though apart from that he was in no way a small man. Because Milton Eisenhower, the Department's Director of Information, had been brought into the Department by the 'Jardine-Hoover clique,' as Peek called it, Peek pointedly refrained from speaking to Eisenhower when they met, on the golf links and in official corridors alike. It irked Peek when Wallace, in driving need of help, found Eisenhower so competent and conscientious as to merit promotion almost immediately to a sort of deputy undersecretariat, and that he kept telling all who would hear him that 'Milton Eisenhower is the best young executive in the Department.' To Peek, this was just another example of what he called young Henry's 'elastic mind.' The following is from Peek's memoirs, under date of May 16, 1936:

> . . . I got out [of the Roosevelt administration] when I saw that I had no chance there to do anything for Agriculture. . . . The administration has committed itself, by a distortion of the lately deceased Agricultural Adjustment Act, to a policy of socialized farming. . . . The major policies of agriculture and foreign trade are in charge of men who have never earned their livings in industry, commerce, finance, or farming, and who have little comprehension as to how such livings are earned. Presenting facts to them is a sheer waste of time. They are long on theories but short on simple arithmetic. They are full of very big thoughts. These thoughts are so big that the United States is not a large enough field for them to operate in. . . .
>
> I found that I was not in a Democratic administration, but in a curious collection of socialists and internationalists. . . . They, fanatic-like, believed that their objectives transcended the objectives of ordinary human beings and therefore could not allow themselves to be hampered by platform pledges or by the Constitution. . . .
>
> The socialists or, more strictly, the collectivists, seemed — for nothing was in the open — to be headed by Felix Frankfurter, Rexford G. Tugwell, and Jerome Frank. They gained the mind of the Secretary of Agriculture and had a good deal of way throughout the Department. The internationalists ruled the State Department, and were headed by Secretary Hull and Assistant Secretary Sayre. Those within the groups had many divergent aims. Secretary Wallace, who had an elastic mind capable of any stretching, alone managed to be in both groups. . . .
>
> The present Secretary of Agriculture had tended rather to specialize in the study of corn and was a dreamy, honest-minded and rather likable sort of fellow. He had a mystical, religious side to him, and, never having been in the real rough and tumble of life — for he simply went on the family paper

as a matter of course — he was apt to view clashes of economic forces as struggles between bad men and good men, and not as between groups, all of whom believed that right was with them. Since Henry was always with the good men, he never quite got the whole of any picture. He believed in low tariffs, for instance, as a moral issue. . . .[8]

In conversation, Peek was a master of the concrete word and of a pointed brevity. In a curious way, for he made no pretense of detachment, his hatreds were seldom personal. 'Blank's all right,' he would say, naming some 'intellectual' of the Department staff, and then tear into the whole crowd that Blank stood with. 'Boys with their hair ablaze! The job's simple. It's just to put up farm prices.' He had unorthodox ideas about money. 'I don't care what we use for money. We can use gold or brass or tin or buffalo chips,' said old George Peek. And as for the Government taking over business: 'Hell! The Government's got more hay down now than it'll get up before it rains.'

Another favorite saying of Triple-A's first administrator was: 'I'm for the profit system if they'll cut the farmers in.' This failed to make as much sense to the city-bred in the Department as it did to the country-bred. Wallace went around repeating it, approvingly. Jerome Frank, Gardner Jackson, Lee Pressman, and other urban liberals found little that Peek said quotable. He had, they said, the sort of 'farm leader' mentality which oversimplifies everything. This was in some part true; but there was truth also, from the administrative standpoint, in Peek's contention that this was the Department of Agriculture, not 'the Department of Everything.'

As a key to the cleavage which threatened to split the Department wide open, and which led to such grievous exhibitions as national figures using the same washroom, shoulder to shoulder, and pretending not to see each other, I recall two stories the country boys put around, with relish, about one of Frank's city lawyers. Taking over the job of drawing a macaroni code, his principal question was: 'Just tell me this; is the code fair to the macaroni growers?' Later, relaxing from labors at a country inn, he is said to have seen his first firefly and cried: 'Good God! What's that?'

Whitney Shepardson, in the same critique previously quoted,

remarks on 'the rather testy self-consciousness' which men of *Land Grant College* training sometimes exhibit in discussing or defending their doings with outsiders. I think there is something to that; but underlying a simple defensiveness there was a wide difference in the accustomed thought and training of most Land Grant College graduates and most liberally educated urbanites, at the time. The city-bred liberals wanted the consumer protected as to prices. They wanted a crack-down on the big milk distributors and packers and other bulges in the distributive chain. They wanted to come down hard on child labor in agriculture, and to protect by methods however unprecedented in agriculture the rights of day-hands, sharecroppers, and tenants. The old-line and the college agrarians were more or less for all these things in principle; but they wanted most of all to go on with Triple-A as if it were a farm strike that they were running, and in large part a *landlord's* farm strike. Land Grant College graduates were extraordinarily land-lord-minded, in the main. And the farm organization and co-oper-ative element had become in general so habituated to playing along with the big distributors, in order to get a penny or more for farmers, while the big commercial operators got dollars, that Wallace was moved at times to speak ironically of 'plutocrats masquerading in overalls.'

With a rare blend of ardor and disdain, Tugwell made one or two attempts to win a general understanding of his character and purposes. For a while he wrote syndicated articles for newspapers. At one time, shortly after he had started this series, as many as fifteen papers were publishing his column. Then, deliberately, he spoke out on the Pure Food and Drug Bill he was backing: 'People are still being swindled, poisoned, and chucked under the chin. I don't like it.' The number of his customers immediately dropped to two. He wrote two more articles, principally for his own amusement. They were remarkable both in form and content, something between a Platonic dialogue and a satirical modern minstrel show. Tugwell was interlocutor. The principal charac-ters were Senator Progressive, from out West, and Beauregarde Boone, a friendly publicist who was trying to lead Tugwell along the paths of popular acclaim. A specimen passage follows:

TUGWELL: I grew up in an American small town and I've never forgot it. No one was very rich there, but no one was very poor, either. . . . I can't make this Park Avenue, country-club life seem right, along with slums and breadlines, ballyhoo, speculation; I can't make this fit into my picture of American institutions. I'm for decentralization, for simplicity of life, along with a recognition of the complexity of industrial and scientific civilization. It seems to me that electricity, vacuum tubes, Diesel engines and all these other things ought to make it possible for us all to approximate that no-riches no-poverty kind of life in which I grew up. I'd certainly set the sleigh bells to jangling again in thousands of village streets if I could. . . .

BEAUREGARDE BOONE (*the publicist*): That's it! Tell 'em how you love the little towns and sleigh bells. . . . Well, got to go. Don't say anything without asking me. . . . Jingle! Jingle!

3. Action

THE FIRST YEAR of Agricultural Adjustment was a driving catch-as-catch-can affair. As critics of the Act had prophesied, planners who go beyond blueprints and step afield to alter the acreage of any major crop take the bear by the tail and travel fast and far, with the need of making farther-reaching plans as they travel. What had not been clearly foreseen was the remarkable behavior of the bear.

Starved and bewildered at the outset, the rampageously individualistic American farmer, having tasted now the bread and honey of adjustment payments and a mild inflation, with a resulting rise in braced prices, sent delegation upon delegation to Washington demanding that the Department have done with such mild tail-twitchings and other gentle gestures of guidance, and assume absolute control. Cotton spokesmen wanted a compulsory sign-up, so that mavericks could not wander from under the price-umbrella and make money by overplanting, to the general ill. A delegation of five Northwestern governors came in to demand of Wallace 'cost of production' guarantees, backed by absolutely mandatory rulings from Washington. 'This,' Wallace wrote in *New Frontiers* a year later, 'precipitated one of the most interesting political thunderstorms I ever watched. . . . The Governors . . . wanted us to license the packers to pay at least eight dollars per hundred for hogs and everything else in proportion. They wanted us to double and treble farm product prices at once by the simple method of licensing all processors and dealers so that they could not purchase farm products except at a very much higher price. It was suggested that this might be illegal or unconstitutional, but one Governor spoke up with a brusque statement, "Hell, what's the Constitution between friends?"

'The Governors had been put on the spot by certain farm spellbinders who had an opening because of the increase in prices under the NRA at the time when farm products were dropping . . . and they came to Washington to put the Administration on the spot instead of themselves. Politically they were in much stronger position than we were. . . . They came from five farm States; we had to take a national view. We knew we would get into a terrible mess if we attempted to go along with the Governors. . . .' [9]

Chief among the 'spellbinders' inciting cost of production agitations and riots was Wallace's old campaign companion of the Hoover-Smith engagement, Milo Reno. Reno expressed no more regard for Wallace now than for Hoover, whom he had called 'the arch-enemy of a square deal for agriculture,' in 1928. Now Wallace's AAA was 'diabolical,' and 'Wallace would make a second-rate county agent if he knew a little more,' Reno cried. He called from the stump for Wallace's resignation, and at Shenandoah, Iowa, on one such occasion, a dummy marked 'Henry Wallace' was spanked by three stout farmers with barrel staves. [10]

Of all these doings Wallace wrote sympathetically: 'The Farm Holiday folks in the Middle West were rarin' to go. A judge was jerked off his bench and confronted with a rope. A lawyer from an insurance company which was about to foreclose on an Iowa farm was tarred and feathered. Harassed debtors, kindly folk driven to desperation, were bound and determined to hold on to their farms and homes, law or no law. . . . These things happened and many more. Sober citizens deplored the violence, but had to admit the depths of the grievance. The Administration could not condone the violence and the defiance of law, but it could and did understand it.' [11]

Wallace traveled far and made thirty-two scheduled pronouncements and publications, not to mention innumerable impromptu exercises in trouble-shooting between the March, 1933, inaugural and New Year's Day, 1934. In August he had flown South and had been flown over the Mississippi Delta to observe the extent of the cotton plow-up. Those in his party said that his gaze was mournful and his eyes were moist when the plane brought him back to the ground. Still earlier in the year, Helen Hill Miller related in her book, *Yours for Tomorrow*: [12] 'A group of New York intelligentsia, planners, technicians, writers for medical journals [had assembled] with a lot of technical questions they wanted to ask him. Finally one of them said, "Mr. Wallace, if you had to pick the quality which you thought most important for a man to have in plant-breeding work, what would it be?" The answer startled them: "Sympathy for the plant!"'

Of the plow-down he said in a speech upon returning: 'There are those, of course, who would say to let the weevil at this cotton and trust to luck. We have been trusting too long to luck. Insects have very small brains. They cannot be counted upon to get us out of troubles of our own making. Clumsily, to be sure, but with a new vigor and an eye to realities, we have started to take hold of this strange situation at both ends in an effort to bring sense and order to our use of land.'

When this plow-down of ten and one-half million acres, a fourth of that year's crop, was being planned, it was suggested to Wallace that the public might be spared shock and eruption if news and movie photographers were discouraged from taking pictures. 'No,' he said sharply. 'We must clear the wreckage before we can build. Rub their noses in the facts.'

At Syracuse, New York, on September 5, he said: 'You had a milk war here this summer. I have seen pictures of it. Not far from where I stand milk was spilled on the roads. Heads were broken by guards and troopers wearing gas-masks, armed with clubs and guns, and by strikers with stones in their hands. In cities, children went hungry. The spectacle did us no credit as a civilized people. I feel that all of us should earnestly examine our own minds and hearts, get at fundamentals, and try to cure the conditions that led to such bewildered haste and waste.'

In the course of the same talk, at Syracuse, he reproached in a more ironical tone the disinclination of dairymen in general to enter into marketing agreements and co-operative compacts designed for more orderly marketing and peace: 'There would seem to be something about the dairy business which leads a man to bury his head in the flank of a cow and lose track of time and space.'

He was far from being a finished speaker then. From the first, however, his speeches and pronouncements attracted attention, not as finished expressions, for he poured them forth in dictation hastily, but for their boldness, candor, and sweep. And at times afield with trouble to mend, he would put by his notes or manuscript and, speaking very slowly, he would say things like this:

'There are, I am told, people here who are accepting relief payments, and yet, anticipating some degree of monetary inflation and price rises, are getting ready to take a flyer in wheat speculation on the Chicago Board of Trade.'

That was the economist in him speaking. Then grandfatherism surged up in him. He threw up his head. It was as if old Uncle Henry stood there again preaching to the wicked. He went on: 'There are such people here. A little, ill-informed, small-minded public, returning like dogs to the vomit you quitted in 1929——'

More gently or wearily on the same trip, he was moved at the end of a prepared address at the Des Moines Coliseum to say a few words more. He crumpled his manuscript in a side pocket, and stood looking at that great crowd of farming people in silence. Knowing their Wallaces, they knew that something was coming and waited patiently: 'Only the merest quarter-turn of the heart separates us from a material abundance beyond the fondest dream of anyone present. . . . Selfishness has ceased to become the mainspring of progress. . . . There is something more. . . . We must learn to live with abundance. . . . There is a new social machinery in the making. . . . Let us maintain sweet and kindly hearts toward each other, however great the difficulties ahead.'

This was in November, with demands for compulsory controls still running high in the Corn Belt. Wallace went to the heart

of the most disaffected area and made three successive talks at
Des Moines, Chicago, and Muncie, Indiana, on the eleventh,
thirteenth, and fourteenth. At Des Moines he said that if the
demand of the five governors were met, it would involve 'a
system of compulsory marketing control, giving monthly marketing quotas to every farmer ... with a system of licensing every
plowed field in the country.' At Muncie he commenced a comparative examination of the 'pain of nationalism' and the 'pain
of internationalism' which led, the year following, to publication
by the Foreign Policy Association of the pamphlet, *America Must
Choose.*

Of this close-of-the-year period, 1933, he has written: 'Every
farmer in danger of foreclosure was invited to write, wire, or telephone the Farm Credit Administration in Washington.: ... A
corn-hog adjustment program involving $350,000,000 in benefit
payments was at last ready for launching. By November the
Corn Belt's rebellion had begun to subside. It was possible once
more to appeal to men's minds. The thunderstorm had cleared
the air. It was possible to explain why the emergency [pig]
slaughter had to be followed by a complicated adjustment both
in hog numbers and in corn acreage in 1934, and to ask the help
of thousands of volunteers in pushing this newest and hardest
program.' [13]

The intricate relationship of corn and hog supplies, as well
as the two months' delay in getting an act passed, held up all
hope of a working plan beyond the time that that year's corn was
planted. 'We might have done with corn as we did with cotton,'
Wallace said in a radio review of 1933 activities, over a CBS
network from Washington on January 17, 1934. 'We might have
organized corn-growing farmers to go out with horses and tractors and destroy a part of the growing crop. One plan we especially considered called not for plowing down, but for going
through part of the field at the first or second cultivation, and
sowing grass, rye, or soybean seed from an end-gate seeder in the
standing corn. The cover crop, coming along, would protect the
soil and smother out that part of the corn crop.

'Perhaps we should have done so, [but] to go and smother a
great excess acreage of corn, as was planned, would have required

an induced slaughter of hogs far greater than our slapdash attempt
in that direction later. Crude as the hog-killing was, it is beginning to help hog prices today; and I have at times regretted that
we did not also begin to take hold of the corn situation, however
crudely, in 1933. . . . No one knows better than I that the livestock farmer this winter is in greater trouble than ever before.
It takes time to control the supply of livestock which has been
several years in the making, and to increase the demand for livestock, which varies so directly with the payrolls of labor. . . .
Our corn-hog programs give us a real chance to reduce [before
birth] the number of hogs coming on the market next fall.'

The sensational death of the little pigs came about thus: Corn
and hog farmer representatives of ten states, meeting in Des
Moines on July 18, named an emergency committee of twenty-
five, with Earl Smith of the Farm Bureau as president and Ralph
H. Moyer, an Iowa farmer, as secretary. The Committee met at
the Union League Club in Chicago on July 24 and 25 and unanimously agreed to urge AAA to contract with the packers to purchase and process pigs weighing from fifty to a hundred and ten
pounds, the product to be disposed of to the Red Cross and other
relief agencies. Earl Smith and a subcommittee of four, including
Ed O'Neal of Alabama, came on for a Washington meeting,
August 10, at the Willard Hotel. There, representatives not
only of the Farm Bureau, but of the Farmers' Union, the
Grange, the Corn Belt Meat Producers, and the Central Co-
Operative Exchange, strongly endorsed the program; and the
Department accepted it, and put it into action.

'The result,' wrote a friendly commentator, Lowell Mellett,
having unearthed these facts when the ghosts of the little pigs
were brought forth to do a political dance anew in the campaign
of 1944, 'was that 6,000,000 surplus pigs were turned into 100,000,-
000 pounds of pork, and the pork was distributed by the government to feed the hungry. . . . If these pigs had been held until
the usual marketing age, they would have eaten about 75,000,000
bushels of corn. That would have produced a bad situation the
following year, since the 1934 corn crop, due to the drought, was
about a billion bushels short.'

In fine, farm organization people thought up this harsh but

perfectly rational plan at the moment.   They urged slaughtering
part of the pig crop a little ahead of time that year, and feeding
the pork to the needy.   Wallace accepted their plan, put it into
effect, and has been taking the rap for it with no attempt to shift
the responsibility ever since.   'The plowing under of ten million
acres of cotton in August, 1933, and the slaughter of six million
little pigs in September, 1933,' he wrote in 1934, 'were not acts
of idealism in any sane society.   They were emergency acts made
necessary by the almost insane lack of world statesmanship during the period 1920 to 1932. . . . To have to destroy a growing
crop is a shocking commentary on civilization.   I could tolerate it
only as a cleaning up of wreckage of the old days of unbalanced
production. . . . [14]

'A wheat carryover three times the normal, no hope for exports,
another crop coming on, and prices far below parity [had also]
suggested drastic action.   One proposal, therefore, was to rent
sufficient wheat land out of the 1933 crop to keep the carryover
down.   That would have involved plowing under growing wheat.

'Fortunately, this proposal was hardly advanced before the
crop reports showed a sensational reduction in winter wheat because of unfavorable weather.   It would not be necessary to
plow under growing wheat; nature had already done it — un-
equally, cruelly, to be sure, but decisively. . . . Our press section
breathed a sigh of relief; it would not be necessary to write about
the logic of plowing under wheat while millions lacked bread.   I
say this, it should be understood, seriously, for our traditional
economy is an economy of scarcity; and it so happens that the
larger the piles of surplus wheat in Kansas, the longer are the
breadlines in New York City.   Crazy, perhaps, but quite orthodox
in a society which still plays the game according to the rules of
scarcity.'

M. L. Wilson had turned in by the time of the 1933 fall planting
the first part of a fairly orderly birth control on wheat. He let the
little patches of wheat go, for the most part, and concentrated on
the plains.   Some Montana and Kansas counties signed up every
acre in the county, a hundred per cent, and reduced their fall
sowings fifteen per cent.   Adjustment payment checks went out
by the millions of dollars' worth, and were distributed by the

local committees of farmers which had supervised the reduction. Some big wheat counties turned in claims for reduction which exceeded the Government's past counts on their total wheat acreage. Often this was because the growers did not know their acreage; again, Government figures were found to be at fault. For the first time now the Government was getting the materials for a farm-by-farm census of production and accurate land measures field-by-field, farm-by-farm, a stupendous job in itself. The technique of measuring farms accurately by airplane photography was not then fully developed. The conflicts, the cries of deception and anguish, the high-hearted pioneer confusion of that first great wheat allotment effort can better be imagined than described. Through it all Wilson seemed extremely unexecutive and absent-minded. He sat on the back of his spine with his feet on the desk, telling all manner of yarns to callers, and firmly shoving every demand for adjudication back into the laps of the county committees. At one time, when a question of field procedure came up and he had no answer for it, he left his desk without leaving a forwarding address, flew out to Montana, and went around visiting farmer committeemen until he found one who had the answer. A key pamphlet for the campaign had to wait. The haste was such that I was sent to meet him on the way in, in Ohio, and clear the proofs from there. He was entirely unperturbed. 'No use in printing anything until we know what it means,' he said.

Assigned to compose a wheat pamphlet that would explain to all the technique of 'a balanced abundance' through acreage reduction, I was often in Wilson's office in those days, and I generally found him thinking and talking about something that seemed to have nothing whatever to do with wheat. But he was, I could see, at times performing a delicate task of highly practical intent. Time and again I found him closeted with some of the business friends who, with large interests in land and wheat, had helped put over the domestic allotment plan. Now that there was a speculative flurry in wheat, and a general feeling of eased tension, these insurance men and bankers were inclined to unload their distressed holdings. This might have meant another wave of farm foreclosures and untold distress. Wilson took it upon himself to talk them out of it, and generally he did. Also, through the turmoil of the wheat sign-up he continued to see as many people who had plans for 'subsistence homesteads' as people who had claims or ideas about wheat.

Partly through the influence of his friend, Henry I. Harriman, a rider, very roughly drawn, went through with the Act establishing the National Industrial Recovery Administration. It provided for aiding the 'redistribution of the overbalance of population in industrial centers' and made $25,000,000 'available to the President . . . for making loans and otherwise aiding in the purchase of subsistence homesteads.' The Act passed in late June, 1933. In July the President delegated administration of the $25,000,000 to Secretary Ickes. In September Wilson went over to the Department of the Interior as Director of the Federal Subsistence Homesteads Corporation, a non-profit corporation set up under the laws of Delaware. He worked for about ten months, until July, 1934, on this job.

Meantime, 'the wheat thing,' as Wilson called it, took hold well and firmly. It reached out to farms representing seventy-seven per cent of the nation's wheat acreage, securing agreement to reduce fall sowings fifteen per cent. Wilson put all possible emphasis on local committees, local responsibility; and in this Wallace backed him to the limit. They sought also to instill into the early drives of agricultural adjustment wider concepts of soil and water conservation, the conveyance of commercially 'surplus' products to the weak and needy, and the rude beginnings of an Ever-Normal Granary. By this time I had risen in the bureaucracy to the rather resounding but still vague title and duties of Chief Information Expert of Triple-A. Paul Porter, who was right-hand man to Oscar Johnson on cotton-option operations by this time, was entitled Principal Information Expert. He used to call me Chief and I would call him Prince. With a number of adventures out into radio, then back into Government at the next crisis, Paul Porter has proved one of the liveliest career men to spring from 1933's informal planting of new blood and brains in official Washington. He ran the publicity for the Democratic National Committee in the Roosevelt-Dewey campaign, went from there to be Chairman of the Federal

Communications Commission, then on to head OPA. A considerable number of green hands who joined up for Triple-A in various rôles in 1933 are still in Government, doing well. Thomas Blaisdell, of the legal staff, is Minister of Economic Affairs at our Embassy in London; Alger Hiss, of the same staff, served as permanent secretary of the San Francisco Peace Conference; Jerome Frank is a federal judge. Tugwell, of course, was Governor of Puerto Rico and President of its University. Thurman Arnold, now in private practice, was for some years Associate Justice of the United States Court of Appeals; Lee Pressman is now principal Counsel for C.I.O.

For my part, though, I felt that I ought to get out while I still had some outside connections as a free lance. I was enjoying the work but there was too much of it, along with outside writing, and I did not discover within myself the makings of even a semi-public man. So in May of 1934 I bought a small, disused farm, 'Thorn Meadow,' in Harford County, Maryland, thirty miles north of Baltimore, seventy miles from the Washington atmosphere, and moved back to my home country. The Secretary's staff gave me the accustomed parting dinner, with the usual rude remarks; and he gave me an inscribed photograph, which I value. The inscription, in his round, sprawling writing, says: *In memory of the happy days when the Deal was new and all the cards were being played haphazardly. Hope to see you again from time to time.*

X I

DISPLACEMENTS AND DEPARTURES

An engineered agriculture is going to require much fewer workers than a mode of living agriculture. It has been estimated that we could easily release two million of the six million farm families now on the land for other productive industry and thereby improve both the status of the four million families remaining on the land and increase the productivity of society as a whole. The question arises, where will the two million families go, especially as we have now between eight and ten million unemployed. How can they be fitted into new walks of life without great human sacrifice? This comes very near to the crux of the agricultural problem. — M. L. WILSON, before the American Economics Association, 1933.

The fluidity of change in society has always been the despair of theorists. — REXFORD G. TUGWELL, in *The Industrial Discipline*, 1933.

1. Dry and Stormy

AN ACT OF GOD embarrassed the agricultural New Dealers in the spring of their second crop year. The winter of 1933–34 had been dry. Snow scouts of the Forest Service reported alarmingly light deposits on the Coast Range and Rockies. Snow on the mountains in the irrigated country is 'next year's rain.' Winter rains on the High Plains were likewise scattered and light. Soil storms there grew worse. The natural cover of grass, deranged in the First World War plow-up, had not been restored. Vast withered stretches of land lay bare, abandoned, untended by ranchers and farming companies that had gone broke. Sandstorms crawled along the ground, cutting at all things living, biting at eyes and nostrils. Storms of lighter soil blew high to shroud the sun and life became a torment. The plainsmen made jokes about it, wrapping their noses in dirty handkerchiefs, spitting soil. 'A raindrop hit a fellow over in the next county yesterday,' they told each other, 'and they had to throw three buckets of dirt on him to bring him to.' 'We'd better get out,' some would say more somberly. 'We've just about wrecked this country and God is sore.' But if anything like that got into the newspapers, the Chambers of Commerce protested and so did the people. 'There's nothing the matter with this country that a little rain won't cure!' they cried. Actually, the rain when it came did the soil as great damage as the wind had done. Over the country as a whole water erosion was far more punishing than the wind erosion. The High Plains were all torn up with overplowing. The powdered soil surface raced off in every cloudburst and shower. But the rain did its damage quietly, whereas wind moaned ruin to heaven and wrote warning of desolation across the sky. Traveling over the Plains in the winter of 1933-34, Rex Tugwell, Assistant Secretary of Agriculture, brought in word that accelerated erosion was out of control and there would be famine and suffering on High Plain and Mountain ranches in 1934.

Early in the second week of May, dust storms, rising in the Panhandles of Texas and Oklahoma and adjacent parts of New Mexico, Colorado, and Kansas, blew together and bore east. The dust clouds crossed the country in four days. Soil on the wing veiled the sky in the great middle country on May 11. On May 12 the dust passed over our Middle Eastern seacoast and far out to sea. This, by an odd coincidence, was the first birthday of the Agricultural Adjustment Act of 1933. The first such storm on record in our East, it made a profound impression.

Farther to the west those clouds of hurtling soil were dark, heavily charged with humus. They were lighter in color, of fine clay particles and colloids, a tawny ocher, when, flying higher, they passed over Maryland. Humus and colloids are the very heart of fertile soil. The wind was blowing the heart out of some of the richest soils in our Southwest. Back on the Plains remained, as Wallace said, 'the skim milk'—sterile, restless sand dunes. The very cream of the land blew out to be lost in the Atlantic or delicately to fleck the decks of ships two hundred miles at sea.

Dust has moved on the wind since this world began. But never in history is there recorded a dust storm such as this. 'That storm,' said Hugh H. Bennett, Chief of the United States Soil Conservation Service, before a Congressional Committee later, 'swept from the Great Plains three hundred million tons of rich soil. It did another thing. It brought to the consciousness of numerous city people the fact that something was going wrong with our agricultural domain. Soils derived from fields two thousand miles away gritting against their teeth presented to them the erosional wastage as a personal experience, not merely as a vague problem of remotely situated farmers. In the Capitol in Washington Congressmen tasted dust.'

Hugh Bennett uttered that last sentence with a certain tone of triumph; and no wonder. For more than a quarter of a century as a soil scientist in the Department of Agriculture he had been crying warning against the waste of our soil by rainwash and blowoff. For the greater part of that time he had won almost no belief and only the feeblest of backing.

Rex Tugwell was the first official to back him strongly. Money had been made available in quantity for purposes of rural relief, apart from Agricultural Adjustment measures, to induce changed plantings. Early in the Roosevelt administration, in the summer of 1933, five million dollars of a Public Works appropriation had been marked off abruptly for erosion control. This was a substantial increase above the initial appropriations made for research during the Hoover administration in 1929, to start ten erosion experiment stations on obviously weather-wounded spots upon the body of this land. First plans for the use of this extra five million dollars called for the construction of miles of terraces. Hearing this, Hugh Bennett, in charge of the erosion experiment stations for the Bureau of Soils, went to Tugwell, as Assistant Secretary in charge of old-line bureaus, and protested. Terracing alone had failed, and always would fail, Bennett said; what was needed was an over-all integrated attack against erosion, using all known methods in varying combination immediately adapted to each individual piece of land. This might, of course, include terracing. Tugwell agreed and backed Bennett's guiding strategy in what later became the Soil Conservation Service. Wallace was interested, but otherwise much occupied. Economic salvage, through Triple-A, had the right of way over soil salvage in the Department of Agriculture at the time. The five million dollars was ticketed off to the Department of the Interior, and Secretary Ickes was glad to add new bureaus, offices, and functions to his departmental array. Tugwell and Wallace loaned him Hugh H. Bennett as Chief of a new Soil Erosion Service in Interior. It was a pleasant gesture, and, ever mindful of longstanding strife between Agriculture and Interior, Mr. Ickes was both surprised and pleased. Later he was more surprised than pleased, and complained vociferously, in a speech before a Conservation Conference, that his false friends, Wallace and Tugwell, had urged him to rest for a while in the April sun of Florida; and then, said Ickes, they had backed up a truck to Interior's back door, stolen this new bureau, hastily rechristened it Soil Conservation Service by Executive Order from the White House, and tucked it into Agriculture, where Hugh Bennett had been working for thirty years. This was on March 25, 1935.

A second dust storm blew over Washington on April 2, 1935. Bennett was up on the Hill again, arguing for more money before the Senate Public Lands Committee, considering Public Bill 46, Seventy-Fourth Congress, when again the dreadful miracle came. As he remembers:

The hearing was dragging a little. I think some of the Senators were sprinkling a few grains of salt on the tail of some of my astronomical figures relating to soil losses by erosion. At any rate, I recall wishing rather intensely, at the time, that the dust storm then reported on its way eastward would arrive. I had followed the progress from its point of origin in northeastern New Mexico, on into the Ohio Valley, and had every reason to believe it would eventually reach Washington.

It did — in sun-darkening proportions — and at about the

right time — for the benefit of Public 46. When it arrived,
while the hearing was still on, we took a little time, off the
record, and moved from the great mahogany table of the
Senate Office Building for a look. Everything went nicely
after that.

The Soil Conservation appropriation, which in Interior had
been fifteen million dollars, was raised to twenty-five million
dollars a year. Public 46, the Act establishing the Soil Conservation Service, took effect on April 27, 1935.

Overstrain on soil hitherto overcropped was somewhat eased
by the initial reduction of tilled land under Triple-A, no doubt;
but this was an incidental purpose and result. Triple-A was set
up initially not to conserve soil, but to buck up prices, and to save
established farmers from sell-out. This in great measure it did,
but it was a to-him-who-hath performance, with allotments and
payments proportioned to each producer's previous acreage and
means. The farming companies got the largest allotments and
payments; the smaller operators got little, less or least, according
to their scale of operation. Even so, it was good to see, while
traveling South after the cotton plow-up, green stretches appearing for the first time amid dim gray and brown expanses of cotton.
Those fresh-plowed patches of bare land in growing weather did
not look right to farmers. They spent their own money, thousands of them, for grass seed to cover that ground. This was a
rude turn toward balanced and decent farming, but it was a
greatly needed turn away from domination by King Cotton. We
may credit even the crudest early methods of rough 'adjustment'
with starting a turn toward more conservative farming, provided
that we do not pretend that was the actual purpose from the first.
The first purpose was to raise the prices of staple farm products by
reducing the total output.

By the end of their first year, in the spring of 1934, the New
Deal agrarians had by various devices raised gross farm income
thirty per cent. Though the degree of measurable recovery attrib-
utable to AAA will be forever debated and never determined, there
can be no doubt that by this time things were picking up the country over, and that AAA had much to do with it. The amount sent

out in definite adjustment payments to the rural regions, where
people *had* to buy things because they had gone so long without,
came that year to two hundred and seventy-seven million dollars.

In West Texas, on a story-trip for *The Country Home* that
spring, I found the cotton nesters celebrating enactment of compulsory allotments under the Bankhead Act. This Act was passed
over Wallace's protests; but he and Chester C. Davis, succeeding
George Peek as Administrator of AAA, agreed later that sometimes the farmers know best what they need. 'Sometimes,' as
Davis said in a press conference, 'a child is not planned for, perhaps not even wanted, but you grow to love it just the same.'

There was no doubt at all of AAA's popularity in Texas that
spring of 1934, and no doubt that things were booming. 'We can
boom on a quarter down here now,' people said. 'We've been
without so long!' And now with the jack rabbits running around
so freely and nobody chasing them, for lack of hog meat, they
quit calling them 'Hoover hogs.'

From Texas back through the Mississippi Delta I found planters worrying because peddlers from Memphis were cleaning out
pawnshops and sending out trucks with all sorts of gimcracks, but
especially any kind of pistol or rifle, to sell for Adjustment money
to the people, especially the day hands and sharecroppers who
were getting a little of it.

But not most of it, by any means. There could be no doubt
whatever, both from the dispersal figures and then by inspection
of the South's cotton terrain, especially, that AAA, as operating,
was shoring up the plantation and large company farming structure, not the deprived substructure of hands and renters.

Further, this new social machinery along with the advancing
use of metal machinery was operating very often to displace
hands, tenants, and operators of low means. This generally was
as bad for the ground as it was for the people. On a new cotton
frontier in Cochran County, Texas, nearly three hundred cotton
farmers nested with their families into new sodded dugouts one
winter. Three-fifths of them arrived broke; they ate three
thousand pounds of relief pork that winter. But they had big
plow rigs and tractors, most of them, on credit from now-booming
machinery companies. And they had 'bought' considerable

acreages of parched short-grass land, no money down, simply on agreement to pay the bankrupt ranching outfit who owned it a bale of cotton for each acre plowed and cropped over a period of thirty years.

These people were mainly displaced refugees from Adjustment farther east. 'Back in East Texas,' one of them told me, 'the landlords are asking forty-five per cent of the crop. I don't sweat much, but what I do, I don't bet it against no blueweed patch and a cut like that to the landlord.' He had a wife and sixteen children there with him. And he was plowing that grassland.

Everywhere I looked other rigs were out plowing; and the dust had started to blow. What kind of Adjustment was this?

It was Wallace's day for a press conference when I passed through Washington returning, and I stopped in. Some of the correspondents were pushing him hard on this displacement question. 'No, the tenants are not faring as well as the Southern land-owners. We must seek out further ways, of greater justice,' he said. Another milk fight was on. 'In some ways,' said Wallace calmly, 'I would be delighted if the courts find the marketing agreements as applied to milk unconstitutional'; and he over-ruled the suggestion of staff lawyers present that this remark be considered off the record.

Some mighty man had, as usual, denounced him as a starry-eyed dreamer. What about that? Again the soft answer, with a sharpening edge to it: 'You know it is very easy for one school of thought to call the other "dreamers." Businessmen, as proved by facts, have been possibly the most idealistic people I have ever heard of.'

At home again in my sheltered Maryland valley, I felt that per-haps after all, as AAA officials claimed, their ministrations were giving small and middle-sized family farmers a greater degree of security in tenure. Looking out from my own place, for instance, I could see two farms of moderate size, whose families did all their own work, and I knew that those two farms at least had been saved from foreclosure by long-term rewriting of Farm Ad-ministration loans, plus Triple-A Adjustment checks. Also, here in mixed-crop country something like a fair share of the money seemed to be getting through to tenants; and a reasonable amount of the extra money seemed to be spent, almost instinctively, for more lime and fertilizer and better grassland culture. Apart from this little Eden, where we had always farmed by rotation and maintained a decent respect for grass, I knew it was not working out that way everywhere. Truck-growing flatlands are not far down from these Piedmont hills of Maryland. To these, as to the vegetable and fruit-growing areas of California, come migrants for the harvest; and it seemed to me that there were more migrants than ever in those horribly dingy camps by the big truck farms, along our bottomlands and creeping up into the hills.

The drought that summer of 1934 seared not only the West and much of the Midland, but hit hard in the Piedmont uplands, too. M. L. Wilson, coming over for a visit, said that the scorched brown landscape made him homesick; it looked so like Montana.

He had just been on a field trip through the Midwest and told of stopping off at the old farm in Cass County, Iowa, where he grew up. The farm had passed from the hands of the Wilsons years since, but an old farmer across the way remembered the Assistant Secretary as a boy. They sat on a shaded porch drinking cold buttermilk and arguing about the New Deal. The old gentleman was dead against it all along the line.

'We sat there,' says Wilson, 'and argued until nearly sundown and I thought maybe I had him softened up. When I left he walked as far as the gate with me and put his hand on my shoulder:

'"Milburn" (nobody has called me that since I was a boy), "I want you to promise me something. I want you to go out and stand for a little while in the old churchyard where your grandfather is buried."'

The Assistant Secretary was moved. He promised.

'"And, Milburn, when you're out there I want you to notice how the sod's all tore up from that old fellow whirling over and over in his grave!"'

There was little good-humored argument about AAA now, however, as the drought settled in to stay. The whole machinery of planning in Washington and throughout the country had to be turned around, headlong. 'In 1934,' Wallace wrote toward the end of that growing season, 'we demonstrated that the Adjustment Act really was an adjustment act and not solely a reduction act. . . . The drought created a new and gigantic relief problem. It compelled AAA to face a situation in 1935 it did not expect to face until 1936 at the earliest; and it set in motion certain imponderables — economic, social, political — the full effect of which no one could foresee.' The drought devoured the surpluses. 'What AAA had planned to do in three years, the drought did — except for cotton and tobacco — in one. . . . In May and June of 1934, AAA began to overhaul its programs.' [1]

Drought nerves led many a stricken farmer and rancher to cry, sincerely, that this was a judgment of God. They saw in the dust swirling above their baked fields the image of tall cotton plants slain in their prime. They heard in the wind the squeal of the little pigs. 'To hear them talk,' said Wallace, 'you'd think that pigs were raised for pets!' He pointed out that the people of western Canada who had not been forced to reduce output had also been stricken by God's weather; and argued on the radio, June 6, 1934, for an Ever-Normal Granary, such as had been used in ancient China and again in Bible times, to carry over the fat yield of good years and provision the people more evenly in times such as these. But 'voodoo-talk,' as Wallace called it, increased and mounted; and the tom-toms of the press and opposition magnified the sound. Deeply troubled, almost angry, Wallace's talks began to acquire a fighting edge; and on August 19 he published in *The New York Times* an agressive defense of the farm program which revealed for the first time his latent abilities as a campaigner:

> Because we have had in the United States this season the worst weather for crops in forty years, advocates of the old order whisper it around the country that the drought is a judgment from Heaven upon us, and they say that the entire program of the Agricultural Adjustment Administration should be abandoned immediately. They are advocates of chaos.
>
> An adjustment program must in its very nature be kept adjustable, and it should at all times be subject to free criticism. But . . . the cry of the opposition is for no course at all. On our course to balanced harvests and an assured

and stable food supply we have met bad weather. In time we shall meet bad weather again. Therefore, these old-deal pilots say that we must abandon distant landmarks, toss all charts overboard, and steer as of old from wave to wave. It was just such childish courses that had us just about on the rocks March 4, 1933, and we have as yet by no means triumphantly weathered the consequences of their heedlessness.

The cry to abolish AAA, he went on to say, was not merely partisan; it was reactionary Democratic as well as reactionary Republican.

And he called for a new party alignment:

> The old party tags do not mean as much as they used to. ... I hope they will mean even less in time to come. We badly need a new alignment: conservatives versus liberals; those who yearn for a return to a dead past, comfortable only for a few, versus those who feel that human intelligence, freed and exercised, can lead us to a far greater abundance and peace between warring groups. With the old crowd shouting the same cries and whimpering the same old incantations, it seems to me that the faster the showdown comes, and the more definite the division between the old dealers and the new dealers of both great present parties, the better.

He predicted the usefulness of AAA in increasing production as well as cutting it down and seemed to foresee the Second World War:

> We have in AAA something new, and still crude; but it is a typically American invention equipped to meet crises, go around or through them. Our agricultural adjustment machinery can be used to spur rather than to check farm production. ... If this country should ever attain to an enlightened tariff policy, reopening world trade, or if there should be war beyond the ocean and other nations clamor for our foods again, it is conceivable that we might offer adjustment payments for more rather than for less acreage of

certain crops. That is the very last use I should want to see
our adjustment machinery put to, but . . . we could provision a war . . . with far less of that plunging, uninformed, and
altogether unorganized overplanting which got us into so
much trouble during and after the first great war.

War is a bad business, a murderous business, and all that
you can collect on it afterward is increasing grief. Another
World War would conceivably destroy us and destroy civilization. . . .

Like drought, earthquakes, flood, fire, and famine, war
remains, however, a recurring reality. Drought is upon us
now. Beyond the seas, nations hurt by the terrible grind of
ungoverned economic forces are in warlike mood. Their
men are arming. We want none of that, but the world is
small.

Wallace said this on August 19, 1934.

2. New Designs

WHEN WE LAMENT, as we often do in this republic, the
lack of a college-trained group of civil servants specifically trained in tasks of administration and statesmanship, we overlook the fact that in one important particular we
are well supplied. The Land Grant Agricultural Colleges, established in the states in the time of Lincoln, have been turning
out year by year not only thousands of trained technicians in the
special branches of agriculture, but economists, sociologists, and
administrators whose approach to events is trained and generally
realistic. And the in-service training which many such men and
women acquire after graduation in the Agricultural Extension
Service, as county agents, state supervisors, and state or regional
administrators, for instance, inclines to instill a considerable degree of skill and competence in public affairs. These men and
women customarily work facing real people, out on the ground.
One reason that Triple-A was able to forward its programs, it may
well be argued, where NRA so largely failed, lies in the fact that

Triple-A could be and was staffed from the very first with specifically trained and, on the whole, educated people.

Charged now, as they had been since early 1933, with remaking the Department of Agriculture, all its field forces, and all the state colleges of agriculture and experiment stations into an active and co-ordinated instrument of ground-line national planning, Wallace, Tugwell, and Wilson could not help but sense a mounting trend toward rigidity and harshness in the plans. As a stay against the economic emergency arising from the loss of foreign markets, the Secretary had been charged with enormous responsibility and power. Centralization of authority was increasing. Parley between Washington and the states would often get just so far, in the face of a state's increasing restlessness and resistance; and, then, because time or patience lacked, the tendency would be to pass another executive miracle, and drive straight through.

Better relations with the states had to be arranged or approached immediately. In the making of a working truce, if not peace, between Washington and the Land Grant deans and directors, Wallace and Wilson, greatly aided by Milton Eisenhower, finally succeeded, in a measure. A pact of understanding known as the Mount Weather Agreement for the purpose of 'Building Agricultural Land Use Programs,' was signed by Wallace, seventeen aides and thirty representatives of the Land Grant Colleges at Mount Weather, Virginia, on July 8, 1938. But initial approaches to this working agreement were stormy; and in this particular Tugwell, who was now the Under-Secretary, was deliberately more irritating than placatory. He had the Land Grant College system, with its State Extension Directors and corps of County Agents, identified, in part correctly, with the ruling caste of farmers, the most conservative Farm Bureau leaders, the cotton barons of the South, the emerging Associated Farmers of California, the banker-farmers of the Middle West. In a University of Georgia Extension circular, *Recollections of Extension History*, T. A. Evans [2] recalls a 1933 conference of federal and of state officials in Wallace's office. In came Rex. He listened a while; then he raised some questions which penetrated like acid such oil as had been spread. He had an appointment at the

White House and rose to hurry there. 'Dr. Tugwell seems to lack confidence in Extension Directors,' said Wallace, smiling. Tugwell, leaving, walked over to Wallace, leaned toward his ear, and spoke cheerfully in a loud whisper, 'No; I haven't a damn bit of confidence in Extension Directors, Henry.'

Between Washington and the Land Grant Colleges, States' Rights is the issue, decidedly, and this is especially so in the South. The South was not in the Union and voting in Congress when the state-federal setup of the Land Grant system was established. This has never been entirely forgotten there. At some state meetings when Wilson was presenting the co-ordination program to college and extension officials there were echoes, not too gently muted, of the rebel yell. In one mid-Southern state a Dean took the platform after Wilson had spoken. For more than an hour he whipped that group into a high excitement. He invoked folded battle-flags. He ranted against these Yankee overseers of Southern civilization and Southern education, come anew. Wilson sat with a stiff face, saying nothing. Next day, reopening the conference, Wilson told without reference to the previous day's ruction, of 'a visit to Einstein at Princeton.' 'As I was leaving, Dr. Einstein took me by the hand and said: "Mr. Wilson, it's in truth a race now between 'education and catastrophe'; between a growing understanding and tolerance, on the one side, and the forces of narrowness and hate on the other."' The Southern audience stood up and cheered.

The Wallaces had always worked with the Land Grant College people, but quite as often to goad them as to praise. H. A. left most of the Extension negotiations to Wilson, himself an old hand at Extension. The States' Rights rift, both Wallace and Wilson felt, would heal with the years; but it would be a slow business.

An immediate and more ominous trouble between Washington and the forces of agriculture afield was a tendency in almost any price emergency for rural commercial pressure groups to shout for democracy and in the same breath demand even more autocratic central control. It was not Washington that led the move to make participation in the cotton program compulsory; it was the Cotton South. Nor was it Washington which suggested potato controls so stringent that Wallace lost patience and flatly

said that if such controls were enacted they would be unen-
forceable, and that he would not attempt to enforce them. Those
suggestions were hardest pressed by 'surplus'-ridden growers in
New England particularly, and by their most conservative representatives in Congress.

Once a drowsily humming mill of information dedicated to
peaceful research, teaching, and demonstration, the Department
of Agriculture now had actively entered the arena of price and
land policies. 'Action programs' increased and multiplied, and
no one could foretell satisfactorily how this increasing maze of
complications and contradictions could be resolved. Plainly the
old setup was not suited to the new or enlarged functions. Preaching co-ordination to the states, the Department itself in this
particular was in bad shape. Clique rose against clique, office
against office, bureau against bureau. And over it all there appeared to be mounting a somewhat terrifying tendency of rural
pressure groups, long denied bounty, to demand more and more.
The Cotton South, in particular, having tasted 'tariff equivalent' pap in Triple-A benefits, was out, as one rough and candid
spokesman put it, 'to get the Civil War debt back,' then get it
again.

To humanize the material clash and the increasing class emphasis, Wallace and Wilson made a number of moves in the fields
of the spirit as unorthodox as their maneuvers toward a planned
crop production democratically controlled. On funds privately
contributed by the late Mrs. Mary Rumsey they brought to
Washington 'AE' — George Russell — the Irish poet and farm
organizer. He read his poetry of evenings at Wallace's and other
apartments, often with brash young realists of the Department
there to snort behind their hands. And Russell held philosophical
conversations, arranged by Wilson, with tense huddles of Triple-
A and Extension executives right in the middle of planning extremely practical courses in a time of needful haste.

These conferences were sometimes funny, but they were not
always so. Russell had campaigned through riotous rural co-
operative times in Ireland. When he faced, say, thirty contending milkshed administrators, with a Syracuse milk strike and
broken heads fresh in their minds, he knew what was bothering

them. He spoke in his grave, musing voice, as from a great distance; an old man, wanting nothing, mellowed, and soon to die. He declared the littleness of conflict and mused on eternal values.

I am sorry that I attended only one of his meetings, and that a brief one. I do not try here to put his words together as he spoke them. He was telling a group of wranglers over a milk-licensing agreement in a Northern milkshed how in an Irish town the dealers had barred him as a co-operative agitator from using the town hall for his meetings. So he drew up a farm wagon on the town square and hoisted a lantern above it. From that platform he spoke; and the farmers stood around and heard him and asked questions. It was early winter and as they stood and reasoned about these troubles, 'A light snow fell and touched our foreheads and blessed us,' he said. I remember that closing sentence word for word. Russell returned to Ireland, remarking confusedly to ship reporters that New Deal America was overorganized and following gods which are not the old gods, or words to that effect. Somewhat perplexed in their own minds and hearts, Wallace and Wilson continued amid headlong action, and in ways most rare among organizers, themselves to raise questions, to spread doubt.

From the first, in putting Triple-A campaign plans before the public, Wallace displayed as often as not the attitude of a man perplexed, debating within himself, and calling continuously for 'widespread public debate on the highest possible plane.'

The area of plowland that had been added to America's tilled domain during the First World War boom exceeded forty million acres. Forecasts of yields for 1934–35 fell off so sharply as the bite of drought tightened that Triple-A, aiming first at fifty million fewer acres of plowland, lowered the goal to forty-three million acres to rest from the plow that crop year. Even that great a reduction, as Howard A. Tolley, then Assistant Administrator of Triple-A, told a Farmers' Week audience at the Ohio State University, called for continuation of a tremendous march of change: 'Considerably more than the area of the State of Illinois, almost one-eighth of all the cultivated land in the United States . . . is to be taken out of commercial, competitive production [of staple crops: corn, cotton, wheat, tobacco] under the allotment method.' Then, speaking at one with Wallace, Davis, and Wilson, Dr. Tolley — himself a leading architect and administrator of the plan in operation — took the whole plan to pieces and displayed grave weaknesses in its development:

> Allotment withdrawals under the present system, crop by crop, are arranged without due regard for correct farm management inter-relations, on farms, and by regions. . . . We are trying now to figure out some method of 'farm-unit' allotments. It may in time be necessary, and even more difficult,' to refine the allotment system to a point where it encourages, rather than upsets, 'sound and appropriate shifts and balances in the entire farm management schemes of whole regions.

As it was, Tolley went on to say, the farmer planting eighty per cent of his land in cotton and the farmer planting only ten per cent of his land in that devastating row crop were alike required to reduce their cotton acreage thirty per cent. To a considerable degree, then, in this and in other one-crop regions, the Triple-A program was perpetuating mistakes and maladjustments and paying out Government money without assuring a defensible social result. At the close of his paper Tolley, who later became Chief of the Bureau of Agricultural Economics, made the first public announcement of a new approach to the 'surplus' problem: What must we have to be well fed and clad? This approach appealed above all others, even then, to Wallace, Tugwell, Wilson, and Tolley himself. Thinking back to the beginnings of the same trend in national and international planning, Wilson said in 1943:

> In 1934, right after I came back to Agriculture from Interior, Henry put me on a Commission to Cuba. We teamed off, we members of this Commission. It was a study of land management and the human consequences. I visited plantations with a man from the Harvard School of Public Health, Dr. Wilson Smiley. He pointed out things. We talked a lot about our South particularly. He convinced me. He said: 'You're an economist. You don't start in the right

place — diet.' He said that he could go to almost any
place in the South, and if it were possible to put the people
there in a pen and feed them right, why, in six months they
would be new people. He said that a lot of people were
nutritionally sick, and if economic recovery isn't under-
written with proper diet it will never amount to much. . . .

Henry and I, in '35 and '36, along in there, talked a great
deal about nutrition. We could see we had in nutrition
something of great interest, and something unifying, binding
together all interests in agriculture, and outside agriculture.
It could be the central thing in a new agricultural policy,
and a policy in reference to low-income people.[3]

The concept of food production in an abundance geared to full
nutritional need appears to derive in point of action from a suggestion that Wallace made to Dr. Louise Stanley, his Chief of the
Bureau of Home Economics, early in his first year as Secretary
of Agriculture, 1933. He suggested that it would be a good idea
to draw up compilations of minimum American food requirements
and maximum possibilities of healthful consumption.

A circular by Hazel K. Steibling, *Diet at Four Levels of Nutritive
Content,* prepared in November of 1933, provided a basis for computations by Dr. F. F. Elliot and others in the Bureau of Agricultural Economics.[4] These initial computations, later refined and
amended by Dr. Elliot, and others, but never substantially altered, were the ones put forward publicly by Dr. Tolley in his
Ohio State University address during Farmers' Week in January,
1934. His figures showed that, if sustained prosperity and a better general knowledge of nutrition co-joined to permit American
consumers a 'liberal diet' recommended as best by nutrition
scientists, *it would then require 'the cultivation of more than three
hundred million acres in crop land and also some increase in range
and pasture land above the amount we now have.'*

*This three-hundred-million-acre figure represented, comparatively,
an increase of twenty or more million acres over the amount of crop
land actually being tilled in the United States during the industrially
prosperous years, 1925–29, before there was any Agricultural Adjustment Administration.* In other words, if the American people

could manage to eat well and wisely, we should need not less land in production, but more.

The *nutritional yardstick* so defined by the agrarian New Dealers in 1934 brought to their hands an invaluable social implement. It cleared the way for advancing programs more generally acceptable than programs of restricted production could ever be. Positive emphasis on a planned abundance helped greatly to gain public consent in the launching of successive advances toward an Ever-Normal Granary, free school lunches and the Food Stamp plan. During the years of this swing away from negative measures, sabotaging completed yields of the earth, reducing yields unborn by abstinence from sowing, these computations showed what people might buy and eat if there were full off-farm employment at good wages. People could understand that. The facts provided, moreover, a rapier of defense which the administrators of Agricultural Adjustment, including Wallace, gladly wielded. They almost quit apologizing for their own actions in the light of charts and tables, all perfectly authentic, demonstrating a close and constant relationship between the rise and fall of total factory payrolls and total farm income. They bade the laborer to rejoice whenever farmers were in the money and the farmer to cry thanks whenever labor got a raise. Even more insistently, the new-agrarian evangelists, with Wallace leading, kept challenging industrial management to sustain full employment and decent wage schedules.

Often, on this score, it must be noted, the new-agrarian rapier swished around in ways quite sharply defensive, especially when those little pigs were mentioned. As to the pigs, Triple-A spokesmen could not convincingly cry to opposition editorial writers, cartoonists, and reporters, 'Thou canst not say I did it. Never shake thy gory locks at me!' They could, however, and did, charge industry with having 'plowed men into the streets' for some years ahead of the little pig liquidation and the surplus cotton plow-down. They could, and did, point out further that even in 1934 with 'recovery' proclaimed, industry was still forty-two per cent under its 1929 level of production, with prices only fifteen per cent below the 1929 level; whereas farmers, even in that year of drought, with prices for their products still far below the 1929 level, produced only fifteen per cent less than in 1929.

Reconsidering now the urban-rural clashes of that interwar adjustment period, it would seem that, while pots calling kettles black is not the highest form of public argument, the agitation over AAA did bring the question of a deliberately restricted production into public notice. And much of the argument proceeded, properly, on a plane above immediate cash considerations. The propriety of restriction was quite generally debated on ethical or moral grounds. 'Only the merest quarter-turn of the human heart,' said Wallace, 'withholds us from a balanced and shared abundance beyond our fondest dreams. It is mean and niggardly in a land so rich and wide to heap up surpluses next door to bitter hunger. It is bad management. We must learn how to live with abundance . . .'

Again, in a series of lectures on Statesmanship and Christianity, he said:

> It is possible for powerful men in positions of financial influence or in control of certain fundamental mechanical processes to pose as hard-headed men of affairs when as a matter of fact they have all too often created temporary illusions; they have merely been blowing bubbles. By the manipulation of money, the floating of bonds, they have distorted the judgment of our people concerning the true state of future demand and future supply. Oftentimes with excellent motives and looking on themselves as realists they are in fact sleight-of-hand performers and short-change artists.
>
> Yes, we have all sinned in one way and another and we are all sick and sore at heart as we look at the misery of so many millions of people, including among them many of our close friends and relatives; and we ask again and again why this should be in a nation so blest with great resources, with nearly half of the world's gold, with great factories, with fertile soil, and no embarrassing external debt. We look at all this and ask what mainspring inside of us is broken . . . and where we can get a new mainspring to drive us forward.

Toward the close of *America Must Choose*, he remarked in the same meditative voice and manner:

> In all civilized lands today we stand appalled by the tragic nonsense of misery and want in the midst of tremendous world stocks of essential goods. . . . Perhaps we can evolve in this country an economy that deals in potentialities instead of in denial. Perhaps in time we shall be able safely to unleash the productive capacity of all our industries, including agriculture, and turn out for the widest distribution imaginable the kind of goods which Americans, and people throughout the world in general, so achingly desire. . . .
>
> That an enforced meanness has throughout modern society become a real menace, no one can deny. The breadlines testify to this reality; a million forced sales of farms in this country tell another part of the wretched story; and then you have only begun to take count of all the millions the world over who live in constant and degrading fear that the same thing may happen to them tomorrow. . . .
>
> In an age when an advanced technology pours forth goods in a smothering abundance, fear of freezing to death and starving to death should be removed as a matter of common decency from the lives of civilized people as a whole. This is not cloudy idealism which has no basis in facts. Only those really close to science can know the abundance that could be ours with even-handed justice and a generous distribution between groups. Our grinding efforts to subsist, in the mass, on the farm and in great cities alike, the world over, would drop into the far background in the light of the attainments we could command.
>
> This nation, and all the developed parts of the world, has been terribly under the weight of the need to subsist, to keep body and soul together, in the past few years. We can throw off that miserable burden. We can stand as free men in the sun. But we cannot dream our way into that future. We must be ready to make sacrifices to a known end. As we wrestle with all the infinite complexities which now beset us, the temptation is to give way to false and easy hopes and to

easy ways of thinking. But we cannot afford to dream again
until we have taken hold of things as they are.

And all the time this same Wallace was vigorously administering an action program which, however they dressed up the press
releases to skirt the drab words 'reduction' or 'restriction,' was
definitely planned to yield a diminished agricultural output.
Was this hypocrisy? If it was, ninety-and-nine of the three million farmers who had then come in on the program were also
hypocrites. Reduction was something they hated doing. They
did it simply because they reasoned or had been told you had to
do it to survive as farmer-citizens with some buying power. To
diminish sowings went against their deepest impulse, as it went
against Wallace's deepest impulse. To have to do so made them
often testy and rather too sharply apt to pronounce moral judgments against other businessmen trying to get along by doing the
corresponding thing in urban callings. 'Enforced meanness,'
Wallace called it somberly, but, in the same pamphlet, *America
Must Choose*, he argued for pressing on under stress of need:

> Much as we all dislike them, the new types of social con-
> trol that we have now in operation are here to stay and to
> grow on a world or national scale. We shall have to go on
> doing all these things we do not want to do. The farmer dis-
> likes production control instinctively. He does not like to
> see land idle and people hungry. The carriers dislike produc-
> tion control because it cuts down loadings. The processors
> dislike it because of the processing tax. The consumer dis-
> likes it because it adds to the price of food. Practically our
> entire population dislikes our basic program of controlling
> farm production; and they will do away with it unless we
> can reach the common intelligence and show the need of
> continuing to plan. We must show that need of continuing
> if we are to save in some part the institutions which we
> prize.

In this fifteen-thousand-word pamphlet, published in the
spring of 1934, Wallace, debating with himself, caught the national and international eye and ear to an extraordinary extent for

the first time. Partly because his publishers, The Foreign Policy Association and the World Peace Foundation, co-operating, had the foresight to print on its flyleaf a complete waiver of copyright, *America Must Choose* was reprinted in a variety of formats by other organizations, reproduced in large part by *The New York Times* and serialized by Scripps-Howard and other newspaper chains and syndicates. Its circulation in English ran into the millions and the pamphlet was later translated into a number of foreign languages, including Italian. The art and craft of pamphleteering, sharply reviving during the F. D. Roosevelt ferment, was measurably advanced by this production, a condensation or distillation, with matured corrections and emendations, of Wallace's public speeches and recorded offhand remarks to smaller gatherings.

The entire first section, I recall from my year as one of his staff men, he delivered extempore, speaking very slowly, feeling his way, before an Outlook Conference of agricultural college field men in applied economics, crowded into a supper room above Child's restaurant, downtown. His father, Secretary Harry, had established these Field Outlook conferences at a time when Government economists especially had to be most circumspect in what they said they foresaw. Free now to egg such civil servants into enlarging thought and aims, as his father had never been, H. A. made, quietly, one of the best off-the-record talks of his first year in public life. When an improvised record of it was shown him, he started to work it over into a pamphlet. At the end of a month or so, working Sundays and betweentimes, he had twenty-five thousand words for the printer. Then he showed it to some of his aides, notably to Arthur P. Chew, senior agricultural writer of the Department, and collaborator on the Secretary's annual report ever since the days of the first Secretary Wallace. 'It sags in places, Arthur,' said the second Secretary Wallace, 'and Monday's deadline.' Chew looked it over that Sunday. 'Just pluck this ten thousand words out of the middle,' said Arthur Chew, suiting the action to the word, 'and it will be fine.' Himself an editor, Wallace saw the point immediately. Forty typed pages went into the wastebasket with a twist of the wrist and the pamphlet came out fine.

H. A. called Arthur Chew his 'dilemma-poser.' Ten years after *America Must Choose* came out, Chew clinched his claim to the title by arguing that the New Deal's agrarian wing, which is commonly supposed to have proceeded Leftward, was really in rapid march toward the Right. The argument, if accepted — and Chew is most persuasive — helps to explain the visible unease and distress of so many earnest men pointing with ardor one way and moving decisively in quite another.

Writing in *The Land*, a quarterly magazine, Chew first showed that Agriculture had no reason to love tariffs, and could not naturally love the tariff-equivalent rigging and reasoning of the initial Triple-A. This was a move Rightward, an unnatural move: for, said Chew:

> Agriculture loves production more than it loves restriction, initiative more than governmental regulation, and trade more than monopoly. With the cynical view that wealth should be acquired rather than produced it has no sympathy. It wants income, not through over-reaching, but through fair exchange, with prices made by markets rather than by governments. It has moved to the Right since World War I, and built up a tremendous apparatus for controlling acreage, stocks, prices, and trade, not from choice but because the interwar breakdown has left it no alternative. ... Making a virtue of necessity doesn't mean liking such rough discipline. ... Beneath agricultural nationalism, Agriculture has developed a longing to be rid of it.
>
> Henry A. Wallace expressed this counter-current in *America Must Choose*. ... As long ago as 1934 he foreshadowed what is now the official philosophy of the Allied nations: World trade instead of trade restrictions, lower tariffs instead of crop controls. I quote from page 11 of his pamphlet:
>
> 'If we go the whole way toward nationalism it may be necessary to have compulsory control of marketing, licensing of plowed land, and base and surplus quotas for every farmer for every product for each month in the year. We may have to have government control of surpluses, and a far greater degree of public ownership than we now have. ... This

whole problem should be debated in such a lively fashion that every citizen . . . will begin definitely to understand the price of withdrawing from world markets, and the price of our going forth for foreign trade again. Not only the price but the practicality of going national should enter into the public's decision.'

Here was criticism of the movement from its head; for the author of the pamphlet was Secretary of Agriculture. He was the man in charge — the leader of the retreat from surplus acres, and of the entire 'nationalistic' program with its government loans, government holding operations, marketing quotas, acreage allotments, and export subsidies. This policy, the agricultural counterpart of our industrial tariff system, had obviously more kinship with the conservative than with the liberal tradition in American life. Mr. Wallace advised the farmers to look where it would lead. . . . The idea in a nutshell was simply that our agricultural restriction program was something we should ditch as soon as possible.[5]

In light of the entire text, it would be fairer to say that in *America Must Choose* Wallace spoke not for ditching the farm program. He argued flatly against ditching any of the then essential features, including a continued immediate restriction of agricultural output. To put it perhaps too simply into another nutshell, he was feeling and arguing his way along toward amending the need of restriction in agriculture and industry alike.

3. Purge

THE FARM ACT charged Wallace's Department not only to control agricultural production by demo-collective actions, but to reduce distribution duplications, tangles, and excessive charges, which take toll of consumer and producer all along the road to market.

In his radioed 'Declaration of Interdependence,' explaining the Act the day after President Roosevelt signed it, Wallace said:

Agriculture and tradesmen must make their way together out of a wilderness of economic desolation and waste.
This new machinery will not work of itself. The farmers
and the distributors of foodstuffs must use it and make it
work. The Government can help map lines of march, and can
see that the interest of no one group is advanced out of line
with the interests of another. But government officials cannot and will not go out and work for private businesses.
A farm is a private business; so is a farmers' co-operative;
and so are all the great links in the food distributing chain.
Government men cannot and will not go out and plow down
old trails for agriculture, or build for the distributing industries new trails out of the woods. The growers, the processors, the carriers and sellers of food, following trade agreements, openly and democratically arrived at, with the consumers represented and protected from gouging — these
industries must work out their own salvation. This emergency Adjustment Act makes it lawful and practical for
them to do so. It provides for the control of production to
accord with actual need, and for an orderly distribution of
essential supplies.

Triple-A had 'codes' for the food trades to administer from the
beginning. Later, when the National Industrial Recovery Act
had passed, and the Blue Eagle soared briefly, Agriculture was
further charged to administer or co-administer certain of its
codes. These codes had to do with the initial processing of farm
commodities, and involved wages, hours of labor, and trade
practices. Attendant negotiations with downright General Hugh
Johnson and his administrative staff were often as stormy as
those with the leaders of the industries in question. In such disputes, as Wallace remarked conversationally in press conference,
to point up a short lecture demonstrating that reporters should
seek as news unexpected points of *agreement* between public
figures: 'In disputes with NRA George Peek and Rex Tugwell
fought shoulder to shoulder, not toe to toe.' But mainly toe-to-
toe encounters here and elsewhere got into the papers; and of
these there were plenty, between Triple-A and NRA, between

Jerome Frank's young urban liberals and men of more specialized 'farm leader' views within the Department and without.

In this lineup they never quite knew where to place Wallace. He listened to all the arguments and then took his stand, often abruptly, one way or the other, sometimes with Tugwell, Frank, and Frank's young lawyers, sometimes with Chester Davis, Edward O'Neal, and others of what the Frank men called 'Henry's father's gang.'

Tugwell lined up almost always with the new group in the Department. He was in fact their chosen leader. M. L. Wilson, of farm-leader background, was enough of a philosopher to serve as a mediating influence between the agrarians and the city liberals. So, in a measure, was Howard R. Tolley. Brought in from the headship of the Gianinni Foundation in California, he had much to do with such progress as was made on his home sector on the Pacific coast.

It was a hard and thankless task. 'The Farm Act,' Dr. Tolley explained in one of his earlier and more hopeful pronouncements, 'places in our hands new weapons: marketing agreements, with licensing provisions, a governmental club behind the door to beat into line the chiseling ten per cent or so who are likely to defeat any agreement among competitors to fit their operations together and wipe out waste.' It proved possible in the earlier years of Triple-A action to get fairly satisfactory agreements operating in the distribution of highly specialized products produced in a compact locality, such as Western canning peaches and citrus fruit. Even here, the young liberal lawyers whom Jerome Frank had recruited, by aid of Felix Frankfurter — men like Alger Hiss, Thurman Arnold, Abe Fortes, and Lee Pressman — were often distressed at the relative willingness of the farm leaders in Triple-A to go easy on the big operators in the matter of final prices, provided the farmer were given a slightly thicker cut than heretofore, however slim that cut remained. Curiously, perhaps, or contrary at least to what might be expected of old-line agrarians who had for years been creating what Wallace called 'personal devils' in the person of the middleman, the farm-bred leaders of Triple-A proved generally far more conciliatory in their attitude toward the existing distributive setup, far less ardent to crack up big combinations or put them out of business, than these young urban liberals newly come to Agriculture.

Jerome·Frank, the most lovable and volatile of them all, discovered, for instance, a shocking waste in the matter of duplicated city milk routes. For a day or so he was all for wiping out that waste. When Land Grant College men who for years had studied the intricacies of this rather strange and unnatural business of bottle-feeding America showed him, with a few strokes of the pencil, what abolishing duplication of the delivery routes would add to total unemployment, he acknowledged that the reform he proposed could probably not be achieved abruptly.

The milk business proved the most recalcitrant of all businesses urged to put their works into better order. The big co-operatives were generally no more amenable than the big corporations were. Co-operative leaders in this field had, quite generally, patched up difficulties by agreements with larger overhead distributing agencies, on their own. During the deepest depression these leaders, to do them justice, brought their dairy farmers through on a higher plane of immediate reward than most other farmers. But even in so doing they had added to their eventual difficulties, for the relatively higher inducements held out to dairy farmers had drawn hundreds of thousands of further farmers into milk production. Consequently, as Wallace pointed out insistently, the national outland tariff on milk, hitherto effective, was effective no longer, while inland areas of the multitudinous milk sheds, attempting 'a local protectionist policy, by sanitary provisions, shipping restrictions, price agreements' of their own were rearing 'little tariff walls.' This, Wallace continued, 'worked up a devil's brew. . . . Gangsters came in to limit competition for their own profit. Disorders assumed in places the proportions of minor guerrilla warfare. . . . Before the end of 1933 we were forced to step in and apply stabilization patchwork to our butter market, and to consider the further proposal of farm leaders that we apply 200 million dollars more to tiding over our dairy and beef cattle situation until we could get on into programs of production control.'

They never did get on into such programs, either for dairy products or beef cattle. The only relief from the pressure of an unbearable and dangerous planlessness in production which these livestock producers and their distributing agencies permitted was an indemnified slaughter and marketing of drought-stricken cattle, as to beef, and, more soundly, the indemnified slaughter of dairy cows infected with tuberculosis and contagious abortion. Milk distribution remained chaotic and remained wastefully cutthroat, with standards in many places closely resembling the law of the jungle. To one Eastern city, with near-by dairymen defending a high retail price at its every border, milk had been bootlegged from lower-priced regions of production, and sneaked into town in hearses. In Chicago, at one period of conflict between milkdrivers' unions, gangsters, and the established monopoly which dominated retail milk distribution there, the gangsters acquired and fortified a city dairy with a beautiful bucolic name — Meadowmoor. Also they fortified and fitted with machine guns at every window the building opposite, and sent forth armored milk trucks with an extra driver, armed, up front. The game was to buy milk high from farmers, sell it cheap as dipped milk, and run up so high a nuisance value that the legitimate dealer combination would pay the gangsters to quit. Quite a few people were killed or disappeared in the course of this muted uproar, but nothing much came of it beyond cheaper and dirtier milk for poor people and a little better price to 'independent' farmer-producers for the while. To seek a moral in the insane proceeding, the gangsters failed to collect because they could not be trusted. The big distributors seemed amenable enough to the idea of paying the gangsters quit-money; only, they asked plaintively, how could they be sure that the gangsters would really quit? Triple-A investigators had complete evidence on the proceeding, but the most concrete part of the evidence was in tapped-wire talk between the gangsters, transcribed by another investigating arm of the Government; and the legal staff of Triple-A decided it would prejudice their case to use such records and decided not to introduce them at the Chicago milk hearing in 1934. Frank, there to conduct this hearing, returned with reports of some stout men who marched in day after day to take their place in the front row of a balcony reserved for spectators. These men never took off their overcoats. 'They were regular walking arsenals. And I thought Agriculture was such a mild, pastoral calling,' Jerry said.

For such disturbances the urban liberals inclined to blame the big dispensing companies or corporations. The agrarians, for their part, saw the hand of the devil most actively working through milk-drivers' unions. These unions were fiercely against any consolidations of milk routes. Such resistance to change worked back through the distributors, and then to the suppliers; and the distribution of milk, that most explosive of commercial liquids, remained for the most part unreformed.

As for tobacco, things went somewhat better. The existing co-operatives in these highly specialized fields of local culture worked out peaceably and quickly, under the adroit technical leadership of John Hutson, Chief of the Triple-A Tobacco Section, a quietly working connection between allotted production and prices collectively bargained for. One of the few harmonious incidents pleasant to recall during those earlier New Deal price bickers was the astonishment of farmer representatives when, having named a better-than-fair asking price on certain grades of cigarette tobacco, the spokesman of the Big Five among the buyers suavely met that figure with hardly a word of protest or argument. Later it appeared that assembled managers of the very biggest companies, figuring that tobacco is but a small part of the cost of a cigarette, anyway, and that their standard fifteen-cent brands could stand that cost much better than a rising horde of depression-bred ten-cent brands, would have paid, perhaps, an even higher figure in the hope of crowding the cheaper brands off the market.

With an informed eye Wallace watched all such sideshows and maneuvers. Market procedures were an old story to him. Grimly amused at times, and at other times more impatient or indignant, he sat through interminable conferences, saying little. Occasionally sitting alone at his dictaphone in the late hours of the night he would bend his head wearily forward and speak slowly, reflecting: 'The more I study our trouble the more I am convinced that it calls for more than emergency action and patch-work on top of patchwork. It is imperative that we get down to fundamentals at the earliest possible moment, that we have a plan in line with our world position and with the genius of our people, and that we stick to this plan through thick and thin, no matter how great the pressure of the opportunists.'

Throughout 1934 cleavage within the Department grew. Tension mounted unsteadily. At times it would seem to relax as the Frank men, generally backed by Tugwell, on the one side, and the Triple-A leaders on the other, came unexpectedly to a passing agreement, or found some outside enemy against whom they could for the moment unite.

As individuals most of these men had worked and argued hard together. Friendships and bonds of mutual respect had formed across the established line of their differences. In number these friendships exceeded the number of enmities; but at critical points, bottlenecks in the entire process of orderly administration, the personal antagonisms became intense beyond endurance.

With the pressures of both inner camps upon him, Wallace fell silent and uncommunicative. A lion for principle, he would not, or could not bring himself at the time, it seemed, to enter into differences when differences became personal. He hated quarreling; it literally made him sick. So he sat silent, and seemed for weeks on end at this critical juncture inept, irresolute, helpless.

To outward appearance, at least, Chester Davis and Rex Tugwell held their differences above the personal level. They did not quarrel or put forth venom stealthily one against the other. But they could not restrain their most excited followers. When, for instance, question of amending the Child Labor Amendment to include all workers on farms came up, Wallace said he could not see how that would be possible. He said he favored writing conditions governing child labor into laws or codes governing operations on large truck, fruit, or 'factory' farms; but it could never be worked on family-size farms, run by the families; and ought never to be. He had done some farm work, himself, he said; and when just a lad in a small town he had pumped up enough bath water for the whole Wallace family every Saturday; and it had all been good for him. 'A certain amount of hard, physical work, performed under family supervision, in the family interest, is good for a growing boy or girl,' said the Secretary. He spoke sincerely, and with all the solemnity of a Puritan patriarch, but not without a twinkling of understanding that he was shocking up-to-date liberals with children in play schools.

The effect aroused by his old-fashioned sentiment was instant.

Young urban liberals of the Department stated openly in restaurants, clubs, and at cocktail parties that Henry Wallace was a reactionary who had no guts. Agrarian leaders, on similar rounds, cried it forth that Tugwell, Frank, Jackson, Pressman, and all had better go over to Russia and see how they liked it there.

Both sides had learned the technique of planting questions in press conference, of trial balloons slipped out under the desk to certain correspondents, of cultivating a given columnist with anonymous tips favoring the cause of their own interest or persuasion. Both sides had learned that saddest and shabbiest of tricks employed by zealots within any organization, public or private — the trick of holding up papers or decisions at bottlenecks, or of burying them in detail, or of tricking them out with such legal or bureaucratic harness or baggage as delays or kills action. Both sides had learned to do good, as each side saw it, on the sly.

If any one man were equipped to compose such differences of view and temperament, while at the same time charged to negotiate agreements between agrarians, come at last to power, and their traditional opponents, the processors, packers, and middlemen, that man was Chester C. Davis. Farm-born in Iowa in 1887, within a year of the birth of Henry A. Wallace, he was educated not specifically in agriculture at a Land Grant College, but more generally at Grinnell. He graduated in 1911, and married Helen Smith, of Montana, in 1913. He was a reporter, then an editor on small-city newspapers in South Dakota and in Montana at Bozeman, the seat of the Montana State College of Agriculture. He became both editor and manager of *The Montana Farmer*, at Great Falls, Montana, from 1917 to 1921. Then, as hard times of the First World War deflation hit first upon Montana, Chester Davis became Commissioner of Agriculture and Labor for the State, and was more and more closely drawn into work and friendship with M. L. Wilson. Some account of their strivings for McNary-Haugenism, of their passing parley with the first Secretary Wallace, Alaska-bound with President Harding, and of their later consultations with Harry Wallace's emissary, H. C. Taylor, has been entered into in chapters VI and VII of this account. It has also been told that younger Henry A. Wallace

roomed more often with Chester Davis than with any other farm
leader when he came to Washington to help lobby in behalf of
equality for agriculture.

Turning from Montana to national fields of agriculture and
trade relations, Davis served in the 'twelve long years' of farm
depression — from his early thirties to his middle forties — as
Director of Grain Marketing for the Illinois Agricultural Association, as Washington Representative of the American Council of
Agriculture, of which George Peek was President, and as Executive Vice President of the National Cornstalk Process Corporation, a concern set up to see if — with corn again being burned as
fuel in the Corn Belt — there might not be some profit in making
paper, cardboard, wallboard from cornstalks; or industrial alcohol to be used as fuel for motors, possibly, as well as for other
needs.

Davis succeeded Peek as Administrator of Agricultural Adjustment in the first month of his fiftieth year. He knew farmers;
his basic sympathies were agrarian; but he was not bound in by
the formulated landlord-agrarianism so often engrafted upon
products of the Land Grant College system. In addition, Davis
knew business, and businessmen, great and small; he had faced
them for years in conferences and price negotiations; he knew that
they were the same kind of people as American farmers, but often
more so, to the extent that the possession of money permits a
man to be more generous, on the one hand, or, again, meaner,
more self-centered, more smug-minded, in the expression of personal quirks and prejudices.

Kind and intelligent, humorously self-deprecatory, cordially
open-minded, and capable of continuing learning, Davis had
developed an extraordinary aptitude for negotiation. The grinding, interminable conferences essential to Triple-A routine became
almost a pleasure, at times, under his guidance. He had prejudices, of course, rather strong prejudices, but in conference he relaxed judicially, departing from his own bias, first this way, then
that, gently prodding the supporters of this angle of the argument,
then that angle; exploring, listening, turning the argument back
into channels, blowing up outbursts of bombast or excesses of
agitation with a quiet laugh. 'Holding their feet to the fire,'

he called it, and it brought out all the evidence. Jerome Frank, who has advanced the idea that the best of judges may be men of no legal training, can hardly be expected to have included Chester Davis under that designation at the time. But a case could be made for it. Davis proved at least a skilled and patient administrator at a time when gentle but firm administration was crucially needed.[6]

Wallace plugged on ahead at the top, keeping more and more to himself. Davis bore on, trying to lessen successive small points of tension with some success. He seemed seldom to dislike the men who so strongly opposed him, and then not for long. Years later, when Frank, ousted from Agriculture, turned from a meteoric Washington career of great usefulness to take the robe of a Federal Judge, Davis sent him in a congratulatory telegram the last stanza of Kipling's 'L'Envoi':

> And only the Master shall praise us, and only the Master shall blame;
> And no one shall work for money, and no one shall work for fame;
> But each for the joy of the working, and each in his separate star,
> Shall draw the Thing as he sees It, for the God of Things as They Are!

But that was in 1941, six years post-'purge.' 'The separate stars' within the United States Department of Agriculture were whirling hotly toward separate orbits as 1934 turned into 1935. Tugwell, still the nominal head of the young liberals, was having less and less to do with Triple-A policies or procedure, partly because of distaste for the Triple-A ideology and his far greater interest in resettlement; again, because wider assignments from the White House or from Wallace kept him traveling. He had been to Puerto Rico on sugar matters involving high departures in Caribbean policy, and after that to Italy as American representative on the International Council of Agriculture. In Rome Under-Secretary Tugwell had been given audience by Mussolini, who did not impress him; and had been shown samples of synthetic clothing, made entirely from wood pulp, without benefit of cotton, which impressed him deeply. 'There may some day be hope,' he remarked upon returning, 'for getting a decent agriculture in the Cotton South.'

With amendments to the Agricultural Adjustment Act impending; with both camps, urban and agrarian, drafting their own and suspecting the other camp of trying to put something over, the liberals kept urging Tugwell to get back in there on the Triple-A Council and fight. But Tugwell had virtually agreed by this time to weld and shoulder variegated and scattered bits of governmental machinery for rural work relief into a new agency, a Resettlement Administration, and he was pressed for time. He confined most of his counseling of Triple-A to speeches that he made around the country. They were straight, plain speeches. Frank and his men had fought to a stalemate a number of Triple-A codes and agreements which let the big canners and packers out from under the Sherman Anti-Trust Law and allowed them, in effect, to fix prices. They held that if combinations and monopolies were to be openly sanctioned by the AAA or the NRA, the Government should have access to the books of private concerns and require the savings effected by controlled competition to be in some part passed around to the farmers and consumers.

Davis had been in the farm fight for a long time, and had found no better way for farmers to get a better price than by giving one point, or possibly three, and taking one point, by bargaining. An ardent internationalist, in his own way a liberal not untouched by yearnings for universal justice, he had formed with the years a stubborn desire for better farm prices, come what may. With Wallace and with Wallace's father, he had plowed that furrow for decades. And now, quite definitely, he, like Wallace, was an administrator with a job to do.

He had invited a number of the most powerful packers to Washington and was trying to bargain with them for better prices. The inner opposition was whispering 'Sell-out' in every corridor of the Department. Out in Iowa, before the Iowa State Bankers' Association, Tugwell made an open, chilly, fighting speech. 'Big canners,' he said, 'have become exceedingly timid about having their books examined. Why this inconsistent and tricky behavior? One of the largest canners is Libby, McNeill & Libby, whose directorate interlocks with one of the biggest meat packers, Swift & Company.' Encouraged by this blast, Frank and his followers renewed sniping. Davis found their attitude and actions definitely obstructive.

But the issue that blew the roof off, finally, had nothing to do with marketing agreements or access to books and records; it was a question, rather, of trying to use Adjustment money to anchor in place the characteristically fluent stream of tenants and day-hands in the Cotton South. No one who knows the South denies that the usual annual bargaining, scrambling, and often fruitless migration of tenants and fieldhands from hut to hut, from place to place, is bad. With large sums of money flowing out to land-lords, everyone saw the danger that this might strengthen land-lord bargaining power and increase displacements. The urban liberals, characteristically, saw a chance to induce or compel by the same payments greater security in tenure for the landless, and a general social gain.

The agrarians, led by Davis (and backed in this by Wallace), did not deny the beauty of this dream; but denied, decidedly, that it was the immediate purpose of the Agricultural Adjustment Act to remedy all ills of the South at a single stroke. The primary intent, the first responsibility of administrators of the Act, they held, was to achieve an economic consequence, a reduced planting of cotton. Anything that could be gained at the same time toward greater security for the insecure, good; but it would be plainly beyond the purpose of the Act, and quite beyond practical possibility, to compel landlords to keep the tenants they had before entering on this adventure in Adjustment.

Two months of inner-office conferences on this point, with Davis presiding, led to what seemed a satisfactory working com-promise. The Cotton Section, the Consumers' Council, and the Legal Division of Triple-A had agreed, as to contracts in the first year of operation, that landlords entering into Adjustment of acreage should not reduce the *number* of their tenants, but provi-sion was made as to extraordinary circumstances in individual cases, and enforcement of the contract was left, in general, to the tact and judgment of local administrators.

With Davis away on a field trip West, and Victor Christgau serving as Acting Administrator, Jerome Frank's Legal Division achieved a fast reinterpretation of the Act, less practical, more radical. Still in Davis's absence, Triple-A shot out a telegram to state administrators in the Cotton Belt commanding them to enforce, in the second year of operation, a ruling which virtually compelled landlords to keep the same tenants in the same houses on the same land. An immediate uproar southward reached Davis afield. He flew in to Washington with his jaw shut tight. The following, written in retrospect, is his own account of his views, mood, and action:

> The new interpretations completely reversed the basis on which cotton contracts had been administered through the first year.
>
> If the contract had been so construed, and if the Department of Agriculture had enforced it, Henry Wallace would have been forced out of the Cabinet within a month. The effects would have been revolutionary.
>
> I laid the contract, the telegram and the legal 'interpretation' before Henry Wallace, and asked him to let me handle it. He agreed. I named the men who would have to go, adding that Paul Appleby would be on that list, too, if he were working in AAA instead of in the Secretary's office.
>
> I then asked Frank, Pressman, Shea, Howe and Jackson to resign, and they did.[7]

Dispute as to the sweep and severity of the opinion endures to this day. The Legal Division regarded its ruling as no reinterpretation of the Farm Act's long-range purposes, but as an opinion consistently in accord with social objectives which Wallace himself held as tenable and had spoken for. Frank's lawyers did not foresee as intolerably severe or insoluble administrative difficulties which the farm-minded element discerned, and in the face of which, they rebelled.

Before an Emergency Council meeting at the White House next day Wallace spoke to the President, announcing the decision; but in the hustle of other Cabinet and Emergency Council members slipping words in sidewise to the Chief, it is doubtful if the Chief gathered more than the fact that Frank was to be transferred, probably promoted, to some other arm of the Government. The press had wind of the story now. Wallace and Davis announced a press conference. I went over.

It was an exceedingly trying conference for Wallace. He was gray-faced and haggard. I never saw at any press conference so many plainly hostile representatives of public opinion, with barbed questions prepared, planted. Wallace was sad and uneasy; his guard was down; his questioners were clamorous and loud. It was not a pleasant occasion. I took notes.

Wallace opened with a low-voiced, hesitating statement:

Yes, Mr. Frank has resigned, or has been asked to resign. Why?

WALLACE: In the interests of the greatest possible harmony. The method we took seemed to make for that. I may say — (*Here he turned to Chester Davis*) I may say that I believe all of us here have the very greatest faith in Mr. Frank's ability and unselfish hard work.

DAVIS: Yes.

Q.: Is this an obit?

Q.: Does that 'in the interests of harmony' apply to the others who are bounced or are going to be bounced?

Q.: Shea . . . Pressman . . . Rotnem . . . Gardner Jackson . . . Hiss?

Q.: There is no objection to Frank's social or economic views, is there?

(*These four questions were delivered almost simultaneously.*)

WALLACE: I haven't any intimation of such objection. It is just a situation which I suppose was almost inevitable. I am quite sure that Mr. Hiss has not resigned. I . . .

DAVIS: There has been no suggestion of Mr. Hiss's resignation, except in the press, as far as I know. Mr. Frank, Mr. Pressman, Mr. Shea, Gardner Jackson, yes; and the Rotnem case is in suspense. In each of these cases, from close association, I want to say that while I agree wholly with the Secretary as to the ability of the men in question;

yet, for an efficiently operating organization in the Triple-A, these changes are desirable in my judgment, and I recommended them to the Secretary on Monday. I think it is important to have in the key positions in the Triple-A men who have some familiarity with farm problems and who have a farm background.

WALLACE: Chester has now made the speech I halted in the midst of making.

Q.: What led up to this thing being crystallized at this time — any one thing determining you to take this step?

DAVIS: No. It was just a mounting difficulty in getting things done, and after all, our job is to get things done.

Q.: Just what does Tugwell do here?

Q.: Travels!

Q.: And writes books!

WALLACE: Your friendship for Dr. Tugwell, your solicitude for him is continuous. He really has a great deal to do here. You may not realize it, and some of you apparently do not, but you are insisting on erecting a mythical man. Dr. Tugwell has an excellent scientific and agricultural background. He has worked very closely with the bureau chiefs. He is very well informed, close in, on the sugar thing. You see, he has visited Puerto Rico, and so he gained knowledge early in the game which made it advisable to keep in close touch with sugar, and he has continued to do so, not in intimate executive supervision at all, but when anything comes along and the whole sugar thing quivers from stem to stern, he is aware of what is going on.

Q.: Mr. Secretary, isn't this something along the lines of what actually happened: A year ago, when the Peek situation was up, the issue was between you and Mr. Peek walked the plank. This time it is a question of Mr. Davis and Mr. Frank, and Mr. Frank walks the plank?

WALLACE: Mr. Frank is a part of Mr. Davis's organization.

Q.: Pursue the middle course, Mr. Secretary!

WALLACE: Well, you see we don't like to have a ship that lists stronger to the left or the right, but one that goes straight ahead.

At the next press conference, on February 20, Wallace looked far more hale and rugged. They could not push him around this time for even a little while. Tugwell, back, had been out West on drought and rural relief assignments and had made another speech in Chicago.

Q.: Alger Hiss has gone. Victor Christgau has gone. (*Both had resigned in the wake of the storm, to both Wallace's and Davis's regret.*) Everybody seems to be going but Tugwell. He seems to stay. I see he is out in Chicago talking on social security. Is that part of the scientific investigation of the Department of Agriculture or has he got a roving commission now that takes him to other subjects? That wasn't unfriendly. I mean, what is the peculiar significance of interpreting the New Deal to a convention of dentists?

WALLACE: Well, I think light should be shed in all various corners, including the dental orifices.

Later, and more gravely, when they asked him to enlarge his expressions of regret on the departure from Agriculture of Victor Christgau, no city liberal, but a Farmer-Labor man from Minnesota, and a former Congressman, 'I don't know where there is any profit in discussing it,' Wallace said.

Q.: Any loss?

WALLACE: I think there is general loss in discussing disagreements and irritations and things of that sort.

Then the session settled down to the more usual tone of a routine Wallace press conference, a 'seminar,' some of the press corps called it, but most of them enjoyed these shirtsleeve seminars. In the field of scientific fact or of abstract ideas Wallace labored cheerfully to instruct them and generally enjoyed it. 'I am trying to educate the daily press up to the levels of the farm press,' he explained at one such conference, 'and to learn from you.' He rarely ducked a question, however difficult. Toward the end of this after-session to the Purge, he summarized his stand on what he conceived to be the central issue, in words so characteristic of his usual middle-way position that I asked for and secured permission to copy the remarks verbatim from the stenographic record:

This is the situation we are in. When you fix farm prices and retail prices you are fixing margins, and when you are fixing margins you are fixing profits. When you abrogate anti-trust laws and are thereby fixing profits, you are responsible for profits to some extent. You are contributing to the profits, and I certainly don't want to be in that position without knowing absolutely, without having access to the books and records. And, really, I think, Chester, that if we place ourselves in that position, then we ought to have more complete powers than we now have. But if we did have the complete power, I am not sure that it would be democracy any more. That is, you would be freezing things all along the line and setting yourself up to be knowing everything that is going on. I think it is legally possible to do this, but I think it is extremely poor public policy to set the price to the farmer or a retail price, and thus determine profits by what all of us do, unless the whole concept of the American people regarding functions of Government changes.

4. Little White Homes

THE FIRST MOVES toward 'subsistence homesteads' and rural migrant relief took start in departments or agencies apart from Agriculture, but within a year or so were gathered under Agriculture's spacious wings, to the considerable increase of Wallace's responsibilities and perplexities. Like soil conservation, which became after 1935 a major goal and justification of the whole Agricultural Adjustment program, the beginnings of what is now known as Farm Security were planted in the Department of the Interior. Again it was Tugwell who had much to do with the planting, then the transplanting. He was more interested in making poor farmers or workmen richer than in increasing the weal of the passably well-to-do. M. L. Wilson, of course, was interested in both. He had worked, it will be recalled, when the New Deal first was forming as a principal social architect both of the commercial farm allotment and subsistence homestead designs. Of the two, the 'Utah idea,' as he called it,

was closest to his heart. So he took leave from Agriculture and
went over to the Interior to make subsistence homestead colonies a reality by use of an appropriation that had been entrusted
to the administration of Secretary Ickes.

With strong White House backing, Senator John H. Bankhead
of Alabama had inserted as Section 208 of the National Industrial
Recovery Act of 1933 an authorization for expending twenty-five
million dollars on 'subsistence homesteads.' This part of the
measure occasioned little discussion or notice and such 'homesteads' became a legal side provision to help Harry Hopkins forward relief from unemployment when the Act passed in May of
the New Deal's first year. Section 208 was 'to aid in the redistribution of the overbalance of population in industrial centers.'
The President was authorized to delegate the use of this fund
'through such agencies as he may establish and under such regu-
lations as he may make, for making loans for and otherwise aiding in the purchase of subsistence homesteads with the moneys
collected to be used as a revolving fund at the President's discretion.'

Some idea of the diversity of interest the subsistence homestead idea aroused may be gained from even a partial list of those
at a supper meeting which Henry I. Harriman called for purposes
of initial discussion at the Shoreham Hotel. Bernarr McFadden
was there, and Tugwell and Ickes and John D. Black and George
Soule of *The New Republic.* Of farm leaders, L. J. Taber of the
Grange; and Ed O'Neal of the Farm Bureau. Of labor people,
Meyer Jacobstein and William Green. Of humanitarians, Dr.
John A. Ryan, Catholic, and Bernard G. Waring, Quaker. And
besides, there were professors and bankers and businessmen, some
of whom had definite projects in mind. Discussion ran unham-
pered and seemed to get nowhere. There were indications of a
tendency among some hardboiled industrialists to favor semi-
rural colonies as convenient places to anchor help until, in their
opinion, such help was needed; and then to pay off not so much in
money as in sunshine and fresh air. There appeared a countering
tendency on the part of labor and labor leaders to suspect a
catch in the subsistence homestead design. There appeared an
unreadiness of business leaders to relocate plants under federal

guidance; and there appeared, inevitably, an immemorial tendency of rural colonization schemes to attract cultists, faddists, intellectual fan dancers, and a certain number of crackpots, along with far more effective humanitarians.

The Subsistence Homestead Division of the Department of the Interior set up modest offices in a dingy old building on Pennsylvania Avenue and tried to keep it fairly quiet that they had twenty-five million dollars to spend. That had seemed a lot of money, but the Division had applications calling for the dispersal of three billion dollars at the end of three months. Wilson's initial staff in the enterprise included Roy Hendrickson, Carl Taylor, Bruce Melvin, Clarence Pickett, Ernest Weiking, Charles Pynchon, and Davis Wickens, all social-minded but all fairly realistic and practical men. As Paul H. Johnstone points out in *A Place on Earth*,[3] open acres have always exerted upon escapists and romantics the appeal of a God-given cushion, to absorb the shocks and disillusionments of urban hustle, commercial strain, and industrial unemployment. The agrarian mind, Dr. Johnstone further indicates — as an agrarian historian he should know — is instinctively skeptical, even hostile, to talk about returning to Mother Nature's soft and welcoming arms; and all of Wilson's first staff men in Subsistence Homesteads were 'agrarians,' said Johnstone, using this term in the sense that we have used it in this book, to denote partisans of agriculture who 'want in,' as Ohioans say, on the goods and goals of a commercialized and industrialized society.

Representation of prevailing farm opinion, in hearings at Washington, in farm organization propaganda, and in the personal fulminations of most professional farm leaders, has been from the first strongly hostile to subsistence homestead colonies, to migrant relief camps and co-operative farm experiments and to tenant rehabilitation alike. Edward Asbury O'Neal, III, of Alabama, for many years president of the American Farm Bureau Federation, used loudly to argue in Wallace's anteroom that young men who bothered about sharecroppers' and tenants' rights were well-meaning but soft-headed do-goodies who simply did not understand the unlimited opportunities still open to all comers, free, white, and twenty-one, in that spacious land, the

Cotton South. He said flatly that anyone who remained a share-cropper or day hand, simply lacked get-up-and-go. A loud and genial talker, Ed would then go in and shout the same sentiments to the Secretary, while the young liberal aides outside squirmed and swore and wondered why Henry bothered to listen to so calloused an oaf.

As a matter of fact, hardly anyone liked, instinctively, the subsistence homestead program, any better than anyone instinctively liked production control. It was another required expedient of a strange, changed time. 'In the pinch of distress,' Paul H. Johnstone continued in his subacid editorial introduction to *A Place on Earth*, 'we lose faith in the bright new world that only recently offered blessings hitherto undreamed of. We despair of handling socially the machines we are so dexterous in contriving. And so we seek to escape our ills by a return to the land, to "nature," or to an older tradition. Thus every panic, every depression, every modern social crisis of major proportion — along with producing plans for making a wholly new, unprecedented, and Utopian world — has brought forth schemes for returning to the real or imagined order of the past.'

The number of farmers who came very close to being subsistence farmers in the United States even then may be indicated in the simple statistic that, year in and year out, on the average, fifty per cent of our farmers receive only about twelve per cent of the national farm income. Critics of Department of Agriculture programs put it the other way, and not without justice, saying that the Department in the past has been run very largely to serve the half of our farm population which already gets eighty-eight per cent of the farm income. As for Triple-A, the critics charged that it operated specifically to increase the well-being of farmers already well-to-do and to increase the distress of the rural poor.

Wallace had to defend Triple-A against such charges as best he honestly could. Early in 1934, when Harry Hopkins as Relief Administrator stated in one of his press conferences that the cotton plow-up had increased unemployment in the South, and the reporters tried, naturally, to stir from that a 'rift' statement, Wallace would not be drawn. The number of rural people on relief, he said, had come down from eight hundred thousand to some six hundred thousand. 'In so far as Harry puts these distressed people on farms, producing agricultural products for sale, he creates a problem for us. In so far as we reduce the number of acres and therefore the number of men required to work these acres, we create a problem for him. But in any event there is a problem that goes back to certain things that are greater than his organization and greater than our organization. There is no method of escape from it. It is just simply a case where we will have to work it out to the best possible advantage.' Later, again in a press conference, Wallace deprecated, in a measure, the fear of commercial farmers and organized farm leaders that subsistence farmers would compete seriously for their markets. 'If it is well worked out and well managed,' he said, 'with an arrangement of little working industries on the side, I don't think it is the part of commercial agriculture to buck this trend. The unemployment problem, combined with our paved roads and the ready transmission of electric power, together with the inherent love of humanity for open spaces, trees, animals, and all that kind of thing, make decentralization inevitable. Such a movement may provide a very modest scale of living, but I do not think we should expect these people to endure all the ancient discomforts of the pioneer farmer. It will take a long time to work it out. There are lots of ups and downs. I think of it as at least a fifty-year kind of program.'

Here Wallace spoke as an official charged to administer policies running counter, in some part, to use of the land as a cushion for urban unemployment. 'We are more than economic men,' he argued, writing personally, in a pronouncement bearing that six-word title, at the end of 1934. 'Somehow, I can't help thinking that the self-subsistence homesteads, if experimented with sufficiently by men of scientific, artistic and religious understanding, will eventually lead us a long way toward a new and finer world. If I were a young man with no other job in prospect, I would try desperately to get into the self-sufficient homestead movement. In the actual work, of course, many petty meannesses will develop. Humanity in a small community is not always lovely ... yet in spite of the disillusionments which may come, the movement deserves the support and the leadership of many strong men. The future seems more and more to favor decentralization.' [9]

Policy decisions in the use of agricultural lands and in directing governmental programs for people engaged in agriculture are forever subject to the pull and tug of what might be called the basic agrarian dilemma. Agriculture is both a business and an escape from business. When land gets scarce, the horns of the dilemma sharpen.

One of President Roosevelt's first executive orders had withdrawn all remaining public lands from private entries under the pre-existing Homestead Acts. The era of simply taking and breaking had ended. For citizens and corporations alike there was to be no more free land. This was belated official recognition that a condition long creeping upon us had come to pass. In 1857 Lord Macaulay, the English historian, wrote in a letter to an American physician that 'institutions, purely democratic, must, sooner or later, destroy liberty or civilization or both.' 'This fate, in America,' he added, 'is deferred by a physical cause.' The physical cause that held our free democracy together and functioning with so little government, as Macaulay saw it, was a vast supply of free or cheap land.

Lord Macaulay's own country has managed, of course, to maintain a decent show of free democracy on land closely held and hard to get; yet only at the cost, perhaps, of a diminished expectancy for the ordinary man. Amid the economic backwash of the First World War the American people were sharply faced for the first time, or forced to feel at length, the lack of a land buffer; and this hard fact served as a shocking check to confidence. It was not that we faced a famine, or even a tightening of belts. It was simply that *in terms of our traditional desires and demands, we now experienced* a sharpening scarcity of good, available land. The American earth is no longer wide enough or rich enough to receive our demobilized or other unemployed and give them a brave new start in life as landlords.

Indisputably, and in the large, our land is still there. We have as many square miles of it as we have had at any time in our history. Figure it in acres to the person, weighing in such probabilities as a declining birth rate, and the figures may seem reassuring.

Our population is only 40 persons to the square mile. Germany proper has 364 persons to the square mile; Japan proper, 462; Italy, 356; England and Wales, 695; and parts of the Nile Valley support considerably more than one thousand human beings to the square mile.

But statistics in themselves can be entirely misleading in determining population pressure or the felt scarcity of soil and earth room. One family to the square mile of an arid mountain plateau may experience, actually and emotionally, a greater lack of nutriment and elbow room than fifty other families huddled as tenants on a square mile of teeming delta soil and inured to low standards.

In the light of actual situations, actual pressures, actual defeats and hopes and passions, statistics cast into acres-per-person terms are all but useless. Where is the acre, what will it grow, and who is the person? A pound is a pound, an inch is an inch, or a kilometer a kilometer the world over, but no one acre is equal to another acre anywhere on earth. What is the slope, the rainfall, the hours of sunlight, the initial endowment of usable fertility, the present endowment or remnant? What about access to market, available machine equipment, the price of this land, the carrying charges? Who are these persons who hold in control fast extending stretches of rich land as individual or corporate owners? What are their capacities, as producers, and as husbandmen? What, on the other hand, are the capacities of a gathering throng, the landless and dispossessed, who rail against the 'land hogs' and move increasingly for a breaking-up of big holdings and a return to little private family farms?

There is still a question, and perhaps the most vital, when it comes to determining a national policy for agriculture and rights of tenure. What do all these people — the great and the small, the possessor and the dispossessed — what do we, all of us, want of this land? What do we expect of it?

Thoreau, in his time, stated the general expectation nobly: 'To rear our lives to an undreamed-of height and meet the expectation of the land.' And for two centuries on end our great gift of soil enabled America to rear to undreamed-of heights, indeed, the estate and holdings of the common man. It has become a commonplace to say that when, around 1890, we ran out of free land, and the frontier virtually closed, we entered upon an era of limited opportunity and diminished expectations. But the thing did not really come on that abruptly. It started happening at the very outset of white agriculture on this shore, a lowering of the general estate, a lessening likelihood that any ordinary citizen could own land in freehold, farm it well, proudly, and profitably, look any man in the eye and tell him where to head in.

The reasons for the diminished expectancy which now so sharply confronts us are principally three: (1) wastrel cultivation over an unbelievably large area, resulting in eroded or depleted soil; (2) technological advances, displacing hands and minds from farming; (3) the combination of farms into larger holdings, in 'strong hands.'

In consequence, the competition for good land has become, in flush times and in hard times, exceedingly severe; and agricultural administrators must make many decisions between the case of relatively well-fixed farmers who demand to be protected from competition and proximity with 'footloose riff-raff,' on the one hand, and the complaints or demands of the migrant or resident dispossessed who rails against 'land hogs,' on the other.

What is the answer? How is our land to be regarded? Strictly as a business proposition, with only the largest, most efficient operators encouraged, and the sign up, 'Keep Out Except on Business'? Or should we follow such policies as regard the land primarily as a homeland, a refuge from the exactions and strains of business, with the business side of the enterprise considered as secondary? Here is a dilemma which has divided men between themselves — and within themselves — since the beginnings of commercial agriculture. Curiously, of late both sides of the argument have come to call their movements 'agrarian.' There are agrarians who want to cut the farmer into the profit system and equal rights or returns in the realm of business. Other 'agrarians' of the Southern intellectual school, or of Ralph Borsodi's following, having contemplated a commercialism and urbanism invading country living, want, in a word, 'out.'

With initial New Deal adventures in 'subsistence homesteads' and in rural migrant relief operating outside of the Department of Agriculture, Wallace had at first little or no responsibility; and he appeared, on the whole, as well pleased. He came, quite definitely, of the 'want-in' school of agrarians. He had many reservations as to the somewhat emotional and haphazard way in which initial stays and catch-alls for displacement and dispossession were set up all over the New Deal lot. With rather a good ear for phrases — *America Must Choose, New Frontiers, Whose Constitution?* — Wallace was not greatly taken with the stark tag, *Subsistence Homesteads* — put into the Act, probably, to reassure existing farm proprietors that these refugees would offer no important competition in commercial farm production. Was this now the boasted land of unlimited opportunity? This new homestead law, proposing subsistence only — was this the measure of the future of the common man? Viewed with all the 'conditioned optimism' that M. L. Wilson could summon, these little white houses, nudging shoulders on scant patches of ground often worn and lean, did not march along with the pipes and trumpets of Rooseveltian New Deal optimism. It sounded rather like the muffled drums of an enforced retreat.

Wallace felt this. He worried about it, often in public. He wrote in *New Frontiers*: 'The New World: at a time of tremendous pressure and distress that phrase rang through Europe to lift the hearts of the defeated, restless, and dissatisfied. It aroused hope of romantic adventure and of sudden riches in gold and furs. But those who came to settle here found that pioneering must be paid for in sweat, blood, and strange diseases, in the suffering of long, slow toil. They paid the price, and the heritage they leave us is rather bitter — a rich land racked and mismanaged, with huge accumulations of goods and wealth, yet with millions of our people deprived and helpless.' [10]

In further speeches and articles Wallace presented accumulating evidence of man-made wasteland throughout America. He cited the sad and almost unbelievable data, brought in and assembled, county by county, and state by state, by Hugh Bennett's soil conservation field reconnaissance corps. This ground-line reconnaissance discovered fifty million acres of soil — an area equal to almost all of England plus all of Scotland — farmed down to the thin edge of abandonment as productive farmland,

and another one hundred and fifty million acres more or less impaired.

To put it in another way: About half of our crop land showed plain signs of abuse by careless or faulty culture when the Soil Conservation Service and its related arms were launching our first great national campaign for soil repair and restitution in the early nineteen-thirties. The yield of all this land had run down, and in varying degree, but discernibly, the quality of the yield had suffered. Not infrequently the diminished quality carried through visibly from stunted plants to scrawny livestock to sagging homes and fences and to sickly, spiritless people. The blight that had settled on such farming communities carried through, moreover, to the whole trading area round about them. When a soil fails, farmers are not the only sufferers. When a soil fails, everything fails.

Not only to conservation groups, to men and women who had fought in the initial Rooseveltian movement with his father, with Gifford Pinchot, Morris L. Cooke, Huston Thompson, and Harry Slattery, to protect and increase our natural resources, but to the general public, through weekly radio talks, the second Secretary Wallace lectured and exhorted. The loss in values now had passed beyond mere surface erosion of 'our great gift of soil,' he said. A depleted soil was delimiting human opportunity and the growth of the people — 'the ultimate crop':

> A whole history of civilized man might be written in terms of population pressing upon soil resources. . . . In no spread-eagle sense of the word but in plain truth, liberty and equality are a natural growth of this soil. If it keeps washing and wearing thinner, what of the ultimate crop? . . . Having played high, wide, and handsome with all our resources, and having in addition lost world trade, we feel the pinch; and an increasing discontent with our modern 'relief' equivalents for a piece of land and an equal chance for everyone is widely evident. It would be, of course, a fanatic view to lay all our present perplexities to a lack of wise land use and conservation. Our man-made wastelands are only one symptom of the trouble, but an important symptom, for in

good times and bad, for all time, the soil is the mother of man, and if we forget her, life weakens. . . .

This country is older now. All of the good land has been taken, and much of it has been worn down. We begin to feel some of the internal pressures which have pinched older nations for many centuries; and the problem of maintaining and governing democratically a land of the free becomes more complicated and challenging. It is perhaps no chance coincidence that share-the-wealth agitations should arise and spread at this time, when we have no longer rich new frontiers to scramble to, when we are just discovering that the United States is not, after all, to remain eternally a place of inexhaustible natural wealth and freebooter opportunity.[11]

For some years before Tugwell first advanced in 1933 the then too-bold concept of a planned resettlement of rural America, a random resettlement under drive of need had been pushing into the back country. A map prepared by economic aides to Wallace from census data showed somewhat in advance of the 1935 population checkup that 523,702 'new' farms had been added to the national total since 1930. These farms were new only in that they were new ventures on old land. They were small farms, almost invariably, and their preponderant general location, dotted in on the map, bore a startling resemblance to population maps of our country in the eighteenth century, in the years just before the westering tide of migration burst over the Allegheny mountain rim into the middle country. The size of these new farm-refugee holdings ranged generally from two acres up to fifty. The greatest increases were in two areas: in New England and the southern Appalachian hill country from Pennsylvania (around where the Wallaces had started in America) down through Birmingham, Alabama. These people were starting again, back where our pioneer grandfathers and great-grandfathers had started, but on worn frontiers this time, on the thinned leavings, on third-, fourth-, and fifth-rate land.

With these figures and the map before him, Wallace went on the air. To the delight of the farm-leader element, he warned the public solemnly that such land as the poor or middling-poor could find and occupy as farms at the time generally offered a rude and doubtful refuge from unemployment. 'Here have come home,' he said, 'unemployed and often penniless, the families of factory workers, miners, lumber workers, and others — unskilled, skilled and highly technical workers, college graduates, teachers and others — to reoccupy the abandoned cabins, shacks, or old farmhouses of persons not known to them. This return to the land, this search of escape from unemployment, has a special, tragic significance. Most of these people are on poor land, hilly, eroded, worn out, or grown up with weeds and brush — land stubborn to the touch of men and their families, who usually have little in the way of equipment to carry on their unequal struggle with nature.'

The first loans for the establishment of subsistence homestead colonies went to places like Austin, Minnesota, and Dayton, Ohio, where industries were willing to promise subsistence homestead colonists part-time and reasonably paid employ. As a sharp scarcity of such locations developed, Wilson put more emphasis upon the need of a peaceful transition from strictly commercial, competitive concepts toward co-operative and community developments, such as he discerned in Denmark at the time. 'There are opportunities for hand-weaving, for woodworking and much handicraft production in the United States provided it can be organized in some guild-like manner,' he told members of the American Farm Economics Association.

'Subsistence homestead colonies can be a sort of new synthesis of present-day ideals and aspirations for community life. ... The pessimists look upon subsistence homesteads as a retreat from the age of machinery and science. Those whom I choose to call the "conditioned optimists" regard the move as natural, sensible adjustment to the machine age, restoring many of the values which were lost in the jazz age.'

Thus, somewhat formally, Wilson staked off the ground which he felt this 'new pattern of rural life' should occupy. Less formally, in a symposium of reflections on the subsistence homestead experience, he said: 'Now this isn't something for everybody. It isn't for well-to-do people and it isn't for poor working people who are willing to go on the way they are, just to be a part of the great jazz-age procession. It isn't a relief proposition, to be applied at random. It's a middle-class movement for selected people, not the top, not the dregs.

'I think that this is one of the bleakest times, right now [1934], in human experience. The present economic system, in agriculture and in industry, is constantly pushing people out of the system, casting them out.

'They say things are going to get better. Maybe. But there will still be fundamental dislocations to contend with. And I think that all these people — the unlimited commercial optimists who really belong to the jazz age, on the one hand, and all the doctrinaire radicals, on the other — all these people who really believe that big things are just ahead again — I think they're in for the biggest bump you could imagine.

'Even if we get world recovery and the curves come up, yet there will not be a great deal in it for a great many people. A lot of them will be left out. It was that way even in good times in Europe before this country was settled. It has been more or less that way even in this country for the past four hundred years. And now, with mechanization and other factors, it will be very sharply so.

'This thing of helping human beings who want to work over toward a new way of life, that will be as big a change for them as the changes the Pilgrims had to make when they came here from England.

'Not all Americans really belong to this jazz-industrial age. We're not all white-lighters, never satisfied, just excited. There are a great many of us, of all degrees of wealth and education, in all walks of life, who feel that they are outcasts of the jazz-industrial age, and who are looking for something more secure and satisfying.' [12]

As Paul Johnstone remarks in the Department of Agriculture study already quoted, the influence of Wilson's 'moderating personality,' brought to bear in Subsistence Homestead, as in Triple-A affairs, was of great effect in healing or repairing wide differences between excited men: 'He was one of the very few leading individuals in the whole movement who by background, training,

actual experience, and character, was a farmer. . . . Like Mr.
Roosevelt, he was not a member of any of the doctrinal groups
that were so prominent in the advocacy of garden homes, subsistence communities, and back-to-the-land programs. He regarded sympathetically the ideals of many of them and, apparently, with some mental reservations of his own, saw at least some
good in all of their theories and cliques. But he always kept his
feet planted solidly on the ground, and his presence was regarded
by many of the more conservative as assurance that the ideas of
zealots and extremists would not dominate a movement in which
he had a hand.'

'This thing can't be made, or even planned, as perfect,' he
would tell his helpers. 'These are imperfect times. The job is to
help these stranded people hew new trails and build homes in the
industrial wilderness. I am very, very doubtful if we are going
to get enough co-operation for enough private industries to make
enough headway. Beyond that, we'll have to proceed on subsidy.' Asked as to the soundness of that economically: 'Economic
problems are moral problems,' he answered.[13]

At the end of four months the Division had approved more
than thirty projects, and the Corporation had authorized loans of
around ten million dollars to local corporations set up under the
laws of the State of Delaware. The first loan was of fifty thousand
dollars to the unit committees of the Dayton County Social
Agencies, Inc., Dayton, Ohio, for the establishment of thirty-
five homesteads on tracts of from two to three acres each, in a
colony barely three miles out of town.

The first of a series of loans had been made on a two hundred-
home project for Jewish garment workers, near Hightstown, New
Jersey. Smaller loans for smaller colony developments had been
arranged with local corporations at Decatur, Indiana; Tygart
Valley, West Virginia; Youngstown, Ohio; Pender County, North
Carolina; Jasper and Putnam Counties, Georgia; and plans were
advancing toward four different colonies, with three hundred
homes in all, out from Birmingham, Alabama.

In points of soil, topography, climate, access to employ, racial
and occupational groups and mixtures, and the heartiness of local
backing and interest, the projects chosen exhibited an all but in-

finite variety. Many of the factors to be considered had to be approximations and most of the questions involved were highly controversial.

Wilson encouraged controversy among his staff and consultants even when it slowed things up. Some of the outside urban consultants upon whom he called were inclined to be dubious of the grouped project or colony approach. They said it was an artificial design, imposed, unsuitable; better spread the people out on small, cheap holdings, or, as to rural rehabilitation, take them and help them as and where they were. Still other experts held that part-time farming is the hardest way of living; that the trend toward imagined pastoral ease was an escapist trend; that the real job was to lead stranded city people to stay where they were and work things out within the urban culture.

There were advisers who felt that the people should be allowed to buy their own homes, over a thirty-year payment period, and then hold individual title to that piece of ground and that home. There were other advisers who held with vigor that the Government should forever hold title; simply renting to settlers for lifetime tenure, or for such period as the settlers met payments, behaved themselves, and treated the land decently.

There were humanitarians who developed dreams of a beneficent 'infiltration' of varying human bloodlines, between colony and colony, between region and region. Good Quaker stock of Pennsylvania, for instance, introduced into Southern colonies, was to intermarry and invigorate the bloodstream of Alabama, Mississippi, Georgia; and there would be a like exchange northward and westward to others of these new colonies. 'What a dream world!' the more pragmatic element in Subsistence Homesteads Division cried.

It required humor — and a humor not embittered — to deal with the most fervent and expectant escape agrarians of our time. 'Window-box agrarians,' Paül Johnstone calls them.

Agrarians of the Borsodi persuasion, seeking escape from the indignities and ugliness of urbanism, a little white home with green shutters, a garden and a goat, do not, however, propose to return to simplicity empty-handed. In respect to subsistence homesteads, they proposed a retreat to nature with a dynamo under one arm, in a manner of speaking, and a watercloset under the other. Actually their proposal makes sense, if one can work it. Old-time pioneering was tough and brutal. We have prettied it up in our memory until it seems completely heroic. To talk now of going back to nature more comfortably, with greater provision for hygienic, medical, and social decencies, does not sound heroic. The subsistence homestead movement of the F. D. Roosevelt administration proceeded in an atmosphere of incongruity which some found bitter and others laughable. What a situation in a land where our great-hearted grandsires sang:

> Our lands are rich and broad enough.
> Don't be alarmed,
> For Uncle Sam is rich enough,
> To give us all a farm!

Or

> What country ever growed up,
> So great in little time,
> Just popping from the nurs'ry
> Right into like it's prime . . .
> Come, take a Quarter-Section
> And I'll be bound you'll say,
> This country takes the rag off,
> This Michigania!

And now — *subsistence* with plumbing!

But ordinary people, dispossessed and driven, who managed to get one of these tight little white houses with modern conveniences and a sizable little tract of tillable land around them, did not find it laughable, or altogether unheroic. Here is part of a latter-day pioneer ballad, made up to be sung to a banjo's strumming by the people resettled on the Tygart Valley Subsistence Homestead project in the mountains of West Virginia:

YOU CAN'T KEEP A GOOD PEOPLE DOWN

> In seventeen fifty-three
> From lands across the sea
> Each with a gun and the strength of one
> In search of liberty
> Those first settlers came,
> Tygarts and Files by name.

But they were too few for the work to do
And the wilds they could not tame.

Chorus

Yet others kep' a comin' and a strummin' and a hummin',
'Cause you can't keep a good people down.

Their trails by others were blazed,
Their crops by others were raised,
'Til they conquered the land by the toil of their hand
And history their efforts has praised.
For they cut, they planted and tied,
They reaped, they built and they tried.
They laid the foundation of a glorious nation
And left it to us when they died.

Chorus

Yet others kep' a comin' and a strummin' and a hummin',
'Cause you can't keep a good people down.

But some people didn't play fair
And some of them just didn't care,
They destroyed the trees and enjoyed their ease
And they left the cupboard bare.
Now the soil must be renewed,
Our resources all reviewed,
To find some other way to make our life pay
And that duty we may not elude.

Chorus

Yet others kep' a comin' and a strummin' and a hummin',
'Cause you can't keep a good people down.

In nineteen thirty-five
We began to arrive
From empty mine and wasted timber-line
And farms that no longer could thrive.
Back to the plow and the land
By the sweat of our brow and our hand,
To build from the start
With faith in our heart
As shoulder to shoulder we stand.

Chorus

Yet others kep' a comin' and a strummin' and a hummin',
'Cause you can't keep a good people down.

Roy Hendrickson, who then was on Wilson's staff, likes charts. One chart which he drew up at the time as a guide in the allocation of subsistence homestead colony loans was a carefully graded array of seventy-six possible, or probable, mistakes. By making only one of the most important mistakes, or two or three mistakes of secondary importance, or a dozen mistakes of minor importance, such projects, he held, would fail. Mistake Number One was 'locating on a base of poor or run-down soil, or with inadequate water for crops or living.' Mistake Number Two: 'Mistaken assumptions of employ.' And so on, up to Mistake Number Seventy-Six. Hendrickson's skepticism proved in many instances justified. Ironically, however, some of the projects which in many ways violated at base the requirements for success thus laid down — those around Birmingham, Alabama, in particular — proved the best paying, simply as housing projects, when the shadow of war sent mills to spinning and the defense boom got under way. 'Well, we got a lot of experience we can apply in the next depression,' says Hendrickson cheerfully; and it was to that end, quite seriously, that M. L. Wilson and Hendrickson asked the Bureau of Agricultural Economics to make a critical study of subsistence homesteads in 1942. I worked with Paul Johnstone on that study. With his sharp memory and extraordinary grasp of detail, Hendrickson was of great assistance. A Midwestern newspaper man, he was covering the Department of Agriculture for the Associated Press when the New Deal started; and his nose for news was so keen as to be disconcerting. Fully a month before the Farm Act had as much as passed he sought out Jerome Frank and blandly asked: 'What tack will you New Deal wizards take, do you think, Mr. Frank, when the Supreme Court declares your law unconstitutional?'

He was both blunt and able; and it seemed best to put his talents working definitely on the side of progress. So Hendrickson became, along with Paul Porter, one of the most stimulating Agricultural career men working for the Government. He worked with Wilson on the Wheat Program, Wilson took him along to Interior on the Subsistence Homestead flurry and back into Agriculture when the Wilsonians there came to a head of differences with Secretary Ickes, principally on the question of centralized control. Back in Agriculture, Hendrickson served successively as Head of Information in the Bureau of Agricultural Economics, Director of Personnel for the Department, Director of the Surplus Marketing Administration, and Deputy Director of the War Food Administration. He went from that to be Deputy Director of UNNRA. An interview he gave *The Land* on his experience in hearing claims for Subsistence Homestead appropriations, with disagreements as to policy, gives a brief account of the needs and perplexities of that era:

First, there was the Macfadden or $150 a year school of thought. You know — fresh air is healthy. The soil is kind. There's lots of land out of the pulsing city, and about $150 a year is all you need. Live in a shack — not too many clothes — clothes are unnatural. And stick to vegetables, roots, herbs; only cave men crave meat. No concern for modern medical facilities; no vaccination. Back to nature!

Next step up were the $500 a year boys. Go out to cutover land, rear cabins; from the extra logs rear a school. Make your own furniture; dig in; and twenty years from now maybe you can get all the settlers together and have a hospital-raising.

There were other little scattered groups a cut beyond that on the up, but the next big school of thought on the question was the $1200 a year bunch. Here the shacks were to be on stubs or some foundation above the ground, cheap, no paint, until paint could somehow be earned, if ever; community baths and waterclosets, if any; and as for electricity or not, let that depend on where the place was — what electricity cost.

Most of us in the first Subsistence Homestead Office wavered somewhere between that and a $1500 minimum, allowing for adjustments upward and downward according to the natural prospects of the people and the place.

We were all with Wilson against strict standardization; we favored local architects and local planning. But in many places we found no local architects who could take on layouts and planning of whole colonies, so we came around to absentee urban architecture and planning, in places.

Besides, whenever you tried to reach a policy decision as to whether subsistence homesteads in a given spot should have water in the kitchen, or in kitchens and in baths, or whether the homes should have electric power and light, the natural tendency was to say that a decent American standard of living required all three.[14]

The First Lady, Eleanor Roosevelt, took a constant interest in these subsistence homesteads, and served powerfully, though she had no official place in the movement, to elevate housing standards. The Roosevelts were never the sort of squires who say that if you give tenants bathtubs they will simply slaughter pigs in them or use them as coal bins. Mrs. Roosevelt's part in directing subsistence homesteads, while indirect, was intense. The Wilson element had her ear; the Ickes element, her husband's. Sometimes Mrs. R.'s exertion of influence upon the Squire could backfire; he had countless projects in mind, and inclined to become irritated if pressure at close hand wearied him of some specific project or detail. The lot of Wilson and his agriculturists in Interior was not a happy one. Wilson did not complain; but when sounds of the reverberations reached Wallace and Tugwell, and they had reviewed between them the sprawled and mixed disbursement of rural housing and relief through so many branches of the Government, they determined to call Wilson back home into Agriculture as Assistant Secretary, with Tugwell as Under-Secretary, shouldering the task of consolidating all such work within a Resettlement Administration.

The Resettlement Administration was established by executive order on April 30, 1935. It was set up first as an agency apart from any department. Tugwell, retaining his title and duties as Under-Secretary of Agriculture, was named by the President as its head. Resettlement took over twenty-four subsistence colonies in twelve states which Wilson had started, and undertook a larger work and relief program under four heads: rural rehabilitation, land utilization, rural resettlement, and urban resettlement. Projects of the fourth sort included satellite or suburban rim communities such as Green Belt, near Washington. Tugwell took a special interest in these. As for the rural projects, he announced

as a general policy a 'greater emphasis . . . upon resettlement projects of the infiltration type, or individual farm, as opposed to
the development of rural communities.'

Tugwell's accession to the head of the movement brought it
into sharper notice, increasingly hostile. With customary *sang-
froid*, he collected, at the request of the President, early New Deal
relief makeshifts — 'everybody else's headaches,' as he expressed
it, into Resettlement; and tried to build a unified working organization and staff. In Resettlement he served in effect as an Assistant President at a time before such a rôle had been authorized
by Congress, maintaining at the same time a sub-cabinet rank in
Agriculture. He found the situation anomalous. So did Wallace.
At the end of eight months, on December 31, 1936, the Resettlement Administration was brought into the Department of Agriculture, with Tugwell continuing momentarily in command. By
September 1, 1937, when Resettlement became the Farm Security
Administration, the organization was administering one hundred
and twenty-two widely various projects throughout the United
States and its dependencies. Great uproar had arisen by this
time to get this Tugwell out of the Government and 'the Government out of the real estate business.' It seemed quite certain
that Congress would not appropriate adequately for a continuation of the program once the period of operation provided for
by executive order had expired. Tired and increasingly restive,
Tugwell was planning to get out of Government and into private
business.

Some of Wallace's closest counselors urged him to let Resettlement go when Tugwell did, to unshoulder responsibility for rural
relief, apart from Triple-A. The Department of Agriculture had
enough to do, as it was, they said. To have let the relief load of
landless tenants or migrants go back to Harry Hopkins or elsewhere would have been a welcome unburdening. It is doubtless
a Christian act, individually or administratively, to 'deliver the
needy when he crieth, the poor also, and him that hath no helper.'[15]
But it is probably the most thankless work in the world. For
reasons that will appear, Wallace decided not to abandon Resettlement. Instead he reorganized it within his Department as the
Farm Security Administration, appointing three men who had

worked closely with Tugwell — Dr. Will Alexander, Benham Baldwin, and Milo Perkins — as co-administrators, to carry the program on.

5. Timber — Unclassified

WALLACE puzzled many people, including writing people. In the earlier nineteen-thirties when almost everything about the New Deal made print, more newspaper and magazine writers composed interview or think-pieces about him, I dare say, than about any other New Deal figure except the President. Some of this material they derived from their subject direct and some from his aides; and the material seldom seemed to gibe. They wrote that he was simple, but exceedingly complex; that he wavered between ardor for the utmost advance of an interdependent civilization, with an abundance of material goods and gimcracks for everyone, and a simple desire to lie on green grass under trees and be let alone. The writers found him further, in general, highly competent intellectually in such widely various fields as plant and animal production, banking, marketing, and in mechanics of government; but in these and in all other matters, a 'mystic.'

Much depended, of course, on how crowded the day was that the writer devoted to the research. Even more depended on what he or she sought audience expecting to find. Admitted as spectator to a secretarial conference with 'a delegation from a Midwestern milling syndicate with uproarious protests against executive action to force the price of wheat up to 1910–1914 level,' Charles Morrow Wilson, representing *The Commercial*, a religious publication, wrote:

> The protestors brought the usual guise and tone of a corporation lobby. They weren't come for selfish interests. Far, far from it. They were come for the good of the commonwealth, for the cause of law, order, and society. They were come with statistics and oily words.

Henry Wallace listened with about as much animation as

AFTER SEVERAL YEARS IN WASHINGTON
Henry A. and Mrs. Wallace

a hitching post. A fat and rather disagreeable member, with a perspiring brow and soft hands, began to gesticulate. He said that God himself . . . couldn't make the domestic allotment plan work. . . . All in an instant Wallace was standing straight with raised head. He spoke easily, but his eyes flashed:

'I have faith that Divine Providence will provide a means to fit the times.'[16]

Gerald W. Johnson, then of *The Baltimore Sun*, is interested in Wallace's 'religious streak,' as he calls it. Of Scotch-Irish origin, himself, Johnson used to ask me many questions about this 'streak' when I worked for Wallace. He feared, he said, that unless it was tempered with humor and with a genuine humility as well as with Wallace's admittedly high intelligence and wide learning, the religious intensity of the man might become, with the passing years, intensified and channeled into 'a dangerous fanaticism, like Bryan's.' Later, in the course of researches for his book, *Roosevelt: Democrat or Dictator?* Gerald Johnson spent a number of hours with Wallace, and wrote a sketch of somewhat altered impressions:

. . . A politician who really does not care about making political 'friends' is, in the opinion of political Washington, a flat contradiction of terms. Hence, in the case of Henry A. Wallace [Washington says] appearances must be deceptive. Behind the figure presented to the public gaze there must be another and very different man; yet no one, not even the most highly trained observers of the nation's press, has perceived that other man. Hence the frank bewilderment. Hence correspondents' confession that although they see him every day, and talk to him, and watch him, they do not know him.

This grows all the more curious when the inquirer encounters Mr. Wallace himself. He doesn't look the least like the Man in the Iron Mask, or like Svengali, or like any other mysterious and incomprehensible figure of history or fiction. He looks like a man from Iowa, which is to say he looks not very different from a small-town resident in any other state. His face is long and rectangular, crowned with rather thick iron-gray hair, rampant, like that of Andrew Jackson. A long nose and keen blue eyes are set above a mouth so sensitive that it may startle the visitor; it is possible at first to believe that the wide, rather thin lips are tremulous, but presently one realizes that they are not really so, but look as if they might become so at any moment. Probably this feature is responsible for the impression that Mr. Wallace is at heart intensely shy. Perhaps he is; but perhaps what passes for shyness is in reality a profound conviction that talking to people is, nine times out of ten, a waste of time, and in the tenth case, imprudent. . . .

Johnson quotes Wallace's insistence on 'two ideas extremely old, so old that the sophisticated have long held them to be outworn and obsolete: (1) "It is my belief that every freedom, every right, every privilege has its price, its corresponding duty without which it cannot be enjoyed." (2) "Satan is turned loose upon the world."' This, Johnson says, puzzles Americans, because:

> It speaks an archaic dialect. That is to say, it is archaic in the ears of the huge population crowded into the urban centers, especially on the two seaboards; but in the rural sections of the country, in the small towns, and even among the older people in the cities, it is familiar enough. This contributes at once to his strength as an author and to his weakness as a leader. When Mr. Wallace speaks of those who 'long for the Kingdom,' of 'conviction of sin,' and of 'spiritual wrestling,' millions of Americans understand him perfectly, but other millions do not understand him at all. . . .
> That Henry A. Wallace is a profoundly religious man is incontestably true, but the charge of fanaticism is hardly sustained by an examination of his writings. 'I know many men,' he says, 'who very rarely attend church, who nevertheless are intensely religious, from the standpoint of my definition, in their daily life. Who am I to criticize a Catholic, a Jew, or a Protestant for the way in which he obtains the spiritual power with which to discipline himself?' . . .[17]

A more volatile *Baltimore Sun* staffman, Paul W. Ward, in an article entitled 'Wallace, the Great Hesitater,' published in *The Nation* for May 8, 1935, likewise departed from the concept of Wallace as a man 'born ahead of his time,' a phrase that was growing in use among more sympathetic commentators, such as Raymond Clapper. Bundling Tugwell with Wallace, and thrusting them back in time as far as the French Revolution and the Middle Ages, respectively, Ward whirled into attack as follows:

> Both Henry Agard Wallace, Secretary of Agriculture, and Rexford Guy Tugwell, his Under-Secretary, were born beyond their time. Tugwell, a third-rate Voltaire trying to be a second-rate Rousseau, would have been a French or English courtier when the Industrial Revolution was in its infancy. Wallace, one of the most admirable and ridiculous figures of the New Deal, should have been born in the Middle Ages and set himself in the quiet of a cloister garden to commune with his soul and the Infinite while finding out the laws of hybridism 'untroubled,' as Bateson says of the nineteenth-century monk, Mendel, 'by any itch to make potatoes larger or bread cheaper.'

Comparing Wallace to Pontius Pilate for 'the manner in which he washed his hands of Frank, Pressman, and Jackson when these champions of the public interest were fired from the Agricultural Adjustment Administration in the "purge" last February,' Ward doubts 'if Wallace, or Tugwell, for that matter, could bring himself to advocate or direct a drastic course of action, even if the White House boss would let them.' They are middle class. 'In the present crisis each is psychologically immobilized by his middle-class roots. Each makes the preservation of "human liberties" a prerequisite to change, mistaking "human liberties" for the minor privileges and creature comforts to which their middle-class rearing has wedded them. . . .'

He analyzes Wallace's inner nature as 'tripartite.' Politician — scientist — Christian mystic, and of these three personalities, the third is dominant. 'Wallace, in short, is a queer duck,' Mr. Ward decided. 'Isadora Duncan would have loved him. So would Gandhi, Krishnamurti, and Bernarr Macfadden. He has almost as many idiosyncrasies as Upton Sinclair.'

Ward further stated that: 'He [Wallace] dabbles in (1) astrology and (2) numerology, consorts with poets ranging from (3) AE down to obscure ones with such *noms de plume* as (4) "The Alabama Wildcat," and corresponds regularly, it is reported, with (5) an Indian medicine man. . . .'

There is more; but this seems a suitable point at which to haul up on this vexed question of Wallace's 'mysticism' and get at some undistorted facts: Wallace has never in his life seriously studied or taken any stock in the mysteries of (1) astrology or (2) numerology. Astronomy and mathematics in relation to planetary movements and their possible bearing on long-time weather forecasting, yes; his interest in such studies dates back almost to 1910, and continues. As for (3) consorting with poets, the record shows him to be a friend not only of the late AE, but of Robert Frost; and he did spend an amusing evening in his own apartment with a number of others listening to the recitations of (4) 'The Alabama Wildcat,' but the acquaintanceship did not ripen into intimacy. As for the charge of corresponding with (5) an Indian medicine man, that is completely false. It paved the way, none the less, toward an undercover circulation of forged 'mystical' letters, rather widely passed from hand to hand in the campaign of 1940. The general context of these remarkable fabrications would have been belittling to the intelligence of an idiot child of ten.[18]

The actual basis and being of Henry A. Wallace's religious convictions are in the man's own statements on the subject. They are singularly clear, uninhibited, and unburdened with the mumbo-jumbo of denominational or ecclesiastical contention.

Less than a year before he came to Washington, H. A. dictated a signed editorial for the family paper and wrote his own headline about it: '*DRAGONS THAT DEVOUR PROSPERITY: The Roads to High Standards of Living.*' The editorial was illustrated with a picture from the 'Frieze of the Prophets,' by Sargent, a bold-typed box below quoted Isaiah, *Woe unto them . . . that take away the right from the poor of my people*; Amos, *Hear this, O ye that swallow up the needy . . .*; Leviticus, *Proclaim liberty throughout all the lands*; Micah, *Nation shall not lift sword against nation; neither shall they learn war any more.* H. A. Wallace wrote: 'The Jewish prophets of old undoubtedly lived in times somewhat like this. They cried out for justice, but knew that justice could not come until the spirit of fairness and understanding permeated the hearts of all the people . . .' [19]

M. L. Wilson, who had read as a boy Uncle Henry's Sunday School Lessons in *Wallaces' Farmer*, was neither shocked nor grieved when the new Secretary in the opening weeks of his first month in Washington offered as an informal discussion guide to topics of the times a ten-page compilation headed, 'Regular and Insurgent Prophets.'

Here were Micah, Isaiah, Hosea, Jeremiah, Ezekiel, Amos, Samuel, and Zephaniah, the kept prophet, all arrayed; with the ageless argument between the comfortable and complacent and the deprived or rebellious more sharply and beautifully stated than in any *Congressional Record*. 'The Bible,' Uncle Henry had written in his book *To the Farm Boy*, more than thirty years before, 'paints men as they are, and not as they should be; and in my feeble way I am trying to do the same thing for you. . . . We are all but abridgements of a perfect humanity. . . .' Of all the farm boys who came under the influence of Uncle Henry's teaching, this Henry Agard Wallace stood first and closest.

'Religious economics!' cried economists of the Secretary's staff. 'Well, economic morality, if you like it better that way,' Wallace replied, smiling. He was amused by the fear of most of his aides when the Chicago Theological Seminary asked him to deliver the Alden-Tuthill Lecture for 1934. Consenting, he went alone with a dictaphone up to his favorite hideout, a cottage at the disused Weather Bureau Station, in Mount Weather, Virginia, to talk about God and the Ways of Man. He came back with three lectures roughed out on the records. These, together with a fourth talk, *Statesmanship and Religion*, delivered before the Federal Council of Churches in New York City, later came out as a book.[20] He had no book in mind when he undertook these lectures; his thought was simply to talk religion in terms of earth and man with theologians, and to show how religion — 'One God, One World,' as he put it, conversationally — may, indeed must, be brought into economics and government, without departure from the traditional separation of Church and State. While the book made him endless trouble, providing marvelous material for distortion by piecemeal quotations torn from context, *Statesmanship and Religion*, if read as a whole, remains the most unstudied, revelatory, and meaningful of Wallace's published works. Here we have his own decent and not too reticent expression of faith. From Chapter I: 'The Spiritual Adventure of the Prophets':

> It happens, fortunately, it seems to me, that the Biblical record is heavily loaded on the side of the Progressive Independents. The fight conducted against the standpatters worshiping Baal and running their commercial affairs according to the ancient respectable Canaanitish traditions, in its inward essence is as strikingly modern as that between the Sons of the Wild Jackass and Wall Street. Of course today most people thoughtlessly look on such vigorous prophets as Elijah, Amos, Micah, and Jeremiah as respectable old grandfathers with long white beards. As a matter of fact, they were as vivid as Senator Norris and at the time they made their pronouncements were as unpopular as the Senator in the Coolidge administration.
>
> I am sure that if we had been trying to earn a living in one of the walled cities of Judah six hundred and twenty years before Christ, most of us would have been respectable worshipers of Baal, genuinely worried about the subversive tendencies of that fellow Jeremiah who was breaking down confidence and saying things that were bad for business. . . . [Amos], telling those crooked priests and businessmen where to get off . . . was more than the professional prophet Amaziah could stand.
>
> Amaziah immediately complained to King Jeroboam with the age-old plaint of respectable men rudely disturbed by a reformer; said Amaziah, concerning Amos, 'The land is not able to bear all his words.' He assumed Amos was one of the kept prophets of Judah and suggested that he go back home and prophesy there for the bread of his own land. Most prophets have been true to their bread, but you can't tell how they will act in a strange land. . . .

In the course of the second lecture, or Chapter II: 'The Spiritual Adventure of the Reformers,' Wallace quietly interjected a personal statement or explanation, here reprinted entire:

> Before going further, I think it might be wise for me to give enough of my own religious background so that you can make due allowance for certain prejudices which may appear in this discussion. It should be obvious that I wish to emphasize those things which unite humanity rather than those which separate humanity and perpetuate hatred, fear, and prejudice.
>
> It happens that I was raised in the United Presbyterian Church and that my grandfather was a United Presbyterian minister. The United Presbyterians were educated men, well grounded in Calvinism, and many of them took delight in occasional sermons against the idolatry of the Papacy. In 1928 I remember a good United Presbyterian and his wife called on me and attempted to demonstrate from the Book of Revelation that the Roman Church was the Whore of Babylon, and that in case Al Smith won the 1928 election, then the last days, in truth, were upon us.

When he read from the lecture script to his theological audience, this ironical passage aroused only a mildly shocked and sympathetic laugh. When the reverend promoters of the lectures spotted book revenue in them, however, and also some syndicate series money for their coffers, and obtained Wallace's permission to go ahead on such publication, trouble started. The syndicated news articles, put out in amateurish fashion, roughhewn, were further hacked down and twisted by hasty or hostile newspaper editors. None, at the time, quite achieved that masterpiece of condensation so widely circulated from hand to hand at the Chicago convention of 1944: 'THE CATHOLIC CHURCH IS THE WHORE OF BABYLON. . . .' HENRY A. WALLACE. But they did what they could in the rush of the moment. When proofs of the proposed book were placed before him, Wallace sought to repair the damage with a footnote:

> This passage is as it was given in the Alden-Tuthill Lectures before the Chicago Theological Seminary on January

30, 1934. When the author discovered that the Round
Table Press had made arrangements for syndication he asked
that the entire personal reference be omitted. Through an
error only the first part was omitted, dealing with the early
religious background of the author. It is obvious, of course,
that the author wishes to emphasize those things which
unite humanity rather than those which separate and per-
petuate hatred, fear, and prejudice.

The text of his personal testimony continued:

As a growing boy and young man, I found considerable
intellectual exercise and interest in following the strictly
Presbyterian sermons. A little later I began to question
many of the points raised by the minister in the course of
his sermon. After a time I felt that a critical attitude in the
House of God on the Sabbath was not proper, and so I
stopped going to church. In college I imbibed the customary
doctrines of *laissez-faire* economics and the 'survival of the
fittest' evolution. Also, one of my college friends interested
me in reading some pamphlets by Ralph Waldo Trine, one of
which was entitled, *Thoughts are Things*. Like all men partially trained in science, I became rather skeptical for a time.
More and more I felt the necessity of believing in a God,
immanent as well as transcendent. About this time I attended a Roman Catholic service and was greatly impressed
by the devotional attitude of all present. I had an instinctive feeling that I, also, would like to *genuflect*, to cross
myself, and remain quietly kneeling after the conclusion of
the Mass, in silent adoration. Some years later I studied,
rather superficially, to be sure, the Aristotelian logic as
developed by St. Thomas Aquinas, and used by the Jesuits
and other neo-scholastic churchmen in support of the present
Roman Catholic position.

Unfortunately, I found that intellectual studies of this
sort tended to destroy for me the spiritual beauty of the
Mass. For some reason the scholastic method of reasoning,
as applied to religious matters, has the same effect on me as
the closely reasoned Calvinistic sermon. I fear both Presby-

terians and Roman Catholics would say that the Lord had hardened my heart. And so it is that I eventually became a member of a so-called High Episcopal parish which, incidentally, is the most poverty-stricken in my home town. It is fair to tell you these things so that you may make allowances when I deal with the men and women who brought on the Reformation. I have read both Catholic and Protestant books about these men and cannot but feel that all of the biographers are prejudiced witnesses. My testimony may be equally prejudiced, but, at any rate, I have given you a certain amount of data so as to put you on guard as to the type of prejudice.

Continuing, Wallace touched on that 'truly dismaying thing . . . the lukewarmness, the wishy-washy, goody-goody-goodiness, the infantile irrelevancy of the Church itself.' He deplored 'a disputatious attitude concerning ethical matters' among churchmen, then passed to consider the plight of 'fine, cultured, tolerant people . . . delightful and enjoyable companions,' departed from the faith of their fathers, 'decidedly materialistic and skeptical about the existence of God or a future life. In the world of business, such people know that they have to "get" if they are not to be "gotten" and, while they don't like this kind of business any better than you and I, they don't know of anything practical to do about it. Therefore, the most decent of the well-educated materialists accept some form of "Lippmanesque" humanism as a way of making the best of a bad job.'

In Iowa, during his years as a grown man there, many of Wallace's friends and associates in the writing and publishing trade — Donald Murphy, James LeCron, and Paul Appleby in particular — were unchurched or unorthodox 'humanists,' as he called them; and now, in Washington, most of his closest helpers were men of good will and intellect of the same strain. He liked to argue with them. Sometimes he abashed them slightly by declaring them, despite their profane objections, to be more 'ardently religious in your own way than any shouting bigot I know.' He never tried to convert his friends to anything, but argued about religion in general as naturally, and used its terminology with as little self-consciousness as Jerome Frank sought to change legal procedures in terms of Freud. It was of such close associates that he was thinking at the close of his second lecture to the clerics at Chicago:

> Now, humanists are, as a rule, superficially agnostic yet resolutely practice the good life as they see it and do their best to bring that life to pass for other people as well. Many of them derive considerable pleasure from making fun of the sacred superstitions of the previous generation and are doubtless a healthful influence in many ways because they puncture the hypocritical pretensions of people who dully profess 'religion' and sharply practice business. In ordinary everyday life, humanists are interesting, amusing, stimulating, and humble. People of this sort will always be very useful in keeping 'religious' people from taking themselves prematurely seriously.

Neither friend nor foe saw in this Wallace a man who took himself too seriously. The enormous seriousness with which he shouldered every responsibility that was thrust upon him stood forth in striking contrast to the unstudied simplicity of his personal demeanor in public or in private. He acted as if everything he turned his hand to — from an improvement in interbureau relationships to an improvement in his tennis — was a matter of immense importance; but he never acted as if he felt himself any more important than anyone else. This was perhaps another reason why writer-analysts found him 'enigmatic,' and inclined either to exalt him beyond reason, or to attack him furiously, with mystified dislike. Sometimes they did both in the same article. In course of the analysis already quoted, Paul W. Ward mixes his strokes in successive sentences thus: 'His sincerity awes all beholders, even when he grows remorseful over the savageness of his tennis strokes, fearing the will to win thus displayed is a departure from the Christian cheek-turning ethic. That there is nothing smug or self-righteous about the man is shown by the way he impresses people in frequent contact with him.' Later, Wallace, 'a man of surpassing candor and dignity . . . shy and sincere . . . looks like a cultured clodhopper.'

The main fact about his tennis is simpler and, thoughtfully considered, more revealing than Ward says. Badminton and volleyball had been Wallace's outdoor games before he came to Washington; tennis, rarely. Neither game had served to develop in him an effective tennis form. He was getting a little fat around the neck — the Wallace men run to fat, if they do not watch it — and he took pains to work it off. Tennis, on near-by public courts, was the most easily available exercise; so he used to call on various men of his staff, mostly country boys themselves, and none too good at the game, to romp through three to five sets with him once or twice a week. Most of the men who played with him at first talked far better tennis than they played. They romped and 'rooted' rudely, rarely tried hard, and took a raucous pleasure in running their Secretary this way and that, even over benches. He would try for a shot anywhere in the court, or even out of it. Ambidextrous, he gripped his racket in the left hand clumsily, and ran himself breathless. Sometimes he would tumble into the backstop while his aides laughed heartily. This did not seem to make him angry; his only expressed chagrin was that he could not, by nature, take tennis or any game lightly; he had to be good at it; he had to win. And he did win, most of the time, over the then opposition, by sheer determination and driving vigor. But his game did not improve. He refused to go over to pitching horseshoes, which game Jim LeCron suggested, and himself played, as one more suitable for 'middle-aged bumpkins.' But Wallace did not give up tennis; he merely gave up playing it with poor players who lacked the will to improve and win. He put himself in the hands of a professional, removed his games to courts where men who took tennis seriously, strove mightily to win. He developed in form and drive until, by the time he was fifty, he could hold his own, and often win. On one occasion he took three games in each of three sets from the then ninth-ranking male player in this land. Wallace plays expert tennis now, but he still plays headlong.

At routine work, he is generally serious, sometimes even somber. He travels or goes to parties eagerly, with zest and a quiet gaiety, and always seems to have a good time. But under heavy tasks of office organization he groans, to himself only, laboring zealously, uncomplaining, but with no evident happiness in it all. An organization can be an awful thing,' he would say in his earlier days as Secretary of Agriculture, as his personnel mounted in number and developed mounting tangles of functions and feuds. But organization was his job, and he set himself to master it. Sherwood Anderson, passing through, sat in Wallace's office through the greater part of a morning's routine, lunched with him and his immediate staff, then wrote an article called 'No Swank' in the curious lumbering, impressionistic style of his later days. He starts: 'In the mountain country . . . they say of a man, meaning to pay him the highest possible compliment . . . they say, "Oh, he's just common."' There follow ruminations on the integrity of mountain poor whites, on 'the great stir and ferment . . . in America,' on loneliness, and finally on Henry Wallace:

> . . . This particular smiling, half shy, half Abraham-Lincoln-looking Henry . . .
>
> I thought he looked tired . . .

So I was looking at him and thinking . . . as anybody would, being with him, thinking . . . 'He's a pretty swell guy but he looks to me too sensitive for the game he's in . . .'

Thinking, 'Jesus, I am pretty strong myself, but I couldn't stand that racket.'

The gimme men who must cluster around him . . .

. . . sugar men . . .

. . . corn men . . .

. . . hog men . . .

Oh, Washington, thou fair capital city . . .

Sugar magnates . . . Smoot of Utah . . . (Oh, I forgot. He ain't there any more) . . . bankers, milk dealers, butter dealers . . . fellows with nice suits of clothes on . . . smooth guys . . . rotten guys . . . angry guys . . .

What I said was, 'How the hell do you stand it?'

'What?' he says.

'All those guys.' I said. 'Gimme, gimme, gimme . . .'

He looked puzzled . . . I was like a child asking some grownups a question when I asked him that. . . .

I was thinking of hungry individualists who have got caught up with during this depression . . . this sudden looking to the government to save us . . . a new relationship in our daily lives . . . most of us being still individualists enough to want, first of all, individual salvation. . . .

A sudden centering of all this upon himself. . . .

Who might as well have been today, a farmer, college professor in some small Midwestern college, country town storekeeper, country town postmaster. I think Will Rogers is the type; there is something in common between Will Rogers and Henry Wallace. There is the same little smile . . . an inner rather than an outward smile . . . perhaps just at bottom sense of the place in life of a civilized man . . . no swank . . . something that gives us confidence.

'I may not solve anything for you, probably won't but I won't let you down, sell you out. I won't lie to you. I won't tell you one thing when I mean another.'

I asked him the question . . . 'How do you stand it? What do you want to do it for?' I wanted to hear what he'd say but he took his time answering —

'I guess I didn't put myself into this. I guess I'm in it. I'll ride along.'

He meant, I think, that if you do not think you are a great poobah, you do not have to worry much whether you turn out to be or not. . . .[21]

The article closes with a story from one of Henry's assistants:

When Henry went to Washington he asked this man to come on down. They had been the kind of friends you see walking about together on back streets in country towns on summer evenings, men who like each other and like to talk together. This man was given a desk in another office. I presume he also had his bells to push, his secretaries and underlings. But then he had to jump for Henry's bell. Jump fast. He was telling me about the first time he ever did it. He said he had been listening to the others and so when he went in he called Henry 'Mister Secretary.' Henry told him in his quiet way what he wanted and he started for the door. 'I was thinking,' he said, 'as I made for the door, of other evenings when I had been with Henry. So I took a look back at him and he was standing by his desk and he was smiling at something and at the same time I saw tears on his cheeks.'

Whatever the general effect of this friendly story, it did not make anyone else cry around the Department at the time. Things were getting organized. Doors which used to stand freely open were now, of necessity, closed and guarded by snippy lady secretaries and young men who had joined up as peacetime privates or corporals highheartedly and were counting each other's desks, phones, and other implements of rising officialdom with a sometimes jaundiced eye. The Secretary's immediate staff had now installed on each desk compact little telephone exchanges that glimmered when buttons were touched with intricate coded connections of green, red, yellow, amber, and (some insisted) purple lights.

'You boys in the front office,' said John R. Fleming, then on the Information Staff, 'may have cried a little when they put those desk-lights in. But how you would bellow now if anybody took them out!' The remark, made in all camaraderie at lunch in a private room off the South Building Cafeteria, where Wallace, his staff men, and almost anyone who came along could eat and converse for ten cents a place service charge above the cafeteria schedule, made Wallace shake with laughter. So did Fleming's report on the outcome of a conference of experts in discussion methods, brought together from all over the country to consider 'How to Discuss.' 'The main thing they argued,' Jack Fleming said, 'was the proper relative weight to be given emotion and logic in discussion. By the end of the second day the boys defending pure logic were beating the table while the boys defending emotion were all tuckered out, icy calm.'

The private-room luncheons of this Ten Cents More Club (known also with mild ribaldry as The Sec's Club) were not only amusing and stimulating, while they lasted, but were important in bringing together men of diverse views and character from within the Government and without. Marriner Eccles used to come there for lunch fairly often during his early days in Washington. Stuart Chase, lecturing in Utah, had sent word to Tugwell that Eccles should be in public service; and soon he was. In this same small room off the Home Economics Cafeteria, Wallace and Tugwell persuaded Ferdinand Silcox that he should return from Labor arbitration to his first love, Forestry, and become

Chief of the Forest Service. Frequently there were striking, even brilliant, non-governmental or anti-governmental figures from the world without. Clarence Darrow came, old now, tired, tired almost to death, humorously despairing, but the old fire was still alive in him, and his talk was brilliant and memorable in short spurts. AE came; and Sherwood Anderson, from time to time; and Robert Frost. Frost despised the whole New Deal show. 'Up where I come from,' he said, 'we don't face Washington when we pray.' But he liked to hear 'the New Deal boys' talk, and he liked to talk with them. He came to one of these Wallace luncheons on a raw and blustery day, and sat in a chair in Wallace's outer waiting room, sending in his name. A great deal was going on that day and the name did not get into Wallace correctly. The old poet sat there musing amid the jangle of phone bells and the bustle of officials. His overshoes made his feet hot, so he kicked them off. In the inner office, waiting, Wallace and Tugwell wondered where he was. Then an aide came hastening to say that Mr. Frost had been out there for nearly half an hour, and they hurried out to greet him and explain. They had to cross to lunch in another building. Frost reached down to retrieve his overshoes. He fumbled with them, talking cheerfully the while. Quite without self-consciousness, Wallace knelt before him and helped him put on his overshoes. I sometimes wonder if that simple act, performed in public, might not have something to do with all the chatter about Wallace's kneeling before strange gods.

Generally, there were no outside visitors at these luncheons. Then the talk was shop talk, intimate, sometimes boisterous — the Secretary and his help blowing off. I recall, from the period when it was becoming fairly certain that the Supreme Court would declare Triple-A unconstitutional, a dissertation on Supreme Court justices by Paul Porter. They are hard to shoot, Paul said, because you can't figure where the robe stops and the man begins. 'It's mighty difficult. It's like trying to guess the weight of a nun.'

Himself refraining, almost invariably, from unkind remarks, either humorous or savage, and from ribaldry or profanity also, Wallace appeared quite definitely on many occasions to experience a sort of relief from godless outbursts among his closest colleagues. Jim LeCron, formerly of the Cowles papers of Des Moines, and perhaps the most intimate of the Secretary's immediate staff, was frequently a great help in this particular. 'No matter how noble a man is, he needs to relax. You can't go on turning the other cheek forever. It gets to be too much of a strain. And you run out of cheeks,' Jim would explain. Jim eased that strain. When his Chief became tired or low in mind, and verbal roughing-up of the most recent disturbing cause or visitor, sharply applied by Jim, did not untense the Secretary, 'Get up out of that chair,' Jim would say, 'I can throw you!' Then they would wrestle — Indian-style, with hand grips only, sometimes; again, in frontier fashion, catch-as-catch-can, for a full throw. For his next appointment the Secretary would be looking a little more than usually rumpled, but more cheerful and composed.

Wallace arranged his life in Washington so that he would live as nearly as possible as if he were still a country editor working near fields in a small town. Rising early, he would walk in almost any weather the two and a half miles from his apartment at the Wardman Park Hotel to his office on the Mall. The route he chose led down along Rock Creek and on through leafy parks, as far as possible away from buildings and people. Sometimes in the early days he would ask Henry Morgenthau, Jr., who then was head of the Farm Credit Administration, to walk to work with him, and they would confer as they strode along. More often, at first, however, Wallace walked it alone. Later, LeCron, with whom Wallace had been walking, it chanced, on the outskirts of Des Moines when he decided to accept a place in the Roosevelt administration, came to Washington as an aide to the Secretary, and walked with him to the office nearly every morning. LeCron is leggy; he can keep up with Wallace's nearly five-miles-an-hour gait without much effort; he is laconic, and that, again, suits Wallace most of the time when he is walking. They knew each other so well that they generally had little need to talk. After 1935, when Milo Perkins had joined the Secretary's official family, the walking party became three or more. In open weather they varied the routine by proceeding afoot to the Mall, near the Washington Monument. Here they were met by the Secretary's official car and chauffeur, and mysterious objects were unloaded from the car. Boomerangs. The Secretary and his friends were learning to throw them with some skill. What a story for the papers; what a boon to cartoonists! Reporters and photographers came unasked to record this odd form of sport and amusement. One photographer who would not stand where he was told crowded in to take a close-up of Wallace throwing the boomerang and was neatly conked and sliced by the returning weapon.

People here and there began to talk about Wallace for President as early as 1933. He paid the talk no outward heed, and would not discuss it. Two informal Wallace-for-President clubs — one in Texas, the other among a group of leftish intellectuals in New York City — made a little spatter of talk in political circles even that early; but the one in Texas was a letterhead organization with a few members only, and the one in New York was just talk. Immediately, however, a number of 'president-makers,' as the press corps called them, arose among Wallace's personal entourage, seeking to guard him more carefully against impulsive utterance, and to give him guidance in political behavior. He paid them little attention, and this was just as well, because most of these advisers were themselves new-come to government and politically inexperienced. They complained, as chiefs of information successively named to handle news for the Secretary and Department invariably complained, that Wallace was a hard, not to say an impossible, man to 'handle.' They all told him the same thing: that a public man may — must — without shame or guile, play a part, assume a rôle, and act that part in public, consistently. Anything else confuses people. A public man's private life and views, if any, must not intrude upon his public appearance and utterance unduly; and, while a public man need not say publicly what he does not believe, he should certainly not spill out anything or everything at the slightest question from a reporter or under thrall of an occasion. Sooner or later, as time and occasion served, Wallace might put all that he believed and yearned for before the public, these handlers of public opinion warned. But only little by little. Be more cautious. Don't crowd them. Operate with a sense of *timing.*

Wallace, possibly, could see some sense in that. He listened at least to all such counsel intently, and tried at times to please. But play a part he would not, or could not.

Whenever on tour he crumpled his manuscript, put it by, and threw up his head to speak extempore, his handlers of opinion there in the audience or grouped around the pressroom radio back in Washington shivered; and once in a while he gave them cause to shiver. In his salad days as Secretary, for example, he was reading a prepared speech, another economic justification of Triple-A reduction policy, before an audience of business men in Chicago. Chicago always seemed to arouse in him something perverse or rebellious. He had arrived there happily enough, handlers with him said, had walked down the lakefront carrying his suitcase two miles to his hotel; then had taken a taxi to the auditorium. In the taxi an old agrarian acquaintance showed him an editorial from that day's Greatest Newspaper. Colonel Mc-Cormick's *Tribune* welcomed to Chicago 'Wallace, The Greatest Butcher in Christendom.'

He started reading his speech haltingly, low-voiced. Then agrarianism with its roots far back in the hill country of Judea flared up in him, and the Wallace temper took fire and blazed. His voice arose to a high pitch and trembled. 'If Chicago,' he cried, 'does not learn to play fair — does not give justice — to the farmers of the great Mississippi Valley, then Chicago will be reduced to an anthill.'

Back in Washington, at press conference, he was asked if that might not go down in history with Bryan's passage on 'grass in the streets' in the Cross of Gold oration. Wallace was contrite. Yes, he said, it was much the same kind of remark; and he hoped it would be forgiven him.

But generally he was at his best when he had his neck out, not too closely guarded; and from another ordeal that he faced, extempore, at Chicago, he emerged chuckling and mildly triumphant. He had been asked to speak at a large luncheon for members of the Union League Club and their guests. This was the very core and center of an all but hysterical New Deal opposition. The chairman of the luncheon, a stout industrialist, had what he considered a smoothly insulting introduction all worked out.

'We have as our speaker today,' he said, in effect, 'a bearer of

the true message from that source of all light and truth to the
East — from Washington, D.C. He comes from the foot of the
Throne of the Great White Father. I introduce you now to . . .
to . . . to . . . [snapping the fingers, as in mental effort to recall].
Oh, yes, Henry A. Wallace.'

Wallace got up. 'Thank you, Mr. Chairman,' he said, 'for
that very thoughtful introduction. I am happy to be here. I
know this club. I have often felt happy and at home here. My
father was a member. He used to bring me here. My father, as
some of you will recall, was Secretary of Agriculture under Presidents Harding and Coolidge. But that was some years ago.
That was back in the happy times of the . . . of the [business of
snapping fingers] — shall we say . . . The Republican Illusion?'[22]

Wallace struggled visibly to discipline his inherited agrarianism,
and at length succeeded. At times, conversing, he would invoke
his father's experience and conviction that, however rough the
trail, there will never in a modern society be fair play for agriculture until business men are 'educated' to the need. But he did
make one more flaming agrarian speech. On May 14, 1935, some
forty-five hundred farmers accompanied by about one hundred
County Agricultural Extension Agents 'marched' peaceably on
Washington, at their own expense, to protest to the President
against an organized effort by some processors and handlers of
farm commodities to disrupt the Adjustment program by destroying or interfering with processing taxes (from which adjustment payments were made to farmers). Wallace and Davis
recognized at once, as administrators, that they would be charged
with having stirred up this political move by use of public moneys.
Indeed, having heard, afield, of agitation for such a march, they
had shot out telegrams to all directors of extension in the states
cautioning them to stand clear of the movement, and to make all
county agents stand clear.

But the farmers and some of their county governmental agents
marched anyway. They put up at low-rate hotels in Washington
and asked Wallace to get the President to receive and address
them on the White House lawn. The President did so, in fine
fettle.

Greatly stirred by the tribute to the New Deal farm program,

the Squire in the White House said that the Opposition was lying
about Triple-A. Wallace and Davis made fighting addresses in
like spirit. It was a sort of postdated Populist outing and everybody enjoyed it. But it took a great deal of paper work to clear
it up afterwards. Senator Daniel O. Hastings of Delaware called
publicly on Wallace for a detailed explanation. With a completely
documented Department release on the affair, Wallace sent a
covering letter showing that no public money had gone into the
excursion, and that its inception had been spontaneous. Then:

> ... Efforts are being made by strong and directly inter-
> ested groups to abolish the processing taxes, which to my
> mind may properly be called 'the farmer's tariff.' These
> processor groups for many years have maintained strong
> lobbies in Washington. To my mind, there is nothing repre-
> hensible in farmers making their voices heard in the capital
> along with that of the processor lobbies. . . .

By the end of his first year as Secretary, Wallace had traveled
forty thousand miles by train, car, ship, and plane through all
forty-eight states. He had made eighty-eight speeches and had
written twenty articles for periodicals, not to mention three books,
one long and two short ones. Then, of course, he was running with
a generally admitted efficiency a key department of the government that was getting on toward a total personnel of one hundred
thousand. But the governing general impression of the man remained that of a shy, meditative philosopher, almost a recluse.
The heavier and more troubled the going, the more detached and
philosophical he would sometimes seem.

'Is he a good executive?' people kept asking, in tones of doubt.
The only possible answer to that at first was yes and no. No, in
the sense of bare-top desk executive display and snap. He brought
with him from journalism the simplest method of journalistic
execution: Put what you have to do on one side of your desk with
a wastebasket handy; get through it; clear the desk. In official
Washington that method had of course to be modified from the
first. There are endless tags, multiplied copies, miles of files.
But Wallace soon found that he could still follow straight-line
methods and let other people attend to the ritual and details.

He went at things very simply, picked his closest aides and key men carefully, then turned them loose, with the warning that they, themselves, were not to get involved exclusively in any one special line of bureaucratic work or ritual. Wallace rather soon had the Department humming at an extraordinarily high pitch of action, confidence, and common understanding of its principal purposes, and nearly everyone was doing an amazing amount of work. As time went on and action widened, he added to his immediate staff young specialists trained especially in the rites of modern organization — Milo Perkins, R. M. Evans, James Mc-Camy, Leon Wolcott. But he never allowed increasing costs and cycles of organization to become impersonal or binding; and no inner circle ever formed around him, or held for long, that could cut him off from contact from without.

He gave little thought to the dignity of his office; in warm weather he would sometimes receive visitors as eminent in sartorial perfection as Senator J. Hamilton Lewis without putting a coat on, in short sleeves and rumpled trousers. One reason his clothes looked so often as if he had slept in them was simply that, through long and tedious conferences, he seemed virtually to sleep, with his eyes open, sprawled almost flat in a tilted desk chair with his feet on the edge of the desk, or on the supporting edge of a near-by wastebasket. This air of profound abstraction, or bored absentmindedness, did not add to his reputation as an alert executive; yet, as a matter of fact, this very habit, or practice, of seeming to go into solitude in the midst of babble partly explains why Wallace can do so much and stand it. Everyone has practiced, perhaps, this form of rest or relaxation, in some measure, during lectures, sermons, or in conference. Some men 'doodle,' making endless meaningless drawings. Wallace when half listening moves not so much as a finger; he simply relaxes, and he has it down to an art.

With personal callers, it all depended on whether the caller was interesting, and had something interesting to talk about; or whether it was simply someone who insisted on coming in. 'Courtesy calls' were frequently something of a trial to Wallace. Wallace was never discourteous, but cordial chat on matters of no moment is not to his liking; he has little talent for small talk.

Ten minutes, duly laid off on his schedule for visits with important people, sometimes passed slowly, in a strained fashion, with long silences on both sides. Wallace never seemed embarrassed by such silences; he simply went on resting, speaking briefly and pleasantly whenever there seemed to be some point to it.

When a man came in angry, that was something else. Then Wallace sat up straight and talked straight. But here, again, his manner with callers was markedly different from that of the master politician, the President. The easy affability, the charm turned on and off so skillfully, simply was not there. Wallace seemed to have no gift or inclination for the rôle in which President Roosevelt, as a political executive, seemed strongest; no power of diplomatic personal placation at all. He had charm — in a quieter way, as much charm as the President, but he could not jolly angry people or soothe hurt pride. Instead of pouring on the oil, he shrank almost morbidly from the most ordinary manifestations of human littleness and spite. But he listened and learned and when he had made up his mind, he acted. He could be tough. Some of his decisions seemed brusque, even ruthless. In the dislocations and realignments that followed, organization morale was shaken, and the just seemed to suffer with the unjust. Wallace worried about that, but, once the decision was announced, he would discuss it with no one. He would shoulder the consequences and stand, even among his intimates, alone. And generally after a while things would go better.

In foreseeing trends, in forming policies, in sticking to first principles under the laws he administered, in securing necessary changes in legislation and administration, and in winning from nearly all who worked with him a highhearted allegiance tinged with awe, Wallace, even in his first four years as a public official, became a highly effective executive. But he still did not look or act like the prevailing public idea of an executive — a stereotype determined in some part, I believe, by those haughty-looking males in the whisky advertisements. For my part, a good executive should be first of all an imaginative, gifted, and active teacher, equipped to impart a human understanding of and an excited sense of participation in the enterprise he heads. Wallace did that. To an extraordinary extent, the people who worked for him felt that they knew not only their own jobs but where their part fitted into the whole, and what the whole business was all about.

'If it fails to work,' the President had said, in submitting the first Farm Act to Congress, 'I shall be the first to inform you.' At all points of partial failures, or doubt, Wallace took this promise literally, as the President's representative. He took the public into his confidence bluntly and ahead of time, before every principal point of swerve and change. In admitting mistakes in detail, as to appointments or policy, within the Department, Wallace was no less forthright to those of his inner councils. Most of the new appointments that he made or authorized in Triple-A, or in old-line bureaus now working along corrclated lines of research and exploration with Triple-A and the Department's other action arms, proved good ones. If he looked at persons and proposals deliberately, cold-bloodedly, and took time to question them evenly about their plans or motives, his powers of penetration even then were remarkably canny; he was seldom deceived. But he had, in his earliest years of public service, rather too high a tolerance for persons ablaze with intentions, or expression of intentions, which struck him as vital to the need of a sick world. For example, there was his appointment of Nicholas Roerich, primarily known as promoter of the Roerich Pact for the promotion of cultural treasures and world peace. He was sent as a member of an expedition of plant explorers seeking new strains of grasses in upland China that might help stitch down the dust storms on our High Plains. Roerich had some knowledge of botany and of the dialects spoken in that far part of the world; but the Banner of Peace meetings that he and his son, who served as his secretary, held upon arrival in China had nothing at all to do with grass seed. Watching the performance from afar, Wallace, who had announced the appointment on his own responsibility, terminated it likewise, with a curt cable dismissing both Roerichs from Government service. Then he called in, one by one, everyone who had counseled him against the venture, and thanked them, saying that they had been right and he had been headstrong.

Lines of defense which men of science draw around their special

confines or parcels of knowledge are sometimes as hard to sur-
mount or penetrate as separating boundaries of geographical location.   All sorts of bureaucratic words apply to such an administrative undertaking: co-operation, co-ordination, integration, co-
implementation, and many more.   But such words are but verbal
embroidery, screening distrust, when a common understanding,
ordinary human sympathy, and a simple friendliness are lacking.
Quite early in his first term as Secretary, Wallace decided that
his warring specialists ought to make friends and a common cause
on the 'central and unifying' ground of an improved general
nutrition.   This required a little sincere and dignified back-
slapping within the Department.   With the Secretary increasingly
confined, a prisoner within his office, the Assistant Secretary,
Wilson, attended to that.   He was good at it.   Wallace's deep
inner qualities of compassion and friendship do not strike readily
through the armor of the spirit, and show in easy, familiar ways.
Wilson's do.   He sprawls and ambles conversationally, exerting
personal persuasion with easy *bonhomie*, and many a homely yarn.
That is one point where Wilson supplemented Wallace so remarkably when they worked together.   They worked rather closely together for more than seven years.   Some of their first attempts
to make various bureau chiefs and holders of Sigma Xi keys
realize the ideal of 'unity amid diversity' in a continuing and
permanent program for the Department bore consequences that
were occasionally ludicrous; but even so it was better to have men
laughing together than standing far apart and giving one another
the fishy eye.

A luncheon for bureau chiefs was planned as an exploratory
step.   The Secretary presided.   Wilson led the talk.   The guest
of honor was a foreign scientist of some eminence.   He had written
a popular book.   The scientists present were suspicious of that.
His English was hard to follow.   His loftier observations smacked
of mysticism on a highly misty level.   As a catalyst invited to
draw warring specialists together, it soon was plain that he was
getting nowhere fast.   With homely tact Wilson drew the talk
down from the infinite to the particular.   Had the Doctor any
suggestions as to nutritional experiments which might unite the
interest of workers, say, in sociology and animal husbandry?

Well, the Doctor had been doing some work with dogs and mice. With what conclusions? Here the Doctor, sensing the atmosphere of scientific men heavy about him, turned cagey and had to be coaxed. Tentatively, however, he had found that well-fed mice inclined in a maze test to be comparatively stupid. Half-starved mice seemed smarter. 'That,' remarked an iconoclastic bureaucrat to his neighbor, audibly, 'would appear to be evidence in justification of the Department's scarcity policy.'

Wallace liked that, and used it quietly as a goad. Conservation of the source and a more rational dispersal of full nutrition were the living heartbeat of his developing, permanent policy for Agriculture and the whole economy from 1934 onward. His first and leading challenge to Milo Perkins, when Perkins came in from the world of business as a policy-making aide in 1935, was simply: 'Help us find some sensible, businesslike, and humane way to cut through the paradox of general want amid abundance.' To Triple-A leaders in private conference during the second and third winter of the New Deal, Wallace was equally plain. 'Triple-A,' he said, 'had got to get honest conservation for its money, or Triple-A will go down the drain.'

Ruction from without as to Triple-A continued, but the organization was no longer sharply divided within itself, and its chief administrators, having developed insensitive hides by this time, bore their troubles less weightedly than before. 'Crises? We thrive on them,' the Secretary told reporters when they questioned him about ten thousand Los Angeles housewives who were bombarding the Department with telegrams protesting against the drought-raised price of meat. And what of pressure from the Cotton South for a twelve-cents-a-pound commodity loan on cotton? Here Wallace was cautious. 'I do not want to say anything that will furnish a tip-sheet for gamblers. But I do not like to see any group overplay its hand. Properly worked through the Commodity Credit Corporation, and properly coupled with production control, these loans-without-recourse can provide us with an Ever-Normal Granary that will be of infinite value. But if the farmers get too greedy, their welfare might explode on them later on.' The loan proposal for that year was settled at eight cents a pound. Huey Long, meantime, had gone up to Wallace's home country and denounced him as 'The Ignoramus from Iowa,' and Gene Talmadge of Georgia had screamed from the same Mid-western platform that for Wallace to have delivered a memorial address to Thomas Jefferson at Atlanta, Georgia, was a 'mock-ery.' Wallace said he was surprised that Huey and Gene had paid him so much attention: 'I thought that I was so far to the Right they couldn't even see me.'

On January 6, 1936, the Supreme Court, six against three, declared the Agricultural Adjustment Act unconstitutional. While the decision was neither unpredictable nor unforeseen, it came sooner and was more sweeping than most partisans of Triple-A anticipated. Now, processing taxes could no longer be collected, adjustment payments to farmers had to be held up, and the sign-up campaign for the 1936 adjustment program was stopped, head-on. Though the Court's decision in the Schechter case as to NRA had forewarned Triple-A officials, the increased severity of the Triple-A decision dealt them a stunning blow. Paul Porter came that day into the Secretary's luncheon room looking dazed. 'What do you make of it, Paul?' his colleagues asked him, as a lawyer. 'Well, I'll tell you,' he said, 'as I was coming down the hall I put my foot on the treadle of a drinking fountain, and the damn' thing still worked.'

Within twenty-four hours Wallace went on the air with a brief, grave statement: 'Both the majority and minority opinions are epochal. I urge that they be read in full and studied carefully in every American home.' On January 13 the Supreme Court or-dered that nearly two hundred million dollars which had been collected in processing taxes be returned to the processors. On the fourteenth, again on the air, Wallace said dryly: 'I do not question the legality of this action, but I certainly do question the justice of it.'

'Thus far,' he went on to say, 'the farmers, like many of the rest of us, are a good bit like the man who has just had the breath knocked out of him. When he comes to, he doesn't know whether to laugh, cry, or cuss. The Administrator of Triple-A, Chester Davis, and I decided to grin and go to work. . . . The important thing . . . is to do some cool, hard, and determined thinking as to what can best be done as soon as possible to repair the damage to farmers and conserve the general welfare. Triple-A is not dead. . . .'

On January 28 he attacked harder, arguing: 'In the Hoosac Mills case, the Supreme Court disapproved the idea that the Government could take money from one group for the benefit of another. Yet in turning over to the processors this two hundred million dollars which came from *all* the people, we are seeing the most flagrant example of expropriation for the benefit of one small group. This is probably the greatest legalized steal in American history.'

Representative Allen Treadway of Massachusetts announced on the floor of the House that Wallace should be impeached for contempt of the Supreme Court. 'Well,' said Wallace, when questioned at his next press conference, 'I simply stated what seems to me the justice of the situation. It is the essence of government to prevent injustice from flowing out of so-called legal acts.'

'Do you think, Mr. Secretary,' asked Felix Belair, Jr., of *The New York Times* in friendly mockery, 'that the Supreme Court follows the election returns?'

Wallace grinned cautiously. 'Belatedly,' he replied. Then he put before the assembled reporters the essence of a new Soil Conservation and Domestic Allotment Bill, drafted in the Department, on the legal basis of an already enacted Act, very broadly drawn to authorize the activities of the Soil Conservation Service in 1934. When this Act, in a changed and enlarged form, had passed, he went on the air again March 3, 1936, and remarked with evident relief:

'I believe that under this new program we can do a more constructive job of putting a firm physical base under our civilization than has ever been done by any great nation with a continental climate. I am confident that if we are able to overcome successfully the very real technical difficulties which now confront us because of the shortage of time, the new plan will be so universally accepted and appreciated by all interests in our society that it will continue for many years.'

In 1936 the drought, which had relented in 1935, struck hard again. 'Meat strikes,' and other agitations of consumer protest, arising in 1935 out of drought reductions in addition to the planned reductions of 1934, continued sporadically, and were somewhat troublesome in a campaign year. In the Roosevelt-Langdon skirmish of 1936, Wallace made some speeches, surely not among his most memorable. He pointed out that, for all their shouting, the Republicans were simply declaring for a continuation of the farm program without substantial change, whereas the Democrats had in process definite changes and improvements.

Gales of opinion aroused by the proposed compulsory Potato Control Act beat in more hotly upon him than did any campaign issue. Republican growers in Maine, oddly, were just as strong for compulsion as were Democratic growers in Florida. Everything was confused. Even as Wallace in press conference was declaring flatly, 'I am going to do all that I can to avoid enforcing the Potato Control Bill; let me make that clear,' a Philadelphia society lady was planting potatoes in her front lawn and daring him to come there in person and tear them out.

A minor diverting incident of the campaign came of the fact that, clinging or reverting to the family's original party tenets, both of Uncle Henry's surviving sons, John P. Wallace and 'Uncle' Daniel A., came out for Landon. Not only that, they traveled with him on his campaign train and gave him advice on his farm speeches. A woman correspondent also of Landon's campaign retinue sent Henry A. a joshing telegram:

AM ON ALF LANDON'S TRAIN ENTIRELY SURROUNDED BY YOUR UNCLES STOP WHAT DO I DO QUERY.

Henry wired back:

HAMLET KNEW WHAT TO DO WITH UNCLES.

As 1936 drew toward an end, Tugwell's departure from public life in Washington was known to be imminent. He had accepted for the while a traveling consultancy in the firm of an old associate, another presidential advisor in Caribbean affairs, Charles Taussig. The firm dealt in molasses. Everybody found it amusing that austere, immaculate Rex should enter the molasses business. 'Our leading brand,' he told friends gleefully, 'is "Grandma." And the slogan on the label, so help me, is "Look for Grandma on the Can"'!'

Soon we shall part from Rex Tugwell in the pages of this narrative. He made a South American business voyage, then became head of planning for the La Guardia administration of New York City. In the four years that he labored in Agriculture he did that Department a great deal of good. Amazing contradictions between the Tugwell you knew and the Tugwell you read about in the papers, as Under-Secretary of Agriculture and later as Governor of Puerto Rico, must always seem to people who worked with him one of the most bewildering examples of a deliberately rigged and distorted public opinion in our time.

Partly because he was not one hundred per cent rural, accustomed to a gradual skinning of farm and range landscapes which seemed to residents to alter little from year to year; largely because he had keen eyes and an outside view when traveling through farmland and rangeland, Tugwell saw that much of our open country, quite apart from gullied wastes, was in fearfully bad shape. He saw that what Hugh Bennett said about imperceptible erosion was true. As has been recorded, it was due to Tugwell more than to anyone else that Bennett and his new corps of soil rangers, the Soil Conservation Service, could 'roll up their sleeves' and go out to 'make America over' along the lines of safer farming in a new design.

Partly, again, because he had not been reared in a completely calloused rural tradition by Old Homestead or rugged pioneer standards, Tugwell could not regard hired men (those lovable, humble, shiftless creatures of rural legend) as something subhuman, beyond hope of advance. With a characteristic combination of chill realism and warm sensitivity he saw plainly that, with the country filled up and farming increasingly industrialized, the day had passed when farm laborers could be part of the family and work their way at all readily up the ladder to farm ownership. He held that farm laborers, fixed and transient, should have a union, and a strong one. He held further that if one arm of the Department, Triple-A, worked for the advantaged element in the farm population, it was the Department's responsibility equally to advance effective programs to improve the lot of the disadvantaged.

It surpasses understanding how completely insensitive most Land Grant College graduates were to the widespread spectacle of a grinding rural poverty and the degradation of rural labor.

Most of the men in the most powerful positions within the Department were of Land Grant College antecedents and training. Only a few changed their minds or enlarged their sympathies. When, at the turn of 1936 into 1937, Wallace had to decide whether to keep an equivalent of Resettlement, an organization under bitter attack, operating in the Department after Tugwell left, practically all the old-line Department men advised their Secretary vehemently to let go, unload. Tugwell and Dr. Will Alexander, whom Tugwell had chosen to succeed him as head of Resettlement, went to Wallace. They challenged him to go afield in the Cotton South, to get out beyond the big houses with tall white pillars into the shacks and roadside slums, to look at the work which the Resettlement Administration had already accomplished, before coming to any decision. Wallace said that he would.

They laid out a two-thousand mile tour for him and he took it. 'What a trip! Two thousand miles of Tobacco Road,' Felix Belair recalls, having covered Wallace's journey of exploration for *The New York Times*. 'Dr. Will Alexander took us over the route he and Tugwell had mapped out. We started down in Arkansas, almost into Texas. We went by car across the Delta and its uplands, working both the Arkansas and Mississippi side. A good part of it was over back roads. We put up for the most part at little country hotels. Wallace would slip off and walk out into the country alone, stopping people, talking with them, visiting them in their homes. Not many people recognized him. And when I would tell some of them who they'd been talking to, not many believed it. They didn't figure it possible that a Cabinet member would be walking in on them, awaiting, just to see how they were getting along. One Sunday he slipped off and walked up into the hills and was gone all day. He said that he had gone to church with the people up there and just visited around afterwards. That was all he would say.

'Along the road in the car he was watching everything, asking questions of whatever R.A. man who was with us, or just brooding, with those bushy eyebrows of his drawn down as if he was seeing more than he could bear. Just when we'd think we were going to push on and roll up a little mileage, he'd see some old people trudging along in the dust, or some kids walking from school, and "Stop for a minute," he'd say. He would get out of the car and go up and talk with these people. Nobody seemed to be shy of him or think it was strange for him to ask the questions he did. He asked the kids how much milk they drank, or how often they had oranges or green vegetables, and what they were learning in school. He asked the older people about T.B. and pellagra and malaria and crops. They all answered him with perfect dignity, black and white. What he learned didn't generally cheer him. "It's incredible," he kept saying, "incredible!"

'At Memphis, in the lobby of the Peabody Hotel, he started to talk, and answer some of the questions I had to ask him. He said he was going to make some changes in the setup of Resettlement, and probably get some of the younger men in the Department to help Dr. Will run it; but he asked me not to print anything until he had gotten in touch with Tugwell. Somebody had sent him a new book by Arthur Raper, *A Preface to Peasantry*, a study of conditions among white and colored tenants in two Georgia counties. "To call these miserable people peasants," he said, "really offends the peasantry of Europe. I have been in the homes of peasants of Czecho-Slovakia and the Balkan countries and they seem now like palaces compared with what we have here in the Cotton Belt."'

The party proceeded to Moultrie, Georgia, where they met Tugwell, who was on his way for a rest in Florida before going to his new work. Next day, from Macon, Belair filed to *The New York Times* his summary report of the trip. He quoted Wallace as saying: 'It is a really marvelous job that Resettlement has done toward reducing tenancy among the underprivileged farmers of the South and toward arresting further destruction of its greatest resource, the soil. Especially is that true when you consider that all this work was done with emergency funds that made operations other than on a month-to-month basis impossible.'

On the last leg of his trip Wallace saw families of three or four who were living on corn bread and molasses and sleeping on the floor, while the only blankets they owned were being used to cover a pile of newly picked tobacco in a corner of the same room. He

was frequently told that some of these families would continue to
sleep on the floor even if the Government bought them beds and
would move a donated bathtub out in the yard so a fire could be
built under it to do the family wash. They were beyond 'rehabilitation' by the Resettlement Administration or any other
agency.

Many of the families themselves told Wallace they would do
anything if given a chance to get one of the neat cottages which
were being built on an experimental scale by the Resettlement Administration. And after one trip off to the home of a tenant who
had received a small loan but was not a member of any of the
regular projects, he said: 'If some of these people live to become
millionaires they probably will never experience anything more
revolutionary than coming into possession of a mule, wagon, and
a wood stove for cooking which an insignificant number have
obtained through the Resettlement Administration.'

Wallace told of finding one sharecropper's shack that had
neither doors nor windows. There was no stove and there were
gaping holes in the roof, floor, and ceiling. The Secretary was
surprised to learn that the occupant was a client of the Resettlement Administration under its rehabilitation program. The man
had borrowed three hundred dollars to buy a mule and farming
equipment. From the standpoint of social advancement, he appeared to be one of the worst clients, but the loan had been repaid
and the barn repaired. The cropper had terraced his heaviest
slopes and carried out the Resettlement Administration plan set
for him.

According to Belair: 'Secretary Wallace's tour virtually
clinched the establishment of the Resettlement Administration
as a part of the Department of Agriculture.'

The Department of Agriculture was a somewhat duller but
more peaceful place with Tugwell gone. On July 22, 1937, a new
rural rehabilitation measure, the Bankhead-Jones Farm Tenancy
Act, was approved. It authorized the Secretary of Agriculture
to (1) lend money to farm tenants for the purchase of farms,
(2) make rehabilitation loans to farmers for subsistence, improvement, and other purposes, (3) develop a program of land utilization, including the retirement of marginal land, (4) complete

SOUTH AMERICAN TRIP, 1943
Two Stops in Ecuador

projects begun by the Resettlement Administration and other agencies. On September 1, 1937, the Farm Security Administration was set up in the Department; and Wallace detailed two of his closest personal aides, Benham Baldwin and Milo Perkins, to work as co-administrators with Dr. Alexander.

After a droughty 1936, 1937 opened with terrific bursts of rain. On January 27, in press conference, Wallace, with Weather Bureau data before him, said: 'Rainfall for the first twenty-six days of January was from five to six times normal. A total of 182 counties seem to have been flooded or partly flooded.' By March floods were exceedingly serious from the mouth of the Potomac to the Mississippi Delta. Closely questioned by Middle-Southerners as to whether floodwater remaining on fields of the Mississippi Valley might delay spring sowing and reduce cotton output, Wallace answered that this was possible; such at least had been a result of the previous great flood of 1927. And would not drought, if it resumed with any such intensity as in previous droughts of 1934 and 1936, lead to a very serious shortage in some crops? Yes, Wallace answered, and, pleading once again for his Ever-Normal Granary, came out flatly for the first time for 'full bins' in 1938, and a slackening of planting restrictions. Drought did recur, but by April it was not as serious as it had been in April of 1934 and 1936. And by the middle of May Wallace could announce: 'For the moment, anyway, the drought is over on the Great Plains.' He continued to ply the spur for fuller production, though not without controls. 'The real story of the 1938 program,' he told representatives of the press on September 1, 1937, 'centers around the word g-o-a-l. Get that, or it will bump you in the face later on.' The country was still in the clutch of the 1937 business depression, more soothingly termed a 'recession,' but in 1936 world prices had started to rise as an international armament race gained furious pace, and raw materials in general seemed to be pointing for a rise. Wallace, discussing such trends on and off the record, seemed to have discounted the sag in wheat and other domestic prices as a lull before a war boom. In any event, he was plainly no longer worrying about crop surpluses. It was the increasing prospect of a bloody and impermanent deliverance from the problems of underemployment and 'superabundance' that principally concerned him now. He had called the turn in August of 1934. Now he bore ahead to fill the nation's bins.

His relationship with the White House at this period was markedly off-and-on. That never seemed to bother him. 'Old Man Common Sense,' the President called him when pleased with him. In the interterm campaign of 1938, however, when Ickes, Hopkins, Corcoran, and others of the immediate inner circle at the White House persuaded the President to come out for purging Senators Tydings of Maryland, George of Georgia, and Gillette of Iowa because they were considerably less than one hundred per cent New Dealers in their voting records, Wallace went twice to the White House to tell the President that such a maneuver would not work; and this pleased neither the President nor the originators of the maneuver. Again, late in 1935, when Wallace wrote an article for *Collier's* arguing for the establishment of an Economic Supreme Court, or a council of non-partisan, continuing membership guided by continuing general referenda, which would help assure a continuing and consistent national policy as to world trade, through all the changes of parties and administrations, he was out of favor for a while.[23]

But although he was surprisingly independent, he was for the most part 'regular.' He made up his own mind, but generally he followed or even anticipated the party line. He backed the Court plan of the President wholeheartedly, to the extent of getting out in 1936, with four collaborators, a book of three hundred and thirty-six pages, *Whose Constitution?* [24] Before the elections of that year, moreover, he and Mrs. Wallace went dutifully to Iowa and at last got around to changing their registration from Republican to Democrat.

With the wraps partly off farm production, with good growing weather and plenty of rain over most of the country in 1937, with the Ever-Normal Granary an established concern and filling up, with free school lunches and a developing Food Stamp Plan channeling momentary gluts of surpluses, the Department of Agriculture rocked along more evenly and efficiently than ever before in the restive nineteen-thirties. It followed a well-established course, listing neither to the right nor to the left. The

Secretary began to take it a little easier. He did not travel as far or make as many speeches in 1937 or 1938 as he had in the years just prior. But the speeches he did make he prepared more thoughtfully and delivered in better form with greater deliberation. He told a General Assembly of State Governments in Washington that if our rural people are in reality the 'backbone' of our national structure, the backbone is weakening. 'We are proceeding with a program of security for industrial workers, while among our farm population security is gradually declining. A million American farm families have an average total income of less than four hundred dollars a year. A half million farm families live on land too poor to warrant continued cultivation.' Again, on a radio program with Harper Sibley, President of the United States Chamber of Commerce, and William Green, President of the American Federation of Labor, he expressed fear of two dangers: 'One is that in their insistence on their own particular rights the largest [pressure] groups, being more skilled in running to Washington, may profit at the expense of the small units in the unorganized groups; and my other fear is that such pressure may bring about a condition of progressive scarcity and therefore a smaller national income.'

In a 1938 New Year's statement to the press, he reported for 1937 the largest agricultural production in the history of the country and challenged industry to take example and raise factory output as well. By the end of January, showing charts with lines wavering upward, he demonstrated to his press seminar that hard times again were ending. 'There has been a real improvement in psychology in the last couple of weeks. But psychology, as you know, is a very tender thing.' Back from the West Coast in March, he reported 'a certain amount of violence' arising from the rural migrant problem, but indicated that some of these Okies, Arkies, and other Grapes of Wrath people were beginning, it seemed, to be absorbed into industrial employ.

Fear of war began to agitate the country even as the enlivening influences of a rising 'defense boom' began to lessen unemployment and invigorate trade.

The revised Farm Program proved far more popular than had the initial drive for tilled-acreage reduction, not only among con-

sumers and the public in general, but among farmers. New York
State and the New England group, for example, which had hung
back in general from reduction programs, now developed excellent
conservation-allotment programs and farmers there came in now
by the thousands and signed agreements to co-operate. In 1934
Wallace, exalting his Triple-A County Agricultural Control Associations as forerunners of a new economic democracy in *New
Frontiers*, could point to four thousand such associations with a
membership of three million farmers. By 1940 six million farmers were reorganized into far more unified county planning and
working groups. There had, moreover, been formed by that
time nearly a thousand county, intercounty, or watershed Soil
Conservation Districts, legally constituted, actually a new unit
of American government, with elected resident farmer district
supervisors directing the work and technicians of the Soil Conservation Service.

All this led, quite naturally, to fear, suspicion, and charges that
Wallace was 'Tammanyizing' agriculture for New Deal political
purposes and building up on federal money an unparalleled political machine of his own. That, of course, is what gave so much
heat to the charges arising after the farm march of forty-five
hundred Triple-A committeemen and some county agents to thank
the President at the White House in 1935. And in 1939 I was
astonished when Gerald W. Johnson, then of *The Baltimore Sun*,
told me flatly that nothing on earth could stop Wallace or some
other agrarian New Dealer from being elected President in 1940.
The organization, he said, was set up and standing ready, with
every county organized, and millions of federal dollars on tap.
'Not only that,' he said, 'they've found the farmers are sick of
talking farming, so they're feeding them philosophy and music,
and they love it; they're eating it up!' In a report for the Carnegie
Foundation on the effects of Agriculture's 'action' programs, *The
Agrarian Revival*, published about that time, I entered Johnson's
observation together with reasons for doubting that anything like
that would happen:

> The command is far from absolute. The ranks are in many
> ways divided. To seek from Washington to impose on the

states and, beyond that, upon all the counties, even a new form of extension report cards arouses such a lively variety of views and such opposition that the prospect of electing a new President by use of the extension machinery seems exceedingly remote. Nowhere at any major agricultural post in Washington have I been able to discover any such ambition or tendency. Nearly all the hotheaded breaks I have come across have been far afield and widely scattered. [And] . . . nowhere do I find . . . feeling channeled along set or partisan lines. . . . Extension workers, taken as a whole, display as little interest in partisan politics as any considerable American group; and they are more deeply imbued with the spirit of civil service than any other American group with which I am acquainted, except employees of the Forest Service and of the Soil Conservation Service. I think it is nonsense to assume that extension workers could be induced in any considerable body to pump for this candidate or that. Nothing could more quickly destroy their efforts or their service. They know that; and Washington knows it.[25]

Later (1940), Gerald Johnson, estimating Wallace as he was before ever facing an election, wrote:

When Wallace is mentioned, political Washington grows strangely vague. The gossipers do not even accuse him of crime, which is almost without precedent; for there is scarcely a felony known to the law that they do not attribute to one prominent figure or another.

'I do not know the man,' said the chief of the Washington bureau of a big metropolitan daily. 'It is an embarrassing confession, for it is my business to know everybody in Washington. Oh, yes, I have interviewed him; I have attended his press conferences when he was Secretary of Agriculture; I have heard him speak; I have read his books. But I am bound to admit that I do not know Wallace.'

This is the answer one gets from the majority of the shrewder observers. . . . They say, 'He has no friends.'

This is, however, merely an example of political Washington's peculiar idiom. It gives to the word 'friends' a sig-

nificance different from that which it carries elsewhere.
Plenty of people invite Mr. Wallace to dinner. He has no
trouble finding a partner when he wishes to play tennis.
The best clubs are open to him and no doubt he could borrow money if he needed it. But in the jargon of political
Washington a politician's friend is a man who gets him a
better job, or who rounds up delegates for him in a convention, or who gives him shrewd advice as to what to think and
do. Of this sort of friends Wallace has none, nor has he ever
had any. Yet for eight years he held an official position, the
Secretaryship of Agriculture, in which the possibility of making that sort of friend is perhaps greater than in any other
post. Obviously then, if he has none, it is because he has
never chosen to make them. . . .

His tenure as Secretary coincided with the period of New
Deal agricultural experimentation, which involved not only
enormous expenditures directly to farmers, but another and
perhaps even greater factor, namely, an unprecedented
amount of indoctrination. During Wallace's régime more
agents of the Department were talking more intimately to
farmers than ever before in its history. One of the minor
activities of the program was the formation of many thousands of Farmers' clubs, covering not merely every county,
but very nearly every voting precinct in the nation. These
clubs devoted only part of their attention to the technicali-
ties of agriculture. They were organized frankly for the
enrichment of rural life culturally, as well as economically,
and any subject whatever that interested farmers and their
wives might be included in the program.

It is doubtful that the history of politics can show an in-
strumentality better suited to the purpose of erecting a
gigantic machine than this organization, penetrating into
every nook and corner of the country, and touching the
people's nearest interests. This instrument Wallace held
in his hands — and he did nothing with it to advance his
political career or to strengthen his position as one of the
dominant party chiefs. What stopped him was plain lack
of interest in that sort of thing. . . .

Mr. Wallace is a man who has come to high office without the usual long and grueling training in the art of being all things to all men; and he is not an expert in that art. More than that, and possibly more important than that, he holds an office for which he has not fought and schemed, dickered and dealt, compromised and contrived through intense and wearying years. He holds an office on which he has never set his heart, so it is reasonable to suppose that he holds it relatively lightly. It is probable that Mr. Wallace sometimes looks around him with mild wonder at what he is doing in the Vice-Presidency anyhow.

Regardless of the turn of fortune's wheel, Henry A. Wallace is one office-holder who will never be defeated. He may be retired to private life at the next election; but if that happens, he will return to Iowa where he will make a better living and probably have a better time than he has for the last ten years. That would be defeat in only a technical sense. On the other hand, if he survives in public life, it will certainly be because the ideas he advocates are pretty much in line with what the people are thinking, not by any Machiavellian strategy on his part. . . .

6. Food Stamps

In 1939, the last full year that Wallace served as Secretary of Agriculture, the situation as to agricultural supplies had come through further trials and changes. The general good growing weather of 1937 led to lower prices to farmers and threat of renewed surplus stocks, unmarketable at a price that would keep farmers buying industrial goods and the amenities of American civilization in 1939.

Wallace considered the directorship of the Surplus Market Administration the key spot in the whole Department at the time. The man who was picked for it was Milo Perkins, who had been co-administrator of the Farm Security Administration since 1935. Wallace challenged Perkins specifically to get a working plan of surplus disposal through regular trade channels to needy people, and then go out and sell his plan to the food trade.

Perkins was thoroughly qualified for this assignment. A born sales executive, he disliked small orders. He despised a philosophy of scarcity. As an evangelist of abundance he exceeded even Wallace in ardor, and his speaking style had the kick of a Texas mule. He went before city business groups, grocerymen, and chain-store executives with simple confidence that these people are just as anxious to see needy people better fed, just as emotional about it, just as decent as farmers are in general.

Perkins had come to Washington under unusual circumstances.

'Milo the bagman,' his friends called him sometimes in Washington; and indeed, his business for fifteen years was bags, gunny sacking. By the time he was twenty-three he was sales manager of the Bemis Bag Company of Houston. At twenty-six he organized it as the King-Perkins Bag Company. They were doing a million-dollar business by 1934.

About this time he was moved one evening as he sat in a hotel room to write a personal letter to Henry A. Wallace, whom he had never met. It was a forthright account of his experience, together with the flat statement that he was tired of simply working for money and would like to work in the New Deal for the ideas in which he believed. 'From childhood,' Perkins wrote Wallace, 'I have wanted to live in the world . . . so that I could leave it happier because I had worked in it. . . . I am going to throw my whole energies into working for the principles of the New Deal. . . . It occurs to me that you may have just the job for a man of my interest.' The letter reached Wallace because it interested LeCron and Appleby; they asked Milo Perkins to come on for a talk, and he was hired at a salary of $5600 a year.

Speaking as President of the Federated Commodities Surplus Corporation at Des Moines on February 20, 1940, Milo Perkins said: 'The term "surpluses" is simply a smug, polite name for a shocking amount of underconsumption. The nightmare of underconsumption — which links with unemployment or underemployment — is the Black Plague of the twentieth century.'

Total unemployment, even then, he reported as close to ten million. Then he gave a recently completed breakdown of 'average income' figures in the United States as determined by the Bureau of Labor Statistics: The average income figure, $1622.

'*But 65 per cent of our people are getting, on an average, only about one half of this amount.*' A survey covering one hundred and twenty-six million persons showed '42 per cent of our families providing only 26 per cent of our food market.' Further: 'Families receiving $312 on the average are spending only slightly more than $1 per person per week for food. With $758 average income, weekly per capita food expenditure rose to about $1.62; and with $1224 income, it rose to $2.18. I should guess the average weekly expenditure for those in this room is around $5.' In sum: 'People with incomes of under $500 have about 5 cents per person per meal for food. Families getting an income of $100 a month have about 10 cents per person per meal. The market for our farmers is doubled, so far as this group is concerned.'

Perkins has always insisted that the tradesmen to whom he took his surplus disposal problem — not he, not Wallace, or any other government official — had most to do with inventing the Food Stamp Plan. The Treasury Department and Post Office Department were of help in inventing actual procedures, but the plan itself was put into action, at first cautiously, along the lines that chain-store and grocery leaders felt were most likely to work. The program in essence was so simple that anyone could grasp it; and its appeal was direct and warming. It was a two-price system, with the 'dumping' not being done overseas, as the McNary-Haugen supporters had planned, nearly a quarter-century previously. This was a beneficent vending of cut-rate necessities, operating through established trade channels, in a way that unloaded price-depressing surpluses from the top-layer market and in the same stroke increased through better nutrition the health and vigor of low-income people.

There were two kinds of food stamps, orange and blue. First through relief agencies and later, experimentally, in some places, upon simple application to the storekeeper, the orange stamps were sold to needy people four for a dollar. For every dollar's worth of orange stamps the buyer received half again as many blue stamps free. The orange stamps were good for any commodity; the blue for foods (chiefly dairy and poultry products, meats, fruits, and vegetables) found momently to be 'in surplus.' Grocers pasted the stamps, each worth twenty-five cents, on five-dollar cards and redeemed them at the Treasury. The effect was that literally millions of city families who had been living on an average of five cents a person a meal could now raise that standard at least one half, to seven and one half cents a meal.

'At any early stage of the New Deal,' Ernest Lindley commented in *The Washington Post*, March 12, 1939, 'the plan would have been launched with fanfare, on a nationwide scale. Instead, after a year of brain-work and several months of discussions with wholesale and retail distributors, it is to be tried experimentally in about six small or medium-small cities.' That is how it was done, starting in Rochester. By the summer of 1940 the plan was operating successfully in nearly one hundred cities and six hundred other cities had applied for it. Food stamps were improving the diets of nearly four million low-income people by the end of 1940, and another 'nearly two million undernourished children are now getting their noonday lunches, in whole or in part, from vitamin-rich surplus foods.' 'We are eating the surplus!' Perkins, as President of the Federal Surplus Commodities Corporation, reported, and added a prediction: 'Some day a like composite approach, the same approach in principle, will be taken to our unemployment problem.'

XII

INTO THE NINETEEN-FORTIES

I told him [President Wilson] that this war must end
sometime; that he was the one man who could attract the
attention of all the world; that probably the time might
come when he would be able to suggest as the basis of
lasting peace the freedom of the seas and their policing by
an international fleet, so that for all time to come the nations of the world, wherever they might be located, could
freely trade with each other without fear of molestation.
I said to him that this was only a vision of mine, a dream;
that I made it to him merely as a suggestion, saying that
it was utterly impractical now and probably would not be
practical until every woman's heart in the warring nations
was broken, until the nations themselves were bankrupt.
I said to him that when that time came, surely the common
people of these nations would not permit themselves to be
crushed under an added burden of taxation, if the ends for
which the navies were built could be subserved without it;
and if the people once clearly came to see this, they would
overturn the government that insisted on breeding men for
the shambles, to carry out the ambition of their leaders.
The President said to me: 'Of course you do not expect
me to give you a definite answer on this point.' I said,
'Certainly not. It is not a plan, simply a vision, which
may mature in time, and if it does mature will give us
world peace for all time.' — From Uncle Henry's own
story of a visit to the White House in October of 1915,
his eightieth year, in *The Wallaces of Iowa*, ch. 6, p. 166.

1. Heir Apparent

Now, with prospect of a more active participation in the
war, Wallace and his aides found it necessary to issue
statement after statement decrying panic buying and food
hoarding. The Ever-Normal Granary was bulging with plenty;
but that never appeared to bother Wallace; he seemed steadily

certain that the utmost product of our land would soon be needed. Also, he foresaw shortages of products such as rubber, not native to our land. At his urging the Department of Agriculture had been pushing exploration of rubber sources since 1935. He had been studying Spanish since 1936 and could now speak the language well enough to be understood in speeches and in conversation. During the closing phases of his work as Secretary of Agriculture he placed all possible emphasis on good-neighborly relations with Pan-America, on the extension of the Ever-Normal Granary, possibly also an extension of the Food Stamp Plan, internationally, and on the continuing need of honest conservation of the country's basic resources.

As campaign time for an unprecedented third term approached, there was a notable holding-back in the usual early rush of conventional party men to climb on the incumbent's band wagon. Unconventionally, H. A. Wallace was the first of Mr. Roosevelt's official family to speak for the President's re-election. He did this on his own, but chose for the utterance a strategic place and political occasion. At a Jackson Day dinner in Des Moines on January 8, 1940, 'I hope the nominee in 1940 will be President Roosevelt,' he said bluntly. The White House issued a mild rebuke. Wallace smiled and did not apologize. The opinion, so generally held, that Wallace lacks political acumen appears to derive more often from the abruptness of his pronouncements than from any lack of pertinence to the time and leading issue. He is not given to the double-talk of routine politics, but what he has to say often proves politic. That proved true this time. The Squire was greatly pleased.

A number of circumstances other than those already suggested led the President to prefer Wallace for a running-mate in 1940, and later to refuse to run, himself, with any other. The Midland farm states, Wallace's homeland, were among the more restive under the continuing Triple-A conservation program. Farmers there, as in the agricultural South, inclined to agree that Triple-A had done some good. Four out of five of all farm families in the country, it must be recalled, were signed up and going ahead under its programs. But there was a boom in the air now, and they scented it. Again, they resented at heart having been in some part saved under compulsion of need by a heightened degree of governance from Washington. Countless irritations necessarily arise from any program in which officials pass on the complex claims and actual payments to six million different individuals. To operate such a system in time of need does not, obviously, make for total and fervent support among all six million beneficiaries of the administration momently in power.

But the main task the vice-presidential candidate faced in the Middle West during that campaign of 1940 was not to appease people who instinctively had disliked his farm program, even while they participated in it voluntarily and received its benefit payments with some pleasure. His main task was to oppose a push there spreading, with a throng of advocates increasingly active — a pro-German push for appeasing Hitler. The President understood that; and Wallace understood it well before the nominees had been determined and the 1940 campaign launched. With this much decided, the detailed approach in opening principal campaign speeches was left largely to Wallace, who made them. Already, with a sort of wise innocence, Wallace in a number of 1939 addresses, quite unlike stump speeches, and certainly non-partisan or bipartisan, had laid down what turned out to be a main line.

He paid tribute to Dr. Franz Boas, for having 'done much to marshal the moral forces of scientists,' on February 12, 1939:

> Claims to racial superiority are not new in this world. Even in such a democratic country as ours there are those who would claim that the American people are superior to all others. But never before in the world's history has such a conscious and systematic effort been made to inculcate the youth of this nation with ideas of racial superiority as are being made in Germany today.

> We must remember that down through the ages one of the most popular political devices has been to blame economic and other troubles on some minority group.

> Superior ability is not the exclusive possession of any one race or any one class. It may arise anywhere, provided men are given the right opportunities.

Along with the plight of Negroes and Jews, Wallace considered that of 'the so-called poor whites':

Now, it is the fashion in many quarters to sneer at those . . .
who suffer from poor education and bad diet . . . live in
tumble-down cabins without mattresses.   And yet I wonder
if any scientist would claim that 100,000 children taken at
birth from these families would rank any lower in inborn
ability than 100,000 children taken at birth from the wealthi-
est one per cent of the parents of the United States.   If both
groups are given the same food, housing, education, and
cultural traditions, would they not turn out to have about
equal mental and moral traits on the average? . . .

The survival and strength of American democracy are
proof that it has succeeded by its deeds thus far.   But we all
know that it contains the seeds of failure.   I for one will not
be confident of the continued survival of American democracy
if millions of unskilled workers and their families are con-
demned to be reliefers all their lives, with no place in our
industrial system.   I will not be confident of the survival of
democracy if half our people must be below the line of a decent
nutrition, while only one tenth succeed in reaching good
nutritional standards.   I will not be confident of the survival
of democracy if most of our children continue to be reared in
surroundings where poverty is highest and education is
lowest. . . .

This address, entitled 'The Genetic Basis of Democracy,'
aroused fervent interest among important leaders, intellectual
and political, of racial minority groups.   Judge Samuel I. Rosenman in particular carried such word to the White House, favoring
Wallace, and the Judge's word at the White House bore weight.
Among more experienced politicians, Ed Flynn had come to
like and admire Wallace; and he pointed out to the President that,
with racial tension on the increase and the Negro vote restless,
Wallace had a quiet but strong following, especially among
Northern Negroes, who had votes.

Rather more than the obvious fact that Wallace had been Secretary of Agriculture, and chanced to come from the right part of the
country, entered, then, into President Roosevelt's stubborn insistence upon Wallace as his 1940 running-mate.   The President had

at that time, it plainly appears, some sense of premonition that his health might break during the four years of a third term. He discussed with various intimates and visitors, merely as a possibility, the outside chance of a midterm retirement, and said he must have to succeed him a Vice-President on whose stature he could depend. This bit of conversational speculation leaked out. Later, amid the storms of the 1940 Democratic convention, hoodlums booing the name and person of the President's choice as vice-presidential nominee, and discontented Southerners phoning the President to ask why one of their men couldn't have it, the President, in the White House, was heard by phone to declare robustly: 'Good God, no!' with a further historical reference to a work-weary president[1] who caught pneumonia at his inauguration and died quickly. 'I've got to have a man I know can do this job: Wallace,' barked F. D. R. in his most commanding quarter-deck manner. So Wallace it was.

At first it was arranged that Wallace would take leave as Secretary to campaign, returning to the same chair for the interim between November and January, and having a hand in the selection of his successor to that chair. When, in his absence, this strategy was abruptly shifted, first within the Department, then without; when it became plain that he would not resume the Secretariat for the post-election interim, Wallace accepted the decision with an air of complete indifference. He resigned his Cabinet post on August 13, 1940. Afield, he made up for the President a private list of five men who might, he said, make good as Secretary of Agriculture. So, closing that door behind him, he never went back.

Final arrangements, resulting in the appointment of Secretary Claude Wickard, were made in hastening scurries within the Department and out to the farm organizations by persons far more immediately concerned as to who would next sit in that big front office of Agriculture than Wallace ever was.

'I confess to a wrench of the heart,' said the Secretary of Agriculture at his closing press conference, 'at leaving this Department where my father worked before me. This is not an easy parting for me.' But he brightened up noticeably during even his first few days of relative freedom. Large when he took it over, the

Department now had grown enormous, both in physical size and enlarged functions.   There were ten and one half miles of corridors in its two main buildings on the Mall now, with seven miles of them in the great south building ('our back forty,' Wallace used to call it) alone.   Washington building laws hold the height of structures along the Mall down to six stories.   But if these two great Agricultural buildings, which join by arcades, were turned on end, they would tower as skyscrapers far above the near-by Washington Monument and dwarf in bulk even the Empire State Building in New York.   'A rather imposing sector of the bureaucratic hierarchy,' Wallace called it at a parting dinner given him at the Press Club by three hundred and fifty of 'the still-imprisoned,' and he spoke in jocund mood of the prospect of only two helpers 'telling me what not to say.'

His campaign aides were James LeCron, who was taking leave from the Department, and David Cushman Coyle, free-lance economist and pamphleteer.   Coyle edited, and supplied with a throbbing introduction for campaign purposes, a revision of Wallace's Home Library pamphlet *Paths to Plenty*, retitled *The Price of Freedom*.   From Coyle's Preface:

> In time of fear, when men feel helpless against the flood of disaster, it is natural to cry to God, but this book is no cry of fear.   Henry Wallace, man of affairs, with knowledge of corn and cattle and forests, of markets and of foreign commerce, manager of billion-dollar enterprises, sets the living religion of America against the path of the living religion of the Conqueror of Europe. . . .
>
> In this month of August, 1940, as we watch the last free country of Europe stand, perhaps only for a moment, against the conqueror's progress, we know that the outcome will not be decided by the number of planes alone, for if that were all, the victim might as well surrender at once.   There is an unseen power of courage and sacrifice and mutual help, a power long unused and corrupted by wealth and selfishness, but roused again and gaining strength.   If the faith and courage of free men can match the miracle-working powers and the material advantage of the conqueror, another miracle

will happen as it did in the time of the Great Armada. Guns and faith together are weighed in the scales of history, and the spiritual is as heavy a counterweight as the material. . . .

There is still decency and good-will, there is still the ideal of freedom, there is still the hope of a world where not only the closed brotherhood of the Dictator's Party, but all sorts and conditions of men, may find tolerance, mutual help, and happiness. All this is left out of the ideal world of the conqueror. And if free men have not lost their ancient virtue, this lack will be the conqueror's defeat. He can overcome the weak but he cannot make his victims love him, and in the end, we still believe, God will not be mocked.

At the campaign's very opening Wallace threw an unexpected punch by 'branding,' as the headlines cried, the Republicans as 'the party of appeasement.' This, in the speech accepting the vice-presidential nomination in his home town, Des Moines, aroused cries of 'foul' and a great furor. The line of attack thus laid down enlivened the campaign enormously; for the challenge struck through strictly party lines to separate those in both parties who wished to stand clear of worldwide explosion and attend so far as possible to our own business, and those who backed the President in strides already taken to join forces, at the imminent risk of actual war, with the Allied powers against the Axis.

Proceeding from a flat statement that 'the dictators have definite designs against this hemisphere,' Wallace spoke of their efforts to set 'class against class,' apparent then on this side of the Atlantic. Then: 'If the Americas present to the Axis powers the same divided front as the democracies of Europe presented to them, we shall assuredly walk the same path of destruction and lost freedom. In the United States, as well as in the other Americas, we find certain men who for purposes of their own profit want England to give up her fight against Hitler and who are strong for economic appeasement between the Americas and a German-controlled Europe. In that direction lies slavery, even though it is sugar-coated with promises of prosperity. Those who stand for business appeasement with Germany are the backbone, even though unwittingly, of the most dangerous of all fifth columns.'

Elsewhere in the same speech and in later ones, Wallace inter-jected the sentence: 'Whether it knows it or not, the Republican party is the party of appeasement.' That sentence stuck in the public mind. Multiplied evidences not only of pro-German oppo-sition and resentment, but of organized efforts for appeasement, came forth clearly as Wallace and his two-man campaign staff worked their way on through the Middle West. The sometimes rowdy demonstrations made Wallace stick his chin out ever more firmly when they tried to howl him down. Sometimes the howls and hisses swept his words from the ears of his immediate hearers; but he kept on repeating them; and the newspapers printed them, in the main. First launched as a simple statement of complete conviction, which he undertook to document later in a pamphlet, *The American Choice*,[2] from sources as various as Hitler, Rauschning, *The New York Herald Tribune*, Veblen, and *Fortune's* 1940 poll of fifteen thousand American business executives, Wallace hammered away along this line over protests to the White House of more orthodox Democratic politicians who felt that such statements might turn out to be a sort of blow below the belt, enraging iso-lationists in both major parties.

The orthodox Democrats turned out to be right about that. But the over-all effect of Wallace's hammering on this theme was such that the master politician in the White House sent him a wire of public congratulation. Even more important, the Republican candidate, Wendell Willkie, immediately was stung to declare that he, too, was one hundred per cent against appeasement. As the campaign leveled off into somewhat steadier going, argument proceeded on a much higher level of leader agreement as to inter-national attitudes than might at first have been expected.

In the President's acceptance speech of third-term candidacy he expressed gratitude that Henry A. Wallace had been chosen by the Democrats as candidate for 'the high office of President of the United States.' This obvious slip of the tongue revived the talk about Wallace really being run for President in the four-year term to come. Representative Andersen of Minnesota declared to the House on September 23, 1940, that if President Roosevelt were re-elected he would turn the presidency over to Wallace 'within the next year or two.' Mr. Roosevelt in press conference declined to comment on this observation at the time, merely tilting his cigarette holder upward, and smiling roguishly. Wallace, of course, had nothing to say on the question. He continued hammering his way westward, branding fewer Republicans as appeasers. The President had thus far likewise continued to parry questions whether he, like Wallace, felt that a considerable part of the opposition to his re-election was being stirred up from Berlin. Early in October, however, the President read, light-heartedly, into the record of one of his press conferences a *New York Times* dispatch from Rome by Herbert Matthews: 'The Axis is out to defeat President Roosevelt. . . . The . . . election is of vast importance to the Axis. Therefore the normal strategy for the Axis is to do something before November 5 that would some-how have a great effect on the electoral campaign.' It was evident that this 'drafted' veteran campaigner was getting restless, yearning for the fray. Toward November, again in press conference, he made passing reference to all that he would have to do in 'the next four years.' A reporter put the question: 'Do, you mean that, if re-elected, you will, God willing, serve the full four-year term?'

'Of course,' said the President. 'You can quote me, if you want.' He gazed at his desk for a moment then lifted his head, and added quietly, 'I'm glad you put in, "God willing."'

Ed Flynn had been in, expressing some doubt as to the outcome in New York and the Northeast, particularly. In mid-October a ten-car Presidential special, with an accompanying party of forty aides and politicos and forty-five reporters and camera-men, moved out of the Washington yards on an 'inspection' tour of points in Ohio and Pennsylvania, important territory that Wendell Willkie had covered as a speaking candidate not long before. At Johns-town, wearing his Navy cape, the President simply waved to the throngs cheering madly above the music of high-school bands. At Akron he made a short off-the-cuff talk, defending what in the First World War was known as 'preparedness,' and now was known as 'defense.' He spoke almost within hearing of the roar and mut-ter of steel mills hammering day and night. At Dayton, in a pre-pared speech, the President declared: 'No combination of dictator

countries of Europe and Asia will stop the help that we are giving
to almost the last free people now fighting to hold them at bay.'

After that there was no holding him, and certainly no loyal
Democrat wanted to. Even opposition reporters and persons of
both parties who feared, distrusted, or disliked Franklin D. Roosevelt could hardly help sharing, in some measure, the high good
time he had when he put on his speaking tour of the Northeast,
the campaign's best and final show. With Willkie laboring hero-
ically and getting hoarse; with Wallace plugging along a following
route in more Western territory, the President touched at Wilmington, skirted Philadelphia by way of factory districts with
millions of people waving flags and yelling, and spoke before
eighteen thousand jam-packed into Convention Hall there that
night.

Back he dashed for quick conferences on foreign affairs in
Washington, then up to New York he rolled to parade through five
boroughs and make six talks in a day, topping it off with a seventh,
carefully and zestfully prepared for delivery, at Madison Square
Garden that evening. Beyond cavil, he was the greatest, most
spirited, and altogether the most captivating demo-aristocratic
campaigner of this land and time, and possibly of all lands and
times. The most captivating feature of the whole performance
was simply that he loved it and enjoyed it so. Franklin Delano
Roosevelt's greater and deeper qualities of mind and character
never got in the way of a gorgeous circus when he rolled forth
magnificently to meet the people and give them a good, stimulating
political show. But he also was deeply interested in getting to
them, somehow, more and better bread, and more than bread.

Once the President stepped out to tour, Wallace's campaign
speeches, initially most important, were ordained both by circumstances and propriety to be of a distinctly secondary importance;
and most of them were. His westward trail followed that of
Wendell Willkie from Indianapolis to Kansas City, then down to
New Mexico, and up through California to the Northwest. The
address in New Mexico was the first that he ever made in Spanish.
He and the Republican candidates exchanged polite expressions
of esteem from time to time and Wallace traveled amicably on a
train for the greater part of a day with Senator Charles McNary,

his old-time McNary-Haugen colleague, who now was the opposing candidate for Vice-President. Throughout his long tour Wallace labored honestly to keep the arguments within the limits of demonstrable fact. His skill as a public speaker improved noticeably. But it was a hard trip. Advance promotion of his meetings along the way was by no means the sort of advance work that is done for a President out campaigning. Sometimes Wallace and his two traveling aides, Coyle and LeCron, would drive into a little town and find that the Democratic committeeman or committeewoman there had made no arrangements. In one such town they picked out a spot by the curb and started to talk with a few people who came up to see who these visitors were. Soon they were holding a really big meeting, with Wallace asking them questions and answering their questions without trying to make a set speech. 'I saw a lot of country and met a lot of fine people,' he said upon return to Washington. 'But, you know,' he added thoughtfully, 'it's a funny way to live.'

2. Vice-President and Envoy Extraordinary

HE TOOK with him to the office of the Vice-President only two of the 146,560 who had worked with him in Agriculture, Mary Huss and Mrs. Mildred Eaton, secretaries. Miss Huss had been his personal secretary ever since he edited *Wallaces' Farmer*. Harold Young of Texas, who had traveled with him in the latter stages of the campaign, was now attached to the Vice-President's office as a special assistant. These three, with two assistant stenographers, were now his entire staff. His principal office was two large rooms and a central anteroom on the main floor of the Senate Office Building; but he sometimes saw people or had them for lunch in the Vice-President's office off the Senators' reception room at the Capitol.

The retiring Vice-President, Mr. Garner, gave his successor lunch in that room with some senatorial cronies, inviting all, as was his genial custom, to make free of bourbon and branch water, thus to 'strike a blow for liberty.' Wallace declined smilingly, saying that no liquor appealed to him except *tequila*, which he had tasted in Mexico. With drinking so fixed a part of the political and diplomatic ritual, Wallace, since removing to Washington, had served cocktails or highballs in his home. The question of his own drinking he handled simply by accepting the proffered glass, touching his lips to the rim, and putting it by. He has nothing against other people's drinking, but he does not care for it himself. After 'Cactus Jack' had gone home to Texas the incoming Vice-President had them take out the private bar and convenient connecting lavatory which Garner had provided for the comfort of callers at his Capitol office, but he left the rest of the furnishings just as they were. Wallace used that office very little. The one in the Senate Office Building, which had the air of a quiet and spacious study, lined with books, except for the window space, suited him better.

'The Vice-President,' owlish Thomas A. Marshall once observed during his own days as such, 'is like a man in a cataleptic state; he cannot speak; he cannot move; he suffers no pain; and yet he is perfectly conscious of everything that is going on about him.' Even robustious Theodore Roosevelt found the vice-presidency somewhat depressing and confining. It soon became apparent that, with the President's favor, no such condition of comparative catalepsy would delimit the action of F. D. Roosevelt's new Vice-President, whom one commentator characterized most aptly as 'this reserved, restless man.' [3]

During the campaign the President had indicated that, with Wallace on the job, wider spheres of vice-presidential usefulness would be opened; and even before the inaugural, by announcement through the State Department, the President named the Vice-President-elect to proceed as Ambassador Extraordinary and Plenipotentiary and attend inaugural ceremonies to install General Avila Camacho as President of Mexico, in Mexico City on December 1, 1940.

It was a delicate mission. Wallace performed it tactfully and graciously. His attendance at Camacho's inaugural was a gesture of tacit recognition. By his authorized presence there the United States recognized the results of an election while results in Mexico still were subject to dispute so violent as to threaten a revolution. Recognition of the Camacho régime was extremely important to our own interest at the moment, for Camacho was ardently anti-German and willing to deal in the matter of our establishing naval and air bases at Tampico, Vera Cruz, Acapulco, and five other key locations in Mexico. In New York, General Andreu Almazan, fraudulently counted out, his followers held, in the Mexican election of the previous July, put out a statement saying that Wallace would find that he, Almazan, was really the people's choice down there.

With only one aide, James LeCron, who had also started studying Spanish when Wallace did in 1936, the Vice-President-elect drove to Mexico City from Washington. Mrs. Wallace and Mrs. LeCron were the other two members of the party. They traveled with no Secret Service men or guards. They stayed at our Embassy with the Ambassador, Josephus Daniels, and made tours from there out through the country. Wallace made talks in Spanish. Some State Department people who had not themselves taken the trouble to learn Spanish expressed amusement at Wallace's 'cornfed' Spanish accent, but the people liked it and were plainly moved by the compliments he paid them with a mild but suitable floridity in their own tongue. Out in the country on routes over which he was announced to pass the people decorated the bridges with cornstalks, to symbolize still another bond they held in common.

The talks with Avila Camacho proceeded satisfactorily; but in Mexico City just before a diplomatic reception at the National Palace, there was a riot, stirred up, apparently, among excited Almazan partisans by German agents working rather openly. Wallace was known to be coming to the American Embassy. A crowd shouting *Viva Almazan!* gathered there. His handlers slipped him into the Embassy quietly by a side way. When the crowd found this out they threw stones, howled murderously and charged the Embassy steps. They were beaten or pushed back by guards and others without much trouble. Almazan, who had flown back to Mexico and renounced the presidency, said that the rioters were no friends of his. Wallace shrugged his shoulders and smiled. Nazis had lots of money and, as for such demonstrations, 'You can buy them any day for twenty dollars.' He went around quite freely after that, unguarded, playing both regular tennis and fronton tennis with some of Mexico's best players, visiting schools, churches, and farms.

Back in Washington he learned almost overnight and without visible strain the rules and droning ritual required of a Vice-President presiding. He found that tall-backed swivel chair on the Senate dais a comfortable place to rest, and his cultivated practice of half-listening until something vital was said saved him many an hour of utter boredom. In the comparative leisure of the vice-presidency he was able to do not more writing than in the past, but more carefully considered writing.

The vice-presidency carries with it, formally, practically no jobs to be assigned or influence in recommendations for governmental posts other than that which the holder of the office chooses to cultivate personally, as a product of his closeness to the President and other high officials. Wallace almost invariably refused to exercise such influence. This took much pressure off his door; at the same time it made for a certain amount of hard feeling. Especially among those who had served him longest and most faithfully in the Department of Agriculture, there were naturally expectations that Henry, now so highly placed, would show a little natural gratitude when, for instance, an open spot on the Federal Reserve Board came up, and say at least a word in their behalf to the President. He did practically nothing of the kind. When pressed from the White House or elsewhere for some recommendation he would as a rule suggest three or four names more or less offhand, and leave it up to them there. Where most statesmen bore a well-developed bump of opportunism or trading zeal in such matters, Wallace, some disappointed friends declared, had deliberately cultivated a hole or a vacuum. He had, in fact, no 'friends' in the ordinary political sense of that word. He neither slapped backs nor scratched them. This he did not regard exactly as a matter of personal rectitude; it was simply not in his nature to trade favors. If a man who chanced also to be a personal friend, he explained, happened to be ideally qualified for a post, then it was all right to engage him or speak up for him. But he, Wallace, would regard it as 'close to dishonorable' to advance or recommend a man for a job simply because that man wanted or needed it. Back in Agriculture, when he had to hire and fire in some quantity, he had felt the responsibility rather keenly; and now that he was happily delivered from such obligation, he thought it was really better for the proper executives to make their own choices since they would have to bear responsibility for the consequences themselves.

Not only old associates who failed to get him to use his influence, but his newer colleagues in the Senate, found such reasoning extremely strange, almost inhuman in a man who, as the saying goes, is only removed by a single heartbeat from the Presidency of the United States of America. But that is how he was, and is. Wallace thought it the simplest thing in the world. A man he had once hired or appointed to do a job had done that job competently and faithfully? Well, that was the idea of the appointment, wasn't it? Wallace honestly felt that apart from the proper amount of praise and gratitude, neither he nor the public owed that man anything; and as for himself, in the way of political debts, he would have blushed to think that he owed anyone a raise at the taxpayers' expense.

Some of his former associates in the Department of Agriculture also found both odd and irksome Wallace's decisive way of closing the door behind him when finished with one job or phase of his life and work and turning to another. This in part was a matter of concentration; he makes a point of rarely looking back in yearning or contemplation. Instead of scattering his energies backward he presses forward eagerly to learn the new setup and explore new possibilities. Again, it was merely a matter of sound procedure and policy, as he saw it, for an official leaving one post to resist all call from friends that he put in a word at the top there for some change or act which they desired of the new Secretary. That door was closed, and, to Wallace's mind, should be. Claude Wickard was in charge there now; let him run it.

The plaint of some of his oldest friends, that to be a friend of Henry's automatically held you down or barred you from receiving his blessing when in quest of advancement, was partly untrue, however. A number of persons with whom he had worked very closely rose to high places on the Federal Reserve system, in the Farm Credit Administration, in the Budget Bureau, and elsewhere; and Wallace himself elevated Milo Perkins, next to LeCron his closest personal friend at the time, to a considerable eminence for a while.

On July 30, 1941, the President set up an Economic Defense Board of eight Cabinet members whose portfolios embraced international affairs and made the Vice-President Chairman of the Board. As such, Wallace was authorized to appoint an executive director and staff to assist this prewar super-Cabinet; and the press in general predicted that the director would be Winfield William Rieffler, a Princeton economist and early New Dealer. But Wallace decided to make Milo Perkins director, and Rieffler his assistant. Circumstances precipitating this decision approached the dramatic.

Milo Perkins, who up to then had spent barely a daylight hour abed, had lately fallen flatly ill from some obscure, undetermined affliction. They had him over at Johns Hopkins in Baltimore for rest and X-rays, but this did not seem to help. Some months later an operation became necessary. The trouble was a coiled stoppage in his intestines. He came to after skillful cutting, but in bad shape. Three weeks later some friends assembled, deeply concerned, for three doctors were disagreeing. Two said operate again; one was dubious. All three said that the patient was probably on the way out anyway and would go rather quickly. Milo came out of his coma and heard them arguing through a partly opened door. He is not, when aroused, an altogether delicate talker. With purple words which gained in force and volume as he proceeded he declared that he would not die, neither would he submit to another operation. 'I got mad; and that opened what was left of my bowels and got the old glands working,' he explained to those who called on him at his home during his rapid convalescence. The doctors simply waved their hands in doubt and a few days later let him be taken home. Wallace, who had not known of the deathwatch at the hospital and so had missed it, came to see Perkins at his suburban home about the problem of a director for the Economic Defense Board and asked him if he felt up to it. That completed the cure, precipitately. Perkins got up out of bed and shortly thereafter went to work. When the Economic Defense Board became the much enlarged Board of Economic Warfare, Perkins continued as director, with Wallace as its chairman. In the interim Wallace served also, rather actively, as Chairman of the Supply Priorities and Allocations Board, set up under the President's direction, with Judge Rosenman acting as the President's special advisor in details of defense reorganization.

The Board of Economic Warfare, recruiting eventually to a personnel exceeding three thousand, operated fairly smoothly and quite decisively almost from the first. Washington headquarters was a large apartment house taken over by the Government in Georgetown with spill-overs into temporary barracks and like emergency structures all over town. Perkins ran that end of it. Wallace directed the program mainly by telephone, through Perkins. From time to time he visited the offices in temporary T and in the Q Street apartments, but most of his administering was done by telephone. Thus, in the nature of things, since Americans in general regard as the greatest executive the most active and effective of front-men hard-pressing the execution, it was generally felt or surmised that Perkins was really the commanding young executive who might even some day be President, whereas that quiet Wallace, sitting up there in his Capitol Hill study, was simply a dreamy figurehead. Perkins, himself, has consistently testified to all who bothered to ask that the truth was quite different: 'Henry could find time to think the whole thing out carefully and really direct it,' he says. 'He directed it vigorously. I was out there in front, pushing and gouging. I was the hatchetman.' They made a good team.

Even as in time of peace Wallace had planned for war, he now directed war strategies of great reach and magnitude, and talked and thought and wrote of 'the shock of peace.' For this he was criticized. *The Atlantic Monthly* asked him to defend his position. He had just finished writing an *Atlantic* article, 'Foundations of the Peace,' when the Japanese struck at Pearl Harbor and this country [4] entered the Second World War.

His article opened in protest against those who were saying that talk of peace was futile until or if the war was won. Wallace argued, rather, that, 'while doing everything we can to speed the drive for victory,' we 'should think hard and often about the future peace, because unless we and the other democracies have confidence in that peace, our resistance to our enemies may not be strong enough to beat them.

'Sometime in the next few years,' he continued, 'if the Allies are successful, the world will have a second chance to organize its affairs on a basis of human decency and mutual welfare. . . . We know now, after our experiences of the past twenty-five years, that the most careful delineation of national boundaries is not in itself enough. . . . Nor can war be prevented simply by the establishment of an international league. We know now that the modern world must be recognized for what it is — an economic unit — and that wise arrangements must be made so that trade will be encouraged.'

The interwar break in the price of raw materials and lack of purchasing power among the producers of such in many countries, Wallace's analysis proceeded, had much to do with a quickly following and 'deadly economic malady afflicting the world, . . . a malady covered up by the billions in private loans floated by foreign borrowers in the United States. . . . Thus they produced a temporary, though basically unsound, prosperity. . . . In very truth, this nation, during those early postwar years, was sowing the wind by its policies of isolation, high tariffs, unwise foreign loans and high-pressure sales abroad. It could not avoid reaping the whirlwind.'

The Economic Defense Board, he indicated, speaking now more cautiously, would in all its actions put moves for victory first. Nevertheless, the Board's activities, now largely secret, might well yield experience along certain basic lines essential to a restored and continued peace. First, 'universality of access to raw materials,' together with 'an economic arrangement to protect the raw-material producers from violent fluctuation in income.' Second, 'the indispensability of markets for goods produced.' Third, a removal of tariffs and other barriers to imports. Fourth and fifth, better use of gold and of credit in stimulating trade. Sixth, close relationship between stable national currencies. 'Seventh, and most important of all, is the essential rôle of adequate purchasing power within the various countries that are trading with each other — for full employment within nations makes broad trade possible with other nations. All these facts and factors are of prime importance in determining the state of the world's health. . . .

'The overthrow of Hitler is only half the battle; we must build a world in which our human and material sources are used to the utmost. . . . In this country we have already made a start. Through the food stamp plan, the school-lunch program, the low-cost milk program . . . and lend-lease . . . the abundance of our farms is being put to use instead of being allowed to go to waste. Similar programs . . . are in effect . . . in a number of South American countries. . . . In England, the government is subsidizing consumption of certain foods — flour, bread, meat, tea, oatmeal, milk, orange juice — to make sure that the population is as well-nourished as possible. . . .'

None of these devices was, of course, 'the final answer,' Wallace granted, but, 'is it not time to recognize that minimum standards of nutrition are as important for growing children as minimum standards of education?' Without plenty of good food, world-wide and full employment, he concluded, there could never be more than a dubious prospect of an enduring — or endurable — peace.

His sons, Robert and Henry, had joined the Army and Navy, respectively. When Robert was commissioned a second lieutenant in Ordnance his father, the Vice-President, came from Washington to make a short talk to that class of new officers at Maryland's Aberdeen Proving Ground:

I have learned something about you during recent months because from time to time on Sundays my son Bob has brought some of you to spend a few hours with us in our home. You have worked hard during the past three months, but work has just begun. Anyone who works hard finds that by doing so he merely earns the privilege to engage in still more difficult work. . . .

Now that we have to fight, we are going to do the job more wholeheartedly than the Germans or the Japs. We shall beat them at their own game, so that we can earn the right to live peacefully, so that the children of the next generation can grow in a world of sunshine, without the black cloud of dictatorial militarism forever threatening free nations and peaceful human beings.

He made this talk to young soldiers on April 18, 1942. On May 8 following, before the Free World Association of New York City, he delivered a far more famous sermon or address: 'The Price of Free World Victory.' The war, which stirred in him great depths of grief, lifted him emotionally to a high exaltation of purpose and power to express it. His voice was slightly tremulous in opening: 'This is a fight between a slave world and a free world.' Then his voice, continuing, rang clear: 'Just as the United States in 1862 could not remain half slave and half free, so in 1942 the world must make its decision for a complete victory one way or the other.'

No public utterance he ever made came forth so easily. Having thought it through, he arose at six in the morning, put it on wax through a dictating machine in his apartment and took it to the office at nine. He changed hardly a word when he saw it in typescript. It was translated and distributed as a pamphlet in twenty different languages.

In the middle part, which was expository and but lightly charged with emotion, he told of a remark he had made to Madame Litvinov, the wife of the Russian Ambassador. 'Half in fun and half seriously, I said: "The object of this war is to make sure that everybody in the world has the privilege of drinking a quart of milk a day." She did not find this as funny as many Americans did. She replied: "Yes, even half a pint."' And this was the speech in which he spoke of the century of the common man:

> Some have spoken of the 'American Century.' I say that the century we are now entering — the century which will come out of this war — can and must be the century of the common man. . . .
>
> Those who write the peace must think of the whole world. There can be no privileged peoples. We ourselves in the United States are no more a master race than the Nazis. And we cannot perpetuate economic warfare without planting the seeds of military warfare.
>
> If we really believe that we are fighting for a people's peace, all the rest becomes easy. . . .
>
> The people's revolution is on the march, and the devil and

all his angels cannot prevail against it. They cannot prevail, for on the side of the people is the Lord.

'He giveth power to the faint; to them that have no might He increaseth strength. . . . They that wait upon the Lord shall mount up with wings as eagles; they shall run, and not be weary; they shall walk and not faint.'

Strong in the strength of the Lord, we who fight in the people's cause will never stop until the cause is won.

In the same spring of 1942, on a trip intended simply for his refreshment by country space and air, along with an offhand talk before a meeting of Friends of the Land at Louisville, the Vice-President aroused a storm of comment by inquiring of industrialists and reporters who were taking him around the city, whether Louisville's great new synthetic rubber industry might not be asking for tariff protection after the war. And if we were to go on with that sort of thing for new war-bloated industries, might not this lead this country into a Third World War.

The press dispatches carried few of Wallace's words on soil care and a 'sustained yield' of all forms of life through endless generations, and many about his unalterable free-trade tendencies. *The New York Times* asked him to write a Sunday article on the rubber question, which he did.[5] This aroused further caustic comment. 'Probably no man in Washington feels it more a personal responsibility to think deep thoughts about the post-war world,' remarked *The Sun* of Baltimore editorially; and found it ironic that Wallace of all people should now express the fear that farmers would be cajoled 'into running political interference' for tariff-seeking oil and alcohol interests in the hope of selling more farm products in the form of synthetics after this war. It was Mr. Wallace, himself, who had taught the farmers pressure-group tactics, *The Sun* observed; and called upon him now as a 'just and humble man' to admit 'that he himself is not blameless.'

Wallace had been worrying about rubber, along with worrying about the increasing voracity of pressure groups, including farmers, for quite a while. As Secretary of Agriculture in February of 1938 he set up an interbureau committee on tropical Latin-American sources and had their first report within a few weeks. This done, he asked of the Budget Bureau, and obtained on April 12, 1938, a special appropriation of sixty-five thousand dollars 'to survey Latin-American countries . . . particularly as pertains to the cultivation of rubber, quinine, and other valuable products . . . to protect our source of supply in time of national emergency.' On June 7, 1938, before a Senate subcommittee on appropriations, he pleaded for more funds for such work, which funds he did not get. On April 10, 1939, he pleaded again for funds, which again he did not get. On July 9, 1939, in a previous article in *The New York Times*, Wallace wrote, 'In case of World War, our lack of this product [rubber] is likely to be our Achilles' heel.' On June 20, 1940, again appearing before the Senate subcommittee, he said, 'I came up because I feel so vigorously at the present time, in connection with international affairs, that this is an exceedingly important matter.'

All this ground was beaten over once more in hearings before the Special Committee to Investigate the National Defense Program, with Senator Harry Truman presiding, on August 10, 1942. The rubber shortage was by this time exceedingly trying. Nothing approaching adequate appropriations were made until after Pearl Harbor. But Wallace, having laid another course, now proposed through the Commodity Credit Corporation to pile up some rubber for war use. He described the trade to the Senate Agricultural Appropriations Committee on April 13, 1939. Commodity Credit, USDA, later carried out the trade and exchanged sixty thousand bales of cotton for ninety thousand bales of rubber — enough to make eighteen million tires — and this rubber was added to the nation's stockpile.

The state paper of 1942 on which he worked most carefully and at length was his Wilson Day proposal of a world council for the enforcement of peace. Twenty-seven years now had passed since the first American Henry Wallace of this line, then in his eightieth year, had talked with a war president, Woodrow Wilson, of a basis for lasting peace — 'not a plan, simply a vision, which may mature in time.' Strongly conscious of what he sometimes calls 'a genetic continuity,' Henry A. Wallace now proposed a world court of economic decisions and a world council to enforce peace. He spoke on December 28, 1942. It would have been Woodrow

ELEGY FOR MILO PERKINS' SON
New London, Connecticut, June, 1943

Wilson's eighty-sixth birthday had Wilson lived that far beyond his time. Wallace said:

> For the people of the United States the war is entering its grimmest phase. At home, we are beginning at last to learn what war privations mean. Abroad, our boys in ever-greater numbers are coming to grips with the enemy. . . .
>
> The situation in the world today is parallel in some ways to that of the United States just before the adoption of the Constitution, when it was realized that the Articles of Confederation had failed and that some stronger union was needed. . . .
>
> In this suddenly-shrunken world . . . the United Nations, like our thirteen American states in 1797, soon will be faced with a fundamental choice. . . . The League of Nations, like our own Union under the Articles of Confederation, was not strong enough. The League never had American support, and at critical moments it lacked the support of some of its own members. The League finally disintegrated under the successive blows of world-wide economic depression and a Second World War. . . .
>
> Woodrow Wilson . . . gave up his health and eventually his life in the first attempt, a generation ago, to preserve the world's peace through united world action. At that time, there were many who said that Wilson had failed. Now we know that it was the world that failed, and the suffering and war of the last few years are the penalty it is paying for its failure. . . .
>
> We cannot now blueprint all the details, but we *can* begin now to think about some of the guiding principles of this world-wide new democracy we of the United Nations hope to build. . . .
>
> Obviously the United Nations must first have machinery which can disarm and keep disarmed those parts of the world which would break the peace. Also there must be machinery for preventing economic warfare and enhancing economic peace among nations. Probably there will have to be an economic court to make decisions in case of dispute. And an international court presupposes some kind of world council,

so that whatever world system evolves will have enough flexibility to meet changing circumstances as they arise.

As a practical matter, we may find that the regional principle is of considerable value in international affairs. For example, European countries, while *concerned* with the problems of Pan-America, should not have to be *preoccupied* with them; likewise Pan-America, while *concerned*, should not have to be *preoccupied* with the problems of Europe. Purely regional problems ought to be left in regional hands. This would leave to any federated world organization problems involving broad principles and those practical matters which affect countries of different regions or which affect the whole world.... The aim should be... unity of purpose in promoting the general welfare of the whole world... in other words, the maximum of home rule that can be maintained along with a minimum of centralized authority that must come into existence to give the necessary protection....

In closing, Wallace quoted Josephus Daniels in *The Life of Woodrow Wilson*, as follows:

> *Wilson never knew defeat, for defeat never comes to any man until he admits it. Not long before the close of his life Woodrow Wilson said to a friend: 'Do not trouble about the things we fought for. They are sure to prevail. They are only delayed.' With the quaintness which gave charm to his sayings he added, 'And I will make this concession to Providence — it may come in a better way than we propose.*

3. Wallace *versus* Jones

A T TIMES,' Wallace confessed before a Senate committee in 1945 when differences between himself and Jesse Holman Jones were given a final public airing, 'I have been almost as much annoyed by Government bureaucrats as any infuriated businessman.' Senator Bailey of North Carolina, presiding, suggested that the witness be more specific. Wallace obliged him:

'Specifically, there was failure to buy in the Dutch East Indies adequate quantities of materials available in the Dutch East Indies — rubber, tin, and quinine — materials that were very vital to our economy in case we got into war. I say, very specifically, it was the fault of certain advisors who should have advised the President more adequately on what the world picture was — *really* was.

'I will say, for my part, since you are pressing me in this way, that in 1939 I felt there was a very great danger of war with Japan.' He told of coming to the Capitol on April 13, 1939, and seeking out Senator Byrnes, who agreed with the idea of trading 600,000 bales of cotton for 90,500 long tons of rubber in England; he told of how the trade was effected: 'Mr. Byrnes and Herbert Feiss [of the State Department] agreed. Herbert Feiss made it possible for me to get clearance. The State Department did not like the idea of commodity interchanges, felt it was not quite the best way of doing business, but the State Department agreed. Joe Kennedy co-operated beautifully. We made the exchange.

'I backed rubber when I was Secretary of Agriculture. I backed rubber when Congress tried to take the appropriations away entirely. Rubber is a hobby of mine. In fact,' Wallace concluded, 'I guess I worked as hard to keep the United States from being caught with its pants down on this question as any other man in the country.'

The picture is inelegant, but a cartoon showing furious Uncle Sam shaking a fist and shouting, 'Just wait 'til I get my pants up!' would have expressed not inaccurately our general sense of grief and humiliation, rage and shame when on December 7, 1941, the Japanese struck at Pearl Harbor. The military aspects of that catastrophe are still under investigation. Here we are concerned only with an established negligence as to laying in adequate stockpiles of vital war materials, or in arranging for supply from alternate sources, before Japan struck. That, too, has been investigated, somewhat lengthily; and on this question the hearings were public, and have been published. A complete chronological recounting of each stage of the conflict between Wallace and Jones — some called it, facetiously, 'The Battle of the Century of the Common Man'—is out of the question or beyond the intention here.   The main facts which seem to emerge, established beyond contention, are these:

Jesse Jones was born in Tennessee on April 5, 1874.   He went to Texas when still young and got into the lumber business.   He soon became head of an important lumber firm, branched out from that into banking and flourished mightily.   He was Chairman of the Board of the National Bank of Houston and owner and publisher of *The Houston Chronicle* and three times an honorary LL.D. already when in 1932 President Hoover brought him to Washington as a director of the newly founded Reserve Finance Corporation.   He became Chairman of the Board of RFC in 1933 and remained so until 1939.   By reason of regional location a Democrat (he was Director of Finance for the Democratic National Committee, 1924–28), Jesse Jones stayed on, naturally, when the New Deal came in, and grew in power as a sort of continuing force with every passing year of the F. D. Roosevelt administrations. In 1939 he was named head of the enlarged Federal Loan Administration.   In September of 1940, President Roosevelt made him, in addition, Secretary of Commerce.   Harry Hopkins had been warming that chair very little; he worked principally at the White House or as a presidential courier; nor did Jones, as Secretary, come often to his offices in Commerce.   Throughout the New Deal, in fact, the Department of Commerce, Hoover's special pride, was all but deliberately neglected and scorned by most of the Rooseveltians.   The Department was allowed to rock along quietly in the routine performance of accustomed chores and used as a catch-all simply to accommodate another Cabinet member on special assignment outside.

As Secretary of Agriculture, Wallace's dealings with Jones were principally related to Jones's power over federal lending; and they got along amicably on the whole.   But when, by executive order of July 30, 1941, the President made the Vice-President head of the Board of Economic Warfare, and assigned to Wallace certain functions hitherto entrusted to RFC and the State Department, ruction started.   Jones's hostility heightened when Wallace made Milo Perkins the executive director of BEW.   Jones and Perkins were both Houston business men, but that was no bond between them; quite the opposite.   No two men could have been more dissimilar; and they detested each other heartily as circumstances brought them together in their work.

Even after Pearl Harbor, with supplies from that part of the world cut off, Jones refused to be concerned about rubber. More than a year later, on February 3, 1942, he assured the House Banking Committee of his belief that the United States 'would be getting all the rubber we need from the Dutch East Indies' by the end of 1943. Quartz crystals from Brazil, to be used in airplane, tank, and submarine radio sets, were another vital need and shortage. RFC and BEW bickered about price. Wallace carried that question to Jones and Will Clayton direct and at length got action; but only part of the ordered Brazilian crystals reached here by the deadline, and quartz fabricators had to raid museums to get usable crystals in the meantime.

It was a crucial shortage in quinine, desperately needed by troops in tropical climates, which more than any other crisis impelled Wallace in the spring of 1942 to demand and get from the President what he hoped was a show-down — a settlement of his differences with Jesse Jones. Quinine is made from the bark of the cinchona tree. Far East cinchona bark contains from seven to ten per cent quinine sulfate; Latin America bark, only around two per cent. It was therefore urgent that Far Eastern trees be planted in South America immediately. This is what Wallace and Perkins said about quinine when finally, around a year later, Wallace determined to have done with behind-the-scenes maneuvers and make the issue public:

On April 14, 1942, General MacArthur wired Washington that two million seeds of a high grade strain [of cinchona] had been brought out of the Philippines, on one of the last planes leaving for Australia; adding that they 'must be planted *without delay.*'

. . . Jesse Jones and Will Clayton stalled for months on this program. As I indicated to the Senate Banking and Currency Committee last December [1941], there are times when we need more fights and fewer shortages.

Lieutenant-Colonel Arthur F. Fischer, who brought these seeds from the Philippines to the United States, came to the

Board of Economic Warfare with his proposal — to plant the seeds in Costa Rica — on August 24, 1942. Within three weeks, the Board of Economic Warfare had worked out a detailed plan and submitted it to the other interested agencies. Reconstruction Finance Corporation representatives at first acquiesced in the proposal when it was first discussed with them on September 11 and 29. Under-Secretary of War Patterson approved it formally on October 7, 1942.

Then, on October 10, the Reconstruction Finance Corporation notified the Board of Economic Warfare that 'the matter requires further consideration.' Those 'considerations' continued for four months . . . right on through the battle with malaria and with Japs at Guadalcanal. Mr. Jones said that our proposal was post-war planning because of the time it takes for cinchona trees to come to full maturity for profitable stripping. The Fischer trees couldn't be harvested for two and one-half years at the earliest; normally, seven years pass before stripping the bark begins.

During 1941 Mr. Jones may have felt that this would be a short war in which we wouldn't become involved; in any event, he did not buy quinine during that period in adequate amounts for government stockpiles. During 1942 he acted as though the war might be over by 1944, if we can take his attitude on this quinine project as a criterion. . . .

In that same spring of 1942, his patience waning, Wallace went to the White House and obtained from the President an order, dated April 13, removing decision as to import purchases from RFC, leaving such decisions up to BEW alone. But Jones was still BEW's banker. He could take his time about signing checks or clearing directives, and he did. By the same presidential order, BEW was given certain functions which hitherto had been those of the Department of State. Secretary Cordell Hull, who was getting increasingly restive with Wallace's acts and pronouncements in foreign trade affairs, stomped over to the White House and had that part of the order rescinded. But Wallace and Perkins did have now, on paper at least, power to operate independently of Jones. Jones took this bitterly to heart and made cabal fairly openly against 'these uplifters' in all of the many places around Washington and elsewhere, where he exercised influence.

Following an inquiry into the matter in the spring of 1942, the Truman Committee found serious delays continuing amid discord and observed by way of report:

> Energetic, aggressive men, striving to meet war needs, will tend to clash when their duties bring them into conflict. But destructive, wasteful feuding must be suppressed.
>
> The task of control and guidance is of utmost importance. Clear leadership in strong hands is required. The influence from above must always be toward unity. Where necessary, heads must be knocked together.

Something more than a year later, heads fell. A forty-day trip to western South American countries which Wallace made in the spring of 1943 helped measurably to precipitate matters. In March the President named him as his Special Representative to make a 'good-will' journey to Costa Rica, Panama, Ecuador, Bolivia, Chile, and Colombia. Attended by Larry Duggan of the State Department, Hector Lazo of the Board of Economic Warfare, and some Secret Service men, the Vice-President flew from Miami on March 13. Wallace insisted that there be as little protocol as possible. His constant striving to keep things informally 'democratic' raised eyebrows and covert snickers among career people in the State Department all along the way. But almost everywhere he went the people and the officials who received him appeared to enjoy it; and Wallace visibly enjoyed most of it. When his plane first touched land, in Costa Rica, he was greeted by a cheering crowd of sixty-five thousand. Next day, speaking in Spanish, he dedicated an Institute of Tropical Agriculture which he had helped to establish when Secretary of Agriculture. 'In order to attain freedom from want,' he said, 'the theory of sustained yield and of the free interchange of products between nations must be accepted and followed. Strength and happiness have a common denominator in adequate diets.' He and his party rode into the back country to inspect the plantings of cinchona seeds that had ben flown in from the Philippines and had

been in the planting so long delayed.   They also inspected recent
plantings of disease-resistant rubber trees.

In Panama they viewed the Canal defenses, then with a few
quick, informal stops flew to Chile.   At Santiago, the capital, in a
huge outdoor stadium, Wallace spoke to a crowd of eighty thousand: 'I have always admired the extraordinary political maturity
of the Chilean people.   You derive from a splendid past a great
capacity, a collective capacity, for judging and meeting the tragic
realities of these modern times — perhaps the gravest that the
Christian world has ever known.   We are of the New World, we
North and South Americans.   We are the repositories of the
worth of Western civilization.'

Here, as in Mexico, old-line diplomats questioned whether a man
whose Spanish plainly fell short of utter perfection should make
speeches in that language; but the people seemed to understand it.
The reception they gave Wallace almost everywhere was extraordinarily ardent.   They understood, too, his repeated and ardent
references to 'the holy plant of the New World' — Indian corn.
Even in countries where the armies, German-trained, or again,
processions of schoolchildren carrying flowers, marched in goose-
step, he had a friendly press, in the main.   Some of the comment
was embarrassingly admiring.   He was compared to both Lincoln
and Jesus Christ on the same day.

The trip was by no means all speech-making, receptions, and
ceremonial dinners on plates of solid gold.   Wallace and his aides
inspected economic developments of the BEW program and did a
little BEW business all along the line.   They spent a week in
Chile, six days in Bolivia, eight days in Ecuador, four days in
Colombia.   In all of these countries Wallace startled conventional
diplomats and sometimes startled the whole body of peoples
accustomed to old Incan rites or the intricacies of receiving Vice-
roys from the Court of Spain.   When it was hot he would take his
coat off and ride in the car in shirtsleeves.   When the car pro-
cessional crept slowly and he felt the need of exercise he would get
out and run on ahead.   Arriving at La Paz, the Bolivian capital,
13,500 feet above sea level, he played two hard sets of tennis, and
was not bothered by the exertion at such an altitude.   Bolivia
was a country he was especially determined to explore beyond the

conventional limits of a journey of state. He wanted to view conditions among the people and among the tin miners particularly; he was having disagreements with our State Department because he insisted that import contracts drawn by BEW should include provision for something more than starvation pay for those degraded Indian miners, as well as for other exploited groups in countries not our own.

Diplomats charged with his routing sought deliberately upon occasion to whisk him through or hasten him around sights of dire poverty. Nevertheless he managed to inspect, rather intimately, actual conditions among the people. He displayed a vast interest in archaeology; he *must* see this ruin or that. Often the ruin turned out to be social as well as historical. Once two Secret Service men whose duty it was to sleep close by him awoke one morning to find him up and gone. He was down by a big lake, laughing and talking with some very poor but gay and pleasant people when his guards rounded him in.

There was constant jockeying, naturally, to make sure that he would not stop at more Catholic institutions than Protestant missions. He wanted especially to see Indian missions of both. In Bolivia he asked that Charles Collier, a young friend then attached to our Embassy there, drive him up into the mountains at the head of an inspecting procession. It was quite a ride on rude mountain roads. Wallace and a small party spent the night at a Protestant mission conducted by Canadian Baptists to advance the civilization of native Indians. Conditions there were of a primitive simplicity. The Indians were sold with the land. The missionary in charge had constant trouble with his Indians' drinking heady liquors and chewing cacao leaves. The Indians, themselves, cheerfully presented Wallace, as a souvenir of his visit, with one of the native whips by which they were accustomed to be chastised. It was a medieval order of life, with but one modern touch — a tractor. With this the mission was growing on common ground the necessary staples for a higher standard of living, and at the same time — much in the manner of our Farm Security Administration — was seeking to induce its charges to acquire small homes and plots of earth that they could call their own. 'It was awful grim,' Wallace said later, recalling the experience, 'but that missionary was a good man, doing the very best he could under almost impossible conditions, and the people he was working with were also doing their best. I was struck with the bravery of their effort.'

In Ecuador he laid a wreath at the statue marking the place where Bolívar and San Martín met and paid a simple ceremonial visit to the tomb of Eloy Alfaro. 'Eloy Alfaro,' he said, 'was a rebel and a conspirator. His conspiracy and his rebellions were devoted to the defeat of hatred, of injustice, of disunity, and of tyranny.'

It was evident that in the light of some of the things he had seen on his South American journey, including some members of our RFC foreign staff at work, the Vice-President was on the verge of feeling somewhat rebellious. But he gave forth no tactless word. He wrote only short speeches in Spanish, and read them carefully word for word.

On April 20, 1943, the day of his departure from Ecuador, *Telegrafo* in Guayaquil ran an article, 'Goodbye Meester Wallace.' The anonymous writer started amusingly by recounting all the different mispronunciations of Wallace's name in Spanish. As for the reception accorded Mr. Wallace in Guayaquil, the account became rather more bitter:

Our people have formed a good opinion of Mr. Wallace but Mr. Wallace cannot possibly have formed a good opinion of us. We have never done so many stupid things in such a short time. From the moment he jumped from the plane we began our silly performances. Whoever had the bright idea of rushing him through the streets in an automobile at full speed? Oh, the unhappy mounted police, mounted on starved and moth-eaten old nags, carrying flags, lances, rifles, whips, swords and all other contraptions, charging to keep up! One horseman lost control of his horse, and horse and rider were catapulted through an open doorway. Another got stuck on a tree limb and finished the ride practically naked. It was better than a movie. . . .

And that famous review: Father in Heaven, what a funeral procession it was! A tragic march, a march which fully ex-

hibited all our miseries. Dirty and ragged people, with
skeleton-like bodies and faces full of hunger. Actually, a
sort of corporal marked time during the march with a leaden
whip, as though he were trying to bring about social justice
by dint of whipping it out of the atmosphere. We saw Mr.
Wallace turn his head and lower his eyes. There was grief in
his face, and bitterness and charity. . . .

Mr. Wallace covered the whole city. And he examined us
with eagle eye, and saw everything, much to the horror and
disgust of the Governor of the Province. At the foot of the
hill he alighted from the car. He entered one of the miserable
houses there. 'Let's see how the people live,' he said, and he
went right in through the back door. It was worse than a
mule stable. On the dirt floor, naked children, skinny, filthy.
Mr. Wallace looked at them with repugnance and sadness.
He asked permission and he entered a room where the women
were. A coal stove, bunches of dirty rags, filth, misery.
That's what Mr. Wallace saw. He didn't say a single word
but we noticed a dimness in his eyes which couldn't help
reflect the sadness in his heart. . . .

Returning to Washington in late April of 1943, the Vice-President made an extended verbal and intimate report to the President. He stressed the fact that the cost of living in most of the
Latin-American countries had far outrun the incomes of the mass
of people; and that Axis agents were doing their utmost to direct
the resulting discontent against the Allies, by blaming all the
trouble on the Yankee Colossus.

What he had seen in the way of active economic warfare, proceeding both under cover and openly in South America, strengthened Wallace's resolution to go ahead with the North American
program faster. A series of events immediately following his
return to these states served to heighten his feelings. BEW,
existing under presidential order, had been authorized by Congress
to continue under the President's War Powers Act; but it depended for its continued existence and expansion, of course, upon
continuing Congressional appropriations. Now Wallace and
Perkins had an appropriation fight on their hands; and Jones,

appearing as a witness before House and Senate committees, openly bucked them. He had previously sought to obtain from Congress resumed right to pass on the Board's expenditures; and now he tried again. 'A day or so ago,' said Senator McKellar of Tennessee, speaking in the Senate on June 4, 'Mr. Jesse Jones testified that Mr. Milo Perkins absolutely ran the entire establishment of two thousand, six hundred and twenty employees; that his word was law, even over him, Mr. Jesse Jones.' And so on. On the basis of this and other of Mr. Jones's representations, before Senator Byrd's Economy Committee, Senator McKellar brought in an amendment to return to Mr. Jones the power to say 'Yes' or 'No,' not simply 'Wait,' to BEW.

Meeting that evening and the evening following, June 4 and 5, Wallace and Perkins drew up a twenty-eight-page documented memorandum as a statement to the Senate Committee on Appropriations. A scathing document, more in Perkins's sharper style than Wallace's, it started by saying that Jones's testimony was 'at variance with the facts,' and proceeded into a bill of particulars which attributed to Mr. Jones 'obstructionist tactics . . . delay of the war effort . . . hamstringing bureaucracy and backdoor complaining.' The cinchona incident was but one of many, all involving vital war materials, which Perkins and Wallace spread on the record.

Perkins wished to release the statement to the press at once. Wallace restrained him. 'After sleeping over the matter for a few nights,' Wallace wrote in a brief preface when the statement was finally made public on June 29, 'I decided not to make it. But [further] misrepresentations which have been called to my attention during the past week have been of such nature that I have decided to release the statement as originally prepared. . . . There are times when the sense of public duty overweighs the natural, personal reluctance to present facts of this nature. This is such a time.'

On June 1, appearing before the House Appropriations Committee, Perkins had said: 'We are going ahead on the conviction that any economic program which will help shorten this war by a month, a week, or even a day is worth any reasonable price. Measured in lives, and remembering the men who died that last morning before the Armistice was signed in 1918, all of us would agree that it is worth any price to shorten the war by a single hour.'

By release of their blast of June 29 Wallace and Perkins put themselves in hazard under a presidential edict, sharply announced on August 21, 1942, that leaders of various agencies must compose their differences between themselves, or at the White House, not air such differences publicly. Now Jones, immediately responding, put himself in like hazard. He issued a statement calling the. Wallace-Perkins charges 'hysterical . . . filled with malice and misstatements . . . dastardly,' and he asserted that 'there has been no serious delay by us of any vital program.'

The day after the statement was issued, the President asked James H. Byrnes to get Wallace and Jones together and see if he could make peace. Wallace displayed at their meeting a mild but troubled demeanor, disclaimed all feeling of personal enmity, and agreed to Mr. Byrnes's suggestion that BEW issue no further statements except at the request of Congressional committees. Mr. Jones stayed angry, and made no attempt to conceal it. And now it was he who broke again beyond the presidential injunction and issued a counterstatement. He said that Wallace was guilty of 'malice, innuendos and half-truths' as well as 'falsehoods out of the whole cloth.' Wallace was out of the city when Jones made his statement. Milo Perkins released to the morning press of July 5 a reply: 'Mr. Jones has thrown up a smoke screen,' adding: 'His Rip Van Winkle approach to a commodity [quinine] that means life or death to our soldiers is simply incredible.'

The sharp language and pointed recriminations initiated by public release of the Perkins-Wallace memorandum on June 29 have puzzled many observers. They felt that, so far at least as Wallace was concerned, the tone of the argument was out of character. A lion for principle and a fighter for causes, Wallace had hitherto shrunk from entering into differences when they became personal. But now, with complete understanding that in so doing he was, as Chairman of the Board of Economic Warfare, putting his neck on the block at the President's pleasure, Wallace stood with Milo Perkins in a feud which, so far as Perkins and Jones were concerned, had become intensely personal.

It is not the intention here deliberately to reopen wounds which have begun to heal a little; but inasmuch as Wallace, the first Vice-President to be given a second large job by his President, was also the first Vice-President to be removed by the President from that second job, the circumstances of the affair, the facts about it, so far as the key facts are obtainable, should certainly be re-entered here on this record.

One highly pertinent fact which since has become generally known is that Milo Perkins and his wife had just lost their second son. Their first son had been killed in a railroad accident on his way to school when he was only fifteen years old. Now came word, on May 21, 1943, that their only remaining child, George Perkins, who had enlisted as a Marine flyer in his eighteenth year, had died in a power-dive crash in Florida. This was what gave so great an emotional thrust to those who knew the facts when Milo Perkins, facing the House Appropriations Committee on June 1, said: 'It is worth any price to shorten the war by a single hour.'

Hitherto, in seeking to settle disputes with Jones, Wallace had carefully observed the President's order that differences be 'submitted to me by the appropriate agencies.' For weeks on end after Wallace's return from South America Wallace called the White House, asking a joint interview with the President for himself and Perkins. The call was shunted around. He received delayed replies, third-hand to fifth-hand, that the President would be glad to see Mr. Wallace, not accompanied by Mr. Perkins, but because of the intense war pressure on his time the President could not now name a day and hour for the appointment.

Wallace had been as close a friend of young George Perkins as of his father. Over the weekend following receipt of the news he dictated an address which he entitled simply 'George,' to be delivered at the commencement exercises of his daughter, Jean, at Connecticut College for Women in early June. It was during the first week of June, on the fourth, remember, that Senator McKellar quoted Jesse Jones in the Senate; and that Perkins and Wallace drafted their memorandum. Perkins had refused to pause in his war work for any formal obsequies. To him, the delays he imputed to Jones now meant just so many more days of war, just so many more boys sent to their death.

Meantime, on Sunday, June 6, Wallace traveled to Connecticut and delivered his commencement address. He did not read it well, for the most part; his emotion toward the end of delivering this commencement funeral oration unsteadied his voice. But he started evenly enough:

> As I meet with you here in the midst of life, where there is so much joy and confidence, I am thinking of a boy. He was such a fine boy, that boy who now is gone. He was a close friend of mine for eight years. Two years ago when he graduated from high school he came to tell me how much opposed he was to the United States getting into the war. He was a pacifist, almost of the Quaker type, and the dignity of the individual, regardless of race, creed, or color, meant everything to him. But he was strong physically, an excellent football player, and a good wrestler, and he had a complete disdain of physical fear. We talked. He said that we Americans were suckers to get into World War I, that it was not our obligation to get involved twice in a European mess. . . .
>
> I told him I disagreed with him, and why. After sketching out for him Germany's five wars of aggression during the past eighty years, I told him that before we could start to work on the kind of world we wanted it would be necessary to destroy the power of the aggressor nations.

George, Wallace continued, joined the Marines, a dive bomber. Then:

> Two weeks ago there came from Florida the telegram announcing his death. I was with George's parents and the girl he was to have married. The father reminded me that two years previously I had given the boy my photograph with the inscription, 'For George, with hope for the future.'
>
> George had supreme confidence in his generation, but less in my generation. He looked on many of the public men of our time as incipient appeasers. He considered them small-minded and shortsighted. He saw them . . . as unlikely to rise to the challenge of the fundamental verities when brought face to face with the job of rebuilding a shattered world.

'Plenty of people who couldn't change fast enough to prevent this war still sit in the seats of the mighty. . . . It's all baloney to talk about this younger generation winning the peace. We won't come to power for twenty years. The same generation that got us into this mess has got to get us out of it,' George said in a letter written shortly before he was killed. . . .

Through George's meteoric life and symbolic death, I was forced into a more complete appreciation of the meaning of the death of Christ to his disciples. Something bright and shining and full of hope had passed from the world. It just couldn't be. Death couldn't end all. Christ must live. He must live in the world forever. Somewhere there must be a perpetual song of resurrection, ringing forth continuously the message of peace and good will. And now I conclude this vivid personal experience by saying: May it so be that my George, your George, and all those who have so sacrificed their lives will so inspire us to effective action that they will not have died in vain.

That was on June 6, 1943. On July 12, Wallace sent to the President at the White House this personal and private letter:

Dear Mr. President:

On July 5, when I was out of town, Mr. Jones released a statement about the Board of Economic Warfare. We are quite willing to ignore his extraordinary adjectives, but we do not feel that we can ignore his intentionally faulty and misleading arithmetic. I am enclosing a preliminary set of observations on the inaccuracies in Mr. Jones's statement of July 5. This shows conclusively that my original charges were understated.

A final report will be sent you within ten days which will include additional documented evidence of serious RFC delays to the war effort. Only July 6, Mr. Byrnes asked me to make no further public statement about this matter unless asked to do so before some Congressional Committee.

It seems to me that this matter should be settled incisively, and settled promptly. Otherwise, it will rise to plague us;

the public has cause to be confused as to the facts of the case. This can become dangerous ammunition in the hands of your opposition at any time during the next fifteen months.

I should like to respectfully suggest that the situation is serious enough to warrant a thorough investigation by an outstanding committee which you might appoint for this purpose. The Baruch Committee faced a similar muddle on rubber, but it met the issues, restored public confidence, and relieved you of what threatened to be continuing embarrassment.

In urging that you consider the completion of such an investigation a year before the next election, I feel that you should differentiate between the man who is Vice-President of the United States and the man who is Chairman of the Board of Economic Warfare.

If it should be proved that the very serious charges which I felt compelled to level at Mr. Jones are in error, then it seems to me that the public interest would be served by removing me as Chairman of the Board of Economic Warfare.

If this approach does not appeal to you, we ought to go ahead promptly with the transfer of the U. S. Commercial Company to BEW. This was the proposal I worked out with Mr. Byrnes the afternoon he met with Mr. Jones and me. Mr. Byrnes authorized my making such an announcement and a copy of it is attached.

Such a move would not wholly eliminate embarrassing questions when we go before the Congress for our appropriations, but this will take place to some extent under any circumstances. Mr. Jones also must go to Congress on RFC money matters and it is certain that we shall be asked to testify in conjunction with his hearings. If you work out the transfer of the USCC to the BEW before such hearings, it would give you a fresh basis for instructing both Mr. Jones and me to give joint support to your administrative determination.

I should like to call your attention to the enclosed letter from Irving Brant. We have heard similar stories from many quarters; the sum and substance of them is that Mr. Jones has been very careful to get your initials on all questionable programs so that he can escape personal responsibility if any serious investigation of RFC activities is ever undertaken by the Congress. This emphasizes the importance of continuing your policy of gradually stripping the RFC of its vast powers.

Donald Nelson has indicated that the BEW job in the import field is one of the outstanding successes of our war effort. Congressional Committees have just gone into BEW activities at length following which the Congress gave us every nickel of your budget estimate. It seems to me that the Board of Economic Warfare has been a distinct asset to you in the conduct of the total war effort of this administration. The immediate transfer of the USCC to the BEW as outlined to you in my letter of June 10 will enable us to do an even more aggressive job in the future than we have done in the past.

Respectfully yours,

H. A. WALLACE

On July 15, employees of the Board of Economic Warfare held a meeting to present the Army, through Milo Perkins, their director, a motor ambulance in memory of his son, George. No reporters were supposed to be present, but a woman reporter of *The Washington Herald* slipped in. Perkins made an intimate talk, thanking his colleagues for their tribute to his son, and added some further fighting remarks about delays and evasions. This part of his talk appeared in the afternoon paper. Next day, July 16, the President issued to the morning papers what *The New York Herald Tribune* called a 'bitter edict' and copies of a letter 'without precedent for sharpness' which he had sent to both Jones and Wallace. He abolished the Economic Warfare Board, sheared Jones of all RFC subsidiaries that engaged in financing foreign purposes; and regrouped these agencies within an enlarged Office of Economic Warfare, to be headed by Leo T. Crowley, a friend and admirer of Jones. The President reminded not only the offenders but all department heads of his order of August 21, 1942, that matters of difference should be submitted to him through the appropriate heads of the conflicting agencies and not aired in the press. He said there was no time to pause in warfare and examine the conflicting claims of RFC and BEW; therefore, 'I transfer these matters into other hands.'

Jones hailed the decision as a personal victory. 'I concur most heartily [and] will render every possible assistance to the new Director.' Wallace made a one-sentence statement: 'In wartime no one should question the over-all wisdom of the Commander in Chief.' When pressed by reporters to say more, he smiled and went out to dig in his backyard garden.

He was scheduled to speak on July 25 before a great labor meeting in Detroit. The speech, which had cleared the White House, contained a somewhat conventional tribute to the President — 'the-man-who' sort of thing. Excited friends brought the manuscript to him as it was about to go up for mimeographing, and asked him if he still intended to say *that*. 'I don't see why not,' he answered. 'Though he slay me, yet will I trust in him,' they mocked. Wallace smiled. 'Well, I'll tell you what I'll do,' he said. 'I'll take it out and do a new first paragraph.' He did so, as follows:

> Three months ago in South America I found the lowliest peon looked on President Roosevelt as a symbol of his dearest aspirations in the peace to come. So it is also in China and occupied Europe. I have known the President intimately for ten years and in the final showdown he always puts human rights first. There are powerful groups who hope to take advantage of the President's concentration on the war effort, to destroy everything he has accomplished on the domestic front for the past ten years.... Sooner or later the machinations of these small but powerful groups which put money and power first and people last will inevitably be exposed to the public eye.

The liberal and radical papers started to make of him a hero and a martyr. The conservative papers started to write him off as completely dead timber politically, yet at the same time use this piece of dead timber as a club with which to beat at the President. Wallace seemed more relaxed and tranquil than he had been for years. For one thing, he observed, he could, simply as Vice-

President, make his speeches entirely his own way now, without always running for permission to the State Department. His Detroit speech with the new opening paragraph was the first of a series of pronouncements which within a year restored him measurably in the President's favor and made him, while still a loyal lieutenant to the President, the fighting spearhead of liberals in the Democratic party or even outside who as yet did not believe that the New Deal had ended.

4. In Partial Conclusion

THE REMOVAL of the Vice-President from his special war work, together with the virtual dismissal of his closest friend and associate from public life in that administration, aroused widespread repercussions.

Liberal publications such as *The Nation* reproved the President severely for his indiscriminating attitude of a 'curse on both your houses.' Conservative papers in general took the stand that Wallace had got his comeuppance by reason of his impulsive recalcitrance and it was a good riddance. Of columnists and commentators none was more acid than Raymond Moley, writing in *The Wall Street Journal:*

> Of all the Roosevelt inept actions, the elevation of Mr. Wallace to the nominal rank of statesman was probably the most inappropriate. . . . Even a competent Vice-President could not perform this dual function. . . .
>
> Mr. Wallace had best enjoy as well as possible his remaining eighteen months as Throttlebottom. There won't be any more. . . . The ideological boys have lost their Gandhi, now that Gandhi has lost his second garment. He was the ideal and inspiration of every little world-planner in Washington. They launched their tiny skiffs in the torrents of his wordy discussion. They burbled their admiration of his cloudy philosophical exercises. . . . They snatched at his curious economic ideas like seal seizing their daily ration of food. All this adulation must go to the catacombs now, for the high priest is out of power. . . .

BEW, with assorted bits of the Jones arsenal, is now safely in charge of a regular Democrat who no doubt realizes that Hottentots will not vote in 1944.[6]

'Steady, Mr. Wallace!' the friendlier *Christian Century* advised, adding with expressions of greatest respect: 'If he speaks for a fourth nomination for Mr. Roosevelt, as he probably will, we will have to take issue with him. . . . Mr. Wallace owes it to his cause to divest his presentation as far as possible of the implications of partisan politics, of all name-calling of his critics, of the assumption that the New Deal is the only vehicle by which his cause can be carried to success, and of every tinge of rabble-rousing. . . .'

Under date of August 10, on a familiar letterhead, the Vice-President was glad to hear as follows from an old friend, then in Colorado:

Dear Henry Wallace:

For a month I have been filling up with good intentions to write you and tell you why I am for you in your fight. Which doesn't mean that I am ever going to support you for President or Vice-President. You shinny on your side, and I'll shinny on my side. God knows there is plenty for us to do in both parties. And the Conservatives are about as plentiful and as mean on one side as the other — little fools led by big scoundrels!

But I have an idea that you missed a very fine piece in *The Christian Century*, which I herewith enclose. I read this paper every week, and it seems to me one of the best publications in the country. The statement of the case that it makes comes nearer the truth than I have seen it stated anywhere else.

I was away from home when the President took action in your difference with Jones. If I had been home, I should have written an editorial something along the lines of *The Christian Century*. One of you men was wrong and one was right. It was the President's job to find out which was right and stand by him. I have upheld the President probably more often than any other Republican editor in the country. But when he is wrong, I am free to say so. And I don't wish to be pharisaical but I thank God I have never been bitter about him and have great respect for what he has done and the great war job that is going on under his administration. But between you and me, twelve years is going to get him. I mean, get his keen sense of justice, get his quick reaction to evil. I know personally from experience that there is a certain zone which when a man has walked through it, he has got to be careful. Maybe Time was the scissors that Delilah used for shearing Samson! After which, 'Samson wist not that God had departed from him!' I am afraid — deeply and mortally afraid — because I love my country and want it to go right, that I can hear Delilah's scissors clicking. . . .

This letter is likely to be too long, so I am going to saw it off. I just want you to know you have my blessing and my prayers.

With warm regards, I am

Most cordially yours,

W. A. WHITE, *Editor and Owner*
The Emporia Gazette

Wallace replied August 19:

Dear William Allen White:

Thanks for yours of August 10. I have no illusions as to which side I was shinnying on and no desire to shinny on the other. I suppose the difference between us is that you think there are more rascals in the Democratic Party and I think there are more rascals in the Republican Party. (Jesse Jones is really just as much Republican as he is Democratic. You will remember that he came in with Hoover.)

Frankly, I think it is much easier to get rid of a certain type of reactionary influence in the Democratic Party than it is to get rid of it in the Republican Party. The tragedy of my father was that he tried to fight the reactionary influence in the Republican Party and, as you know, we both stood for the same things.

With all good wishes, I am

Sincerely yours,

H. A. WALLACE

White explained in a later letter that the difference between their respective parties was not in the quantity of the rascals, but the quality:

> It boils down to this: my fellow rascals are greedy pluto-crats; yours are hill-billy democrats. Both hate the kind of democracy that we love. Mine are greedy, yours are igno-rant. I just happen to get more satisfaction fighting greed than ignorance — and I believe better results. Iowa and Kansas are more civilized than Mississippi and Georgia.
>
> I have been in and out of the Republican Party and slammed the door both ways, going and coming, and will do it again if it seems necessary. In the meantime, don't let them kid you out of it. You are on the side of the angels, and in the long run and by and large, you are bound to win. And when you do, I shall be there to applaud you.

Wallace to White, August 31:

> The rank and file of the people in both parties are fine and decent. The rascals are those who work behind the scenes to try and control each party. I believe that rascals in the Republican Party have objectives of such a nature that it would be a very great calamity for them to come back into power.
>
> Well, we shall each keep fighting in our own way and per-haps between us we can produce results.

In a succession of speeches, addressed in the main to labor groups, as 1943 turned into 1944, the Vice-President reiterated 'the four duties of the people's revolution,' which he had formu-lated the year before, as follows:

> 1. The duty to produce to the limit. 2. The duty to trans-port as rapidly as possible to the field of battle. 3. The duty to fight with all that is in us. 4. The duty to build a peace — just, charitable and enduring.

Now he added:

> But if war has its duties, peace has its responsibilities.

Three outstanding peacetime requirements as I see them today are these: 1. The responsibility for the enlightenment of the people. 2. The responsibility for mobilizing peacetime production for full employment. 3. The responsibility for planning world co-operation.

Turning from the North to Texas, he made a fighting speech on a theme which had been a Wallace family favorite ever since the days when old Uncle Henry, crusading for an Interstate Commerce Commission, started off, as he liked to phrase it, 'by putting the fire under Pete Hepburn's tail.' And at the Jackson Day dinner in Washington, January 22, 1944, with the party chiefs assembled to 'draft' Franklin D. Roosevelt for a fourth term, Wallace made far and away the most aggressive talk. The President had been giving some comfort to those in his party who held that wartime was no time whatever for simultaneously pushing liberal policies of domestic reform. Old Doctor New Deal had outworn his needful time, the President said. This was the time for another doctor, Doctor-Win-the-War.

Wallace said flatly to those hundred-dollar-a-plate diners, in a ringing voice:

> The New Deal is not dead. If it were dead the Democratic Party would be dead and well dead. But the Democratic Party is not dead and the New Deal has yet to attain to its full strength. The New Deal is as old as the wants of man. The New Deal is Amos proclaiming the needs of the poor in the land of Israel. The New Deal is New England citizens dumping tea in Boston Harbor. The New Deal is Andrew Jackson marching in the twentieth century. The New Deal is Abraham Lincoln preaching freedom for the oppressed. The New Deal is the New Freedom of Woodrow Wilson fighting the cartels as they tried to establish national and international fascism. The New Deal is Franklin D. Roosevelt. . . .
>
> One man more than any other in all history has given dynamic power and economic expression to the ageless New Deal. That man is Roosevelt. Roosevelt has never denied the principles of the New Deal, and he never will. They are a part of his very being. Roosevelt, God willing, will in the

future give the New Deal a firmer foundation than it has ever had before.

The Vice-President wrote and published in 1944, under imprint of the American Council of Pacific Relations, a fifty-six-page pamphlet, *Our Job in the Pacific*.[7]   There was also published, in boards, that year, an annotated collection of his principal public papers, *Democracy Reborn*.[8]   'Japan,' he wrote in his Pacific pamphlet, 'disrupted the old imperial-colonial pattern of Asia and the Pacific and we must choose whether to aid in restoring the old pattern or to aid in creating a new one. . . . Industrialization will raise the standards of living of Asiatic peoples and create new markets for American goods and opportunities for American investments, but all this will be possible only if accompanied by improvements in Asiatic agriculture. . . . Rural areas, left in a backwash of primitive agriculture, are breeding grounds for social unrest and revolution.'

In April, 1944, the President asked him to fly to eastern Asia over the north-to-the-Orient route to visit New Siberia, and proceed from there to China, bearing personal messages of vital importance to Generalissimo Chiang Kai-shek. 'I have asked the Vice-President of the United States,' the President said, making news of this mission public, 'to serve as a messenger for me in China.   He is taking with him Mr. John Carter Vincent, chief of the Division of Chinese affairs, State Department; Mr. Owen Lattimore, deputy director of the Overseas Branch, Office of War Information, and Mr. John Hazard, chief liaison officer, Division for Soviet Supply, Foreign Economic Administration.'

FEA, the last-named agency, was Mr. Crowley's revamped Board of Economic Warfare, from command of which Wallace and Perkins had been relieved. 'Eastern Asia,' the President continued, 'will play a very important part in the future history of the world.   Forces are being unleashed there which are of the utmost importance to our future peace and prosperity.   The Vice-President, because of his present position as well as his training in economics and agriculture, is unusually well fitted to bring both to me and the people of the United States a most valuable first-hand report.'

The bland air of the statement indicated careful composition, something the President had little time or inclination for under existing pressure. That little word 'present' in the phrase 'present position' raised questions at press conference. Of course, Henry would be back in time for the Convention, said the President. That, too, was taken care of smoothly in the closing paragraph of the formally issued announcement:

'For the time being nothing more can be said of certain aspects of the Vice-President's trip. Suffice it to say that he will be visiting a dozen places which I have long wanted to see. He left today (May 20) and will report to me upon his return, which is expected about the middle of July.'

The opening day of the National Democratic Convention at Chicago had been set for July 19. Wallace, not oblivious to the connotations of the calendar, but to all appearances indifferent, prepared to set forth with a vast interest and eagerness. He figured his maximum load of personal belongings most carefully, so that he could carry many new seeds, vitamins, and medical supplies to eastern Asia. Examining the proofs of *Democracy Reborn* at his desk in Washington on April 11, he dictated an end-note for this collection of his state papers. The gist of the note he dictated was that, while our foreign trade investments after the First World War had been largely wrong — 'We made the wrong investments in the wrong places' — there was still going to be a real need of pushing American exports after the Second World War. 'I have become more and more convinced that the deeply intrenched business habits of the American public will not permit any very rapid lowering of tariffs, a complete investment of savings or sufficiently large-scale government construction based on deficit financing,' he said. 'But the American people are perhaps willing to buy full employment and prosperity on the basis of a large volume of exports. They are willing to accept payments in gold and services to tourists. Eventually they will be willing to accept imports in excess of exports, provided that both they and the world at large are benefiting from a full flow of prosperity.'

Here he reverted to his reiterated central theme of *America Must Choose:*

America will be called upon to make a new choice after this war. Our people, if they really want to do so, could raise their standard of living 50 per cent; but in so doing they would violate many of their cherished convictions. The easiest way to avoid violating the prejudices which have come down to us out of the past would be to rely for full employment in considerable measure on a large volume of exports. Moreover, by pushing in this direction we help the whole world toward the attainment of ease and prosperity. The limit beyond which we must not go in pushing for full exports is the point where, by increasing exports, we increase unemployment elsewhere in the world. We cannot hope to export our unemployment to other nations without an inevitable backlash. Therefore, we must be sure that our exports in the main tend to increase both the productivity and the standard of living of the world.

... We must also be firmly prepared not to take such irresponsible and dangerous action as we did when we enacted the tariff acts of 1922 and 1930. To take such action is simply to declare to the world that a creditor nation is irrevocably committed to the insane policy of never receiving anything in return for its investments. ... Every time our thoughtlessness plants a Hitler seed abroad, the germ of depression is planted within the United States.

Wallace concluded this slowly dictated final footnote to his collected words to that date with the suggestion — 'not fully thought out' — that private concerns might be led under some type of United Nations authority which would provide a guarantee of repayment provided certain conditions were met. 'In brief ... a mechanism like the Federal Housing Authority might give the necessary courage and wisdom to private capital to do an adequate job at a modest fee.'

With this much said, he turned his thoughts to travel, and dictated a statement for the press, to be released with the President's, on May 20, the day of his departure:

The President has asked me to visit Asia. The President is a symbol of hope for hundreds of millions of people throughout the world and I am proud to serve as one of his messengers.

There will be no press or other public representatives with me. The object of the trip is to let our Asiatic friends know the spirit of the American people and the beliefs and hopes of their Commander in Chief.

Asia is just as important to the United States as is Europe. We are fighting a determined enemy in the north, south, and middle Pacific. We fight because of Pearl Harbor. We fight to preserve our freedom, and for the democracies of Australia, New Zealand, and Canada. We fight so that permanent peace and its blessings may become safe for the half of humanity which has its being on the shores of the world's greatest ocean.

The two great lands of China and Russia are glorious in the present. Siberia is the great arsenal without which the Russian victories over Germany could not have occurred. The Chinese will to survive and their resistance has its only counterpart in the defense of Stalingrad, Moscow, and Leningrad. If I may carry to these working and fighting peoples of Asia something of the confidence and pride which the American people and their President feel in their magnificent effort, I know the journey is well undertaken.

The truth which China has been writing on the pages of history for forty centuries is simply that hundreds of millions of peaceful people have never permanently been conquered by war aggression. . . .

Neither the swamps of Burma nor the Himalaya Mountains nor Japanese warships shall stop America from bringing all possible and prompt aid to this great and enduring people. Our President's message to China is just that. . . .

It is with great anticipation that I approach the Siberian experience. This country embraces one eighth of all the land of the world. Under the Tsars it miserably supported fewer people than the State of Pennsylvania — one-hundredth of its size.

A scant twenty-five years have passed. Over 40,000,000 busy people have taken the place of the 7,000,000 — mostly convicts — who miserably existed there under Imperial Russia. So the detractors of Russia must pause before the fact of the Soviet Asia of today.

Soviet Asia in American terms may be called the Wild East
of Russia. America after the Civil War developed her Wild
West, pushing triumphantly to the Pacific — creating what
Los Angeles, San Francisco, Portland, Seattle, and Denver
mean now. The Soviet Asia cities of Novo-Sibirsk, Tashkent,
Krasnoyark, Stalinsk, Semipalantinsk and Alma-Ata are as
equally well known in Moscow and Leningrad as American
West Coast cities are known in Washington and New York.
I shall see these cities. I shall feel the grandeur that comes
when men wisely work with nature.

He saw all of that, and more — cities as great as Pittsburgh, of
shining modern construction, reared on a bleak and deeply frozen
prairie within the past twenty years. At far outland farms and
experiment stations he talked corn and cotton. He had learned
enough Russian to make himself understood in most places if he
phrased it very simply and wrote it out ahead of time. He talked
to a few tremendous gatherings and at a number of elaborate
banquets, but most of his talks were made to small groups of
country people, young and old, in their schools. He kept a diary,
later to be published as a journal.[9] It was quite a while since
1909, when as the family cub of twenty-one, Henry took his first
travel assignment as a farm reporter, going all the way to California, to learn the experience of Iowa farmers who had pushed on
West. He had more space and background now to cover — half
a world in the perspective of all time. The following notes are
typical:

As these Soviet executives talked of towns that would one
day rival Alma-Ata, a question came to mind: Is there a
symbolic comparison between their visions and the outlook of
pioneer America? There is. Think of the opening of the
railroads, and the poet of the 'steam whistle,' Walt Whitman,
who saw the 'countless masses debouch upon vast trackless
spaces.' And even earlier there was Johnny Appleseed, who
crossed the Appalachian barrier, carrying the 'seeds and tree-
souls' of today's American Midwest, 'a state capital in each
apple, all America in each apple.' In our age of the airplane
and itinerant machine tools, the trans-Ural peoples of Soviet

Asia are on the move in a way that is easy for Americans to understand.

We met Katrina Trifovna in Komsomolsk. We were driving from factory to mill in the new town on the Amur. It was Sunday afternoon and everybody appeared to be out either walking or working in victory gardens. Seeing roadside fields that needed to be spaded, I brought the cars to a stop and set the boys to work in various gardens. The exercise was good for us, and the Russians were delighted to be helped out so much. After we had been digging for some time, an old woman came over from her garden near-by. She was Katrina Trifovna, who had lost her husband in a mine accident. In the war her two sons had been killed — one an infantryman, the other a fighter pilot. Most of her teeth were gone, but she still had plenty of spirit.

'My tools are all I have left,' she said as we moved into her garden. She showed us a *palata*, which is a short-handled shovel, not as efficient as an American spade. 'This tool,' she went on, 'will help me grow enough to eat.' Some of our boys began spading her garden. She didn't know who we were, nor did she inquire. Katrina was critical of the local officialdom, giving them a vigorous tongue-lashing. 'Bureaucrats!' she snapped. By the time we left, her garden was spaded. Bowing, she bade us farewell, saying: 'Thank you most heartily.'

He was for three weeks in Siberia. The Russian press carried word of his speeches and of most of the things he saw and did; but little or no news about him was sent outside. Then he flew into China. His first stop was at Tihwa, the capital of Sinkiang Province in Chinese Turkestan. Great crowds of Chinese, Mohammedans, Uigurs, Usbeks, Kazaks, and Kueihuas turned out to see him there. The Governor of the province gave him two bright native rugs, one for himself and one for President Roosevelt. Wallace gave the Governor's wife some strawberries that he had flown in with him from Alma-Ata in Siberia.

Flying on to Chungking, he spent five days with the Generalissimo and Madame Chiang at the presidential villa. Such account of their talks as was put out to the press was exceedingly brief and guarded. In his five days on that ground Wallace went out into the country quite a little. Once they sought to ease him and do him honor by having two coolies carry him in a sedan chair. He flushed and refused almost abruptly. 'I have two strong legs,' he said, 'I want no man to carry me.' The whole party walked to near-by farms together. He had brought forty-three kinds of seed with him to China and wished as far as possible to see where they would be planted. He stripped to the waist to play volleyball with G.I.'s stationed at Chungking and was feted that same evening at a state dinner. After the war, it came out that his principal state mission was to persuade the Generalissimo to permit officers of the United States Army to visit the Chinese communists in the north; and in this Wallace succeeded.

He flew home. It was a twelve-thousand-mile trip in all. Reaching Seattle, he made a speech, extolling Chinese tenacity and Russian achievement, but firmly dissociating himself from belief in communism as a form of government suitable for us. Harold Young, his principal political advisor, who had flown to Seattle to meet him, insisted on that. The 'inside boys' at the White House, Young told Wallace, had moved in on him, against him, as to the vice-presidency; and this, together with the continuing protest of the professional bosses, plus the uproar of rebellious Southern Democrats, in Texas particularly, Young said, made things look bad. Judge Rosenman, speaking from or for the White House, had phoned Wallace in Seattle, saying he had to see him the minute he reached town. Wallace asked Young few questions. He seemed little interested. They had a rough flight to Washington with a forced landing at midnight. Wallace was thin, worn, and rumpled. Too much travel with too many strange and different dishes in the tents of herdsmen, and in Siberian frontier log cabins, and at palatial banquet halls in otherwise half-starved China, had upset his system. He was low in his mind, he told Young, and sick at heart. 'I have just seen a great people desperately waging a death-struggle,' he said, 'in a world fire.' Young's assurances as to all the delegates they had, while gratifying, did not seem of world-shaking importance to him at the moment. From the Washington Airport Wallace drove directly to his apartment at the Wardman Park Hotel and closed the door. He said he did not think he would go to the office that day.

In a narrative such as this one, which reaches back to facts fairly well stratified if not crystalized yet as rocks in the stream of history, but which presses forward most closely now toward whirls and pools, immediate, contemporary, there comes a point where the careful writer will not claim too explicitly to explain just what has happened, or why it happened exactly as it did.

What happened at the Democratic National Convention in Chicago in July, 1944, is such a point. After the event men can and generally do talk with greater honesty, analytically; and that is true even in Washington, an exceedingly talkative town. Congenitally, I take little interest in politics; but I spent two solid months there during the winter just passed, 1945-46, to talk with a considerable number of persons who sat close up on one side and on the other, in the 'Missouri Compromise.'

When of, say, twenty interested and variously biased accounts of the arrangements and proceedings, weighed and sifted, a dozen different patterns connect, check, and agree, here, I figure roughly, we enter the realm of probability; and when around eighteen of the twenty coincide, we may assert facts of a reasonable probability.

The President, it should first be remembered, was an aging, tiring man, still of great spirit and vigor, but bearing a load possibly heavier than any other American in previous history. At one time he had forty-seven different war agencies reporting to him directly. He hated to unload anything, but, as we have seen, he tried to; and the Wallace-Jones bombshell was only one of a number that exploded embarrassingly in his lap. He had no love for Jones, by this time. In general conversation with friends, the President said that he had had enough of old 'Jesus H. Jones,' and was going to shelve him after the next election.

As for Wallace, he sometimes irritated the President; but they greatly liked and respected each other. The vehemence of the presidential 'curse on both your houses,' when the President publicly rebuked them both in 1943, arose, it appears, not only from the natural irritation of an overworked Commander in Chief who had to turn from world plans to a squabble in his anteroom.

Courtesy of Acme Photo

DEMOCRATIC NATIONAL CONVENTION, CHICAGO, 1944
Wallace listening to broadcast of President Roosevelt's address

The President was also sharply aware that the widening rift between old-time Southern Democrats and Wallace Democrats represented an increasing danger to his party and program.

In the earlier days of his administrations, when the President had time for talk and plans in domestic politics — and a great zest in it — he would sometimes compare himself as party head with a man driving at least four wild horses: Liberals, Labor, City Machines, and Southerners. (Not to mention the torn Agrarian mule.) In those days, with more time and zest for such considerations, he would probably never have believed the city 'boys' who kept telling him throughout 1943 that if it were Wallace again for Vice-President, the first three horses would turn and rend each other and the Southerners would bolt. It is doubtful if he believed this even by the beginning of 1944; but the boys, especially after Robert Hannegan of Missouri became National Chairman of the party, kept telling him that was how it was.

They told him that at an informal evening caucus in his study at the White House very early in January of 1944. Three of the men present were city bosses; there were no outstanding New Deal liberals there, that time. He let them talk. They trotted out a string of prospects. First, Judge Douglas; but it was generally agreed that, while perhaps possessed of potential political 'oomph,' Bill Douglas had no important visible following at the moment, except Harold Ickes. Sherman Minton of Indiana was then considered, but the suggestion aroused no spark. Jimmy Byrnes? The President remained noncommittal. Harry Truman? The President said he thought there might be an idea there; but let it cook.

Thus, more than six months before the Convention, the first lines were laid. Hannegan went out, working openly and hard for Truman. Harold Young was out, working just as hard and openly to get delegates for Wallace. Senator Truman said that he was going to be for the 'Assistant President,' Jimmy Byrnes, and would probably make the nominating speech for him at the Convention.

The President said nothing at that time. He had not thus far, it seems, made up his mind. When, however, during Wallace's journey to Asia, Judge Rosenman and Harold Ickes came to him saying that the practical politicos were right; that Wallace on the ticket would split the party wide open, the President was impressed. These men were good New Deal liberals. The Judge, it will be remembered, had backed Wallace for drafting as Vice-President in 1940. It was different now, 'Sammy the Rose' reported sadly; especially in view of the revolt now apparent in the South.

At this juncture, the President vacillated. Only three weeks or so before the Convention, Governor Ellis Arnall of Georgia came in to see him and ask to whom should be delivered the votes of the Georgia delegation. The President told him to make it for Wallace as Vice-President right down the line.

With Wallace's return imminent, and sure to be heralded in headlines, not only because of the glamour and importance of the journey, but by reason of the major speech he was to make at Seattle, the opposition to Wallace, both the practical operators and the White House guardsmen, pressed for decision. The President told Judge Rosenman and Harold Ickes to go to Wallace immediately upon his arrival and tell Wallace what they had been telling him.

Perhaps — probably — the President went further. 'Harry S. Truman,' Judge Rosenman stated in a memorial article in *The New York Times* for April 7, 1946, 'was picked by Franklin D. Roosevelt and by no one else. I make that statement not on information or belief or hearsay. I make it as a matter of personal knowledge.'

On the day of Wallace's arrival back from Asia, Rosenman and Ickes went to the Wardman Park and had lunch with him at his apartment. They told him they admired him greatly; he knew that; but that for him to run for Vice-President again would weaken the ticket. They indicated that this was the view of the White House also and urged him to announce that he would not run.

Wallace replied simply. He said that he would not run unless the President wanted him to and that he would go at once and talk about it with the President. He went that afternoon and had two hours with the President. Much of their talk was about affairs in Asia. Then the President said that a number of people had been in, telling him this and that. What about it? Wallace told the President what he had told the scurrying aides, that he would not run for the Vice-Presidency again unless the President thought it would help the ticket and wanted him to. They arranged to meet for lunch the day following.

At this lunch Wallace showed Roosevelt the list of state delegations Harold Young and he figured on, a total of 290 delegates, at least. The President whistled with surprise. It was news to the President, also, that a forthcoming Gallup poll (published July 20) would show 65 per cent of Democratic voters for Wallace, 17 per cent for Barkley, 5 per cent for Rayburn, 4 per cent for Byrd, 3 per cent for Byrnes, 2 per cent for Douglas, 2 per cent for Truman, and 2 per cent for Stettinius. 'Well, I'll be damned!' the President said.

They discussed tactics. Wallace definitely did not want to be thrust down the throats of another convention simply by the President's favor. He suggested that the President make it known that if he were a delegate, he would vote for the then Vice-President to continue as such, or words to that effect, then leave it open to a fight on the convention floor. Having agreed to this, the two men, who were really deeply fond of each other, and who stimulated each other's minds most usefully and agreeably, talked of many other matters.

As Wallace left, the President reached an arm up from his wheelchair and gave him half a hug, half a pat on the shoulder, 'I hope it's the same team again, Henry,' he said.

But the lines were already set. The others came in for another informal caucus that very night; the projected letter became a letter with a postscript above the signature; and then another letter; and then another. Wallace, himself, was neither surprised nor bitter about the shenanigans which followed. 'I had a much better time at that Convention than I had at the one before,' he says.

And, despite all the gyrations and indirections, the recriminations and the catcalls, the ill-coached CIO young stock, bawling; despite all the talk of presidential perfidy and of presidential obsolescence or dotage which ensued, may we not grant, at this later date, a certain amount of surviving political skill, and even of long-range statesmanship, somewhere hidden in the President's decision?

It was not simply a matter of possible party disunity which he had to decide. He had also to make peace in some measure between the administrative and legislative arms of our Government in order to expect with some assurance to get a better Treaty of Peace with world-wide implications than Woodrow Wilson was able to obtain.

It might not be a better peace; but it might be possible to place fairly firmly upon a better treaty, or approach to peace, the seal of approval of the Senate.

Not since Harding, it must be remembered, had there been a President who had served actively and convivially as a member of that august Club. Coolidge was an honorary member, much as was Wallace; but Hoover had never belonged at all; nor had F. D. Roosevelt, any more than had Woodrow Wilson. Already in the Senate knives were being sharpened. And F. D. Roosevelt had vivid cause to remember what the Senate did to Wilson's, his first Chief's, peace proposals after the First World War.

These are personal surmises, only. Possibly no such thoughts ever occurred to the wide-ranging, hard-driving, infinitely calculating mind of our Commander in Chief and President. But possibly they did. Let us press on.

Late in the week before the Convention the President left Washington for an inspection tour of Western defense works, a journey shrouded in wartime secrecy as to detail. Saturday saw his private car parked in the Chicago railyards. Here, somewhat furtively, making their way through guards, up and coming stalwarts of the new order, Hannegan especially, clambered aboard to get further instructions. This was the first national convention Hannegan had ever managed and he was rather jumpy. His fellow Missourian, Harry Truman, the man for whom he had labored so hard and ardently, was acting, unaccountably, innocent or unbelieving as to all the prearrangements, and pumping hard for Byrnes, who was most receptive. The President's train rolled on toward San Diego, and on Wednesday, July 19, the Convention opened.

The war was storming toward a climax. The banner headlines on page one of *The New York Herald Tribune* that morning of July 19 read:

BRITISH CROSS ORNE, BREAK LINES BELOW CAEN
AMERICANS SEIZE ST. LO; REDS DRIVE ON LWOW

Wallace Goes to Chicago to Fight for Renomination

He motored out to a suburban station on the main line of the
B & O to Chicago and reached Chicago that morning. He put up
in a two-room suite at the Hotel Sherman, which he used very
little. Some of the press complained a shade bitterly that of
course Wallace would never think of it, but Young, being from
Texas and of political experience, should have known better than
to neglect to lay in any liquor at Wallace headquarters in a
reception room downstairs.

Wallace and Young held a press conference just the same,
attended by about one hundred and fifty reporters. 'I am in
this fight to the finish,' Wallace told them. They asked him
what he thought his chances were. 'I really haven't the slightest
idea,' he answered. 'I told the President in justice to himself and
to myself that there should not be anything in the nature of dictation to the convention. The letter did what I suggested.'

This was the first letter publicly released, and generally headlined as the 'Kiss of Death.' Addressed to Senator Samuel D.
Jackson at the Stevens Hotel, Chicago, typed on White House
stationery, but dated at Hyde Park, New York, July 14, 1944, it
read:

My dear Senator Jackson:

In the light of the probability that you will be chosen as
Permanent Chairman of the Convention, and because I know
that many rumors accompany all Conventions, I am wholly
willing to give you my own personal thought in regard to the
selection of a candidate for Vice-President. I do this at this
time because I expect to be away from Washington for the
next few days.

The easiest way of putting it is this: I have been associated
with Henry Wallace during his past four years as Vice-President, for eight years earlier while he was Secretary of Agriculture, and well before that. I like him and I respect him, and
he is my personal friend. For these reasons, I personally

would vote for his renomination if I were a delegate to the Convention.

At the same time, I do not wish to appear in any way as dictating to the Convention. Obviously the Convention must do the deciding. And it should — and I am sure it will — give great consideration to the pros and cons of its choice.

Very sincerely yours,

FRANKLIN D. ROOSEVELT

Governor Robert S. Kerr of Oklahoma placed in nomination for President, somewhat floridly and at too great length, the name of Franklin Delano Roosevelt.

Henry A. Wallace seconded the nomination, as follows, on Thursday, July 20:

As chairman of the Iowa delegation I am deeply honored to second the nomination of the greatest living American — Franklin D. Roosevelt.

The strength of the Democratic Party has always been the people — plain people like so many of those here in this convention — ordinary folks, farmers, workers, and businessmen along Main Street. Jefferson, Jackson, and Woodrow Wilson knew the power of the plain people. All three laid down the thesis that the Democratic Party can win only if and when it is the liberal party.

Now we have come to the most extraordinary election in the history of our country. Three times the Democratic Party has been led to victory by the greatest liberal in the history of the United States. The name Roosevelt is revered in the remotest corners in this earth. The name Roosevelt is cursed only by Germans, Japs, and certain American troglodytes.

The first issue which transcends all others is that complete victory be won quickly. Roosevelt, in a world sense, is the most experienced military strategist who has ever been President of the United States. Roosevelt is the only person in the United States who can meet on even terms the other great leaders in discussions of war and peace. The voice of our New World liberalism must carry on.

It is appropriate that Roosevelt should run on the basis of his record as a war leader. He is successfully conducting a war bigger than all the rest of our wars put together. We must finish this job before the Nation can breathe in safety. The boys at the front know this better than anyone else.

The future belongs to those who go down the line unswervingly for the liberal principles of both political democracy and economic democracy regardless of race, color, or religion. In a political, educational, and economic sense there must be no inferior races. The poll tax must go. Equal educational opportunities must come. The future must bring equal wages for equal work regardless of sex or race.

Roosevelt stands for all this. That is why certain people hate him so. That, also, is one of the outstanding reasons why Roosevelt will be elected for a fourth time.

President Roosevelt has long known that the Democratic Party in order to survive, must serve men first and dollars second. That does not mean that the Democratic Party is against business — quite the contrary. But if we want more small businessmen, as the Democratic Party undoubtedly does, we must modify our taxation system to encourage risk capital to invest in all rapidly growing small business. We want both a taxation system and a railroad rate structure which will encourage new business and the development of the newer industrial regions of the South and the West. Rate discrimination must go.

The Democratic Party in convention assembled is about to demonstrate that it is not only a free party but a liberal party. The Democratic Party cannot long survive as a conservative party. The Republican Party has a monopoly on the conservative brains and the conservative dollars.

Democrats who try to play the Republican game inside the Democratic Party always find that it just can't work on a national scale.

In like manner Republicans who try to play the Democratic game inside the Republican Party find that while it may work on a State basis, it can never work nationally. I know because my own father tried it. Perhaps Wendell Willkie may have learned in 1940 a little of that which my own father learned in 1924. The old elephant never changes and never forgives.

By nominating Franklin Roosevelt the Democratic Party is again declaring its faith in liberalism. Roosevelt is a greater liberal today than he has ever been. His soul is pure. The high quality of Roosevelt liberalism will become more apparent as the war emergency passes. The only question ever in Roosevelt's mind is how best to serve the cause of liberalism in the long run. He thinks big. He sees far.

There is no question about the renomination of President Roosevelt by this convention. The only question is whether the convention and the party workers believe wholeheartedly in the liberal policies for which Roosevelt has always stood. Our problem is not to sell Roosevelt to the Democratic convention but to sell the Democratic Party and the Democratic convention to the people of the United States.

The world is peculiarly fortunate that in times like these the United States should be blessed with a leader of the caliber of Roosevelt. With the spirit of Woodrow Wilson but avoiding the pitfalls which beset that great statesman, Roosevelt can and will lead the United States in co-operation with the rest of the world toward that type of peace which will prevent World War Number 3. It is this peace for which the mothers and fathers of America hope and work.

Issues that will be with us for a generation — perhaps even for a hundred years—will take form at this convention and at the November election. The Democratic Party and the independent voters will give Roosevelt their wholehearted support because of his record in peace and war.

As head of the Iowa delegation, in the cause of liberalism, and with a prayer for prompt victory in this war, permanent peace, and full employment, I give you Franklin D. Roosevelt.

Early that evening the voice of Roosevelt, coming in on tiny loudspeakers from some undesignated Western military base, accepted the nomination for President — an 'eerie' performance, as *Time* reported.

Newspaper wirephotos of the President reading his acceptance speech, crouched over an improvised desk in his private car, reinforced the same foreboding note of eeriness. He looked ghastly. But such were his spurts of high energy and spirit, at this stage, that even those closest around him were inclined to lay to the tricks that flashbulb photography plays an occasional haunting resemblance to the shriveling, dying countenance and frame of Woodrow Wilson.

Returning to that evening session, Wallace supporters, even some of the mightiest, found their places taken by minions of Boss Kelly and their badges or credentials challenged or rejected at the doors. 'This convention is in the hands of the enemy!' stout Harold Young shouted. Harold Ickes, revolting now at the turn things were taking in his native habitat of reform politics, Chicago, plugged hard for Wallace, and sent the President a five-page telegram of protest. But the President was inaccessible.

Only a few hours after the convention had heard his acceptance speech ('like a voice from beyond,' an impressionable Southerner said), Hannegan released the second letter:

White House, July 19.

Mr. Robert E. Hannegan,
Blackstone Hotel, Chicago

Dear Bob:

You have written me about Harry Truman and Bill Douglas. I should, of course, be very glad to run with either of them and believe that either one of them would bring real strength to the ticket.

Always sincerely,
FRANKLIN D. ROOSEVELT

There seems to have been a third letter, of a sort, even briefer, and undated. According to Frank McNaughton and Walter Hehmeyer, collaborating authors of *This Man Truman*[10] (chapter X, 'The Nomination,' pages 148 and 149):

The convention was to meet the next day, and Truman, since his arrival on the preceding Friday, had been talking up Jimmy Byrnes day and night.... Truman was living alone in a suite on the seventeenth floor of the noisy, over-crowded Stevens Hotel. The telephone rang sharply ... Hannegan. ... When he arrived at Truman's room [he] was blunt and direct: 'Harry, the President wants you for Vice-President.' Truman turned a shade pale, his mouth opened and he said, 'I told you, Bob, I don't believe the President wants me for a running mate. I don't believe it.'

'Harry, I can show you,' Hannegan replied. He fished in his pocket, pulled out a note and thrust it over to Truman. It was written in pencil, and it said, 'Bob, I think Truman is the right man. FDR.'

Truman's face registered surprise, incredulity, and some consternation. This disclosure jolted him, and despite the authoritative note and the handwriting which he well recognized, he found it hard to believe. He burst out:

'Bob, I don't want the darned thing.'

Whether authorized or not, this account of Senator Truman's notification, like most accounts of everything that went on that week in Chicago, would seem rather too high-pitched. Talk in the corridors, reflected by talk in the columns, had him weeping, praying, wringing his hands in anguish, doing everything but crawl under the rug. Harry Truman was surely not so green, naïve or scary as that. But it does seem true that he and his wife gave the nod of acceptance to his immediate fate unwillingly.

On the first ballot for the vice-presidential candidate the vote ran: Wallace, 429½; Truman, 319½; Bankhead, 98; Barkley, 49; all others, 280.

At the second ballot, with all the switches thrown, the complete vote, as finally straightened out, after a stampede midway in the balloting, ran thus:

Truman, 1031; Wallace, 105; Douglas, 4; Governor Prentice Cooper of Tennessee, 26; Barkley, 6; Paul V. McNutt, 1.

Then they pulled down the flags and banners and danced in the streets and finally all went home. Henry Wallace sent a wire of congratulations to Harry Truman. His wire was delayed in delivery, because of a bureaucratic dispute within Western Union as to flexing a wartime stay against messages of congratulations.

The President's wire from San Diego congratulating Wallace for his 'magnificent fight' in the convention got through promptly. 'Please tell Ilo,' his message continued, 'not to make any plans for leaving Washington in January.' Ilo is Mrs. Wallace. Henry showed the wire to Harold Young, laughing, and they went out and walked around in a quieter part of that great city for a little fresh air and relaxation. Wallace was headed for his home town, Des Moines, for a week's sleep and rest. He walked alone to his train, carrying his bag. Only one man, a reporter who liked him, recognized him and came up at the station to speak to him. 'I really think,' said Wallace, 'that I can do more for the cause of liberalism this way.'

'The significant event of the Convention,' the *New Statesman and Nation*, London, observed editorially, on August 19, 'was the struggle that raged around the person of Mr. Wallace.'

This English editor went on to say:

> The Democratic Party has always been a Janus that faces both ways. . . . It must always enlist Southern States, which are, with rare exceptions, Conservative and often reactionary. On this occasion the more advanced half of organized Labour, the C.I.O., intervened in the contest with a decision and interest new in American politics, and it, of course, supported Mr. Wallace. The President, who has swung perceptibly to the Right since the last election, did not, on the balance, help his chances . . . . Mr. Wallace, while opposition rolled up from many quarters, definitely refused to lower his flag or play at politics . . . . He campaigned for the social programme of the New Deal and for a planned economy in the international field as well as at home. But his startling act of courage was that he defied the South by calling for the abolition of the Poll Tax, with which it disfranchises its Negroes and the poorest of its white share-croppers. . . .

> The Convention was deeply impressed, and had the vote been taken then it is likely that Mr. Wallace would have been nominated, once again, for the Vice-Presidency. The Machine managed to get it delayed, and in the interval used all its arts to secure the victory of its own choice, Senator Truman, a Southerner. . . .

In recent years, this rather shy and retiring man [Mr.
Wallace] has learned to speak in public with a warmth that
wins affection as well as assent. We should like to think
that his influence will survive this defeat and that some position can be found for him in which he can still exercise his gifts
as a leader and intellectual pioneer. But he is not a Senator,
and will have no recognized place in the life of the Republic
when he steps down from the high office he now holds. The
same thing is true of Mr. Willkie. America often wastes her
leaders. . . .

Back in Washington in the Vice-President's office, which still
was to serve as his base for some months while he traveled and
campaigned for the new ticket, Wallace found awaiting him an
enormous stack of mail. More than two thousand personal
letters were received in a single week and acknowledged by an
expanded staff. Editorials which eulogized him (there were
many, even among more numerous editorial hosannas of praise
for relief and deliverance) did not move him. The great salt tears
of political columnists such as Frank Kent, wailing for the moment
that so simple and saintly a man as Wallace should have been so
mercilessly decapitated, moved him only to quiet laughter. 'Any
stick will do to beat F. D. with. But they can't beat him!' he
remarked. On the other hand, he was deeply moved by far and
away the greatest outpouring of mail from the great mass and
variety of our people ever to reach him up to that time, to express
faith in him and hope for the future.

To one such who had known his family a long while, he wrote,
'I'll be seeing you soon so there is not much need to reply to
yours of July 22. Curiously enough, my grandfather was about
my age when he took a fresh start.' [11]

Of all the letters which came pouring in to him during this
interim, one from George W. Norris, from McCook, Nebraska,
July 31, 1944, pleased him most deeply. It has never been
printed before:

> I listened to the radio and heard every word of your speech
> made in the Democratic Convention, seconding the nomina-
> tion of Mr. Roosevelt. I thought this was one of the best

speeches I ever heard.   It was an exhibition of statesmanship
and courage that I have never seen surpassed.

I do not suppose it would be considered a proper speech for
that occasion by the politicians.   If you had been trying to
appease somebody you made a mistake, but you were talking
straight into the faces of your enemies who were trying to
defeat you, and no matter what they may think or what
effect it may have on them, the effect on the country and all
those who will read that speech is that it was one of the most
courageous exhibitions ever seen at a political convention in
our country.   I was delighted with every word of it, and
regardless of what effect it may have upon those who are
fighting you, it certainly must bring commendation and praise
from every human being who believes in better government
and is opposed to machine politics controlling the national
convention.

I think I ought to add that I am not classifying Senator
Truman as one of the enemies.   I think his nomination was a
very good one.   He came into public life with somewhat of a
cloud because he was probably first elected to the Senate by
the influence of the noted Boss Pendergast.   I watched him in
his public service more than I otherwise would, and I must say
that in all the time I knew him, I never knew of an instance,
I knew of no time that the bosses or the machine controlled
his official work.   I think he has done some very good work.

I congratulate you on the speech you made and I congratulate you on the way you have taken your defeat.   You have
grown mightily in my estimation.   I want you to continue to
grow.

With best wishes, I am,

Yours very truly,

G. W. NORRIS

The old Senator was eighty-three years old.   He died soon after.
G. W. Norris and H. A. Wallace never met again.   But they corresponded.   Norris wrote as follows to Wallace, August 19, 1944:

Why this awful fight over the Vice-Presidency?   Why do so
many other men, good men, able men, like Barkley, for

instance, want to become Democratic Vice-Presidential candidate?... Under the Constitution the Vice-President has very little to do in an official way. Only one contingency makes the office nationally important, the death of the President....

Was this unprecedented clawing for second place on the ticket as ghoulish, Norris asked, as it sometimes seemed to him, now, at his age and at that distance? 'Is it true that the burdens of the presidential office under the terrible stress that war brings are going to kill the President? What are the chances that he will live through the next term of office if he is re-elected? I know that the burdens of this office are terrible at this time. I know too that few men who try to do their duty would be able to stand up under those burdens, and while there [is?] was a greater chance of Roosevelt dying during the four years than under ordinary circumstances, I have not regarded this as a strong probability.

'I am wondering if I am wrong about this. I am wondering if the gambling chances are that he is going to die before he serves out his next term if he is re-elected.... Is this why the machine was so anxious to defeat you?... Coldblooded politicians that handle the various political machines are not moved by any patriotic sentiment. These are the gamblers in the world of politics....'

But, Norris reiterated sharply and warmly toward the end of this long letter, his feeling that the 'gamblers' had bet wrong on Harry Truman; he was not their kind of man:

He has done a very fine progressive work... steered a very fine progressive course... done a wonderful work, I think, in the Committee of which he is Chairman, investigating our various war efforts. Such a man would not be the selection of the machine which nominated him.

Norris's letter to Wallace of this date ended thus:

I come now to another proposition, and that is the attitude of Roosevelt himself. I know that many progressives are angry at Roosevelt and disgusted with him because he did not take a greater part than he did take in attempting to secure **your** renomination for the Vice-Presidency. I do not agree with these people myself, but it is quite evident that he could have secured your renomination had he stood fervently for it, and been rather dictatorial in his action.

Personally I have never believed that the candidate on the national ticket for President had the right to arbitrarily dominate the convention in its action over the nomination of a Vice-Presidential candidate. I think his wishes ought to have carried weight, and ought to be given consideration, but to take away from the convention the absolute right to nominate a Vice-President and place that in the control of one man is a step toward dictatorship.

On August 29 Wallace had lunch at the White House. It was the first time he and the President had met since the Convention. WALLACE LUNCHES WITH ROOSEVELT; 'FAMILY THERE,' SO POLITICS IS OUT, *The New York Herald Tribune* headlined the story, and reported chattily:

> ... The circumstances left most observers agreeing that politics is a funny business. ... Asked as he left the White House whether he and Mr. Roosevelt had talked politics, Mr. Wallace sort of shrugged and said, 'Well, the family was there,' and the impression reporters got was that no politics had been talked because of that fact. They further conjectured that the luncheon may have been planned that way to prevent mention of politics and of Mr. Roosevelt's acquiescence to the demand of Democratic bosses, that Mr. Wallace be dropped from the ticket as a political liability.
>
> Mr. Wallace was referring to the presence, at the luncheon under the Andrew Jackson magnolia tree, of the President's daughter, Mrs. John Boettiger; her children, Anna Eleanor Dall Boettiger and Curtis Dall Boettiger, and a distant cousin of the President, Miss Margaret Suckley. 'Mrs. Roosevelt had lunch elsewhere, but came in for some of the talk before Mr. Wallace left.
>
> Mr. Wallace said that he talked primarily with Mr. Roosevelt about his recent trips into New England, Texas, and Georgia, reporting on his talks with 'a great many mayors'

about the problems to be faced with returning service men and dislocated war workers.

Asked about his future plans, Mr. Wallace said: 'Nothing particular, but I will be active.'

'In a political sense?' he was asked.

'From the standpoint of the welfare of the country as I see it,' he said.

He said he knew of no plans for future trips outside the country, saying: 'The thing to do now is get November 7 out of the way.'

He was asked how he found the political winds blowing in his recent trips, and his reply was: 'The Democrats in Maine were remarkably hopeful.'

Later a correspondent asked Mr. Roosevelt at a press conference, 'Did you talk about the schedule of his coming speeches?' and Mr. Roosevelt replied that he did—yes, right in front of the family, too.

One of the family, at least, had become since the Convention rather more of a supporter of Wallace than she had been before. Reviewing his book of public papers, *Democracy Reborn*, in *The New Republic* for August 7, 1944, Eleanor Roosevelt wrote of him as 'a human being who has become a statesman; . . . driving into the minds of the American people certain truths made clear as no other statesman in this period has done.' Her review continued:

> Mr. Wallace's extensive training in journalism and in the technique of scientific experiment help one to understand the patience which he showed as Secretary of Agriculture. Mr. Wallace never was a politician and is not a very good one now, but he has long been a thinker and writer. That is why his speeches, until very recently, read much better than they sound. He has had to become a speaker.
>
> If one were to pick out the one outstanding and continuing theme of all that Wallace says, it is his belief that whatever is done, must be done for the general welfare of the majority of the people. This belief colors his attitude on domestic as well as international problems.
>
> You will hear people say that they are afraid of Henry Wallace because he is a dreamer, an impractical person, a

mystic. No one who reads these speeches attentively would be afraid on any of these counts. They would recognize instead a man of curiosity, of deep religious feeling, not bound by any particular doctrine. They would know that he had to be practical because his scientific training was too intense to allow loose thinking. They would know that out of his background, nothing which was not truly American could possibly grow. He has traditional American attitudes on so many things that this fear of him which has been implanted in some people's minds, will seem strange to anyone who reads him carefully.

He is a realist. In 1933 he recognized that he could not embark on the realization of his own theory of abundance until he had cleared away the wreckage left by the past, and changed the political and economic philosophy which had preceded him. That is the attitude of a practical, straight-thinking person. There is a unity of thought in what he writes about the hopes the American people have for the future. It runs through every year of his life. Back in 1933 we find him saying:

'In brief, then, we wish a wider and better controlled use of engineering and science to the end that man may have a much higher percentage of his energy left over to enjoy the things which are non-material and non-economic, and I would include in this not only music, painting, literature and sport for sport's sake, but I would particularly include the idle curiosity of the scientist himself. Even the most enthusiastic engineers and scientists should be heartily desirous of bending their talents to serve these higher human ends. If the social will does not recognize these ends, at this particular stage in history, there is grave danger that Spengler may be proved right after all, and a thousand years hence a new civilization will be budding forth after this one has long lain fallow in a relative Middle Ages. . . .'

It was at the luncheon on August 29, under the Andrew Jackson magnolia, that Franklin Roosevelt told Henry Wallace to choose any cabinet post he wanted except Secretary of State. Wallace chose Commerce. Later, when the President sent his name up to Congress for that post, and Wallace was asked by reporters why he preferred Commerce to Labor, War, Navy or another go at Agriculture, Wallace replied: 'My father found as Secretary of Agriculture, and told me, that he could never get economic justice for Agriculture until we educate the business men of the country that this is necessary; and that unless we get such justice for all groups, there will be no assurance of peace and plenty for all of us. In eight years at the same job in the Department of Agriculture I found out that my father was right. That is why I told the President I would be Secretary of Commerce; and I think that we ought to be able to do some good work toward full employment, the building up of small businesses, and healthy international trade, in that Department.'

Wallace took a small, hard part in the campaign of 1944, which really was not much of a campaign. His remark that, while he hated to say it, every vote for Dewey would be considered pleasing in Berlin, aroused in a minor way the same indignation and excitement that his definition of the Republican Party as the party of appeasement stirred up in the previous campaign. He traveled a long, hard schedule under wartime travel conditions. On one jump Midwest, he stood in a jam-packed daycoach from six in the evening until two the following morning. No one recognized him and no one offered him a seat. He came in tired but well.

On the day of his fourth inaugural the President, addressing Mr. Jones as 'Dear Jesse,' sent him a letter which, he confessed in his opening paragraph, he found 'very difficult' to write. With thanks for Jones's 'splendid services,' he asked for Jones's resignation as Secretary of Commerce, explaining:

> Henry Wallace deserves almost any service which he believes he can satisfactorily perform. I told him this at the end of the campaign, in which he displayed the utmost devotion to our cause, traveling almost incessantly and working for the success of the ticket in a great many parts of the country. Though not on the ticket himself, he gave of his utmost toward the victory which ensued.
>
> He has told me that he thought he could do the greatest

amount of good in the Department of Commerce, for which he is fully suited. And I feel, therefore, that the Vice-President should have this post in the new Administration.

It is for this reason only that I am asking you to relinquish this present post to Henry, and I want to tell you that it is in no way a lack of appreciation for all that you have done, and that I hope you will continue to be a part of the Government.

The letter closed with a hasty and airy suggestion that Jones drop around some time and see Ed Stettinius at the State Department; they might have something in the way of an ambassadorship for him there. Stung and defiant, aging Jesse Jones — he was now seventy-one — made immediate public reply:

It is difficult to reconcile [your] encomiums with your avowed purpose to replace me. While I want to be of any further service, I would not want a diplomatic assignment.

I have had satisfaction in my Government service because I have had the confidence of the Congress, as well as your own. I have had that confidence because I have been faithful to the responsibilities that have been entrusted to me. For you to turn over all these assets and responsibilities to a man inexperienced in business and finance will, I believe, be hard for the business and financial world to understand. . . .

Old-line Southern leaders in the Senate swung at once into line with most of the Republicans. On the day that the President flew for Yalta to confer with Stalin and Churchill, George of Georgia, Chairman of the Senate Finance Committee, introduced a bill to sever all lending agencies from the Department of Commerce. This and the question of confirming Wallace as Secretary of Commerce were referred jointly to the Commerce Committee, of which Josiah Bailey of North Carolina was Chairman. Senator Bailey made it known that he favored the George bill and called hearings which opened on January 24.

In his pamphlet, *An Uncommon Man: Henry Wallace and Sixty Million Jobs*, Frank Kingdon, a publicist and radio commentator, remarks that the contrast between the testimony of Jones and Wallace on successive days, January 24 and 25, was such as might

challenge the satirical powers of a George Bernard Shaw or
Jonathan Swift; and yet, Kingdon adds, there was discernible
throughout the performance an undercurrent of serious drama —
'The Nation's Choice for the Future Charting of Its Course.' [12]
Of the ensuing debate on the Senate floor, *The Times*, London, on
January 30, took a similar solemn view:

> There is a sense in which this particular struggle . . . is
> nearer to the realities of American life than the recent presi-
> dential election.   In that contest, Mr. Dewey, the Republican
> candidate, did not challenge the New Deal, and indeed
> chagrined his more reactionary supporters by his domestic
> liberalism. . . .
> But the Wallace-Jones debate may well come to rank in
> American history with the Hayne-Webster debate as pregnant
> with significance in the future.   It involves all those mighty
> issues which agitate men's minds when they look forward to
> the world after the war — the true function of Government in
> a democratic state; the yearning to be rid of the scourge of
> unemployment; the conflict between the social conscience
> and the nostalgia for the old ways; the strenuous attempt to
> reconcile freedom and control, to prevent the one from
> becoming self-destructive, and the other from becoming
> tyrannical. . . .
> Mr. Wallace has emerged as the apostle of full employment
> at home and of an expansionist trade policy abroad.   He
> believes that if, by the co-operation of the State and private
> industry, 60,000,000 Americans can be found jobs, not only
> the United States but the whole world will benefit.   He is
> convinced that if the standard of living in such countries as
> India and China can be raised even slightly there will be such
> an abundance of demand as to keep the wheels turning in all
> the industrial communities of the West.   Whatever his limi-
> tations, Mr. Wallace's conception of a world set free from
> hunger, want, and fear through a deliberately fostered policy
> of expansion is one that commends itself to the sympathies of
> many people outside the United States.
> The issue which antagonizes Mr. Wallace and Mr. Jones is

the issue which divided Jefferson and Hamilton, Washington's Secretary of State and his Secretary of the Treasury — the rights of the 'common man' as against the privileges of the money power. At Cleveland's second nomination his proposer said: 'We love him for the enemies he has made.' That is the feeling that most of his supporters entertain for Mr. Wallace. The fascination of this debate is the fashion in which it strikes to the roots of the central political conflict that has agitated the Republic since its birth — even though in its modern context the advocate of a strong and a weak central authority have changed sides. In the hands of a man with the political principles of Mr. Wallace the Department of Commerce, together with the mobilized power of the Federal Government, can be made into the vehicle of full employment policies internally and liberal trade policies externally. It seems likely at the moment, however, that in the next few weeks either the Department of Commerce will be shorn of its lending powers or the appointment of Mr. Wallace will be blocked. But however the decision of the Senate may go it should not be imagined that the debate will thus be ended. Principles and personalities are too closely entangled for the decision to be clear-cut or final, and the underlying question of future economic policy is too important for America and the world to be answered upon side-issues.

The hearings provided an amazing side-show before the more formal debate. On the opening day Jones made entrance with a jest about 'the gate receipts.' A packed chamber of loyal satellites found this charming. Senator George, favoring Jones, read off a list of the federal financial structures Jones commanded, a staggering number, transferred to his management as Secretary of Commerce and head of the RFC by the Reorganization Act of 1939. It took Senator George twenty minutes to encompass, even in strictest summary, the 'loan powers' wielded by Jones. Jones listened complacently. Then, helpfully, Chairman Bailey asked him, 'Have you ever used your powers as Loan Administrator and RFC Chairman for the purpose of determining the economic character or the social character of the country?'

'I certainly have not!'

In his prepared statement, Jones had spoken of Wallace, inferentially, as 'willing to jeopardize the country's future with untried ideas and idealistic schemes.' Led now by friendly questioners, he rambled on and rumbled on, quite at ease and comfortable before an audience who heard him, for the most part, sympathetically, with rapt approval, with even a sort of awe: 'I have been honored by Congress a great deal and by the President. You have passed laws enough . . . to make me lie awake nights and worry, and as a result I have found it necessary to lie awake nights and worry. . . . RFC is bigger than General Motors and General Electric and Montgomery Ward and everything else put together, and you don't hear much about it by business men, men who haven't any idea about remaking the world. [*Laughter and applause.*] Plodders — not smart, just plodders, trying to do a job honestly and constructively; and they have done it.'

He was asked reverentially about the extent of his power to lend public money. 'For general purposes, up to fourteen billion dollars. . . . For the war effort, eighteen billion dollars,' up to then, 'with thirty-two or thirty-three billion dollars authorized; it hasn't all been used. We have not held anybody up one minute. . . . Back in 1940 we started building plants and we would do it on the telephone. Knudsen would call up, " Can you do this; can you do that — a hundred million dollars here, two hundred million dollars there?" " Yes." That is the way we have run the business.'

The Chairman asked: 'What are the limits? How far can you go?'

'We can lend anything that we think that we should. Any amount, any length of time, or any rate of interest . . . to anybody that we feel is entitled to the loan.'

Senator Pepper of Florida asked the witness whether, if the George bill were enacted, he would expect to stay on as Federal Loan Administrator. That would be up to the President, Jones replied. Continuing with unfriendly questioning, Senator Pepper nettled Jones by implying that his was a sort of 'squatter's sovereignty.' Then Pepper asked:

'Out of your experience, Mr. Jones, is it not your opinion that these two offices [Commerce and the loan powers] can be administered by one man, assuming the competence of that man?'. . .

'If you are trying to ask me if Henry Wallace is qualified for both jobs, I will say, " No."' [*Applause.*]

He seemed never, to the very verge of his complete and cruel dismissal by the President from public life, to be able to understand that he was being discarded. Now at this hearing he brought forth further friendly laughter when, in rumbling derision of Wallace's known concern for small businesses, he described himself as ' a little business man . . . and I also know the big fellows . . . they are awfully smart. Men come to us drawing $100,000 a year salary, maybe; and they talk to our boys who are getting $6000, $7000 or $8000, and they do not run away with anything. You know, we are the sugar, and there is where the flies are. Where the money is, that is where the moochers are, and the moochers have not all been in WPA; they are in business.'

Senator Pepper returned to his main question: If one man, Jones, could do both the jobs, might not another?

'I do not believe there is another fellow in the world that will do it except me.'

Again the crowd applauded.

Next day a different crowd of equal size assembled in the same hearing chamber. They cheered for Wallace when he entered, smiling but tense. Wallace brought forth a long prepared statement and made a rather edgy start in reading it. But at the end of the first paragraph he had written two sentences that hit home:

'You know and I know that it is not a question of my lack of experience. Rather, it is a case of not liking the experience I have.' [*Applause.*]

More than six billion dollars had been loaned under his supervision as Secretary of Agriculture, his prepared statement continued — 11,500,000 separate commodity credit loans, 1,208,000 rural rehabilitation loans, with a very high rate of recovery. But that was not the real issue:

> The real motive underlying these suggestions for stripping the Department of Commerce of its vast financial power has, of course, nothing to do with my competence. The real issue

is whether the powers of the Reconstruction Finance Corporation and its giant subsidiaries are to be used to help only big
business or whether these powers are also to be used to help
little businesses and to help carry out the President's commitment of 60,000,000 jobs. . . .

This is not any petty question of personalities. This is a
question of fundamental policy. It is the question of the
path which America will follow in its future. . . .

Reverting to Jones's expressed contempt for 'a man willing to
jeopardize the country's future with untried ideas and idealistic
schemes,' Wallace read:

These people think they are realists. Actually, they are the
persons of limited vision and stunted imagination. These
people are of the same breed of 'sound business men' who
haggled over pennies in the purchase of strategic stockpiles
before the war, only to leave the materials for the Japs to use
against us. . . .

These people think the same as those who said the President was dreaming when he declared in 1940 that the American people would produce 50,000 planes in one year. Do
these Monday morning quarterbacks have the great faith in
the American people, and in their way of life, which is required to understand the meaning of America?

No soldier on the battlefield can do less than carry out his
assignment. Certainly we on the home front cannot hesitate
to do anything less. Both must give their all in the common
cause. [*Applause.*]

That was at the morning session. The resumed session that
afternoon was in a number of ways noteworthy. First Senator
Pepper, for the defense, having forewarned Wallace that they
would have to 'brag' — as Wallace expressed it later — that the
seed-corn business he had founded and still held part in was
making a gross of around four million dollars a year, put a friendly
question: 'You have been able to manage your own private affairs
in a frugal way, so that you have been able to stay off of the WPA,
or to live other than on the public salary which you have received?'

'I am not one really to talk about private affairs. What have they been saying about me?' Wallace blushed and squirmed like a schoolboy taken in some misdemeanor. Then:

'You think the feeling of the American public is that only a millionaire should be Secretary of Commerce? Is that the idea?' [*Applause.*] Then, starting wryly, 'If it is any assurance to this Committee, the only institution with which I have any business responsibility is a seed-corn company,' he put on the record testimony which startled a great many people out of fixed images of him as a completely other-worldly dreamer. Toward the end of this passing small ordeal — but to him a highly serious one — he seemed to sense in the audience not only astonishment but friendly interest, and really bragged a little, with heightening spirit:

... The thing was my idea; it was based on my own corn-breeding work. I had started experiments in 1906 ... had greatly expanded them in 1919, incorporated the business in 1926. I had very little money myself at the time, due to the farm depression. I raised the money myself. In co-operation with a lawyer I wrote out the articles of incorporation myself. I selected all the key people in the company myself. The farm manager, all the folks that are key people in the company today, are people that I picked at the time. I determined every step of the organization of the concern as it went along. It was genuinely a small business in its initiation.

I know the problems of the small business man because I have lived with them. My name has been on the note at the bank for more money than I could possibly pay unless the seed-corn were sold. I know what that experience is. I have been up against that more than many men who claim that they are hard-headed realistic business men and I am not. I know what this is because I have been up against it.

Last year this company sold more than $4,000,000 worth of seed-corn. I resigned as president of the concern when I came to Washington, and shortly thereafter I got my brother into the business. Last night he called me up to wish me luck at this hearing and I asked just out of curiosity how much money the concern owed the banks at the present time and was told it was $800,000. Of course if the sales of corn go up well between now and next May all of that money will be paid off. Last year, I believe, they borrowed something like $1,000,000. They have always paid off the money they borrowed at the banks.

I won't go into any more detail on that. If any of you have any questions about any aspects of my business, either in my private life or in Government, I will be pleased to answer them. I have always felt this kind of talk more or less beside the point, and that it dignified propaganda too much.

The remainder of the hearing that afternoon was on an unusually high plane. The Chairman, Josiah Bailey of North Carolina, a man of no mean mental caliber, engaged with the witness in an extended argument, conducted with mutual respect, on the soundness of governments going deeply into debt in wartime and during reconstruction periods afterwards.

'In the decade of the twenties,' Wallace pointed out, 'when we were going into debt we had full employment. I think we must give the administration of that day credit.'

'Would you give the administration credit or would you give the people credit?' Senator Bailey asked.

'You have asked a question that would take quite a long time to answer. Your questions, Senator, always have the deepest philosophical implications.'

Then Wallace quoted Macaulay to controvert Bailey's quotations from the elder Pitt; then they clashed on the question of internal production controls, for which controls Bailey expressed a resolute disfavor. Wallace scored mildly at this point:

> I remember how eager the Senator was to have restrictions put on the potato crop some years ago. At that time, the Senator may remember that I referred to a Bible story: When the Children of Israel came to Samuel and he said, 'It's up to you — a king will do many bad things to you but if you want a king go ahead and have one.' I think that is exactly what I said to the Senator.

As for export and import limitations, Wallace said:

I must say that the problem was not quite as simple as I thought it was when I left the Republican Party. After World War I, when we emerged as a creditor nation, and a very powerful foreign trade drive, very skillfully done, was put on through the Department of Commerce, I felt very critical because almost simultaneously . . . we raised our tariff. . . .

Then we put a pitchfork against the bellies of these foreign nations, saying, 'No, you don't, you so-and-so; stay away from here; we won't let you pay up.' I said that kind of thing was bound to produce irritation; bound to create the most serious kind of trouble. . . . I really think it was the fundamental cause of the rise of Hitler, the fundamental cause for a great deal of disturbances we have had all over the world. I have felt that most deeply.

Now, here we come after this war. Again, we are a creditor nation. I want to say that I have considerable sympathy with Herbert Hoover's problem as Secretary of Commerce right now, because I can say that I am going to go all out to get the maximum of use of whatever powers may reside in the Bureau of Foreign and Domestic Commerce to foster and develop trade here and abroad. I am going to use those powers to the maximum to get an increase in foreign trade and, undoubtedly, for a period of five or possibly ten years after the war there will be a great excess of exports over imports. As Secretary of Commerce I would be contributing perhaps as much as any single individual to producing a situation like that for which I criticized the Republican Party back in the decade of the twenties.

I say from the standpoint of the United States and the whole world, that there should for a time be an excess over imports, but we should embark on this policy with our eyes open, with the idea that eventually we will receive more goods than we export. Those men who are in Congress who are going to be here for a period of years; and that means, of course, the Southern Senators, should keep this in mind.

Senator Bailey interjected drily: 'They change.'

Wallace was on the stand for nearly five hours. When Senator Brewster of Maine objected to the President's bald statement that he was removing Jones to pay a debt to Wallace, Wallace replied that, in a sense, he was grateful: 'I never felt I was primarily a political figure, but I am glad to be recognized as having some competence in the political field, which hasn't always been recognized hitherto.' But did not such transactions smack of Farleyism? 'Senator,' said Wallace, still replying to Brewster, 'I can't help hoping that maybe the Democrats will get the same percentage of jobs as they got of the national vote in the last election, namely 53.6 per cent. If 53.6 per cent of the people of the United States are Democrats, it seems to me they have a right to 53.6 per cent of the jobs.

'It is only good administration that in policy positions there be men administering policy who are in sympathy with the policy of the administration. I feel that definitely and clearly, from the standpoint of appointments. I would hope that the Democratic National Committee, under its present management, would show the same high sense of morality Jim Farley used to show.

'Jim never forced a man on me at any time. Jim thought that if there were a Democrat with equally high qualifications, he should be given a break. If the same high standards followed by Jim Farley in his relation to the Department of Agriculture were generally followed, I am sure that the Government would be well served.'

The entire hearings, with full documentation, are entered in Senate Document, No. 68424.[13] Most of it is quite readable; this was a lively hearing. 'Wallace,' I. F. Stone, a sharply pro-Wallace observer, wrote in *The Nation* for February 3, 1945, 'did not seek to placate the committee, to trim his sails, to gloss over his fundamental beliefs. He laid out his post-war full-employment program with courage, zest, and a passionate sincerity. He has Jefferson's wide-ranging mind and Lincoln's homely human goodness, and the committee was impressed despite itself. . . . Wallace is a hard man to hate face to face, and the hearing must have disappointed the Jones supporters.'

Westbrook Pegler, on the other hand, saw in this 'not too bright, and, by himself, an amiable and harmless bleeding heart,' a really dangerous character, who had fooled 'a small group of Washington journalists, some of them innocent dupes of their own sentimentalism.'

These 'yearning essayists,' Pegler continued in his syndicated column for February, 1945, 'forever seeking another Lincoln ... overlook Lincoln's many faults, including his frequent contempt for law and his unmanly submission to the rule of a vixen in his home even to the extent of keeping his own son safe from war while he was rounding up by force the sons of other mothers to die horribly in battle. Such Lincoln-seekers pounce eagerly on any untidy man with a bang over his eyes, not unlike Hitler's, if it comes to that, knee-sprung pants and a clumsy, fumbling public manner, which may be sheer political affectation. Given these properties and some generalities stolen from Jesus Christ, such as the brotherhood of all mankind and the great virtue of the poor, and the people can be fooled. Hitler, too,' Pegler concluded, 'was humble in his early days.'

The debate in the Senate was valuable principally in revealing the remarkable extent to which the most ardent vilification and adulation which in pre-war New Deal times had been directed at the President, now bore directly upon Wallace, staunchest of the confessed surviving New Dealers, and the most important. Senator Taft made the principal speech against Wallace's confirmation. Senator Hill of Alabama made the most fervid closing plea in Wallace's behalf. The George bill got intricately tangled up in parliamentary machinery, but test votes indicated plainly that confirmation of Wallace as Secretary of Commerce would be impossible without a separation of the loan powers. The President sent word from Yalta to put the confirmation through without the loan powers.

Confirmation as Secretary without the loan powers was given, fifty-six for and thirty-two against, on March 1, 1945. Wallace went to work at his new post March 4. He walked to the office as usual. It was a slightly shorter walk than it used to be to Agriculture. The great bulk of the gigantic Department of Commerce building covering eight acres, three full city blocks, was built during Hoover's secretariat, and was Hoover's special pride. Now it was taken over very largely by jamming war agencies. The Department personnel was 32,339 in number, with but 10,102 of them in Washington. But the Secretary's private office and anteroom, each about the size of a tennis court, stood empty. Wallace slipped in a side entrance by way of the north court and took over.

To a friend the new Secretary pointed out, engraved above the portals of the Fifteenth Street north entrance, these words: *Commerce defies every wind, outrides every tempest, and invades every zone.* — Bancroft. 'That's what my father used to say about Mr. Hoover and his Department of Commerce,' said Secretary Wallace. 'It's curious, but I'm going to try to do here just what Hoover tried to do hardest — push exports. Only, I'm going to push even harder for imports.'

His only book in 1945 was *Sixty Million Jobs*, published jointly by an unprecedented arrangement between two houses,[14] one in cloth and one in paper, with the text identical. He set up a small foundation to expend for economic studies any money the book made. It was his ninth major book or pamphlet up to that time. He had started work on it the previous January when the month's unreadiness on the part of Congress to confirm him as a fit Secretary of Commerce gave him a spell of unaccustomed leisure. Considering that he himself was technically unemployed and facing a trying public hearing at the time, not only his opening chapters but the work as a whole breathe forth an altogether extraordinary serenity and good humor. In opening he says flatly: 'We can attain the goal of sixty million jobs and a national income of two hundred billion dollars without a " planned economy," without disastrous inflation, and without an unbalanced budget that will endanger our national credit.' The matter, he adds, is of such gravity that it 'allows for no quibbling or demagoguery' and his sixty million jobs must be regarded as symbolic of full employment, 'not arithmetically exact'; it may be fifty-nine million or again sixty-one million; but sixty million, he is persuaded, is about right.

Much of the argument will be familiar to those who have come thus far in this chronicle of his family and their times; but this work, *Sixty Million Jobs*, is for the most part the most refreshingly and delightfully written of all Henry A. Wallace's books to date.

Even as far as he needs must go into intricate matters of governmental budgeting, he pleads for financing, public and private, in terms of real and enduring values; and at almost every point he keeps the argument close to the ground. 'The Wallaces always have tilled the land,' he writes toward the end. '"Uncle Henry," my grandfather, and my father taught me this one basic fact — the farmer, if he is worth the seed he sows, is a humanitarian.'

He set himself to cleaning up an Augean clutter of neglect in the Department of Commerce. On April 12, 1945, President Roosevelt died. Reporters, sensing drama in the deeply sorrowing countenance of this man who might have been the bearer of the heaviest load in our history, asked Henry Wallace where he had heard the news. 'In the dentist's chair,' he answered shortly.

Later, and more privately, he said that he had thought or hoped Franklin D. Roosevelt probably would live to the war's end, or even to the end of his fourth term, or longer. He had gravely feared for the President's life, Wallace said, the previous August, when even in public utterance the President gave the appearance of a man stricken and worn beyond all possible restoration. 'But the campaign revived him. The old war horse seemed to be almost well then — quite himself again.'

For a symposium of appraisals issued by *The New Republic*, April 15, 1946, to commemorate the first anniversary (April 12) of the death of Franklin Delano Roosevelt, Wallace hastily dictated a short article entitled, 'He Led the Common Man':

> To those of us who worked with Roosevelt day by day, the outstanding thing about him was his ability to lift the spirits of those around him. No matter how difficult the problem, he always had a worthwhile suggestion.
>
> His leadership was always on behalf of the common man both in the United States and the world. In his airplane flights abroad he was impressed by the miserable living conditions in certain backward areas. He was convinced that it would eventually prove profitable to the United States to furnish engineering leadership to these areas.
>
> He was completely shocked by imperialistic exploitation of backward peoples and felt that in some way he could do something about it.

His vision was always worldwide. As a boy he loved post-age stamps, maps, and boats — symbols of things which would take him everywhere in the world. No other man had such a detailed, personal, vivid understanding of world geography.

The first time I met Roosevelt he started talking to me about the shelter belt of trees to be planted in the Great Plains all the way from Texas, through Nebraska, to North Dakota. Those were the days of the dust storms and he felt that if trees were planted the weather would change. To me some of his agricultural ideas seemed fanciful; nevertheless, experience proved many of them to be far more practical than I had expected. His love for trees equaled his affection for maps and boats. When he registered to vote, he gave his occupation as that of 'tree planter.'

He might also have called himself an architect and dam builder. He loved to draw plans of just how things should be built. No President except, perhaps, Jefferson was so precisely conscious of space relationships. The engineering aspects of the TVA fascinated him. But in the final analysis, the TVA interested him most as a demonstration of how the living standards of people might be raised.

Roosevelt was not a scientist, but he had an intuition which made him respond in a remarkable way to the suggestions of scientists. The outstanding example, of course, was the way he acted at once on Einstein's atomic-bomb suggestion in the fall of 1939. It took the highest order of executive courage to pour more than two billion dollars into an utterly untried project. No President ever had such a remarkable combination of courage and imagination. Without that imaginative courage, America would not today be the world's greatest democratic nation.

No one in the United States will ever again be elected four times to the presidency with the support of a party victory in seven successive congressional elections. Undoubtedly, Roosevelt made many political mistakes, but the essential fact remains that he held the Democratic Party together, as an effective political force, at a time when no one else could have done it. He made it an instrument of progress without completely alienating the conservative elements in his own party. Many accused him of duplicity when he was merely reconciling in a practical way conflicting elements. He played his politics by ear. Or perhaps we should say that he composed as he went along. He never wavered in his desire to serve the plain people, but his political methods and political advisers might change in the twinkling of an eye. In making these changes he was as impressionable as a woman and responded sometimes to the pressure of the last person who saw him. Yet, he always prided himself on being a hard-headed stubborn Dutchman. And at times he was exactly that. This combination of adaptability and stubbornness baffled everyone. Henry Morgenthau, when I first saw him fourteen years ago, summed it all up briefly by saying — 'This man Roosevelt is lucky.'

Yes, he was lucky. He came on the national scene at a time when his unique qualities could best serve the world. He died as soon as he had made his essential contribution. He missed the bitterness of postwar wrangling. He missed the Woodrow Wilson tragedy of seeing his mental and physical powers slip away when the world need for those powers was greatest.

His passing was our loss but his gain. His name will live as long as the memory of man.

HENRY A. WALLACE

AFTERWORD

December 1, 1946

THE PLAN OF THIS BOOK as laid down in its first chapter, first drafted early in 1940, was to treat of the Henry Wallace who is born in Chapter V, not as a stray, unpredictable character thrust by odd circumstances upon the world's attention, but as a man born and reared to fulfill definite purposes in his time. He is no chance growth. The product of an extraordinary heritage and upbringing, deeply — almost broodingly — aware of a genetic continuity in his every act, he lives, moves, and grows as a continuing force.

But how do you end a book about a continuing force, or when? That has been a problem for some years now. Originally, the publisher's contract called for a completed production by the end of 1942. In ordinary times, with ordinary schedules holding, that might have been possible. But, with war imminent, the President broke precedent doubly, first by consenting to be 'drafted' for a third term, second by so consenting only if he could have Wallace as official heir apparent. The harsh, accompanying displacement of expectant Presidents and Vice-Presidents seemed certain to arouse robust political repercussions later, and so it proved. Next to the President himself, Wallace became during the war years probably the most discussed, abused, adored, and derided man in the land. His detractors kept shouting that he was about to pass into complete obscurity, but all the time he kept growing less obscure.

They are saying again now that he is through, but the very intensity of the clamor predicting his obliteration in national and world affairs seems to make such obliteration unlikely.

That 'fluidity of change in Society,' which is, according to Tugwell, 'the despair of theorists,' raises problems for the contemporary biographer too. Never, perhaps, have the waves of change beat higher and faster the world over than in the past six months, since May, 1946, when this manuscript was sent to its

publishers. On September 20, 1946, Wallace was forced to resign from President Truman's Cabinet.

This set him some three months ahead upon a new course. He
had expected to stay through the November elections and through
the consequent reshuffling of personnel, then resign, in January
of 1947, and carry his 'fight for peace' out to the country. Only
his wife and closest friends were aware of this determination. He
came to it definitely and, as he saw it, inevitably, during the
summer of 1946.

'There are cycles in all things,' he had observed as a geneticist and statistician, far back in the nineteen-twenties. Later
he found pleasure in working on computations that foretell with
an amazing approach to certainty election day headlines a year
or more ahead of time. Discussing such matters in the middle
years of the New Deal, Wallace more than once expressed a
sort of awed interest in F. D. R.'s special genius for stoking
anew the fires of the Progressive spirit just at the times when
a quenching back wave of reaction would ordinarily have been
expected. But no political charm and skill could ward off forever the dampening backwash. As a longtime student of economic cycles, fundamentally, Wallace knew quite well that as
soon as the New Deal's basic program of full employment and
a generally shared prosperity were somehow or other attained,
then *this* New Deal and its recurrent crop of eternal New Dealers
at heart would be thrust out of office. He said as much in ad-
monitions to 'young liberals ... between eighteen and thirty
years of age' when the Roosevelt New Deal was at its peak of
hope and fervor, at the end of its first year:

> The New Deal spirit ebbs and flows. ... So-called young
> liberals of today received their first political inspiration be-
> tween 1906 and 1915 from Woodrow Wilson and Theodore
> Roosevelt. They saw liberalism go out of date in the nine-
> teen-twenties and wondered if the American people had
> permanently accepted a Belly-God. Young men who today
> are anxious to see America built over fundamentally and
> completely in line with their dreams will perhaps also watch
> the conservatives get back into power. This may not come

for eight, twelve, or sixteen years, but it will come almost as surely as prosperity returns. . . .

Twelve years plus 1934 is 1946. He hit it in the middle. Continuing:

> People like to be comfortable and 'let alone.' The conservative is bound to triumph fully half the time.
> But . . . there is something inherently inadequate and often rotting about comfort. The conservative type of mind is constitutionally incapable of understanding the inevitability of certain changes; . . . [it] is so instinctively and continuously self-centered that it is always being surprised by changing forces. . . . Only by forthright attack and counter-attack can the people be stimulated really to think . . .
> I am deeply concerned that the leadership of the future, whether liberal or conservative, should grapple more definitely and clearly with the facts and forces involved. . . . There are tremendously important problems to be put before the people. It may not be good politics to conduct this education, but it is absolutely vital if our democracy is to survive.[1]

These three Henry Wallaces have always held 'education' well above job-holding on the family agenda. Their minds never would stand tied. The first Henry, it will be recalled, shook off strictly denominational harness to become a free-lance minister. As a public leader he displayed a distinguished inability either to take his politics straight or leave it alone. In his late fifties, when he was almost exactly the age of the present Henry A., 'He shook off old entanglements,' said H. A., talking with friends recently, 'and struck out on his own. It was a time of great upset for him. But once he stood free he realized his greatest opportunities and reached greater fields of usefulness, and had more fun.'

Through the war years Wallace did whatever task that fell to hand with an increased capacity and dispatch, but he was gloomy and restless. With his wartime speeches before us there is no

[1] *New Frontiers*, pp. 16–18, 1934.

need here to pry further into his heights of enforced exaltation and depths of sorrow and foreboding during the slaughter. As America's tremendous skill and strength at arms increased and became each month more manifest, his forebodings deepened. He began to speak sharply against 'jingoism,' against dreams of 'manifest destiny' revived, as phenomena naturally to be expected among the professional military, but exceedingly wrong and dangerous as policies of State. When powerful journals and journalistic combinations took up the cry first sounded by Henry Luce of *Life*, *Time*, and *Fortune*, Wallace struck back with the best-remembered and most-derided of his wartime speeches: 'Some have spoken of the "American Century." I say that out of this war can and must come the Century of the Common Man.' (*The Price of Free World Victory*, New York, May 8, 1942.)

Imperialism was a phenomenon to which he had long given thought. With far-flung new bases established, with armed forces great beyond all precedent, seeming for the while to solve in glory the problem of complete employment (which the New Deal in peace had failed to solve), might not our postwar cycle of ambition this time take in a great deal more territory than it had in 1919? The public temper ran against territorial expansion then, as Wallace recalled it, writing *America Must Choose* fifteen years after, in 1934:

> With an empire of our own to possess and conquer (domestically), America has never as yet displayed a consistently imperialistic temper, in the broadly expansive sense of that term. After the World War, the Allies divided the world up, with a shrewd, contending eye for the deficit areas; and the United States said it didn't want any. Disillusioned and confused ⸍by terrific adventures in our first war beyond the water and by the struggle at Versailles afterwards, we yearned only to come home quietly, expand some more within our own borders, and contend thereafter only among ourselves for the old, spacious, separate spoils of 'normalcy' (page 5).

In the same pamphlet, arguing for a 'planned middle course'

between 'rampant nationalism' and 'freebooter internationalism,' he weighed alternatives:

> A rampant nationalist feeling grows by what it feeds on,
> and it swells to unpredictable proportions with marvelous
> speed. Once it gets going headlong it puts down objections
> brutally; and the speed of the march is thus accelerated.
> That might prove just as true in this country as elsewhere.
> Regimentation without stint might indeed, I sometimes
> think, go farther and faster here than anywhere else. We
> are a people given to excesses. . . . (page 15).
> Some say that world trade leads to world-mindedness,
> world sympathies, world peace. Others say that world
> trade just gets you out among strangers who trim you, and
> step on your feet, and have you fighting before you know it.
> All such talk seems to me, if weighed in the balance, to
> come to nothing either way. The real question is how the
> trading is done. If it is done blindly in response to ex-
> pansive greed, without planning or governance, it is likely
> to get you into serious trouble, whether you are trading at
> home or abroad.

Continuing, he compared the half-hearted or pseudo-imperial-
ism of our first post-World War era with policies of the Good
Neighbor and of Reciprocal Trade enunciated by President
Roosevelt and Secretary of State Hull:

> A clean-cut program of planned international trade or
> barter would be far less likely to get us into war, I think,
> than the attempts to function internationally as sellers, yet
> nationalistically as buyers, inaugurated under Presidents
> Harding and Coolidge and followed by President Hoover.
> Such tactics, pursued in the past by older nations, led to
> bloody foreclosure proceedings, at the point of guns. Not
> dissimilar current programs in other countries have created
> a dangerous degree of tension throughout the civilized
> world, and there are many who think that sooner or later
> the pressure will be bound to blow itself off in another orgy
> of human killing. We have blown off pressure that way
> very often in the past. . . .

Straight, cool-headed thinking about the sort of economic
warfare which is followed by actual warfare was never more
needed than now [1934]. This time, it would seem, it is
nationalistic pressure that is heading us toward the abyss.
The last time, it was supposed to be international pressures,
expressed in dreams and deeds of imperialism, intricately
bound up with foreign loans . . . (page 19).

The methods of reciprocal trade . . . lead to peace. It
makes no sales without providing opportunity for the buyers
to pay the bill. Since the bill does not remain outstanding
indefinitely, and does not have to be collected at the point
of a gun, it makes new business easy to get and profitable
(page 20).

Plainly, there is a consistent line of growth between the fore-
going premonitions, Wallace's steady adherence to the Roosevelt-
Hull policies, and his outburst against the Luce line in 1942.
In the same year, 'Think hard and often,' he urged, 'about the
future peace. Daily actions being taken now by both Britain
and ourselves are determining to a large extent the kind of
postwar world we can have later on.' (*The Atlantic Monthly*,
January, 1942.)

Ten months later, before the Congress of American-Soviet
Friendship in New York November 8, 1942, he said:

Democracy by definition is internationally minded and
supremely interested in raising the productivity, and therefore the standard of living, of all the peoples of the world.
First comes transportation, and this is followed by improved
agriculture, industrialization, and rural electrification. The
big planes and skilled pilots which will be ours when the
war comes to an end will lead us to a remarkable future as
surely as day follows night. We can make it a future of new
democracy based on peace.

On March 8, 1943, he spoke to farmers assembled at Columbus,
Ohio:

I am not urging Ohio farmers or any other farmers to give
a bottle of milk a day to the Hottentots. This weird and

manifestly impossible idea has been peddled up and down the land — why, I will leave it to you to guess.

People of other countries can enjoy higher standards of living when they learn to use their soils and their resources more effectively to produce the things they need. We in the United States can help them learn how to do these things, and also can help build the factories they need to get started. Our technical experts and industrial equipment can aid them to raise their own standards of production and of consumption — and so, along with other good things, have plenty of milk for themselves, producing it from their own pastures through their own efforts.

Again, July 25, 1943, before labor groups at Chicago, immediately after President Roosevelt had dismissed him as Chairman of the Board of Economic Warfare, he said:

We must continue our teamwork with the British. We must become better acquainted with our new friends, the Russians. We can live peacefully in the same world with the Russians if we demonstrate to ourselves and the world after the war that we have gone in for all-out peace production and total consumer use of our products.

In 1944, when Governor Dewey of New York, Republican presidential-aspirant, came out guardedly for a postwar alliance with Great Britain against Russia, Wallace and his Chief made note of it quietly, but held their fire.

In January of 1945, after his rejection for a second term as Vice-President, and some delay on the part of Congress to confirm him as President Roosevelt's new choice for Secretary of Commerce, Wallace started writing in his hotel apartment in Washington still another pamphlet, *60,000,000 Jobs*. To friends calling, such as Louis H. Bean, who had served as his economic advisor in the Department of Agriculture, he showed the penciled draft of the opening section. In part:

...When thirteen million of our people are Negroes, twenty-three million are Catholics, and five million are Jews

— a total equal to about one third of our total population, ... America cannot afford the social chaos of racial and religious discrimination. ...

We have learned — and we have paid for that knowledge in life and treasure — that whosoever willfully harms any part of society irreparably damages all of it. ...

Just as lasting peace at home cannot thrive in a climate of social tensions, so can there be no lasting peace in the world if our relations with foreign countries are founded on prejudice, ignorance, and suspicion. There can be no question as to the necessity of full participation with the United Nations in helping other countries help themselves toward better living standards, for I believe this good-neighborliness spreads benefits both ways. And I want here to emphasize the necessity of avoiding and removing the defeatist tension in international relations that are caused by constantly expecting the other fellow to take a poke at us. I have in mind particularly at this juncture our attitude toward Russia.

There is altogether too much irresponsible defeatist talk about the possibility of war with Russia. In my opinion, such talk, at the time when the blood of our boys shed on the fields of Europe has scarcely dried, is criminal. There are certain people — and they are the rankest kind of un-Americans — who are anxious to see the United States and Russia come to blows. I do not deny that in the past Russia has given the United States some provocation — just as the United States has given provocation to Russia. But anyone who has studied the relations of western Europe and Poland — anyone acquainted with the bungling policy of non-recognition blindly followed by this country until Franklin Roosevelt ended it in 1933 — surely can understand the background of Russian suspicions. ...

The job for all of us is to understand ... the basic lack of conflict ... [and do our part] toward developing a co-operative and harmonious relationship with Russia. I am assuming, of course, that the Russians will come halfway. I think they will. From what I have learned through long and hard study of the Soviet Russian mind in action — from my own personal acquaintanceship with a wide range of Russian citizens from officials to factory workers — I firmly believe that the people of Russia have a great admiration and friendship for the people of the United States and that they want to live with us and prosper with us in peace.

Of course, the Russian system of government is not for us. It is probable that the Russian Government will not, for a number of years, permit its citizens certain basic freedoms that we prize so dearly. . . . The Russians undoubtedly feel now that without Stalin and the Soviet system, Russia would have been destroyed in this war. . . . We must respect the Russian attitude — and they also must respect our attitude with regard to preserving our own form of government. It is this mutual respect that means peace. . . . The world looks to its great powers for co-operation and for political, economic, and moral leadership, not for suspicion, hate, and war.

. . . We have nothing to fear from Communism in this country if our free-enterprise system lives up to its opportunities. . . .

Wallace's friends, the economists and others, asked him whether it was not both a distortion and impolitic to put in a pamphlet on domestic re-employment all this about Russia up front. The pamphlet could not, they pointed out, be finished and published for some months to come; and how could he know what the situation would be by then? 'This Russian question,' said the author, mildly stubborn, 'will be the most vital of all questions, not only for months but for years.' The passage appeared unaltered, even as to the somewhat dashing punctuation, in the published pamphlet-book, issued soon after V–J Day, August, 1945.

Wallace went to work as Secretary of Commerce on March 4, 1945. President Roosevelt died on April 12. That he and Wallace saw eye to eye on general questions of Russian, British, and other postwar relationships seems doubly likely in the light of recent books by Elliott Roosevelt and Frances Perkins. (*As He Saw It* and *The Roosevelt I Knew*, respectively, both published in October, 1946.)

Miss Perkins's memoir reveals further, and for the first time, why Wallace feels, perhaps, an especially heavy burden of responsibility as to the future use of atomic energy: 'He [President Roosevelt] gave the signal to go ahead on . . . the atomic bomb because of his hunch that Einstein, like his fellow scientists, was truthful and wise. He had seen him on Henry Wallace's recommendation, and he knew Wallace, a man of scientific understanding, was also truthful and wise' (pages 164–65).

Wallace stayed for about a year and a half in the Truman Cabinet. Little was heard from him publicly the first year. It was a melancholy task that he had asked for and received from his departed Chief: the task of making something real and vital, postwar, of the sprawling and neglected Department of Commerce. 'There he is in the crypt of Hoover, with the bones of Jones around him!' one former associate, a tiring liberal, said. Wallace worked mainly with the personnel he found there, and managed to invigorate them in zeal and hope considerably, as well as to make a number of ardent converts for full employment among consulting business men.

Such victories! the detritus among New Dealers mocked, moaning low, with an eye to the clouds of reaction and a foot in the hand: 'Now they're looking for help, they'll give you the pious nod and mean it, but once the pinch comes, they'll turn their help out on the street again.'

Completely lacking in cynicism, but with a growing caginess, Wallace bore ahead. Privately, he said that he did not think honest exhortation was ever wholly wasted, but he really placed more weight on an unemployment bill drawn in his Department. It wasn't a perfect measure, but it was a long step forward. President Truman stood behind this bill, and it passed. Wallace took solid satisfaction, too, in the ardent backing that his old foe, Senator Bailey of North Carolina, and other Southern conservatives gave legislative proposals looking toward the encouragement of small decentralized industries, a move designed to cushion the shock of a probable decline or collapse of tyrannous King Cotton in the Deep South.

By the end of his first year as Secretary of Commerce, early in 1946, he had regathered under that aegis most of the functions that had been taken from him upon his wartime dismissal as Chairman of the Board of Economic Warfare; and he was working these programs over with a long-time peaceful bent toward balanced trade, stressing imports as well as exports. Congress, perceiving this, struck at him, and cut appropriations, reducing the personnel so engaged by four hundred men and women. Wallace recognized the propriety of some peacetime reduction; but he also recognized the hand of the State Department; and this added to his unease.

It was all rather heavy going, but he continued to invigorate public discussion in a torpid time. An offhand suggestion, delivered extempore to a Democratic Women's Club in Washington, that both political parties work out an American adaptation of the British parliamentary system so they could act decisively in meeting key problems during critical times certainly ahead, proved so stimulating as partly to obscure his first public pronouncement on Russian policy early in the spring of 1946.

The Baltimore Sun of March 20, for example, played up an hour's denunciation of Wallace in the Senate ['He can't write me out of the party and let Mr. Joe Stalin take my place!' — Senator Johnson, Democrat, South Carolina] above an Associated Press dispatch from New York:

> ... Speaking at a dinner honoring W. Averell Harriman, retired Ambassador to Russia, Secretary Wallace said, 'The Soviets may feel that the only road to peace and security is to give the capitalistic nations tit for tat.
> 'They have gone farther and given their tats first. They are out to make every boundary secure. They fear capitalistic encirclement. They are hungry for science and machines, and feel that time is short to prepare for a possible capitalist-provoked war.
> 'But granting that Russia is wrong on every count,' Wallace went on, 'I still say that the United States has nothing to gain, but, on the contrary, everything to lose, by beating the tom-toms against Russia. . . .'

'We must make it clear . . . that we have no intention of creating blocs or special axes inside or outside the United Nations Organization. We are opposed to any ideas of the "American Century" or the "Anglo-Saxon Century."

'If the English-speaking people have any destiny at all, it is to serve the world, not to dominate it. The same is true of the Soviet people. . . .

'Our joint chance of success lies in developing the maximum trade between the two countries.'

In a prepared address, Harriman said he shared with other Americans 'disappointment and concern over the direction that some Soviet Government policies appear to be taking.'

Harriman added that he, personally, endorsed 'the positions that have been taken by our Government.' . . .

The incident aroused no enduring reverberations. The President, so far as he was aware of it, was said to incline to Wallace's view. Certainly, he and Wallace stood as one, at the time, against an atomic energy control bill drafted by a special Senate Committee. In a statement opposing this measure (March 12) Wallace said it

. . . has the potentiality of delivering us into the hands of military fascism. . . . It places control of atomic energy, in effect, in the hands of the military.

The Committee had voted 6 to 1. Chairman McMahon, Connecticut, cast the dissenting vote. Wallace commented:

I hope that when the American people realize the significance of this development, they will rise up in their wrath. . . .

The peacetime uses of atomic energy can be much more significant than its use in war. . . . I hope we can get the President's program through the Senate. The President (who has said the program should be under civilian control) is everlastingly right on this subject. He deserves the backing of all the people.

'The President's program' passed in the form of the McMahon Act.

Wallace gave further evidence of a springtime restiveness, and of a growing impatience with existing partisan divisions and coalitions last April, May, and June. With the La Follette Progressives in Wisconsin about to disband and rejoin the Republicans on the far chance of liberalizing that party from within, or simply because they saw no other place to go, he again cited the tragic experience of his father, and also that of Wendell Willkie. The Democratic Party, he said, offered better prospect for liberals; nothing special, to be sure, at the moment; but for the long pull the Democrats were 'ten times as likely to serve a progressive cause as the Republicans.' After twelve years in power, of course, the Democrats had lost some of their original zest, and might need 'chastening.' But the South, especially, he felt, would turn out to be a 'reservoir of liberalism.'

Some delegates at the Wisconsin Progressives' sad final convention advanced a like line of argument, and called upon that dispersing group to follow the leadership of Wallace; but the suggestion aroused more boos than cheers; and the delegates voted overwhelmingly to return to the Republican fold.

With Harold Ickes out of the Cabinet now, and snorting around on all sorts of maneuvers with Independent Citizens' Committees and the Political Action Committee, talk of a third party grew louder. Wallace was often named and approached as a natural candidate. An analysis of mail on such matters addressed to him at the Department of Commerce and tallied up by Harold Young in April and May showed an almost equal division between those calling for Wallace to stand free of the Truman administration and fight, and those counseling him to stay where he was and fight for the liberal cause from within.

Speaking before liberals at a meeting sponsored by the P.A.C. in St. Louis, June 14, Wallace said:

> It would be simply impossible for a third party to get on the ballot in enough states to make anything approaching an effective challenge. Too many states have restrictive

election laws that either outlaw a third party or put big obstacles in its way. It is time for third party advocates to stop kidding themselves.

'Too few people know about this,' he added. Strangely few. This tightening rigidity in our political machinery, accomplished piecemeal, little by little, in State Legislatures whose acts are seldom reported as news of national importance, becomes a fact of historic moment. And the situation will probably be slow to change. Wallace continued:

Thinking even of 1952 instead of 1948, I believe it is unrealistic to expect that we could bring about a change in the election laws in enough states to build a really effective national organization. And as far as 1948 is concerned, a third party effort would insure beyond all doubt the election of a reactionary Republican — give him the name of Bricker or whatever name you want. . . .

The independent progressive voter who turned to the Democratic Party for national leadership — after full disillusionment elsewhere — well knows the facts of political life. He knows all about the obstructionists to progress in high Democratic councils. He knows all about the shameful, yet brazen, coalition of reactionaries in both parties. And he knows that this coalition is no newfound symptom of bipartisan reaction — for this coalition was at work against Franklin Roosevelt and against the people's program even before we were forced into World War II. . . .

I am a New Deal Democrat who believes that this is no time to surrender to any force of defeatism, whether in Washington or anywhere else. . . .

The course of honest men must be broad enough for honest differences. There always have been and there always will be honest differences in the councils of government. That is part of the give-and-take of our free life.

I have sat in the Cabinet of the President of the United States ever since that historic day of March 4, 1933 — that day when Franklin Roosevelt stripped away the people's fear of national disaster, and put them back once more on the road of national progress. In the years since then, I have had many honest differences and have participated in many honest controversies. I have done this because the Cabinet of the President was never meant to be — and can never be — a meeting of closed minds. No President has ever found strength in the blind acquiescence of members of his Cabinet. And no President — worth his salt or the people's salt — wants blind acquiescence. Franklin Roosevelt never asked for it and Harry Truman has never asked for it.

And as long as blind acquiescence is not a condition of service in the Cabinet of the President — and, of more importance, as long as there is an opportunity in that Cabinet to serve the cause of the people's progress without sacrifice of personal integrity and without compromise of personal principles — I shall continue to do my part in the fight for progressivism inside the councils of the Government in Washington.

Winston Churchill, whose rôle in history as he saw and played it was never to dismember the British Empire, came to this country for a visit. At the President's request, he consented to make an address at Westminster College, at Fulton, in the President's home state of Missouri. The President went along in the private car to introduce him to the folks. It has never been established whether he saw the script of the speech before he heard Mr. Churchill deliver it after introducing him ['I know he will say something constructive'], next day.

'A shadow has fallen over the scenes so lately lighted by the Allied victory,' Britain's wartime Prime Minister said in a majestic rumble. 'Nobody knows what Soviet Russia and its Communist international organization intend to do or what are the limits, if any, to their expansive tendencies.' He called for an Anglo-American alliance against Russia while the President of the United States sat there on the same platform looking mildly worried and playing with the tassels of his mortar-board hat.

In the United States Senate, Arthur Vandenberg, speaking from the Republican side, called for a tougher policy as to Russia:

'If we abandon the miserable fiction that we somehow jeopardize the peace if our candor is as firm as Russia's always is, and if we assume a moral leadership . . . we must have positive foreign policies.' The military were enchanted. Close-in White House advisors such as the redoubtable Admiral William D. Leahy urged Secretary Byrnes, who had started by following the conciliatory line laid down by Roosevelt, and who was getting mighty tired of it, to be just as tough as Vandenberg; and soon Byrnes was. With demobilization, reconversion, recruiting, and stockpiling proceeding simultaneously, the popular mind was dazed and restive, rueful, yet excited, and talk of war with Russia was heard at every hand. The people didn't want it, but there it was. They didn't blame the White House: 'Don't shoot the piano player; he's doing his best.' Another gibe of the moment, widely repeated, had a discharged soldier in a new civilian suit, saying, 'Like it? It's prewar. Bought it yesterday.'

Wallace and others spoke sharply against the Byrnes-Vandenberg line in Cabinet. The President shared their concern. He asked all of his official family to give him counsel and put it in writing. Wallace's long letter on Russia and the atomic bomb, later published, reached the President privately on July 23.

The summer wore on. Congress recessed and the President was often absent from Washington. With active campaigning for the mid-elections of 1946 due to start with cooler weather, Wallace was asked to speak before a mass meeting to be jointly sponsored by the National Citizens' Political Action Committee and the Independent Citizens' Committee of the Arts, Sciences and Professions, set for Madison Square Garden, New York City, September 12.

The same Bob Hannegan who had helped put Truman over, above Wallace, at Chicago in 1944, had now become intensely anxious to use Wallace as a spark plug of administration support from liberal Democrats and Independents. Hannegan had become, moreover, not insensitive to the common saying that the new President, seeking competent aides, had searched 'East and West — all the way from Kansas City to St. Louis.' Here, in a most important Eastern State, was a chance to woo the left-wing element, with an old-time New Deal speaker of national eminence; and the White House urged Wallace to make a good speech.

Wallace wrote it around the general line and argument of his previous private letter to the President, much modified as to detail. He took two copies to the President at the White House on September 10. President Truman held one copy while Wallace held the other. They spent thirty minutes in going over the script, point by point. Wallace was sure that parts of the speech would not be popular with left-wingers in his audience, and certainly not with extreme right-wingers. He suggested as much to the President, who told him that was all right; go ahead. Callers further along the President's schedule that day remarked later, with some amusement, that the President told them he stood firmly as neither pro-British nor anti-British, pro-Russian nor anti-Russian.

With advance copies of the speech out, the President said at press conference on Thursday, September 12, that he approved of it in every particular and saw in it no departure from the policies being forwarded by Secretary Byrnes.

Wallace made his speech that night. In some part it followed the line he had indicated in his public remarks at the Averell Harriman dinner the previous March, but it was much sharper in tone. Amid the roaring cheers from the leftist crowd of 20,000 assembled in the Garden came cries of 'Wallace for President' as he rose to speak.

He started by saying that to get world peace we must rid ourselves of prejudice, hatred, fear, and ignorance of other races. He denounced the Georgia lynchings. The audience liked that. He defended the British loan and called for a larger volume of world trade. As for our part, 'low tariffs by creditor nations are a part of the price of peace.' This met with no vociferous objection.

Again as to Britain, he rejected the idea of an alliance of mutual defense with Great Britain as a key to our foreign policy:

> ... To the military men the British Isles are our advanced air base against Europe ... We must not let reactionary leadership force us into that position. We must

not let British balance-of-power manipulations determine whether and when the United States gets into war.

Make no mistake about it — the British imperialistic policy in the Near East alone, combined with Russian retaliation, would lead the United States straight to war unless we have a clearly defined and realistic policy of our own. (*Cheers and scattered hisses.*)

Neither of these two great powers wants war now, but the danger is that whatever their intentions may be, their current policies may eventually lead to war. To prevent war and insure our survival in a stable world, it is essential that we look abroad through our own American eyes and not through the eyes of either the British Foreign Office or a pro-British or anti-Russian press . . .

I am neither anti-British nor pro-British — neither anti-Russian nor pro-Russian. And just two days ago, when President Truman read these words, he said that they represented the policy of his administration.

Hissing became so vehement at this point that he had to pause. But for the next two minutes, denouncing a 'get-tough-with-Russia' policy, he had them with him.

The tougher we get, the tougher the Russians will get. . . . We must not let our Russian policy be guided or influenced by those inside or outside the United States who want war with Russia. This does not mean appeasement.

We most earnestly want peace with Russia — but we want to be met halfway. We want co-operation. And I believe we can get co-operation once Russia understands that our primary objective is neither saving the British Empire nor purchasing oil in the Near East with the lives of American soldiers. . . .

Now he came to the part that raised the stormiest outcry from that immediate audience:

. . . We may not like what Russia does in Eastern Europe. Her type of land reform, industrial expropriation, and suppression of basic liberties offends the great majority of the people of the United States. . . .

Hissing rose to such a pitch that Wallace's shouted interjection could be heard only over the radio, not in the hall: 'I'm talking about people outside New York City when I say that,' he shouted. 'Every Gallup poll will show it!' He read the remainder of the speech doggedly, thrusting his words against a buzzing tumult:

> The Russians have no more business in stirring up native communists to political activity in Western Europe, Latin America, and the United States than we have in interfering in the politics of Eastern Europe and Russia. We know what Russia is up to in Eastern Europe, for example, and Russia knows what we are up to. We cannot permit the door to be closed against our trade in Eastern Europe.... However, the open door to trade and to opportunities for economic development in China are meaningless unless there is a unified and peaceful China — built on the co-operation of the various groups in that country and based on a hands-off policy of the outside powers. . . .

Audience interruptions were cutting more and more into radio time. It all was on the record; his script had been given to the papers; so he made some short cuts as he read. Skipping, he omitted one of the bluntest paragraphs in the latter part of his speech:

> . . . The Russians should stop teaching that their form of communism must, by force if necessary, ultimately triumph over democratic capitalism — while we should close our ears to those among us who would have us believe that Russian communism and our free enterprise system cannot live, one with another, in a profitable and productive peace.

He concluded:

> How we meet this issue will determine whether we live not in 'one world' or 'two worlds' — but whether we live at all.

There was only the slightest ripple of applause.

To sympathizers who came up to him afterward to decry the ill-mannered response, 'It was to be expected,' he said; 'I was following straight American policy.'

Press reactions were predominantly irritated, shocked, or hostile. But initial repercussions from abroad were relatively gentle, and the whole thing might have ended there but for the fantastic succession of mixups.

Initially, in September 13 dispatches from various European capitals, an unnamed spokesman for the British Foreign Office expressed 'pained surprise.' From Paris, at the Peace Conference, Mr. Byrnes was reported 'disturbed.' 'Tomorrow's morning papers,' *The New York Times*' Clifton Daniel cabled from London, 'will print reassuring dispatches from Washington to the effect that Mr. Wallace is "notoriously emotional and notoriously independent" and that what counts is not what he says but what the United States is doing — that is, resisting Russian expansion at every turn.'

Back in Washington, Wallace told reporters he would stand by his New York speech, every word of it; and planned soon to make another. That was Friday, September 13. On Saturday, at a special press conference, President Truman read a prepared statement saying that by his previously expressed O.K. he had meant to approve only Wallace's right to make it, not what Wallace had said. A 'clumsy . . . lie,' *Time* called this disclaimer in its running account of developing circumstances the week following. Excitement over 'the Wallace incident' continued to mount. From Paris, Secretary Byrnes was said to have sent word to the President that if remarks from other officials at home kept pulling the rug out from under him, he might have to come home. An elderly retired admiral on the Pacific Coast got off the reservation and made a speech saying that Wallace ought to be shot for giving aid and comfort to the enemy.

On the following Tuesday, September 17, it was reported that a copy of the personal letter Wallace had written to the President some two months back had come into the hands of Drew Pearson, news columnist and radio commentator, who planned to make it public. Wallace said that if this 'filched' letter were made public, he would sue. Pearson retorted, and satisfied Wallace that the 'leak' was (by columnist ethics) legitimate spoil. Press Secretary Ross, at the White House, was likewise persuaded that at least one other correspondent had managed to get hold of a copy of the letter; so Ross hastily authorized general release of the text as a whole. The President, when informed of this, was reported to be 'near hysterics'; too late, he forbade the release and could only express 'disapproval.'

The letter, thus released by accident, was a far less labored utterance, an infinitely simpler, more personal, yet more convincingly objective document than the speech; and it led to a considerable amelioration of previously set and thoroughly angry attitudes, both in this country and abroad.

July 23, 1946

My dear Mr. President:

...I am increasingly...troubled by the apparently growing feeling among the American people that another war is coming and the only way we can head it off is to arm ourselves to the teeth. Yet all of past history indicates that an armaments race does not lead to peace but to war. The months just ahead may well...decide whether the civilized world will go down in destruction after the five or ten years needed for several nations to arm themselves with atomic bombs. Therefore I want to give you my views on how the present trend toward conflict might be averted.

Acknowledging the difficulties of treating with Russia and praising the 'patience that has been exercised by our various negotiators,' Wallace argued that the very intensity of the 'aggravation' made greater patience necessary.

Continued manufacture of the atomic bomb and other militant stockpiling impose upon us a staggering cost, in terms of both taxes at home and mistrust abroad. Our budget estimate for 1947 demands thirteen billion dollars for the War and Navy Departments, another fifteen billion dollars for liquidation activities and veterans' benefits — 'primarily the continuing cost of past wars'— *and only eight billion dollars for all other government costs.*

Observing us, the world's most powerful people, still spending four fifths of our public money on warlike purposes; observing such shows of martial strength as the Bikini tests; observing our continuing effort 'to secure air bases spread over half the globe from which the other half of the globe can be bombed, how must this look to other nations? How would it look to us if Russia had the atomic bomb and we did not, if Russia had ten-thousand-mile bombers and air bases within a thousand miles of our coast lines and we did not?' Wallace asked the President.

All such show of force is not only dangerous but futile. Predominance of force, a prevailing notion among certain of the military, is no longer possible. The reasons are clear: (1) 'Atomic warfare is cheap and easy.' Atomic bombs cut down the unit cost of killing. Even a small nation can afford to plan war now, and to launch the first stroke. (2) If this happens, what good would a towering stockpile of the bombs do us? Wallace wrote:

> If another nation had enough bombs to eliminate all our principal cities and our heavy industry, it wouldn't help us very much if we had ten times as many bombs as we needed to do the same to them.

And (3)

> 'Most important, the very fact that several nations have atomic bombs will inevitably result in a neurotic, fear-ridden, itching-trigger psychology in all the peoples of the world, and because of our wealth and vulnerability we would be among the most seriously affected.'

> Another school of military thinking, recognizing that... no nation or combination of nations can win such a war ...therefore advocates a 'preventive war,' an attack on Russia *now* before Russia has atomic bombs.

> This scheme is not only immoral but stupid.

> If we should attempt to destroy all the principal Russian cities and her heavy industry, we might well succeed. But the immediate countermeasure which such an attack would call forth is the prompt occupation of all Continental Europe by the Red Army. Would we be prepared to destroy the cities of all Europe in trying to finish what we had started? This idea is so contrary to all the basic instincts and principles of the American people that any such action would be possible only under a dictatorship at home. . . .

> The only solution is the one which you [Mr. President] have so wisely advanced and which forms the basis of the

Moscow statement on atomic energy. That solution consists of mutual trust and confidence, atomic disarmament, and an effective system of enforcing that disarmament.

There is, however, a fatal defect in the Moscow statement, in the Atcheson report, and in the American plan recently presented to the United Nations Atomic Energy Commission. . . .

Here Wallace started another tempest of controversy, to be noted later. His letter was given to the press on Tuesday, September 17. On Wednesday his name appeared on the President's calling list, and more than a hundred reporters were there to see what would come of it. Wallace was closeted with the President for two hours and forty minutes. When he came out he told the thronging pressmen buoyantly that he had enjoyed 'a most detailed and friendly conversation' and would 'make no public statements or speeches until the Foreign Ministers' conference in Paris is concluded.' He read this from a brief penciled statement that he and the President had worked out between them, inside. And after Paris? Then he would speak again, he said.

Soon after he left the White House, Bernard Baruch and several aides went in. The President was reported unable to reach Paris by telephone that day or the next; atmospheric conditions blocked the calls; but on Thursday he 'talked' with Secretary Byrnes for twenty minutes by teletype.

Friday morning, September 20, Wallace was fired. Or, more precisely, the President, telephoning him, asked, with hasty expressions of friendliness, for his resignation; and, 'Why, yes, Mr. President, if that is your wish; certainly!' Wallace answered; and they both issued brief statements to the press. Wallace's press aides in the Department immediately had visions of a hippodrome press conference, such as that marking the departure of Harold Ickes. Wallace said no; none of that; but he consented finally to make a short broadcast that night:

Winning the peace is more important than high public office. It is more important than any consideration of party politics.

The success or failure of our foreign policy will mean the difference between life and death for our children and our grandchildren. It will mean the difference between the life and death of our civilization. It may mean the difference between the existence and the extinction of man and of the world . . .

The action taken by the President this morning relieves me of my obligation of last Wednesday. I feel that our present foreign policy does not recognize the basic realities which led to two wars and which now threatens another war — this time an atomic war. . . . I do not wish to abuse the freedom granted me by the President this morning by saying anything that might interfere with the success of the Paris Peace Conference. But . . . I intend to carry on the fight for peace.

The following Monday, September 23, he held a farewell reception in his Department office, set up a temporary staff at his hotel apartment to help handle more than seven thousand personal letters which even then had poured in, and came no more to Commerce thereafter. President Truman made W. Averell Harriman Secretary of Commerce.

The confused controversy between Wallace and Bernard Baruch which flared into print during the first week of October had to do with Wallace's statement in his July 23 letter to the President that:

. . . We are telling the Russians that if they are 'good boys' we may eventually turn over our knowledge of atomic energy to them and to other nations. But there is no objective standard of what will qualify them as being 'good' nor any specified time for sharing our knowledge. . . .

The step-by-step plan in any such one-sided form is not workable. The entire agreement will have to be worked out and wrapped up in a single package. . . . We must be prepared to reach an agreement which will commit us to disclosing information and destroying our bombs at a specified time or in terms of specified actions by other countries, rather than at our unfettered discretion.

Mr. Baruch held, angrily, that he *was* in accord with the 'single-package' idea; neither was his Commission pursuing a course timed to 'our unfettered discretion.' Wallace replied, with unwonted impatience, that Mr. Baruch was quibbling over procedural points only, and:

> Nothing in our discussion could cause me to revise the basic tenets of my letter concerning the ways to peace and atomic energy controls. . . .
>
> The stalemate we have reached in the United States Energy Commission arises from two basic points of disagreement. The first relates to whether the United States should continue its production of atomic bombs while the transition to full international controls, which would outlaw such production, is in progress. The second has to do with Russian reservations as to international inspection and control of atomic energy production.
>
> For some time the work of the Atomic Energy Commission has been deadlocked over these basic differences. And at this writing [October 7] the Commission still is deadlocked over these very same issues.
>
> We are now in the second year of the atomic armaments race. Time passes perilously — and there is still no peace. . . .
>
> I believe the American people — if given full and constant access to the facts — will make the right choice, without doubt or fear. Above all else, let us not fear full and free debate.

The above paragraphs are from Wallace's introduction to a pamphlet, *The Fight for Peace*, containing the New York speech, the July 23 letter, and other relevant documents. (Reynal and Hitchcock, October, 1946.)

On October 12, when it was announced that Wallace would become editor of *The New Republic* as of December 16, he said: 'I shall have the opportunity of saying exactly what I think at a time when a bipartisan bloc mouthing the phrase "One World" is really driving the world into two armed camps.'

THE END

NOTES AND REFERENCES

CHAPTER I

SPRING MOUNT

1. (Page 3.) *Corn and horse sense.* Old neighbors told this story on John Wallace to his son, Henry, when 'Uncle' Henry paid them a visit back East in 1914. He put it on record in dictated notes preserved by the family.

2. (Page 9.) *Of men and livestock.* Daniel A. Wallace, whose contributions of family lore are further cited under head of Acknowledgments, page x, is now in charge of field work for the Farmers Union Grain Terminal Association, 1923 University Avenue, Saint Paul 4, Minnesota.

3. (Page 12.) *'Fortune' analyzes Henry A.* Under title of 'The Vice-President: A Top Maker of War Policy, he believes that the Kingdom of Heaven is within our grasp,' the article starts on page 135, October, 1942.

4. (Page 13.) *'Uncle Henry's Own Story or Personal Reminiscences,'* hereafter referred to in these Notes as *Reminiscences*, was dictated over a period of six years starting in the fall of 1910, when Uncle Henry was seventy-four. The letters began running in *Wallaces' Farmer* after his death in 1916 and were republished by Wallaces' Publishing Company in three paper-bound volumes totaling 362 pages, 1917–19. Young Henry A., just out of college and breaking in as associate editor, urged his grandfather to make this record, remarking, in the Introduction to vol. I of the pamphlet series: 'The ordinary biography, or even autobiography, fails to tell the things that most people like to learn. His great-grandchildren (I suggested) would like to know of the manners and customs of the people with whom he grew up and lived. Such letters would reveal his own personality as no biographer could.' Uncle Henry lived long enough to hold on his knee the first of the great-grandchildren to whom he addressed these letters. See frontispiece.

5. (Page 18.) *'A good land, a land of brooks and waters . . .'* Deut. VIII, 7–9.

CHAPTER II

SEMINARY VEAL

1. (Page 26.) *Sinful anger as a sign of vealiness. Uncle Henry's Letters to a Farm Boy.* 4th Edition. The MacMillan Company, New York, 1906, pp. 18–19.

2. (Page 30) *Porridge and catechism. Ibid.*, p. 161.

3. (Page 33.) *Aristocratical Uncle Daniel* plays a large part in the early chapters of Uncle Henry's *Reminiscences.* Later he removed to Pittsburgh and became a man of considerable means.

4. (Page 37.) *Make something worth polishing. Letters to a Farm Boy*, p. 88.

CHAPTER III

THE YEARS OF THE GREAT REBELLION

1. (Page 52.) *'Dance, Jeanie!' Ibid.*, p. 175.

2. (Page 58.) *Moody*, Wallace was careful to add in *Reminiscences*, mellowed with age into a reasonable and companionable human being; but that time was not yet.

CHAPTER IV

MORNING SUN AND WINTERSET

1. (Page 80.) *Quick on the prairie. One Man's Life*, p. 18.

2. (Page 87.) *Childhood at Winterset.* These notes derive from an unpublished memoir, *Recollections of Henry Cantwell Wallace*, written for the family annals by Daniel A. Wallace, April 7, 1939.

3. (Page 88.) *'Tama Jim.'* A biography by Earley Vernon Wilcox with the collaboration of Flora H. Wilson. The Stratford Company, 1930.

4. (Page 88.) *Seaman Knapp.* Much has been written of the Founder of Farm Demonstration. Joseph Cannon Bailey's recent (1945) *Seaman Knapp: American Schoolmaster*, published by the Columbia University Press, is the first complete and authoritative book.

5. (Page 89.) *Knapp as a stockman.* The quotation is from a talk by his daughter, Mrs. A. M. Mayo, recorded in Proceedings of the Silver Anniversary Co-operative Demonstration Work 1903–1928, p. 46, Texas Agricultural and Mechanical College, 1929.

6. (Page 94.) *Andrew D. White's tribute to Morrill* is quoted from p. 259, The Life and Public Services of Justin Smith Morrill, Houghton Mifflin Company, 1924.

7. (Page 96.) *Roberts at Ames. Autobiography of a Farm Boy*, by Isaac Phillips Roberts. Cornell University Press, 1946, pp. 91–105.

CHAPTER V

THE TORCH AND THE LAMP

1. (Page 104.) *'Convictions of the best people.' Reminiscences*, vol. I, p. 48.
2. (Page 106.) *How the Harry Wallaces started.* From a talk with Mrs. H. C. Wallace, Des Moines, Dec. 10, 1940.
3. (Page 110.) *'Tom Watson: Agrarian Rebel,'* by C. Vann Woodward. The Macmillan Company, 1938, pp. 173–174.
4. (Page 112.) *'Sacred' populism. Ibid.,* p. 138.
5. (Page 114.) *Father Clarkson's Retreat.* Quick's *One Man's Life,* pp. 231–235.
6. (Page 122.) *George Washington Carver.* The account here derives partly from Rackham Holt's *George Washington Carver,* with certain additions from members of the Wallace family who knew Carver well when he was at Ames.

CHAPTER VI

'WALLACES' FARMER'

1. (Page 126.) *Hardmans and Goodmans. Letters to a Farm Boy,* p. 115 ff.
2. (Page 131.) *A platform for his father.* H. C. Taylor was among H. C. Wallace's closest professional friends and associates. He enters this remark of Harry's in *A Farm Economist in Washington, 1919–1935,* a memoir privately reproduced by multigraph. Request for permission to examine this document should be addressed to Dr. Taylor as Director of the Farm Foundation, 600 S. Michigan Avenue, Chicago.
3. (Page 133.) *James G. Mitchell* is now engaged in the practice of law in New York City. These are notes from an interview at his office, 305 Lexington Avenue, November 25, 1944.
4. (Page 135.) *'Keep Wilson.'* Wilcox's *Tama Jim,* p. 4. Donald Murphy of the staff of *Wallaces' Farmer* recal's that Uncle Henry took active part in stirring up such pressure at the time.
5. (Page 137.) *Tama Jim and the martial spirit. Tama Jim,* p. 85.
6. (Page 140.) *The happiest days.* The story of this happy summer, here set down as Dan Wallace told it on a Friends of the Land tour in the Tennessee Valley, Oct. 13, 1942, he later supplemented with a written reminiscence entitled 'Partners in Iniquity or Life Without Women' in *The Land* (vol. IV, no. 2; 1945).

7. (Page 142.) *The strength and quietness of grass:* 'I have always had a great affection for grass. It seems to stand for quietness and strength. A countryside shorn and stripped of thick, green grass, it seems to me, is weakened just as Samson was. An agriculture without grass loses a primary source of strength. . . .' H. A. W. in a three-minute radio talk, June 21, 1940. *Democracy Reborn,* an anthology of public papers. Reynal & Hitchcock, New York, 1944, p. 175.

8. (Page 142.) *The Aztecs as geneticists.* H. A. W. in *Wallaces' Farmer,* Dec. 12, 1908.

9. (Page 143.) *Indian crops take revenge.* H. A. W. in *The Land,* vol. I, no. 1, 1941, p. 48.

10. (Page 143.) *The Eighth Annual Spragg Memorial Lecture,* delivered April 21, 1938 and published as a pamphlet by the Department of Farm Crops, Michigan State College, East Lansing.

11. (Page 152.) *Correlation and Machine Calculation* was first issued as Official Publication vol. 23, no. 35, Jan. 28, 1925, by the Iowa State College of Agriculture and Mechanic Arts, Ames. Revised by George W. Snedecor, 71 pp., in the same series, June 24, 1931.

12. (Page 154.) *T. R.'s conservative side.* Wilcox's *Tama Jim,* p. 84.

13. (Page 156.) *Country Life Commission.* The Commission's Report, first issue as Senate Document no. 705, Sixtieth Congress, Second Session, 1909, was reprinted as a book by the University of North Carolina Press in 1944. The quotation here is from pp. 19–20 of the Senate document.

14. (Page 161.) *Uncle Henry on the common man.* He made this speech in February of 1912 before students of the New York State College of Agriculture, assembled during Farmer's Week at Cornell University, Ithaca. Mrs. Henry A. Wallace has preserved the manuscript, parts of which were printed in *The Cornell Countryman* for April, 1912. The advice given there to the young follows in general the line of a letter likewise carefully preserved in the family. From Uncle Henry to Young Henry A. on his twenty-first birthday:

Des Moines, Iowa, Oct. 7, 1909

My dear grandson:

How time flies! As we boys used to say at college, 'How tempus fugits!' It seems but yesterday that your grandmother and I were rejoicing over the telegram announcing your birth. I am now twenty-one years older than then, and your grandmother has gone to her reward.

You have a great future before you, if you keep yourself well in hand. I must say you have started out well. We are proud of you, but 'better is the end of a thing than the beginning thereof.' The history of no man can be truly written until he is dead. There are few boys that have the opportunities that are coming to you. None of us realize the possibilities that will come to us in life, provided we are prepared to deal with them properly. The world is waiting for men who can do her work, and there is always a bigger job ahead of the man who performs faithfully the job that he is at now.

You have far greater opportunities than your father had at your age, and very much greater than I had at twenty-one. The world has been advancing by leaps and bounds; and the greater the advance, the bigger the man that is required to solve the problems of his age.

You must not expect to be a really big man unless you live a sincere, earnest, religious life. In other words, you want always to be on the side of the great Power that rules this world, and that we have learned to call 'Our Father.' In solving the questions that come up from year to year and from day to day, the man who is on God's side is really on the side of the majority, although the world will not think so and he may for a time himself doubt it. Nevertheless, posterity will appreciate the man who does the right as he sees the right, and who has an eye single for righteousness.

The fact is that we are really bigger than we know, although not quite so big as we sometimes think; that is, while sometimes we overestimate our capacities as measured by those of our fellowmen, we are prone to underestimate them, or rather, we fail to improve them. We are really in a great big world, the servants of a God who is infinitely bigger than we can possibly comprehend; and if we are in right relation to him, and improve our opportunities, there is a great big work for us to do before we pass away, leaving others to carry it on.

Affectionately,
Your Grandfather,
HENRY WALLACE

15. (Page 163). *Uncle Henry's editorial method.* DeWitt C. Wing in *The Land*, vol. II, no. 3, 1943, p. 202.

16. (Page 165.) *'Grandfather feared war.'* *Fortune*, October, 1942, p. 135.

CHAPTER VII

THE FIRST WORLD WAR BOOM AND CRASH

1. (Page 171.) *Dr. H. C. Taylor Remembers*. See footnote 2, chapter VI.

2. (Page 174.) *The change had struck*. America's swing from a debtor to a creditor position is well summarized in *Farmers in a Changing World*, the United States Department of Agriculture Yearbook for 1940, p. 20 ff.

3. (Page 174.) *Education of a Princess*, by the Grand Duchess Marie. The Viking Press, New York, 1930, p. 286 ff.

4. (Page 185.) *Young Henry's business plans for corn*. From an article he wrote for *Wallaces' Farmer*, issue of Jan. 21, 1923.

5. (Page 185.) *'I saw I was fooling away my time.'* *Wallaces' Farmer*, March 7, 1919.

6. (Page 186.) *A Seminar in Economics*. This extemporaneous talk, taken down stenographically, is included in his collection of public papers, *Democracy Reborn*, pp. 96–103.

7. (Page 187.) *The mystery of milk*. Secretary Wilson's complaint as to lack of knowledge is quoted in Wilcox's *Tama Jim*, p. 48.

8. (Page 189.) *Statistics have no 'mystical values.'* Extempore, in seminar at Ames. *Democracy Reborn*, p. 107.

9. (Page 189.) *H. A. W. on Veblen*. In *Democracy Reborn* he treats of Veblen as an economist (p. 98) and as an author (p. 132). In August of 1929 when Veblen died, Wallace wrote editorially in his 'Odds & Ends' column of the family paper, prophesying: 'One hundred years from now people will read Thorstein Veblen's books and realize that he was one of the few men of the early twentieth century who really knew what was going on. I don't feel sad because of Veblen's death, because his books were his real life, and they will live for centuries.'

10. (Page 197.) *'The great fat fight.'* *Saturday Evening Post*, May 12 and 19, 1928.

11. (Page 197.) *Agricultural Prices*, by Henry A. Wallace. Wallace Publishing Company, Des Moines, 1920, p. 27 ff.

12. (Page 200.) *'Down to defeat.'* *Ibid.*, p. 35.

13. (Page 201.) *'A Mistaken Daily.'* H. C. W. in *Wallaces' Farmer*, March 5, 1920.

14. (Page 203.) *For a Farmers' University*. H. C. W., Editorial, Sept. 27, 1918.

15. (Page 209.) *Speculators: unangelic but useful*. H. A. W.'s *Agricultural Prices*, pp. 8–10.

16. (Page 211.) *'Farmers will . . . practice sabotage.'* *Ibid.*, pp. 17–18.

17. (Page 215.) *'Farmers fear . . . Hoover's ability.'* H. C. W., *Wallaces' Farmer*, April 23, 1920.

18. (Page 215.) *Against Hooveresque Democrats?* Guilty!' H. C. W. editorially, Jan. 26, 1920.

19. (Page 216.) *Our Debt and Duty to the Farmer*, by Henry C. Wallace. The Century Company, New York, 1925.

20. (Page 219.) *A managed deflation. Ibid.*, p. 60.

21. (Page 223.) *Notes on George Norris* in this chapter derive largely from *Democracy's Norris: The Biography of a Lonely Crusader* by Alfred Leif, Stackpole Sons, New York, 1939. The material here has been somewhat supplemented, however, with data obtained by interview from Harry Slattery, Gifford Pinchot, Morris L. Cooke, Huston Thompson, and other crusading conservationists of that era.

22. (Page 227.) *Contention over naval oil* had extended back through the Wilson administration. In his memoir *The Wilson Era* (The University of North Carolina Press, 1944, pp. 368–381) Josephus Daniels tells how he and his Assistant Secretary of the Navy, Franklin D. Roosevelt, sat up nights at the closing of the Wilson era to make sure that oil resources would not be captured by the forces then forming to move in, under Harding.

23. (Page 227.) *Fall's Threatening Letter* was addressed to Arthur Ringland, then Regional Forester in the Southwest, now with the War Relief Control Board, Washington Building, Washington, D.C.

24. (Page 228.) *In Cabinet meeting 'a row ensued.'* Leif's *Democracy's Norris*, p. 264.

25. (Page 228.) *The record of a meeting* held at the Cosmos Club, Washington, June 25, 1932, in Honor of Harry Slattery's Twenty-Five Years of Public Service.

26. (Page 229.) *'Wallace finally won, but . . .'* H. C. W.'s unsigned dispatch to *Wallaces' Farmer*, Feb. 8, 1924.

CHAPTER VIII

REAPING THE WHIRLWIND

1. (Page 233.) *An Ever-Normal Granary.* H. A. W., *Wallaces' Farmer*, March 3, 1922.

2. (Page 233.) *Who plays the part of Joseph?* Initial approach to the Ever-Normal Granary. *Ibid.*, Sept. 27, 1912.

3. (Page 234.) *Economic principles of Confucius.* Chen Huan-Chang describes the 'Constantly Normal Granary' in chapter 30 of his thesis, pp. 568–585.

4. (Page 235.) *Hoover's demarcation: Agriculture and Commerce.* Testimony before the Second Session House Agricultural Committee, recorded in CC13, p. 456.

5. (Page 239.) '*Peek was his customary battling self.*' H. A. W., *New Frontiers*, Reynal & Hitchcock, New York, 1934, pp. 144–146.

6. (Page 239.) *A Farm Economist in Washington, 1919–1935*, H. C. Taylor. See footnote 2, chapter VI.

7. (Page 240.) *Norris charges a sell-out.* Leif's *Democracy's Norris*, p. 248.

CHAPTER IX

OUTSIDERS

1. (Page 269.) *Pressure Groups: A Review of Experience.* H. A. W., *New Frontiers*, pp. 55–56.

2. (Page 270.) *Wooing the South.* Chester Davis, p. 310 ff., *Farmers in a Changing World.* Yearbook of the United States Department of Agriculture, 1940.

3. (Page 273.) *Export dumping outdated.* H. A. W., *New Frontiers*, p. 157.

4. (Page 275.) *For a third party?* H. A. W., *Wallaces' Farmer*, June 15, 1928.

5. (Page 277.) '*Hoover will carry Iowa . . . plunk for Smith.*' H. A. W., *Ibid.*, September 28, 1928.

6. (Page 277.) '*Asserts Hoover Saved Farmers.*' Headline *New York World-Telegram*, May 10, 1928.

7. (Page 290.) *A. W. Ashby*, for years head of Agricultural Economics at the College of North Wales, has recently (1945) removed to a like post at Oxford.

8. (Page 290.) '*Tailspin . . . with a vengeance.*' Hearings, Senate Committee of Commerce, Seventy-Ninth Congress, First Session on S. 375. Document 68424, 1945, pp. 102–103.

9. (Page 305.) *Genesis of Agricultural Adjustment Act.* H. A. W., *New Frontiers*, pp. 156–157.

10. (Page 306.) *Spillman's 'Use of the Exponential Yield Curve in Fertilizer,*' U.S.D.A. Technical Bulletin no. 348, was published in April, 1933, some two years after his death at the age of sixty-eight.

11. (Page 308.) *Wilson to Tugwell to F. D. R.* How the Domestic Allotment Plan became a campaign issue. *New Frontiers*, p. 157.

12. (Page 310.) *Land Utilization.* Wilson's broadcast, published as Lecture no. 25 by the National Advisory Committee on Radio, University of Chicago, April, 1932.

CHAPTER X

WHEN THE DEAL WAS NEW

1. (Page 331.) *First Triple-A: Authors. New Frontiers*, pp. 164–167.
2. (Page 338.) *Pressures. Ibid.*, pp. 169–170.
3. (Page 343.) *Peek on Frank. Saturday Evening Post*, May 16, 1936.
4. (Page 343.) *Declaration of Interdependence.* H. A. W., *Democracy Reborn*, p. 43 ff.
5. (Page 345.) *'Challenge to Science.'* H. A. W., *Ibid.*, p. 47 ff.
6. (Page 347.) *The Tugwell furor.* Some part of this material appeared as a two-part 'Profile' in *The New Yorker*, starting March 23, 1935.
7. (Page 356.) *Wallace on Peek. New Frontiers*, p. 146.
8. (Page 358.) *Peek on Wallace. Saturday Evening Post*, May 23, 1936.
9. (Page 361.) *'Political thunderstorm.'* H. A. W., *New Frontiers*, pp. 56–58.
10. (Page 361.) *Spanked in effigy. Time*, November 6, 1933, p. 18.
11. (Page 362.) *'Rarin' to go.'* H. A. W., *New Frontiers*, pp. 188–189.
12. (Page 362.) *'Yours for Tomorrow,'* by Helen Hill Miller. Farrar & Rinehart, New York, 1943.
13. (Page 364.) *Thunder cleared the air.* H. A. W., *New Frontiers*, pp. 189–190.
14. (Page 366.) *'Almost insane' acts. Ibid.*, pp. 171–175; 200.

CHAPTER XI

DISPLACEMENTS AND DEPARTURES

1. (Page 378.) *'Not solely . . . reduction.' Ibid.*, p. 203.
2. (Page 381.) *Evans's Recollections* were issued as Extension Circular no. 224 by the University of Georgia, Athens, 1938.
3. (Page 386.). *Nutrition as 'the central thing': Wilson. The Land*, vol. II, no. 4, p. 309.
4. (Page 386.) *Diet at four levels: Steibling.* U.S.D.A. Circular no. 296.
5. (Page 393.) *Triple-A moved rightward: Chew. The Land*, vol. III, no. 1, (1943), p. 33.
6. (Page 402.) *How Davis operated: Stedman.* Having worked most closely with Davis as his Chief of Information for Triple-A, Alfred Stedman, now with *The Pioneer Press*, Saint Paul, wrote this personal footnote in a letter, April 20, 1946. Stedman had been called back to Washington for a brief spell at the time, to help Davis and Herbert Hoover in the administration of Famine Relief:

'Early in our Triple-A association, when Chester proposed some minor concession to the opposition in framing a piece of legislation, I burst out with, "I'm opposed to compromise." He looked at me sidewise with that glancing smile he has. "Why, Sted," he said, "I thought that compromise was the very essence of the legislative process."

'For all his flexibility in the formative stage of program-making, there is nothing weak or infirm about him once the program has been determined. His understanding of people and their motives and his readiness to show respect for others' ideas explained much of his success in legislative and administrative negotiations. He was on good terms even with "Cotton Ed" Smith when the old Senator was boiling mad at about everybody else in the administration that tried to purge him. As Chairman of the Senate Agricultural Committee, Cotton Ed had declared opposition to the Triple-A marketing amendments. That would have been fatal.

'The day the Senate Committee hearings opened Chester took hold. He went up and testified, then sat down by Cotton Ed. The Senator said nothing pro or con, but just chewed tobacco. Chester asked for a chew and they sat there side by side chewing and spitting like a couple of buddies, and in the end the Senator got up and allowed that he guessed he would support the bill.

'Chester Davis showed his grasp of the huge and complicated problems of food that were coming upon the country with the approach of World War II, and his understanding of the basic principles that would have to guide a successful attempt to meet these problems. That understanding explained his recommendation of one unified War Food Administration [when F. D. R. made him Food Administrator in wartime] — one unified agency, clothed with the power and having the responsibility for developing food policies and operating food programs that would mobilize all the food industries to help win the war.

'Failure to establish such a unified administration, and the consequent scatteration of authority, the lack of any centralized federal agency to deal with food, is the biggest reason for this country's conspicuous delay in moving to meet the world famine, now [April, 1946] in a crisis stage.'

7. (Page 405.) '*I was tired . . . of sharp tricks.*' From a letter, written in retrospect, by Chester C. Davis, President of the Federal Reserve Bank of Saint Louis, October 31, 1946, with the manuscript of this section of chapter XI before him.

8. (Page 411.) *A Place on Earth: A Critical Appraisal of Subsistence Homesteads*, 202 pages, multigraphed. The Bureau of Agricultural Economics, United States Department of Agriculture, Washington, 1942.

9. (Page 414.) *We are more than economic men*, by H. A. W., *Scribner's Magazine*, December, 1934, p. 321.

10. (Page 417.) '*The heritage is . . . bitter*': H. A. W., *New Frontiers*, p. 9.

11. (Page 419.) '*The ultimate crop.*' H. A. W. before the Upstream Engineering Conference, Washington, 1936.

12. (Page 421.) *Wilson on subsistence*. *The Land*, vol. I, no. 4 (1941), p. 339.

13. (Page 422.) *Wilson as a moderator: Johnstone*. *A Place on Earth*, p. 21.

14. (Page 428.) *Hendrickson on Subsistence*. *The Land*, vol. I, no. 4 (1941), p. 346.

15. (Page 429.) '*The needy when He crieth . . .*' Psalms LXXII, 12.

16. (Page 431.) '*I have faith*': H. A. W., 'Iowa Cycle' by Charles Morrow Wilson, *The Commonweal* for November 10, 1933.

17. (Page 432.) *Gerald Johnson on H. A. W.* Hitherto unpublished. Prepared at the suggestion of a weekly of national circulation, Mr. Johnson's manuscript failed to please the editors.

18. (Page 434.) *Of ghostly matters*. The legend of the mystic letters lingered on. In a memoir prepared after retirement as publicity chief for the Democratic Party (*The Ghost Talks*, issued by G. P. Putnam's Sons, in 1944, another campaign year), Charles Michelson, or his ghost, mischievously chuckles to recall how upset Harry Hopkins was in 1940 over these letters and the anti-Wallace whispering campaign. Hopkins, says Michelson, kept running to 'the Boss . . . with suggested expedients that would have made admirable chapters in an Oppenheim novel.' With no love for 'the Palace Guard' in general, or Hopkins in particular, Michelson cites this as an instance of 'Hopkins' . . . political ineptitude.' Wallace was never of the Palace Guard. In the light of events since, there can be no doubt that this agitation of the Inner Guardsmen at the White House, whether sincere or simulated, together with the covert sneers of Old Guard Democratic political hacks, was designed to do Wallace political harm.

19. (Page 435.) *Dragons that devour prosperity*: H. A. W., *Wallaces' Farmer*, May 14, 1932.

20. (Page 435.) *Statesmanship and Religion*: H. A. W., The Round Table Press, New York, 1934.

21. (Page 443.) *Sherwood Anderson on Wallace*. 'No Swank' in *Today* for November 11, 1933.

22. (Page 449.) '*The Republican Illusion.*' According to the recollection of E. J. Condon, Assistant to the President of Sears Roebuck, who was among those present.

23. (Page 464.) *For an 'economic Supreme Court.'* Wallace presented the idea at the annual dinner meeting of the Aca⌐ ¬ny of Political Science, November 14, 1935, in New York. As to tariffs, especially, he held that alternating policies, conditioned in part by Democratic administrations taking over from Republican and vice versa, get nowhere; and there is need in interior economics also of a continuing policy placing the General Welfare above the jostling contentions of pressure groups. To such ends he proposed the establishment of a nonpartisan Council of the General Welfare, chartered as a sort of economic Supreme Court, to study Federal legislation, recommend changes, and promote as a continuing body through all the administrations an 'increased balanced production.'

This Council 'might be composed of four or five of our most eminent economic statesmen . . . appointed for overlapping terms, say, from five to eleven years. Appointment could be by the President, with the advice and approval of Congress, but with the appointments so arranged that no one President could determine the economic complexion of the Council. . . . If, in the mature judgment of the Council, our national economic objectives were being endangered or violated, it would be the duty of the Council to inform the people of this opinion. If, nevertheless, the appropriate branch of the government took no action, it would be the further duty of the Council, after a proper and ample interval, to submit the question to the people. . . . The result of the referendum might then serve as a guide to the government for future policies and acts.

'The sole power of the Council would be to refer, in a proper and deliberate manner, issues of grave national importance directly to the people. . . . Obviously, the power should be used sparingly.'

24. (Page 464.) *Whose Constitution? An Inquiry Into the General Welfare.* H. A. W., with acknowledgments of collaboration to John R. Fleming, Morris L. Ernst, Philip Glick, and Irving Brant. Reynal & Hitchcock, New York, 1936.

25. (Page 467.) *The Agrarian Revival: A Study of Agricultural Extension*, published by the American Association for Adult Education, New York, 1939. The quotation is from pp. 216–218.

CHAPTER XII

INTO THE NINETEEN-FORTIES

1. (Page 477.) *Must have Wallace: F. D. R.* His reference to early death in office was to William Henry Harrison, the ninth President, elected in 1840 over Van Buren; inaugurated March 4, died April 4.

Recent memoirs add items of interest to Roosevelt's insistence on Wallace as his running-mate in 1940. In *The Roosevelt I Knew* (Viking, 1946)

Frances Perkins quotes his pre-convention cogitations: 'He [Wallace] ... would be a good man if something happened to the President. He is no isolationist. He knows what we are up against in this war that is so rapidly engulfing the world' (p. 130). Later, by long-distance phone to Miss Perkins at the Convention in Chicago: 'I think Wallace is good. I like him. He is the kind of man I like to have around. He is good to work with and he knows a lot, you can trust his information. He digs to the bottom of things and gets the facts. He is honest as the day is long. He thinks right. He has the general ideas we have. He is the kind of man who can do something in politics. He can help the people with their political thinking. . . . Yes, it's Wallace, I guess. Yes, it will be Wallace. I think I'll stick to that. . . . Would you mind going over to tell Harry [Hopkins]? . . . Better go over yourself and tell him. Will you? That I have decided on Wallace' (pp. 132–133)?

Still later, as resistance developed in the Convention, and resentment of deprived Southern Democrats, particularly, raised cries of a 'phony draft,' Vice-Admiral Ross T. McIntire relates in *White House Physician* (Copyright, 1946, by Ross T. McIntire and George Creel, Courtesy of G. P. Putnam's Sons), 'The President's reaction was instant and angry. Overwork had left him tired and edgy. . . . Hell was poppin'. The Boss . . . had his Dutch up, and was going to refuse to run. It was not only the "phony draft" attack, but the bedlam of disapproval that broke out when Henry Wallace's name was placed in nomination. But for rapid action of the Chairman, Paul McNutt would have been named, a direct blow at the President. . . .

'Entering the study (Pa Watson, Steve Early, and I) found F. D. R., set of jaw, writing away on a desk pad. Missy Le Hand, Grace Tully, and Sam Rosenman, huddled in a corner, gaped helplessly. He waved us off impatiently when we tried to talk, and after throwing down his pencil, handed the sheet to Judge Rosenman.

'"Put that in shape, Sam," he ordered, "give it out. No," he continued, turning to us, "I've made up my mind. I did not want to run, and now some of the very people who urged me the most are putting me in the position of an office-hungry politician, scheming and plotting to keep his job. I'm through . . ."'

They carried his written refusal from the room, the Surgeon-General of the Navy continues, then marched back in to 'lay down a barrage of argument . . . for the best part of an hour. . . . In the end he smiled somewhat sheepishly and admitted he had gone off half-cocked' (pp. 124–126).

2. (Page 480.) *The American Choice: A Foreign and Domestic Policy for America Now*, by H. A. W., Reynal & Hitchcock, New York, 1940.

3. (Page 484.) '*This reserved and restless man.*' John MacCormac,

reviewing H. A. W.'s *The Century of the Common Man*, Reynal & Hitchcock, 1943, in *The New York Times Book Review*, July 11, 1943.

4. (Page 489.) *Foundations of the Peace:* H. A. W., *The Atlantic Monthly*, January, 1942.

5. (Page 493.) *The Quest for Rubber.* Statements by Doctor Earl Bressman before a Special Committee to Investigate the National Defense Program and a subcommittee of the Senate Committee on Agriculture investigating industrial alcohol and synthetic rubber. Doctor Bressman cites and documents Wallace's long fight for rubber supplies. Printed in *The Congressional Record*, August 10 and 17, 1942.

6. (Page 515.) '*The ideological boys have lost their Gandhi*': Raymond Moley in *The Wall Street Journal*, July 19, 1943.

7. (Page 519.) *Our job in the Pacific:* H. A. W. Institute of Pacific Relations Pamphlet no. 12, 1944.

8. (Page 519.) *Again, America must choose.* Wallace challenges private capital to show 'courage and wisdom.' *Democracy Reborn*, pp. 273–274.

9. (Page 523.) *East Asia Mission, 12,000 Air Miles Through the New Soviet Orient.* H. A. W. in collaboration with Andrew J. Steiger. Reynal & Hitchcock, 1946.

10. (Page 535.) *This Man Truman*, by Frank McNaughton and Walter Hehmeyer, Whittlesey House, 1945. Mr. McNaughton is of the staff of *Time*; Mr. Hehmeyer worked intimately with Mr. Truman as one of his staff on the Truman Committee, investigating National Defense. The quotation is from pp. 148–149.

11. (Page 538.) '*A fresh start.*' To another friend, C. F. Palmer of Atlanta, Georgia, who wrote Wallace after the convention, quoting Kipling: *If you can bear to hear the truth you've spoken twisted by knaves to make a trap for fools. . . .* Wallace replied in a note, August 11, 1944:
'I have never been too keen about Kipling's poem, because it seemed to me to foster a kind of martyrdom-egotism. I prefer to look on adversity as opportunity, provided you are willing to look around hard enough to find the opportunity which adversity almost invariably presents.'

12. (Page 546.) *An Uncommon Man: Henry Wallace and 60 Million Jobs*, by Frank Kingdon. Readers Press, New York, 1945.

13. (Page 554.) *Proceedings of the Jones-Wallace Hearings before the Committee of Commerce*, United States Senate, January 24 and 25, 1945. Printed for the use of the Committee, 144 pages, Document 68424, United States Government Printing Office.

14. (Page 556.) *60,000,000 Jobs*, by H. A. W., Reynal & Hitchcock and Simon & Schuster, New York, 1945.

INDEX